Cisco IOS 12.0 Configuration Fundamentals

Cisco Systems, Inc.

Cisco Press
201 W 103rd Street
Indianapolis, IN 46290

Cisco IOS 12.0 Configuration Fundamentals

Cisco Systems, Inc.

Copyright© 1999 Cisco Systems, Inc.

Cisco Press logo is a trademark of Cisco Systems, Inc.

Published by:
Cisco Press
201 West 103rd Street
Indianapolis, IN 46290 USA

Printed in the United States of America 1 2 3 4 5 6 7 8 9 0

Library of Congress Cataloging-in-Publication Number 99-60054

ISBN: 1-57870-155-4

Warning and Disclaimer

This book is designed to provide information about **Cisco IOS 12.0 Configuration Fundamentals**. Every effort has been made to make this book as complete and as accurate as possible, but no warranty or fitness is implied.

The information is provided on an "as is" basis. The author, Cisco Press, and Cisco Systems, Inc. shall have neither liability nor responsibility to any person or entity with respect to any loss or damages arising from the information contained in this book or from the use of the discs or programs that may accompany it.

The opinions expressed in this book belong to the author and are not necessarily those of Cisco Systems, Inc.

Trademark Acknowledgments

All terms mentioned in this book that are known to be trademarks or service marks have been appropriately capitalized. Cisco Press or Cisco Systems, Inc. cannot attest to the accuracy of this information. Use of a term in this book should not be regarded as affecting the validity of any trademark or service mark.

Feedback Information

At Cisco Press, our goal is to create in-depth technical books of the highest quality and value. Each book is crafted with care and precision, undergoing rigorous development that involves the unique expertise of members from the professional technical community.

Readers' feedback is a natural continuation of this process. If you have any comments regarding how we could improve the quality of this book, or otherwise alter it to better suit your needs, you can contact us through email at ciscopress@mcp.com. Please make sure to include the book title and ISBN in your message.

We greatly appreciate your assistance.

Associate Publisher	Jim LeValley
Executive Editor	Alicia Buckley
Cisco Systems Program Manager	H. Kim Lew
Managing Editor	Patrick Kanouse
Acquisitions Editor	Tracy Hughes
Copy Editor	Michael Hughes
Team Coordinator	Amy Lewis
Book Designer	Scott Cook
Cover Designer	Karen Ruggles
Page Layout	Eric S. Miller
Proofreader	Sheri Replin
Indexer	Chris Wilcox

Acknowledgments

The Cisco IOS Reference Library is the result of collaborative efforts of many Cisco technical writers and editors over the years. This bookset represents the continuing development and integration of user documentation for the ever-increasing set of Cisco IOS networking features and functionality.

The current team of Cisco IOS technical writers and editors includes Katherine Anderson, Hugh Bussell, Melanie Cheng, Christy Choate, Sue Cross, Meredith Fisher, Tina Fox, Sheryl Kelly, Marsha Kinnear, Doug MacBeth, Lavanya Mandavilli, Mary Mangone, Andy Mann, Bob Marburg, Greg McMillan, Madhu Mitra, Vicki Payne, Jeremy Pollock, Patricia Rohrs, Teresa Oliver Schick, Wink Schuetz, Grace Tai, Brian Taylor, Jamianne Von-Prudelle, and Amanda Worthington.

The writing team wants to acknowledge the many engineering, customer support, and marketing subject-matter experts for their participation in reviewing draft documents and, in many cases, providing source material from which this bookset is developed.

Contents at a Glance

Table of Contents

Configuration Fundamentals Overview

This introduction provides an overview of Cisco IOS software configuration, describes the chapters in this book, and suggests sections to read based on various situations. This introduction contains the following sections:

- Overview of Router Configuration Tasks
- Cisco IOS User Interfaces
- File Management
- System Management
- Guide to This Book
- About the Cisco IOS 12.0 Reference Library
- Using Cisco IOS Software

Overview of Router Configuration Tasks

To configure your router or access server, you must perform several tasks. Initially, you must determine the following:

- Which network protocols you are supporting (for example, AppleTalk, IP, Novell IPX, and so on)
- The addressing plan for each network protocol
- Which routing protocol you will use for each network protocol
- Which WAN protocols you will run on each interface (for example, Frame Relay, HDLC, SMDS, X.25, and so on)

Set up the hardware as described in the documentation shipped with your product. Configure any user interface, file management, or interface management tasks as described in this book. Configure protocol-specific features on your router or access server as described in the appropriate chapters of the other Cisco IOS software configuration guides.

Cisco IOS User Interfaces

The user interface chapters describe the different methods of entering commands into the router and altering the user environment.

The Cisco IOS software provides a command line interface that allows you to configure and manage the router or access server. If you are unfamiliar with the Cisco IOS command line interface, you should read Chapter 1, "Using the Command Line Interface." This chapter discusses the different command modes, context-sensitive help, and editing features. This chapter also describes the Web browser interface, which can be used to configure and monitor the router as well.

Cisco provides some configuration alternatives to the command line interface. If you wish to use AutoInstall to configure a new router to change the configuration, read Chapter 3, "Using Configuration Tools." This chapter also mentions other configuration tools that are available, but it does not provide detailed documentation.

To use the command line interface, your terminal must be connected to the router through the console port or one of the TTY lines. By default, the terminal is configured to a basic configuration, which should work for most terminal sessions. However, you may want to alter the terminal settings. Refer to Chapter 5, "Configuring Operating Characteristics for Terminals," for information.

You can also make connections to other hosts from the router. Chapter 7, "Managing Connections, Menus, and System Banners," describes how to manage these connections. Alternately, users can connect to your router. You can display messages to the terminals of these users.

File Management

The file management chapters describe the different types of files you can manipulate on the router, such as configuration files, images, and microcode.

Chapter 13, "Modifying, Downloading, and Maintaining Configuration Files," discusses how to modify configuration files, download configuration files for servers, store configuration files on servers, and configure the router to load a configuration file at system startup. In order to customize your router's operation to your needs, you will need to alter the configuration file. This chapter describes how to do this task.

Chapter 15, "Loading and Maintaining System Images and Microcode," discusses how to download images from servers, store images on servers, specify which image is loaded at system startup, and specify which microcode images to use. If you are not storing or upgrading your system image and you do not wish to change image booting procedures, you do not need to read this chapter.

Chapter 17, "Maintaining Router Memory," deals with the different types of memory your router may have and how to use this memory to manage files. This chapter also contains information on how to upgrade images on some platforms. Read this chapter if you are upgrading your system image or deleting files in Flash memory.

Chapter 19, "Rebooting a Router," focuses on tasks related to the rebooting procedure. Read this chapter if you wish to change which image or configuration file is loaded at system startup. This chapter also discusses ROM Monitor mode, which allows you to boot the router manually.

Chapter 21, "Configuring Additional File Transfer Functions," describes how to configure your router to be a server or use rsh and rcp. As a TFTP server, your router can provide other routers with images and configuration files over the network. The remote shell and remote copy functions allow users to remotely execute commands or copy files to or from another host.

System Management

The system management chapters discuss tasks that allow you to maintain your router after it is configured with the network, routing, and WAN protocols. These chapters discuss ways you can fine-tune the router and maintain it over time.

SNMP, RMON, Cisco Discovery Protocol, and Response Time Reporter are described in Chapter 23, "Monitoring the Router and Network." You can use these protocols to gather information about the router and network usage.

Chapter 25, "Troubleshooting the Router," provides an introduction to troubleshooting techniques, error message logging, and debugging commands. If you are troubleshooting a particular protocol, read this chapter to learn how to log system error messages and use debugging commands.

Chapter 27, "Performing Basic System Management," discusses basic optional tasks. For example, you can change the name of the router, create command aliases, enable minor services, and set time and calendar services.

Chapter 29, "Configuring the System Controller and Managed Shelves," describes the system controller, a Cisco IOS-based device that aids in the monitoring and management of a number of access servers and routers. Access servers and routers managed by the system controller are called shelves.

Guide to This Book

The previous sections listed common tasks found in each chapter. However, some common tasks require information in more than one chapter. This section suggests sections in different chapters that are useful to read based on your situation.

Learning the Cisco IOS Command Line Interface

If you are not familiar with the Cisco IOS command line interface, read the following sections to gain a basic understanding of the user interface and basic configuration tasks:

In Chapter 1, "Using the Command Line Interface":

- Access Each Command Mode
- Using the No and Default Forms of Commands
- Get Context-Sensitive Help
- Check Command Syntax

- Use the Command History Features
- Use the Editing Features

In Chapter 13, "Modifying, Downloading, and Maintaining Configuration Files":

- Display Configuration File Information
- Understand Configuration Files
- Enter Configuration Mode and Select a Configuration Source
- Configure the Cisco IOS Software from the Terminal
- Reexecute the Configuration Commands in Startup Configuration
- Clear the Configuration Information

In Chapter 27, "Performing Basic System Management":

- Set the Router Name

Storing or Obtaining Configuration Files or Images from a Server

You might want to save a configuration or image on a server or upgrade your image to a different release. If you will be storing or obtaining configuration files or images from a server, read the following sections:

In Chapter 13, "Modifying, Downloading, and Maintaining Configuration Files":

- Copy Configuration Files from the Router to a Network Server
- Copy Configuration Files from a Network Server to the Router
- Maintain Configuration Files Larger than NVRAM
- Copy Configuration Files between Different Locations

In Chapter 17, "Maintain Router Memory":

- Partition Flash Memory
- Use Flash Load Helper to Upgrade Software on Run-from-Flash Systems

Changing the Image or Configuration File Loaded by the Router

If you wish to change the image or configuration file used when the system reloads, read the following sections:

In Chapter 13, "Modifying, Downloading, and Maintaining Configuration Files":

- Specify the Startup Configuration File

In Chapter 15, "Loading and Maintaining System Images and Microcode":

- Specify the Startup System Image in the Configuration File

In Chapter 19, "Rebooting a Router":

- Display Booting Information
- Rebooting Procedures
- Modify the Configuration Register Boot Field
- Set Environment Variables

About the Cisco IOS 12.0 Reference Library

The Cisco IOS 12.0 Reference Library books are Cisco documentation that describe the tasks and commands necessary to configure and maintain your Cisco IOS network.

The Cisco IOS software bookset is intended primarily for users who configure and maintain access servers and routers, but are not necessarily familiar with the tasks, the relationship between tasks, or the commands necessary to perform particular tasks.

Cisco IOS Reference Library Organization

The Cisco IOS 12.0 Reference Library consists of 11 books. Each book contains technology-specific configuration chapters with corresponding command reference chapters. Each configuration chapter describes Cisco's implementation of protocols and technologies, related configuration tasks, and contains comprehensive configuration examples. Each command reference chapter complements the organization of its corresponding configuration chapter and provides complete command syntax information.

Other Books Available in the Cisco IOS 12.0 Reference Library

- *Cisco IOS 12.0 Solutions for Network Protocols, Volume I*, 1-57870-154-6; Available March 1999

  This book is a comprehensive guide detailing available IP and IP routing alternatives. It describes how to implement IP addressing and IP services and how to configure support for a wide range of IP routing protocols including BGP for ISP networks and basic and advanced IP Multicast functionality.

- *Cisco IOS 12.0 Interface Configuration*, 1-57870-156-2; Available March 1999

  This book is a comprehensive guide detailing how to configure physical and virutal interfaces—the two types of interfaces supported on Cisco routers. It provides readers with the most current router task and commands information for their network environments and teaches how to effectively implement these techniques and commands on their networks.

- *Cisco IOS 12.0 WAN Solutions*, 1-57870-158-9; Available April 1999

  This book offers thorough, comprehensive coverage of internetworking technologies, particularly ATM, Frame Relay, SMDS, LAPB, and X.25, teaching the reader how to configure the technologies in a LAN/WAN environment.

- *Cisco IOS 12.0 Switching Services*, 1-57870-157-0; Available April 1999

  This book is a comprehensive guide detailing available Cisco IOS switching alternatives. Cisco's switching services range from fast switching and Netflow switching to LAN emulation. This book describes how to configure routing between virtual LANs (VLANs) and teaches how to effectively configure and implement VLANs on switches.

- *Cisco IOS 12.0 Solutions for Multiservice Applications*, 1-57870-159-7; Available April 1999

  This book shows you how to configure your router or access server to support voice, video, and broadband transmission. Cisco's voice and video support is implemented using voice packet technology. In voice packet technology, voice signals are packetized and transported in compliance with ITU-T specification H.323, which is the ITU-T specification for transmitting multimedia (voice, video, and data) across a local-area network (LAN).

- *Cisco IOS 12.0 Network Security*, 1-57870-160-0; Available May 1999

  This book documents security configuration from a remote site and for a central enterprise or service provider network. It describes AAA, Radius, TACACS+, and Kerberos network security features. It also explains how to encrypt data across enterprise networks. The book includes many illustrations that show configurations and functionality, along with a discussion of network security policy choices and some decision-making guidelines.

- *Cisco IOS 12.0 Solutions for Quality of Service*, 1-57870-161-9; Available May 1999

  This comprehensive guide details the available Cisco IOS quality of service (QoS) features. This book suggests benefits you can gain from implementing Cisco IOS QoS features and describes how to effectively configure and implement the various QoS features. Some of the features described in this book include Committed Access Rate (CAR), Weighted Fair Queueing (WFQ), and Weighted Random Early Detection (WRED), as well as many other features.

- *Cisco IOS 12.0 Solutions for Network Protocols, Volume II*, 1-57870-164-3; Available June 1999

  This book is a comprehensive guide detailing available network protocol alternatives. It describes how to implement various protocols in your network. This book includes documentation of the latest functionality for the IPX and AppleTalk desktop protocols as well as the following network protocols: Apollo Domain, Banyan VINES, DECNet, ISO CLNS, and XNS.

- *Cisco IOS 12.0 Bridging and IBM Network Solutions*, 1-57870-162-7; Available June 1999

  This book describes Cisco's support for networks in IBM and bridging environments. Support includes the following: transparent and source-route transparent bridging; source-route bridging; remote source-route bridging; data-link switching plus; serial tunnel and block serial tunnel; SDLC and LLC2 parameter; IBM network media translation; downstream physical unit and SNA service point; SNA Frame Relay access support; Advanced Peer-to-Peer Networking; and native client interface architecture.

- *Cisco IOS 12.0 Dial Solutions*, 1-57870-163-5; Available June 1999

This book provides readers with real-world solutions and how to implement them on a network. Customers interested in implementing dial solutions across their network environment include remote sites dialing in to a central office, Internet service providers (ISPs), ISP customers at home offices, and enterprise WAN system administrators implementing dial-on-demand routing (DDR).

Book Conventions

The Cisco IOS documentation set uses the following conventions:

Convention	Description
^ or Ctrl	Represents the Control key. For example, when you read ^D or *Ctrl-D*, you should hold down the Control key while you press the D key. Keys are indicated in capital letters but are not case sensitive.
string	A string is defined as a nonquoted set of characters. For example, when setting an SNMP community string to public, do not use quotation marks around the string; otherwise, the string will include the quotation marks.

Examples use the following conventions:

Convention	Description
screen	Shows an example of information displayed on the screen.
boldface screen	Shows an example of information that you must enter.
< >	Nonprinting characters, such as passwords, appear in angled brackets.
!	Exclamation points at the beginning of a line indicate a comment line. They are also displayed by the Cisco IOS software for certain processes.
[ ]	Default responses to system prompts appear in square brackets.

The following conventions are used to attract the reader's attention:

CAUTION   Means *reader be careful*. In this situation, you might do something that could result in equipment damage or loss of data.

NOTE   Means *reader take note*. Notes contain helpful suggestions or references to materials not contained in this manual.

TIMESAVER   Means the *described action saves time*. You can save time by performing the action described in the paragraph.

Within the Cisco IOS 12.0 Reference Library, the term *router* is used to refer to both access servers and routers. When a feature is supported on the access server only, the term *access server* is used.

Within examples, routers and access servers are alternately shown. These products are used only for example purposes; that is, an example that shows one product does not indicate that the other product is not supported.

Command Syntax Conventions

Command descriptions use the following conventions:

Convention	Description
boldface	Indicates commands and keywords that are entered literally as shown.
italics	Indicates arguments for which you supply values; in contexts that do not allow italics, arguments are enclosed in angle brackets (< >).
[**x**]	Keywords or arguments that appear within square brackets are optional.
{**x** | **y** | **z**}	A choice of required keywords (represented by **x**, **y**, and **z**) appears in braces separated by vertical bars. You must select one.
[**x** {**y** | **z**}]	Braces and vertical bars within square brackets indicate a required choice within an optional element. You do not need to select one. If you do, you have some required choices.

Cisco Connection Online

Cisco Connection Online (CCO) is Cisco Systems' primary, real-time support channel. Maintenance customers and partners can self-register on CCO to obtain additional information and services.

Available 24 hours a day, 7 days a week, CCO provides a wealth of standard and value-added services to Cisco's customers and business partners. CCO services include product information, product documentation, software updates, release notes, technical tips, the Bug Navigator, configuration notes, brochures, descriptions of service offerings, and download access to public and authorized files.

CCO serves a wide variety of users through two interfaces that are updated and enhanced simultaneously: a character-based version and a multimedia version that resides on the World Wide Web (WWW). The character-based CCO supports Zmodem, Kermit, Xmodem, FTP, and Internet e-mail, and it is excellent for quick access to information over lower bandwidths. The WWW version of CCO provides richly formatted documents with photographs, figures, graphics, and video, as well as hyperlinks to related information.

You can access CCO in the following ways:

- WWW: http://www.cisco.com

- WWW: http://www-europe.cisco.com

- WWW: http://www-china.cisco.com

- Telnet: cco.cisco.com

- Modem: From North America, 408 526-8070; from Europe, 33 1 64 46 40 82. Use the following terminal settings: VT100 emulation; databits: 8; parity: none; stop bits: 1; and connection rates up to 28.8 kbps.

Using Cisco IOS Software

This section provides helpful tips for understanding and configuring Cisco IOS software using the command-line interface (CLI).

Getting Help

Entering a question mark (?) at the system prompt displays a list of commands available for each command mode. You can also get a list of any command's associated keywords and arguments with the context-sensitive help feature.

To get help specific to a command mode, a command, a keyword, or an argument, use one of the following commands:

Command	Purpose
help	Obtains a brief description of the help system in any command mode.

Command	Purpose
*abbreviated-command-entry***?**	Obtains a list of commands that begin with a particular character string. (No space between the command and the question mark.)
abbreviated-command-entry<**Tab**>	Completes a partial command name.
?	Lists all commands available for a particular command mode.
command **?**	Lists a command's associated keywords. (Space between the command and the question mark.)
command keyword **?**	Lists a keyword's associated arguments. (Space between the keyword and the question mark.)

Example: How to Find Command Options

This section provides an example of how to display syntax for a command. The syntax can consist of optional or required keywords. To display keywords for a command, enter a question mark (**?**) at the configuration prompt, or after entering part of a command followed by a space. The Cisco IOS software displays a list of keywords available along with a brief description of the keywords. For example, if you were in global configuration mode, typed the command **arap**, and wanted to see all the keywords for that command, you would type **arap ?**.

Table I-1 shows examples of how you can use the question mark (**?**) to assist you in entering commands. It steps you through entering the following commands:

- **controller t1 1**

- **cas-group 1 timeslots 1-24 type e&m-fgb dtmf**

Table I-2 *How to Find Command Options*

Command	Comment

`Router>` **`enable`**
`Password: <password>`
`Router#`
	Enter the **enable** command and password to access privileged EXEC commands.
	
	You have entered privileged EXEC mode when the prompt changes to `Router#`.

`Router#` **`config terminal`**
`Enter configuration commands, one per line. End with CTRL-Z.`
`Router(config)#`
	Enter global configuration mode.
	
	You have entered global configuration mode when the prompt changes to `Router(config)#`.

Table I-2 *How to Find Command Options (Continued)*

Command	Comment

`Router(config)# `**`controller t1 ?`**
  `<0-3>  Controller unit number`
`Router(config)# `**`controller t1 1`**
`Router(config-controller)#`
	Enter controller configuration mode by specifying the T1 controller that you want to configure using the **controller t1** global configuration command.
	
	Enter **?** to display what you must enter next on the command line. In this example, you must enter a controller unit number from 0 to 3.
	
	You have entered controller configuration mode when the prompt changes to `Router(config-controller)#`.

`Router(config-controller)# `**`?`**
`Controller configuration commands:`
  `cablelength   Specify the cable length for a DS1 link`
  `cas-group     Configure the specified timeslots for CAS`
  `              (Channel Associate Signals)`
  `channel-group Specify the timeslots to channel-group`
  `              mapping for an interface`
  `clock         Specify the clock source for a DS1 link`
  `default       Set a command to its defaults`
  `description   Controller specific description`
  `ds0           ds0 commands`
  `exit          Exit from controller configuration mode`
  `fdl           Specify the FDL standard for a DS1 data`
  `              link`
  `framing       Specify the type of Framing on a DS1 link`
  `help          Description of the interactive help`
  `              system`
  `linecode      Specify the line encoding method for a DS1`
  `              link`
  `loopback      Put the entire T1 line into loopback`
  `no            Negate a command or set its defaults`
  `pri-group     Configure the specified timeslots for PRI`
  `shutdown      Shut down a DS1 link (send Blue Alarm)`
`Router(config-controller)#`
	Enter **?** to display a list of all the controller configuration commands available for the T1 controller.

continues

Table I-2 *How to Find Command Options (Continued)*

Command	Comment

`Router(config-controller)# `**`cas-group ?`**
`  <0-23>          Channel number`
`Router(config-controller)# cas-group`
	Enter the command that you want to configure for the controller. In this example, the **cas-group** command is used.

	Enter **?** to display what you must enter next on the command line. In this example, you must enter a channel number from 0 to 23.
	Because <cr> is not displayed, it indicates that you must enter more keywords to complete the command.

`Router(config-controller)# `**`cas-group 1 ?`**
`  timeslots      List of timeslots in the cas-group`
`Router(config-controller)# cas-group 1`
	After you enter the channel number, enter **?** to display what you must enter next on the command line. In this example, you must enter the **timeslots** keyword.

	Because <cr> is not displayed, it indicates that you must enter more keywords to complete the command.

`Router(config-controller)# `**`cas-group 1 timeslots ?`**
`  <1-24>          List of timeslots which comprise the cas-`
`                  group`
`Router(config-controller)# cas-group 1 timeslots`
	After you enter the **timeslots** keyword, enter **?** to display what you must enter next on the command line. In this example, you must enter a list of timeslots from 1 to 24.

	You can specify timeslot ranges (for example, 1–24), individual timeslots separated by commas (for example 1, 3, 5), or a combination of the two (for example 1–3, 8, 17–24). The 16th time slot is not specified in the command line, because it is reserved for transmitting the channel signaling.
	Because <cr> is not displayed, it indicates that you must enter more keywords to complete the command.

Table I-2 *How to Find Command Options (Continued)*

Command	Comment

Router(config-controller)# **cas-group 1 timeslots 1-24 ?**
  service   Specify the type of service
  type   Specify the type of signaling
Router(config-controller)# cas-group 1 timeslots 1-24
	After you enter the timeslot ranges, enter **?** to display what you must enter next on the command line. In this example, you must enter the **service** or **type** keyword.
	
	Because <cr> is not displayed, it indicates that you must enter more keywords to complete the command.

Router(config-controller)# **cas-group 1 timeslots 1-24 type ?**
  e&m-fgb   E & M Type II FGB
  e&m-fgd   E & M Type IIFGD
  e&m-immediate-start E & M Immediate Start
  fxs-ground-start   FXS Ground Start
  fxs-loop-start   FXS Loop Start
  sas-ground-start   SAS Ground Start
  sas-loop-start   SAS Loop Start
Router(config-controller)# cas-group 1 timeslots 1-24 type
	In this example, the **type** keyword is entered. After you enter the **type** keyword, enter **?** to display what you must enter next on the command line. In this example, you must enter one of the signaling types.
	
	Because <cr> is not displayed, it indicates that you must enter more keywords to complete the command.

Router(config-controller)# **cas-group 1 timeslots 1-24 type e&m-fgb ?**
  dtmf   DTMF tone signaling
  mf   MF tone signaling
  service   Specify the type of service
  <cr>
Router(config-controller)# cas-group 1 timeslots 1-24 type e&m-fgb
	In this example, the **e&m-fgb** keyword is entered. After you enter the **e&m-fgb** keyword, enter **?** to display what you must enter next on the command line. In this example, you can enter the **dtmf**, **mf**, or **service** keyword to indicate the type of channel-associated signaling available for the **e&m-fgb** signaling type.
	
	Because <cr> is displayed, it indicates that you can enter more keywords or enter **<cr>** to complete the command.

continues

Table I-2 *How to Find Command Options (Continued)*

Command	Comment
```Router(config-controller)# cas-group 1 timeslots 1-24 type e&m-fgb dtmf ? dnis DNIS addr info provisioned service Specify the type of service <cr> Router(config-controller)# cas-group 1 timeslots 1-24 type e&m-fgb dtmf```	In this example, the **dtmf** keyword is entered. After you enter the **dtmf** keyword, enter **?** to display what you must enter next on the command line. In this example, you can enter the **dnis** or **service** keyword to indicate the options available for **dtmf** tone signaling. Because <cr> is displayed, it indicates that you can enter more keywords or enter **<cr>** to complete the command.
```Router(config-controller)# cas-group 1 timeslots 1-24 type e&m-fgb dtmf Router(config-controller)#```	In this example, enter **<cr>** to complete the command.

Understanding Command Modes

The Cisco IOS user interface is divided into many different modes. The commands available to you at any given time depend on which mode you are currently in. Entering a question mark (**?**) at the system prompt allows you to obtain a list of commands available for each command mode.

When you start a session on the router, you begin in user mode, often called EXEC mode. Only a limited subset of the commands are available in EXEC mode. In order to have access to all commands, you must enter privileged EXEC mode. Normally, you must enter a password to enter privileged EXEC mode. From privileged mode, you can enter any EXEC command or enter global configuration mode. Most of the EXEC commands are one-time commands, such as **show** commands, which show the current status of something, and **clear** commands, which clear counters or interfaces. The EXEC commands are not saved across reboots of the router.

The configuration modes allow you to make changes to the running configuration. If you later save the configuration, these commands are stored across router reboots. In order to get to the various configuration modes, you must start at global configuration mode. From global configuration mode, you can enter interface configuration mode, subinterface configuration mode, and a variety of protocol-specific modes.

ROM monitor mode is a separate mode used when the router cannot boot properly. If your router or access server does not find a valid system image when it is booting, or if its configuration file is corrupted at startup, the system might enter read-only memory (ROM) monitor mode.

Summary of Main Command Modes

Table I-2 summarizes the main command modes of the Cisco IOS software.

Table I-3 *Summary of Main Command Modes*

Command Mode	Access Method	Prompt	Exit Method
User EXEC	Log in.	`Router>`	Use the **logout** command.
Privileged EXEC	From user EXEC mode, use the **enable** EXEC command.	`Router#`	To exit back to user EXEC mode, use the **disable** command.
			To enter global configuration mode, use the **configure terminal** privileged EXEC command.
Global configuration	From privileged EXEC mode, use the **configure terminal** privileged EXEC command.	`Router(config)#`	To exit to privileged EXEC mode, use the **exit** or **end** command or press **Ctrl-Z**.
			To enter interface configuration mode, enter an **interface** configuration command.
Interface configuration	From global configuration mode, enter by specifying an interface with an **interface** command.	`Router(config-if)#`	To exit to global configuration mode, use the **exit** command.
			To exit to privileged EXEC mode, use the **exit** command or press **Ctrl-Z**.
			To enter subinterface configuration mode, specify a subinterface with the **interface** command.
Subinterface configuration	From interface configuration mode, specify a subinterface with an **interface** command.	`Router(config-subif)#`	To exit to global configuration mode, use the **exit** command.
			To enter privileged EXEC mode, use the **end** command or press **Ctrl-Z**.
ROM monitor	From privileged EXEC mode, use the **reload** EXEC command. Press the Break key during the first 60 seconds while the system is booting.	`>`	To exit to user EXEC mode, type **continue**.

Using the No and Default Forms of Commands

Almost every configuration command also has a **no** form. In general, use the **no** form to disable a function. Use the command without the keyword **no** to reenable a disabled function or to enable a function that is disabled by default. For example, IP routing is enabled by default. To disable IP routing, specify the **no ip routing** command and specify **ip routing** to reenable it. The Cisco IOS software command references provide the complete syntax for the configuration commands and describe what the **no** form of a command does.

Configuration commands can also have a **default** form. The **default** form of a command returns the command setting to its default. Most commands are disabled by default, so the **default** form is the same as the **no** form. However, some commands are enabled by default and have variables set to certain default values. In these cases, the **default** command enables the command and sets variables to their default values. The Cisco IOS software command references describe what the **default** form of a command does if the command is not the same as the **no** form.

Saving Configuration Changes

Enter the **copy system:running-config nvram:startup-config** command to save your configuration changes to your startup configuration so that they will not be lost if there is a system reload or power outage. For example:

```
Router# copy system:running-config nvram:startup-config
Building configuration...
```

It might take a minute or two to save the configuration. After the configuration has been saved, the following output appears:

```
[OK]
Router#
```

On most platforms, this step saves the configuration to nonvolatile random-access memory (NVRAM). On the Class A Flash file system platforms, this step saves the configuration to the location specified by the CONFIG_FILE environment variable. The CONFIG_FILE variable defaults to NVRAM.

PART I

Cisco IOS User Interfaces

## CHAPTER 1

Using the Command Line Interface

Cisco IOS commands can be entered at a terminal connected to the access server or router using the command line interface (CLI). Commands may also be entered using the Cisco Web browser interface. This chapter describes how to use the Cisco IOS command line interface and Web page interface. It describes command modes, help features, command editing and history features, and menus.

For a complete description of the user interface commands in this chapter, refer to Chapter 2, "Basic Command Line Interface Commands." To locate documentation of specific commands, you can search online at www.cisco.com.

User Interface Task List

You can perform the tasks in the following sections to familiarize yourself with the Cisco IOS user interface. If you are not familiar with the Cisco IOS command line interface, read the first six sections to gain a basic understanding of the user interface.

- Access Each Command Mode
- Using the No and Default Forms of Commands
- Get Context-Sensitive Help
- Check Command Syntax
- Use the Command History Features
- Use the Editing Features
- Use the Cisco Web Browser Interface to Issue Commands
- Customize the User Interface on a Web Browser
- Display 8-bit and Multibyte Character Sets

Access Each Command Mode

The Cisco IOS user interface is divided into many different modes. The commands available to you at any given time depend on which mode you are currently in. Entering a question mark (**?**) at the system prompt allows you to obtain a list of commands available for each command mode.

When you start a session on the router, you begin in user mode, often called EXEC mode. Only a limited subset of the commands are available in EXEC mode. In order to have access to all commands, you must enter privileged EXEC mode. Normally, you must enter a password to enter privileged EXEC mode. From privileged mode, you can enter any EXEC command or enter global configuration mode. Most of the EXEC commands are one-time commands, such as **show** commands, which show the current configuration status, and **clear** commands, which clear counters or interfaces. The EXEC commands are not saved across reboots of the router.

The configuration modes allow you to make changes to the running configuration. If you later save the configuration, these commands are stored across router reboots. In order to access the various configuration modes, you must start at global configuration mode. From global configuration mode, you can enter interface configuration mode, subinterface configuration mode, and a variety of protocol-specific modes.

ROM monitor mode is a separate mode used when the router cannot boot properly. If your router or access server does not find a valid system image when it is booting, or if its configuration file is corrupted at startup, the system might enter read-only memory (ROM) monitor mode.

The following sections describe how to access each of the Cisco IOS command modes:

- User EXEC Mode
- Privileged EXEC Mode
- Global Configuration Mode
- Interface Configuration Mode
- Subinterface Configuration Mode
- ROM Monitor Mode

User EXEC Mode

After you log in to the router or access server, you are automatically in user EXEC command mode. The EXEC commands available at the user level are a subset of those available at the privileged level. In general, the user EXEC commands allow you to connect to remote devices, change terminal settings on a temporary basis, perform basic tests, and list system information.

To list the user EXEC commands, use the following command:

Command	Purpose
?	Lists the user EXEC commands.

The user-level prompt consists of the host name followed by the angle bracket (>):

```
Router>
```

The default host name is `Router` unless it has been changed during initial configuration using the **setup** command. Refer to the product user guide for information on the **setup** facility. You can also change the host name using the **hostname** global configuration command described in the Chapter 28, "Basic System Management Commands."

To list the commands available in user EXEC mode, enter a question mark (**?**) as shown in the following example:

```
Router> ?
Exec commands:
  <1-99>            Session number to resume
  connect           Open a terminal connection
  disconnect        Disconnect an existing telnet session
  enable            Turn on privileged commands
  exit              Exit from the EXEC
  help              Description of the interactive help system
  lat               Open a lat connection
  lock              Lock the terminal
  login             Log in as a particular user
  logout            Exit from the EXEC
  menu              Start a menu-based user interface
  mbranch           Trace multicast route for branch of tree
  mrbranch          Trace reverse multicast route to branch of tree
  mtrace            Trace multicast route to group
  name-connection   Name an existing telnet connection
  pad               Open a X.29 PAD connection
  ping              Send echo messages
  resume            Resume an active telnet connection
  show              Show running system information
  systat            Display information about terminal lines
  telnet            Open a telnet connection
  terminal          Set terminal line parameters
  tn3270            Open a tn3270 connection
  trace             Trace route to destination
  where             List active telnet connections
  x3                Set X.3 parameters on PAD
  xremote           Enter XRemote mode
```

The list of commands might vary slightly from this example, depending on the software feature set and configuration of the product.

Privileged EXEC Mode

Because many of the privileged commands set operating parameters, privileged access should be password protected to prevent unauthorized use. The privileged command set includes those commands contained in user EXEC mode, as well as the **configure** command through which you can access the remaining command modes. Privileged EXEC mode also includes high-level testing commands, such as **debug**.

The privileged EXEC mode prompt consists of the devices's host name followed by the pound sign (#). (If the router or access server was named with the **hostname** command, that name would appear as the prompt instead of "Router.")

```
Router#
```

To access and list the privileged EXEC commands, use the following commands:

Step	Command	Purpose
1	**enable** [*password*]	Enters the privileged EXEC mode.
2	**?**	Lists privileged EXEC commands.

To return from privileged EXEC mode to user EXEC mode, use the following command:

Command	Purpose
disable	Moves from privileged EXEC mode to user EXEC mode.

If the system administrator has set a password, you are prompted to enter it before being allowed access to privileged EXEC mode. The password is not displayed on the screen and is case sensitive. If an enable password has not been set, enable mode can be accessed only from the router console. The system administrator uses the **enable password** global configuration command to set the password that restricts access to privileged mode.

The following example shows how to access privileged EXEC mode:

```
Router> enable
Password:letmein
Router#
```

From the privileged level, you can access global configuration mode. For instructions, see the "Global Configuration Mode" section, which follows this section.

Global Configuration Mode

Global configuration commands apply to features that affect the system as a whole, rather than just one protocol or interface. Use the **configure terminal** privileged EXEC command to enter global configuration mode. Commands to enable a particular routing or bridging function are also global configuration commands.

To access and list the global configuration commands, use the following commands:

Step	Command	Purpose
1	**configure terminal**	At the terminal, from the privileged EXEC mode, enters global configuration mode.
2	**?**	Lists the global configuration commands.

The following example shows how to access global configuration mode:

```
Router# configure terminal
Enter configuration commands, one per line. End with Ctrl-Z.
Router(config)#
```

To exit global configuration command mode and return to privileged EXEC mode, use one of the following commands:

Command	Purpose
exit end Ctrl-Z	Exits global configuration mode.

From global configuration mode, you can access a number of other command modes. These command modes are described in the sections that follow. For a complete list of these modes, see the section "Other Configuration Modes."

Interface Configuration Mode

Many features are enabled on a per-interface basis. Interface configuration commands modify the operation of an interface such as an Ethernet, FDDI, or serial port. Interface configuration commands always follow an **interface** global configuration command, which defines the interface type.

To access and list the interface configuration commands, use the following commands:

Step	Command	Purpose
1	**interface** *type number*	From global configuration mode, enters interface configuration mode.
2	**?**	Lists the interface configuration commands.

In the following example, serial interface 0 is about to be configured. The new prompt `Router(config-if)#` indicates interface configuration mode.

```
Router(config)# interface serial 0 <Return>
Router(config-if)#
```

To exit interface configuration mode and return to global configuration mode, enter the **exit** command. To exit configuration mode and return to privileged EXEC mode, use the **end** command or press **Ctrl-Z**.

Subinterface Configuration Mode

You can configure multiple virtual interfaces (called subinterfaces) on a single physical interface. Subinterfaces appear to be distinct physical interfaces to the various protocols. For example, Frame Relay networks provide multiple point-to-point links called permanent virtual circuits (PVCs). PVCs can be grouped under separate subinterfaces that, in turn, are configured on a single physical interface. From a bridging spanning-tree viewpoint, each subinterface is a separate bridge port, and a frame arriving on one subinterface can be sent out on a another subinterface.

Subinterfaces also allow multiple encapsulations for a protocol on a single interface. For example, a router or access server can receive an ARPA-framed IPX packet and forward the packet back out the same physical interface as a SNAP-framed IPX packet.

For detailed information on how to configure subinterfaces, see the appropriate module for a specific protocol in the Cisco IOS software documentation.

To access and list the subinterface configuration commands, use the following commands:

Step	Command	Purpose
1	See the example that follows. For information on interface commands that allow subinterface implementation, see Chapter 2 for protocol specific info.	From interface configuration mode, configures a virtual interface.
2	?	Lists the subinterface configuration commands.

In the following example, a subinterface is configured for serial line 2, which is configured for Frame Relay encapsulation. The subinterface is called 2.1 to indicate that it is subinterface 1 of serial interface 2. The new prompt Router(config-subif)# indicates that you are in subinterface configuration mode. The subinterface can be configured to support one or more Frame Relay PVCs.

```
Router(config)# interface serial 2
Router(config-if)# encapsulation frame-relay
Router(config-if)# interface serial 2.1
Router(config-subif)#
```

To exit subinterface configuration mode and return to global configuration mode, enter the **exit** command. To exit configuration mode and return to privileged EXEC mode, press **Ctrl-Z**.

ROM Monitor Mode

If your router or access server does not find a valid system image, or if you interrupt the boot sequence, the system might enter read-only memory (ROM) monitor mode. From ROM monitor mode, you can boot the device or perform diagnostic tests.

You can also enter ROM monitor mode by entering the **reload** EXEC command and then pressing the Break key during the first 60 seconds of startup. If you have changed the configuration, use the **copy running-config startup-config** command and then issue the **reload** command to save your configuration changes.

To access and list the ROM monitor configuration commands, use the following commands:

Step	Command	Purpose
1	**reload** Press the Break key during the first 60 seconds while the system is booting.	Enters ROM monitor mode from privileged EXEC mode.
2	**?**	Lists the ROM monitor commands.

The ROM monitor prompt is the angle bracket (>):

```
> ?
$ state      Toggle cache state (? for help)
B [filename] [TFTP Server IP address ¦ TFTP Server Name]
             Load and execute system image from ROM or from TFTP server
C [address]  Continue execution [optional address]
D /S M L V   Deposit value V of size S into location L with modifier M
E /S M L     Examine location L with size S with modifier M
G [address]  Begin execution
H            Help for commands
I            Initialize
K            Stack trace
L [filename] [TFTP Server IP address ¦ TFTP Server Name]
             Load system image from ROM or from TFTP server, but do not
             begin execution
O            Show configuration register option settings
P            Set the break point
S            Single step next instruction
T function   Test device (? for help)
Deposit and Examine sizes may be B (byte), L (long) or S (short).
Modifiers may be R (register) or S (byte swap).
Register names are: D0-D7, A0-A6, SS, US, SR, and PC
```

To return to user EXEC mode, type **continue**. To initialize the router or access server, enter the **i** command. The **i** command causes the bootstrap program to reinitialize the hardware, clear the contents of memory, and boot the system. (It is best to issue the **i** command before you run any tests or boot software.) To boot the system image file, use the **b** command (see Chapter 19, "Rebooting a Router"). For details on ROM monitor mode commands, refer to the appropriate hardware installation guide.

Summary of Basic Command Modes

Table 1-1 summarizes the main command modes of the Cisco IOS software.

Table 1-1 *Summary of Basic Command Modes*

Command Mode	Access Method	Prompt	Exit Method
User EXEC	Log in.	`Router>`	Use the **logout** command.
Privileged EXEC	From user EXEC mode, use the **enable** EXEC command.	`Router#`	To exit back to user EXEC mode, use the **disable** command. To enter global configuration mode, use the **configure terminal** privileged EXEC command.
Global configuration	From privileged EXEC mode, use the **configure terminal** privileged EXEC command.	`Router(config)#`	To exit to privileged EXEC mode, use the **exit** or **end** command or press **Ctrl-Z**. To enter interface configuration mode, enter an **interface** configuration command.
Interface configuration	From global configuration mode, enter by specifying an interface with an **interface** command.	`Router(config-if)#`	To exit to global configuration mode, use the **exit** command. To exit to privileged EXEC mode, use the **exit** command or press **Ctrl-Z**. To enter subinterface configuration mode, specify a subinterface with the **interface** command.
Subinterface configuration	From interface configuration mode, specify a subinterface with an **interface** command.	`Router(config-subif)#`	To exit to global configuration mode, use the **exit** command. To enter privileged EXEC mode, use the **end** command or press **Ctrl-Z**.
ROM monitor	From privileged EXEC mode, use the **reload** EXEC command. Press the Break key during the first 60 seconds while the system is booting.	`>`	To exit to user EXEC mode, type **continue**.

Other Configuration Modes

The following sections describe the other configuration modes:

- Access-List Configuration Mode
- APPN Command Modes
- CAS-Custom Configuration Mode
- Certificate Authorities Configuration Mode
- Certificate Chain Configuration Mode
- Controller Configuration Mode
- Crypto Map Configuration Mode
- Crypto Transform Configuration Mode
- Dial-Peer Configuration Mode
- Hex Input Mode
- Hub Configuration Mode
- IBM Channel Attach Command Modes
  - Interface Channel Configuration Mode
  - Internal LAN Configuration Mode
  - Internal Adapter Configuration Mode
- Interface-ATM-VC Configuration Mode
- IPX-Router Configuration Mode
- ISAKMP Policy Configuration Mode
- Key Chain Configuration Mode
  - Key Chain Key Configuration Mode
- LANE Database Configuration Mode
- Line Configuration Mode
- Map-Class Configuration Mode
- Map-List Configuration Mode
- Modem Pool Configuration Mode
- MPC Configuration Mode
- MPS Configuration Mode

- Poll-Group Configuration Mode
- Public Key Configuration Mode
    - Public Key Chain Configuration Mode
- Response Time Reporter Configuration Mode
- Route-Map Configuration Mode
- Router Configuration Mode
- TN3270 Server Command Modes
- VC-Class Configuration Mode
- Voice-Port Configuration Mode

Most of these modes can be entered from global configuration mode. In these modes, the **exit** command returns you to the global configuration mode. Other modes must be entered from another configuration mode. Entering the **exit** command in one of these modes returns you to the configuration mode you used to enter the mode.

In any configuration mode, to enter privileged EXEC mode and leave configuration mode entirely, use the **end** command or press **Ctrl-Z**.

Table 1-2 in the "Summary of Configuration Command Modes" section lists how to enter each mode.

Access List Configuration Mode

All IP and IPX access lists can be identified by a number. Alternatively, some IP and IPX access lists can be identified by a name. Use access-list configuration mode when you are creating a named IP or IPX access list.

APPN Command Modes

Advanced Peer-to-Peer Networking (APPN) is the second generation of SNA. APPN provides support for client/server applications and offers more dynamics than traditional hierarchical SNA, such as dynamic directory and routing services.

APPN allows you to define attributes of the APPN network that can become quite complex. To easily manage the details of APPN, special configuration command modes and conventions have been developed.

Because APPN offers a large number of configuration options, specific configuration dialogs are used for each major APPN configuration item. When you define the major item, you will automatically enter the detailed configuration mode for that item. There are two options to exit the detailed configuration mode. Use the **complete** command to exit the detailed configuration mode and update the APPN subsystem with the changes. Use the **exit** command to leave the definition in "no complete" state without updating the APPN subsystem.

- APPN Control Point Mode
- APPN Port Mode
- APPN Link Station Mode
- APPN Connection Network Mode
- APPN Class of Service Mode
- APPN Mode Configuration Mode
- APPN Partner LU Location Mode
- APPN Subsystem Mode

CAS-Custom Configuration Mode

R2 signaling is an international signaling standard common to channelized E1 networks. However, there is no single signaling standard for R2. The ITU-T Q.400-Q.490 recommendation defines R2, but a number of countries and geographic regions implement R2 in entirely different ways.

Use CAS-custom configuration mode to customize E1 R2 signaling parameters for a particular E1 channel group on a channelized E1 line. Some switches require you to fine-tune your R2 settings. However, do not tamper with these special signaling commands unless you understand exactly how your switch will be affected.

Certificate Authorities Configuration Mode

Performing the **crypto ca identity** command puts you into the ca-identity configuration mode. In this mode, you can specify characteristics for certificate authorities (CAs).

Certificate Chain Configuration Mode

The **crypto ca certificate chain** global configuration command puts you into certificate chain configuration mode. In this mode, you can delete certificates using the **certificate** command.

Controller Configuration Mode

You can configure channelized T1 in the controller configuration mode.

Crypto Map Configuration Mode

Use crypto map configuration mode to create or alter the definition of a crypto-map. Crypto-maps are part of an authentication/encryption router configuration.

Crypto Transform Configuration Mode

Using the **crypto ipsec transform-set** command puts you into crypto transform configuration mode. While in this mode, you can change the initialization vector length for the esp-rfc1829 transform, or you can change the mode to tunnel or transport.

Dial-Peer Configuration Mode

Use dial-peer configuration mode to configure dial peers for Voice over IP, Voice over ATM, Voice over Frame Relay, and Voice over HDLC.

Hex Input Mode

Use hex input mode to enter a public key for an encrypting peer router. The public key data is entered in hexadecimal form, and it will take more than one command line to enter. To continue entering the public key data on a new line, press Return. When the public key is completely entered, press Return to get a new line, then type **quit** to return to the global configuration mode.

Hub Configuration Mode

Hub configuration commands configure hub functionality for an Ethernet interface on the Cisco 2500. They always follow a **hub** global configuration command.

IBM Channel Attach Command Modes

The Channel Interface Processor (CIP) supports the IBM channel attach feature. This configuration is an ideal connectivity hub for large corporate networks that provide routing services between mainframes and LANs.

Interface Channel Configuration Mode

Before you configure your channel attach interface, you must select an interface. The following mode is valid only for port 2 on a CIP board. Ports 0 and 1 represent real, physical ports. Port 2 is an internal, virtual port.

Internal LAN Configuration Mode

Use the IBM channel internal LAN configuration mode to configure an internal LAN on a CIP interface and configure Cisco Systems Network Architecture (CSNA) parameters.

Internal Adapter Configuration Mode

Internal adapter commands allow you to configure the link characteristics for the internal LAN adapter and name the internal LAN adapter.

To configure an internal adapter interface, you must first use the bridge-group internal LAN configuration command or the source-bridge internal LAN configuration command to configure bridging type.

Interface-ATM-VC Configuration Mode

When you create an ATM PVC or SVC, you will enter the interface-ATM-VC configuration submode which allows you to configure various parameters that will apply when the VC is active.

IPX-Router Configuration Mode

Internet Packet Exchange (IPX) is a Novell network-layer protocol. The IPX-router configuration mode is used to configure IPX routing.

ISAKMP Policy Configuration Mode

When you enter the **crypto isakmp policy** command, you are put into the ISAKMP policy configuration command mode. In this mode, you can specify IKE policy parameters.

Key Chain Configuration Mode

From key chain configuration mode, you can manage authentication keys.

Key management controls the authentication keys that routing protocols use. To enter key chain configuration mode, identify or define a key chain using the **keychain** command. From key chain configuration mode, you can identify or define key numbers.

Key Chain Key Configuration Mode

Once you define a key chain, use the key chain key configuration mode to configure the keys on the key chain.

LANE Database Configuration Mode

LAN Emulation (LANE) clients consult the LANE configuration server for information such as the location of the LANE server. The configuration server looks up the configuration information in its name database.

A LANE database contains entries that bind an emulated LAN name to the ATM address of the LANE server, bind LANE client MAC addresses to an emulated LAN name, and bind LANE client ATM address templates to an emulated LAN name.

In LANE database configuration mode, you can use the **client-atm-address name**, **default name**, **mac-address name**, and **name server-atm-address** commands to create entries in the specified database.

Line Configuration Mode

Line configuration commands modify the operation of an auxiliary, console, physical, or virtual terminal line. Line configuration commands always follow a **line** command, which defines a line number. These commands are generally used to connect to remote routers or access servers, change terminal parameter settings either on a line-by-line basis or for a range of line, and set up the auxiliary port modem configuration to support dial-on-demand routing (DDR).

Map-Class Configuration Mode

Cisco IOS Frame Relay software allows you to specify parameters that control the traffic that the source router will send over a switched virtual circuit (SVC). Use the map-class configuration mode to configure these parameters.

Map-List Configuration Mode

Cisco IOS Frame Relay software supports static mapping schemes that identify the protocol addresses of remote hosts or routers. Use the map-list configuration mode to define the protocol addresses and associate each protocol address with a specific map class.

Modem Pool Configuration Mode

A modem pool is a group of modems inside an access server that are assigned a single dialed number identification service number (DNIS). After you enter modem pool configuration mode, you can create multiple pools of physical modems, assign unique DNIS numbers to each modem pool, and set maximum simultaneous connect limits.

MPC Configuration Mode

When you configure/create an MPOA client (MPC), you automatically enter the MPC configuration mode. Using the MPC configuration mode is optional. You can use the MPC configuration mode only when you need to change certain operating parameters. If you choose not to change any parameters, just exit and the default values will be used.

MPS Configuration Mode

When you configure/create an MPOA server (MPS), you automatically enter the MPS configuration mode. Using the MPS configuration mode is optional. You can use the MPS configuration mode only when you need to change certain operating parameters. If you choose not to change any parameters, just exit and the default values will be used.

Poll-Group Configuration Mode

Use the **syscon poll-group** command to enable data collection for a specific poll group. The poll-group configuration mode is required for Performance Data Collection, which allows a system controller to collect and store SNMP MIB data from its managed router and dial shelves.

You can enter any of the following commands while in poll-group configuration mode:

- **enable (poll-group configuration)**
- **oid**
- **poll-interval**
- **samples**
- **shelf-type**
- **transfer-mode**

You must specify the desired Object IDs and the transfer mode. If you do not specify the **shelf-type** command, the system controller collects data from all discovered shelves. The default data collection interval is 10 minutes. The default maximum number of samples is 10. To begin the data collection process, specify the **enable** command.

Public Key Configuration Mode

Using the **addressed-key** or **named-key** public key chain configuration commands puts you into public key configuration mode. In this mode, you can specify RSA or DSS public keys.

Public Key Chain Configuration Mode

Using the **crypto key pubkey-chain rsa** command puts you into public key chain configuration mode. In this mode, you can manually specify other IPSec peers' RSA or DSS public keys.

Response Time Reporter Configuration Mode

Use the response time reporter configuration mode to configure a probe to measure response times and availability. Refer to Chapter 23, "Monitoring the Router and Network."

Route-Map Configuration Mode

Use the route-map configuration mode to configure routing table and source and destination information.

Router Configuration Mode

Router configuration commands configure an IP routing protocol and always follow a **router** command.

TN3270 Server Command Modes

The TN3270 server provides a set of command modes. The TN3270 server can be configured only on Port 2, the internal LAN port, of a Channel Interface Processor (CIP) card.

The following are the TN3270 server command modes:

- TN3270 server configuration mode
- DLUR configuration mode
- DLUR SAP configuration mode
- PU configuration mode

VC-Class Configuration Mode

A VC class is a set of preconfigured VC parameters that you configure and apply to a particular VC or ATM interface. You may apply a VC class to an ATM main interface, subinterface, PVC or SVC. For example, you can create a VC class that contains VC parameter configurations that you will apply to a particular PVC or SVC. You might create another VC class that contains VC parameter configurations that you will apply to all VCs configured on a particular ATM main interface or subinterface.

Use VC-class configuration mode to configure a set of VC parameters that will apply to an ATM main interface, subinterface, PVC, or SVC.

Voice-Port Configuration Mode

Use voice port configuration mode to configure voice port settings on the Cisco 3600 and Cisco MC3810.

Summary of Configuration Command Modes

Table 1-2 lists the command modes, how to access and exit each mode, the prompt while in each mode, and an example of how to get to the mode. The exit method is only listed if the **exit** command does not return you to global configuration mode or you must use a different command to exit the mode. The prompts listed assume that the default device name is "Router."

Table 1-2 *Summary of Command Modes*

Command Mode	Access and Exit Method	Prompt	Example

Access list configuration	From global configuration mode, use the **ip access-list** or **ipx access-list** command. **ip access-list {standard | extended}** *name*
	
	 or
	
	 ipx access-list {standard | extended | sap | summary} *name*
		`Router(config-std-nacl)#`
		 or
		 `Router(config-ext-nacl)#`
			`Router(config)# ip` `access-list` `extended flag`
			
			 `Router(config-ext-nacl)#`

APPN configuration	From global configuration mode, use the **appn mode** command.	`Router(appn)#`	`Router(config)#` `appn mode` `Router(appn)#`
Ca-identity configuration	From global configuration mode, use the **crypto ca identity** command.	`Router(ca-identity)#`	`Router(config)#` `crypto ca identity` `Router(ca-identity)#`

CAS-custom configuration	From controller E1 configuration mode, use the **cas-custom** *channel* command.	`Router(config-ctrl-cas)#`	`Router(config-controller)# cas-custom 1`
			 `router(config-ctrl-cas)# ?`
			 `CAS custom commands:`
			 `  ani-digits`
			 `  answer-signal`
			 `  caller-digits`
			 `  ...`

Continues

Table 1-2 *Summary of Command Modes (Continued)*

Command Mode	Access and Exit Method	Prompt	Example
Certificate chain configuration	From global configuration mode, use the **crypto ca certificate** chain command.	`Router(config-cert-chain)#`	`Router(config)#` **`crypto ca certificate`** `Router(config-cert-chain)#`
Controller configuration	From global configuration mode, use the **controller t1** *slot/port* command to configure a channelized T1 interface.	`Router(config-controller)#`	`Router(config)#` **`controller t1 0/0`** `Router(config-controller)#`
Crypto map configuration	From global configuration mode, use the **crypto map** *map-name* [*seq-num*] command.	`Router(config-crypto-map)#`	`Router(config)#` **`crypto map Research 10`** `Router(config-crypto-map)#`
Crypto transform configuration	From global configuration mode, use the **crypto ipsec transform-set** command.	`Router(config-crypto-trans)#`	`Router(config)#` **`crypto ipsec transform-set`** `Router(config-crypto-trans)#`
Dial peer voice configuration	From global configuration mode, use the **dial peer voice** *tag* {**pots** | **voip** | **vofr**|**voatm**|**vohdlc**} command.	`Router(config-dialpeer)#`	`Router(config)#` **`dial peer voice 1 pots`** `Router(config-dialpeer)#`

Hex input	From global configuration mode, use the **crypto public-key** command. **crypto public-key** *key-name serial-number*
	
	 To exit hex input mode, use the **quit** command.
		`Router(config-pubkey)#`	`Router(config)#` **`crypto public-key BananaCryptoEngine 01709644`**
			
			 `Enter a public key as a hexadecimal number ....`
			
			 `Router(config-pubkey)#` **`C31260F4 BD8A5ACE 2C1B1E6C 8B0ABD27 01493A50`**
			
			 `Router(config-pubkey)#` **`A6A66946`**
			
			 `Router(config-pubkey)#` **`quit`**
			
			 `Router(config)#`

Table 1-2 *Summary of Command Modes (Continued)*

Command Mode	Access and Exit Method	Prompt	Example
Hub configuration	From global configuration mode, enter by specifying a hub with the **hub** *number port* [*port*] command.	`Router(config-hub)#`	`Router(config)#` **hub ethernet 0 1 3** `Router(config-hub)#`
Interface-ATM-VC configuration	From interface configuration mode, use the **pvc** *vpi/vci* or **svc nsap** *address* command.	`Router(config-if-atm-vc)#`	`Router(config-if)#` **pvc 0/33** `Router(config-if-atm-vc)#` or `Router(config-if)#` **svc nsap AB.CDEF.01.234567. 890A.BCDE.F012.345 6.7890.1234.12** `Router(config-if-atm-vc)#`
Interface channel configuration	From global configuration mode, use the **interface channel** *slot/port* command.	`Router(config)#`	`Router(config)#` **interface channel 0/1** `Router(config)#`
Internal LAN configuration	From interface configuration mode, use the **lan [ethernet	tokenring	fddi]** *lan-id* command. To exit to interface configuration mode, use the **exit** command.	`Router(config-if)#`	`Router(config)#` **lan ethernet 10** `Router(cfg-lan-Ether 10)#`
Internal adapter configuration	From internal LAN configuration mode, enter the **adapter** *adapter-number mac-address* command. To exit to Internal LAN configuration mode, use the **exit** command.	`Router(config-lan)#`	`Router(config)#` **lan ethernet 10** `Router(cfg-lan-Ether 10)#` **adapter 1 4.5.6** `Router(cfg-adap-Ether 10-1)#`

Continues

Table 1-2 *Summary of Command Modes (Continued)*

Command Mode	Access and Exit Method	Prompt	Example
IPX-router configuration	From global configuration mode, enter by issuing the **ipx routing** command, then a command that begins with **ipx router** (such as **ipx router eigrp**). **ipx router** {**eigrp** *autonomous-system-number* | **nlsp** [*tag*] | **rip**}	`Router(config-ipx-router)#`	`Router(config)#` **ipx router rip** `Router(config-ipx-router)#`
ISAKMP policy configuration	From global configuration mode, use the **crypto isakmp policy** command.	`Router(config-isakmp)#`	`Router(config)#` **crypto isakmp policy** `Router(config-isakmp)#`
Key chain configuration	From global configuration mode, use the **keychain** command. **keychain** *name-of-chain*	`Router(config-keychain)#`	`Router(config)#` **keychain blue** `Router(config-keychain)#`
Key chain key configuration	From key chain configuration mode, use the **key** *number* command. To exit to key chain configuration mode, use the **exit** command.	`Router(config-keychain-key)#`	`Router(config)#` **keychain blue** `Router(config-keychain)#` **key 10** `Router(config-keychain-key)#`
LANE database configuration	From global configuration mode, use the **lane database** command. **lane database** [*database-name*]	`Router(lane-config-datab)#`	`Router(config)#` **lane database red** `Router(lane-config-datab)#`
Line configuration	From global configuration mode, enter by specifying a line with a **line** {**aux** | **con** | **tty** | **vty**} *line-number* [*ending-line-number*] command.	`Router(config-line)#`	`Router(config)#` **line vty 0 4** `Router(config-line)#`
Map-class configuration	From global configuration mode, configure a map class with the **map-class** *encapsulation class-name* command.	`Router(config-map-class)#`	`Router(config)#` **map-class atm aaa** `Router(config-map-class)#`

Table 1-2 *Summary of Command Modes (Continued)*

Command Mode	Access and Exit Method	Prompt	Example
Map-list configuration	From global configuration mode, define a map list with the **map-list** *name* command.	`Router(config-map-list)#`	`Router(config)#` **`map-list atm`** `Router(config-map-list)#`
Modem pool configuration	From global configuration mode, use the **modem-pool** *name* command.	`Router(config-modem-pool)#`	`Router(config)#` **`modem-pool v90service`** `Router(config-modem-pool)#` **`pool-range 30-50`** `Router(config-modem-pool)#` **`called-number 2000`** `Router(config-modem-pool)#` **`exit`** `Router(config)`
MPC configuration mode	From global configuration mode, use the **mpoa client config name** command.	`Router(config)#`	`Router(config)#` **`mpoa client config name`** *ip_mpc* `Router(mpoa-client-config)#`
MPS configuration mode	From global configuration mode, use the **mpoa server config name** command.	`Router(config)#`	`Router(config)#` **`mpoa server config name`** *ip_mps* `Router(mpoa-server-config)#`
Poll-group configuration	From global configuration mode, enter poll-group configuration mode with the **syscon poll-group** command.	`Router(config-poll-gr)#`	`Router(config)#` **`syscon poll-group cmlineinfo`** `Router(config-poll-gr)#`
Public key configuration	Using the **addressed-key** or **named-key** public key chain configuration commands puts you into public key configuration mode. In this mode, you can specify RSA or DSS public keys.	`Router(config-pubkey)#`	`Router(config)#` **`addressed-key`** `Router(config-pubkey)#`

Continues

Table 1-2 *Summary of Command Modes (Continued)*

Command Mode	Access and Exit Method	Prompt	Example
Public key chain configuration	From global configuration mode, enter public key chain configuration mode with the **crypto key pubkey-chain rsa** command.	`Router(config-pubkey-key)#`	`Router(config)#` **`crypto key pubkey-chain rsa`** `Router(config-pubkey-key)#`
Response time reporter configuration	From global configuration mode, use the **rtr** command, **rtr** *probe*.	`Router(config-rtr)#`	`Router(config)#` **`rtr 1`** `Router(config-rtr)#`
Route-map configuration	From global configuration mode, enter by specifying the **route-map** [*map-tag*] command.	`Router(config-route-map)#`	`Router(config)#` **`route-map arizona`** `Router(config-route-map)#`
Router configuration	From global configuration mode, enter by issuing the **router** [*keyword*] command (such as **router igrp**).	`Router(config-router)#`	`Router(config)#` **`router rip`** `Router(config-router)#`
TN3270 server configuration	From interface configuration mode, use the **tn3270-server** command. To exit to interface configuration mode, use the **exit** command.	`Router(tn3270-server)#`	`Router(config)#` **`tn3270-server`** `Router(tn3270-server)#`
DLUR configuration	From TN3270 configuration mode, use the **dlur** command. To exit to TN3270 configuration mode, use the **exit** command.	`Router(tn3270-dlur)#`	`Router(config)#` **`tn3270-server`** `Router(tn3270-server)#` **`dlur`** `Router(tn3270-dlur)#`

Table 1-2 *Summary of Command Modes (Continued)*

Command Mode	Access and Exit Method	Prompt	Example
DLUR SAP configuration	From DLUR configuration mode, use the **lsap** command. To exit to DLUR configuration mode, use the **exit** command.	`Router(tn3270-dlur-sap)#`	`Router(config)#` **tn3270-server** `Router(tn3270-server)#` **dlur** `Router(tn3270-dlur)#` **lsap** `Router(tn3270-dlur-sap)#`
PU configuration	From TN3270 server configuration mode or from DLUR configuration mode, use the **PU** command. To exit PU configuration mode, use the **exit** command.	`Router(tn3270-pu)#` `Router(tn3270-dlur-pu)#`	`Router(config)#` **tn3270-server** `Router(tn3270-server)#` **pu PU1 05d00001 10.0.0.1 token-adapter 1 8 rmac 4000.0000.0001 rsap 4** `Router(tn3270-pu)#`
VC-class configuration	From interface configuration mode, use the **vc-class atm** *name* command.	`Router(config-vc-class)#`	`Router(config-if)#` **vc-class atm pvc1** `Router(config-vc-class)#`
Voice-port configuration	From global configuration mode, enter by issuing the **voice port** *slot/sub-unit/port* command for the Cisco 3600 series, or **voice port** *slot/port* for the Cisco MC3810.	`Router(config-voiceport)#`	`Router(config)#` **voice port 1/1/2** `Router(config-voiceport)`

Using the No and Default Forms of Commands

Almost every configuration command has a **no** form. In general, use the **no** form to disable a feature or function. Use the command without the keyword **no** to reenable a disabled feature or to enable a feature that is disabled by default. For example, IP routing is enabled by default. To disable IP routing, specify the **no ip routing** command and specify **ip routing** to reenable it. The Cisco IOS software command reference*s* provides the complete syntax for the configuration commands and describes what the **no** form of a command does.

Configuration commands can also have a **default** form. The **default** form of a command returns the command setting to its default. Most commands are disabled by default, so the **default** form is the same as the **no** form. However, some commands are enabled by default and have variables set to certain default values. In these cases, the **default** command enables the command and sets variables to their default values. The Cisco IOS software command reference*s* describe what the **default** form of a command does if the command is not the same as the **no** form.

Get Context-Sensitive Help

Entering a question mark (**?**) at the system prompt displays a list of commands available for each command mode. You can also get a list of any command's associated keywords and arguments with the context-sensitive help feature.

To get help specific to a command mode, a command, a keyword, or an argument, perform one of the following commands:

Step	Command	Purpose
1	**help**	Obtains a brief description of the help system in any command mode.
2	*abbreviated-command-entry***?**	Obtains a list of commands that begin with a particular character string.
3	*abbreviated-command-entry*<**Tab**>	Completes a partial command name.
4	**?**	Lists all commands available for a particular command mode.
5	*command* **?**	Lists a command's associated keywords.
6	*command keyword* **?**	Lists a keyword's associated arguments.

When using context-sensitive help, the space (or lack of a space) before the **?** is significant. To obtain a list of commands that begin with a particular character sequence, type in those characters followed immediately by the **?**. Do not include a space. This form of help is called *word help*, because it completes a word for you.

To list keywords or arguments, enter a **?** in place of a keyword or argument. Include a space before the **?**. This form of help is called *command syntax help*, because it reminds you which keywords or arguments are applicable based on the command, keywords, and arguments you already have entered.

You can abbreviate commands and keywords to the number of characters that allow a unique abbreviation. For example, you can abbreviate the **show** command to **sh**.

Enter the **help** command (which is available in any command mode) for a brief description of the help system:

```
Router# help
Help may be requested at any point in a command by entering
a question mark '?'. If nothing matches, the help list will
be empty and you must back up until entering a '?' shows the
available options.
```

```
Two styles of help are provided:
1. Full help is available when you are ready to enter a
   command argument (e.g. 'show ?') and describes each possible
   argument.
2. Partial help is provided when an abbreviated argument is entered
   and you want to know what arguments match the input
   (e.g. 'show pr?').
```

As described in the **help** command output, you can enter a partial command name and a **?** to obtain a list of commands beginning with a particular character set. (See the section "Complete a Partial Command Name" later in this chapter for more details.)

Example of Context-Sensitive Help

The following example illustrates how the context-sensitive help feature enables you to create an access list from configuration mode.

Enter the letters **co** at the system prompt followed by a question mark (**?**). Do not leave a space between the last letter and the **?**. The system provides the commands that begin with **co**.

```
Router# co?
configure  connect  copy
```

Enter the **configure** command followed by a space and a **?** to list the command's keywords and a brief explanation:

```
Router# configure ?
  memory    Configure from NV memory
  network   Configure from a TFTP network host
  terminal  Configure from the terminal
  <cr>
```

Enter the **terminal** keyword to enter configuration mode from the terminal:

```
Router# configure terminal
Enter configuration commands, one per line. End with Ctrl-Z.
Router(config)#
```

Enter the **access-list** command followed by a space and a **?** to list the command's keywords:

```
Router(config)# access-list ?
  <1-99>       IP standard access list
  <100-199>    IP extended access list
  <1000-1099>  IPX SAP access list
  <1100-1199>  Extended 48-bit MAC address access list
  <200-299>    Protocol type-code access list
  <300-399>    DECnet access list
  <400-499>    XNS standard access list
  <500-599>    XNS extended access list
  <600-699>    Appletalk access list
  <700-799>    48-bit MAC address access list
```

```
<800-899>    IPX standard access list
<900-999>    IPX extended access list
```

The two numbers within the angle brackets represent an inclusive range. Enter the access list number **99** and then enter another **?** to see the arguments that apply to the keyword and their brief explanations:

```
Router(config)# access-list 99 ?
  deny    Specify packets to reject
  permit  Specify packets to forward
```

Enter the **deny** argument followed by a **?** to list additional options:

```
Router(config)# access-list 99 deny ?
  A.B.C.D  Address to match
```

Generally, uppercase letters represent variables, though this is not always the case. Enter the IP address followed by a **?** to list additional options:

```
Router(config)# access-list 99 deny 131.108.134.0 ?
  A.B.C.D  Mask of bits to ignore
  <cr>
```

The <cr> symbol appears in the list to indicate that one of your options is to press Return to execute the command.

The other option is to add a wildcard mask. Enter the wildcard mask followed by a **?** to list further options.

```
Router(config)# access-list 99 deny 131.108.134.0 0.0.0.255 ?
<cr>

Router(config)# access-list 99 deny 131.108.134.0 0.0.0.255
```

The <cr> symbol by itself indicates there are no more keywords or arguments. Press Return to execute the command. The system adds an entry to access list 99 that denies access to all hosts on subnet 131.108.134.0.

Display Help for All User-Level Commands

To configure a line to display help for the full set of user-level commands during all sessions, use the following commands in line configuration mode:

Command	Purpose
full-help	Configures a line or lines to receive help for the full set of user-level commands when a user presses **?**.

To configure the current session to display help for the full set of user-level commands, use the following command in user **exec** mode:

Command	Purpose
terminal full-help	Configures this session to provide help for the full set of user-level commands.

The **full-help** and **terminal full-help** commands enable (or disable) a display of all help messages available from the terminal. They are used with the **show** command.

The following example is output for **show ?** with **terminal full-help** disabled and then enabled:

```
Router> show ?
  bootflash  Boot Flash information
  calendar   Display the hardware calendar
  clock      Display the system clock
  context    Show context information
  dialer     Dialer parameters and statistics
  history    Display the session command history
  hosts      IP domain-name, lookup style, nameservers, and host table
  isdn       ISDN information
  kerberos   Show Kerberos Values
  modemcap   Show Modem Capabilities database
  ppp        PPP parameters and statistics
  rmon       rmon statistics
  sessions   Information about Telnet connections
  snmp       snmp statistics
  terminal   Display terminal configuration parameters
  users      Display information about terminal lines
  version    System hardware and software status

Router> terminal full-help
Router> show ?
  access-expression  List access expression
  access-lists       List access lists
  aliases            Display alias commands
  apollo             Apollo network information
  appletalk          AppleTalk information
  arp                ARP table
  async              Information on terminal lines used as router interfaces
  bootflash          Boot Flash information
  bridge             Bridge Forwarding/Filtering Database [verbose]
  bsc                BSC interface information
  bstun              BSTUN interface information
  buffers            Buffer pool statistics
  calendar           Display the hardware calendar
  cdp                CDP information
  clns               CLNS network information
  clock              Display the system clock
  cls                DLC user information
  cmns               Connection-Mode networking services (CMNS) information
  ...
```

```
x25              X.25 information
xns              XNS information
xremote          XRemote statistics
```

Check Command Syntax

The user interface provides error isolation in the form of an error indicator, a caret symbol (^). The ^ symbol appears at the point in the command string where you have entered an incorrect command, keyword, or argument.

In the following example, suppose you want to set the clock. Use context-sensitive help to check the syntax for setting the clock.

```
Router# clock ?
  set  Set the time and date
Router# clock
```

The help output shows that the **set** keyword is required. Check the syntax for entering the time:

```
Router# clock set ?
hh:mm:ss   Current time
Router# clock set
```

Enter the current time:

```
Router# clock set 13:32:00
% Incomplete command.
```

The system indicates that you need to provide additional arguments to complete the command. Press ·**Ctrl-P** (see the next section, "Use the Command History Features") to automatically repeat the previous command entry. Then add a space and question mark (**?**) to reveal the additional arguments:

```
Router# clock set 13:32:00 ?
  <1-31>     Day of the month
  January    Month of the year
  February
  March
  April
  May
  June
  July
  August
  September
  October
  November
  December
```

Now you can complete the command entry:

```
Router# clock set 13:32:00 23 February 97
                                    ^
% Invalid input detected at '^' marker.
```

The ^ and help response indicate an error at 97. To list the correct syntax, enter the command up to the point where the error occurred and then enter a **?**:

```
Router# clock set 13:32:00 23 February ?
  <1993-2035> Year
Router# clock set 13:32:00 23 February
```

Enter the year using the correct syntax and press Return to execute the command.

```
Router# clock set 13:32:00 23 February 1997
```

Use the Command History Features

With the current Cisco IOS release, the user interface provides a history or record of commands that you have entered. This feature is particularly useful for recalling long or complex commands or entries, including access lists. With the command history feature, you can complete the tasks in the following sections:

● Set the Command History Buffer Size

● Recall Commands

● Disable the Command History Feature

Set the Command History Buffer Size

By default, the system records 10 command lines in its history buffer. To set the number of command lines that the system will record during the current terminal session, use the following command in EXEC mode:

Command	Purpose
terminal history [**size** *number-of-lines*]	Enables the command history feature for the current terminal session.

The **terminal no history size** command resets the number of lines saved in the history buffer to the default of 10 lines.

To configure the number of command lines the system will record for all sessions on a particular line, use the following command in line configuration mode:

Command	Purpose
history [**size** *number-of-lines*][1]	Enables the command history feature.

1. The **no history** command turns off command history for the line.

Recall Commands

To recall commands from the history buffer, use one of the following commands:

Command	Purpose
Press **Ctrl-P** or the up arrow key.[1]	Recalls commands in the history buffer, beginning with the most recent command. Repeat the key sequence to recall successively older commands.
Press **Ctrl-N** or the down arrow key.[1]	Returns to more recent commands in the history buffer after recalling commands with Ctrl-P or the up arrow key. Repeat the key sequence to recall successively more recent commands.
show history	While in EXEC mode, it lists the last several commands you have just entered.

1. The arrow keys function only on ANSI-compatible terminals such as VT100s.

Disable the Command History Feature

The command history feature is automatically enabled. To disable it during the current terminal session, use the following EXEC mode command:

Command	Purpose
terminal no history	Disables the command history feature for the current session.

To configure a specific line so that the command history feature is disabled, use the following command in line configuration mode:

Command	Purpose
no history	Configures the line so that the command history feature is disabled.

Use the Editing Features

The current software release includes an enhanced editing mode that provides a set of editing key functions similar to those of the emacs editor.

You can enter commands in uppercase, lowercase, or mixed case. Only passwords are case sensitive. You can abbreviate commands and keywords to the number of characters that allow a unique abbreviation. For example, you can abbreviate the **show** command to **sh**. After entering the command line at the system prompt, press the Return key to execute the command.

The following subsections are included in this section:

● Enable Enhanced Editing Mode

● Move Around on the Command Line

● Complete a Partial Command Name

● Paste in Buffer Entries

● Edit Command Lines that Wrap

● Delete Entries

● Scroll Down a Line or a Screen

● Redisplay the Current Command Line

● Transpose Mistyped Characters

● Control Capitalization

● Designate a Keystroke as a Command Entry

● Disable Enhanced Editing Mode

Enable Enhanced Editing Mode

Although enhanced editing mode is automatically enabled with the current Cisco IOS release, you can disable it and revert to the editing mode of previous Cisco IOS releases. (See the section "Disable Enhanced Editing Mode" later in this chapter.)

To re-enable the enhanced editing mode for the current terminal session, use the following command in EXEC mode:

Command	Purpose
terminal editing	Enables the enhanced editing features for the current terminal session.

To reconfigure a specific line to have enhanced editing mode, use the following command in line configuration mode:

Command	Purpose
editing	Enables the enhanced editing features.

Move Around on the Command Line

Use the following commands to move the cursor around on the command line to make corrections or changes:

Step	Keystrokes	Purpose
1	Press **Ctrl-B** or press the left arrow key.[1]	Moves the cursor back one character.
2	Press **Ctrl-F** or press the right arrow key.[1]	Moves the cursor forward one character.
3	Press **Ctrl-A**.	Moves the cursor to the beginning of the command line.
4	Press **Ctrl-E**.	Moves the cursor to the end of the command line.
5	Press **Esc B**.	Moves the cursor back one word.
6	Press **Esc F**.	Moves the cursor forward one word.

1. The arrow keys function only on ANSI-compatible terminals such as VT100s.

Complete a Partial Command Name

If you cannot remember a complete command name, press the Tab key to allow the system to complete a partial entry. To do so, use the following command:

Keystrokes	Purpose
Enter the first few letters and press the Tab key.	Completes a command name.

If your keyboard does not have a Tab key, press **Ctrl-I** instead.

In the following example, when you enter the letters **conf** and press the Tab key, the system provides the complete command:

```
Router# conf<Tab>
Router# configure
```

If you enter a set of characters that could indicate more than one command, the system beeps to indicate an error. Enter a question mark (**?**) to obtain a list of commands that begin with that set of characters. Do not leave a space between the last letter you enter and the **?**.

For example, there are three commands in privileged mode that start with co. To see what they are, type **co?** at the privileged EXEC prompt:

```
Router# co?
configure  connect  copy
Router# co
```

Paste in Buffer Entries

The system provides a buffer that contains the last 10 items you deleted. To recall these items and paste them in the command line, use the following commands:

Step	Keystrokes	Purpose
1	Press **Ctrl-Y**.	Recalls the most recent entry in the buffer.
2	Press **Esc Y**.	Recalls the next buffer entry.

The buffer contains only the last 10 items you have deleted or cut. If you press **Esc Y** more than 10 times, you will cycle back to the first buffer entry.

Edit Command Lines that Wrap

The new editing command set provides a wraparound feature for commands that extend beyond a single line on the screen. When the cursor reaches the right margin, the command line shifts 10 spaces to the left. You cannot see the first 10 characters of the line, but you can scroll back and check the syntax at the beginning of the command. To scroll back, use the following command:

Keystrokes	Purpose
Press **Ctrl-B** or the left arrow key repeatedly until you scroll back to the beginning of the command entry, or press **Ctrl-A** to return directly to the beginning of the line.[1]	Returns to the beginning of a command line to verify that you have entered a lengthy command correctly.

1. The arrow keys function only on ANSI-compatible terminals such as VT100s.

In the following example, the **access-list** command entry extends beyond one line. When the cursor first reaches the end of the line, the line is shifted 10 spaces to the left and redisplayed. The dollar sign ($) indicates that the line has been scrolled to the left. Each time the cursor reaches the end of the line, the line is again shifted 10 spaces to the left.

```
Router(config)# access-list 101 permit tcp 131.108.2.5 255.255.255.0 131.108.1
Router(config)# $ 101 permit tcp 131.108.2.5 255.255.255.0 131.108.1.20 255.25
Router(config)# $t tcp 131.108.2.5 255.255.255.0 131.108.1.20 255.255.255.0 eq
Router(config)# $108.2.5 255.255.255.0 131.108.1.20 255.255.255.0 eq 45
```

When you have completed the entry, press **Ctrl-A** to check the complete syntax before pressing the Return key to execute the command. The $ appears at the end of the line to indicate that the line has been scrolled to the right:

```
Router(config)# access-list 101 permit tcp 131.108.2.5 255.255.255.0 131.108.1$
```

The Cisco IOS software assumes you have a terminal screen that is 80 columns wide. If you have a width other than that, use the **terminal width** command to set the width of your terminal.

Use line wrapping in conjunction with the command history feature to recall and modify previous complex command entries. See the section "Recall Commands" in this chapter for information about recalling previous command entries.

Delete Entries

Use any of the following commands to delete command entries if you make a mistake or change your mind:

Keystrokes	Purpose
Press the Delete or Backspace key.	Erases the character to the left of the cursor.
Press **Ctrl-D**.	Deletes the character at the cursor.
Press **Ctrl-K**.	Deletes all characters from the cursor to the end of the command line.
Press **Ctrl-U** or **Ctrl-X**.	Deletes all characters from the cursor to the beginning of the command line.
Press **Ctrl-W**.	Deletes the word to the left of the cursor.
Press **Esc D**.	Deletes from the cursor to the end of the word.

Scroll Down a Line or a Screen

When you use the help facility to list the commands available in a particular mode, the list is often longer than the terminal screen can display. In such cases, a More prompt is displayed at the bottom of the screen, assuming that the **length** or **terminal length** command is configured correctly. To view the next line or screen, use the following commands:

Keystrokes	Purpose
Press the Return key.	Scrolls down one line.
Press the Space bar.	Scrolls down one screen.

NOTE   The More prompt is used for any output that has more lines than can be displayed on the terminal screen, including **show** command output. You can use the keystrokes listed above whenever you see the More prompt.

Redisplay the Current Command Line

If you are entering a command and the system suddenly sends a message to your screen, you can easily recall your current command line entry. To do so, use the following command:

Keystrokes	Purpose
Press **Ctrl-L** or **Ctrl-R**.	Redisplays the current command line.

Transpose Mistyped Characters

If you have mistyped a command entry, you can transpose the mistyped characters by using the following command:

Keystrokes	Purpose
Press **Ctrl-T**.	Transposes the character to the left of the cursor with the character located at the cursor.

Control Capitalization

You can capitalize or lowercase words or capitalize a set of letters with simple keystroke sequences. To do so, use the following commands:

Keystrokes	Purpose
Press **Esc C**.	Capitalizes at the cursor.
Press **Esc L**.	Changes the word at the cursor to lowercase.
Press **Esc U**.	Capitalizes letters from the cursor to the end of the word.

Designate a Keystroke as a Command Entry

Sometimes you might want to use a particular keystroke as an executable command, perhaps as a shortcut. Use the following keystroke to insert a system code for this purpose:

Keystrokes
Press **Ctrl-V** or **Esc Q**.

Disable Enhanced Editing Mode

To globally disable enhanced editing mode and revert to the editing mode of previous software releases, use the following command in line configuration mode:

Command	Purpose
no editing	Disables the enhanced editing features for a particular line.

To disable enhanced editing mode and revert to the editing mode of software releases before Cisco IOS release 9.21 for the current terminal session, use the following command in EXEC mode:

Command	Purpose
terminal no editing	Disables the enhanced editing features for the local line.

For example, you might disable enhanced editing if you have prebuilt scripts that conflict when enhanced editing is enabled. You can re-enable enhanced editing mode with the **editing** command or **terminal editing** command.

The editing keys and functions of software releases before 9.21 are listed in Table 1-3.

Table 1-3 *Editing Keys and Functions for Software Release 9.21 and Earlier*

Key	Function
Delete or Backspace	Erases the character to the left of the cursor.
Ctrl-W	Erases a word.
Ctrl-U	Erases a line.
Ctrl-R	Redisplays a line.
Ctrl-Z	Ends configuration mode and returns to the EXEC prompt.
Return	Executes single-line commands.

Use the Cisco Web Browser Interface to Issue Commands

You can issue most of the Cisco IOS commands using a Web browser. This Cisco IOS feature is accessed by using the Cisco Web browser interface, which is accessed from the router's home page. (All Cisco routers and access servers loaded with the latest version of Cisco IOS software have a home page, which is password protected.)

From the router's home page, you click on a hypertext link titled "Monitor the Router." This link takes you to a Web page that has a "Command" field. You can type commands in this field as if you were entering commands at a terminal connected to the router. The page also displays a list of commands. You can execute these commands by clicking on them, as if you were clicking on hypertext links.

Cisco Web Browser Interface Task List

To use the Cisco Web browser interface to issue commands, use the tasks in the following sections:

● Configure the Cisco Web Browser Interface

● Use the Correct Hardware and Software

● Access Your Router's Home Page

● Issue Commands Using the Cisco Web Browser Interface

  — Enter Commands Using Hypertext Links

  — Enter Commands Using the Command Field

  — Enter Commands Using the URL Window

Configure the Cisco Web Browser Interface

You can enable the Cisco Web browser interface on any router running Cisco IOS Release 11.0(6) or later software. Once enabled, you will be able to issue Cisco IOS commands to your router using a Web browser.

The Web browser interface is automatically enabled when you use ClickStart to configure a Cisco 1003, Cisco 1004, or Cisco 1005 router.

If you have any other Cisco router, you must enable the Web browser interface by altering the routers' configuration. To do this, use the tasks in the following list. The first task is required; the remaining are optional.

● Enable the Cisco Web Browser Interface

● Change the Cisco Web Browser Interface Port Number

● Control Access to the Cisco Web Browser Interface

● Specify the Method for User Authentication

Enable the Cisco Web Browser Interface

To enable a Cisco router to be configured from a browser using the Cisco Web browser interface, use the following command in global configuration mode:

Command	Purpose
ip http server	Enables a router to be reconfigured using the Cisco Web browser interface.

Now that the Cisco Web browser interface is enabled, you can use any of the optional tasks or proceed to configure a router using the Cisco Web browser interface.

Change the Cisco Web Browser Interface Port Number

By default, the Cisco Web browser interface uses port 80 on the router. To assign the Cisco Web browser interface to a different port, use the following command in global configuration mode:

Command	Purpose
ip http port *number*	Assigns a port number to be used by the Cisco Web browser interface.

Control Access to the Cisco Web Browser Interface

To control which hosts can access the http server used by the Cisco Web browser interface, use the following command in global configuration mode:

Command	Purpose
ip http access-class {*access-list-number* | *name*}	Controls access to the http server used by the Cisco Web browser interface.

Specify the Method for User Authentication

To specify how HTTP server users are authenticated, use the following command in global configuration mode:

Command	Purpose
ip http authentication {**aaa** | **enable** | **local** | **tacacs**}	Specifies how HTTP server users are authenticated.

Use the Correct Hardware and Software

To use the Cisco Web browser interface, your computer must have a World Wide Web browser. The Cisco Web browser interface works with most browsers, including Netscape Navigator. Your Web browser must be able read and submit forms. The original versions of Mosaic might have problems using the Cisco Web browser interface, because they either cannot submit forms or have difficulty doing so.

The computer must be connected to the same network that the router or access server is on.

Access Your Router's Home Page

Cisco IOS Release 11.0(6) or later software allows users with a default privilege level of 15 to access a predefined home page for a router or access server. If you have been assigned a privilege level other than 15, Cisco IOS Release 11.3 or later software allows you to issue Cisco IOS commands from a Web page where the commands defined for your specific user privilege level will be displayed.

To access the home page for your router or access server with a default privilege level of 15, use the following steps:

Step 1   Enter the following command in the URL field of your Web browser and press Return: **http://***router-name*/. (For example, to access a Cisco router named *cacophony* with a default privilege level of 15, type http://cacophony/.) The browser then prompts you for the password.

Step 2   Enter the password.

NOTE   The name and password for your router and access server are designated in their configuration. Contact your network administrator if you do not have this information.

The browser should display the home page for your router or access server.

The router's home page looks something like the Cisco 7200 home page shown in Figure 1-1.

Figure 1-1   *Example of a Home Page for a Cisco 7200*

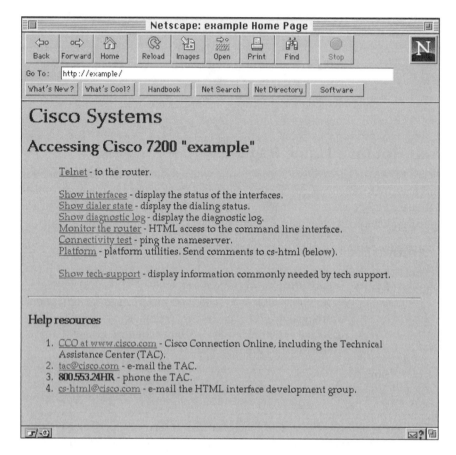

To access a router Web page for a preassigned privilege level other than the default of 15, use the following steps:

        Step 1   Enter the following command in the URL field of your Web browser and press Return: **http://***router-name***/level/***level***/ ***mode***/***command***. (For example, to request a user privilege level of 12 on a Cisco router named *cacophony*, type http:// cacophony/level/12/exec).The browser then prompts you for the username and/or password.

        Step 2   Depending on your authentication method, enter your username and/or password and press Return. The Web browser should display a Web page specific to your user privilege level, mode, and the command you have requested.

Table 1-4 lists the URL arguments you must use when requesting a Web page.

Table 1-4   *Description of the URL Arguments*

Argument	Description
router-name	The name of the router being configured.
level	The privilege level you are requesting.
mode	The mode the command will be executed in, such as exec, configure, and interface.
command	(Optional) The command you want to execute. If you specify a command, your browser will display a Web page showing the results of the requested command. If you do not specify a command in the URL, your browser will display a Web page listing all of the commands available for your privilege level.

Issue Commands Using the Cisco Web Browser Interface

To issue commands using the Cisco Web browser interface, click the link "Monitor the router" in the first list of hypertext links on the home page. This displays the Web page shown in Figure 1-2.

Figure 1-2 *The "Command" Field Web Page for a Router Named "example"*

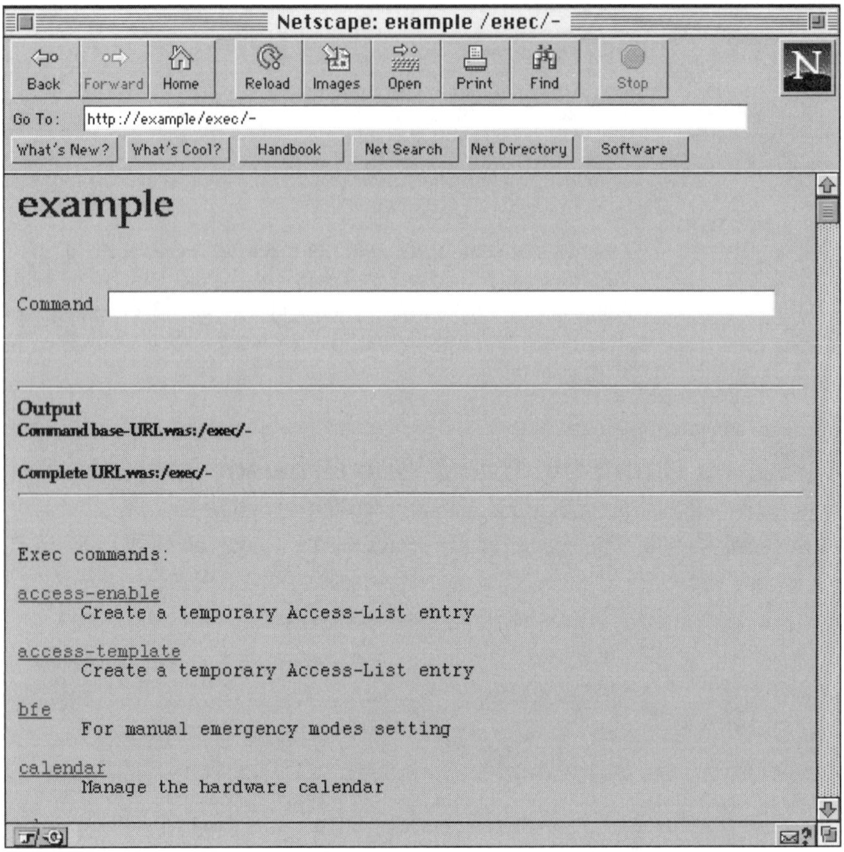

Enter Commands Using Hypertext Links

To enter a command using hypertext links, scroll through the commands listed at the bottom of the screen and click the one you want to execute. If the link is a complete command, it is executed. If the command has more parameters, another list of command hypertext links is displayed. Scroll through this second list and click the one you want to execute.

If the command is a request for information, like a **show** command, the information is displayed in the Web browser window.

If the command requires a variable, a form in which you can enter the variable is displayed.

Enter Commands Using the Command Field

Entering the command in the command field is just like entering it at a terminal console. Enter the command using the syntax documented in the Cisco IOS command reference. If you are uncertain of the options available for a particular command, type a question mark (**?**).

For example, entering **show ?** in the command field displays the parameters for the **show** command. The Cisco Web browser interface displays the parameters as hypertext links. To select a parameter, you can either click on one of the links, or you can enter the parameter in the command field.

Enter Commands Using the URL Window

You can issue a command using the URL window for the Web browser.

For example, to execute a **show configuration** command on a router named *example*, you would enter the following in the URL window:

```
http://example/exec/show/configuration
```

The Web browser then displays the configuration for the "example" router. To save effort, modify the URL in the URL window in the browser control bar instead of retyping the entire URL.

The difference between entering a command in the command field and entering a command in the URL window is that in the URL window, command modes, keywords, and options should be separated by slashes, not spaces.

Customize the User Interface on a Web Browser

You can customize HTML pages to display Cisco IOS command output and Cisco IOS platform-specific variables (for example, a router host name or router address typically used in router setup pages) for a Web browser. You can display this information using HTML formatted Server Side Includes (SSIs) that you insert into your custom HTML pages. SSIs are a Cisco IOS software feature described in the following sections.

Definition of SSIs

SSIs are HTML-formatted commands or variables that you insert into HTML pages when you customize Cisco IOS platform configuration pages for a Web browser. These SSI commands and SSI variables display Cisco IOS command output and Cisco IOS platform-specific variables.

The Cisco IOS software supports two HTML SSI commands defined for customizing HTML pages: the SSI EXEC command and the **SSI ECHO** command. The HTML format of the SSI EXEC command is **<!--#exec cmd="*xxx*"-->**, and the HTML format of the **SSI ECHO** command is **<!--#echo var="*yyy*"-->**. (See the section "Customize HTML Pages Using SSIs" later in this chapter for a description of how to use these commands.)

In addition to the two SSI commands, the Cisco IOS software supports several SSI variables defined for customizing HTML pages. SSI variables are used with the **SSI ECHO** command. There is one SSI variable defined for all Cisco IOS platforms (SERVER_NAME) and other SSI variables specifically defined for ISDN, Frame Relay, and asynchronous serial platforms. The format and a description of all the available SSI variables are provided in Table 1-5.

The SSI EXEC command is supported on all platforms. The SSI ECHO command, used with SSI variables, is supported on all platforms listed in Table 1-5.

Table 1-5 *Description of SSI Variables*

HTML Format of SSI Variable	Description of Variable Displayed on Browser Page	Cisco IOS Platform(s) This SSI Is Supported On
SERVER_NAME	Host name of the HTTP server.	All Cisco IOS platforms
EZSETUP_PASSWORD	Enable password (currently left blank).	Cisco 1000 series
EZSETUP_PASSWORD_VERIFY	Repeat of the enable password to verify accuracy (currently left blank).	Cisco 1000 series
EZSETUP_ETHERNET0_ADDRESS	IP address of the Ethernet 0 interface.	Cisco 1000 series
EZSETUP_ETHERNET0_MASK	IP mask of the Ethernet 0 interface.	Cisco 1000 series
EZSETUP_DNS_ADDRESS	DNS address used by the router.	Cisco 1000 series
EZSETUP_STANDARD_DEBUG_Y	Standard debug variable. Returns CHECKED if set to TRUE; otherwise, it is blank.	Cisco 1000 series
EZSETUP_STANDARD_DEBUG_N	Standard debug variable. Returns CHECKED if set to FALSE; otherwise, it is blank.	Cisco 1000 series
EZSETUP_ISDN_SWITCHTYPE	ISDN Switch type.	Cisco 1003 and Cisco 1004
EZSETUP_ISDN_REMOTE_NAME	Name of remote ISDN system.	Cisco 1003 and Cisco 1004
EZSETUP_ISDN_REMOTE_NUMBER	Phone number of remote ISDN system.	Cisco 1003 and Cisco 1004
EZSETUP_ISDN_CHAP_PASSWORD	CHAP password of remote ISDN system.	Cisco 1003 and Cisco 1004
EZSETUP_ISDN_SPID1	ISDN SPID 1.	Cisco 1003 and Cisco 1004

Table 1-5 *Description of SSI Variables (Continued)*

HTML Format of SSI Variable	Description of Variable Displayed on Browser Page	Cisco IOS Platform(s) This SSI Is Supported On
EZSETUP_ISDN_SPID2	ISDN SPID 2.	Cisco 1003 and Cisco 1004
EZSETUP_ISDN_SPEED_56	Speed of ISDN interface. Returns CHECKED if set to 56k; otherwise, it is blank.	Cisco 1003 and Cisco 1004
EZSETUP_ISDN_SPEED_64	Speed of ISDN interface. Returns CHECKED if set to 64k; otherwise, it is blank.	Cisco 1003 and Cisco 1004
EZSETUP_FR_ADDRESS	Frame Relay IP address.	Cisco 1005
EZSETUP_FR_MASK	Frame Relay IP mask.	Cisco 1005
EZSETUP_FR_DLCI	Frame Relay DLCI.	Cisco 1005
EZSETUP_ASYNC_REMOTE_NAME	Name of remote system.	Cisco 1005
EZSETUP_ASYNC_REMOTE_NUMBER	Phone number of remote system.	Cisco 1005
EZSETUP_ASYNC_CHAP_PASSWORD	CHAP password for remote system.	Cisco 1005
EZSETUP_ASYNC_LINE_PASSWORD	Async line password.	Cisco 1005
EZSETUP_ASYNC_MODEM_SPEED	Speed of async modem (either 14.4k or 28.8k).	Cisco 1005
EZSETUP_ASYNC_MODEM_SPEED_144K	Returns CHECKED if async modem speed is 14.4k; otherwise it is blank.	Cisco 1005
EZSETUP_ASYNC_MODEM_SPEED_288K	Returns CHECKED if async modem speed is 28.8k; otherwise it is blank.	Cisco 1005

How SSIs Work

Once you have designed a set of HTML pages that include SSIs, you can copy these pages to a Cisco IOS platform's Flash memory. (See the section "Copy HTML Pages to Flash Memory" for instructions on storing HTML pages in Flash memory later in this section.) When you retrieve these pages from Flash memory and display them using a Web browser, any SSI command that was designed into these pages will either display Cisco IOS command output or display a current variable or identifier defined in Table 5. For example, the **SSI ECHO** command with the variable SERVER_NAME will display the current host name of the HTTP server you are using, and the **SSI ECHO** command with the variable EZSETUP_ISDN_SWITCHTYPE will display the current ISDN switch type you are using.

Benefits of Customizing Web Pages with SSIs

Using SSIs, you can customize one set of international HTML pages (for example, in Japanese) and copy these pages to Flash memory on multiple Cisco IOS platforms. When you retrieve these pages from the Flash memory of a Cisco IOS platform, current variables and identifiers associated with the platform you are currently using are displayed. SSIs save you from having to duplicate these international pages (considered relatively large images that contain 8-bit or multibyte characters) and store them in the source code for each platform you are using. (Refer to Table 1-5 to determine which Cisco IOS platforms support which SSIs variables.)

User Interface Customization Task List

To customize your HTML pages and view them for the user interface, use the tasks in the following sections:

- Customize HTML Pages Using SSIs
- Copy HTML Pages to Flash Memory
- Enable the Cisco Web Browser Interface
- View Your HTML File Containing SSIs

Customize HTML Pages Using SSIs

When you are customizing an HTML page for a Web browser, type **<!--#exec cmd="***xxx***"-->** in your HTML file where you want Cisco IOS command output to appear on the browser page. Replace *xxx* with a Cisco IOS command that can be executed in the router's EXEC mode. (See the "**SSI EXEC** Command Example" section later in this chapter.)

When you are customizing an HTML page for a Web browser, type **<!--#echo var="***yyy***"-->** in your HTML file where you want a value or identifier associated with a particular Cisco IOS platform (for example, an ISDN or Frame Relay platform) to appear on the browser page. Replace *yyy* with an SSI variable described in Table 1-5. (See the "**SSI ECHO** Command Example" section later in this chapter.)

Copy HTML Pages to Flash Memory

Once you have customized HTML pages using SSIs, copy your HTML pages to a Cisco IOS platform's Flash memory. To do this, save your pages using a filename appended with .shtml (for example, *filename*.shtml) and copy your file to Flash memory using a **copy** command (for example, the **copy tftp flash** command).

Enable the Cisco Web Browser Interface

To view the HTML pages you have just customized, you must first enable the Cisco Web browser interface. To enable the Cisco Web browser interface, use the following command in global configuration mode:

Command	Purpose
ip http server	Enables the Cisco Web browser interface.

Refer to the section "Configure the Cisco Web Browser Interface" earlier in this chapter for further information on configuring the Cisco Web browser interface.

View Your HTML File Containing SSIs

Once the Cisco Web browser interface is enabled, you can retrieve your HTML page from Flash memory and view it on the Cisco Web browser by typing the URL **http://**router/**flash/**filename in the URL window. Replace router with the host name or IP address of the current Cisco IOS platform you are using, and replace filename with the name of the file you created with .shtml appended. For example, http://myrouter/flash/ssi_file.shtml.

SSI Configuration Examples

This section provides the following configuration examples:

● **SSI EXEC** Command Example

● **SSI ECHO** Command Example

SSI EXEC Command Example

The following is an example of the **HTML SSI EXEC** command used to display the Cisco IOS **show users** EXEC command output:

Contents of the HTML file in Flash memory:

```
<HTML>
<HEAD>
<TITLE> SSI EXEC Command Example</TITLE>
</HEAD>
<BODY>
This is an example of the SSI EXEC command
<HR>
<PRE>
<!--#exec cmd="show users"-->
</PRE>
<HR>
</BODY>
</HTML>
```

Contents that the Web browser receives when the HTML file is retrieved from Flash memory:

```
<HTML>
<HEAD>
<TITLE> SSI EXEC Command Example</TITLE>
</HEAD>
<BODY>
This is an example of the SSI EXEC command
<HR>
<PRE>

Line    User   Host(s) Idle  Location
0 con 0        idle     12
2 vty 0        idle      0   router.cisco.com

</PRE>
<HR>
</BODY>
</HTML>
```

SSI ECHO Command Example

The following is an example of the **HTML SSI ECHO** command used with the SSI variable *SERVER_NAME* (see Table 5) to display the Cisco IOS platform host name *rain*:

Contents of the HTML file in Flash memory:

```
<HTML>
<HEAD>
<TITLE>SSI Echo Command Example</TITLE>
</HEAD>
<BODY>
This is an example of the SSI echo command
<HR>
<!--#echo var="SERVER_NAME"-->
<HR>
</BODY>
</HTML>
```

Contents that the Web browser receives when the HTML file is retrieved from Flash memory:

```
<HTML>
<HEAD>
<TITLE>SSI Echo Command Example</TITLE>
</HEAD>
<BODY>
This is an example of the SSI echo command
<HR>
rain
<HR>
</BODY>
</HTML>
```

Display 8-Bit and Multibyte Character Sets

Your Cisco IOS platform will automatically display 8-bit and multibyte character sets and print the ESC character as a single character instead of as the caret and bracket symbols (^[) when the Cisco Web browser interface is enabled with the **ip http server** command. (Refer to the section "Configure the Cisco Web Browser Interface" for further information on configuring the Cisco Web browser interface.)

If you are Telneting to a Cisco IOS platform, use the following command in line configuration mode to display 8-bit and multibyte international character sets and print the ESC character as a single character instead of ^[:

Command	Purpose
international	Configures a router to display 8-bit and multibyte international character sets and prints the ESC character as a single character instead of ^[when Telneting to a Cisco IOS platform.

If you are Telneting to a Cisco IOS platform, use the following command in EXEC mode to display 8-bit and multibyte international characters sets and print the ESC character as a single character instead of ^[for the current Telnet session:

Command	Purpose
terminal international	Configures a router to display 8-bit and multibyte international character sets and prints the ESC character as a single character instead of ^[when Telneting to a Cisco IOS platform for the current session.

## CHAPTER 2

Basic Command Line Interface Commands

This chapter describes the commands used to enter and exit the various Cisco IOS configuration command modes. It provides a description of the **help** command and help features, lists the command editing keys and functions, and details the command history feature.

You can abbreviate the syntax of Cisco IOS configuration commands. The software recognizes a command when you enter enough characters of the command to uniquely identify it.

For user interface task information and examples, see Chapter 1, "Using the Command Line Interface."

disable

To exit privileged EXEC mode and return to user EXEC mode, enter the **disable** EXEC command.

> **disable** [*level*]

Syntax	Description
level	(Optional) Specifies the user-privilege level.

NOTE	The **disable** command is associated with privilege level 0. If you configure AAA authorization for a privilege level greater than 0, this command will not be included in the command set for that privilege level.

Command Mode
EXEC

Usage Guidelines
This command first appeared in Cisco IOS Release 10.0.

Use this command with the **level** option to reduce the user-privilege level. If a level is not specified, it defaults to the user EXEC mode, which is level 1.

Example

In the following example, entering the **disable** command causes the system to exit privileged EXEC mode and return to user EXEC mode as indicated by the angle bracket (>):

```
Router# disable
Router>
```

Related Commands

To locate documentation of related commands, you can search online at www.cisco.com.

enable

editing

To enable enhanced editing mode for a particular line, use the **editing** line configuration command. To disable the enhanced editing mode, use the **no** form of this command.

> **editing**
> **no editing**

Syntax Description

This command has no arguments or keywords.

Default

Enabled

Command Mode

Line configuration

Usage Guidelines

This command first appeared in Cisco IOS Release 10.0.

Table 2-1 provides a description of the keys used to enter and edit commands. Ctrl indicates the Control key. It must be pressed simultaneously with its associated letter key. Esc indicates the Escape key. It must be pressed first, followed by its associated letter key. Keys are case sensitive.

Table 2-1 *Editing Keys and Functions for Cisco IOS Release 9.21 and Later*

Keys	Function
Tab	Completes a partial command name entry. When you enter a unique set of characters and press the Tab key, the system completes the command name. If you enter a set of characters that could indicate more than one command, the system beeps to indicate an error. Enter a question mark (?) immediately following the partial command (no space). The system provides a list of commands that begin with that string.
Delete or Backspace	Erases the character to the left of the cursor.
Return	At the command line, pressing the Return key performs the function of processing a command. At the More prompt on a terminal screen, pressing the Return key scrolls down a line.
Space Bar	Allows you to see more output on the terminal screen. Press the space bar when you see the More prompt on the screen to display the next screen.
Left Arrow[1]	Moves the cursor one character to the left. When you enter a command that extends beyond a single line, you can press the Left Arrow key repeatedly to scroll back toward the system prompt and verify the beginning of the command entry.
Right Arrow[1]	Moves the cursor one character to the right.
Up Arrow[1] or Ctrl-P	Recalls commands in the history buffer, beginning with the most recent command. Repeat the key sequence to recall successively older commands.
Down Arrow[1] or Ctrl-N	Return to more recent commands in the history buffer after recalling commands with the Up Arrow or Ctrl-P. Repeat the key sequence to recall successively more recent commands.
Ctrl-A	Moves the cursor to the beginning of the line.
Ctrl-B	Moves the cursor back one character.
Ctrl-D	Deletes the character at the cursor.
Ctrl-E	Moves the cursor to the end of the command line.
Ctrl-F	Moves the cursor forward one character.
Ctrl-K	Deletes all characters from the cursor to the end of the command line.
Ctrl-L and Ctrl-R	Redisplays the system prompt and command line.
Ctrl-T	Transposes the character to the left of the cursor with the character located at the cursor.
Ctrl-U and Ctrl-X	Deletes all characters from the cursor back to the beginning of the command line.
Ctrl-V and Esc Q	Inserts a code to indicate to the system that the keystroke immediately following should be treated as a command entry, *not* as an editing key.
Ctrl-W	Deletes the word to the left of the cursor.

Continues

Table 2-1   *Editing Keys and Functions for Cisco IOS Release 9.21 and Later (Continued)*

Keys	Function
Ctrl-Y	Recalls the most recent entry in the delete buffer. The delete buffer contains the last ten items you have deleted or cut. Ctrl-Y can be used in conjunction with Esc Y.
Ctrl-Z	Ends configuration mode and returns you to the EXEC prompt.
Esc B	Moves the cursor back one word.
Esc C	Capitalizes the word from the cursor to the end of the word.
Esc D	Deletes from the cursor to the end of the word.
Esc F	Moves the cursor forward one word.
Esc L	Changes the word to lowercase at the cursor to the end of the word.
Esc U	Capitalizes from the cursor to the end of the word.
Esc Y	Recalls the next buffer entry. The buffer contains the last ten items you have deleted. Press Ctrl-Y first to recall the most recent entry. Then press Esc Y up to nine times to recall the remaining entries in the buffer. If you bypass an entry, continue to press Esc Y to cycle back to it.

1. The arrow keys function only with ANSI-compatible terminals.

Table 2-2 lists the editing keys and functions of the earlier software release.

Table 2-2   *Editing Keys and Functions for Cisco IOS Release 9.1 and Earlier*

Key	Function
Delete or Backspace	Erases the character to the left of the cursor.
Ctrl-W	Erases a word.
Ctrl-U	Erases a line.
Ctrl-R	Redisplays a line.
Ctrl-Z	Ends configuration mode and returns to the EXEC prompt.
Return	Executes single-line commands.

Example

In the following example, enhanced editing mode is disabled on line 3:

```
line 3
no editing
```

Related Commands

To locate documentation of related commands, you can search online at www.cisco.com.

terminal editing

enable

To enter privileged EXEC mode, use the **enable** EXEC command.

> **enable** [*level*]

Syntax	Description
level	(Optional) Privileged level on which to log in.

NOTE	The **enable** command is associated with privilege level 0. If you configure AAA authorization for a privilege level greater than 0, this command will not be included in the command set for that privilege level.

Command Mode

EXEC

Usage Guidelines

This command first appeared in Cisco IOS Release 10.0.

Because many of the privileged commands set operating parameters, privileged access should be password-protected to prevent unauthorized use. If the system administrator has set a password with the **enable password** global configuration command, you are prompted to enter it before being allowed access to privileged EXEC mode. The password is case sensitive.

If an enable password has not been set, enable mode only can be accessed from the router console. If a level is not specified, it defaults to the privileged EXEC mode, which is level 15.

Example

In the following example, the user enters the **enable** command and is prompted to enter a password. The password is not displayed on the screen. After the user enters the correct password, the system enters privileged command mode as indicated by the pound sign (#).

```
Router> enable
Password:
Router#
```

Related Commands

To locate documentation of related commands, you can search online at www.cisco.com.

disable
enable password

end

To exit configuration mode, or any of the configuration submodes, use the **end** global configuration command.

> **end**

Syntax Description

This command has no arguments or keywords.

Command Mode

Global configuration

Usage Guidelines

This command first appeared in Cisco IOS Release 10.0.

You can also press **Ctrl-Z** to exit configuration mode.

Example

In the following example, the name is changed to *george* using the **hostname** global configuration command. Entering the **end** command causes the system to exit configuration mode and return to EXEC mode.

```
Router(config)# hostname george
george(config)# end
george#
```

Related Commands

To locate documentation of related commands, you can search online at www.cisco.com.

hostname

exit

To exit any configuration mode or close an active terminal session and terminate the EXEC, use the **exit** command at the system prompt.

> **exit**

Syntax Description

This command has no arguments or keywords.

Command Mode

Available in all command modes.

Usage Guidelines

This command first appeared in Cisco IOS Release 10.0.

Use the **exit** command at the EXEC levels to exit the EXEC mode. Use the **exit** command at the configuration level to return to privileged EXEC mode. Use the **exit** command in interface, line, router, IPX-router, and route-map command modes to return to global configuration mode. Use the **exit** command in subinterface configuration mode to return to interface configuration mode. You also can press **Ctrl-Z**, or use the **end** command, from any configuration mode to return to privileged EXEC mode.

NOTE   The **exit** command is associated with privilege level 0. If you configure AAA authorization for a privilege level greater than 0, this command will not be included in the command set for that privilege level.

Examples

In the following example, the user exits subinterface configuration mode to return to interface configuration mode:

```
Router(config-subif)# exit
Router(config-if)#
```

The following example shows how to exit an active session:

```
Router> exit
```

Related Commands

To locate documentation of related commands, you can search online at www.cisco.com.

disconnect
end
logout

full-help

To get help for the full set of user-level commands, use the **full-help** line configuration command.

> **full-help**

Syntax Description

This command has no arguments or keywords.

Default

Disabled

Command Mode

Line configuration

Usage Guidelines

This command first appeared in Cisco IOS Release 10.0.

The **full-help** command enables (or disables) an unprivileged user to see all of the help messages available. It is used with the **show ?** command.

Example

The following example is output for the **show ?** command with **full-help** disabled and then enabled:

```
Router> show ?
  bootflash  Boot Flash information
  calendar   Display the hardware calendar
  clock      Display the system clock
```

```
context    Show context information
dialer     Dialer parameters and statistics
history    Display the session command history
hosts      IP domain-name, lookup style, nameservers, and host table
isdn       ISDN information
kerberos   Show Kerberos Values
modemcap   Show Modem Capabilities database
ppp        PPP parameters and statistics
rmon       rmon statistics
sessions   Information about Telnet connections
snmp       snmp statistics
terminal   Display terminal configuration parameters
users      Display information about terminal lines
version    System hardware and software status

Router> enable
Password:
Router# configure terminal
Enter configuration commands, one per line.  End with CNTL/Z.
Router(config)# line console 0
Router(config-line)# full-help
Router(config-line)# end
Router#
%SYS-5-CONFIG_I: Configured from console by console
Router# disable
Router> show ?
  access-expression  List access expression
  access-lists       List access lists
  aliases            Display alias commands
  apollo             Apollo network information
  appletalk          AppleTalk information
  arp                ARP table
  async              Information on terminal lines used as router interfaces
  bootflash          Boot Flash information
  bridge             Bridge Forwarding/Filtering Database [verbose]
  bsc                BSC interface information
  bstun              BSTUN interface information
  buffers            Buffer pool statistics
  calendar           Display the hardware calendar
  ...
  translate          Protocol translation information
  ttycap             Terminal capability tables
  users              Display information about terminal lines
  version            System hardware and software status
  vines              VINES information
  vlans              Virtual LANs Information
  whoami             Info on current tty line
  x25                X.25 information
  xns                XNS information
  xremote            XRemote statistics
```

Related Commands

To locate documentation of related commands, you can search online at www.cisco.com.

help

help

To display a brief description of the help system, enter the **help** command.

> **help**

Syntax Description

This command has no arguments or keywords.

Command Mode

Available in all command modes.

Usage Guidelines

This command first appeared in Cisco IOS Release 10.0.

The **help** command provides a brief description of the context-sensitive help system.

- To list all commands available for a particular command mode, enter a question mark (?) at the system prompt.

- To obtain a list of commands that begin with a particular character string, enter the abbreviated command entry immediately followed by a question mark (?). This form of help is called word help, because it lists only the keywords or arguments that begin with the abbreviation you entered.

- To list a command's associated keywords or arguments, enter a question mark (?) in place of a keyword or argument on the command line. This form of help is called command syntax help because it lists the keywords or arguments that apply based on the command, keywords, and arguments you have already entered.

NOTE   The **help** command is associated with privilege level 0. If you configure AAA authorization for a privilege level greater than 0, this command will not be included in the command set for that privilege level.

Examples

Enter the **help** command for a brief description of the help system:

```
Router# help
Help may be requested at any point in a command by entering
a question mark '?'. If nothing matches, the help list will
be empty and you must backup until entering a '?' shows the
available options.
Two styles of help are provided:
1. Full help is available when you are ready to enter a
   command argument (e.g. 'show ?') and describes each possible
   argument.
2. Partial help is provided when an abbreviated argument is entered
   and you want to know what arguments match the input
   (e.g. 'show pr?'.)
```

The following example shows how to use word help to display all the privileged EXEC commands that begin with the letters "co":

```
Router# co?
configure  connect  copy
```

The following example shows how to use command syntax help to display the next argument of a partially complete **access-list** command. One option is to add a wildcard mask. The <cr> symbol indicates that the other option is to press Return to execute the command.

```
Router(config)# access-list 99 deny 131.108.134.234 ?
  A.B.C.D  Mask of bits to ignore
<cr>
```

Related Commands

To locate documentation of related commands, you can search online at www.cisco.com.

full-help

history

To enable the command history function, or to change the command history buffer size for a particular line, use the **history** line configuration command. To disable the command history feature, use the **no** form of this command.

> **history** [**size** *number-of-lines*]
> **no history** [**size** *number-of-lines*]

Syntax	Description
size *number-of-lines*	(Optional) Specifies the number of command lines that the system will record in its history buffer. The range is 0 to 256.

Default

10 lines

Command Mode

Line configuration

Usage Guidelines

This command first appeared in Cisco IOS Release 10.0.

The **history** command without the **size** keyword and the *number-of-lines* argument enables the history function with the last buffer size specified or with the default of 10 lines, if there was not a prior setting.

The **no history** command without the **size** keyword and the *number-of lines* argument disables the history feature but remembers the buffer size if it was something other than the default. The **no history size** command resets the buffer size to 10.

NOTE	The **history size** command only sets the size of the buffer; it does not re-enable the history feature. If the **no history** command is used, the **history** command must be used to re-enable this feature.

The command history feature provides a record of EXEC commands that you have entered. This feature is particularly useful for recalling long or complex commands or entries, including access lists.

Table 2-3 lists the keys and functions you can use to recall commands from the command history buffer.

Table 2-3 *History Keys*

Key	Function
Ctrl-P or Up Arrow[1]	Recalls commands in the history buffer in a backward sequence, beginning with the most recent command. Repeat the key sequence to recall successively older commands.
Ctrl-N or Down Arrow[1]	Returns to more recent commands in the history buffer after recalling commands with Ctrl-P or the Up Arrow. Repeat the key sequence to recall successively more recent commands.

1.The arrow keys function only with ANSI-compatible terminals such as VT100s.

Example

In the following example, line 4 is configured with a history buffer size of 35 lines:

```
line 4
history size 35
```

Related Commands

To locate documentation of related commands, you can search online at www.cisco.com.

show history
terminal history size

international

If you are Telneting to a Cisco IOS platform and you want to display 8-bit and multibyte international characters (for example, Japanese) and print the ESC character as a single character instead of as the caret and bracket symbols (^[ ]), use the **international** line configuration command. Use the **no** form of this command to display characters in 7-bit format.

> **international**
> **no international**

Syntax Description

This command has no arguments or keywords.

Default

Disabled

Command Mode

Line configuration

Usage Guidelines

This command first appeared in Cisco IOS Release 11.3.

If you are configuring a Cisco IOS platform using the Cisco Web browser interface, this feature is enabled automatically when you enable the Cisco Web browser using the **ip http server** command.

Example

The following example enables a Cisco IOS platform to display 8-bit and multibyte characters and print the ESC character as a single character instead of as the caret and bracket symbols (^[) when you are Telneting to the platform:

```
international
```

Related Commands

To locate documentation of related commands, you can search online at www.cisco.com.

terminal international

ip http access-class

To assign an access list to the HTTP server used by the Cisco IOS ClickStart software or the Cisco Web browser interface, use the **ip http access-class** global configuration command. To remove the assigned access list, use the **no** form of this command.

> **ip http access-class** {*access-list-number* | *name*}
> **no ip http access-class** {*access-list-number* | *name*}

Syntax	Description
access-list-number	Standard IP access list number in the range 0 to 99, as configured by the **access-list (standard)** command.
name	Name of a standard IP access list, as configured by the **ip access-list** command.

Default

There is no access list applied to the HTTP server.

Command Mode

Global configuration

Usage Guidelines

This command first appeared in Cisco IOS Release 11.2.

If this command is configured, the specified access list is assigned to the HTTP server. Before the HTTP server accepts a connection, it checks the access list. If the check fails, the HTTP server does not accept the request for a connection.

Example

The following example assigns the access list named *marketing* to the HTTP server:

```
ip http access-class marketing
ip access-list standard marketing
 permit 192.5.34.0  0.0.0.255
 permit 128.88.0.0  0.0.255.255
 permit 36.0.0.0  0.255.255.255
! (Note: all other access implicitly denied)
```

Related Commands

To locate documentation of related commands, you can search online at www.cisco.com.

ip access-list
ip http server

ip http authentication

Use the **ip http authentication** global configuration command to specify a particular authentication method for HTTP server users. Use the **no** form of this command to disable a configured authentication method.

ip http authentication {aaa | enable | local | tacacs}
no ip http authentication {aaa | enable | local | tacacs}

Syntax	Description
aaa	Indicates that the AAA facility is used for authentication.
enable	Indicates that the enable password method, which is the default method of HTTP server user authentication, is used for authentication.
local	Indicates that the local user database as defined on the Cisco router or access server is used for authentication.
tacacs	Indicates that the TACACS or XTACACS server is used for authentication.

Default

The default method of authentication for the HTTP server interface is the enable password method.

Command Mode

Global configuration

Usage Guidelines

This command first appeared in Cisco IOS Release 11.2 F.

The **ip http authentication** command enables you to specify a particular authentication method for HTTP server users. The HTTP server uses the enable password method to authenticate a user at privilege level 15. The **ip http authentication** command now lets you specify enable, local, TACACS, or AAA HTTP server user authentication.

Example

The following example specifies TACACS as the method of HTTP server user authentication:

```
ip http authentication tacacs
```

Related Commands

To locate documentation of related commands, you can search online at www.cisco.com.

ip http server

ip http port

To specify the port to be used by the Cisco IOS ClickStart software or the Cisco Web browser interface, use the **ip http port** global configuration command. To use the default port, use the **no** form of this command.

> **ip http port** *number*
> **no ip http port**

Syntax

Syntax	Description
number	Port number for use by ClickStart or the Cisco Web browser interface.

Default

80

Command Mode

Global configuration

Part
I

Command Reference

Usage Guidelines

This command first appeared in Cisco IOS Release 11.2.

Use this command if ClickStart or the Cisco Web browser interface cannot use port 80.

Example

The following example configures the router so that you can use ClickStart or the Cisco Web browser interface via port 60:

```
ip http server
ip http port 60
```

Related Commands

To locate documentation of related commands, you can search online at www.cisco.com.

ip http server

ip http server

To enable a Cisco 1003, Cisco 1004, or Cisco 1005 router to be configured from a browser using the Cisco IOS ClickStart software, and to enable any router to be monitored or have its configuration modified from a browser using the Cisco Web browser interface, use the **ip http server** global configuration command. To disable this feature, use the **no** form of this command.

> **ip http server**
> **no ip http server**

Syntax Description

This command has no arguments or keywords.

Default

This feature is enabled on Cisco 1003, Cisco 1004, and Cisco 1005 routers that have not yet been configured. For Cisco 1003, Cisco 1004, and Cisco 1005 routers that have already been configured, and for all other routers, this feature is disabled.

Command Mode

Global configuration

Usage Guidelines

This command first appeared in Cisco IOS Release 11.2.

Example

The following example configures the router so that you can use the Cisco Web browser interface to issue commands to it:

```
ip http server
```

Related Commands

To locate documentation of related commands, you can search online at www.cisco.com.

ip http access-class
ip http port

menu (EXEC)

Use the **menu** EXEC command to invoke a user menu.

> **menu** *name*

Syntax   Description

name   The name of the menu.

Command Mode

User EXEC mode or privileged EXEC mode

Usage Guidelines

This command first appeared in Cisco IOS Release 10.0.

A menu can be invoked at either the user or privileged EXEC level, but if an item in the menu contains a privileged EXEC command, the user must be logged in at the privileged level for the command to succeed.

When a particular line should always display a menu, that line can be configured with an **autocommand** line configuration command. The menu should not contain any exit paths that leave users in an unfamiliar interface environment.

Menus can be run on a per-user basis by defining a similar **autocommand** command for that local username.

Example

The following example invokes the menu named Access1:

```
menu Access1
```

Related Commands

To locate documentation of related commands, you can search online at www.cisco.com.

autocommand
menu command
menu prompt
menu text
menu title
no menu

menu clear-screen

Use the **menu** global configuration command to clear the terminal screen before displaying a menu.

> **menu** *name* **clear-screen**

Syntax	Description
name	The configuration name of the menu.

Default

Disabled

Command Mode

Global configuration

Usage Guidelines

This command first appeared in Cisco IOS Release 10.0.

This command uses a terminal-independent mechanism based on termcap entries defined in the router and the terminal type configured for the user's terminal. This command allows the same menu to be used on multiple types of terminals instead of having terminal-specific strings embedded within menu titles. If the termcap entry does not contain a clear string, the menu system enters 24 new lines, causing all existing text to scroll off the top of the terminal screen.

Examples

The following example clears the terminal screen before displaying the menu named Access1:

```
menu Access1 clear-screen
```

Related Commands

To locate documentation of related commands, you can search online at www.cisco.com.

menu (EXEC)
menu command
menu default
menu line-mode
menu options
menu prompt
menu single-space
menu status-line
menu text
menu title
no menu

menu command

Use the **menu command** global configuration command to specify underlying commands for user interface menus.

menu *name* **command** *item command*

Syntax	Description
name	The configuration name of the menu. You can specify a maximum of 20 characters.
item	Number, character, or string used as the key for the item. The key is displayed to the left of the menu item text. You can specify a maximum of 18 menu entries. When the tenth item is added to the menu, the line-mode and single-space options are activated automatically.
command	Command to issue when the user selects an item.

Default
Disabled

Command Mode
Global configuration

Usage Guidelines
This command first appeared in Cisco IOS Release 10.0.

Use this command to assign actions to items in a menu. Use the **menu text** command to assign text to items. These commands must use the same menu name and menu selection key.

The **menu command** command has a special keyword for the *command* argument, **menu-exit**, that is available only within menus. It is used to exit a submenu and return to the previous menu level or exit the menu altogether and return to the EXEC command prompt.

You can create submenus that are opened by selecting entries in another menu. Use the **menu** EXEC command as the *command* for the submenu item.

NOTE   If you nest too many levels of menus, the system prints an error message on the terminal and returns to the previous menu level.

When a menu allows connections (their normal use), the command for an entry activating the connection should contain a **resume** command, or the line should be configured to prevent users from escaping their sessions with the **escape-char none** command. Otherwise, when they escape from a connection and return to the menu, there will be no way to resume the session, and it will sit idle until the user logs off.

Specifying the **resume** command as the action that is performed for a selected menu entry permits a user to resume a named connection or connect using the specified name, if there is no active connection by that name. As an option, you can also supply the connect string needed to connect initially. When you do not supply this connect string, the command uses the specified connection name.

You can also use the **resume/next** command, which resumes the next connection in the user's list of connections. This function allows you to create a single menu entry that steps through all of the user's connections.

Example

The following example specifies the commands to be issued when a user enters the selection number associated with the menu entry for the menu named Access1:

```
menu Access1 command 1 tn3270 vms.cisco.com
menu Access1 command 2 rlogin unix.cisco.com
menu Access1 command 3 menu-exit
```

Related Commands

To locate documentation of related commands, you can search online at www.cisco.com.

menu (EXEC)
menu clear-screen
menu default
menu-exit
menu line-mode
menu options
menu prompt
menu single-space
menu status-line
menu text
menu title
no menu
resume

menu default

Use the **menu default** global configuration command to specify the menu item to use as the default.

       menu *name* **default** *item*

Syntax   Description

Syntax	Description
name	The name of the menu. You can specify a maximum of 20 characters.
item	Number, character, or string key of the item to use as the default.

Default

Disabled

Command Mode

Global configuration

Usage Guidelines

This command first appeared in Cisco IOS Release 10.0.

Use this command to specify which menu entry is used when the user presses Enter without specifying an item. The menu entries are defined by the **menu command** and **menu text** commands.

Example

The following example exits the menu when a user presses Enter without selecting an item:

```
menu Access1 9 text Exit the menu
menu Access1 9 command menu-exit
menu Access1 default 9
```

Related Commands

To locate documentation of related commands, you can search online at www.cisco.com.

menu (EXEC)
menu command
menu prompt
menu text
menu title
no menu

menu-exit

Use the **menu-exit** command within a **menu command** command to allow a user to exit the menu.

menu-exit

Syntax Description

This command has no arguments or keywords.

Command Mode

This command can only be used within a **menu command** command.

Usage Guidelines

This command first appeared in Cisco IOS Release 10.0.

Use this command to provide a way for menu users to return to a higher-level menu or exit the menu system.

Example

The following example allows a menu user to exit a menu by entering "Exit" at the menu prompt:

```
menu Access1 text Exit Exit
menu Access1 command Exit menu-exit
```

Related Commands

To locate documentation of related commands, you can search online at www.cisco.com.

menu command

menu line-mode

Use the **menu line-mode** global configuration command to require the user to press Enter after specifying an item.

> **menu** *name* **line-mode**

Syntax

name

Description

The configuration name of the menu.

Default

Enabled for menus with more than nine items. Disabled for menus with nine or fewer items.

Command Mode

Global configuration

Usage Guidelines

This command first appeared in Cisco IOS Release 10.0.

In a menu of nine or fewer items, you ordinarily select a menu item by entering the item number. In line mode, you select a menu entry by entering the item number and pressing Enter. Line mode allows you to backspace over the selected number and enter another number before pressing Enter to issue the command.

This option is activated automatically when more than nine menu items are defined but also can be configured explicitly for menus of nine or fewer items.

In order to use strings as keys for items, the **menu line-mode** command must be configured.

Examples

The following example enables the line-mode option for the menu named Access1:

```
menu Access1 line-mode
```

Related Commands

To locate documentation of related commands, you can search online at www.cisco.com.

menu (EXEC)
menu clear-screen
menu command
menu default
menu options
menu prompt
menu single-space
menu status-line
menu text
menu title
no menu

menu options

Use the **menu options** global configuration command to set options for items in user interface menus.

> **menu** *name* **options** *item* {**login** | **pause**}

Syntax	Description
name	The name of the menu. You can specify a maximum of 20 characters.
item	Number, character, or string key of the item affected by the option.
login	Requires a login before issuing the command.
pause	Pauses after the command is entered before redrawing the menu.

Default

Disabled

Command Mode

Global configuration

Usage Guidelines

This command first appeared in Cisco IOS Release 10.0.

Use the **menu command** and **menu text** commands to define a menu entry.

Example

The following example requires a login before issuing the command specified by menu entry 3 of the menu named Access1:

```
menu Access1 options 3 login
```

Related Commands

To locate documentation of related commands, you can search online at www.cisco.com.

menu (EXEC)
menu clear-screen
menu command
menu default
menu line-mode
menu prompt
menu single-space
menu status-line
menu text
menu title
no menu

menu prompt

Use the **menu prompt** global configuration command to specify the prompt for a user interface menu.

> **menu** *name* **prompt** *delimiter prompt delimiter*

Syntax	Description
name	The name of the menu. You can specify a maximum of 20 characters.
delimiter	Characters that mark the beginning and end of the prompt. Text delimiters are characters that do not ordinarily appear within the text of a title, such as slash (/), double quote ("), and tilde (~). Ctrl-C is reserved for special use and should not be used in the text of the title.
prompt	Prompt string for the menu.

Default
Disabled

Command Mode
Global configuration

Usage Guidelines
This command first appeared in Cisco IOS Release 10.0.

Press Enter after entering the first delimiter. The router will prompt you for the text of the prompt. Type the text followed by the delimiter, and press Enter.

Use the **menu command** and **menu text** commands to define the menu selections.

Example
The following example configures the prompt as "Select an item.":

```
Router(config)# menu Access1 prompt /
Enter TEXT message.  End with the character '/'.
Select an item. /
Router(config)#
```

Related Commands
To locate documentation of related commands, you can search online at www.cisco.com.

menu (EXEC)
menu command
menu default
menu text
menu title
no menu

menu single-space

Use the **menu single-space** global configuration command to display menu items single-spaced rather than double-spaced.

> **menu** *name* **single-space**

Syntax	Description
name	The configuration name of the menu.

Default

Enabled for menus with more than nine items; disabled for menus with nine or fewer items.

Command Mode

Global configuration

Usage Guidelines

This command first appeared in Cisco IOS Release 10.0.

When more than nine menu items are defined, the menu is displayed single-spaced. To configure the menus with nine or fewer items to display single-spaced, use this command.

Example

The following example displays single-spaced menu items for the menu named Access1:

```
menu Access1 single-spaced
```

Related Commands

To locate documentation of related commands, you can search online at www.cisco.com.

menu (EXEC)
menu clear-screen
menu command
menu default
menu line-mode
menu options
menu prompt
menu status-line
menu text
menu title
no menu

menu status-line

Use the **menu status-line** global configuration command to display a line of status information about the current user at the top of a menu.

menu *name* **status-line**

Syntax

Syntax	Description
name	The configuration name of the menu.

Default

Disabled

Command Mode

Global configuration

Usage Guidelines

This command first appeared in Cisco IOS Release 10.0.

This command displays the status information at the top of the screen before the menu title is displayed. This status line includes the router's host name, the user's line number, and the current terminal type and keymap type (if any).

Example

The following example displays the status information using the **status-line** option for the menu named Access1:

```
menu Access1 status-line
```

Related Commands

To locate documentation of related commands, you can search online at www.cisco.com.

menu (EXEC)
menu clear-screen
menu command
menu default
menu line-mode

menu options
menu prompt
menu single-space
menu text
menu title
no menu

menu text

Use the **menu text** global configuration command to specify the text of a menu item in a user interface menu.

> **menu** *name* **text** *item text*

Syntax

Description

Syntax	Description
name	The configuration name of the menu. You can specify a maximum of 20 characters.
item	Number, character, or string used as the key for the item. The key is displayed to the left of the menu item text. You can specify a maximum of 18 menu items. When the tenth item is added to the menu, the **menu line-mode** and **menu single-space** commands are activated automatically.
text	Text of the menu item.

Default

No text appears for the menu item.

Command Mode

Global configuration

Usage Guidelines

This command first appeared in Cisco IOS Release 10.0.

Use this command to assign text to items in a menu. Use the **menu command** command to assign actions to items. These commands must use the same menu name and menu selection key.

You can specify a maximum of 18 items in a menu.

Example

The following example specifies the descriptive text for the three entries in the menu named Access1:

```
menu Access1 text 1 IBM Information Systems
menu Access1 text 2 UNIX Internet Access
menu Access1 text 3 Exit menu system
```

Related Commands

To locate documentation of related commands, you can search online at www.cisco.com.

menu (EXEC)
menu clear-screen
menu command
menu default
menu line-mode
menu options
menu prompt
menu single-space
menu status-line
menu text
menu title
no menu

menu title

Use the **menu title** global configuration command to create a title, or banner, for a user menu.

menu *name* **title** *delimiter title delimiter*

Syntax	Description
name	The configuration name of the menu. You can specify a maximum of 20 characters.
delimiter	Characters that mark the beginning and end of a title. Text delimiters are characters that do not ordinarily appear within the text of a title, such as slash (/), double quote ("), and tilde (~). Ctrl-C is reserved for special use and should not be used in the text of the title.
title	The lines of text to appear at the top of the menu.

Default

The menu does not have a title.

Command Mode

Global configuration

Usage Guidelines

This command first appeared in Cisco IOS Release 10.0.

The **menu title** command must use the same menu name used with the **menu text** and **menu command** commands used to create a menu.

You can position the title of the menu horizontally by preceding the title text with blank characters. You can also add lines of space above and below the title by pressing Enter.

Follow the **title** keyword with one or more blank characters and a delimiting character of your choice. Then enter one or more lines of text, ending the title with the same delimiting character. You cannot use the delimiting character within the text of the message.

When you are configuring from a terminal and are attempting to include special control characters, such as a screen-clearing string, you must use Ctrl-V before the special control characters so that they are accepted as part of the title string. The string ^[[H^[[J is an escape string used by many VT100-compatible terminals to clear the screen. To use a special string, you must enter **Ctrl-V** before each escape character.

You also can use the **menu clear-screen** command to clear the screen before displaying menus and submenus, instead of embedding a terminal-specific string in the menu title. The **menu clear-screen** command allows the same menu to be used on different types of terminals.

Example

The following example specifies the title that will be displayed when the menu named Access1 is invoked. Press Enter after the second slash (/) to display the prompt.

```
Router(config)# menu Access1 title /^[[H^[[J
Enter TEXT message.  End with the character '/'.
            Welcome to Access1 Internet Services

                Type a number to select an option;
                    Type 9 to exit the menu.
/
Router(config)#
```

Related Commands

To locate documentation of related commands, you can search online at www.cisco.com.

menu (EXEC)
menu clear-screen

menu command
menu default
menu line-mode
menu options
menu prompt
menu single-space
menu status-line
menu text
no menu

no menu

Use the **no menu** global configuration command to delete the specified menu from the configuration.

> **no menu** *name*

Syntax

Description

name   The configuration name of the menu.

Default

menu commands, if any, remain in the configuration.

Command Mode

Global configuration

Usage Guidelines

This command first appeared in Cisco IOS Release 10.0.

Use this command to remove any **menu** commands for a particular menu from the configuration.

Example

The following example deletes the menu named Access1:

```
no menu Access1
```

Related Commands

To locate documentation of related commands, you can search online at www.cisco.com.

menu (EXEC)
menu command
menu prompt
menu text
menu title
no menu

show history

To list the commands you have entered in the current EXEC session, use the **show history** EXEC command.

> **show history**

Syntax Description

This command has no arguments or keywords.

Command Mode

EXEC

Usage Guidelines

This command first appeared in Cisco IOS Release 10.0.

The command history feature provides a record of EXEC commands you have entered. The number of commands that the history buffer will record is determined by the **history size** line configuration command or the **terminal history size** EXEC command.

Table 2-4 lists the keys and functions you can use to recall commands from the command history buffer.

Table 2-4 *History Keys*

Key	Function
Ctrl-P or Up Arrow	Recalls commands in the history buffer in a backward sequence, beginning with the most recent command. Repeat the key sequence to recall successively older commands.
Ctrl-N or Down Arrow	Returns to more recent commands in the history buffer after recalling commands with Ctrl-P or the Up Arrow. Repeat the key sequence to recall successively more recent commands.

Sample Display

The following is sample output from the **show history** command, which lists the commands the user has entered in EXEC mode for this session:

```
Router# show history
  help
  where
  show hosts
  show history
Router#
```

Related Commands

To locate documentation of related commands, you can search online at www.cisco.com.

history size
terminal history size

terminal editing

To enable the enhanced editing mode on the local line, use the **terminal editing** EXEC command. To disable the enhanced editing mode on the current line, use the **no** form of this command.

> **terminal editing**
> **terminal no editing**

Syntax Description

This command has no arguments or keywords.

Default

Enabled

Command Mode

EXEC

Usage Guidelines

This command first appeared in Cisco IOS Release 10.0.

Table 2-5 provides a description of the keys used to enter and edit commands. Ctrl indicates the Control key. It must be pressed simultaneously with its associated letter key. Esc indicates the Escape key. It must be pressed first, followed by its associated letter key. Keys are *not* case sensitive.

Table 2-5 *Command Editing Keys and Functions*

Key	Function
Tab	Completes a partial command name entry. When you enter a unique set of characters and press the Tab key, the system completes the command name. If you enter a set of characters that could indicate more than one command, the system beeps to indicate an error. Enter a question mark (?) immediately following the partial command (no space). The system provides a list of commands that begin with that string.
Delete or Backspace	Erases the character to the left of the cursor.
Return	At the command line, pressing the Return key performs the function of processing, or carrying out, a command. At the More prompt on a terminal screen, pressing the Return key scrolls down a line.
Space Bar	Scrolls down a page on the terminal screen. Press the space bar when you see the More prompt on the screen to display the next screen.
Left arrow[1]	Moves the cursor one character to the left. When you enter a command that extends beyond a single line, you can continue to press the left arrow key at any time to scroll back toward the system prompt and verify the beginning of the command entry.
Right arrow[1]	Moves the cursor one character to the right.
Up arrow[1] or Ctrl-P	Recalls commands in the history buffer, beginning with the most recent command. Repeat the key sequence to recall successively older commands.
Down arrow[1] or Ctrl-N	Return to more recent commands in the history buffer after recalling commands with the up arrow or Ctrl-P. Repeat the key sequence to recall successively more recent commands.
Ctrl-A	Moves the cursor to the beginning of the line.
Ctrl-B	Moves the cursor back one character.
Ctrl-D	Deletes the character at the cursor.
Ctrl-E	Moves the cursor to the end of the command line.
Ctrl-F	Moves the cursor forward one character.
Ctrl-K	Deletes all characters from the cursor to the end of the command line.
Ctrl-L or Ctrl-R	Redisplays the system prompt and command line.
Ctrl-T	Transposes the character to the left of the cursor with the character located at the cursor.

Table 2-5   *Command Editing Keys and Functions (Continued)*

Key	Function
Ctrl-U or Ctrl-X	Deletes all characters from the cursor back to the beginning of the command line.
Ctrl-V or Esc Q	Inserts a code to indicate to the system that the key stroke immediately following should be treated as a command entry, not as an editing key.
Ctrl-W	Deletes the word to the left of the cursor.
Ctrl-Y	Recalls the most recent entry in the delete buffer. The delete buffer contains the last 10 items you have deleted or cut. Ctrl-Y can be used in conjunction with Esc Y.
Ctrl-Z	Ends configuration mode and returns you to the EXEC prompt.
Esc B	Moves the cursor back one word.
Esc C	Capitalizes the word at the cursor.
Esc D	Deletes from the cursor to the end of the word.
Esc F	Moves the cursor forward one word.
Esc L	Changes the word at the cursor to lowercase.
Esc U	Capitalizes from the cursor to the end of the word.
Esc Y	Recalls the next buffer entry. The buffer contains the last ten items you have deleted. Press Ctrl-Y first to recall the most recent entry. Then press Esc Y up to nine times to recall the remaining entries in the buffer. If you bypass an entry, continue to press Esc Y to cycle back to it.

1.The arrow keys function only with ANSI-compatible terminals.

The editing keys and functions for Software Release 9.1 and earlier are listed in Table 2-6.

Table 2-6   *Editing Keys and Functions for Software Release 9.1 and Earlier*

Key	Function
Delete or Backspace	Erases the character to the left of the cursor.
Ctrl-W	Erases a word.
Ctrl-U	Erases a line.
Ctrl-R	Redisplays a line.
Ctrl-Z	Ends configuration mode and returns to the EXEC prompt.
Return	Executes single-line commands.

Example

In the following example, enhanced mode editing is re-enabled for the current terminal session:

```
terminal editing
```

Related Commands

To locate documentation of related commands, you can search online at www.cisco.com.

editing

terminal full-help

To get help for the full set of user-level commands, use the **terminal full-help** EXEC command.

> **terminal full-help**

Syntax Description

This command has no arguments or keywords.

Default

Disabled

Command Mode

EXEC

Usage Guidelines

This command first appeared in Cisco IOS Release 10.0.

The **terminal full-help** command enables (or disables) a user to see all of the help messages available from the terminal. It is used with the **show ?** command.

Example

The following example is output for the **show ?** command with **terminal full-help** disabled and then enabled:

```
Router> show ?
  bootflash  Boot Flash information
  calendar   Display the hardware calendar
  clock      Display the system clock
```

```
    context    Show context information
    dialer     Dialer parameters and statistics
    history    Display the session command history
    hosts      IP domain-name, lookup style, nameservers, and host
    isdn       ISDN information
    kerberos   Show Kerberos Values
    modemcap   Show Modem Capabilities database
    ppp        PPP parameters and statistics
    rmon       rmon statistics
    sessions   Information about Telnet connections
    snmp       snmp statistics
    terminal   Display terminal configuration parameters
    users      Display information about terminal lines
    version    System hardware and software status
Router> terminal full-help
Router> show ?
    access-expression  List access expression
    access-lists       List access lists
    aliases            Display alias commands
    apollo             Apollo network information
    appletalk          AppleTalk information
    arp                ARP table
    async              Information on terminal lines used as router interfaces
    bootflash          Boot Flash information
    bridge             Bridge Forwarding/Filtering Database [verbose]
    bsc                BSC interface information
    bstun              BSTUN interface information
    buffers            Buffer pool statistics
    calendar           Display the hardware calendar
    cdp                CDP information
    clns               CLNS network information
    clock              Display the system clock
    cls                DLC user information
    cmns               Connection-Mode networking services (CMNS) information
    compress           Show compression statistics.
    ...
    x25                X.25 information
    xns                XNS information
    xremote            XRemote statistics
```

Related Commands

To locate documentation of related commands, you can search online at www.cisco.com.

full-help
help

terminal history

To enable the command history feature for the current terminal session or change the size of the command history buffer for the current terminal session, use the **terminal history** EXEC command. To disable the command history feature or reset the command history buffer to its default size, use the **no** form of this command.

> **terminal history** [**size** *number-of-lines*]
> **terminal no history** [**size**]

Syntax

Syntax	Description
size	(Optional) Sets command history buffer size.
number-of-lines	(Optional) Specifies the number of command lines that the system will record in its history buffer. The range is 0 to 256.

Default

10 lines

Command Mode

EXEC

Usage Guidelines

This command first appeared in Cisco IOS Release 10.0.

The **terminal history** command without the **size** keyword and argument enables the command history feature with the last buffer size specified or the default size. The **terminal no history** command without the **size** keyword disables the command history feature. The **terminal no history size** command resets the buffer size to the default of 10 command lines.

The **terminal history** command provides a record of EXEC commands you have entered. This feature is particularly useful to recall long or complex commands or entries, including access lists.

Table 2-7 lists the keys and functions you can use to recall commands from the history buffer.

Table 2-7 *History Keys*

Key	Function
Ctrl-P or up arrow[1]	Recalls commands in the history buffer in a backward sequence, beginning with the most recent command. Repeat the key sequence to recall successively older commands.
Ctrl-N or down arrow[1]	Returns to more recent commands in the history buffer after recalling commands with Ctrl-P or the up arrow. Repeat the key sequence to recall successively more recent commands.

1. The arrow keys function only with ANSI-compatible terminals such as VT100s.

Example

In the following example, the number of command lines recorded is set to 15 for the local line:

```
terminal history size 15
```

Related Commands

To locate documentation of related commands, you can search online at www.cisco.com.

history
show history

terminal international

If you are Telneting to a Cisco IOS platform and you want to display 8-bit and multibyte international characters (for example, Japanese) and print the ESC character as a single character instead of as the caret and bracket symbols (^[) for a current Telnet session, use the **terminal international** EXEC command. Use the **no** form of this command to display characters in 7-bit format for a current Telnet session.

> **terminal international**
> **no terminal international**

Syntax Description

This command has no arguments or keywords.

Default

Disabled

Command Mode
EXEC

Usage Guidelines
This command first appeared in Cisco IOS Release 11.3.

If you are configuring a Cisco IOS platform using the Cisco Web browser interface, this feature is enabled automatically when you enable the Cisco Web browser using the **ip http server** command.

Example
The following example enables a Cisco IOS platform to display 8-bit and multibyte characters and print the ESC character as a single character instead of as the caret and bracket symbols (^[) when you are Telneting to the platform for the current Telnet session:

```
terminal international
```

Related Commands
To locate documentation of related commands, you can search online at www.cisco.com.

international

## CHAPTER 3

Using Configuration Tools

Cisco IOS software includes a number of configuration tools that simplify the process of setting up the initial configuration of a router or access server. This chapter describes the following configuration tools:

- Using AutoInstall
- Using Setup for Configuration Changes
- Using Other Configuration Tools

For a complete description of the configuration tools commands in this chapter, refer to Chapter 4, "Configuration Tools Commands." To locate documentation of other commands, you can search online at www.cisco.com.

Using AutoInstall

This section provides information about AutoInstall, a procedure that allows you to configure a new router automatically and dynamically. The AutoInstall procedure involves connecting a new router to a network where an existing router is preconfigured, turning on the new router, and enabling it with a configuration file that is automatically downloaded from a Trivial File Transfer Protocol (TFTP) server.

The following sections provide the requirements for AutoInstall and an overview of how the procedure works. To start the procedure, see the "Perform the AutoInstall Procedure" section.

AutoInstall Requirements

For the AutoInstall procedure to work, your system must meet the following requirements:

- Routers must be physically attached to the network using one or more of the following interface types: Ethernet, Token Ring, Fiber Distributed Data Interface (FDDI), serial with High-Level Data Link Control (HDLC) encapsulation, or serial with Frame Relay encapsulation. HDLC is the default serial encapsulation. If the AutoInstall process fails over HDLC, the Cisco IOS software automatically configures Frame Relay encapsulation.

- The existing preconfigured router must be running Software Release 9.1 or later. For AutoInstall over Frame Relay, this router must be running Cisco IOS Release 10.3 or later.

- The new router must be running Software Release 9.1 or later. For AutoInstall over Frame Relay, the new router must be running Cisco IOS Release 10.3 or later.

NOTE	Of Token Ring interfaces, only those that set ring speed with physical jumpers support AutoInstall. AutoInstall does not work with Token Ring interfaces for which the ring speed must be set with software configuration commands. If the ring speed is not set, the interface is set to shutdown mode.

- You must complete procedure 1 and either procedure 2 or 3:

    — Procedure 1: A configuration file for the new router must reside on a TFTP server. This file can contain the full configuration or the minimum needed for the administrator to Telnet into the new router for configuration. In addition, make sure to complete one of the following procedures.

    — Procedure 2: A file named *network-confg* also must reside on the server. The file must have an Internet Protocol (IP) host name entry for the new router. The server must be reachable from the existing router.

    — Procedure 3: An IP address-to-host name mapping for the new router must be added to a Domain Name System (DNS) database file.

- If the existing router is to help automatically install the new router via an HDLC-encapsulated serial interface using Serial Line Address Resolution Protocol (SLARP), that interface must be configured with an IP address whose host portion has the value 1 or 2. (AutoInstall over Frame Relay does not have this address constraint.) Subnet masks of any size are supported.

- If the existing router is to help automatically install the new router using a Frame Relay-encapsulated serial interface, that interface must be configured with the following:

    — An IP helper address pointing to the TFTP server. In the following example, 171.69.2.75 is the address of the TFTP server:

    ```
    ip helper 171.69.2.75
    ```

    — A Frame Relay map pointing back to the new router. In the following example, 172.21.177.100 is the IP address of the *new* router's serial interface, and 100 is the PVC identifier:

    ```
    frame-relay map ip 172.21.177.100 100 dlci
    ```

- If the existing router is to help automatically install the new router via an Ethernet, Token Ring, or FDDI interface using BOOTP or Reverse Address Resolution Protocol (RARP), a BOOTP or RARP server also must be set up to map the new router's Media Access Control (MAC) address to its IP address.

- IP helper addresses might need to be configured to forward the TFTP and DNS broadcast requests from the new router to the host that is providing those services.

Using a DOS-Based TFTP Server

AutoInstall over Frame Relay and other WAN encapsulations support downloading configuration files from UNIX-based and DOS-based TFTP servers. Other booting mechanisms such as RARP and SLARP also support UNIX-based and DOS-based TFTP servers.

The DOS format of the UNIX network-confg file that must reside on the server must be eight characters or fewer, with a three-letter extension. Therefore, when an attempt to load network-confg fails, AutoInstall automatically attempts to download the file *cisconet.cfg* from the TFTP server.

If cisconet.cfg exists and is downloaded successfully, the server is assumed to be a DOS machine. The AutoInstall program then attempts to resolve the host name for the router through host commands in cisconet.cfg.

If cisconet.cfg does not exist, cannot be downloaded, or the program is unable to resolve a host name, DNS attempts to resolve the host name. If DNS cannot resolve the host name, the router attempts to download ciscortr.cfg. If the host name is longer than eight characters, it is truncated to eight characters. For example, a router with a host name "australia" will be treated as "australi" and AutoInstall will attempt to download australi.cfg.

The format of cisconet.cfg and ciscortr.cfg is to be the same as that described for network-confg and hostname-confg.

If neither network-confg nor cisconet.cfg exists and DNS is unable to resolve the host name, AutoInstall attempts to load router-confg and then ciscortr.cfg if router-confg does not exist or cannot be downloaded. The cycle is repeated three times.

How AutoInstall Works

Once the requirements for using AutoInstall are met, the dynamic configuration of the new router occurs in the following order:

1   The new router acquires its IP address. Depending on the interface connection between the two routers and/or access servers, the new router's IP address is dynamically resolved by either SLARP requests or BOOTP or RARP requests.

2   The new router resolves its name through network-confg, cisconet.cfg, or DNS.

3   The new router automatically requests and downloads its configuration file from a TFTP server.

4   If a host name is not resolved, the new router attempts to load router-confg or ciscortr.cfg.

Acquiring the New Router's IP Address

The new router (*newrouter*) resolves its interface's IP addresses by one of the following means:

• If *newrouter* is connected by an HDLC-encapsulated serial line to the existing router (*existing*), *newrouter* sends a SLARP request to *existing*.

- If *newrouter* is connected by an Ethernet, Token Ring, or FDDI interface, it broadcasts BOOTP and RARP requests.

- If *newrouter* is connected by a Frame Relay-encapsulated serial interface, it first attempts the HDLC automatic installation process and then attempts the BOOTP or RARP process over Ethernet, Token Ring, or FDDI. If both attempts fail, the new router attempts to automatically install over Frame Relay. In this case, a BOOTP request is sent over the lowest numbered serial or HSSI interface.

The existing router (*existing*) responds in one of the following ways depending on the request type:

- In response to a SLARP request, *existing* sends a SLARP reply packet to *newrouter*. The reply packet contains the IP address and netmask of *existing*. If the host portion of the IP address in the SLARP response is 1, *newrouter* configures its interface using the value 2 as the host portion of its IP address and vice versa. (See Figure 3-1.)

Figure 3-1 *Using SLARP to Acquire the New Router's IP Address*

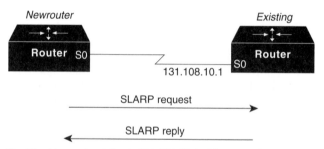

- In response to BOOTP or RARP requests, an IP address is sent from the BOOTP or RARP server to *newrouter*.

    A BOOTP or RARP server must have already been set up to map *newrouter*'s MAC address to its IP address. If the BOOTP server does not reside on the directly attached network segment, routers between *newrouter* and the BOOTP server can be configured with the **ip helper-address** command to allow the request and response to be forwarded between segments, as shown in Figure 3-2.

    AutoInstall over Frame Relay is a special case in that the existing router acts as a BOOTP server and responds to the incoming BOOTP request. Only a helper address and a Frame Relay map need to be set up. No MAC-to-IP address map is needed on the existing router.

Figure 3-2   *Using BOOTP or RARP to Acquire the New Router's IP Address*

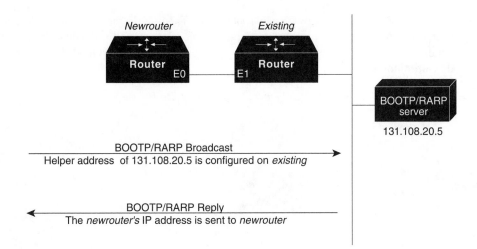

As of Software Release 9.21, routers can be configured to act as RARP servers.

Because the router attempts to resolve its host name as soon as one interface resolves its IP address, only one IP address needs to be set up with SLARP, BOOTP, or RARP.

Resolving the IP Address to the Host Name

The new router resolves its IP address-to-host name mapping by sending a TFTP broadcast requesting the file network-confg, as shown in Figure 3-3.

The network-confg file is a configuration file generally shared by several routers. In this case, it is used to map the IP address of the new router (just obtained dynamically) to the name of the new router. The file network-confg must reside on a reachable TFTP server and must be globally readable.

The following is an example of a minimal network-confg file that maps the IP address of the new router (131.108.10.2) to the name *newrouter*. The address of the new router was learned via SLARP and is based on *existing*'s IP address of 131.108.10.1.

```
ip host newrouter 131.108.10.2
```

If you are not using AutoInstall over Frame Relay, the host portion of the address must be 1 or 2. AutoInstall over Frame Relay does not have this addressing constraint.

If *newrouter* does not receive a network-confg or a cisconet.cfg file, or if the IP address-to-host-name mapping does not match the newly acquired IP address, *newrouter* sends a DNS broadcast. If DNS is configured and has an entry that maps *newrouter*'s SLARP, BOOTP, or RARP-acquired IP address to its name, *newrouter* successfully resolves its name.

If DNS does not have an entry that maps the new router's SLARP, BOOTP, or RARP-acquired address to its name, the new router cannot resolve its host name. The new router attempts to download a default configuration file as described in the next section, and failing that, enters **setup** mode—or enters user EXEC mode with AutoInstall over Frame Relay.

Figure 3-3 *Dynamically Resolving the New Router's IP Address-to-Host Name Mapping*

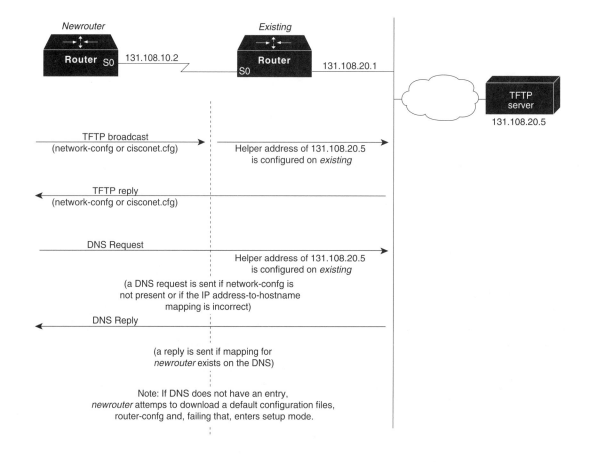

Downloading the New Router's Host Configuration File

After the router successfully resolves its host name, *newrouter* sends a TFTP broadcast requesting the file newrouter-confg or newrouter.cfg. The name *newrouter-confg* must be in all lowercase letters, even if the true host name is not. If *newrouter* cannot resolve its host name, it sends a TFTP broadcast requesting the default host configuration file router-confg. The file is downloaded to *newrouter*, where the configuration commands take effect immediately.

When using AutoInstall over Frame Relay, you are put into **setup** mode while the AutoInstall process is running. If the configuration file is successfully installed, the **setup** process is terminated. If you expect the AutoInstall process to be successful, either do *not* respond to the **setup** prompts or respond to the prompts as follows:

```
Would you like to enter the initial configuration dialog? [yes]: no
Would you like to terminate autoinstall? [yes]: no
```

If you do not expect the AutoInstall process to be successful, create a configuration file by responding to the **setup** prompts. The AutoInstall process is terminated transparently.

You will see the following display as the AutoInstall operation is in progress:

```
Please Wait. AutoInstall being attempted!!!!!!!!!!!!!!!!!!!!
```

If the host configuration file contains only the minimal information, you must connect using Telnet into *existing,* from there connect via Telnet to *newrouter*, and then run the **setup** command to configure *newrouter*. Refer to the "Using Setup for Configuration Changes" section later in this chapter for details on the **setup** command.

If the host configuration file is complete, *newrouter* should be fully operational. You can enter the **enable** command (with the system administrator password) at the system prompt on *newrouter*, and then issue the **copy running-config startup-config** command to save the information in the recently obtained configuration file into nonvolatile random-access memory (NVRAM) or to the location specified by the CONFIG_FILE environment variable. If it must reload, *newrouter* simply loads its configuration file from NVRAM.

If the TFTP request fails, or if *newrouter* still has not obtained the IP addresses of all its interfaces, and those addresses are not contained in the host configuration file, then *newrouter* enters **setup** mode automatically. **Setup** mode prompts you for manual configuration of the Cisco IOS software at the console. The new router continues to issue broadcasts in an attempt to learn its host name and obtain any unresolved interface addresses. The broadcast frequency will dwindle to every 10 minutes after several attempts. Refer to the "Using Setup for Configuration Changes" section later in this chapter for details on the **setup** command.

Perform the AutoInstall Procedure

To dynamically configure a new router using AutoInstall, complete the following commands. Steps 1, 2, and 3 are completed by the central administrator. Step 4 is completed by the person at the remote site.

Step 1 Modify the existing router's configuration to support the AutoInstall procedure.

Step 2 Set up the TFTP server to support the AutoInstall procedure.

Step 3 Set up the BOOTP or RARP server if needed. A BOOTP or RARP server is required for AutoInstall using an Ethernet, Token Ring, FDDI, or Frame Relay-encapsulated serial interface. With a Frame Relay-encapsulated serial interface, the existing router acts as the BOOTP server. A BOOTP or RARP server is not required for AutoInstall using an HDLC-encapsulated serial interface.

Step 4 Connect the new router to the network.

Modify the Existing Router's Configuration

You can use any of the following types of interfaces:

● An HDLC-encapsulated serial line (the default configuration for a serial line)

● An Ethernet, Token Ring, FDDI interface

● A Frame Relay-encapsulated serial line

Use an HDLC-Encapsulated Serial Interface Connection

To set up AutoInstall via a serial line with HDLC encapsulation (the default), you must configure the existing router. Use the following commands, beginning in global configuration mode:

Step	Command	Purpose
1	**interface serial** *interface-number*	Configures the serial interface that connects to the new router with HDLC encapsulation (the default), and enters interface configuration mode.
2	**ip address** *address mask*	Enters an IP address for the interface. The host portion of the address must have a value of 1 or 2. (AutoInstall over Frame Relay does not have this address constraint.)
3	**ip helper-address** *address*	Configures a helper address for the serial interface to forward broadcasts associated with the TFTP, BOOTP, and DNS requests.

Step	Command	Purpose
4	**clock rate** *bps*	Optionally, configures a DCE clock rate for the serial line, unless an external clock is being used. This step is needed only for DCE appliques.
5	**Ctrl-Z**	Exits configuration mode.
6	**copy running-config startup-config**	Saves the configuration file to your startup configuration. On most platforms, this step saves the configuration to NVRAM. On the Cisco 7000 family, this step saves the configuration to the location specified by the CONFIG_FILE environment variable.

In the following example, the existing router's configuration file contains the commands needed to configure the router for AutoInstall on a serial line using HDLC encapsulation:

```
Router# configure terminal
interface serial 0
 ip address 172.31.10.1 255.255.255.0
 ip helper-address 172.31.20.5
 Ctrl-Z
Router(config)# copy running-config startup-config
```

Use an Ethernet, Token Ring, or FDDI Interface Connection

To set up AutoInstall using an Ethernet, Token Ring, or FDDI interface, you must modify the configuration of the existing router. Use the following commands, beginning in global configuration mode:

Step	Command	Purpose
1	**interface {ethernet | tokenring | fddi}** *interface-number*	Configures a LAN interface, and enters interface configuration mode.
2	**ip address** *address mask*	Enters an IP address for the interface.
3	**ip helper-address** *address*	Optionally, configures a helper address to forward broadcasts associated with the TFTP, BOOTP, and DNS requests.
4	**Ctrl-Z**	Exits configuration mode.
5	**copy running-config startup-config**	Saves the configuration file to your startup configuration. On most platforms, this step saves the configuration to NVRAM. On the Cisco 7000 family, this step saves the configuration to the location specified by the CONFIG_FILE environment variable.

Typically, the local-area network (LAN) interface and IP address are already configured on the existing router. You might need to configure an IP helper address if the TFTP server is not on the same network as the new router.

In the following example, the existing router's configuration file contains the commands needed to configure the router for AutoInstall on an Ethernet interface:

```
Router# configure terminal
interface Ethernet 0
 ip address 172.31.10.1 255.255.255.0
 ip helper-address 172.31.20.5
 Ctrl-Z
Router(config)# copy running-config startup-config
```

Use a Frame Relay-Encapsulated Serial Interface Connection

To set up AutoInstall via a serial line with Frame Relay encapsulation, you must configure the existing router. Use the following commands beginning in global configuration mode:

Step	Command	Purpose
1	**interface serial 0**	Configures the serial interface that connects to the new router, and enters interface configuration mode.
2	**encapsulation frame-relay**	Configures Frame Relay encapsulation on the interface that connects to the new router.
3	**frame-relay map ip** *ip-address dlci* or **frame-relay interface-dlci** *dlci option* [**protocol ip** *ip-address*]	Creates a Frame Relay map pointing back to the new router. or For point-to-point subinterfaces, assigns a data link connection identifier (DLCI) to the interface that connects to the new router, and provide the IP address of the serial port on the new router.
4	**ip address** *address mask*	Enters an IP address for the interface. This step sets the IP address of the existing router.
5	**ip helper-address** *address*	Configures a helper address for the TFTP server.
6	**clock rate** *bps*	Optionally, configures a DCE clock rate for the serial line, unless an external clock is being used. This step is needed only for DCE appliques.
7	**Ctrl-Z**	Exits configuration mode.
8	**copy running-config startup-config**	Saves the configuration file to your startup configuration. On most platforms, this step saves the configuration to NVRAM. On the Cisco 7000 family, this step saves the configuration to the location specified by the CONFIG_FILE environment variable.

You must use a DTE interface on the new router because the network always provides the clock signal.

In the following example, the existing router's configuration file contains the commands needed to configure the router for Frame Relay AutoInstall on a serial line:

```
Router# configure terminal
interface serial 0
 ip address 172.31.20.20 255.255.255.0
 encapsulation frame-relay
 frame-relay map ip 172.31.10.1 255.255.255.0 48
 ip helper-address 172.31.20.5
```

Set Up the TFTP Server

For AutoInstall to work correctly, the new router must be able to resolve its host name and then download a *name*-confg or a *name*.cfg file from a TFTP server. The new router can resolve its host name by using a network-confg or a cisconet.cfg file downloaded from a TFTP server or by using the DNS.

To set up a TFTP server to support AutoInstall, use the following commands. Step 2 includes two ways to resolve the new router's host name. Use the first method if you want to use a network-config file to resolve the new router's host name. Use the second method if you want to use DNS to resolve the new router's host name.

Step	Command	Purpose
1	Consult your host vendor's TFTP server documentation and RFCs 906 and 783.	Enables TFTP on a server.
2	**ip host** *hostname address* or	If you want to use a network-confg or cisconet.cfg file to resolve the new router's name, create the network-confg or cisconet.cfg file containing an IP address-to-host name mapping for the new router. Enter the **ip host** command into the TFTP config file, not into the router. The IP address must match the IP address that is to be dynamically obtained by the new router.
	Contact the DNS administrator or refer to RFCs 1101 and 1183.	If you want to use DNS to resolve the new router's name, create an address-to-name mapping entry for the new router in the DNS database. The IP address must match the IP address that is to be dynamically obtained by the new router.
3	See the appropriate chapter in this guide for specific commands.	Creates the *name*-confg or *name*.cfg file, which should reside in the tftpboot directory on the TFTP server. The *name* part of *name*-confg or *name*.cfg filename must match the host name you assigned for the new router in the previous step. Enter configuration commands for the new router into this file.

The *name*-confg or the *name*.cfg file can contain either the new router's full configuration or a minimal configuration.

The minimal configuration file is a virtual terminal password and an enable password. It allows an administrator to Telnet into the new router to configure it. If you are using BOOTP or RARP to resolve the address of the new router, the minimal configuration file must also include the IP address to be obtained dynamically using BOOTP or RARP.

You can use the **copy running-config tftp** command to help you generate the configuration file that you will download during the AutoInstall process.

NOTE   The existing router might need to forward TFTP requests and response packets if the TFTP server is not on the same network segment as the new router. When you modified the existing router's configuration, you specified an IP helper address for this purpose.

You can save a minimal configuration under a generic newrouter-confg file. Use the **ip host** command in the network-confg or cisconet.cfg file to specify *newrouter* as the host name with the address you will be dynamically resolving. The new router should then resolve its IP address, host name, and minimal configuration automatically. Use Telnet to connect to the new router from the existing router and use the **setup** facility to configure the rest of the interfaces. For example, the line in the network-confg or cisconet.cfg file could be similar to the following:

```
ip host newrouter 131.108.170.1
```

The following host configuration file contains the minimal set of commands needed for AutoInstall using SLARP or BOOTP:

```
enable-password letmein
!
line vty 0
password letmein
!
end
```

The preceding example shows a minimal configuration for connecting from a router one hop away. From this configuration, use the **setup** facility to configure the rest of the interfaces. If the router is more than one hop away, you also must include routing information in the minimal configuration.

The following minimal network configuration file maps the new router's IP address, 131.108.10.2, to the host name *newrouter*. The new router's address was learned via SLARP and is based on the existing router's IP address of 131.108.10.1.

```
ip host newrouter 131.108.10.2
```

Set Up the BOOTP or RARP Server

If the new router is connected to the existing router using an Ethernet, Token Ring, or FDDI interface, you must configure a BOOTP or RARP server to map the new router's MAC address to its IP address. If the new router is connected to the existing router using a serial line with HDLC encapsulation or if you are configuring AutoInstall over Frame Relay, the tasks in this section are not required.

To configure a BOOTP or RARP server, use one of the following commands:

Command	Purpose
Refer to your host vendor's manual pages and to RFCs 951 and 1395	If BOOTP is to be used to resolve the new router's IP address, it configures your BOOTP server.
Refer to your host vendor's manual pages and to RFC 903	If RARP is to be used to resolve the new router's IP address, it configures your RARP server.

NOTE	If the RARP server is not on the same subnet as the new router, use the **ip rarp-server** command to configure the existing router to act as a RARP server. See the "Configure a Router as a RARP Server" section.

The following host configuration file contains the minimum set of commands needed for AutoInstall using RARP. It includes the IP address that will be obtained dynamically via BOOTP or RARP during the AutoInstall process. When RARP is used, this extra information is needed to specify the proper netmask for the interface.

```
interface ethernet 0
 ip address 131.108.10.2 255.255.255.0
enable-password letmein
!
line vty 0
 password letmein
!
end
```

Connect the New Router to the Network

Connect the new router to the network using either an HDLC-encapsulated or Frame Relay-encapsulated serial interface or an Ethernet, Token Ring, or FDDI interface. After the router successfully resolves its host name, *newrouter* sends a TFTP broadcast requesting the file *name*-confg or *name*.cfg. The router name must be in all lowercase, even if the true host name is not. The file is downloaded to the new router, where the configuration commands take effect immediately. If the configuration file is complete, the new router should be fully operational. To save the complete configuration to NVRAM, use the following commands in privileged EXEC mode:

Step	Command	Purpose
1	**enable** *password*	Enters privileged mode at the system prompt on the new router.
2	**copy running-config startup-config**	Saves the information from the *name*-config file into your startup configuration. On most platforms, this step saves the configuration to NVRAM. On the Cisco 7000 family, this step saves the configuration to the location specified by the CONFIG_FILE environment variable.

CAUTION   Verify that the existing and new routers and/or access servers are connected before entering the **copy running-config startup-config** EXEC command to save configuration changes. Use the **ping** EXEC command to verify connectivity. If an incorrect configuration file is downloaded, the new router will load NVRAM configuration information before it can enter AutoInstall mode.

If the configuration file is a minimal configuration file, the new router comes up with only one interface operational. Use the following commands to connect to the new router and configure it:

Step	Command	Purpose
1	**telnet** *existing*	Establishes a Telnet connection to the existing router.
2	**telnet** *newrouter*	From the existing router, establishes a Telnet connection to the new router.
3	**enable** *password*	Enters privileged EXEC mode.
4	**setup**	Enters **setup** mode to configure the new router.

Using Setup for Configuration Changes

The **setup** command facility is an interactive facility that allows you to perform first-time configuration and other basic configuration procedures on all routers. The facility prompts you to enter basic information needed to start a router functioning quickly and uneventfully.

Although the **setup** command facility is a quick way to "set up" a router, you can also use it after first-time startup to perform basic configuration changes. This section focuses on the following:

● How to use the **setup** command facility after first-time startup

● How to use the streamlined **setup** facility

Refer to your hardware platform's user guide for more information on how to use **setup** for first-time startup.

Whenever you use the **setup** command facility, be sure that you know the following:

- Interfaces the router has

- Protocols the router is routing

- Whether the router is to perform bridging

- Network addresses for the protocols being configured

- Password strategy for your environment

Setup Command Facility Task List

You can use the tasks in the following sections to make configuration changes using the **setup** command facility. Both tasks are optional.

- Use Setup after First-Time Startup

- Use the Streamlined Setup Facility

Use Setup after First-Time Startup

The command parser allows you to make very detailed changes to your configurations. However, some major configuration changes do not require the granularity provided by the command parser. In these cases, you can use the **setup** command facility to make major enhancements to your configurations. For example, you might want to use **setup** to add a protocol suite, to make major addressing scheme changes, or to configure a newly installed interface. Although you can use the command parser to make these major changes, the **setup** command facility provides you with a high-level view of the configuration and guides you through the configuration change process.

Additionally, if you are not familiar with Cisco products and the command parser, the **setup** command facility is a particularly valuable tool because it asks you the questions required to make configuration changes.

NOTE   If you use **setup** to modify a configuration because you have added or modified the hardware, be sure to verify the physical connections using the **show version** command. Also, verify the logical port assignments using the **show running-config** command to ensure that you configure the proper port. Refer to your platform's hardware publications for details on physical and logical port assignments.

To enter the **setup** command facility, use the following command in privileged EXEC mode:

Command	Purpose
setup	Enters the **setup** command facility.

When you enter the **setup** command facility after first-time startup, an interactive dialog called the System Configuration Dialog appears on the system console screen. The System Configuration Dialog guides you through the configuration process. It prompts you first for global parameters and then for interface parameters. The values shown in brackets next to each prompt are the default values last set using either the **setup** command facility or the **configure** command.

NOTE   The prompts and the order in which they appear on the screen vary depending on the platform and the interfaces installed in the device.

You must run through the entire System Configuration Dialog until you come to the item that you intend to change. To accept default settings for items that you do not want to change, press the Return key.

To return to the privileged EXEC prompt without making changes and without running through the entire System Configuration Dialog, press **Ctrl-C**.

The facility also provides help text for each prompt. To access help text, press the question mark (?) key at a prompt.

When you complete your changes, the **setup** command facility shows you the configuration command script that was created during the **setup** session. It also asks you if you want to use this configuration. If you answer Yes, the configuration is saved to NVRAM. If you answer No, the configuration is not saved and the process begins again. There is no default for this prompt; you must answer either Yes or No.

NOTE   If any problems exist with the configuration file pointed to in NVRAM, or if the ignore NVRAM bit is set in the configuration register, the router enters the streamlined **setup** command facility. See the "Use the Streamlined Setup Facility" section for more information.

The following example shows how to use the **setup** command facility to configure interface serial 0 and to add ARAP and IP/IPX PPP support on the asynchronous interfaces:

```
Router# setup

        --- System Configuration Dialog ---

At any point you may enter a question mark '?' for help.
Use ctrl-c to abort configuration dialog at any prompt.
Default settings are in square brackets '[]'.

Continue with configuration dialog? [yes]:

First, would you like to see the current interface summary? [yes]:

Interface          IP-Address      OK?  Method  Status                  Protocol
Ethernet0          172.16.72.2     YES  manual  up                      up
Serial0            unassigned      YES  not set administratively down   down
Serial1            172.16.72.2     YES  not set up                      up

Configuring global parameters:

  Enter host name [Router]:

The enable secret is a one-way cryptographic secret used
instead of the enable password when it exists.

  Enter enable secret [<Use current secret>]:

The enable password is used when there is no enable secret
and when using older software and some boot images.

  Enter enable password [ww]:
  Enter virtual terminal password [ww]:
  Configure SNMP Network Management? [yes]:
    Community string [public]:
  Configure DECnet? [no]:
  Configure AppleTalk? [yes]:
    Multizone networks? [no]: yes
  Configure IPX? [yes]:
  Configure IP? [yes]:
    Configure IGRP routing? [yes]:
      Your IGRP autonomous system number [15]:
  Configure Async lines? [yes]:
    Async line speed [9600]: 57600
    Configure for HW flow control? [yes]:
    Configure for modems? [yes/no]: yes
      Configure for default chat script? [yes]: no
    Configure for Dial-in IP SLIP/PPP access? [no]: yes
      Configure for Dynamic IP addresses? [yes]: no
      Configure Default IP addresses? [no]: yes
      Configure for TCP Header Compression? [yes]: no
      Configure for routing updates on async links? [no]:
    Configure for Async IPX? [yes]:
    Configure for Appletalk Remote Access? [yes]:
      AppleTalk Network for ARAP clients [1]: 20
      Zone name for ARAP clients [ARA Dialins]:
```

```
Configuring interface parameters:

Configuring interface Ethernet0:
  Is this interface in use? [yes]:
  Configure IP on this interface? [yes]:
    IP address for this interface [172.16.72.2]:
    Number of bits in subnet field [8]:
    Class B network is 172.16.0.0, 8 subnet bits; mask is /24
  Configure AppleTalk on this interface? [yes]:
    Extended AppleTalk network? [yes]:
    AppleTalk starting cable range [1]:
    AppleTalk ending cable range [1]:
    AppleTalk zone name [Sales]:
    AppleTalk additional zone name:
  Configure IPX on this interface? [yes]:
    IPX network number [1]:

Configuring interface Serial0:
  Is this interface in use? [no]: yes
  Configure IP on this interface? [no]: yes
  Configure IP unnumbered on this interface? [no]: yes
    Assign to which interface [Ethernet0]:
  Configure AppleTalk on this interface? [no]: yes
    Extended AppleTalk network? [yes]:
    AppleTalk starting cable range [2]: 3
    AppleTalk ending cable range [3]: 3
    AppleTalk zone name [myzone]: ZZ Serial
    AppleTalk additional zone name:
  Configure IPX on this interface? [no]: yes
    IPX network number [2]: 3

Configuring interface Serial1:
  Is this interface in use? [yes]:
  Configure IP on this interface? [yes]:
  Configure IP unnumbered on this interface? [yes]:
    Assign to which interface [Ethernet0]:
  Configure AppleTalk on this interface? [yes]:
    Extended AppleTalk network? [yes]:
    AppleTalk starting cable range [2]:
    AppleTalk ending cable range [2]:
    AppleTalk zone name [ZZ Serial]:
    AppleTalk additional zone name:
  Configure IPX on this interface? [yes]:
    IPX network number [2]:
Configuring interface Async1:
    IPX network number [4]:
    Default client IP address for this interface [none]: 172.16.72.4
Configuring interface Async2:
    IPX network number [5]:
    Default client IP address for this interface [172.16.72.5]:
Configuring interface Async3:
    IPX network number [6]:
    Default client IP address for this interface [172.16.72.6]:
Configuring interface Async4:
    IPX network number [7]:
```

```
    Default client IP address for this interface [172.16.72.7]:
Configuring interface Async5:
    IPX network number [8]:
    Default client IP address for this interface [172.16.72.8]:
Configuring interface Async6:
    IPX network number [9]:
    Default client IP address for this interface [172.16.72.9]:
Configuring interface Async7:
    IPX network number [A]:
    Default client IP address for this interface [172.16.72.10]:
Configuring interface Async8:
    IPX network number [B]:
    Default client IP address for this interface [172.16.72.11]:
Configuring interface Async9:
    IPX network number [C]:
    Default client IP address for this interface [172.16.72.12]:
Configuring interface Async10:
    IPX network number [D]:
    Default client IP address for this interface [172.16.72.13]:
Configuring interface Async11:
    IPX network number [E]:
    Default client IP address for this interface [172.16.72.14]:
Configuring interface Async12:
    IPX network number [F]:
    Default client IP address for this interface [172.16.72.15]:
Configuring interface Async13:
    IPX network number [10]:
    Default client IP address for this interface [172.16.72.16]:
Configuring interface Async14:
    IPX network number [11]:
    Default client IP address for this interface [172.16.72.17]:
Configuring interface Async15:
    IPX network number [12]:
    Default client IP address for this interface [172.16.72.18]:
Configuring interface Async16:
    IPX network number [13]:
    Default client IP address for this interface [172.16.72.19]:

The following configuration command script was created:

hostname Router
enable secret 5 $1$krIg$emfYm/1OwHVspDuS8Gy0K1
enable password ww
line vty 0 4
password ww
snmp-server community public
!
no decnet routing
appletalk routing
ipx routing
ip routing
!
line 1 16
speed 57600
flowcontrol hardware
```

```
modem inout
!
arap network 20 ARA Dialins
line 1 16
arap enable
autoselect
!
! Turn off IPX to prevent network conflicts.
interface Ethernet0
no ipx network
interface Serial0
no ipx network
interface Serial1
no ipx network
!
interface Ethernet0
ip address 172.16.72.2 255.255.255.0
appletalk cable-range 1-1 1.204
appletalk zone Sales
ipx network 1
no mop enabled
!
interface Serial0
no shutdown
no ip address
ip unnumbered Ethernet0
appletalk cable-range 3-3
appletalk zone ZZ Serial
ipx network 3
no mop enabled
!
interface Serial1
no ip address
ip unnumbered Ethernet0
appletalk cable-range 2-2 2.2
appletalk zone ZZ Serial
ipx network 2
no mop enabled
!
Interface Async1
ipx network 4
ip unnumbered Ethernet0
peer default ip address 172.16.72.4
async mode interactive
!
Interface Async2
ipx network 5
ip unnumbered Ethernet0
peer default ip address 172.16.72.5
async mode interactive
!
Interface Async3
ipx network 6
ip unnumbered Ethernet0
peer default ip address 172.16.72.6
```

```
async mode interactive
!
Interface Async4
ipx network 7
ip unnumbered Ethernet0
peer default ip address 172.16.72.7
async mode interactive
async dynamic address
!
Interface Async5
ipx network 8
ip unnumbered Ethernet0
peer default ip address 172.16.72.8
async mode interactive
!
Interface Async6
ipx network 9
ip unnumbered Ethernet0
peer default ip address 172.16.72.9
async mode interactive
!
Interface Async7
ipx network A
ip unnumbered Ethernet0
peer default ip address 172.16.72.10
async mode interactive
!
Interface Async8
ipx network B
ip unnumbered Ethernet0
peer default ip address 172.16.72.11
async mode interactive
!
Interface Async9
ipx network C
ip unnumbered Ethernet0
peer default ip address 172.16.72.12
async mode interactive
!
Interface Async10
ipx network D
ip unnumbered Ethernet0
peer default ip address 172.16.72.13
async mode interactive
!
Interface Async11
ipx network E
ip unnumbered Ethernet0
peer default ip address 172.16.72.14
async mode interactive
!
Interface Async12
ipx network F
ip unnumbered Ethernet0
peer default ip address 172.16.72.15
```

```
async mode interactive
!
Interface Async13
ipx network 10
ip unnumbered Ethernet0
peer default ip address 172.16.72.16
async mode interactive
!
Interface Async14
ipx network 11
ip unnumbered Ethernet0
peer default ip address 172.16.72.17
async mode interactive
!
Interface Async15
ipx network 12
ip unnumbered Ethernet0
peer default ip address 172.16.72.18
async mode interactive
!
Interface Async16
ipx network 13
ip unnumbered Ethernet0
peer default ip address 172.16.72.19
async mode interactive
!
router igrp 15
network 172.16.0.0
!
end

Use this configuration? [yes/no]: yes

Building configuration...

Use the enabled mode 'configure' command to modify this configuration.

Router#
```

Use the Streamlined Setup Facility

The streamlined **setup** command facility is available only if your router is running from a ROM monitor and has RXBOOT ROMs installed. The following routers can have this type of ROM installed:

- Cisco 2500 running the IGS-RXBOOT image

- Cisco 3000 running the IGS-RXBOOT image

- Cisco 4000 running the XX-RXBOOT image

- Other routers running the RXBOOT image

The streamlined **setup** command facility permits your router to load a system image from a network server when there are problems with the startup configuration. The Cisco IOS software automatically puts you in the streamlined **setup** command facility when your router is accidentally or intentionally rebooted (or you are attempting to load a system image from a network server) after any of the following circumstances:

● You issued an **erase startup-config** command, thereby deleting the startup configuration file.

● You have bit 6 (ignore NVRAM configuration) set in the configuration register.

● Your startup configuration has been corrupted.

● You configured the router to boot from a network server (the last four bits of the configuration register are not equal to 0 or 1) and there is no Flash or no valid image in Flash.

● You configured the router to boot the RXBOOT image.

The streamlined **setup** command facility differs from the standard **setup** command facility because the streamlined facility does not ask you to configure global router parameters. You are prompted only to configure interface parameters, which permit your router to boot.

The following example shows a router entering the streamlined **setup** command facility:

```
        --- System Configuration Dialog ---

Default settings are in square brackets '[]'.

Configuring interface IP parameters for netbooting:
```

NOTE   The message "Configuring interface IP parameters for netbooting" only appears if you are booting over a network server and your configuration has insufficient IP information.

The streamlined **setup** command facility continues by prompting you for interface parameters for each installed interface. The facility asks if an interface is in use. If so, the facility then prompts you to provide an IP address and subnet mask bits for the interface. Enter the subnet mask bits as a decimal value, such as 5.

The following example shows the portion of the streamlined **setup** command facility that prompts for interface parameters. In the example, the facility is prompting for Ethernet0 interface parameters and Serial0 interface parameters:

```
Configuring interface Ethernet0:
  Is this interface in use? [yes]:
  Configure IP on this interface? [yes]:
    IP address for this interface: 192.195.78.50
    Number of bits in subnet field [0]: 5
    Class C network is 192.195.78.0, 5 subnet bits; mask is 255.255.255.248
```

```
Configuring interface Serial0:
  Is this interface in use? [yes]:
  Configure IP on this interface? [yes]:
    IP address for this interface: 192.195.78.34
    Number of bits in subnet field [5]:
    Class C network is 192.195.78.0, 5 subnet bits; mask is 255.255.255.248
```

The configuration information you provide on this screen is *temporary* and exists only so that you can proceed with booting your system. When you reload the system, your original configuration is left intact. If your startup configuration is corrupted, enter the **setup** command facility, and configure the basic parameters. Then issue the **copy running-config startup-config** command to write this configuration to NVRAM.

Using Other Configuration Tools

You can also you configure the Cisco IOS using one of the following tools:

● ClickStart

● ConfigMaker

For more information on using these configuration tools, refer to the documentation shipped with your product or configuration tool.

ClickStart

ClickStart enables you to configure and monitor a router using a World Wide Web browser. ClickStart can be used to configure a router to connect a small office or home PC to the Internet or to another network. In this environment, your PC is connected to the router via an Ethernet connection. You configure the router to dial your Internet service provider, and your Internet service provider supplies an ISDN, Frame Relay, or Asynchronous Serial connection to the Internet. You do not need to have an extensive background in networks and routers to configure your router using ClickStart.

You can use ClickStart to configure a Cisco 1003 or Cisco 1004 ISDN router running Cisco IOS Release 11.0(6) or later software, or Cisco IOS Release 11.1(2) or later software. You can also use ClickStart to configure a Cisco 1005 Frame Relay or Asynchronous Serial router running Cisco IOS Release 11.1(5) or later software. ClickStart is also available for the Cisco 1600 series and Cisco 700 series.

ConfigMaker

Use Cisco ConfigMaker on a Windows 95 or Windows NT system to quickly and easily configure Cisco 1000 series, Cisco 1600 series, Cisco 2500 series, and Cisco 3600 series routers and access servers from a single PC. Use this application to create a network of devices, make connections between devices, automatically assign addresses, and deliver configurations to routers by using the COM port on the computer. Cisco ConfigMaker is designed for resellers and network administrators of small to medium-sized businesses who are proficient in LAN fundamentals and basic network design.

ConfigMaker makes configuring a High-Level Data Link Control (HDLC), Frame Relay or ISDN wide-area network connection between routers or the Internet as easy as drawing a network diagram. The tool guides users step-by-step through network design and addressing tasks and automatically delivers configuration files to individual routers on the network. ConfigMaker provides a graphical view of the entire network and lets the user build network diagrams using standard copy/paste, drag/drop and online editing functions. ConfigMaker enables the user to monitor router and network configuration status at a glance with simple color codes.

CHAPTER 4

Configuration Tools Commands

AutoInstall and Setup are facilities that assist in setting up the initial configuration of a Cisco product.

The AutoInstall facility has no unique commands. Its functionality is built on other Cisco IOS commands.

The **setup** command facility is an interactive facility that allows you to perform first-time configuration and other basic configuration procedures on all routers. The facility prompts you to enter basic information needed to start a router functioning quickly and uneventfully.

While the **setup** command facility is a quick way to "set up" a router, you can also use it after first-time startup to perform basic configuration changes. The command in this chapter focuses on using **setup** after first-time startup.

Refer to your hardware platform's user guide for details on how to use **setup** for first-time startup.

setup

To enter the **setup** command facility, use the **setup** privileged EXEC command.

setup

Syntax Description

This command has no arguments or keywords.

Command Mode

Privileged EXEC

Usage Guidelines

This command first appeared in Cisco IOS Release 11.1.

You can use the **setup** command facility to make major enhancements to your configurations. For example, you might want to use **setup** to add a protocol suite, to make major addressing scheme changes, or to configure a newly installed interface. While you can use the command parser to make these major changes, the **setup** command facility provides you with a high-level view of the configuration and guides you through the configuration change process.

Additionally, if you are not familiar with Cisco products and the command parser, the **setup** command facility is a particularly valuable tool because it asks you the questions required to make configuration changes.

NOTE   If you use **setup** to modify a configuration because you have added or modified the hardware, be sure to verify the physical connections using the **show version** command. Also, verify the logical port assignments using the **show running-config** command to ensure that you configure the correct port. Refer to your platform's hardware publications for details on physical and logical port assignments.

Whenever you use the **setup** command facility, be sure that you have the following information:

● Interfaces the router has

● Protocols the router is routing

● Whether the router is to perform bridging

● Network addresses for the protocols being configured

● Password strategy for your environment

When you enter the **setup** command facility after first-time startup, an interactive dialog called the System Configuration Dialog appears on the system console screen. The System Configuration Dialog guides you through the configuration process. It prompts you first for global parameters and then for interface parameters. The values shown in brackets next to each prompt are the default values last set using either the **setup** command facility or the **configure** command.

NOTE   The prompts and the order in which they appear on the screen vary depending on the platform and the interfaces installed in the device.

You must run through the entire System Configuration Dialog until you come to the item that you intend to change. To accept default settings for items that you do not want to change, press the Return key.

To return to the privileged EXEC prompt without making changes and without running through the entire System Configuration Dialog, press **Ctrl-C**.

The facility also provides help text for each prompt. To access help text, press the question mark (?) key at a prompt.

When you complete your changes, the **setup** command facility shows you the configuration command script that was created during the **setup** session. It also asks you if you want to use this configuration. If you answer Yes, the configuration is saved to NVRAM. If you answer No, the configuration is not saved and the process begins again. There is no default for this prompt; you must answer either Yes or No.

The Cisco IOS software automatically puts you in the streamlined **setup** command facility when your router is accidentally or intentionally rebooted (or you are attempting to load a system image from a network server) after any of the following circumstances:

- You issued an **erase startup-config erase nvram:** command, thereby deleting the startup configuration file.

- You have bit 6 (ignore NVRAM configuration) set in the configuration register.

- Your startup configuration has been corrupted.

- You configured the router to boot from a network server (the last four bits of the configuration register are not equal to 0 or 1) and there is no Flash or no valid image in Flash.

- You configured the router to boot the RXBOOT image.

The streamlined **setup** command facility permits your router to load a system image from a network server when there are problems with the startup configuration.

The streamlined **setup** command facility differs from the standard **setup** command facility because the streamlined facility does not ask you to configure global router parameters. You are prompted only to configure interface parameters, which permit your router to boot.

The streamlined **setup** command facility is available only if your router is running from ROM monitor and has RXBOOT ROMs installed. The following routers can have this type of ROM installed:

- Cisco 2500 running the IGS-RXBOOT image

- Cisco 3000 running the IGS-RXBOOT image

- Cisco 4000 running the XX-RXBOOT image

- Other routers running the RXBOOT image

Examples

The following example shows how to use the **setup** command facility to configure interface serial 0 and to add ARAP and IP/IPX PPP support on the asynchronous interfaces.

```
Router# setup

        --- System Configuration Dialog ---

At any point you may enter a question mark '?' for help.
Use ctrl-c to abort configuration dialog at any prompt.
Default settings are in square brackets '[]'.

Continue with configuration dialog? [yes]:

First, would you like to see the current interface summary? [yes]:
```

```
Interface          IP-Address      OK?  Method   Status                  Protocol
Ethernet0          172.16.72.2     YES  manual   up                      up
Serial0            unassigned      YES  not set  administratively down   down
Serial1            172.16.72.2     YES  not set  up                      up
```

Configuring global parameters:

  Enter host name [Router]:

The enable secret is a one-way cryptographic secret used
instead of the enable password when it exists.

  Enter enable secret [<Use current secret>]:

The enable password is used when there is no enable secret
and when using older software and some boot images.

  Enter enable password [ww]:
  Enter virtual terminal password [ww]:
  Configure SNMP Network Management? [yes]:
    Community string [public]:
  Configure DECnet? [no]:
  Configure AppleTalk? [yes]:
    Multizone networks? [no]: **yes**
  Configure IPX? [yes]:
  Configure IP? [yes]:
    Configure IGRP routing? [yes]:
      Your IGRP autonomous system number [15]:
  Configure Async lines? [yes]:
    Async line speed [9600]: **57600**
    Configure for HW flow control? [yes]:
    Configure for modems? [yes/no]: **yes**
      Configure for default chat script? [yes]: **no**
    Configure for Dial-in IP SLIP/PPP access? [no]: **yes**
      Configure for Dynamic IP addresses? [yes]: **no**
      Configure Default IP addresses? [no]: **yes**
      Configure for TCP Header Compression? [yes]: **no**
      Configure for routing updates on async links? [no]:
    Configure for Async IPX? [yes]:
    Configure for Appletalk Remote Access? [yes]:
      AppleTalk Network for ARAP clients [1]: **20**
      Zone name for ARAP clients [ARA Dialins]:

Configuring interface parameters:

Configuring interface Ethernet0:
  Is this interface in use? [yes]:
  Configure IP on this interface? [yes]:
    IP address for this interface [172.16.72.2]:
    Number of bits in subnet field [8]:
    Class B network is 172.16.0.0, 8 subnet bits; mask is /24
  Configure AppleTalk on this interface? [yes]:
    Extended AppleTalk network? [yes]:
    AppleTalk starting cable range [1]:
    AppleTalk ending cable range [1]:
```
```

```
     AppleTalk zone name [Sales]:
     AppleTalk additional zone name:
   Configure IPX on this interface? [yes]:
     IPX network number [1]:

Configuring interface Serial0:
   Is this interface in use? [no]: yes
   Configure IP on this interface? [no]: yes
   Configure IP unnumbered on this interface? [no]: yes
     Assign to which interface [Ethernet0]:
   Configure AppleTalk on this interface? [no]: yes
     Extended AppleTalk network? [yes]:
     AppleTalk starting cable range [2]: 3
     AppleTalk ending cable range [3]: 3
     AppleTalk zone name [myzone]: ZZ Serial
     AppleTalk additional zone name:
   Configure IPX on this interface? [no]: yes
     IPX network number [2]: 3

Configuring interface Serial1:
   Is this interface in use? [yes]:
   Configure IP on this interface? [yes]:
   Configure IP unnumbered on this interface? [yes]:
     Assign to which interface [Ethernet0]:
   Configure AppleTalk on this interface? [yes]:
     Extended AppleTalk network? [yes]:
     AppleTalk starting cable range [2]:
     AppleTalk ending cable range [2]:
     AppleTalk zone name [ZZ Serial]:
     AppleTalk additional zone name:
   Configure IPX on this interface? [yes]:
     IPX network number [2]:
Configuring interface Async1:
     IPX network number [4]:
     Default client IP address for this interface [none]: 172.16.72.4
Configuring interface Async2:
     IPX network number [5]:
     Default client IP address for this interface [172.16.72.5]:
Configuring interface Async3:
     IPX network number [6]:
     Default client IP address for this interface [172.16.72.6]:
Configuring interface Async4:
     IPX network number [7]:
     Default client IP address for this interface [172.16.72.7]:
Configuring interface Async5:
     IPX network number [8]:
     Default client IP address for this interface [172.16.72.8]:
Configuring interface Async6:
     IPX network number [9]:
     Default client IP address for this interface [172.16.72.9]:
Configuring interface Async7:
     IPX network number [A]:
     Default client IP address for this interface [172.16.72.10]:
```

```
Configuring interface Async8:
    IPX network number [B]:
    Default client IP address for this interface [172.16.72.11]:
Configuring interface Async9:
    IPX network number [C]:
    Default client IP address for this interface [172.16.72.12]:
Configuring interface Async10:
    IPX network number [D]:
    Default client IP address for this interface [172.16.72.13]:
Configuring interface Async11:
    IPX network number [E]:
    Default client IP address for this interface [172.16.72.14]:
Configuring interface Async12:
    IPX network number [F]:
    Default client IP address for this interface [172.16.72.15]:
Configuring interface Async13:
    IPX network number [10]:
    Default client IP address for this interface [172.16.72.16]:
Configuring interface Async14:
    IPX network number [11]:
    Default client IP address for this interface [172.16.72.17]:
Configuring interface Async15:
    IPX network number [12]:
    Default client IP address for this interface [172.16.72.18]:
Configuring interface Async16:
    IPX network number [13]:
    Default client IP address for this interface [172.16.72.19]:

The following configuration command script was created:

hostname Router
enable secret 5 $1$krIg$emfYm/1OwHVspDuS8Gy0K1
enable password ww
line vty 0 4
password ww
snmp-server community public
!
no decnet routing
appletalk routing
ipx routing
ip routing
!
line 1 16
speed 57600
flowcontrol hardware
modem inout
!
arap network 20 ARA Dialins
line 1 16
arap enable
autoselect
!
! Turn off IPX to prevent network conflicts.
interface Ethernet0
no ipx network
```

```
interface Serial0
no ipx network
interface Serial1
no ipx network
!
interface Ethernet0
ip address 172.16.72.2 255.255.255.0
appletalk cable-range 1-1 1.204
appletalk zone Sales
ipx network 1
no mop enabled
!
interface Serial0
no shutdown
no ip address
ip unnumbered Ethernet0
appletalk cable-range 3-3
appletalk zone ZZ Serial
ipx network 3
no mop enabled
!
interface Serial1
no ip address
ip unnumbered Ethernet0
appletalk cable-range 2-2 2.2
appletalk zone ZZ Serial
ipx network 2
no mop enabled
!
Interface Async1
ipx network 4
ip unnumbered Ethernet0
peer default ip address 172.16.72.4
async mode interactive
!
Interface Async2
ipx network 5
ip unnumbered Ethernet0
peer default ip address 172.16.72.5
async mode interactive
!
Interface Async3
ipx network 6
ip unnumbered Ethernet0
peer default ip address 172.16.72.6
async mode interactive
!
Interface Async4
ipx network 7
ip unnumbered Ethernet0
peer default ip address 172.16.72.7
async mode interactive
async dynamic address
!
```

```
Interface Async5
ipx network 8
ip unnumbered Ethernet0
peer default ip address 172.16.72.8
async mode interactive
!
Interface Async6
ipx network 9
ip unnumbered Ethernet0
peer default ip address 172.16.72.9
async mode interactive
!
Interface Async7
ipx network A
ip unnumbered Ethernet0
peer default ip address 172.16.72.10
async mode interactive
!
Interface Async8
ipx network B
ip unnumbered Ethernet0
peer default ip address 172.16.72.11
async mode interactive
!
Interface Async9
ipx network C
ip unnumbered Ethernet0
peer default ip address 172.16.72.12
async mode interactive
!
Interface Async10
ipx network D
ip unnumbered Ethernet0
peer default ip address 172.16.72.13
async mode interactive
!
Interface Async11
ipx network E
ip unnumbered Ethernet0
peer default ip address 172.16.72.14
async mode interactive
!
Interface Async12
ipx network F
ip unnumbered Ethernet0
peer default ip address 172.16.72.15
async mode interactive
!
Interface Async13
ipx network 10
ip unnumbered Ethernet0
peer default ip address 172.16.72.16
async mode interactive
!
```

```
Interface Async14
ipx network 11
ip unnumbered Ethernet0
peer default ip address 172.16.72.17
async mode interactive
!
Interface Async15
ipx network 12
ip unnumbered Ethernet0
peer default ip address 172.16.72.18
async mode interactive
!
Interface Async16
ipx network 13
ip unnumbered Ethernet0
peer default ip address 172.16.72.19
async mode interactive
!
router igrp 15
network 172.16.0.0
!
end

Use this configuration? [yes/no]: yes

Building configuration...

Use the enabled mode 'configure' command to modify this configuration.

Router#
```

The following example shows a router entering the streamlined **setup** command facility:

```
--- System Configuration Dialog ---

Default settings are in square brackets '[]'.

Configuring interface IP parameters for netbooting:
```

NOTE   The message "Configuring interface IP parameters for netbooting" only appears if you are booting over a network server and your configuration has insufficient IP information.

The streamlined **setup** command facility continues by prompting you for interface parameters for each installed interface. The facility asks if an interface is in use. If so, the facility then prompts you to provide an IP address and subnet mask bits for the interface. Enter the subnet mask bits as a decimal value, such as 5. Continuing with the streamlined **setup** command facility example, the following output shows the portion of the facility that prompts for interface parameters. In the example, the facility is prompting for Ethernet 0 interface parameters and Serial 0 interface parameters:

```
Configuring interface Ethernet0:
  Is this interface in use? [yes]:
  Configure IP on this interface? [yes]:
    IP address for this interface: 192.195.78.50
    Number of bits in subnet field [0]: 5
    Class C network is 192.195.78.0, 5 subnet bits; mask is 255.255.255.248

Configuring interface Serial0:
  Is this interface in use? [yes]:
  Configure IP on this interface? [yes]:
    IP address for this interface: 192.195.78.34
    Number of bits in subnet field [5]:
    Class C network is 192.195.78.0, 5 subnet bits; mask is 255.255.255.248
```

The configuration information you provide on this screen is *temporary* and exists only so that you can proceed with booting your system. When you reload the system, your original configuration is left intact. If your startup configuration is corrupted, enter the **setup** command facility, and configure the basic parameters. Then issue the **copy running-config startup-config or copy system:running-config nvram:startup-config** command to write this configuration to NVRAM.

Related Commands

To locate documentation of related commands, you can search online at www.cisco.com.

copy running-config startup-config
erase nvram:
more system:running-config
show version

## CHAPTER 5

Configuring Operating Characteristics for Terminals

This chapter describes how to configure operating characteristics for terminals. For a complete description of the terminal operation commands in this chapter, refer to Chapter 6, "Terminal Operating Characteristics Commands." To locate documentation of other commands that appear in this chapter, you can search online at www.cisco.com.

To configure operating characteristics for terminals, perform any of the tasks in the following sections:

- Display Information about Current Terminal Session
- Set Local Terminal Parameters
- Save Local Settings between Sessions
- End a Session
- Change Terminal Session Parameters
- Record the Device Location
- Change the Retry Interval for a Terminal Port Queue
- LPD Protocol Support

Display Information about Current Terminal Session

The **show whoami** command displays information about the current user's terminal line, including hostname, line number, line speed, and location. To display line information, use the following command at the EXEC prompt:

Command	Purpose
show whoami *text*	Displays line information.

If text is included as an argument in the command, that text is displayed as part of the additional data about the line.

The following example shows sample output of the **show whoami** command:

```
Router> show whoami

Comm Server "Router", Line 0 at 0bps.  Location "Second floor, West"
```

```
--More--              .
Router>
```

To prevent the information from being lost, this command always displays a More prompt before returning. Press the space bar to return to the prompt.

Set Local Terminal Parameters

The **terminal** EXEC commands enable or disable features for the current session only. You can use these commands to temporarily change terminal line settings without changing the stored configuration file.

To see a list of the commands for setting terminal parameters for the current session, use the following command in user EXEC mode:

Command	Purpose
terminal ?	Lists the commands for setting terminal parameters.

The following example shows the type of output **terminal ?** could generate:

```
Router> terminal ?
  autohangup             Automatically hangup when last connection closes
  data-character-bits    Size of characters being handled
  databits               Set number of data bits per character
  dispatch-character     Define the dispatch character
  dispatch-timeout       Set the dispatch timer
  download               Put line into 'download' mode
  editing                Enable command line editing
  escape-character       Change the current line's escape character
  exec-character-bits    Size of characters to the command exec
  flowcontrol            Set the flow control
  full-help              Provide help to unprivileged user
  help                   Description of the interactive help system
  history                Enable and control the command history function
  hold-character         Define the hold character
  ip                     IP options
  keymap-type            Specify a keymap entry to use
  lat                    DEC Local Area Transport (LAT) protocol-specific
                         configuration
  length                 Set number of lines on a screen
  no                     Negate a command or set its defaults
  notify                 Inform users of output from concurrent sessions
  padding                Set padding for a specified output character
  parity                 Set terminal parity
  rxspeed                Set the receive speed
  special-character-bits Size of the escape (and other special) characters
  speed                  Set the transmit and receive speeds
  start-character        Define the start character
  stop-character         Define the stop character
```

```
stopbits              Set async line stop bits
telnet                Telnet protocol-specific configuration
telnet-transparent    Send a CR as a CR followed by a NULL instead of a CR
                      followed by a LF
terminal-type         Set the terminal type
transport             Define transport protocols for line
txspeed               Set the transmit speeds
width                 Set width of the display terminal
```

Throughout this chapter, many terminal settings can be configured for all terminal sessions or for just the current terminal session. The commands will be in two forms. The basic form will be in line configuration mode and can be saved permanently so that all terminal sessions are affected. The **terminal** form of the command is entered in EXEC mode and only affects the current session.

Save Local Settings between Sessions

You can configure the Cisco IOS software to save local parameters set with **terminal** EXEC commands between sessions. Saving local settings ensures that the parameters the user sets will remain in effect between terminal sessions. This function is useful for servers in private offices. To save local settings between sessions, use the following command in line configuration mode:

Command	Purpose
private	Saves local settings between sessions.

By default, user-set terminal parameters are cleared when the session ends with either the **exit** EXEC command, or when the interval set with the **exec-timeout** line configuration command has passed.

End a Session

To end a session, use the following command:

Command	Purpose
quit	Uses the quit EXEC command.

Refer to Chapter 7, "Managing Connections, Menus, and System Banners," for more information on exiting sessions and closing connections.

Change Terminal Session Parameters

This section explains how to change terminal and line settings both for a particular line and locally. The local settings are set with the EXEC **terminal** commands. They temporarily override the settings made by the system administrator and remain in effect only until you exit the system. In line configuration mode, you can set terminal operation characteristics that will be in operation for that line until the next time you change the line parameters.

The following sections describe the more common changes to the terminal and line settings:

- Define Escape Character and Other Key Sequences
- Specify Telnet Operation Characteristics
- Configure Data Transparency for File Transfers
- Specify an International Character Display

The following sections describe the less common changes to the terminal and line settings:

- Set Character Padding
- Specify the Terminal and Keyboard Type
- Change the Terminal Screen Length and Width
- Change Pending Output Notification
- Create Character and Packet Dispatch Sequences
- Display Debug Messages on the Console and Terminals
- Change Flow Control for the Current Session
- Set a Terminal-Locking Mechanism
- Configure Automatic Baud Rate Detection
- Set a Line as Insecure
- Configure Communication Parameters for Terminal Ports

Define Escape Character and Other Key Sequences

You can define or modify the default key sequences to execute functions for system escape, terminal activation, disconnect, and terminal pause.

Globally Define Escape Character and Other Key Sequences

To define or change the default key sequence, use one or more of the following commands in line configuration mode:

Command	Purpose
escape-character *ascii-number*	Changes the system escape sequence. The escape sequence indicates that the codes that follow have special meaning. The default escape sequence is Ctrl-^.[1]
activation-character *ascii-number*	Defines a session activation sequence or character. Entering this sequence at a vacant terminal begins a terminal session. The default activation sequence is the Return key.
disconnect-character *ascii-number*	Defines the session disconnect sequence or character. Entering this sequence at a terminal ends the session with the router. There is no default disconnect sequence.
hold-character *ascii-number*	Defines the hold sequence or character that causes output to the terminal screen to pause. To continue the output, enter any character after the hold character. To use the hold character in normal communications, precede it with the escape character. There is no default sequence.

1. Pressing **Ctrl** displays a caret (^) character. The escape sequence is **Ctrl-Shift-6**.

You can reinstate the default value for the escape character or activation character by using the **no** form of the command. For example, issuing the **no escape-character** line configuration command returns the escape character to Ctrl-^.

NOTE   If you are using the **autoselect** function, the activation character should not be changed from the default value of Return. If you change this default, the **autoselect** feature may not function immediately.

Define Escape and Pause Characters for the Current Session

For the current terminal session, you can modify key sequences to execute functions for system escape and terminal pause. To modify these sequences, use one or more of the following commands in EXEC mode:

Command	Purpose
terminal escape-character *ascii-number*	Changes the system escape sequence for the current session. The escape sequence indicates that the codes that follow have special meaning. The default sequence is Ctrl-^.

Command	Purpose
terminal hold-character *ascii-number*	Defines the hold sequence or character that causes output to the terminal screen to pause for this session. There is no default sequence. To continue the output, type any character after the hold character. To use the hold character in normal communications, precede it with the escape character. You cannot suspend output on the console terminal.

The **terminal escape-character** command is useful, for example, if you have the default escape character defined for a different purpose in your keyboard file. Entering the escape character followed by the X key returns you to EXEC mode when you are connected to another computer.

Specify Telnet Operation Characteristics

The following sections discuss telnet operation characteristics tasks:

● Generate a Hardware Break Signal for a Reverse Telnet Connection

● Set the Line to Refuse Full-Duplex, Remote Echo Connections

● Allow Transmission Speed Negotiation

● Synchronize the Break Signal

● Change the End-of-Line Character

Generate a Hardware Break Signal for a Reverse Telnet Connection

To cause the router to generate a hardware Break signal on the EIA/TIA-232 line that is associated with a reverse Telnet connection for the current line and session, use the following command in EXEC mode:

Command	Purpose
terminal telnet break-on-ip	Generates a hardware Break signal on the EIA/TIA-232 line that is associated with a reverse Telnet connection for the current line and session.

The hardware Break signal occurs when a Telnet Interrupt-Process command is received on that connection. This command can be used to control the translation of Telnet IP commands into X.25 Break indications.

This command is also a useful workaround in the following situations:

● Several user Telnet programs send an Interrupt-Process command, but cannot send a Telnet Break signal.

● Some Telnet programs implement a Break signal that sends an Interrupt-Process command.

Some EIA/TIA-232 hardware devices use a hardware Break signal for various purposes. A hardware Break signal is generated when a Telnet Break command is received.

NOTE	This command applies only to access server products. It is not supported on standalone routers.

Set the Line to Refuse Full-Duplex, Remote Echo Connections

You can set the line to allow the Cisco IOS software to refuse full-duplex, remote echo connection requests from the other end. This refusal suppresses negotiation of the Telnet Remote Echo and Suppress Go Ahead options. To set the current line to refuse to negotiate full-duplex for the current session, remote echo options on incoming connections, use the following command in EXEC mode:

Command	Purpose
terminal telnet refuse-negotiations	Sets the current line to refuse to negotiate full-duplex for the current session.

NOTE	This command applies only to access server products. It is not supported on standalone routers.

Allow Transmission Speed Negotiation

To allow the Cisco IOS software to negotiate transmission speed for the current line and session, use the following command in EXEC mode:

Command	Purpose
terminal telnet speed *default-speed maximum-speed*	Allows the Cisco IOS software to negotiate transmission speed for the current line and session.

You can match line speeds on remote systems in reverse Telnet, on host machines that connect to the network through an access server, or on a group of console lines hooked up to an access server, when disparate line speeds are in use at the local and remote ends of the connection. Line speed negotiation adheres to the Remote Flow Control option, defined in RFC 1080.

NOTE   This command applies only to access server products. It is not supported on standalone routers.

Synchronize the Break Signal

You can set lines on the access server to cause a reverse Telnet line to send a Telnet Synchronize signal when it receives a Telnet Break signal. The TCP Synchronize signal clears the data path, but interprets incoming commands. To cause the Cisco IOS software to send a Telnet Synchronize signal when it receives a Telnet Break signal on the current line and session, use the following command in EXEC mode:

Command	Purpose
terminal telnet sync-on-break	Causes the Cisco IOS software to send a Telnet Synchronize signal when it receives a Telnet Break signal on the current line and session.

NOTE   This command applies only to access server products. It is not supported on standalone routers.

Change the End-of-Line Character

The end of each line typed at the terminal is ended with a Return (CR). To cause the current terminal line to send a CR as a CR followed by a NULL instead of a CR followed by a line feed (LF), use the following command in EXEC mode:

Command	Purpose
terminal telnet transparent	Causes the current terminal line to send a CR as a CR followed by a NULL instead of a CR followed by a line feed (LF).

This command ensures interoperability with different interpretations of end-of-line handling in the Telnet protocol specification.

NOTE   This command applies only to access servers. It is not supported on standalone routers.

Configure Data Transparency for File Transfers

Data transparency enables the Cisco IOS software to pass data on a terminal connection without the data being interpreted as a control character.

During terminal operations, some characters are reserved for special functions. For example, **Ctrl-Shift-6-X** (^^x) suspends a session. When transferring files over a terminal connection (using the Xmodem or Kermit protocols, for example), you must suspend the recognition of these special characters to allow a successful file transfer. This process is called *data transparency*.

You can set a line to act as a transparent pipe so that programs such as Kermit, Xmodem, or CrossTalk can download a file across a terminal line. To temporarily configure a line to act as a pipe for file transfers, use the following command in EXEC mode:

Command	Purpose
terminal download	Sets up the terminal line to act as a transparent pipe for file transfers.

The **terminal download** command is equivalent to using all the following commands:

- **terminal telnet transparent**
- **terminal no escape-character**
- **terminal no hold-character**
- **terminal no padding 0**
- **terminal no padding 128**
- **terminal parity none**
- **terminal databits 8**

Specify an International Character Display

The classic U.S. ASCII character set is limited to 7 bits (128 characters), which adequately represents most displays in the U.S. Most defaults on the modem router work best on a 7-bit path. However, international character sets and special symbol display can require an 8-bit wide path and other handling.

You can use a 7-bit character set (such as ASCII), or you can enable a full 8-bit international character set (such as ISO 8859). This allows special graphical and international characters for use in banners and prompts, and adds special characters such as software flow control. Character settings can be configured globally, per line, or locally at the user level. Use the following criteria for determining which configuration mode to use when you set this international character display:

- If a large number of connected terminals support nondefault ASCII bit settings, use the global configuration commands.

- If only a few of the connected terminals support nondefault ASCII bit settings, use line configuration commands or the EXEC local terminal setting commands.

NOTE	Setting the EXEC character width to an 8-bit character set can cause failures. If a user on a terminal that is sending parity enters the **help** command, an "unrecognized command" message appears because the system is reading all eight bits, although the eighth bit is not needed for **help**.

NOTE	If you are using the **autoselect** function, the activation character should be set to the default Return, and the EXEC character bit should be set to 7. If you change these defaults, the application does not recognize the activation request.

Specify the International Character Display for All Lines

To specify a character set for all lines, use one or both of the following commands in global configuration mode:

Command	Purpose
default-value exec-character-bits {7	8}	Specifies the character set used in EXEC and configuration command characters.
default-value special-character-bits {7	8}	Specifies the character set used in special characters such as software flow control, hold, escape, and disconnect characters.

Specify the International Character Display on a Hardware, Software, or Per-line Basis

To specify a character set based on hardware, software, or on a per-line basis, use any of the following commands in line configuration mode:

Command	Purpose
databits {5	6	7	8}	Sets the number of data bits per character that are generated and interpreted by hardware.
data-character-bits {7	8}	Sets the number of data bits per character that are generated and interpreted by software.

Command	Purpose
exec-character-bits {7 | 8}	Specifies the character set used in EXEC and configuration command characters on a per-line basis.
special-character-bits {7 | 8}	Specifies the character set used in special characters such as software flow control, hold, escape, and disconnect characters on a per-line basis.

Specify an International Character Display for the Current Session

To specify a character set based on hardware, software, or on a per-line basis for the current terminal session, use the following appropriate commands in EXEC mode:

Step	Command	Purpose
1	**terminal databits** {5 | 6 | 7 | 8}	Sets the number of data bits per character that are generated and interpreted by hardware for the current session.
2	**terminal data-character-bits** {7 | 8}	Sets the number of data bits per character that are generated and interpreted by software for the current session.
3	**terminal exec-character-bits** {7 | 8}	Specifies the character set used in EXEC and configuration command characters on a per-line basis for the current session.
4	**terminal special-character-bits** {7 | 8}	Specifies the character set used in special characters (such as software flow control, hold, escape, and disconnect characters) on a per-line basis for the current session.

Set Character Padding

Character padding adds a number of null bytes to the end of the string and can be used to make a string an expected length for conformity. You can change the character padding on a specific output character.

Globally Set Character Padding

To set character padding, use the following command in line configuration mode:

Command	Purpose
padding *ascii-number count*	Sets padding on a specific output character for the specified line.

Change Character Padding for the Current Session

To change character padding on a specific output character for the current session, use the following command in EXEC mode:

Command	Purpose
terminal padding *ascii-number count*	Sets padding on a specific output character for the specified line for this session.

Specify the Terminal and Keyboard Type

You can specify the type of terminal connected to a line. This feature has two benefits: it provides a record of the type of terminal attached to a line, and it can be used in Telnet terminal negotiations to inform the remote host of the terminal type for display management.

Globally Specify the Terminal Type

To specify the terminal type, use the following command in line configuration mode:

Command	Purpose
terminal-type {*terminal-name*	*terminal-type*}	Specifies the terminal type.

This feature is used by TN3270 terminal to identify the keymap and ttycap passed by the Telnet protocol to the end host.

Change the Terminal and Keyboard Type for the Current Session

To specify the type of terminal connected to the current line for the current session, use the following command in EXEC mode:

Command	Purpose
terminal terminal-type *terminal-type*	Specifies the terminal type for this session.

Indicate the terminal type if it is different from the default of VT100. This default is used by TN3270 for display management and by Telnet and rlogin to inform the remote host of the terminal type.

To specify the current keyboard type for a session, use the following command in EXEC mode:

Command	Purpose
terminal keymap-type *keymap-name*	Specifies the keyboard type for this session.

You must specify the keyboard type when you use a keyboard other than the default of VT100. The system administrator can define other keyboard types and give you their names.

Change the Terminal Screen Length and Width

By default, the Cisco IOS software provides a screen display of 24 lines by 80 characters. You can change these values if they do not meet the requirements of your terminal. The screen values you set are passed during rsh and rlogin sessions.

The screen values set can be learned by some host systems that use this type of information in terminal negotiation. To disable pausing between screens of output, set the screen length to a zero.

The screen length specified can be learned by remote hosts. For example, the rlogin protocol uses the screen length to set up terminal parameters on a remote UNIX host. The width specified also can be learned by remote hosts.

Globally Change the Terminal Screen Length and Width

To set the terminal screen length and width, use the following commands in line configuration mode:

Step	Command	Purpose
1	**length** *screen-length*	Sets the screen length.
2	**width** *characters*	Sets the screen width.

Change the Terminal Screen Length and Width for the Current Session

To set the number of lines or character columns on the current terminal screen for the current session, use one of the following commands in EXEC mode:

Command	Purpose
terminal length *screen-length*	Sets the screen length for the current session.
terminal width *characters*	Sets the screen width for the current session.

Change Pending Output Notification

You can set up a line to inform a user who has multiple, concurrent Telnet connections when output is pending on a connection other than the active one. For example, you might want to know when another connection receives mail or a message.

Globally Set Pending Output Notification

To set pending output notification, use the following command in line configuration mode:

Command	Purpose
notify	Sets up a line to notify a user of pending output.

Set Pending Output Notification for the Current Session

To set pending output notification for the current session, use the following command in EXEC mode:

Command	Purpose
terminal notify	Sets up a line to notify a user of pending output for the current session.

Create Character and Packet Dispatch Sequences

The Cisco IOS software supports dispatch sequences and TCP state machines that transmit data packets only when they receive a defined character or sequence of characters. You can set up dispatch characters that allow packets to be buffered, then transmitted upon receipt of a character. You can set up a state machine that allows packets to be buffered and then transmitted upon receipt of a sequence of characters. This feature enables packet transmission when the user presses a function key, which is typically defined as a sequence of characters, such as "Esc I C."

TCP state machines can control TCP processes with a set of predefined character sequences. The current state of the device determines what happens next, given an expected character sequence. The state-machine commands configure the server to search for and recognize a particular sequence of characters, then cycle through a set of states. The user defines these states—up to eight states can be defined. (Think of each state as a task that the server performs based on the assigned configuration commands and the type of character sequences received.)

The Cisco IOS software supports user-specified state machines for determining whether data from an asynchronous port should be sent to the network. This functionality extends the concept of the dispatch character and allows the equivalent of multicharacter dispatch strings.

Up to eight states can be set up for the state machine. Data packets are buffered until the appropriate character or sequence triggers the transmission. Delay and timer metrics allow for more efficient use of system resources. Characters defined in the TCP state machine take precedence over those defined for a dispatch character.

Set Character and Packet Dispatch Sequences for a Line

Use the following commands in line configuration mode, as needed, for your particular system needs:

Step	Command	Purpose
1	**state-machine** *name state firstchar lastchar* [*nextstate* | **transmit**]	Specifies the transition criteria for the states in a TCP state machine.
2	**dispatch-machine** *name*	Specifies the state machine for TCP packet dispatch.
3	**dispatch-character** *ascii-number* [*ASCII-number2 . . . ascii-number*]	Defines a character that triggers packet transmission.
4	**dispatch-timeout** *milliseconds*	Sets the dispatch timer.

Change the Packet Dispatch Character for the Current Session

To change the packet dispatch character for the current session, use the following command in EXEC mode:

Command	Purpose
terminal dispatch-character *ascii-number1* [*ascii-number2 . . . ascii-number*]	Defines a character that triggers packet transmission for the current session.

Display Debug Messages on the Console and Terminals

To display **debug** command output and system error messages in EXEC mode on the current terminal, use the following command in privileged EXEC mode:

Command	Purpose
terminal monitor	Displays debug command output and system error messages in EXEC mode on the current terminal.

Remember that all terminal parameter-setting commands are set locally and do not remain in effect after a session is ended. You must use this command at the privileged-level EXEC prompt at each session to see the debugging messages.

Change Flow Control for the Current Session

To configure flow control between the router and attached device for this session, use one of the following commands in EXEC mode:

Command	Purpose
terminal flowcontrol {**none** | **software** [**in** | **out**] | **hardware**}	Sets the terminal flow control for this session.
terminal start-character *ascii-number*[1]	Sets the flow control start character in the current session.
terminal stop-character *ascii-number*[1]	Sets the flow control stop character in the current session.

1.This command is seldom used. Typically, you only need to use the **terminal flowcontrol** command.

Set a Terminal-Locking Mechanism

You can enable a terminal-locking mechanism that allows a terminal to be temporarily locked by using the following command in line configuration mode:

Command	Purpose
lockable	Enables a temporary terminal locking mechanism.

After you configure the line as lockable, you must still issue the **lock** EXEC command to lock the keyboard.

Configure Automatic Baud Rate Detection

You can configure a terminal to detect the baud rate being used over an asynchronous serial line automatically. To set up automatic baud detection, use the following command in line configuration mode:

Command	Purpose
autobaud	Sets the terminal to automatically detect the baud rate.

NOTE	Do not use the **autobaud** command with the **autoselect** command.

To start communications using automatic baud detection, use multiple Returns at the terminal. A 600-, 1800-, or 19200- baud line requires three Returns to detect the baud rate. A line at any other baud rate requires only two Returns. If you use extra Returns after the baud rate is detected, the EXEC facility simply displays another system prompt.

Set a Line as Insecure

You can set up a terminal line to appear as an insecure dial-up line. The information is used by the LAT software, which reports such dial-up connections to remote systems.

To set a line as insecure, use the following command in line configuration mode:

Command	Purpose
insecure	Sets the line as a dial-up line.

In the previous releases of Cisco IOS software, any line that used modem control was reported as dial-up connection through the LAT protocol; this feature allows more direct control of your line.

Configure Communication Parameters for Terminal Ports

You can change these parameters as necessary to meet the requirements of the terminal or host to which you are attached. To do so, use one or more of the following commands in EXEC mode:

Command	Purpose
terminal speed *bps* **terminal txspeed** *bps* **terminal rxspeed** *bps*	Sets the line speed for the current session. Choose from line speed, transmit speed, or receive speed.
terminal databits {5 | 6 | 7 | 8}	Sets the data bits for the current session.
terminal stopbits {1 | 1.5 | 2}	Sets the stop bits for the current session.
terminal parity {**none** | **even** | **odd** | **space** | **mark**}	Sets the parity bit for the current session.

Record the Device Location

You can record the location of a serial device. The text provided for the location appears in the output of the EXEC monitoring commands. To record the device location, use the following command in line configuration mode:

Command	Purpose
location *text*	Records the location of a serial device.

Change the Retry Interval for a Terminal Port Queue

If you attempt to connect to a remote device (such as a printer) that is busy, the connection attempt is placed in a terminal port queue. If the retry interval is set too high, and several routers or other devices are connected to the remote device, your connection attempt can have long delays. To change the retry interval for a terminal port queue, use the following command in global configuration mode:

Command	Purpose
terminal-queue entry-retry-interval *interval*	Changes the retry interval for a terminal port queue.

LPD Protocol Support

The Cisco IOS software supports a subset of the Berkeley UNIX Line Printer Daemon (LPD) protocol used to send print jobs between UNIX systems. This subset of the LPD protocol permits the following:

- Improved status information

- Cancellation of print jobs

- Confirmation of successful printing and automatic retry for common print failures

- Use of standard UNIX software

The Cisco implementation of LPD permits you to configure a printer to allow several types of data to be sent as print jobs (for example, PostScript or raw text).

To configure a printer for the LPD protocol, use the following command in global configuration mode:

Command	Purpose
printer *printername* {**line** *number* | **rotary** *number*} [**newline-convert**]	Configures printer and specify a TTY line (or lines) for the device.

If you use the **printer** command, you also must modify the */etc/printcap* file on the UNIX system to include the definition of the remote printer on the router. Use the optional **newline-convert** keyword on UNIX systems that do not handle single character line terminators to convert a new line to a character Return, line-feed sequence.

The following example includes the configuration of the printer Saturn on the host Memphis:

```
comm1pt¦Printer on cisco AccessServer:\
    :rm=memphis:rp+saturn:\
    :sd+/usr/spool/lpd/comm1pt:\
    :lf=?var/log/lpd/comm1pt:
```

The content of the actual file may differ, depending on the configuration of your UNIX system.

To print, use the standard UNIX lpr command.

Support for the LPD protocol allows you to display a list of currently defined printers and current usage statistics for each printer. To do so, use the following command in EXEC mode:

Command	Purpose
show printer	Lists currently defined printers and their usage statistics.

To provide access to LPD features, your system administrator must configure a printer and assign a TTY line (or lines) to the printer. The administrator must also modify */etc/printcap* on your UNIX system to include the definition of the remote printer in the Cisco IOS software.

CHAPTER 6

Terminal Operating Characteristics Commands

This chapter describes the commands used to control terminal operating characteristics.

For terminal operating characteristic task information and examples, refer to Chapter 5, "Configuring Operating Characteristics for Terminals."

activation-character

To define the character you enter at a vacant terminal to begin a terminal session, use the **activation-character** line configuration command. Use the **no** form of this command to make any character activate a terminal.

> **activation-character** *ascii-number*
> **no activation-character**

Syntax

Syntax	Description
ascii-number	Decimal representation of the activation character.

Default
Return (decimal 13)

Command Mode
Line configuration

Usage Guidelines
This command first appeared in Cisco IOS Release 10.0.

See Appendix A, "ASCII Character Set," for a list of ASCII characters.

NOTE	If you are using the **autoselect** function, set the activation character to the default, Return, and exec-character-bits to seven. If you change these defaults, the application will not recognize the activation request.

Example

The following example sets the activation character for the console to Delete, which is decimal 127:

```
line console
 activation-character 127
```

autobaud

To set the line for automatic baud detection, use the **autobaud** line configuration command. Use the **no** form of this command to restore the default.

> **autobaud**
> **no autobaud**

Syntax Description

This command has no arguments or keywords.

Default

No autobaud detection

Command Mode

Line configuration

Usage Guidelines

This command first appeared in Cisco IOS Release 10.0.

The autobaud detection supports a range from 300 to 19200 baud. A line set for autobaud cannot be used for outgoing connections, nor can you set autobaud capability on a line using 19200 baud when the parity bit is set (because of hardware limitations).

Example

The following example sets the auxiliary port for autobaud detection:

```
line 5
 autobaud
```

databits

To set the number of data bits per character that are interpreted and generated by the router hardware, use the **databits** line configuration command. Use the **no** form of the command to restore the default value.

databits {5 | 6 | 7 | 8}
no databits

Syntax	Description
5	Five data bits per character.
6	Six data bits per character.
7	Seven data bits per character.
8	Eight data bits per character.

Default
Eight data bits per character

Command Mode
Line configuration

Usage Guidelines
This command first appeared in Cisco IOS Release 10.0.

The **databits** line configuration command can be used to mask the high bit on input from devices that generate 7 data bits with parity. If parity is being generated, specify 7 data bits per character. If no parity generation is in effect, specify 8 data bits per character. The other keywords are supplied for compatibility with older devices and generally are not used.

Example
The following example sets the number of data bits per character to seven on line 4:

```
line 4
 databits 7
```

Part I

Command Reference

Related Commands

To locate documentation of related commands, you can search online at www.cisco.com.

data-character-bits
terminal databits
terminal data-character-bits

data-character-bits

To set the number of data bits per character that are interpreted and generated by the Cisco IOS software, use the **data-character-bits** line configuration command. Use the **no** form of the command to restore the default value.

> **data-character-bits** {7 | 8}
> **no data-character-bits**

Syntax	Description
7	Seven data bits per character.
8	Eight data bits per character.

Default

Eight data bits per character

Command Mode

Line configuration

Usage Guidelines

This command first appeared in Cisco IOS Release 10.0.

The **data-character-bits** line configuration command is used primarily to strip parity from X.25 connections on routers with the protocol translation software option. The **data-character-bits** line configuration command does not work on hard-wired lines.

Example

The following example sets the number of data bits per character to seven on virtual terminal line 1:

```
line vty 1
 data-character-bits 7
```

Related Commands

To locate documentation of related commands, you can search online at www.cisco.com.

terminal data-character-bits

default-value exec-character-bits

To define the EXEC character width for either 7 bits or 8 bits, use the **default-value exec-character-bits** global configuration command. Use the **no** form of the command to restore the default value.

> **default-value exec-character-bits {7 | 8}**
> **no default-value exec-character-bits**

Syntax	Description
7	Selects the 7-bit ASCII character set.
8	Selects the full 8-bit ASCII character set.

Default

7-bit ASCII character set

Command Mode

Global configuration

Usage Guidelines

This command first appeared in Cisco IOS Release 10.0.

Configuring the EXEC character width to 8 bits allows you to add graphical and international characters in banners, prompts, and so forth. However, setting the EXEC character width to 8 bits can also cause failures. If a user on a terminal that is sending parity enters the command **help**, an "unrecognized command" message appears because the system is reading all 8 bits, although the eighth bit is not needed for the **help** command.

Example

The following example selects the full 8-bit ASCII character set for EXEC banners and prompts:

```
default-value exec-character-bits 8
```

Related Commands

To locate documentation of related commands, you can search online at www.cisco.com.

default-value special-character-bits
exec-character-bits
length
terminal exec-character-bits
terminal special-character-bits

default-value special-character-bits

To configure the flow control default value from a 7-bit width to an 8-bit width, use the **default-value special-character-bits** global configuration command. Use the **no** form of the command to restore the default value.

> **default-value special-character-bits {7 | 8}**
> **no default-value special-character-bits**

Syntax	Description
7	Selects the 7-bit character set.
8	Selects the full 8-bit character set.

Default

7-bit character set

Command Mode

Global configuration

Usage Guidelines

This command first appeared in Cisco IOS Release 10.0.

Configuring the special character width to 8 bits allows you to add graphical and international characters in banners, prompts, and so forth.

Example

The following example selects the full 8-bit special character set:

```
default-value special-character-bits 8
```

Related Commands

To locate documentation of related commands, you can search online at www.cisco.com.

default-value exec-character-bits
exec-character-bits
length
terminal exec-character-bits
terminal special-character-bits

disconnect-character

To define a character to disconnect a session, use the **disconnect-character** line configuration command. Use the **no** form of this command to remove the disconnect character.

> **disconnect-character** *ascii-number*
> **no disconnect-character**

Syntax   Description

ascii-number   Decimal representation of the session disconnect character.

Default
No disconnect character is defined.

Command Mode
Line configuration

Usage Guidelines
This command first appeared in Cisco IOS Release 10.0.

The Break character is represented by zero; NULL cannot be represented.

To use the session-disconnect character in normal communications, precede it with the escape character. See Appendix A, "ASCII Character Set" for a list of ASCII characters.

Example

The following example sets the disconnect character for virtual terminal line 4 to Escape, which is decimal character 27:

```
line vty 4
 disconnect-character 27
```

dispatch-character

To define a character that causes a packet to be sent, use the **dispatch-character** line configuration command. Use the **no** form of this command to remove the definition of the specified dispatch character.

> **dispatch-character** *ascii-number1* [*ascii-number2 . . . ascii-number*]
>
> **no dispatch-character** *ascii-number1* [*ascii-number2 . . . ascii-number*]

Syntax	Description
ascii-number	Decimal representation of the character, such as Return (decimal 13) for line-at-a-time transmissions.

Default

No dispatch character is defined.

Command Mode

Line configuration

Usage Guidelines

This command first appeared in Cisco IOS Release 10.0.

The **dispatch-character** command defines a dispatch character that causes a packet to be sent even if the dispatch timer has not expired. It causes the Cisco IOS software to attempt to buffer characters into larger-sized packets for transmission to the remote host.

Enable the **dispatch-character** command from the session that initiates the connection, not from the incoming side of a streaming Telnet session.

This command can take multiple arguments, so you can define any number of characters as dispatch characters.

Example

The following example specifies the Return character (decimal 13) as the dispatch character:

```
line vty 4
 dispatch-character 13
```

Related Commands

To locate documentation of related commands, you can search online at www.cisco.com.

dispatch-machine
dispatch-timeout
state-machine
terminal dispatch-character

dispatch-machine

To specify an identifier for a TCP packet dispatch state machine on a particular line, use the **dispatch-machine** line configuration command. Use the **no** form of the command to disable a state machine on a particular line.

> **dispatch-machine** *name*
> **no dispatch-machine**

Syntax	Description
name	Name of the state machine that determines when to send packets on the asynchronous line.

Default

No dispatch state machine identifier is defined.

Command Mode

Line configuration

Usage Guidelines

This command first appeared in Cisco IOS Release 10.0.

When the **dispatch-timeout** command is specified, a packet being built will be sent when the timer expires, and the state will be reset to zero.

Any dispatch characters specified using the **dispatch-character** command are ignored when a state machine is also specified.

If a packet becomes full, it will be sent regardless of the current state, but the state is not reset. The packet size depends on the traffic level on the asynchronous line and the dispatch-timeout value. There is always room for 60 data bytes. If the dispatch-timeout value is greater than or equal to 100 ms, a packet size of 536 (data bytes) is allocated.

Example

The following example specifies the name *linefeed* for the state machine:

```
state-machine linefeed 0 0 9 0
state-machine linefeed 0 11 255 0
state-machine linefeed 0 10 10 transmit

line 1
 dispatch-machine linefeed
```

Related Commands

To locate documentation of related commands, you can search online at www.cisco.com.

dispatch-character
dispatch-timeout
state-machine

dispatch-timeout

To set the character dispatch timer, use the **dispatch-timeout** line configuration command. Use the **no** form of this command to remove the timeout definition.

> **dispatch-timeout** *milliseconds*
> **no dispatch-timeout**

Syntax

milliseconds

Description

Integer that specifies the number of milliseconds that the Cisco IOS software waits after putting the first character into a packet buffer before sending the packet. During this interval, more characters might be added to the packet, which increases the processing efficiency of the remote host.

Default

No dispatch timeout is defined.

Command Mode

Line configuration

Usage Guidelines

This command first appeared in Cisco IOS Release 10.0.

The **dispatch-timeout** line configuration command causes the software to buffer characters into packets for transmission to the remote host. The Cisco IOS software sends a packet a specified amount of time after the first character is put into the buffer. You can use the **dispatch-timeout** and **dispatch-character** line configuration commands together. In this case, the software dispatches a packet each time the dispatch character is entered, or after the specified dispatch timeout interval, depending on which condition is met first.

NOTE	The software's response might appear intermittent if the timeout interval is greater than 100 ms and remote echoing is used. For lines with a reverse-Telnet connection, use a dispatch-timeout value less than 10 ms.

Example

The following example sets the dispatch timer to 80 ms:

```
line vty 0 4
 dispatch-timeout 80
```

Related Commands

To locate documentation of related commands, you can search online at www.cisco.com.

dispatch-character
dispatch-machine
state-machine

escape-character

To define a system escape character, use the **escape-character** line configuration command. Use the **no** form of this command to set the escape character to Break.

> **escape-character** {*ascii-number* | **none**}
> **no escape-character**

Syntax	Description
ascii-number	Either the decimal representation of the character or a control sequence (Ctrl-E, for example).
none	Disables escape entirely.

Default

Ctrl-^

Command Mode

Line configuration

Usage Guidelines

This command first appeared in Cisco IOS Release 10.0.

The Break key cannot be used as an escape character on the console terminal because the Cisco IOS software interprets Break as an instruction to halt the system. To send the escape character to the other side, press **Ctrl-^** twice.

See Appendix A, "ASCII Character Set," for a list of ASCII characters.

Example

The following example sets the escape character to Ctrl-P, which is decimal character 16:

```
line console
 escape-character 16
```

Related Commands

To locate documentation of related commands, you can search online at www.cisco.com.

terminal escape-character

exec-character-bits

To configure the character widths of EXEC and configuration command characters, use the **exec-character-bits** line configuration command. Use the **no** form of the command to restore the default value.

exec-character-bits {7 | 8}
no exec-character-bits

Syntax	Description
7	Selects the 7-bit character set.
8	Selects the full 8-bit character set for use of international and graphical characters in banner messages, prompts, and so forth.

Default

7-bit ASCII character set

Command Mode

Line configuration

Usage Guidelines

This command first appeared in Cisco IOS Release 10.0.

Setting the EXEC character width to 8 allows you to use special graphical and international characters in banners, prompts, and so forth. However, setting the EXEC character width to 8 bits can cause failures. If a user on a terminal that is sending parity enters the **help** command, an "unrecognized command" message appears because the system is reading all 8 bits, and the eighth bit is not needed for the **help** command.

NOTE   If you are using the **autoselect** function, set the activation-character to the default, Return, and **exec-character-bits** to 7. If you change these defaults, the application will not recognize the activation request.

Example

The following example enables full 8-bit international character sets, except for the console, which is an ASCII terminal. It illustrates use of the **default-value exec-character-bits** global configuration command and the **exec-character-bits** line configuration command.

```
default-value exec-character-bits 8
line 0
 exec-character-bits 7
```

Related Commands

To locate documentation of related commands, you can search online at www.cisco.com.

default-value exec-character-bits
default-value special-character-bits
length
terminal exec-character-bits
terminal special-character-bits

hold-character

To define the local hold character used to pause output to the terminal screen, use the **hold-character** line configuration command. Use the **no** form of this command to restore the default.

> **hold-character** *ascii-number*
> **no hold-character**

Syntax	Description
ascii-number	Either the decimal representation of the hold character or a control sequence (for example, Ctrl-P).

Default

No hold character is defined.

Command Mode

Line configuration

Usage Guidelines

This command first appeared in Cisco IOS Release 10.0.

The Break character is represented by zero; NULL cannot be represented. To continue the output, enter any character after the hold character. To use the hold character in normal communications, precede it with the escape character. See Appendix A, "ASCII Character Set" for a list of ASCII characters.

Example

The following example sets the hold character to Ctrl-S, which is decimal 19:

```
line 8
 hold-character 19
```

Related Commands

To locate documentation of related commands, you can search online at www.cisco.com.

terminal hold-character

insecure

To set the line as an insecure location, use the **insecure** line configuration command. Use the **no** form of this command to disable this feature.

> **insecure**
> **no insecure**

Syntax Description

This command has no arguments or keywords.

Default

Disabled

Command Mode

Line configuration

Usage Guidelines

This command first appeared in Cisco IOS Release 10.0.

Example

The following example sets up line 10 as a dial-up line that is used by the LAT software to report the line as available to remote hosts:

```
line 10
 insecure
```

length

To set the terminal screen length, use the **length** line configuration command. Use the **no** form of the command to restore the default value.

> **length** *screen-length*
> **no length**

Syntax	Description
screen-length	Number of lines on the screen. A value of zero disables pausing between screens of output.

Default

24 lines

Command Mode

Line configuration

Usage Guidelines

This command first appeared in Cisco IOS Release 10.0.

The Cisco IOS software uses the value of this command to determine when to pause during multiple-screen output. Not all commands recognize the configured screen length. For example, the **show terminal** command assumes a screen length of 24 lines or more.

Example

The following example disables the screen pause function on the terminal connected to line 6:

```
line 6
 terminal-type VT220
 length 0
```

Related Commands

To locate documentation of related commands, you can search online at www.cisco.com.

terminal length

location

To record the location of a serial device, use the **location** line configuration command. Use the **no** form of this command to remove the description.

> **location** *text*
> **no location**

Syntax	Description
text	Location description.

Command Mode
Line configuration

Usage Guidelines
This command first appeared in Cisco IOS Release 10.0.

The **location** command enters information about the device location and status. Use the **show users all** EXEC command to display the location information.

Example
The following example identifies the location of the console:

```
line console
 location Building 3, Basement
```

lockable

To enable the **lock** EXEC command, use the **lockable** global configuration command. Use the **no** form of this command to reinstate the default—the terminal cannot be locked.

> **lockable**
> **no lockable**

Syntax Description
This command has no arguments or keywords.

Default
Not lockable

Command Mode
Global configuration

Usage Guidelines

This command first appeared in Cisco IOS Release 10.0.

This command activates a temporary password, which is set up with the **lock** EXEC command, so that a terminal is temporarily inaccessible.

Example

The following example sets the terminal to the lockable state:

```
lockable
```

Related Commands

To locate documentation of related commands, you can search online at www.cisco.com.

lock

logout-warning

To warn users of an impending forced timeout, use the **logout-warning** line configuration command. Use the **no** form of this command to restore the default.

logout-warning [*number*]

Syntax	Description
number	(Optional) Number of seconds that are counted down before session termination. If no number is specified, the default of 20 seconds is used.

Default

No warning is sent to the user.

Command Mode

Line configuration

Usage Guidelines

This command first appeared in Cisco IOS Release 10.3.

This command notifies the user of an impending forced timeout, set by using the **absolute-timeout** command, or another method such as ARAP.

Example

The following example sets a countdown value of 30 seconds:

```
line 5
 logout-warning 30
```

Related Commands

To locate documentation of related commands, you can search online at www.cisco.com.

absolute-timeout
session-timeout

notify

To enable terminal notification about pending output from other Telnet connections, use the **notify** line configuration command. Use the **no** form of this command to end notification.

> **notify**
> **no notify**

Syntax Description

This command has no arguments or keywords.

Default

Disabled

Command Mode

Line configuration

Usage Guidelines

This command first appeared in Cisco IOS Release 10.0.

This command sets a line to inform a user who has multiple, concurrent Telnet connections when output is pending on a connection other than the current one.

Example

The following example sets up notification of pending output from connections on virtual terminal lines 0 to 4:

```
line vty 0 4
 notify
```

Related Commands

To locate documentation of related commands, you can search online at www.cisco.com.

terminal notify

padding

To set the padding on a specific output character, use the **padding** line configuration command. Use the **no** form of this command to remove padding for the specified output character.

> **padding** *ascii-number count*
> **no padding** *ascii-number*

Syntax

Syntax	Description
ascii-number	Decimal representation of the character.
count	Number of NULL bytes sent after that character, up to 255 padding characters in length.

Command Mode

Line configuration

Usage Guidelines

This command first appeared in Cisco IOS Release 10.0.

Use this command when the attached device is an old terminal that requires padding after certain characters (such as ones that scrolled or moved the carriage). See Appendix A, "ASCII Character Set," for a list of ASCII characters.

Example

The following example pads a Return (decimal 13) with 25 NULL bytes:

```
line console
 padding 13 25
```

Related Commands

To locate documentation of related commands, you can search online at www.cisco.com.

terminal padding

parity

To define generation of a parity bit, use the **parity** line configuration command. Use the **no** form of the command to specify no parity.

> **parity** {**none** | **even** | **odd** | **space** | **mark**}
> **no parity**

Syntax	Description
none	No parity.
even	Even parity.
odd	Odd parity.
space	Space parity.
mark	Mark parity.

Default

No parity

Command Mode

Line configuration

Usage Guidelines

This command first appeared in Cisco IOS Release 10.0.

Communication protocols provided by devices such as terminals and modems often require a specific parity bit setting.

Example

The following example changes the default of no parity to even parity:

```
line 34
 parity even
```

Related Commands

To locate documentation of related commands, you can search online at www.cisco.com.

terminal parity

printer (LPD)

To configure a printer and assign a server TTY line (or lines) to it, use the **printer** global configuration command. Use the **no** form of the command to disable printing on a TTY line.

> **printer** *printer-name* {**line** *number* | **rotary** *number*} [**newline-convert** | **formfeed**]
> **no printer**

Syntax	Description
printer-name	Printer name.
line *number*	Assigns a TTY line to the printer.
rotary *number*	Assigns a rotary group of TTY lines to the printer.
newline-convert	(Optional) Converts newline (linefeed) characters to a two-character sequence "carriage-return, linefeed."
formfeed	(Optional) Causes the Cisco IOS software to send a form-feed character (ASCII 0x0C) to the printer TTY line immediately following each print job received from the network.

Default

No printers are defined by default.

Command Mode

Global configuration

Usage Guidelines

This command first appeared in Cisco IOS Release 10.3.

This command enables you to configure a printer for operations and assign either a single TTY line or a group of TTY lines to it. To make multiple printers available through the same printer name, specify the number of a rotary group.

In addition to configuring the printer with the **printer** command, you must also modify the file */etc/printcap* on your UNIX system to include the definition of the remote printer in the Cisco IOS software.

Use the optional **newline-convert** keyword in UNIX environments that cannot handle single-character line terminators. This converts newline characters to a carriage-return linefeed sequence. Use the **formfeed** keyword when using the line printer daemon (lpd) protocol to print and your system is unable to separate individual output jobs with a form feed (page eject). You can enter the **newline-convert** and **formfeed** keywords together and in any order.

Example

The following example configures a printer named printer1 and assigns its output to the single TTY line 4:

```
printer printer1 line 4
```

Related Commands

To locate documentation of related commands, you can search online at www.cisco.com.

clear line
show printer

private

To save user EXEC command changes between terminal sessions, use the **private** line configuration command. Use the **no** form of this command to restore the default condition.

> **private**
> **no private**

Syntax Description

This command has no arguments or keywords.

Default

User-set configuration options are cleared with the EXEC command **exit** or when the interval set with the **exec-timeout** line configuration command has passed.

Command Mode

Line configuration

Usage Guidelines

This command first appeared in Cisco IOS Release 10.0.

This command ensures that the terminal parameters set by the user remain in effect between terminal sessions. This behavior is desirable for terminals in private offices.

Example

The following example sets up virtual terminal line 15 to keep all user-supplied settings at system restarts:

```
line 15
 private
```

Related Commands

To locate documentation of related commands, you can search online at www.cisco.com.

exec-timeout
exit

show whoami

To display information about the current user's terminal line, including host name, line number, line speed, and location, use the **show whoami** EXEC command.

> **show whoami** [*text*]

Syntax	Description
text	(Optional) Additional data to print to the screen.

Command Mode

EXEC

Usage Guidelines

This command first appeared in Cisco IOS Release 10.0.

If text is included as an argument in the command, that text is displayed as part of the additional data about the line.

To prevent the information from being lost if the menu display clears the screen, this command always displays a More prompt before returning. Press the spacebar to return to the prompt.

Sample Display

The following example is sample output from the **show whoami** command:

```
Router> show whoami


Comm Server "Router", Line 0 at 0bps.  Location "Second floor, West"

--More--
Router>
```

special-character-bits

To configure the number of data bits per character for special characters such as software flow control characters and escape characters, use the **special-character-bits** line configuration command. Use the **no** form of the command to restore the default value.

> **special-character-bits** {**7** | **8**}
> **no special-character-bits**

Syntax / Description

Syntax	Description
7	Selects the 7-bit ASCII character set.
8	Selects the full 8-bit character set for special characters.

Default

7-bit ASCII character set

Command Mode

Line configuration

Usage Guidelines

This command first appeared in Cisco IOS Release 10.0.

Setting the special character bits to 8 allows you to use twice as many special characters as with the 7-bit ASCII character set. The special characters affected by this setting are the escape, hold, stop, start, disconnect, and activation characters.

Example

The following example allows the full 8-bit international character set for special characters on line 5:

```
line 5
 special-character-bits 8
```

Related Commands

To locate documentation of related commands, you can search online at www.cisco.com.

default-value exec-character-bits
default-value special-character-bits
exec-character-bits
terminal exec-character-bits
terminal special-character-bits

state-machine

To specify the transition criteria for the state of a particular state machine, use the **state-machine** global configuration command. Use the **no** form of the command to delete a particular state machine.

> **state-machine** *name state firstchar... lastchar* [*nextstate* | **transmit**]
> **no state-machine** *name*

Syntax	Description
name	Specifies the name for the state machine (used in the **dispatch-machine** line command). The user can specify any number of state machines, but each line can have only one state machine associated with it.
state	Defines which state is being modified. There are a maximum of eight states per state machine. Lines are initialized to state 0 and return to state 0 after a packet is transmitted.
firstchar... lastchar	Specify a range of characters. If the state machine is in the indicated state, and the next character input is within this range, the process goes to the specified next state. Full 8-bit character comparisons are done, so the maximum value is 255. Take care that the line is configured to strip parity bits (or not generate them), or duplicate the low characters in the upper half of the space.
nextstate	(Optional) Defines the state to enter if the character is in the specified range.
transmit	(Optional) Causes the packet to be transmitted and the state machine to be reset to state 0. Recurring characters that have not been explicitly defined to have a particular action return the state machine to state 0.

Default

No transition criteria are specified.

Command Mode

Global configuration

Usage Guidelines

This command first appeared in Cisco IOS Release 10.0.

This command is paired with the **dispatch-machine** line configuration command, which defines the line on which the state machine is effective.

Example

The following example uses a dispatch machine named *function* to ensure that the function key characters on an ANSI terminal are lumped together in one packet. Because the default in the example is to remain in state 0 without transmitting anything, normal key signals are transmitted immediately.

```
line 1 20
 dispatch-machine function
 !
state-machine function 0 0 255 transmit
```

Related Commands

To locate documentation of related commands, you can search online at www.cisco.com.

dispatch-character
dispatch-machine
dispatch-timeout

stopbits

To set the number of the stop bits transmitted per byte, use the **stopbits** line configuration command. Use the **no** form of the command to restore the default value.

stopbits {1 | 1.5 | 2}
no stopbits

Syntax	Description
1	One stop bit.
1.5	One and one-half stop bits.
2	Two stop bits.

Default
Two stop bits

Command Mode
Line configuration

Usage Guidelines
This command first appeared in Cisco IOS Release 10.0.

Communication protocols provided by devices such as terminals and modems often require a specific stop-bit setting.

Example
The following example changes the default from two stop bits to one as a performance enhancement:

```
line 4
 stopbits 1
```

Related Commands
To locate documentation of related commands, you can search online at www.cisco.com.

terminal stopbits

terminal databits

To change the number of data bits per character for the current terminal line for this session, use the **terminal databits** EXEC command.

terminal databits {5 | 6 | 7 | 8}

Syntax	Description
5	Five data bits per character.
6	Six data bits per character.
7	Seven data bits per character.
8	Eight data bits per character.

Default
Eight data bits per character

Command Mode
EXEC

Usage Guidelines
This command first appeared in a release prior to Cisco IOS Release 10.0.

Communication protocols provided by devices such as terminals and modems often require a specific data bit setting. The **terminal databits** command can be used to mask the high bit on input from devices that generate 7 data bits with parity. If parity is being generated, specify 7 data bits per character. If no parity generation is in effect, specify 8 data bits per character. The other keywords (**5** and **6**) are supplied for compatibility with older devices and are generally not used.

Example
The following example changes the databits per character to 7:

```
Router> terminal databits 7
```

Related Commands
To locate documentation of related commands, you can search online at www.cisco.com.

databits

terminal data-character-bits

To set the number of data bits per character that are interpreted and generated by the Cisco IOS software for the current line and session, use the **terminal data-character-bits** EXEC command.

terminal data-character-bits {**7** | **8**}

Syntax	Description
7	Seven data bits per charcter.
8	Eight data bits.

Default

Eight data bits per character

Command Mode

EXEC

Usage Guidelines

This command first appeared in a release prior to Cisco IOS Release 10.0.

This command is used primarily to strip parity from X.25 connections on routers with the protocol translation software option. The **terminal data-character-bits** command does not work on hard-wired lines.

Example

The following example sets the data bits per character to 7 on the current line :

```
terminal data-character-bits 7
```

Related Commands

To locate documentation of related commands, you can search online at www.cisco.com.

data-character-bits

terminal dispatch-character

To define a character that causes a packet to be sent for the current session, use the **terminal dispatch-character** EXEC command.

> **terminal dispatch-character** *ascii-number1* [*ascii-number2 . . . ascii-number*]

Syntax	Description
ascii-number	The ASCII decimal representation of the character, such as Return (ASCII character 13) for line-at-a-time transmissions. The command can take multiple arguments, so you can define any number of characters as the dispatch character.

Command Mode
EXEC

Usage Guidelines
This command first appeared in a release prior to Cisco IOS Release 10.0.

At times, you might want to queue up a string of characters until they fill a complete packet and then transmit the packet to a remote host. This can make more efficient use of a line, because the access server or router normally dispatches each character as it is entered.

Example
The following example defines the characters Ctrl-D (ASCII decimal character 4) and Ctrl-Y (ASCII decimal character 25) as the dispatch characters:

```
terminal dispatch-character 4 25
```

Related Commands
To locate documentation of related commands, you can search online at www.cisco.com.

dispatch-character

terminal dispatch-timeout
To set the character dispatch timer for the current terminal line for the current session, use the **terminal dispatch-timeout** EXEC command.

terminal dispatch-timeout *milliseconds*

Syntax	Description
milliseconds	An integer that specifies the number of milliseconds that the router waits after it puts the first character into a packet buffer before sending the packet. During this interval, more characters can be added to the packet, which increases processing efficiency of the remote host.

Command Mode
EXEC

Usage Guidelines

This command first appeared in a release prior to Cisco IOS Release 10.0.

Use this command to increase the processing efficiency of the remote host.

> **NOTE**   The router's response might appear intermittent if the timeout interval is greater than 100 milliseconds and remote echoing is used.

Example

The following example sets the dispatch timer to 80 milliseconds:

```
terminal dispatch-timeout 80
```

Related Commands

To locate documentation of related commands, you can search online at www.cisco.com.

dispatch-timeout

terminal download

To temporarily set the ability of a line to act as a transparent pipe for file transfers for the current session, use the **terminal download** EXEC command.

terminal download

Syntax Description

This command has no arguments or keywords.

Default

Disabled

Command Mode

EXEC

Usage Guidelines

This command first appeared in a release prior to Cisco IOS Release 10.0.

You can use this feature to run a program such as KERMIT, XMODEM, or CrossTalk that downloads a file across an access server or router line. This command sets up the terminal line to transmit data and is equivalent to entering all the following commands:

- **terminal telnet transparent**

- **terminal no escape-character** (see **terminal escape-character**)

- **terminal no hold-character** (see **terminal hold-character**)

- **terminal no padding 0** (see **terminal padding**)

- **terminal no padding 128** (see **terminal padding**)

- **terminal parity none**

- **terminal databits 8**

Example

The following example configures a line to act as a transparent pipe:

```
terminal download
```

terminal escape-character

To set the escape character for the current terminal line for the current session, use the **terminal escape-character** EXEC command.

> **terminal escape-character** *ascii-number*

Syntax

ascii-number

Description

Either the ASCII decimal representation of the escape character or a control sequence (Ctrl-P, for example). Entering the escape character followed by X returns you to the EXEC when you are connected to another computer. See Appendix A, "ASCII Character Set," for a list of ASCII characters.

Default

Ctrl-^ (which is **Ctrl-Shift-6**)

Command Mode

EXEC

Usage Guidelines

This command first appeared in a release prior to Cisco IOS Release 10.0.

This command is useful, for example, if you have the default escape character defined for a different purpose in your keyboard file. Entering the escape character followed by the X key returns you to EXEC mode when you are connected to another computer.

NOTE   The Break key cannot be used as an escape character on the console terminal because the operating software interprets BREAK as an instruction to halt the system.

Example

The following example sets the escape character to Ctrl-P (ASCII decimal 16):

```
terminal escape-character 16
```

Related Commands

To locate documentation of related commands, you can search online at www.cisco.com.

escape-character

terminal exec-character-bits

To locally change the ASCII character set used in EXEC and configuration command characters for the current session, use the **terminal exec-character-bits** EXEC command.

terminal exec-character-bits {7 | 8}

Syntax   Description

7   Selects the 7-bit ASCII character set.

8   Selects the full 8-bit character set.

Default

7-bit ASCII character set (unless set otherwise in global configuration mode)

Command Mode

EXEC

Usage Guidelines

This command first appeared in a release prior to Cisco IOS Release 10.0.

This EXEC command overrides the **default-value exec-character-bits** global configuration command. Configuring the EXEC character width to 8 bits enables you to add special graphical and international characters in banners, prompts, and so forth.

When the user exits the session, the character width is reset to the default value established by the default value EXEC-character-bits global configuration command. However, setting the EXEC character width to 8 bits can also cause failures. If a user on a terminal that is sending parity enters the **help** command, an "unrecognized command" message appears because the system is reading all 8 bits, and the eighth bit is not needed for the **help** command.

Example

The following example temporarily configures a router to use a full 8-bit user interface for system banners and prompts, allowing the use of additional graphical and international characters.

```
terminal exec-character-bits 8
```

Related Commands

To locate documentation of related commands, you can search online at www.cisco.com.

exec-character-bits

terminal flowcontrol

To set flow control for the current terminal line for the current session, use the **terminal flowcontrol** EXEC command.

terminal flowcontrol {none | software [in | out] | hardware}

Syntax	Description
• **none**	Prevents flow control.
software	Sets software flow control.
**in	out**	(Optional) Specifies the direction: **in** causes the router to listen to flow control from the attached device, and **out** causes the router to send flow control information to the attached device. If you do not specify a direction, both directions are assumed.
hardware	Sets hardware flow control. For information about setting up the EIA/TIA-232 line, see the manual that was shipped with your product.

Command Mode
EXEC

Usage Guidelines
This command first appeared in a release prior to Cisco IOS Release 10.0.

Flow control enables you to regulate the rate at which data can be transmitted from one point so that it is equal to the rate at which it can be received at another point. Flow control protects against loss of data because the terminal is not capable of receiving data at the rate it is being sent. You can set up data flow control for the current terminal line in one of two ways: software flow control, which you do with control key sequences, and hardware flow control, which you do at the device level.

For software flow control, the default stop and start characters are Ctrl-S and Ctrl-Q (XOFF and XON). You can change them with the **terminal stop-character** and **terminal start-character** commands.

Example
The following example sets incoming software flow control:

```
terminal flowcontrol software in
```

Related Commands
To locate documentation of related commands, you can search online at www.cisco.com.

flowcontrol

terminal hold-character

To set or change the hold character for the current session, use the **terminal hold-character** EXEC command. Use the **terminal no hold-character** command to delete the hold character.

> **terminal hold-character** *ascii-number*
> **terminal no hold-character**

Syntax	Description
ascii-number	Either the ASCII decimal representation of the hold character or a control sequence (for example, Ctrl-P). By default, no local hold character is set. The Break character is represented by zero; NULL cannot be represented.

Command Mode

EXEC

Part I

Command Reference

Usage Guidelines

This command first appeared in Cisco IOS Release 10.0.

You can define a local hold character that temporarily suspends the flow of output on the terminal. When information is scrolling too quickly, you can enter the hold character to pause the screen output, then enter any other character to resume the flow of output.

You cannot suspend output on the console terminal. To send the hold character to the host, precede it with the escape character.

Example

The following example removes the previously set hold character:

```
terminal no hold-character
```

Related Commands

To locate documentation of related commands, you can search online at www.cisco.com.

hold-character

terminal keymap-type

To specify the current keyboard type for the current session, use the **terminal keymap-type** EXEC command.

terminal keymap-type *keymap-name*

Syntax	Description
keymap-name	Name defining the current keyboard type.

Default

VT100

Command Mode

EXEC

Usage Guidelines

This command first appeared in Cisco IOS Release 11.2.

You must use this command when you are using a keyboard other than the default of VT100. The system administrator can define other keyboard types and give you their names.

Example

The following example specifies a VT220 keyboard as the current keyboard type:

```
terminal keymap-type vt220
```

terminal length

To set the number of lines on the current terminal screen for the current session, use the **terminal length** EXEC command.

> **terminal length** *screen-length*

Syntax   Description

screen-length   Your desired number of lines on the screen. The router uses this value to determine when to pause during multiple-screen output. A value of zero prevents the router from pausing between screens of output. When the output exceeds the screen length, it scrolls past.

Default

24 lines

Command Mode

EXEC

Usage Guidelines

This command first appeared in a release prior to Cisco IOS Release 10.0.

Some types of terminal sessions do not require you to specify the screen length because the screen length specified can be learned by some remote hosts. For example, the rlogin protocol uses the screen length to set up terminal parameters on a remote UNIX host.

Part

I

Command Reference

Example

The following example prevents the router from pausing between multiple screens of output:

```
terminal length 0
```

Related Commands

To locate documentation of related commands, you can search online at www.cisco.com.

length

terminal monitor

To display **debug** command output and system error messages for the current terminal and session, use the **terminal monitor** EXEC command.

> **terminal monitor**

Syntax Description

This command has no arguments or keywords.

Default

Disabled

Command Mode

EXEC

Usage Guidelines

This command first appeared in a release prior to Cisco IOS Release 10.0.

Remember that all terminal parameter-setting commands are set locally and do not remain in effect after a session is ended. You must perform this task at the privileged-level EXEC prompt at each session to see the debugging messages.

For more information about privileged-level EXEC mode, refer to Chapter 1, "Using the Command Line Interface."

Example

The following example displays **debug** command output and error messages during the current terminal session:

```
terminal monitor
```

terminal notify

To configure a line to inform a user who has multiple concurrent Telnet connections when output is pending on a connection other than the current one, use the **terminal notify** EXEC command.

terminal notify

Syntax Description

This command has no arguments or keywords.

Command Mode

EXEC

Usage Guidelines

This command first appeared in a release prior to Cisco IOS Release 10.0.

You might want to know, for example, when another connection receives mail or a message.

Example

The following example configures a line to inform a user with multiple connections when output is pending on a non-current connection:

```
terminal notify
```

Related Commands

To locate documentation of related commands, you can search online at www.cisco.com.

notify

terminal padding

To change the character padding on a specific output character for the current session, use the **terminal padding** EXEC command.

terminal padding *ascii-number count*

Syntax	Description
ascii-number	The ASCII decimal representation of the character.

Syntax	Description
count	The number of NULL bytes sent after that character, up to 255 padding characters in length.

Default
No padding

Command Mode
EXEC

Usage Guidelines
This command first appeared in a release prior to Cisco IOS Release 10.0.

Character padding adds a number of null bytes to the end of the string and can be used to make a string an expected length for conformity.

Example
The following example pads Ctrl-D (ASCII decimal character 4) with 164 NULL bytes:

```
terminal padding 4 164
```

Related Commands
To locate documentation of related commands, you can search online at www.cisco.com.

padding

terminal parity

To define the generation of the parity bit for the current terminal line for the current session, use the **terminal parity** EXEC command.

> **terminal parity** {**none** | **even** | **odd** | **space** | **mark**}

Syntax	Description
none	No parity. This is the default.

Syntax	Description
even	Even parity.
odd	Odd parity.
space	Space.
mark	Mark.

Command Mode
EXEC

Usage Guidelines
This command first appeared in a release prior to Cisco IOS Release 10.0.

Communication protocols provided by devices such as terminals and modems often require a specific parity bit setting.

Example
The following example sets the parity bit to odd:

```
terminal parity odd
```

Related Commands
To locate documentation of related commands, you can search online at www.cisco.com.

parity

terminal-queue entry-retry-interval

To change the retry interval for a terminal port queue, use the **terminal-queue** global configuration command. Use the **no** form of this command to restore the default terminal port queue interval.

> **terminal-queue entry-retry-interval** *interval*
> **no terminal-queue**

Syntax	Description
interval	Number of seconds between terminal port retries.

Default
60 seconds

Command Mode
Global configuration

Usage Guidelines
This command first appeared in Cisco IOS Release 11.1.

If a remote device (such as a printer) is busy, the connection attempt is placed in a terminal port queue. If you want to decrease the waiting period between subsequent connection attempts, decrease the default of 60 to an interval of 10 seconds. Decrease the time between subsequent connection attempts when, for example, a printer queue stalls for long periods.

Example
The following example changes the terminal port queue retry interval from the default of 60 seconds to 10 seconds:

```
terminal-queue entry-retry-interval 10
```

terminal rxspeed

To set the terminal receive speed (how fast information is sent to the terminal) for the current line and session, use the **terminal rxspeed** EXEC command.

> **terminal rxspeed** *bps*

Syntax	Description
bps	Baud rate in bits per second (bps).

Default
9600 bps

Command Mode
EXEC

Usage Guidelines
This command first appeared in a release prior to Cisco IOS Release 10.0.

Example
The following example sets the current auxiliary line receive speed to 115200 bps:

```
terminal rxspeed 115200
```

Related Commands
To locate documentation of related commands, you can search online at www.cisco.com.

rxspeed

terminal special-character-bits

To change the ASCII character widths to accept special characters for the current terminal line and session, use the **terminal special-character-bits** EXEC command.

terminal special-character-bits {7 | 8}

Syntax	Description
7	Selects the 7-bit ASCII character set.
8	Selects the full 8-bit ASCII character set. Configuring the width to 8 bits enables you to use twice as many special characters as with the 7-bit setting. This selection enables you to add special graphical and international characters in banners, prompts, and so forth.

Default
7-bit ASCII character set

Command Mode
EXEC

Usage Guidelines
This command first appeared in a release prior to Cisco IOS Release 10.0.

This command is useful, for example, if you want the router to provide temporary support for international character sets. It overrides the **default-value special-character-bits** global configuration command and is used to compare character sets typed by the user with the special character available during a data connection, which includes software flow control and escape characters.

When you exit the session, the character width is reset to the default value established by the global configuration command. However, setting the EXEC character width to eight bits can cause failures. If a user on a terminal that is sending parity enters the **help** command, an "unrecognized command" message appears because the Cisco IOS software is reading all eight bits, and the eighth bit is not needed for the **help** command.

Example
The following example temporarily configures a router to use a full 8-bit user interface for system banners and prompts. When you exit the system, character width is reset to the width established by the **default-value exec-character-bits** global configuration command.

```
terminal special-character-bits 8
```

Related Commands
To locate documentation of related commands, you can search online at www.cisco.com.

special-character-bits

terminal speed

To set the transmit and receive speeds of the current terminal line for the current session, use the **terminal speed** EXEC command.

> **terminal speed** *bps*

Syntax	Description
bps	The baud rate in bits per second (bps).

Default
9600 bps

Command Mode
EXEC

Usage Guidelines

This command first appeared in a release prior to Cisco IOS Release 10.0.

Set the speed to match the transmission rate of whatever device you have connected to the port. Some baud rates available on devices connected to the port might not be supported on the router. The router indicates whether the speed you selected is not supported.

Example

The following example restores the transmit and receive speed on the current line to 9600 bps.

```
terminal speed 9600
```

Related Commands

To locate documentation of related commands, you can search online at www.cisco.com.

speed

terminal start-character

To change the flow control start character for the current session, use the **terminal start-character** EXEC command.

> **terminal start-character** *ascii-number*

Syntax	Description
ascii-number	The ASCII decimal representation of the start character.

Default

Ctrl-Q (ASCII decimal character 17)

Command Mode

EXEC

Usage Guidelines

This command first appeared in a release prior to Cisco IOS Release 10.0.

The flow control start character signals the start of data transmission when software flow control is in effect.

Example

The following example changes the start character to Ctrl-O (ASCII decimal character 15):

```
terminal start-character 15
```

Related Commands

To locate documentation of related commands, you can search online at www.cisco.com.

start-character

terminal stopbits

To change the number of stop bits transmitted per byte by the current terminal line during an active session, use the **terminal stopbits** EXEC command.

terminal stopbits {1 | 1.5 | 2}

Syntax	Description
1	One stop bit.
1.5	One and a half stop bits.
2	Two stop bits.

Default

Two stop bits

Command Mode

EXEC

Usage Guidelines

This command first appeared in a release prior to Cisco IOS Release 10.0.

Communication protocols provided by devices such as terminals and modems often require a specific stop-bit setting.

Example

The following example changes the stop bits to one:

```
terminal stopbits 1
```

Related Commands

To locate documentation of related commands, you can search online at www.cisco.com.

stopbits

terminal stop-character

To change the flow control stop character for the current session, use the **terminal stop-character** EXEC command.

terminal stop-character *ascii-number*

Syntax	Description
ascii-number	The ASCII decimal representation of the stop character.

Default

Ctrl-S (ASCII character 19)

Command Mode

EXEC

Usage Guidelines

This command first appeared in a release prior to Cisco IOS Release 10.0.

The flow control stop character signals the end of data transmission when software flow control is in effect.

Example

The following example changes the stop character to Ctrl-E (ASCII character 5):

```
terminal stop-character 5
```

Related Commands

To locate documentation of related commands, you can search online at www.cisco.com.

stop-character

terminal telnet break-on-ip

To cause the access server to generate a hardware Break signal on the EIA/TIA-232 line, which is associated with a reverse Telnet connection, for the current line and sessions, use the **terminal telnet break-on-ip** EXEC command.

terminal telnet break-on-ip

Syntax Description

This command has no arguments or keywords.

Default

Disabled

Command Mode

EXEC

Usage Guidelines

This command first appeared in a release prior to Cisco IOS Release 10.0.

The hardware Break signal occurs when a Telnet Interrupt-Process (IP) command is received on that connection. The **terminal telnet break-on-ip** command can be used to control the translation of Telnet IP commands into X.25 Break indications.

This command is also a useful workaround in the following situations:

● Several user Telnet programs send an IP command, but cannot send a Telnet break signal.

● Some Telnet programs implement a Break signal that sends an IP command.

Some EIA/TIA-232 hardware devices use a hardware Break signal for various purposes. A hardware Break signal is generated when a Telnet Break command is received.

NOTE   This command applies only to access servers. It is not supported on standalone routers.

Example

The following example generates a Break signal on the asynchronous TTY line 4:

```
line tty 4
terminal telnet break-on-ip
```

terminal telnet refuse-negotiations

To set the current line to refuse to negotiate full-duplex, remote echo options on incoming connections for current sessions, use the **terminal telnet refuse-negotiations** EXEC command.

terminal telnet refuse-negotiations

Syntax Description

This command has no arguments or keywords.

Default

Disabled

Command Mode

EXEC

Usage Guidelines

This command first appeared in a release prior to Cisco IOS Release 10.0.

You can set the line to allow the access server to refuse full-duplex, remote echo connection requests from the other end. This task suppresses negotiation of the Telnet Remote Echo and Suppress Go Ahead options.

NOTE   This command applies only to access servers. It is not supported on standalone routers.

Example

The following example sets an asynchronous interface to refuse full-duplex, remote echo requests:

```
line async 1
terminal telnet refuse-negotiations
```

terminal telnet speed

To allow the access server to negotiate transmission speed for the current line and session, use the **terminal telnet speed** EXEC command.

terminal telnet speed *default-speed maximum-speed*

Syntax	Description
default-speed	Line speed (in bps) that the access server will use if the device on the other end of the connection has not specified a speed.
maximum-speed	Maximum line speed (in bps) that the device on the other end of the connection can use.

Default

9600 bps (unless otherwise set using the **speed**, **txspeed** or **rxspeed** line configuration commands)

Command Mode

EXEC

Usage Guidelines

This command first appeared in a release prior to Cisco IOS Release 10.0.

You can match line speeds on remote systems in reverse Telnet, on host machines hooked up to an access server to access the network, or on a group of console lines hooked up to the access server, when disparate line speeds are in use at the local and remote ends of the connection. Line speed negotiation adheres to the Remote Flow Control option, defined in RFC 1080.

NOTE   This command applies only to access servers. It is not supported on standalone routers.

Example

The following example enables the access server to negotiate a bit rate on the line using the Telnet option. If no speed is negotiated, the line will run at 2400 bps. If the remote host requests a speed greater than 9600 bps, then 9600 bps will be used.

```
line async 7
terminal telnet speed 2400 9600
```

terminal telnet sync-on-break

To cause the access server to send a Telnet Synchronize signal when it receives a Telnet Break signal on the current line and session, use the **terminal telnet sync-on-break** EXEC command.

terminal telnet sync-on-break

Syntax Description

This command has no arguments or keywords.

Default

Disabled

Command Mode

EXEC

Usage Guidelines

This command first appeared in a release prior to Cisco IOS Release 10.0.

You can set the line to cause a reverse Telnet line to send a Telnet Synchronize signal when it receives a Telnet Break signal. The TCP Synchronize signal clears the data path, but it still interprets incoming commands.

NOTE	This command applies only to access servers. It is not supported on standalone routers.

Example

The following example sets an asynchronous line to cause the access server to send a Telnet Synchronize signal:

```
line async 15
terminal telnet sync-on-break
```

terminal telnet transparent

To cause the current terminal line to send a Return character (CR) as a CR followed by a NULL instead of a CR followed by a Line Feed (LF) for the current session, use the **terminal telnet transparent** EXEC command.

terminal telnet transparent

Syntax Description

This command has no arguments or keywords.

Default

CR followed by an LF

Command Mode

EXEC

Usage Guidelines

This command first appeared in a release prior to Cisco IOS Release 10.0.

The end of each line typed at the terminal is ended with a Return (CR). This command permits interoperability with different interpretations of end-of-line demarcation in the Telnet protocol specification.

NOTE   This command applies only to access server products. It is not supported on standalone routers.

Example

The following example configures a line to send a CR as a CR followed by a NULL:

```
terminal telnet transparent
```

terminal terminal-type

To specify the type of terminal connected to the current line for the current session, use the **terminal terminal-type** EXEC command.

terminal terminal-type *terminal-type*

Syntax	Description
terminal-type	Defines the terminal name and type and permits terminal negotiation by hosts that provide that type of service.

Default
VT100

Command Mode
EXEC

Usage Guidelines
This command first appeared in a release prior to Cisco IOS Release 10.0.

Indicate the terminal type if it is different from the default of VT100. The terminal type name is used by TN3270 for display management and by Telnet and rlogin to inform the remote host of the terminal type.

Example
The following example defines the terminal on line 7 as a VT220:

```
terminal terminal-type VT220
```

Related Commands
To locate documentation of related commands, you can search online at www.cisco.com.

terminal keymap-type
terminal-type

terminal txspeed

To set the terminal transmit speed (how fast the terminal can send information) on the current line and session, use the **terminal txspeed** EXEC command.

> **terminal txspeed** *bps*

Syntax	Description
bps	Baud rate in bits per second (bps).

Default
9600 bps

Command Mode
EXEC

Usage Guidelines

This command first appeared in Cisco IOS Release 10.0.

Example

The following example sets the current auxiliary line transmit speed to 2400 bps:

```
terminal txspeed 2400
```

Related Commands

To locate documentation of related commands, you can search online at www.cisco.com.

terminal keymap-type
terminal terminal-type
txspeed

terminal-type

To specify the type of terminal connected to a line, use the **terminal-type** line configuration command. Use the **no** form of this command to remove any information about the type of terminal and reset the line to the default terminal emulation.

> **terminal-type** {*terminal-name* | *terminal-type*}
> **no terminal-type**

Syntax	Description
terminal-name	Terminal name.
terminal-type	Terminal type.

Default

VT100

Command Mode

Line configuration

Usage Guidelines

This command first appeared in Cisco IOS Release 10.0.

This command records the type of terminal connected to the line. The argument *terminal-name* provides a record of the terminal type and allows terminal negotiation of display management by hosts that provide that type of service.

For TN3270 applications, this command must follow the corresponding ttycap entry in the configuration file.

Example

The following example defines the terminal on line 7 as a VT220:

```
line 7
 terminal-type VT220
```

terminal width

To set the number of character columns on the terminal screen for the current line for a session, use the **terminal width** EXEC command.

> **terminal width** *characters*

Syntax

Description

characters   Number of character columns displayed on the terminal.

Default

80 characters

Command Mode

EXEC

Usage Guidelines

This command first appeared in a release prior to Cisco IOS Release 10.0.

By default, the route provides a screen display width of 80 characters. You can reset this value if it does not meet the needs of your terminal. The width specified can be learned by remote hosts.

Example

The following example sets the terminal character columns to 132:

```
terminal width 132
```

Related Commands

To locate documentation of related commands, you can search online at www.cisco.com.

width

width

To set the terminal screen width, use the **width** line configuration command. This command sets the number of character columns displayed on the attached terminal. Use the **no** form of this command to return to the default screen width.

> **width** *characters*
> **no width**

Syntax   Description

characters   Number of character columns displayed on the terminal.

Default

80 character columns

Command Mode

Line configuration

Usage Guidelines

This command first appeared in Cisco IOS Release 10.0.

The rlogin protocol uses the *characters* argument to set up terminal parameters on a remote host.

Some hosts can learn the values for both length and width specified with the **line** and **width** commands.

Example

The following example changes the character columns to 132 for the terminal on line 7:

```
line 7
 location console terminal
 width 132
```

Related Commands

To locate documentation of related commands, you can search online at www.cisco.com.

terminal width

CHAPTER **7**

Managing Connections, Menus, and System Banners

This chapter describes how to manage connections to other hosts, create menus of specific user tasks, and set banner messages for router users. For a complete description of the connections, menu, and system banner commands in this chapter, refer to Chapter 8, "Connection and System Banner Commands." To locate documentation of other commands that appear in this chapter, you can search online at www.cisco.com.

The following sections describe the connections and system banners tasks:

- Manage Connections
- Create Menus
- Set Up Terminal Banners
- Set Up Terminal Messages

Manage Connections

This section describes session-management activities. The following sections describe connection-management activities that apply to all supported connection protocols:

- Escape to the EXEC Prompt
- Switch to Another Connection
- Assign a Logical Name to a Connection
- Change a Login Name
- Lock Access to a Terminal
- Specify a TACACS Host
- Send Messages to Other Terminals
- Clear TCP/IP Connections
- Exit a Session Started from a Router
- Log Out of a Router
- Disconnect a Line

Escape to the EXEC Prompt

After you have started a connection, you can escape out of the current session and return to the EXEC prompt by using the escape sequence command (**Ctrl-Shift-6** then **x** [**Ctrl^x**] by default). You can type the command character as you hold down the **Ctrl** key or with the **Ctrl** key released.

NOTE   In screen output examples that show two caret (^^) symbols together, the first caret represents the Control key (**Ctrl**) and the second caret represents the keystroke sequence **Shift-6**. The double-caret combination (^^) means hold down the **Ctrl** key while you press the **Shift** and the **6** key.

By default, the escape sequence is **Ctrl^x**. If you press the Escape key (**Escape-Char**), you change the **Shift-Ctrl-6** sequence to whatever you want. For example, if you press **Escape-Char Break**, the **Break** key becomes the new escape character to suspend a session and to access the EXEC prompt.

Switch to Another Connection

You can have several concurrent sessions open and switch back and forth between them.

The number of sessions that can be open is defined by the **session-limit** command.

To switch between sessions by escaping one session and resuming a previously opened session, use the following commands:

Step	Command	Purpose
1	**Ctrl-Shift-6** then **x** (**Ctrl^x**) by default	Escapes the current connection and returns to the EXEC prompt.
2	**where**	Lists the open sessions. All open sessions associated with the current terminal line are displayed.
3	**resume** [*connection*] [*keyword*]	Makes the connection.

The **Ctrl^x**, **where**, and **resume** commands are available with all supported connection protocols.

You could also make a new connection while you are at the EXEC prompt.

Assign a Logical Name to a Connection

To assign a logical name to a connection, use the following command in EXEC mode:

Command	Purpose
name-connection	Assigns a logical name to a connection.

The logical name can be useful for keeping track of multiple connections.

You are prompted for the connection number and name to assign. The **where** command displays a list of the assigned logical connection names.

Change a Login Name

You can change a login username if you must match outgoing access list requirements or other login prompt requirements. To change a login username, use the following command in user EXEC mode:

Command	Purpose
login	Changes a login username.

When you enter this command, the system prompts you for a username and password. Enter the new username and the original password. If the username does not match, but the password does, the Cisco IOS software updates the session with the new username used by **login** command attempt.

If no username and password prompts appear, the network administrator did not specify that a username and password be required at login time. If both the username and password are entered correctly, the session becomes associated with the specified username.

When you access a system with TACACS security, you can enter your login name or specify a TACACS server by using the following argument when the "Username:" prompt appears:

> *user @tacacs-server*

The router must be one of the routers defined in a router configuration. For more information, refer to the "Specify a TACACS Host" section later in this chapter.

If you do not specify a host, the router tries each of the TACACS servers in the list until it receives a response.

If you specify a host that does not respond, no other TACACS server will be queried. The router either denies access or function, according to the action specified by the **tacacs-server last-resort** command if it is configured.

If you specified a TACACS server host with the *user @tacacs-server* argument, the TACACS server specified is used for all subsequent authentication or notification queries with the possible exception of SLIP address queries.

For an example of changing a login name, see the "Change a Login Name Example" section at the end of this chapter.

Lock Access to a Terminal

You can prevent access to your terminal session while keeping your connection open by setting up a temporary password. To lock access to the terminal, use the following commands in EXEC mode:

Step	Command	Purpose
1	**lock**	Issues the **lock** command. The system prompts you for a password.
2	*password*	Enters a password, which can be any arbitrary string. The screen clears and displays the message "Locked."
3	*password*	To regain access to your sessions, re-enter the password.

The Cisco IOS software honors session timeouts on a locked line. You must clear the line to remove this feature. The system administrator must set up the line to allow use of the temporary locking feature.

Specify a TACACS Host

You can specify a TACACS host when you dial in or use the **login** command. Only the specified host is accessed for user authentication information.

To specify the name of a TACACS host at login, use the following command in EXEC mode:

Command	Purpose
user@hostname	Specifies the name of a TACACS host at login.

For an example of specifying a TACACS host, see the "Specify a TACACS Host Example" section at the end of this chapter.

Send Messages to Other Terminals

You can send messages to one or all terminal lines. A common reason for doing this is to inform users of an impending shutdown. To send a message to other terminals, use the following command in EXEC mode:

Command	Purpose
send {*line-number*	*}	Sends a message to other terminals.

The system prompts for the message, which can be up to 500 characters long. Enter **Ctrl-Z** to end the message. Enter **Ctrl-C** to abort the command.

Clear TCP/IP Connections

To clear a TCP connection, use the following command in privileged EXEC mode:

Command	Purpose
clear tcp {**line** *line-number*	**local** *host-name port* **remote** *host-name port*	**tcb** *address*}	Clears a TCP connection.

The **clear tcp** command is particularly useful for clearing hung TCP connections.

The **clear tcp line** *line-number* command terminates the TCP connection on the specified TTY line. Additionally, all TCP sessions initiated from that TTY line are terminated.

The **clear tcp local** *host-name port* **remote** *host-name port* command terminates the specific TCP connection identified by the host name/port pair of the local and remote router.

Exit a Session Started from a Router

The protocol used to initiate a session determines how you exit that session.

To exit XRemote, you must quit all active X connections with a command supported by your X client system. Usually, when you quit the last connection (all client processes are stopped), XRemote closes, and you return to the EXEC prompt. Check your X client system documentation for specific information about exiting an XRemote session.

To exit a SLIP and PPP, you must hang up the dial-in connection, usually with a command that your dial-in software supports.

To exit a LAT, Telnet, rlogin, TN3270, and X.3 PAD session that began from the router to a remote device, enter the escape sequence (**Ctrl-Shift-6** then **x** [**Ctrl^x**] by default) and enter the **disconnect** command at the EXEC prompt. You can also log off the remote system.

Except for XRemote, you also can escape to the EXEC prompt and enter either of the following commands to terminate an active terminal session:

- **exit**

- **logout**

To exit a Telnet session *to* a router, see the next section.

Log Out of a Router

The method you use to disconnect from a router depends on where you are located in relation to the router and the port on the router to which you log in. Keep the following in mind:

- If your terminal or computer running a terminal-emulation application is connected physically to the console port of the router, you can disconnect from the console port by physically disconnecting the cable from the console port of the router.

- If your terminal or computer running a terminal-emulation application is remotely connected to the console port of the router, you disconnect by issuing the command or key sequence used by your terminal-emulation package. For example, if you are on a Macintosh computer running the application "TCP/Connect" from InterCon Corporation, you would press **Ctrl-]** at the user or privileged EXEC prompt to disconnect.

- If you are on a remote terminal and connect to a VTY line through a synchronous interface on the router, you can issue any of the following commands to disconnect:

  - **close**
  - **exit**
  - **logout**
  - **quit**

Disconnect a Line

To disconnect a line, use the following command in EXEC mode:

Command	Purpose
disconnect [*connection*]	Disconnects a line.

Avoid disconnecting a line to end a session. Instead, log off the host to allow the router to clear the connection. Then end the session. Only if you cannot log out of an active session should you disconnect the line.

Create Menus

A menu is a displayed list of actions from which you can select without having to know anything about the underlying command-level details. A menu system effectively controls which functions a user can access. Figure 7-1 illustrates the parts that make up a typical menu.

Figure 7-1   *Typical Menu Example*

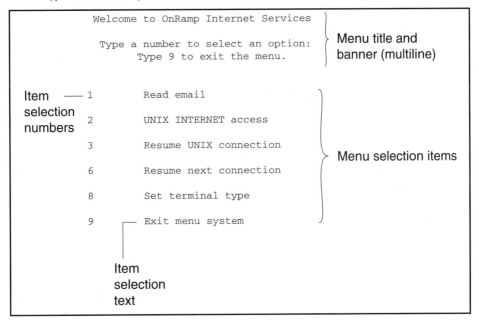

Create a Menu Task List

To create menus, perform the tasks in the following sections:

- Understand Menu Guidelines
- Specify the Menu Title
- Specify the Menu Prompt
- Specify the Menu Item Text
- Specify the Underlying Command for the Menu Item
- Specify the Default Command for the Menu
- Create a Submenu
- Create Hidden Menu Entries

- Specify Menu Display Configuration Options

- Specify Per-Item Menu Options

- Invoke the Menu

- Delete the Menu from the Configuration

Understand Menu Guidelines

Anyone who can enter configuration mode can create these menus. Keep the following guidelines in mind when you create menus:

- Each menu item represents a single user command.

- The menu system default is a standard "dumb" terminal that only displays text in a 24-line-by-80-column format.

- A menu can have a maximum of 18 menu items. Menus containing more than 9 menu items are automatically configured as single-spaced menus; menus containing 9 or fewer menu items are automatically configured as double-spaced menus, but they can be configured as single-spaced menus using the **menu single-space** command. (For more information about menu display configuration options, refer to the section "Specify Menu Display Configuration Options" later in this chapter.)

- Item keys can be numbers, letters, or strings. If you use strings, you must configure the **menu line-mode** command.

- When you construct a menu, always specify how a user exits a menu and where the user goes. If you do not provide an exit from a menu—such as with the **menu-exit** command (described in the section "Specify the Underlying Command for the Menu Item" later in this section), there is no way to exit the menu.

- The **exec-timeout** command can be used to close and clean up an idle menu; the **session-timeout** command can be used to clean up a menu with an open connection.

Specify the Menu Title

You can specify an identifying title for the menu. To specify the menu title, use the following command in global configuration mode:

Command	Purpose
menu *name* **title** *delimiter title delimiter*	Specifies the title for the menu.

The following example specifies the title that is displayed when the OnRamp menu is selected. The following four main elements create the title:

- The **menu title** command
- Delimiter characters that open and close the title text
- Escape characters to clear the screen (optional)
- Title text

The following example shows the command used to create the title for the menu shown in Figure 7-1, at the beginning of this section:

```
Router(config)# menu OnRamp title /^[[H^[[J
Enter TEXT message.  End with the character '/'.
                    Welcome to OnRamp Internet Services

        Type a number to select an option;
            Type 9 to exit the menu.
/
Router(config)#
```

You can position the title of the menu horizontally by preceding the title text with blank characters. You can also add lines of space above and below the title by pressing Enter.

In this example, the title text consists of the following:

- One-line title
- Space
- Two-line menu instruction banner

Title text must be enclosed within text delimiter characters—the slash character (/) in this example. Title text delimiters are characters that do not ordinarily appear within the text of a title, such as slash (/), double quote ("), or tilde (~). You can use any character that is not likely to be used within the text of the title as a delimiter character. Ctrl-C is reserved for special use and should not be used in the text of the title.

This title text example also includes an escape character sequence to clear the screen before displaying the menu. In this case the string ^[[H^[[J is an escape string used by many VT100-compatible terminals to clear the screen. To enter it, you must enter **Ctrl-V** before each escape character (^[).

You can also use the **menu clear-screen** command to clear the screen before displaying menus and submenus, instead of embedding a terminal-specific string in the menu title. This option uses a terminal-independent mechanism based on termcap entries defined in the router and the terminal type configured for the user's terminal. The **menu clear-screen** command allows the same menu to be used on multiple types of terminals instead of having terminal-specific strings embedded within menu titles. If the termcap entry does not contain a clear string, the menu system inserts 24 new lines, causing all existing text to scroll off the top of the terminal screen.

To clear the screen before displaying the menu, use the following command in global configuration mode:

Command	Purpose
menu *name* **clear-screen**	Specifies screen clearing before displaying menus and submenus.

The following example clears the screen before displacing the OnRamp menu or a submenu:

```
Router(config)# menu OnRamp clear-screen
```

Specify the Menu Prompt

You can specify a prompt for the menu. To specify the menu prompt, use the following command in global configuration mode:

Command	Purpose
menu *name* **prompt** *delimiter prompt delimiter*	Specifies the prompt for the menu.

Specify the Menu Item Text

Each displayed menu entry consists of the selection key (number, letter, or string) and the text describing the action to be performed. You can specify descriptive text for a maximum of 18 menu items. Because each menu entry represents a single user interface command, you must specify the menu item text one entry at a time. To specify the menu item text, use the following command in global configuration mode:

Command	Purpose
menu *name* **text** *item text*	Specifies the text for the menu item.

The following example specifies the text that is displayed for the three entries in the OnRamp menu:

```
Router(config)# menu OnRamp text 1 Read email
Router(config)# menu OnRamp text 2 UNIX Internet Access
Router(config)# menu OnRamp text 9 Exit menu system
```

You can provide access to context-sensitive help by creating a "help server" host and using a menu entry to make a connection to that host.

Menu selection keys do not need to be contiguous. You can provide consistency across menus by assigning a particular number, letter, or string to a special function—such as Help or Exit—regardless of the number of menu entries in a given menu. For example, menu entry H could be reserved for help across all menus.

When more than nine menu items are defined in a menu, the **menu line-mode** and **menu single-space** commands are activated automatically. The commands can be configured explicitly for menus of nine items or fewer. For more information on these commands, refer to the section "Specify Menu Display Configuration Options" later in this chapter.

Specify the Underlying Command for the Menu Item

Each displayed menu entry issues a user interface command when the user enters its key. Each menu entry can have only a single command associated with it. To specify the menu item command, use the following command in global configuration mode:

Command	Purpose
menu *name* **command** *item command*	Specifies the command to be performed when the menu item is selected.

The following example specifies the commands that are associated with the three entries in the OnRamp menu:

```
Router(config)# menu OnRamp command 1 rlogin mailsys
Router(config)# menu OnRamp command 2 rlogin unix.cisco.com
Router(config)# menu OnRamp command 9 menu-exit
```

The **menu-exit** command is available only from within menus. This command provides a way to return to a higher-level menu or to exit the menu system.

When a menu item allows you to make a connection, the menu item should also contain entries that can be used to resume connections; otherwise, when you try to escape from a connection and return to the menu, there is no way to resume the session. It will sit idle until you log off.

You can build the **resume connection** EXEC command into a menu entry so that the user can resume a connection, or you can configure the line using the **escape-char none** command to prevent users from escaping their sessions.

To specify connection resumption as part of the menu item command, use the following command in global configuration mode:

Command	Purpose
menu *name* **command** *item* **resume** [*connection*] **/connect** [*connect string*]	Specifies the command to be performed when the menu item is selected.

Embedding the **resume** command within the **menu** command permits a user to resume the named connection or make another connection using the specified name if there is no active connection by that name. As an option, you can also supply the connect string needed to connect initially. When you do not supply this connect string, the command uses the specified connection name.

You can use the **resume** command in the following menu entries:

- Embedded in a menu entry

- As a separate, specific menu entry

- As a "rotary" menu entry that steps through several connections

In the following example, the **resume** command is embedded in the **menu** command so that selecting the menu item either starts the specified connection session (if one is not already open) or resumes the session (if one is already open):

```
Router(config)# menu Duluth text 1 Read email
Router(config)# menu Duluth command 1 resume mailsys /connect rlogin mailsys
```

In the following example, the **resume** command is used in a separate menu entry (entry 3) to resume a specific connection:

```
Router(config)# menu Duluth text 3 Resume UNIX Internet Access
Router(config)# menu Duluth command 3 resume unix.cisco.com
```

You use the **resume/next** command to resume the next open connection in the user's list of connections. This command allows you to create a single menu entry that steps through all of the user's connections. To specify the **resume/next** connection resumption as part of the menu item command, use the following command in global configuration mode:

Command	Purpose
menu *name* **command** *item* **resume /next**	Specifies **resume/next** connection resumption.

The following example shows a menu entry (entry 6) created to step through all of the user's connections:

```
Router(config)# menu Duluth text 6 Resume next connection
Router(config)# menu Duluth command 6 resume /next
```

Specify the Default Command for the Menu

When a user presses Enter without specifying an item, the router performs the command for the default item. To specify the default item, use the following command in global configuration mode:

Command	Purpose
menu *name* **default** *item*	Uses the command to be performed when no item is specified.

Create a Submenu

To create submenus that are opened by selecting a higher-level menu entry, use the **menu** command to invoke a menu in a line menu entry. To specify a submenu item command, use the following commands in global configuration mode:

Step	Command	Purpose
1	**menu** *name* **text** *item text*	Specifies the menu item that invokes the submenu.
2	**menu** *name* **command** *item* **menu** *name2*	Specifies the command to be used when the menu item is selected.
3	**menu** *name2* **title** *delimiter title2 delimiter*	Specifies the title for the submenu.
4	**menu** *name2* **text** *item text*	Specifies the submenu item.
5	**menu** *name2* **command** *item command*	Specifies the commands to be used when the submenu item is selected.

The following example specifies that the menu item (entry 8) activates the submenu in the OnRamp menu:

```
Router(config)# menu OnRamp text 8 Set terminal type
```

The following example specifies the command that is performed when the menu item (entry 8) is selected in the OnRamp menu:

```
Router(config)# menu OnRamp command 8 menu Terminals
```

The following example specifies the title for the Terminals submenu:

```
Router(config)# menu Terminals title /
                    Supported Terminal Types

        Type a number to select an option;
        Type 9 to return to the previous menu.
```

The following example specifies the submenu items for the Terminals submenu:

```
Router(config)# menu Terminals text 1 DEC VT420 or similar
Router(config)# menu Terminals text 2 Heath H-19
Router(config)# menu Terminals text 3 IBM 3051 or equivalent
Router(config)# menu Terminals text 4 Macintosh with gterm emulator
Router(config)# menu Terminals text 9 Return to previous menu
```

The following example specifies the commands associated with the items in the Terminals submenu:

```
Router(config)# menu Terminals command 1 term terminal-type vt420
Router(config)# menu Terminals command 2 term terminal-type h19
Router(config)# menu Terminals command 3 term terminal-type ibm3051
Router(config)# menu Terminals command 4 term terminal-type gterm
Router(config)# menu Terminals command 9 menu-exit
```

When you select entry 8 on the main menu, the Terminals submenu appears:

```
        Supported Terminal Types

   Type a number to select an option;
Type 9 to return to the previous menu.

1       DEC VT420 or similar

2       Heath H-19

3       IBM 3051 or equivalent

4       Macintosh with gterm emulator

9       Return to previous menu
```

NOTE   If you nest too many levels of menus, the system prints an error message on the terminal and returns to the previous menu level.

Create Hidden Menu Entries

A hidden menu entry is a menu item that contains a selection key but no associated text describing the action to be performed. Include this type of menu entry to aid system administrators who help users. The normal procedure is to specify a menu command but omit specifying any text for the item. To specify a hidden menu item, use the following command in global configuration mode:

Command	Purpose
menu *name* **command** *item command*	Specifies the command to be used when the hidden menu entry is selected.

The following example shows the command associated with the submenu entry in the OnRamp menu:

```
Router(config)# menu OnRamp command 7 show whoami
```

The **show whoami** command can be included in menus to aid system administrators who help users. If text is included as an argument in the command, that text is displayed as part of the additional data about the line and helps identify exactly which menu or submenu the user is accessing. Because the **show whoami** command is hidden inside the menu entry, this information might not be otherwise available. For example, the hidden menu entry created by the line in the configuration file menu OnRamp command 7 show whoami Terminals submenu of OnRamp Internet Access menu might display information similar to the following:

```
Comm Server "cs101", Line 0 at 0 bps. Location "Second floor, West"
Additional data: Terminals submenu of OnRamp Internet Access menu
```

To prevent the information from being lost if the menu display clears the screen, this command always displays a More prompt before returning.

Specify Menu Display Configuration Options

In addition to the **menu clear-screen** command, described in the section "Specify the Menu Title," the following are the three other **menu** commands that define menu functions:

● **menu line-mode**

● **menu single-space**

● **menu status-line**

Using Line Mode in Menus

In a menu of nine or fewer items, you ordinarily select a menu item by entering the item number or a letter. In line mode, you select a menu entry by entering the item key and pressing Enter. The line mode allows you to backspace over the selection and enter another before pressing Enter to issue the command. This function allows you to change the selection before you invoke the command.

To invoke the **line-mode** option, use the following command in global configuration mode:

Command	Purpose
menu *name* **line-mode**	Specifies line-mode operation.

The line-mode option is invoked automatically when more than nine menu items are defined, but it can also be configured explicitly for menus of nine items or fewer.

In order to use strings as selection keys, you must enable the **menu line-mode** command.

Displaying Single-Spaced Menus

If there are nine or fewer menu items, the Cisco IOS software ordinarily displays the menu items double-spaced. In a menu of more than nine items, the **single-space** option is activated automatically to fit the menu into a normal 24-line terminal screen. However, the single-space option also can be configured explicitly for menus of nine or fewer items.

To invoke the **single-space** option, use the following command in global configuration mode:

Command	Purpose
menu *name* **single-space**	Specifies single-space operation.

Displaying an Informational Status Line

The **status-line** option displays a line of status information about the current user at the top of the terminal screen before the menu title is displayed. This status line includes the router's host name, the user's line number, and the current terminal type and keymap type (if any).

To display the **status-line** option, use the following command in global configuration mode:

Command	Purpose
menu *name* **status-line**	Displays a status line when using a menu.

Specify Per-Item Menu Options

To configure per-item options, use either or both of the following commands in global configuration mode:

Command	Purpose
menu *name* **options** *item* **pause**	After the command is issued, it pauses before redrawing the menu. Enter this command once for each menu item that pauses.
menu *name* **options** *item* **login**	Requires a login before the command. Enter this command once for each menu item that requires a login.

Invoke the Menu

To invoke the menu, use the following command at the EXEC prompt:

Command	Purpose
menu *name*	Invokes the menu by specifying the name of the menu.

You can define menus containing privileged EXEC commands, but users must have privileged access when they start up the menu.

To ensure that a menu is automatically invoked on a line, make sure the menu does not have any exit paths that leave users in an interface they cannot operate, then configure that line with the command **autocommand menu** *menu_name*.

Menus also can be invoked on a per-user basis by defining an **autocommand** for that local username.

Invoke a Menu Example

The following example invokes the OnRamp menu:

```
Router> menu OnRamp

      Welcome to OnRamp Internet Services

      Type a number to select an option;
          Type 9 to exit the menu.

1     Read email

2     UNIX Internet access

3     Resume UNIX connection

6     Resume next connection

9     Exit menu system
```

Delete the Menu from the Configuration

To delete the menu from the configuration, use the following command in global configuration mode:

Command	Purpose
no menu *name*	Deletes the menu by specifying the menu name.

In order to use the menu again, you must reconfigure the entire menu again.

The following example deletes the OnRamp menu from the configuration:

```
Router(config)# no menu OnRamp
```

Set Up Terminal Banners

The types of banners that can be displayed to terminal users who connect to the router are described in the following sections:

- Configure a Message-of-the-Day (MOTD) Banner

- Configure a Login Banner

- Configure a Line-Activation Banner

- Configure an Incoming Banner

You also can turn off message displays, as described in the "Enable or Disable the Display of Banners" section.

For an example of displaying terminal banner messages, see the "Banner Example" section at the end of this chapter.

Configure a Message-of-the-Day (MOTD) Banner

You can configure a message-of-the-day (MOTD) banner to be displayed on all connected terminals. This banner is displayed at login and is useful for sending messages that affect all network users (such as impending system shutdowns). To do so, use the following command in global configuration mode:

Command	Purpose
banner motd *d message d*	Configures a MOTD banner.

Configure a Login Banner

You can configure a login banner to be displayed on all connected terminals. This banner is displayed after the MOTD banner and before the login prompts.

To configure a login banner, use the following command in global configuration mode:

Command	Purpose
banner login *d message d*	Configures a login banner.

The login banner cannot be disabled on a per-line basis. To globally disable the login banner, you must delete the login banner with the **no banner login** command.

Configure a Line-Activation Banner

You can configure a line-activation banner to be displayed when an EXEC process (such as a line-activation or incoming connection to a VTY line) is created. To do so, use the following command in global configuration mode:

Command	Purpose
banner exec *d message d*	Configures a banner to be displayed on terminals with an interactive EXEC session.

Configure an Incoming Banner

You can configure a banner to be displayed on terminals connected to reverse Telnet lines. This banner is useful for providing instructions to users of these types of connections.

To configure a banner that is sent on incoming connections, use the following command in global configuration mode:

Command	Purpose
banner incoming *d message d*	Configures a banner to display on terminals connected to reverse Telnet lines.

Enable or Disable the Display of Banners

You can control display of the message-of-the-day (MOTD) and line-activation (EXEC) banners. By default, these banners are displayed on all lines. To suppress or reinstate the display of such banners, use one of the following commands in line configuration mode:

Command	Purpose
no exec-banner	Suppresses MOTD and EXEC banner display.
exec-banner	Reinstates the display of the EXEC or MOTD banners.
no motd-banner	Suppresses MOTD banner display only.
motd-banner	Reinstates the display of the MOTD banners.

These commands determine whether the router will display the EXEC banner and the message-of-the-day (MOTD) banner when an EXEC session is created. These banners are defined with the **banner motd** and **banner exec** commands. By default, the MOTD banner and the EXEC banner are enabled on all lines.

Disable the EXEC and MOTD banners using the **no exec-banner** command.

The MOTD banners can also be disabled by the **no motd-banner** line configuration command, which disables MOTD banners on a line. If the **no exec-banner** command is configured on a line, the MOTD banner will be disabled regardless of whether the **motd-banner** command is enabled or disabled. Table 7-1 summarizes the effects of the **exec-banner** command and the **motd-banner** command.

Table 7-1 *Banners Displayed*

	exec-banner (default)	no exec-banner
	MOTD banner	none
motd-banner (default)	EXEC banner	
no motd-banner	EXEC banner	none

For reverse Telnet connections, the EXEC banner is never displayed. Instead, the incoming banner is displayed. The MOTD banner is displayed by default, but it is disabled if either the **no exec-banner** command or **no motd-banner** command is configured. Table 7-2 summarizes the effects of the **exec-banner** command and the **motd-banner** command for reverse Telnet connections.

Table 7-2 *Banners Displayed—Reverse Telnet Session to Async Lines*

	exec-banner (default)	no exec-banner
	MOTD banner	incoming banner
motd-banner (default)	incoming banner	
no motd-banner	incoming banner	incoming banner

Set Up Terminal Messages

The types of messages that can be displayed to terminal users who connect to the router are described in the following sections:

● Configure an Idle Terminal Message

● Display a "Line in Use" Message

● Display a "Host Failed" Message

Configure an Idle Terminal Message

You can configure messages to be displayed on a console or terminal not in use. Also called a *vacant message*, this message is different from the banner message displayed when an EXEC process is activated. To configure an idle terminal message, use the following command in line configuration mode:

Command	Purpose
vacant-message [*d message d*]	Displays an idle terminal message.

Display a "Line in Use" Message

You can display a "line in use" message when an incoming connection is attempted and all rotary group or other lines are in use. Use the following command in line configuration mode:

Command	Purpose
refuse-message *d message d*	Displays a "line in use" message.

If you do not define such a message, the user receives a system-generated error message when all lines are in use. You also can use this message to provide the user with further instructions.

Display a "Host Failed" Message

You can display a "host failed" message when a Telnet connection with a specific host fails. Use the following command in line configuration mode:

Command	Purpose
busy-message *hostname d message d*	Displays a "host failed" message.

Managing Connections and System Banners Examples

This section contains the following examples:

- Change a Login Name Example
- Specify a TACACS Host Example
- Clear TCP/IP Connection Examples
- Menu Configuration Example
- Banner Example

Change a Login Name Example

The following example shows how login usernames and passwords can be changed. In this example, a user currently logged on under the username *user1* attempts to change that login name to *user2*. After entering the **login** command, the user enters the new username but enters an incorrect password. Because the password does not match the original password, the system rejects the attempt to change the username.

```
Router> login
Username: user2
Password:
% Access denied
Still logged in as "user1"
```

Next, the user attempts the login change again, with the username *user2* but enters the correct (original) password. This time the password matches the current login information, the login username is changed to *user2*, and the user is allowed access to the EXEC at the user-level.

```
router> login
Username: user2
Password:
router>
```

Specify a TACACS Host Example

In the following example, *user1* specifies the TACACS host *host1* to authenticate the password:

```
router> login
Username: user1@host1
Translating "HOST1"...domain server (131.108.1.111) [OK]
```

Clear TCP/IP Connection Examples

The following example clears a TCP connection using its TTY line number. The **show tcp** command displays the line number (tty2) that is used in the **clear tcp** command.

```
Router# show tcp

    tty2, virtual tty from host router20.cisco.com
    Connection state is ESTAB, I/O status: 1, unread input bytes: 0
    Local host: 171.69.233.7, Local port: 23
    Foreign host: 171.69.61.75, Foreign port: 1058

    Enqueued packets for retransmit: 0, input: 0, saved: 0

    Event Timers (current time is 0x36144):
    Timer          Starts    Wakeups         Next
    Retrans          4          0            0x0
    TimeWait         0          0            0x0
    AckHold          7          4            0x0
    SendWnd          0          0            0x0
```

```
KeepAlive          0          0          0x0
GiveUp             0          0          0x0
PmtuAger           0          0          0x0

iss: 4151109680  snduna: 4151109752  sndnxt: 4151109752   sndwnd:   24576
irs: 1249472001  rcvnxt: 1249472032  rcvwnd:         4258 delrcvwnd:   30

SRTT: 710 ms, RTTO: 4442 ms, RTV: 1511 ms, KRTT: 0 ms
minRTT: 0 ms, maxRTT: 300 ms, ACK hold: 300 ms
```
```
Router# clear tcp line 2
    [confirm]
    [OK]
```

The following example clears a TCP connection by specifying its local router host name and port and its remote router host name and port. The **show tcp brief** command displays the local (Local Address) and remote (Foreign Address) host names and ports to use in the **clear tcp** command.

```
Router# show tcp brief
    TCB        Local Address        Foreign Address       (state)
    60A34E9C   router1.cisco.com.23     router20.cisco.1055   ESTAB
```
```
Router# clear tcp local router1 23 remote router20 1055
    [confirm]
    [OK]
```

The following example clears a TCP connection using its TCB address. The **show tcp brief** command displays the TCB address to use in the **clear tcp** command.

```
Router# show tcp brief
    TCB        Local Address        Foreign Address       (state)
    60B75E48   router1.cisco.com.23     router20.cisco.1054   ESTAB
```
```
Router# clear tcp tcb 60B75E48
    [confirm]
    [OK]
```

Menu Configuration Example

The following example allows menu users to Telnet to one of three different machines. The user can also view the output of the **show user** command and exit the menu. One hidden menu item, specified by the selection here, allows system administrators to view the current software version.

```
menu new title ^C


            Telnet Menu


^C
menu new prompt ^C
```

```
Please enter your selection: ^C
menu new text 1 telnet system1
menu new command 1 telnet system1
menu new options 1 pause
menu new text 2 telnet system2
menu new command 2 telnet system2
menu new options 2 pause
menu new text b telnet systemblue
menu new command b telnet systemblue
menu new options b pause
menu new text me show user
menu new command me show user
menu new options me pause
menu new command here show version
menu new text Exit Exit
menu new command Exit menu-exit
menu new clear-screen
menu new status-line
menu new default me
menu new line-mode
!
```

Banner Example

The following example shows how to use the **banner** global configuration commands and the **no exec-banner** line configuration command to notify your users that the server is going to be reloaded with new software:

```
! The EXEC and MOTD banners are inappropriate for the VTYs.
line vty 0 4
 no exec-banner
!
banner exec /
 This is Cisco Systems training group router.

 Unauthorized access prohibited.
 /
!
banner incoming /
 You are connected to a Hayes-compatible modem.

 Enter the appropriate AT commands.
 Remember to reset anything to change before disconnecting.
 /
!
banner motd /
 The router will go down at 6pm for a software upgrade
 /
```

When someone connects to the router, the MOTD banner appears before the login prompt. After the user successfully logs in to the router, the EXEC banner or incoming banner will be displayed, depending on the type of connection. For a reverse Telnet login, the incoming banner will be displayed. For all other connections, the router will display the EXEC banner.

## CHAPTER 8

Connection and System Banner Commands

This chapter describes the connection and system banner commands.

For connection and system banner task information and examples, refer to Chapter 7, "Managing Connections, Menus, and System Banners."

banner exec

To display a banner on terminals with an interactive EXEC, use the **banner exec** global configuration command. This command specifies a message to be displayed when an EXEC process is created (a line is activated, or an incoming connection is made to a VTY line). The **no** form of this command deletes the EXEC banner.

banner exec *d message d*
no banner exec

Syntax	Description
d	Delimiting character of your choice—a pound sign (#) for example. You cannot use the delimiting character in the banner message.
message	Message text.

Default
No banner is displayed.

Command Mode
Global configuration

Usage Guidelines
This command first appeared in Cisco IOS Release 10.0.

Follow this command with one or more blank spaces and a delimiting character of your choice. Then enter one or more lines of text, terminating the message with the second occurrence of the delimiting character.

When someone connects to the router, the MOTD banner appears before the login prompt. After the user successfully logs in to the router, the EXEC banner or incoming banner will be displayed, depending on the type of connection. For a reverse Telnet login, the incoming banner will be displayed. For all other connections, the router will display the EXEC banner.

To disable the EXEC banner on a particular line, use the **no exec-banner** line configuration command.

Example

The following example sets an EXEC banner. The dollar sign ($) is used as a delimiting character.

```
banner exec $
Session activated. Enter commands at the prompt.
$
```

Related Commands

To locate documentation of related commands, you can search online at www.cisco.com.

banner incoming
banner login
banner motd
exec-banner

banner incoming

To specify a banner used when you have an incoming connection to a line from a host on the network, use the **banner incoming** global configuration command. The **no** form of this command deletes the incoming connection banner.

> **banner incoming** *d message d*
> **no banner incoming**

Syntax   Description

Syntax	Description
d	Delimiting character of your choice—a pound sign (#) for example. You cannot use the delimiting character in the banner message.
message	Message text.

Default

No banner is specified.

Command Mode

Global configuration

Usage Guidelines

This command first appeared in Cisco IOS Release 10.0.

Follow this command with one or more blank spaces and a delimiting character of your choice. Then enter one or more lines of text, terminating the message with the second occurrence of the delimiting character.

An *incoming connection* is one initiated from the network side of the router. Incoming connections are also called reverse Telnet sessions. These sessions can display MOTD banners and incoming banners, but they do not display EXEC banners. Use the **no motd-banner** line configuration command to disable the MOTD banner for reverse Telnet sessions on asynchronous lines.

When a user connects to the router, the MOTD banner appears before the login prompt. After the user successfully logs in to the router, the EXEC banner or incoming banner will be displayed, depending on the type of connection. For a reverse Telnet login, the incoming banner will be displayed. For all other connections, the router will display the EXEC banner.

Incoming banners cannot be suppressed. If you do not want the incoming banner to appear, you must delete it with the **no banner incoming** command.

Example

The following example sets an incoming connection banner. The pound sign (#) is used as a delimiting character.

```
banner incoming #
Welcome to Reuses.
#
```

Related Commands

To locate documentation of related commands, you can search online at www.cisco.com.

banner exec
banner login
banner motd
motd-banner

banner login

To display a login banner, use the **banner login** global configuration command. This command specifies a message to be displayed before the username and password login prompts. The **no** form of this command deletes the login banner.

> **banner login** *d message d*
> **no banner login**

Syntax

Syntax	Description
d	Delimiting character of your choice—a pound sign (#) for example. You cannot use the delimiting character in the banner message.
message	Message text.

Default

No login banner is displayed.

Command Mode

Global configuration

Usage Guidelines

This command first appeared in Cisco IOS Release 10.0.

Follow this command with one or more blank spaces and a delimiting character of your choice. Then enter one or more lines of text, terminating the message with the second occurrence of the delimiting character.

When someone connects to the router, the MOTD banner (if configured) appears first, followed by the login banner and prompts. After the user successfully logs in to the router, the EXEC banner or incoming banner will be displayed, depending on the type of connection. For a reverse Telnet login, the incoming banner will be displayed. For all other connections, the router will display the EXEC banner.

Example

The following example sets a login banner. The dollar sign ($) is used as a delimiting character.

```
banner login $
Welcome to Bob's Router
$
```

Related Commands

To locate documentation of related commands, you can search online at www.cisco.com.

banner exec
banner incoming
banner motd

banner motd

To specify a message-of-the-day (MOTD) banner, use the **banner motd** global configuration command. The **no** form of this command deletes the MOTD banner.

> **banner motd** *d message d*
> **no banner motd**

Syntax	Description
d	Delimiting character of your choice—a pound sign (#) for example. You cannot use the delimiting character in the banner message.
message	Message text.

Default

No MOTD banner is specified.

Command Mode

Global configuration

Usage Guidelines

This command first appeared in Cisco IOS Release 10.0.

Follow this command with one or more blank spaces and a delimiting character of your choice. Then enter one or more lines of text, terminating the message with the second occurrence of the delimiting character.

This MOTD banner is displayed to all terminals connected and is useful for sending messages that affect all users (such as impending system shutdowns). Use the **no exec-banner** or **no motd-banner** command to disable the MOTD banner on a line. The **no exec-banner** command also disables the EXEC banner on the line.

When someone connects to the router, the MOTD banner appears before the login prompt. After the user successfully logs in to the router, the EXEC banner or incoming banner will be displayed, depending on the type of connection. For a reverse Telnet login, the incoming banner will be displayed. For all other connections, the router will display the EXEC banner.

The **banner** command without any keywords specified defaults to the **banner motd** command. When a new **banner motd** command is added to the configuration, it overwrites the existing **banner** command if no keyword is specified. Similarly, if a **banner** command is added to the configuration, any existing **banner motd** command is overwritten.

Example

The following example sets a MOTD banner. The pound sign (#) is used as a delimiting character.

```
banner motd #
Building power will be off from 7:00 AM until 9:00 AM this coming Tuesday.
#
```

Related Commands

To locate documentation of related commands, you can search online at www.cisco.com.

banner exec
banner incoming
banner login
exec-banner
motd-banner

busy-message

To create a "host failed" message that displays when a connection fails, use the **busy-message** global configuration command. Use the **no** form of this command to disable the "host failed" message from displaying on the specified host.

> **busy-message** *hostname d message d*
> **no busy-message** *hostname*

Syntax	Description
hostname	Name of the host that cannot be reached.
d	Delimiting character of your choice—a pound sign (#) for example. You cannot use the delimiting character in the message.
message	Message text.

Default
No message is displayed.

Command Mode
Global configuration

Usage Guidelines
This command first appeared in Cisco IOS Release 10.0.

This command applies only to Telnet connections.

Follow the **busy-message** command with one or more blank spaces and a delimiting character of your choice. Then enter one or more lines of text, terminating the message with the second occurrence of the delimiting character.

Defining a "host failed" message for a host prevents all Cisco IOS software-initiated user messages, including the initial message that indicates the connection is "Trying...". The **busy-message** command can be used in the **autocommand** command to suppress these messages.

Example
The following example displays a message on the terminal whenever an attempt to connect to the host named *dross* fails. The pound sign (#) is used as a delimiting character.

```
busy-message dross #
Cannot connect to host. Contact the computer center.
#
```

clear tcp
To clear a TCP connection, use the **clear tcp** privileged EXEC command.

> **clear tcp** {**line** *line-number* | **local** *host-name port* **remote** *host-name port* | **tcb** *address*}

Syntax	Description
line *line-number*	TTY line number of the TCP connection to clear.
local *host-name port* **remote** *host-name port*	Local router's host name and port and remote router's host name and port of the TCP connection to clear.

Syntax	Description
tcb *address*	Transmission Control Block (TCB) address of the TCP connection to clear. The TCB address is an internal identifier for the end point.

Command Mode

Privileged EXEC

Usage Guidelines

This command first appeared in Cisco IOS Release 11.1.

The **clear tcp** command is particularly useful for clearing hung TCP connections.

The **clear tcp line** *line-number* command terminates the TCP connection on the specified TTY line. Additionally, all TCP sessions initiated from that TTY line are terminated.

The **clear tcp local** *host-name port* **remote** *host-name port* command terminates the specific TCP connection identified by the host name/port pair of the local and remote router.

The **clear tcp tcb** *address* command terminates the specific TCP connection identified by the TCB address.

Examples

The following example clears a TCP connection using its TTY line number. The **show tcp** command displays the line number (tty2) that is used in the **clear tcp** command.

```
Router# show tcp

    tty2, virtual tty from host router20.cisco.com
    Connection state is ESTAB, I/O status: 1, unread input bytes: 0
    Local host: 171.69.233.7, Local port: 23
    Foreign host: 171.69.61.75, Foreign port: 1058

    Enqueued packets for retransmit: 0, input: 0, saved: 0

    Event Timers (current time is 0x36144):
    Timer          Starts    Wakeups          Next
    Retrans           4         0             0x0
    TimeWait          0         0             0x0
    AckHold           7         4             0x0
    SendWnd           0         0             0x0
    KeepAlive         0         0             0x0
    GiveUp            0         0             0x0
    PmtuAger          0         0             0x0

    iss: 4151109680  snduna: 4151109752  sndnxt: 4151109752    sndwnd:  24576
    irs: 1249472001  rcvnxt: 1249472032  rcvwnd:       4258  delrcvwnd:     30
```

```
    SRTT: 710 ms, RTTO: 4442 ms, RTV: 1511 ms, KRTT: 0 ms
    minRTT: 0 ms, maxRTT: 300 ms, ACK hold: 300 ms
Router# clear tcp line 2
    [confirm]
     [OK]
```

The following example clears a TCP connection by specifying its local router host name and port and its remote router host name and port. The **show tcp brief** command displays the local (Local Address) and remote (Foreign Address) host names and ports to use in the **clear tcp** command.

```
Router# show tcp brief
    TCB        Local Address        Foreign Address        (state)
    60A34E9C   router1.cisco.com.23    router20.cisco.1055   ESTAB

Router# clear tcp local router1 23 remote router20 1055
    [confirm]
     [OK]
```

The following example clears a TCP connection using its TCB address. The **show tcp brief** command displays the TCB address to use in the **clear tcp** command.

```
Router# show tcp brief
    TCB        Local Address        Foreign Address        (state)
    60B75E48   router1.cisco.com.23    router20.cisco.1054   ESTAB

Router# clear tcp tcb 60B75E48
    [confirm]
     [OK]
```

Related Commands

To locate documentation of related commands, you can search online at www.cisco.com.

show tcp
show tcp brief

exec

To allow an EXEC process on a line, use the **exec** line configuration command. Use the **no** form of this command to turn off the EXEC process for the specified line.

exec
no exec

Syntax Description

This command has no arguments or keywords.

Default

The EXEC processes start is activated automatically on all lines.

Command Mode

Line configuration

Usage Guidelines

This command first appeared in Cisco IOS Release 10.0.

When you want to allow an outgoing connection *only* for a line, use the **no exec** command. When a user tries to Telnet to a line with the **no exec** command configured, the user will get no response when pressing the Return key at the login screen.

Example

The following example turns off the EXEC on line 7. You might want to do this on the auxiliary port if the attached device (for example, the control port of a rack of modems) sends unsolicited data. If this happens, an EXEC process starts, which makes the line unavailable.

```
line 7
 no exec
```

exec-banner

To display EXEC and MOTD banners, use the **exec-banner** line configuration command. Use the **no** form of this command to suppress the banners.

> **exec-banner**
> **no exec-banner**

Syntax Description

This command has no arguments or keywords.

Default

Enabled on all lines.

Command Mode

Line configuration

Usage Guidelines

This command first appeared in Cisco IOS Release 10.0.

This command determines whether the router will display the EXEC banner and the message-of-the-day (MOTD) banner when an EXEC session is created. These banners are defined with the **banner exec** and **banner motd** commands. By default, these banners are enabled on all lines. Disable the EXEC and MOTD banners using the **no exec-banner** command.

This command has no effect on the incoming banner, which is controlled by the **banner incoming** command.

The MOTD banners can also be disabled by the **no motd-banner** line configuration command, which disables MOTD banners on a line. If the **no exec-banner** command is configured on a line, the MOTD banner will be disabled regardless of whether the **motd-banner** command is enabled or disabled. Table 8-1 summarizes the effects of the **exec-banner** command and the **motd-banner** command.

Table 8-1 *Banners Displayed*

	exec-banner (default)	**no exec-banner**
motd-banner (default)	MOTD banner EXEC banner	none
no motd-banner	EXEC banner	none

For reverse Telnet connections, the EXEC banner is never displayed. Instead, the incoming banner is displayed. The MOTD banner is displayed by default, but it is disabled if either the **no exec-banner** command or **no motd-banner** command is configured. Table 8-2 summarizes the effects of the **exec-banner** command and the **motd-banner** command for reverse Telnet connections.

Table 8-2 *Banners Displayed—Reverse Telnet Session to Async Lines*

	exec-banner (default)	**no exec-banner**
motd-banner (default)	MOTD banner incoming banner	incoming banner
no motd-banner	incoming banner	incoming banner

Example

The following example suppresses the EXEC and MOTD banners on virtual terminal lines 0 to 4:

```
line vty 0 4
 no exec-banner
```

Related Commands

To locate documentation of related commands, you can search online at www.cisco.com.

banner exec
banner incoming
banner motd
motd-banner

exec-timeout

To set the interval that the EXEC command interpreter waits until user input is detected, use the **exec-timeout** line configuration command. Use the **no** form of this command to remove the timeout definition.

> **exec-timeout** *minutes* [*seconds*]
> **no exec-timeout**

Syntax	Description
minutes	Integer that specifies the number of minutes.
seconds	(Optional) Additional time intervals in seconds.

Default

10 minutes

Command Mode

Line configuration

Usage Guidelines

This command first appeared in Cisco IOS Release 10.0.

If no input is detected during the interval, the EXEC facility resumes the current connection. If no connections exist, the EXEC facility returns the terminal to the idle state and disconnects the incoming session.

To specify no timeout, enter the **exec-timeout 0 0** command.

Examples

The following example sets a time interval of 2 minutes, 30 seconds:

```
line console
 exec-timeout 2 30
```

The following example sets a time interval of 10 seconds:

```
line console
 exec-timeout 0 10
```

motd-banner

To display message-of-the-day (MOTD) banners, use the **motd-banner** line configuration command. Use the **no** form of this command to suppress the MOTD banners.

> **motd-banner**
> **no motd-banner**

Syntax Description

This command has no arguments or keywords.

Default

Enabled on all lines.

Command Mode

Line configuration

Usage Guidelines

This command first appeared in Cisco IOS Release 11.1.

This command determines whether the router will display the MOTD banner when an EXEC session is created. The MOTD banner is defined with the **banner motd** command. By default, the MOTD banner is enabled on all lines. Disable the MOTD banner using the **no motd-banner** command.

The MOTD banners can also be disabled by the **no exec-banner** line configuration command, which disables both MOTD banners and EXEC banners on a line. If the **no exec-banner** command is configured on a line, the MOTD banner will be disabled regardless of whether the **motd-banner** command is enabled or disabled. Table 8-3 summarizes the effects of the **exec-banner** command and the **motd-banner** command.

Table 8-3 *Banners Displayed*

	exec-banner (default)	**no exec-banner**
	MOTD banner	none
motd-banner (default)	EXEC banner	
no motd-banner	EXEC banner	none

For reverse Telnet connections, the EXEC banner is never displayed. Instead, the incoming banner is displayed. The MOTD banner is displayed by default, but it is disabled if either the **no exec-banner** command or **no motd-banner** command is configured. Table 8-4 summarizes the effects of the **exec-banner** command and the **motd-banner** command for reverse Telnet connections.

Table 8-4 *Banners Displayed—Reverse Telnet Session to Async Lines*

	exec-banner (default)	**no exec-banner**
	MOTD banner	incoming banner
motd-banner (default)	incoming banner	
no motd-banner	incoming banner	incoming banner

Example

The following example suppresses the MOTD banner on virtual terminal lines 0 to 4:

```
line vty 0 4
 no motd-banner
```

Related Commands

To locate documentation of related commands, you can search online at www.cisco.com.

banner exec
banner incoming
banner motd
motd-banner

name-connection

To assign a logical name to a connection, use the **name-connection** user EXEC command.

name-connection

Syntax Description

This command has no arguments or keywords.

Default

No logical name is defined.

Command Mode

User EXEC

Usage Guidelines

This command first appeared in a release prior to Cisco IOS Release 10.0.

This command can be useful for keeping track of multiple connections.

You are prompted for the connection number and name to assign. The **where** command displays a list of the assigned logical connection names.

Example

The following example assigns the logical name *blue* to the connection:

```
Router> where
Conn Host              Address            Byte  Idle Conn Name
*  1 doc-2509          172.30.162.131        0     0 doc-2509

Router> name-connection
Connection number: 1
Enter logical name: blue
Connection 1 to doc-2509 will be named "BLUE" [confirm]
```

Related Commands

To locate documentation of related commands, you can search online at www.cisco.com.

where

refuse-message

To define a line-in-use message, use the **refuse-message** line configuration command. Use the **no** form of this command to disable the message.

refuse-message *d message d*
no refuse-message

Syntax

Syntax	Description
d	Delimiting character of your choice—a pound sign (#) for example. You cannot use the delimiting character in the message.
message	Message text.

Default

No line-in-use message is defined.

Command Mode

Line configuration

Usage Guidelines

This command first appeared in Cisco IOS Release 10.0.

Follow this command with one or more blank spaces and a delimiting character of your choice. Then enter one or more lines of text, terminating the message with the second occurrence of the delimiting character. You cannot use the delimiting character within the text of the message.

When you define a message using this command, the Cisco IOS software does the following:

1 Accepts the connection.

2 Prints the custom message.

3 Clears the connection.

Example

In the following example, line 5 is configured with a line-in-use message, and the user is instructed to try again later:

```
line 5
refuse-message  /The dial-out modem is currently in use.

Please try again later./
```

send

To send messages to one or all terminal lines, use the **send** EXEC command.

send {*line-number* | * | **aux** *number* | **console** *number* | **tty** *number* | **vty** *number*}

Syntax	Description
line-number	Line number to which the message will be sent.
*	Sends a message to all TTY lines.
aux *number*	Sends a message to the AUX port.
console *number*	Sends a message to the console port.
tty *number*	Sends a message to an asynchronous line.
vty *number*	Sends a message to a VTY line.

Default

No messages are sent.

Command Mode

EXEC

Usage Guidelines

This command first appeared in Cisco IOS Release 11.2.

The system prompts for the message, which can be up to 500 characters long. Enter **Ctrl-Z** to end the message. Enter **Ctrl-C** to abort this command.

Example

The following example sends a message to all lines:

```
2509# send *
Enter message, end with Ctrl-Z; abort with Ctrl-C:
The system 2509 will be shut down in 10 minutes for repairs.^Z
Send message? [confirm]
2509#


***
***
*** Message from tty0 to all terminals:
```

```
***
The system 2509 will be shut down in 10 minutes for repairs.

2509#
```

service linenumber

To configure the Cisco IOS software to display line number information after the EXEC or incoming banner, use the **service linenumber** global configuration command. Use the **no** form of this command to disable this function.

> **service linenumber**
> **no service linenumber**

Syntax Description

This command has no arguments or keywords.

Default

Disabled

Command Mode

Global configuration

Usage Guidelines

This command first appeared in Cisco IOS Release 10.0.

With the **service linenumber** command, you can have the Cisco IOS software display the host name, line number, and location each time an EXEC process is started, or an incoming connection is made. The line number banner appears immediately after the EXEC banner or incoming banner. This feature is useful for tracking problems with modems, because the host and line for the modem connection are listed. Modem type information can also be included.

Example

In the following example, a user Telnets to Router2 before and after the **service linenumber** command is enabled. The second time, information about the line is displayed after the banner.

```
Router1> telnet Router2
Trying Router2 (172.30.162.131)... Open
```

```
Welcome to Router2.

User Access Verification

Password:
Router2> enable
Password:
Router2# configure terminal
Enter configuration commands, one per line.  End with Ctrl-Z.
Router2(config)# service linenumber
Router2(config)# end
Router2# logout

[Connection to Router2 closed by foreign host]
Router1> telnet Router2
Trying Router2 (172.30.162.131)... Open

Welcome to Router2.

Router2 line 10


User Access Verification

Password:
Router2>
```

Related Commands

To locate documentation of related commands, you can search online at www.cisco.com.

show users

show hosts

To display the default domain name, the style of name lookup service, a list of name server hosts, and the cached list of host names and addresses on the network to which you can connect, use the **show hosts** user EXEC command.

> **show hosts**

Syntax Description

This command has no arguments or keywords.

Command Mode

User EXEC

Usage Guidelines

This command first appeared in a release prior to Cisco IOS Release 10.0.

Sample Display

The following is sample output from the **show hosts** command:

```
Router# show hosts

Default domain is CISCO.COM
Name/address lookup uses domain service
Name servers are 255.255.255.255
Host                Flags        Age    Type     Address(es)
SLAG.CISCO.COM      (temp, OK)   1      IP       131.108.4.10
CHAR.CISCO.COM      (temp, OK)   8      IP       192.31.7.50
CHAOS.CISCO.COM     (temp, OK)   8      IP       131.108.1.115
DIRT.CISCO.COM      (temp, EX)   8      IP       131.108.1.111
DUSTBIN.CISCO.COM   (temp, EX)   0      IP       131.108.1.27
DREGS.CISCO.COM     (temp, EX)   24     IP       131.108.1.30
```

Table 8-5 describes significant fields shown in the display.

Table 8-5 *show hosts Field Descriptions*

Field	Description
Host	Name of server host.
Flags	A temporary entry is entered by a name server; the server removes the entry after 72 hours of inactivity.
	A permanent entry is entered by a configuration command and is not timed out. Entries marked "OK" are believed to be valid. Entries marked "??" are considered suspect and subject to revalidation. Entries marked "EX" are expired.
Age	Indicates the number of hours since the Cisco IOS software last referred to the cache entry.
Type	Identifies the type of address (for example, IP, CLNS, or X.121). If you used the **ip hp-host** global configuration command, the **show hosts** command displays these host names as type HP-IP.
Address(es)	Shows the address of the host. One host can have up to eight addresses.

systat

The *show users* command replaces the **systat** command. Refer to the description of the **show users** command for more information.

vacant-message

To display an idle terminal message, use the **vacant-message** line configuration command. Use the **no** form of this command to remove the default vacant message or any other vacant message that may have been set.

> **vacant-message** [*d message d*]
> **no vacant-message**

Syntax	Description
d	(Optional) A delimiting character of your choice—a pound sign (#), for example. You cannot use the delimiting character in the banner message.
message	(Optional) Vacant terminal message.
d	(Optional) A delimiting character of your choice.

Default

The format of the default vacant message is as follows:

```
<blank lines>
hostname tty# is now available
<blank lines>
Press RETURN to get started.
```

This message is generated by the system.

Command Mode

Line configuration

Usage Guidelines

This command first appeared in Cisco IOS Release 10.0.

This command enables the banner to be displayed on the screen of an idle terminal. The **vacant-message** command without any arguments restores the default message.

Follow this command with one or more blank spaces and a delimiting character of your choice. Then enter one or more lines of text, terminating the message with the second occurrence of the delimiting character.

NOTE	For a rotary group, you only need to define the message for the first line in the group.

Example

The following example turns on the system banner and displays this message:

```
line 0
vacant-message #
                Welcome to Cisco Systems, Inc.
                 Press Return to get started.
```

## CHAPTER 9

Using the Cisco Web Browser

The Cisco IOS software includes a Web browser from which you can issue Cisco IOS commands. This Cisco IOS feature is accessed from the router's home page and can be customized for your business environment. For example, you can view pages in different languages and save them in Flash memory for easy retrieval. You can also configure the Web Cache Control Protocol (WCCP) to handle Web traffic and increase the efficiency of your time spent on the Web.

For a complete description of the Cisco Web browser configuration commands in this chapter, refer to Chapter 10, "Cisco IOS Web Browser Commands." To locate documentation of other commands that appear in this chapter, you can search online at www.cisco.com.

Cisco Web Browser Task List

Use of the Cisco Web browser is optional. To use and customize the Cisco Web browser, complete the tasks in the following sections:

- Use the Cisco Web Browser Interface to Issue Commands

- Customize the User Interface on a Web Browser

- Configure the Web Cache Control Protocol

Use the Cisco Web Browser Interface to Issue Commands

You can issue most of the Cisco IOS commands using a Web browser. This Cisco IOS feature is accessed by using the Cisco Web browser interface, which is accessed from the router's home page. (All Cisco routers and access servers loaded with the latest version of Cisco IOS software have a home page, which is password protected.)

From the router's home page, you click on a hypertext link titled "Monitor the Router." This link takes you to a Web page that has a "Command" field. You can type commands in this field as if you were entering commands at a terminal connected to the router. The page also displays a list of commands. You can execute these commands by clicking on them, as if you were clicking on hypertext links.

Cisco Web Browser Interface Task List

To use the Cisco Web browser interface to issue commands, use the commands in the following sections:

- Configure the Cisco Web Browser Interface
- Use the Correct Hardware and Software
- Access Your Router's Home Page
- Issue Commands Using the Cisco Web Browser Interface
    - Enter Commands Using Hypertext Links
    - Enter Commands Using the Command Field
    - Enter Commands Using the URL Window

Configure the Cisco Web Browser Interface

The Web browser interface is automatically enabled when you use ClickStart to configure a Cisco 1003, Cisco 1004, or Cisco 1005 router. You must enable the Cisco Web browser interface on all other Cisco IOS routers. Once enabled, you will be able to issue Cisco IOS commands to your router using a Web browser.

If you have any other Cisco router, you must enable the Web browser interface by altering the router's configuration. To do this, perform the tasks in the following list. The first task is required; the remaining are optional.

- Enable the Cisco Web Browser Interface
- Change the Cisco Web Browser Interface Port Number
- Control Access to the Cisco Web Browser Interface
- Specify the Method for User Authentication

Enable the Cisco Web Browser Interface

To enable a Cisco router to be configured from a browser using the Cisco Web browser interface, use the following command in global configuration mode:

Command	Purpose
ip http server	Enables a router to be reconfigured using the Cisco Web browser interface.

Now that the Cisco Web browser interface is enabled, you can perform any of the optional tasks or proceed to configure a router using the Cisco Web browser interface.

Change the Cisco Web Browser Interface Port Number

By default, the Cisco Web browser interface uses port 80 on the router. To assign the Cisco Web browser interface to a different port, use the following command in global configuration mode:

Command	Purpose
ip http port *number*	Assigns a port number to be used by the Cisco Web browser interface.

Control Access to the Cisco Web Browser Interface

To control which hosts can access the HTTP server used by the Cisco Web browser interface, use the following command in global configuration mode:

Command	Purpose
ip http access-class {*access-list-number*	*name*}	Controls access to the HTTP server used by the Cisco Web browser interface.

Specify the Method for User Authentication

To specify how HTTP server users are authenticated, use the following command in global configuration mode:

Command	Purpose
ip http authentication {**aaa**	**enable**	**local**	**tacacs**}	Specifies how HTTP server users are authenticated.

Use the Correct Hardware and Software

To use the Cisco Web browser interface, your computer must have a World Wide Web browser. The Cisco Web browser interface works with most browsers, including Netscape Navigator. Your Web browser must be able to read and submit forms. The original versions of Mosaic might have problems using the Cisco Web browser interface, because they either cannot submit forms or have difficulty doing so.

The computer must be connected to the same network that the router or access server is on.

Access Your Router's Home Page

Cisco IOS software allows users with a default privilege level of 15 to access a predefined home page for a router or access server. If you have been assigned a privilege level other than 15, Cisco IOS Release 11.3 or later software allows you to issue Cisco IOS commands from a Web page where the commands defined for your specific user privilege level will be displayed.

To access the home page for your router or access server with a default privilege level of 15, perform the following steps:

> **Step 1** Enter the following command in the URL field of your Web browser and press return: http://*router-name/*. (For example, to access a Cisco router named *cacophony* with a default privilege level of 15, type http://cacophony/.) The browser then prompts you for the password.
>
> **Step 2** Enter the password.

NOTE The name and password for your router and access server are designated in their configuration. Contact your network administrator if you do not have this information.

The browser should display the home page for your router or access server.

The router's home page looks something like the Cisco 7200 home page shown in Figure 9-1.

To access a router Web page for a preassigned privilege level other than the default of 15, perform the following steps:

> **Step 1** Enter the following command in the URL field of your Web browser and press return: http://*router-name/*level/*level/* *mode/command*. (For example, to request a user privilege level of 12 on a Cisco router named *cacophony*, type http://cacophony/level/12/exec.) The browser then prompts you for the username and/or password.

Figure 9-1   *Example of a Home Page for a Cisco 7200*

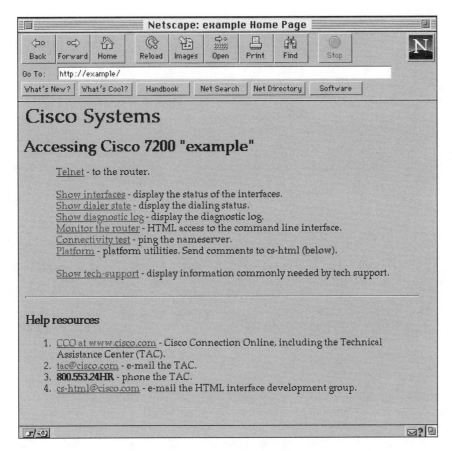

Step 2   Depending on your authentication method, enter your username and/or password and press return. The Web browser should display a Web page specific to your user privilege level, mode, and the command you have requested.

Table 9-1 lists the URL arguments you must use when requesting a Web page.

Table 9-1   *Description of the URL Arguments*

Argument	Description
router-name	Name of the router being configured.
level	The privilege level you are requesting.
mode	The mode the command will be executed in, such as exec, configure, and interface.
command	(Optional) The command you want to execute. If you specify a command, your browser will display a Web page showing the results of the requested command. If you do not specify a command in the URL, your browser will display a Web page listing all of the commands available for your privilege level.

Issue Commands Using the Cisco Web Browser Interface

To issue commands using the Cisco Web browser interface, click the link "Monitor the router" in the first list of hypertext links on the home page. This displays the Web page shown in Figure 9-2.

Enter Commands Using Hypertext Links

To enter a command using hypertext links, scroll through the commands listed at the bottom of the screen and click the one you want to execute. If the link is a complete command, it is executed. If the command has more parameters, another list of command hypertext links is displayed. Scroll through this second list and click the one you want to execute.

If the command is a request for information, such as a **show** command, the information is displayed in the Web browser window.

If the command requires a variable, a form where you can enter the variable is displayed.

Figure 9-2   *The "Command" Field Web Page for a Router Named "example"*

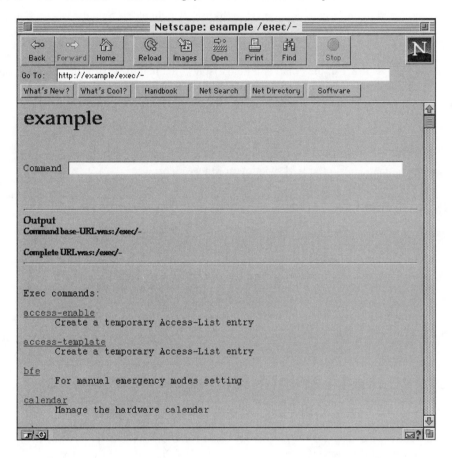

Enter Commands Using the Command Field

Entering the command in the command field is just like entering it at a terminal console. Enter the command using the syntax documented in the Cisco IOS command reference. If you are uncertain of the options available for a particular command, type a question mark (**?**).

For example, entering **show ?** in the command field displays the parameters for the **show** command. The Cisco Web browser interface displays the parameters as hypertext links. To select a parameter, you can either click on one of the links, or you can enter the parameter in the command field.

Enter Commands Using the URL Window

You can issue a command using the URL window for the Web browser.

For example, to execute a **show configuration** command on a router named *example*, you would enter the following in the URL window:

```
http://example/exec/show/configuration
```

The Web browser then displays the configuration for the "example" router. To save effort, modify the URL in the URL window in the browser control bar instead of retyping the entire URL.

The difference between entering a command in the command field and entering a command in the URL window is that in the URL window, command modes, keywords, and options should be separated by slashes, not spaces.

Customize the User Interface on a Web Browser

You can customize HTML pages to display Cisco IOS command output and Cisco IOS platform-specific variables (for example, a router host name or router address typically used in router setup pages) for a Web browser. You can display this information using HTML formatted Server Side Includes (SSIs) that you insert into your custom HTML pages. The SSIs are a Cisco IOS software feature described in the following sections.

Definition of SSIs

SSIs are HTML formatted commands or variables that you insert into HTML pages when you customize Cisco IOS platform configuration pages for a Web browser. These SSI commands and SSI variables display Cisco IOS command output and Cisco IOS platform-specific variables.

The Cisco IOS software supports two HTML SSI commands defined for customizing HTML pages: the SSI EXEC command and the **SSI ECHO** command. The HTML format of the **SSI EXEC** command is **<!--#exec cmd="***xxx***"-->**, and the HTML format of the SSI ECHO command is **<!--#echo var="***yyy***"-->**. (See the section "Customize HTML Pages Using SSIs" later in this chapter for a description of how to use these commands.)

In addition to the two SSI commands, the Cisco IOS software supports several SSI variables defined for customizing HTML pages. SSI variables are used with the SSI ECHO command. There is one SSI variable defined for all Cisco IOS platforms (SERVER_NAME) and other SSI variables specifically defined for ISDN, Frame Relay, and asynchronous serial platforms. The format and a description of all the available SSI variables are provided in Chapter 1, Table 1-5. (See the section "Customize HTML Pages Using SSIs" later in this chapter for a description of how to use these SSI variables with the SSI ECHO command.)

The SSI EXEC command is supported on all platforms. The SSI ECHO command, used with SSI variables, is supported on all platforms listed in Table 9-2.

Table 9-2 *Description of SSI Variables*

HTML Format of SSI Variable	Description of Variable Displayed on Browser Page	Cisco IOS Platform(s) This SSI Is Supported On
SERVER_NAME	Host name of the HTTP server.	All Cisco IOS platforms
EZSETUP_PASSWORD	Enable password (currently left blank).	Cisco 1000 series
EZSETUP_PASSWORD_VERIFY	Repeat of the enable password to verify accuracy (currently left blank).	Cisco 1000 series
EZSETUP_ETHERNET0_ADDRESS	IP address of the Ethernet 0 interface.	Cisco 1000 series
EZSETUP_ETHERNET0_MASK	IP mask of the Ethernet 0 interface.	Cisco 1000 series
EZSETUP_DNS_ADDRESS	DNS address used by the router.	Cisco 1000 series
EZSETUP_STANDARD_DEBUG_Y	Standard debug variable. Returns CHECKED if set to TRUE; otherwise, it is blank.	Cisco 1000 series
EZSETUP_STANDARD_DEBUG_N	Standard debug variable. Returns CHECKED if set to FALSE; otherwise, it is blank.	Cisco 1000 series
EZSETUP_ISDN_SWITCHTYPE	ISDN Switch type.	Cisco 1003 and Cisco 1004
EZSETUP_ISDN_REMOTE_NAME	Name of remote ISDN system.	Cisco 1003 and Cisco 1004
EZSETUP_ISDN_REMOTE_NUMBER	Phone number of remote ISDN system.	Cisco 1003 and Cisco 1004

Continues

Table 9-2 *Description of SSI Variables (Continued)*

HTML Format of SSI Variable	Description of Variable Displayed on Browser Page	Cisco IOS Platform(s) This SSI Is Supported On
EZSETUP_ISDN_CHAP_PASSWORD	CHAP password of remote ISDN system.	Cisco 1003 and Cisco 1004
EZSETUP_ISDN_SPID1	ISDN SPID 1.	Cisco 1003 and Cisco 1004
EZSETUP_ISDN_SPID2	ISDN SPID 2.	Cisco 1003 and Cisco 1004
EZSETUP_ISDN_SPEED_56	Speed of ISDN interface. Returns CHECKED if set to 56k; otherwise, it is blank.	Cisco 1003 and Cisco 1004
EZSETUP_ISDN_SPEED_64	Speed of ISDN interface. Returns CHECKED if set to 64k; otherwise, it is blank.	Cisco 1003 and Cisco 1004
EZSETUP_FR_ADDRESS	Frame-Relay IP address.	Cisco 1005
EZSETUP_FR_MASK	Frame-Relay IP mask.	Cisco 1005
EZSETUP_FR_DLCI	Frame-Relay DLCI.	Cisco 1005
EZSETUP_ASYNC_REMOTE_NAME	Name of remote system.	Cisco 1005
EZSETUP_ASYNC_REMOTE_NUMBER	Phone number of remote system.	Cisco 1005
EZSETUP_ASYNC_CHAP_PASSWORD	CHAP password for remote system.	Cisco 1005
EZSETUP_ASYNC_LINE_PASSWORD	Async line password.	Cisco 1005
EZSETUP_ASYNC_MODEM_SPEED	Speed of async modem (either 14.4k or 28.8k).	Cisco 1005
EZSETUP_ASYNC_MODEM_SPEED_144K	Returns CHECKED if async modem speed is 14.4k; otherwise, it is blank.	Cisco 1005
EZSETUP_ASYNC_MODEM_SPEED_288K	Returns CHECKED if async modem speed is 28.8k; otherwise, it is blank.	Cisco 1005

How SSIs Work

Once you have designed a set of HTML pages that include SSIs, you can copy these pages to a Cisco IOS platform's Flash memory. (See the section "Copy HTML Pages to Flash Memory" for instructions on storing HTML pages in Flash memory later in this section.) When you retrieve these pages from Flash memory and display them using a Web browser, any SSI command that was designed into these pages either displays Cisco IOS command output or displays a current variable or identifier as defined in Table 9-2. For example, the SSI ECHO command with the variable SERVER_NAME will display the current host name of the HTTP server you are using, and the SSI ECHO command with the variable EZSETUP_ISDN_SWITCHTYPE will display the current ISDN switch type you are using.

Benefits of Customizing Web Pages with SSIs

Using SSIs, you can customize one set of international HTML pages (for example, in Japanese) and copy these pages to Flash memory on multiple Cisco IOS platforms. When you retrieve these pages from the Flash memory of a Cisco IOS platform, current variables and identifiers associated with the platform you are currently using are displayed. SSIs save you from having to duplicate these international pages (considered relatively large images that contain 8-bit or multibyte characters) and store them in the source code for each platform you are using. (Refer to Table 9-2 to determine which Cisco IOS platforms support which SSIs variables.)

User Interface Customization Task List

To customize your HTML pages and view them for the user interface, perform the tasks in the following sections:

- Customize HTML Pages Using SSIs

- Copy HTML Pages to Flash Memory

- Enable the Cisco Web Browser Interface

- View Your HTML File Containing SSIs

- Display 8-Bit and Multiple Character Sets

Customize HTML Pages Using SSIs

When you are customizing an HTML page for a Web browser, type **<!--#exec cmd="***xxx***"-->** in your HTML file where you want Cisco IOS command output to appear on the browser page. Replace *xxx* with a Cisco IOS command that can be executed in the router's EXEC mode. (See the "SSI EXEC Command Example" section later in this chapter.)

When you are customizing an HTML page for a Web browser, type **<!--#echo var="***yyy***"-->** in your HTML file where you want a value or identifier associated with a particular Cisco IOS platform (for example, an ISDN or Frame Relay platform) to appear on the browser page. Replace *yyy* with an SSI variable described in Table 9-2. (See the "SSI ECHO Command Example" section later in this chapter.)

Copy HTML Pages to Flash Memory

After you have customized HTML pages using SSIs, copy your HTML pages to a Cisco IOS platform's Flash memory. To do this, save your pages using a filename appended with ".shtml" (for example, *filename*.shtml) and copy your file to Flash memory using a **copy** command (for example, the **copy tftp flash** command). (Refer to the Cisco IOS command references for a **copy** command compatible with your Cisco IOS platform.)

Enable the Cisco Web Browser Interface

To view the HTML pages you have just customized, you must first enable the Cisco Web browser interface. To enable the Cisco Web browser interface, use the following command in global configuration mode:

Command	Purpose
ip http server	Enables the Cisco Web browser interface.

Refer to the section "Configure the Cisco Web Browser Interface" earlier in this chapter for further information on configuring the Cisco Web browser interface.

View Your HTML File Containing SSIs

After the Cisco Web browser interface is enabled, you can retrieve your HTML page from Flash memory and view it on the Cisco Web browser by typing the URL **http://***router***/flash/***filename* in the URL window. Replace *router* with the host name or IP address of the current Cisco IOS platform you are using, and replace *filename* with the name of the file you created with ".shtml" appended. For example, http://myrouter/flash/ssi_file.shtml.

Display 8-Bit and Multibyte Character Sets

Your Cisco IOS platform will automatically display 8-bit and multibyte character sets and print the ESC character as a single character instead of as the caret and bracket symbols (^[) when the Cisco Web browser interface is enabled with the **ip http server** command.

If you are Telneting to a Cisco IOS platform, use the following command in line configuration mode to display 8-bit and multibyte international character sets and print the ESC character as a single character instead of "^[":

Command	Purpose
international	Configures a router to display 8-bit and multibyte international character sets and prints the ESC character as a single character instead of "^[" when Telneting to a Cisco IOS platform.

If you are Telneting to a Cisco IOS platform, use the following command in EXEC mode to display 8-bit and multibyte international characters sets and to print the ESC character as a single character instead of "^[" for the current Telnet session:

Command	Purpose
terminal international	Configures a router to display 8-bit and multibyte international character sets and prints the ESC character as a single character instead of "^[" when Telneting to a Cisco IOS platform for the current session.

Configure the Web Cache Control Protocol

The Web Cache Control Protocol (WCCP) feature allows you to use a Cisco Cache Engine to handle Web traffic, thus reducing transmission costs and downloading time. This traffic includes user requests to view pages and graphics on World Wide Web servers, whether internal or external to your network, and the replies to those requests. Figure 9-3 shows a sample WCCP network configuration.

Figure 9-3   *Sample Cisco Cache Engine Network Configuration*

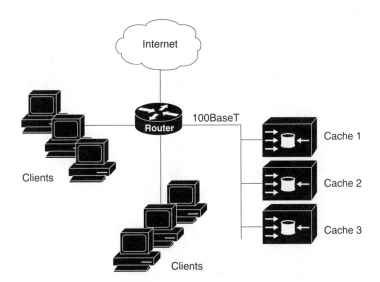

When a user (client) requests a page from a Web server (located in the Internet, in this case), the router sends the request to a Cisco Cache Engine (Cache 1, Cache 2, or Cache 3). If the cache engine has a copy of the requested page in storage, the engine sends the user that page. Otherwise, the engine gets the requested page and the objects on that page from the Web server, stores a copy of the page and its objects (caches them), and forwards the page and objects to the user.

WCCP transparently redirects HTTP requests from the intended server to a Cisco Cache Engine. End users do not know that the page came from the cache engine rather than the originally requested Web server.

Benefits of Using WCCP

Web caches reduce transmission costs and the amount of time required to download Web files. If a client requests a Web page that is already cached, the request and data only have to travel between the Cisco Cache Engine and the client. Without a Web cache, the request and reply must travel over the Internet or wide-area network. Cached pages can be loaded faster than non-cached pages and do not have to be transmitted from the Internet to your network.

Cisco IOS support of WCCP provides a transparent Web cache solution. Users can benefit from Web proxy caches without having to configure clients to contact a specific proxy server to access Web resources. Many Web proxy caches require clients to access Web resources through a specific proxy Web server rather than use the originally requested Web server URL. With WCCP, the clients send Web requests to the desired Web server URL. Cisco IOS routers intelligently intercept HTTP requests and transparently redirect them to a Cisco Cache Engine.

When a Web Cache Control Protocol-enabled router receives an IP packet, the router determines if the packet is a request that should be directed to a Cisco Cache Engine. The router looks for TCP as the protocol field in the IP header and for 80 as the destination port in the TCP header. If the packet meets these criteria, it is redirected to a Cisco Cache Engine.

Through communication with the Cisco Cache Engines, the routers running WCCP are aware of available cache engines.

Platforms Supported

WCCP is supported on the following platforms:

- Cisco 2500 series
- Cisco 3600 series
- Cisco 4000 series
- Cisco 4500 series
- Cisco 4700 series
- Cisco 5200 series
- Cisco 5300 series
- Cisco 7000 series with RSP7000
- Cisco 7200 series

- Cisco 7500 series
- Catalyst 5000

Web Cache Control Protocol Configuration Task List

To use the Web Cache Control Protocol, IP must be configured on the interface connected to the Internet and the interface connected to the Cisco Cache Engine.

The interface connected to the Cisco Cache Engine must be an Ethernet or Fast Ethernet interface.

To configure the Web Cache Control Protocol on the router, you must use the following tasks. The first task is required, while the rest are optional.

- Enable the Web Cache Control Protocol on the Router
- Monitor the Web Cache Control Protocol

Enable the Web Cache Control Protocol on the Router

To enable an interface to redirect Web traffic to the Cisco Cache Engine using the Web Cache Control Protocol, use the following commands beginning in global configuration mode:

Step	Command	Purpose
1	**ip wccp enable**	Enables the router to use the Web Cache Control Protocol.
2	**ip wccp redirect-list** {*number*	*name*}	(Optional) Specifies the redirect access list. Only packets that match this access list are redirected. If you do not configure this command, all Web-based packets are redirected.
3	**interface** *interface*	Enters interface configuration mode.
4	**ip web-cache redirect**	Configures the interface connected to the Internet to redirect Web traffic to the Cisco Cache Engine.
5	**ip route-cache same-interface**	(Optional) Configures the router to use the fast switching path on the interface if the client and a Cisco Cache Engine are located on the same network.
6	**end**	Exits configuration mode.
7	**copy running-config startup-config**	Saves the configuration.

Monitor the Web Cache Control Protocol

To monitor the Web Cache Control Protocol, use any of the following commands in EXEC mode:

Step	Command	Purpose
1	**show ip wccp**	Displays global Web Cache Control Protocol statistics.
2	**show ip wccp web-caches**	Displays information about all known Cisco Cache Engines.
3	**show ip interface**	Shows whether Web cache redirecting is enabled on an interface.

The **show ip wccp** and **show ip wccp web-caches** commands display a count of the number of packets redirected. Use the **clear ip wccp** EXEC command to clear this counter.

What to Do Next

To use WCCP, the Cisco Cache Engine must be properly configured. Keep these important points in mind:

● The IP address of the router must be configured as the home router for the Cisco Cache Engine.

● Versions of software on the Cisco Cache Engines must be compatible with the router.

● The Cisco Cache Engines must not have their packets encrypted or compressed and should be part of the "inside" Network Address Translation if one is present.

● Placing a Cisco Cache Engine beyond a Web-cache-redirect enabled interface and along the route to the server will not cause the IP route cache to be populated with an entry.

Cisco Web Browser Configuration Examples

This section provides the following configuration examples:

● SSI EXEC Command Example

● SSI ECHO Command Example

● WCCP Configuration Example

SSI EXEC Command Example

The following is an example of the HTML SSI EXEC command used to display the Cisco IOS **show users** EXEC command output:

Contents of the HTML file in Flash memory:

```
<HTML>
<HEAD>
<TITLE> SSI EXEC Command Example</TITLE>
</HEAD>
<BODY>
This is an example of the SSI EXEC command
<HR>
<PRE>
<!--#exec cmd="show users"-->
</PRE>
<HR>
</BODY>
</HTML>
```

Contents that the Web browser receives when the HTML file is retrieved from Flash memory:

```
<HTML>
<HEAD>
<TITLE> SSI EXEC Command Example</TITLE>
</HEAD>
<BODY>
This is an example of the SSI EXEC command
<HR>
<PRE>

Line    User   Host(s) Idle  Location
0 con 0        idle     12
2 vty 0        idle      0   router.cisco.com

</PRE>
<HR>
</BODY>
</HTML>
```

SSI ECHO Command Example

The following is an example of the HTML SSI ECHO command used with the SSI variable *SERVER_NAME* (refer to Chapter 1, Table 1–5) to display the Cisco IOS platform host name *rain*:

Contents of the HTML file in Flash memory:

```
<HTML>
<HEAD>
<TITLE>SSI Echo Command Example</TITLE>
</HEAD>
<BODY>
This is an example of the SSI echo command
<HR>
<!--#echo var="SERVER_NAME"-->
<HR>
</BODY>
</HTML>
```

Contents that the Web browser receives when the HTML file is retrieved from Flash memory:

```
<HTML>
<HEAD>
<TITLE>SSI Echo Command Example</TITLE>
</HEAD>
<BODY>
This is an example of the SSI echo command
<HR>
rain
<HR>
</BODY>
</HTML>
```

WCCP Configuration Example

The following example configures a router to support the Web Cache Control Protocol and to redirect Web-related packets from Ethernet interface 0 to the Cisco Cache Engine:

```
Router# configure terminal
Router(config)# ip wccp enable
Router(config)# interface Ethernet 0
Router(config-if)# ip web-cache redirect
Router(config-if)# end
Router#
%SYS-5-CONFIG_I: Configured from console by console.
Router# copy running-config startup-config
```

After the router has been configured, use the **show ip wccp web-cache** command to verify that Web Cache Control Protocol is enabled and is aware of Cisco Cache Engines. In this example, the **show ip wccp web-cache** command is entered immediately after the router has been configured. After a few seconds, the cache engine becomes usable, as seen in the second output.

```
Router# show ip wccp web-cache

WCCP Web-Cache information:
        IP Address:           192.168.51.102
        Protocol Version:     0.3
        State:                NOT Usable
        Initial Hash Info:    FFFFFFFFFFFFFFFFFFFFFFFFFFFFFFFF
                              FFFFFFFFFFFFFFFFFFFFFFFFFFFFFFFF
        Assigned Hash Info:   00000000000000000000000000000000
                              00000000000000000000000000000000
        Hash Allotment:       0 (0.00%)
        Packets Redirected:   0
        Connect Time:         00:00:06

Router# show ip wccp web-cache

WCCP Web-Cache information:
        IP Address            192.168.51.102
        Protocol Version:     0.3
```

```
State:                  Usable
Initial Hash Info:      FFFFFFFFFFFFFFFFFFFFFFFFFFFFFFFF
                        FFFFFFFFFFFFFFFFFFFFFFFFFFFFFFFF
Assigned Hash Info:     FFFFFFFFFFFFFFFFFFFFFFFFFFFFFFFF
                        FFFFFFFFFFFFFFFFFFFFFFFFFFFFFFFF
Hash Allotment:         256 (100.00%)
Packets Redirected:     0
Connect Time:           00:00:31
```

Cisco IOS Web Browser Commands

This chapter provides detailed descriptions of the commands used to issue Cisco IOS commands from the Cisco Web browser accessible from your router's home page.

For configuration tasks and examples, refer to Chapter 9, "Using the Cisco Web Browser."

clear ip wccp

To clear the counter for packets redirected by the Web Cache Control Protocol, use the **clear ip wccp** EXEC command.

> **clear ip wccp**

Syntax Description

This command has no arguments or keywords.

Command Mode

EXEC

Usage Guidelines

This command first appeared in Cisco IOS Release 11.2 P and Cisco IOS Release 11.1 CA.

The "Packets Redirected" count is displayed by the **show ip wccp** and **show ip wccp web-caches** commands.

Sample Display

The following is sample output from the **show ip wccp web-caches** command before and after the **clear ip wccp** command is used:

```
Router# show ip wccp web-caches

WCCP Web-Cache information:
        IP Address:            192.168.88.11
        Protocol Version:      1.0
        State:                 Usable
```

```
        Initial Hash Info:    AAAAAAAAAAAAAAAAAAAAAAAAAAAAAAAA
                              AAAAAAAAAAAAAAAAAAAAAAAAAAAAAAAA
        Assigned Hash Info:   FFFFFFFFFFFFFFFFFFFFFFFFFFFFFFFF
                              FFFFFFFFFFFFFFFFFFFFFFFFFFFFFFFF
        Hash Allotment:       256 (100.00%)
        Packets Redirected:   21345
        Connect Time:         00:13:46

Router# clear ip wccp
Router# show ip wccp web-caches

WCCP Web-Cache information:
        IP Address:           192.168.88.11
        Protocol Version:     1.0
        State:                Usable
        Initial Hash Info:    AAAAAAAAAAAAAAAAAAAAAAAAAAAAAAAA
                              AAAAAAAAAAAAAAAAAAAAAAAAAAAAAAAA
        Assigned Hash Info:   FFFFFFFFFFFFFFFFFFFFFFFFFFFFFFFF
                              FFFFFFFFFFFFFFFFFFFFFFFFFFFFFFFF
        Hash Allotment:       256 (100.00%)
        Packets Redirected:   0
        Connect Time:         00:13:46
```

Related Commands

To locate documentation of related commands, you can search online at www.cisco.com.

show ip wccp
show ip wccp web-caches

international

If you are Telneting to a Cisco IOS platform and you want to display 8-bit and multibyte international characters (for example, Japanese) and print the ESC character as a single character instead of as the caret and bracket symbols (^[), use the **international** line configuration command. Use the **no** form of this command to display characters in 7-bit format.

> **international**
> **no international**

Syntax Description

This command has no arguments or keywords.

Default

Disabled

Command Mode

Line configuration

Usage Guidelines

This command first appeared in Cisco IOS Release 11.3.

If you are configuring a Cisco IOS platform using the Cisco Web browser interface, this feature is enabled automatically when you enable the Cisco Web browser using the **ip http server** command.

Example

The following example enables a Cisco IOS platform to display 8-bit and multibyte characters and print the ESC character as a single character instead of as the caret and bracket symbols (^[) when you are Telneting to the platform:

```
international
```

Related Commands

To locate documentation of related commands, you can search online at www.cisco.com.

terminal international

ip http access-class

To assign an access list to the HTTP server used by the Cisco IOS ClickStart software or the Cisco Web browser interface, use the **ip http access-class** global configuration command. To remove the assigned access list, use the **no** form of this command.

> **ip http access-class** {*access-list-number* | *name*}
> **no ip http access-class** {*access-list-number* | *name*}

Syntax	Description
access-list-number	Standard IP access list number in the range 0 to 99, as configured by the **access-list (standard)** command.
name	Name of a standard IP access list, as configured by the **ip access-list** command.

Default

There is no access list applied to the HTTP server.

Command Mode

Global configuration

Usage Guidelines

This command first appeared in Cisco IOS Release 11.2.

If this command is configured, the specified access list is assigned to the HTTP server. Before the HTTP server accepts a connection, it checks the access list. If the check fails, the HTTP server does not accept the request for a connection.

Example

The following example assigns the access list named *marketing* to the HTTP server:

```
ip http access-class marketing
ip access-list standard marketing
 permit 192.5.34.0  0.0.0.255
 permit 128.88.0.0  0.0.255.255
 permit 36.0.0.0  0.255.255.255
! (Note: all other access implicitly denied)
```

Related Commands

To locate documentation of related commands, you can search online at www.cisco.com.

ip access-list
ip wccp enable

ip http authentication

Use the **ip http authentication** global configuration command to specify a particular authentication method for HTTP server users. Use the **no** form of this command to disable a configured authentication method.

> **ip http authentication** {aaa | enable | local | tacacs}
> **no ip http authentication** {aaa | enable | local | tacacs}

Syntax	Description
aaa	Indicates that the AAA facility is used for authentication.
enable	Indicates that the enable password method, which is the default method of HTTP server user authentication, is used for authentication.

Syntax	Description
local	Indicates that the local user database as defined on the Cisco router or access server is used for authentication.
tacacs	Indicates that the TACACS or XTACACS server is used for authentication.

Default

The default method of authentication for the HTTP server interface is the enable password method.

Command Mode

Global configuration

Usage Guidelines

This command first appeared in Cisco IOS Release 11.2 F.

The **ip http authentication** command enables you to specify a particular authentication method for HTTP server users. The HTTP server uses the enable password method to authenticate a user at privilege level 15. The **ip http authentication** command now lets you specify enable, local, TACACS, or AAA HTTP server user authentication.

Example

The following example specifies TACACS as the method of HTTP server user authentication:

```
ip http authentication tacacs
```

Related Commands

To locate documentation of related commands, you can search online at www.cisco.com.

ip wccp enable

ip http port

To specify the port to be used by the Cisco IOS ClickStart software or the Cisco Web browser interface, use the **ip http port** global configuration command. To use the default port, use the **no** form of this command.

> **ip http port** *number*
> **no ip http port**

Syntax   Description

number   Port number for use by ClickStart or the Cisco Web browser interface.

Default

80

Command Mode

Global configuration

Usage Guidelines

This command first appeared in Cisco IOS Release 11.2.

Use this command if ClickStart or the Cisco Web browser interface cannot use port 80.

Example

The following example configures the router so that you can use ClickStart or the Cisco Web browser interface via port 60:

```
ip http server
ip http port 60
```

Related Commands

To locate documentation of related commands, you can search online at www.cisco.com.

ip wccp enable

ip http server

To enable a Cisco 1003, Cisco 1004, or Cisco 1005 router to be configured from a browser using the Cisco IOS ClickStart software, and to enable any router to be monitored or have its configuration modified from a browser using the Cisco Web browser interface, use the **ip http server** global configuration command. Use the **no** form of this command to disable this function.

> **ip http server**
> **no ip http server**

Syntax Description

This command has no arguments or keywords.

Default

This command is enabled on Cisco 1003, Cisco 1004, and Cisco 1005 routers that have not yet been configured. For Cisco 1003, Cisco 1004, and Cisco 1005 routers that have already been configured, and for all other routers, this command is disabled.

Command Mode

Global configuration

Usage Guidelines

This command first appeared in Cisco IOS Release 11.2.

Example

The following example configures the router so that you can use the Cisco Web browser interface to issue commands to it:

```
ip http server
```

Related Commands

To locate documentation of related commands, you can search online at www.cisco.com.

ip http access-class
ip http port

ip wccp enable

To enable the router to support the Web Cache Control Protocol, use the **ip wccp enable** global configuration command. The **no** form of this command disables support for the Web Cache Control Protocol.

> **ip wccp enable**
> **no ip wccp enable**

Syntax Description

This command has no arguments or keywords.

Default

The Web Cache Control Protocol is disabled on the router.

Command Mode

Global configuration

Usage Guidelines

This command first appeared in Cisco IOS Release 11.2 P and Release 11.1 CA.

This command and the **ip web-cache redirect** interface command are the only commands required to start redirecting requests to the Cisco Cache Engine using the Web Cache Control Protocol. To see if the Web Cache Control Protocol is enabled on the router, use the **show ip wccp** command.

When this command is enabled but the **ip web-cache redirect** command is disabled, the router is aware of caches but does not use them.

Use the **ip wccp redirect-list** command to limit the redirection of packets to those matching an access list.

Example

The following example configures a router to support the Web Cache Control Protocol and redirects web-related packets from Ethernet interface 0 to the Cisco Cache Engine:

```
Router# configure terminal
Router(config)# ip wccp enable
Router(config)# interface Ethernet 0
Router(config-if)# ip web-cache redirect
Router(config-if)# end
Router#
%SYS-5-CONFIG_I: Configured from console by console.
```

Related Commands

To locate documentation of related commands, you can search online at www.cisco.com.

ip wccp redirect-list
ip web-cache redirect
show ip wccp
show ip wccp web-caches

ip wccp redirect-list

To specify which packets are redirected to a Cisco Cache Engine, use the **ip wccp redirect-list** global configuration command. The **no** form of this command enables redirection of all packets.

ip wccp redirect-list {*number* | *name*}

Syntax	Description
number	Standard or extended IP access list number from 1 to 199.
name	Standard or extended IP access list name. This argument is only available in Release 11.2 P.

Default

All HTTP packets are redirected to the Cisco Cache Engine.

Command Mode

Global configuration

Usage Guidelines

This command first appeared in Cisco IOS Release 11.2 P and Release 11.1 CA.

Use this command to specify which packets should be redirected to the Cisco Cache Engine. When WCCP is enabled but this command is not configured, all web-related packets are redirected to the Cisco Cache Engine. When you enter this command, only packets that match the access list are redirected.

Some Web sites use the source IP address of packets for authentication. The Cisco Cache Engine uses its own IP address when sending requests to Web sites. Thus, the requests from the Cisco Cache Engine may not be authenticated. Use this command to bypass the Cisco Cache Engine in these cases.

Use the **ip wccp enable** and **ip web-cache redirect** commands to configure WCCP.

Example

The following example configures a router to redirect web-related packets without a destination of 192.168.196.51 to the Cisco Cache Engine:

```
Router# configure terminal
Router(config)# access-list 100 deny ip any host 192.168.196.51
Router(config)# access-list 100 permit ip any any
Router(config)# ip wccp enable
Router(config)# ip wccp redirect-list 100
Router(config)# interface Ethernet 0
Router(config-if)# ip web-cache redirect
Router(config-if)# end
Router#
%SYS-5-CONFIG_I: Configured from console by console.
```

Related Commands

To locate documentation of related commands, you can search online at www.cisco.com.

clear ip wccp
ip wccp enable
ip web-cache redirect
show ip wccp

ip web-cache redirect

To instruct an interface to check for appropriate outgoing packets and redirect them to a Cisco Cache Engine, use the **ip web-cache redirect** interface configuration command. The **no** form of this command disables the redirection of messages to the Cisco Cache Engine.

> **ip web-cache redirect**
> **no ip web-cache redirect**

Syntax Description

This command has no arguments or keywords.

Default

The interface does not redirect messages to the Cisco Cache Engine.

Command Mode

Interface configuration

Usage Guidelines

This command first appeared in Cisco IOS Release 11.2 P and Release 11.1 CA.

This command and the **ip wccp enable** interface command are the only commands required to start redirecting requests to the Cisco Cache Engine using the Web Cache Control Protocol.

Example

The following example configures a router to support the Web Cache Control Protocol and redirects web-related packets from Ethernet interface 0 to the Cisco Cache Engine:

```
Router# configure terminal
Router(config)# ip wccp enable
Router(config)# interface Ethernet 0
Router(config-if)# ip web-cache redirect
Router(config-if)# end
Router#
%SYS-5-CONFIG_I: Configured from console by console.
```

Related Commands

To locate documentation of related commands, you can search online at www.cisco.com.

clear ip wccp
ip wccp enable
ip wccp redirect-list
show ip interface
show ip wccp
show ip wccp web-caches

show ip interface

To display the usability status of interfaces configured for IP, use the **show ip interface** EXEC command.

> **show ip interface** [*type number*]

Syntax	Description
type	(Optional) Interface type.
number	(Optional) Interface number.

Command Mode

EXEC

Usage Guidelines

This command first appeared in Cisco IOS Release 10.0.

The Cisco IOS software automatically enters a directly connected route in the routing table if the interface is usable. A usable interface is one through which the software can send and receive packets. If the software determines that an interface is not usable, it removes the directly connected routing entry from the routing table. Removing the entry allows the software to use dynamic routing protocols to determine backup routes to the network (if any).

If the interface can provide two-way communication, the line protocol is marked "up." If the interface hardware is usable, the interface is marked "up." If you specify an optional interface type, you will see only information on that specific interface. If you specify no optional arguments, you will see information on all the interfaces.

When an asynchronous interface is encapsulated with PPP or SLIP, IP fast switching is enabled. A **show ip interface** command on an asynchronous interface encapsulated with PPP or SLIP displays a message indicating that IP fast switching is enabled.

Sample Display

The following is sample output from the **show ip interface** command:

```
Router# show ip interface

Ethernet0 is up, line protocol is up
  Internet address is 192.195.78.24, subnet mask is 255.255.255.240
  Broadcast address is 255.255.255.255
  Address determined by non-volatile memory
  MTU is 1500 bytes
  Helper address is not set
  Secondary address 131.192.115.2, subnet mask 255.255.255.0
  Directed broadcast forwarding is enabled
  Multicast groups joined: 224.0.0.1 224.0.0.2
  Outgoing access list is not set
  Inbound  access list is not set
  Proxy ARP is enabled
  Security level is default
  Split horizon is enabled
  ICMP redirects are always sent
  ICMP unreachables are always sent
  ICMP mask replies are never sent
  IP fast switching is enabled
  IP fast switching on the same interface is disabled
  IP SSE switching is disabled
  Router Discovery is disabled
  IP output packet accounting is disabled
  IP access violation accounting is disabled
  TCP/IP header compression is disabled
  Probe proxy name replies are disabled
  Web Cache Redirect is enabled
```

Table 10-1 describes the fields shown in this display.

Table 10-1 *Show IP Interface Field Descriptions*

Field	Description
Ethernet0 is up	If the interface hardware is usable, the interface is marked "up." For an interface to be usable, both the interface hardware and line protocol must be up.
line protocol is up	If the interface can provide two-way communication, the line protocol is marked "up." For an interface to be usable, both the interface hardware and line protocol must be up.
Broadcast address	Shows the broadcast address.
Address determined by...	Indicates how the IP address of the interface was determined.
MTU	Shows the MTU value set on the interface.
Helper address	Shows a helper address, if one has been set.
Secondary address	Shows a secondary address, if one has been set.
Directed broadcast forwarding	Indicates whether directed broadcast forwarding is enabled.
Multicast groups joined	Indicates the multicast groups this interface is a member of.
Outgoing access list	Indicates whether the interface has an outgoing access list set.
Inbound access list	Indicates whether the interface has an incoming access list set.
Proxy ARP	Indicates whether Proxy ARP is enabled for the interface.
Security level	Specifies the IPSO security level set for this interface.
ICMP redirects	Specifies whether redirects will be sent on this interface.
ICMP unreachables	Specifies whether unreachable messages will be sent on this interface.
ICMP mask replies	Specifies whether mask replies will be sent on this interface.
IP fast switching	Specifies whether fast switching has been enabled for this interface. It is generally enabled on serial interfaces, such as this one.
IP SSE switching	Specifies whether IP SSE switching is enabled.
Router Discovery	Specifies whether the discovery process has been enabled for this interface. It is generally disabled on serial interfaces.
IP output packet accounting	Specifies whether IP accounting is enabled for this interface and what the threshold (maximum number of entries) is.
TCP/IP header compression	Indicates whether compression is enabled or disabled.
Probe proxy name	Indicates whether HP Probe proxy name replies are generated.
Web Cache Redirect	Indicates whether HTTP packets are redirected to a Cisco Cache Engine.

show ip wccp

To display global statistics related to the Web Cache Control Protocol, use the **show ip wccp** EXEC command.

> **show ip wccp**

Syntax Description

This command has no arguments or keywords.

Command Mode

EXEC

Usage Guidelines

This command first appeared in Cisco IOS Release 11.2 P and Release 11.1 CA.

Use the **clear ip wccp** command to reset the counter for the "Packets Redirected" information.

Sample Display

The following example is sample output from the **show ip wccp** command:

```
Router# show ip wccp

Global WCCP information:
        Number of web-caches:           2
        Total Packets Redirected:       101
        Redirect access-list:           no_linux
        Total Packets Denied Redirect:  88
        Total Packets Unassigned:       0
```

Table 10-2 describes fields shown in this display.

Table 10-2 *Show IP WCCP Field Descriptions*

Field	Description
Number of web-caches	Number of Cisco Cache Engines using the router as their home router.
Total Packets Redirected	Total number of packets redirected by the router.
Redirect access-list	Name or number of the redirect access list. Only packets matching the access list are redirected.
Total Packets Denied Redirect	Total number of packets that were not redirected because they did not match the access list.

Table 10-2 *Show IP WCCP Field Descriptions (Continued)*

Field	Description
Total Packets Unassigned	Number of packets that were not redirected because they were not assigned to any web cache. Packets may not be assigned during initial discovery of Cisco Cache Engines or when a cache is dropped from a farm.

Related Commands

To locate documentation of related commands, you can search online at www.cisco.com.

clear ip wccp
ip wccp enable
ip wccp redirect-list
ip web-cache redirect
show ip interface
show ip wccp web-caches

show ip wccp web-caches

To display information about the router's known Cisco Cache Engines, use the **show ip wccp web-caches** EXEC command.

show ip wccp web-caches

Syntax Description

This command has no arguments or keywords.

Command Mode

EXEC

Usage Guidelines

This command first appeared in Cisco IOS Release 11.2 P and Release 11.1 CA.

Use the **clear ip wccp** command to reset the counter for the "Packets Redirected" information.

Sample Display

The following example is sample output from the **show ip wccp web-caches** command:

```
Router# show ip wccp web-caches

WCCP Web-Cache information:
        IP Address:          192.168.88.11
        Protocol Version:    1.0
        State:               Usable
        Initial Hash Info:   AAAAAAAAAAAAAAAAAAAAAAAAAAAAAAAA
                             AAAAAAAAAAAAAAAAAAAAAAAAAAAAAAAA
        Assigned Hash Info:  FFFFFFFFFFFFFFFFFFFFFFFFFFFFFFFF
                             FFFFFFFFFFFFFFFFFFFFFFFFFFFFFFFF
        Hash Allotment:      256 (100.00%)
        Packets Redirected:  21345
        Connect Time:        00:13:46
```

Table 10-3 describes the fields shown in this display.

Table 10-3   *Show IP WCCP Web-Caches Field Descriptions*

Field	Description
IP Address	IP address of the Cisco Cache Engine.
Protocol Version	Version of the Web Cache Control Protocol the Cisco Cache Engine is running.
State	State of the Cisco Cache Engine. Possible values are "Usable" and "NOT Usable."
Initial Hash Info	Initial contents of the hash field. The hash field contains information about how the router intends to use the Cisco Cache Engine.
Assigned Hash Info	Current hash information of the Cisco Cache Engine. The hash information field contains information about how the router intends to use the Cisco Cache Engine.
Hash Allotment	Percentage of all possible Web servers for which the router redirects HTTP requests to this Web cache. In this example, there is only one Cisco Cache Engine, so all HTTP requests are redirected to it.
Packets Redirected	Number of packets redirected to this Cisco Cache Engine.
Connect Time	Indicates how long the Cisco Cache Engine has used this router as its home router.

Related Commands

To locate documentation of related commands, you can search online at www.cisco.com.

clear ip wccp
ip wccp enable
ip web-cache redirect
show ip interface
show ip wccp

terminal international

If you are Telneting to a Cisco IOS platform and you want to display 8-bit and multibyte international characters (for example, Japanese) and print the ESC character as a single character instead of as the caret and bracket symbols (^[) for a current Telnet session, use the **terminal international** EXEC command. Use the **no** form of this command to display characters in 7-bit format for a current Telnet session.

> **terminal international**
> **no terminal international**

Syntax Description

This command has no arguments or keywords.

Default

Disabled

Command Mode

EXEC

Usage Guidelines

This command first appeared in Cisco IOS Release 11.3.

If you are configuring a Cisco IOS platform using the Cisco Web browser interface, this feature is enabled automatically when you enable the Cisco Web browser using the **ip http server** command.

Example

The following example enables a Cisco IOS platform to display 8-bit and multibyte characters and print the ESC character as a single character instead of as the caret and bracket symbols (^[) when you are Telneting to the platform for the current Telnet session:

```
terminal international
```

Related Commands

To locate documentation of related commands, you can search online at www.cisco.com.

international

PART II

File Management

## CHAPTER 11

Using the Cisco IOS File System

This chapter describes the Cisco IOS File System (IFS) feature, which provides a single interface to all the file systems a router uses, including:

- Flash memory file systems

- Network file systems (TFTP, rcp, and FTP)

- Any other endpoint for reading or writing data (such as NVRAM, the running configuration, ROM, raw system memory, system bundled microcode, Xmodem, Flash load helper log, modems, and BRI MUX interfaces)

For a complete description of the IFS commands in this chapter, refer to Chapter 12, "Cisco IOS File System Commands." To locate documentation of other commands that appear in this chapter, you can search online at www.cisco.com.

IFS Use and Management Task List

This chapter describes how to use the Cisco IFS feature and the tasks you can perform to manage file systems related to IFS. Information about IFS and its optional file management tasks are described in the following sections:

- Understanding IFS

- Copy Files Using URLs

- Use URLs in Commands

- File System Management Task List

Understanding IFS

This section describes the following IFS capabilities and benefits:

- File Viewing and Classification

- Platform-Independent Commands

- Minimal Prompting for Commands

- Directory Navigation and Creation

File Viewing and Classification

With IFS, all files can be viewed and classified (image, text file, and so forth), including files on remote servers. For example, you may want to determine the size and type of an image on a remote server before you copy it to ensure that it is a valid image. You can also view a configuration file on a remote server to verify that it is the correct configuration file before you load the file on the router.

Platform-Independent Commands

With IFS, the file system user interface is no longer platform specific. Commands have the same syntax, regardless of which platform is used. Thus, you can use the same commands for all of your routers.

However, not all commands are supported on all platforms and file systems. Because different types of file systems support different operations, certain commands are not available for all file systems. Platforms will support commands for the file systems they use.

Minimal Prompting for Commands

IFS minimizes the required prompting for many commands, such as the **copy** command. You can enter all of the required information in the command line, rather than having to provide information when the system prompts you for it. For example, if you want to copy a file to an FTP server, you can specify the specific location on the router of the source file, the specific location of the destination file on the FTP server, and the username and password to use when connecting to the FTP server, all on a single line. However, if you wish to have the router prompt you for the needed information, you can still enter the minimum form of the command.

Depending on the current configuration of the **file prompt** command and the type of command you entered, the router may prompt you for confirmation, even if you have provided all the information in the command. In these cases, the default value will be the value entered in the command. Press Return to confirm the values.

Directory Navigation and Creation

With IFS, you can move around to different directories and list the files in a directory. On newer platforms, you can create subdirectories in Flash memory or on a disk.

Copy Files Using URLs

The new file system interface uses Uniform Resource Locators (URLs) to specify the location of a file. URLs are commonly used to specify files or locations on the World Wide Web. However, on Cisco routers, they can now be used to specify the location of files on the router or remote file servers.

On Cisco routers, use URLs in commands to specify the location of the file or directory. For example, if you want to copy a file from one location to another, use the **copy** *source-url destination-url* command.

The format of URLs used by the routers can vary from the format you may be used to using. There are also a variety of formats that can be used, based on the location of the file.

This section provides the following information for copying files using URLs:

- Specify Files on a Network Server
- Specify Local Files
- URL Prefixes

Specify Files on a Network Server

When you want to specify a file on a network server, use one of the following forms:

ftp:[[//[*username*[:*password*]@]*location*]/*directory*]/*filename*

rcp:[[//[*username*@]*location*]/*directory*]/*filename*

tftp:[[//*location*]/*directory*]/*filename*

The location can be an IP address or a host name. The username variable, if specified, overrides the username specified by the **ip rcmd remote-username** or **ip ftp username** commands. The password overrides the password specified by the **ip ftp password** command.

The file path (directory and filename) is specified relative to the directory used for file transfers. For example, on UNIX file servers, TFTP pathnames start in the /tftpboot directory, and rcp and FTP paths start in the home directory associated with the username.

The following example specifies the file c7200-j-mz.112-current on the TFTP server myserver.cisco.com. The file is located in the directory called /tftpboot/master.

```
tftp://myserver.cisco.com/master/c7200-j-mz.112-current
```

The following example specifies the file ship-config on the server enterprise.cisco.com. The router uses the username jeanluc and the password secret to access this server via FTP.

```
ftp://jeanluc:secret@enterprise.cisco.com/ship-config
```

Specify Local Files

Use the following syntax to specify a file located on the router:

*prefix***:**[*directory*/]*filename*

You can use this form to specify a file in Flash memory or NVRAM.

The following example specifies the startup configuration in NVRAM:

```
nvram:startup-config
```

The following example specifies the file backup-config in the configs directory of Flash memory:

```
flash:configs/backup-config
```

When referring to a file system instead of a file, the form is

*prefix***:**

This form specifies the file system itself, rather than a file in the file system. Use this form to perform commands on file systems themselves, such as listing the files in a file system or formatting the file system.

The following example specifies the first PCMCIA Flash memory card:

```
slot0:
```

URL Prefixes

The URL prefix specifies the file system. File system prefixes are listed in Table 11-1. The list of available file systems differs by platform and operation. Refer to your product documentation or use the **show file systems** command to determine which prefixes are available on your platform.

Table 11-1 *File System Prefixes*

Prefix	File System
bootflash:	Boot Flash memory.
disk0:	Rotating media.
flash:	Flash memory. This prefix is available on all platforms. For platforms that do not have a device named flash:, the prefix **flash:** is aliased to **slot0:**. Therefore, you can use the prefix **flash:** to refer to the main Flash memory storage area on all platforms.
flh:	Flash load helper log files.
ftp:	File Transfer Protocol (FTP) network server.
null:	Null destination for copies. You can copy a remote file to null to determine its size.
nvram:	NVRAM.
rcp:	Remote copy protocol (rcp) network server.
slavebootflash:	Internal Flash memory on a slave RSP card of a router configured for HSA.
slavenvram:	NVRAM on a slave RSP card of a router configured for HSA.
slaveslot0:	First PCMCIA card on a slave RSP card of a router configured for HSA.
slaveslot1:	Second PCMCIA card on a slave RSP card of a router configured for HSA.
slot0:	First PCMCIA Flash memory card.

Table 11-1 *File System Prefixes (Continued)*

Prefix	File System
slot1:	Second PCMCIA Flash memory card.
system:	Contains the system memory, including the running configuration.
tftp:	Trivial File Transfer Protocol (TFTP) network server.
xmodem:	Obtain the file from a network machine using the Xmodem protocol.
ymodem:	Obtain the file from a network machine using the Ymodem protocol.

NOTE   MOP servers are no longer supported as file systems.

In all commands, the colon is required after the file system name. However, commands that did not require the colon previously will continue to be supported, although they will not be available in the context-sensitive help.

URL Prefix for Partitioned Devices

For partitioned devices, the prefix includes the partition number. The syntax for the prefix on a partitioned device is *device:partition-number:*.

For example, **flash:2:** refers to the second partition in Flash memory.

URL Component Lengths

Table 11-2 lists the maximum lengths, in characters, of the different URL components.

Table 11-2 *URL Component Lengths*

Component	Length (Number of Characters)
Prefix	31
Username	15
Password	15
Hostname	31
Directory	63
Filename	63

Use URLs in Commands

Depending on which command you are using, different file systems are available. Some file systems can only serve as a source for files, not a destination. For example, you cannot copy to another machine using Xmodem. Other operations, such as **format** and **erase**, are only supported by certain file systems on certain platforms.

The following sections provide hints for using URLs in commands:

- Determine File Systems Supporting a Command
- Use the Default File System
- Use Tab Completion
- List Files in a File System

Determine File Systems Supporting a Command

Use the context-sensitive help to determine which file systems can be used for a particular command. In the following example, the context-sensitive help displays which file systems can be used as sources for the **copy** command. The output will vary based on the platform.

```
Router# copy ?
  /erase      Erase destination file system.
  bootflash:  Copy from bootflash: file system
  flash:      Copy from flash: file system
  ftp:        Copy from ftp: file system
  null:       Copy from null: file system
  nvram:      Copy from nvram: file system
  rcp:        Copy from rcp: file system
  system:     Copy from system: file system
  tftp:       Copy from tftp: file system
```

Use the Default File System

For most commands, if no file system is specified, the file is assumed to be in the default directory, as specified by the **cd** command.

```
Router# pwd
slot0:
Router# dir
Directory of slot0:/

  1  -rw-     4720148   Aug 29 1997 17:49:36  hampton/nitro/c7200-j-mz
  2  -rw-     4767328   Oct 01 1997 18:42:53  c7200-js-mz
  5  -rw-         639   Oct 02 1997 12:09:32  foo
  7  -rw-         639   Oct 02 1997 12:37:13  the_time

20578304 bytes total (3104544 bytes free)
Router# cd nvram:
```

```
Router# dir
Directory of nvram:/

   1  -rw-       2725              <no date>  startup-config
   2  ----          0              <no date>  private-config
   3  -rw-       2725              <no date>  underlying-config

129016 bytes total (126291 bytes free)
```

Use Tab Completion

You can use tab completion to reduce the number of characters you need to type for a command. Type the first few characters of the filename, and press the Tab key. If the characters are unique to a filename, the router will complete the filename for you. Continue entering the command as usual, and press Return to execute the command.

In the following example, the router completes the filename startup-config, because it is the only file in the nvram: file system that starts with "s":

```
Router# show file info nvram:s<tab>
Router# show file info nvram:startup-config<Enter>
```

If you use tab completion without specifying any characters, the router uses the first file in the file system.

```
Router# show file info nvram:<tab>
Router# show file info nvram:private-config<Enter>
```

List Files in a File System

For many commands, you can get a listing of the files in a file system on the router by using the context-sensitive help. In the following example, the router lists the files in NVRAM:

```
Router# show file info nvram:?
nvram:private-config  nvram:startup-config  nvram:underlying-config
```

File System Management Task List

This section describes the following tasks related to file system management and IFS:

● General File System Management Tasks

● Flash Memory File System Management Tasks

● Remote File System Management Tasks

● NVRAM File System Management Tasks

● System File System Management Tasks

General File System Management Tasks

This section describes general tasks you can perform to use the different file systems.

List Available File Systems

Not all file systems are supported on every platform. To list the file systems available on your platform, use the following EXEC mode command:

Command	Purpose
show file systems	Lists the file systems available on your platform. This command also displays information about each file system.

Set the Default File System

You can specify the file system or directory that the system uses as the default file system. Setting the default file system allows you to omit an optional *filesystem*: argument from related commands. For all EXEC commands that have an optional *filesystem*: argument, the system uses the file system specified by the **cd** command when you omit the optional *filesystem*: argument. For example, the **dir** command contains an optional *filesystem*: argument and displays a list of files on the file system.

To specify a default file system, use the following EXEC mode command:

Command	Purpose
cd *filesystem*:	Sets a default Flash memory device.

The following example sets the default file system to the Flash memory card inserted in slot 0:

```
cd slot0:
```

Display the Current Default File System

To display the current default file system, as specified by the **cd** command, use the following EXEC mode command:

Command	Purpose
pwd	Displays the current file system.

The following example shows that the default file system is slot 0:

```
Router> pwd
slot0:
```

The following example uses the **cd** command to change the default file system to system and then uses the **pwd** command to verify that the default file system was changed:

```
Router> cd system:
Router> pwd
system:
```

Display Information about Files on a File System

You can view a list of the contents of a file system before manipulating its contents. For example, before copying a new configuration file to Flash memory, you may want to verify that the file system does not already contain a configuration file with the same name. Similarly, before copying a Flash configuration file to another location, you may want to verify its filename for use in another command.

To show display information about files on a file system, use one of the following EXEC mode commands:

Command	Purpose
dir [**/all**] [*filesystem:*][*filename*]	Displays a list of files on a file system.
show filesystems	Displays more information about each of the files on a file system.
show file information *file-url*	Displays information about a specific file.
show file descriptors	Displays a list of open file descriptors.

The following example compares the different commands used to display information about files for the PCMCIA card in the first slot. Notice that deleted files appear in the **dir /all** output but not in the **dir** output.

```
Router# dir slot0:
Directory of slot0:/

  1  -rw-     4720148    Aug 29 1997 17:49:36  hampton/nitro/c7200-j-mz
  2  -rw-     4767328    Oct 01 1997 18:42:53  c7200-js-mz
  5  -rw-          639    Oct 02 1997 12:09:32  foo
  7  -rw-          639    Oct 02 1997 12:37:13  the_time

20578304 bytes total (3104544 bytes free)

Router# dir /all slot0:
Directory of slot0:/

  1  -rw-     4720148    Aug 29 1997 17:49:36  hampton/nitro/c7200-j-mz
  2  -rw-     4767328    Oct 01 1997 18:42:53  c7200-js-mz
  3  -rw-     7982828    Oct 01 1997 18:48:14  [rsp-jsv-mz]
  4  -rw-          639    Oct 02 1997 12:09:17  [the_time]
  5  -rw-          639    Oct 02 1997 12:09:32  foo
  6  -rw-          639    Oct 02 1997 12:37:01  [the_time]
  7  -rw-          639    Oct 02 1997 12:37:13  the_time
```

```
20578304 bytes total (3104544 bytes free)

Router# show slot0:
-#- ED --type-- --crc--- -seek-- nlen -length- -----date/time------ name
1   .. unknown  317FBA1B 4A0694   24   4720148 Aug 29 1997 17:49:36 hampton/nitz
2   .. unknown  9237F3FF 92C574   11   4767328 Oct 01 1997 18:42:53 c7200-js-mz
3   .D unknown  71AB01F1 10C94E0  10   7982828 Oct 01 1997 18:48:14 rsp-jsv-mz
4   .D unknown  96DACD45 10C97E0   8       639 Oct 02 1997 12:09:17 the_time
5   .. unknown  96DACD45 10C9AE0   3       639 Oct 02 1997 12:09:32 foo
6   .D unknown  96DACD45 10C9DE0   8       639 Oct 02 1997 12:37:01 the_time
7   .. unknown  96DACD45 10CA0E0   8       639 Oct 02 1997 12:37:13 the_time

3104544 bytes available (17473760 bytes used)
```

Display a File

To display the contents of any readable file, including a file on a remote file system, use the following EXEC mode command:

Command	Purpose
more [**/ascii**	**/binary**	**/ebcdic**] *file-url*	Displays a file.

The following example displays the contents of a configuration file on a TFTP server:

```
Router# more tftp://serverA/hampton/savedconfig

!
! Saved configuration on server
!
version 11.3
service timestamps log datetime localtime
service linenumber
service udp-small-servers
service pt-vty-logging
!
...
end
```

Flash Memory File System Management Tasks

The methods used for erasing, deleting, and recovering files depend on the class of the Flash file system.

Flash Memory File System Types

Cisco platforms use one of three different Flash memory file system types. Some commands are supported on only one or two file system types. The command reference documentation notes commands that are not supported on all file system types.

See Table 11-3 to determine which Flash memory file system type your platform uses.

Table 11-3 *Flash Memory File System Types*

Type	Platforms
Class A	Cisco 7000 family, C12000, LS1010
Class B	Cisco 1003, Cisco 1004, Cisco 1005, Cisco 2500 series, Cisco 3600 series, Cisco 4000 series, Cisco AS5200
Class C	Cisco MC3810, disk0 of SC3640

Class A Flash File Systems

On Class A Flash file systems, you can delete individual files using the **delete** command and later recover these files with the **undelete** command. The delete command marks the files as "deleted," but the files still take up space in Flash memory. To permanently delete the files, use the **squeeze** command. The **squeeze** command removes all of the files marked "deleted" from the specified Flash memory device. These files can no longer be recovered. To erase all of the files on a Flash device, use the **format** command.

Delete Files on a Flash Device

When you no longer need a file on a Flash memory device, you can delete it. When you delete a file, the router simply marks the file as deleted, but it does not erase the file. This feature allows you to recover a "deleted" file, as discussed in the following section. You may want to recover a "deleted" image or configuration file if the new image or configuration file becomes corrupted.

To delete a file from a specified Flash device, use the following EXEC mode command:

Command	Purpose
delete [*device***:**] *filename*	Deletes a file from a Flash memory device.

If you omit the device, the router uses the default device specified by the **cd** command.

If you attempt to delete the file specified by the CONFIG_FILE or BOOTLDR environment variable, the system prompts you to confirm the deletion. Also, if you attempt to delete the last valid system image specified in the BOOT environment variable, the system prompts you to confirm the deletion.

The following example deletes the file myconfig from a Flash memory card inserted in slot 0:

```
delete slot0:myconfig
```

Recover Deleted Files on a Flash Device

You can undelete a deleted file. For example, you may want to revert to a previous configuration file because the current one is corrupt.

To undelete a deleted file on a Flash memory device, use the following commands in EXEC mode:

Step	Command	Purpose
1	**dir /all** [*filesystem***:**]	Determines the index of the deleted file.
2	**undelete** *index* [*filesystem***:**]	Undeletes a deleted file on a Flash memory device.

You must undelete a file by its index because you can have multiple deleted files with the same name. For example, the "deleted" list could contain multiple configuration files with the name router-config. You undelete by index to indicate which of the many router-config files from the list to undelete. Use the **dir** command with the **/all** option to learn the index number of the file you want to undelete.

You cannot undelete a file if a valid (undeleted) one with the same name exists. Instead, first delete the existing file and then undelete the file you want. For example, if you had an undeleted version of the router-config file and you wanted to use a previous, deleted version instead, you cannot simply undelete the previous version by index. You must first delete the existing router-config file and then undelete the previous router-config file by index. You can undelete a file as long as the file has not been permanently erased with the **squeeze** command. You can delete and undelete a file up to 15 times.

The following example recovers the deleted file whose index number is 1 to the Flash memory card inserted in slot 0:

```
undelete 1 slot0:
```

Permanently Delete Files on a Flash Device

When a Flash memory device is full, you may need to rearrange the files so that the space used by the "deleted" files can be reclaimed. To determine whether a Flash memory device is full, use the **dir** command.

To permanently delete files on a Flash memory device, use the following command from privileged EXEC mode:

Command	Purpose
squeeze *filesystem***:**	Permanently deletes all files marked "deleted" in Flash memory.

When you issue the **squeeze** command, the router copies all valid files to the beginning of Flash memory and erases all files marked "deleted." At this point, you cannot recover "deleted" files, and you can now write to the reclaimed Flash memory space.

NOTE	The squeeze operation can take as long as several minutes because it can involve erasing and rewriting almost an entire Flash memory space.

Verify Flash

To recompute and verify the checksum of a file in Flash memory on a Class A Flash file system, use the **verify** command.

Class A Flash File System Examples

In the following example, the image c7200-js-mz is deleted and undeleted. Note that the deleted file does not appear in the output for the first **dir** command, but it appears in the output for the **dir /all** command.

```
Router# delete slot1:
Delete filename []? c7200-js-mz
Delete slot1:c7200-js-mz? [confirm]
Router# dir slot1:
Directory of slot1:/

No such file

20578304 bytes total (15754684 bytes free)
Router# dir /all slot1:
Directory of slot1:/

   1  -rw-    4823492   Dec 17 1997 13:21:53  [c7200-js-mz]

20578304 bytes total (15754684 bytes free)
Router# undelete 1 slot1:
Router# dir slot1:
Directory of slot1:/

   1  -rw-    4823492   Dec 17 1997 13:21:53  c7200-js-mz

20578304 bytes total (15754684 bytes free)
```

In the following example, the image is deleted. In order to reclaim the space taken up by the deleted file, the **squeeze** command is issued.

```
Router# delete slot1:c7200-js-mz
Delete filename [c7200-js-mz]?
Delete slot1:c7200-js-mz? [confirm]
Router# squeeze slot1:
All deleted files will be removed. Continue? [confirm]
Squeeze operation may take a while. Continue? [confirm]
Erasing squeeze log
Squeeze of slot1: complete
Router# dir /all slot1:
```

```
Directory of slot1:/

No such file

20578304 bytes total (20578304 bytes free)
```

Class B Flash File Systems

On Class B Flash file systems, you can delete individual files with the **delete** command. The **delete** command marks the file as "deleted." The file is still present in Flash memory and takes up space. To recover the file, use the **undelete** command. To reclaim any space in Flash memory, you must erase the entire Flash file system with the **erase** command.

Delete Files on a Flash Device

When you no longer need a file on a Flash memory device, you can delete it. When you delete a file, the router simply marks the file as deleted, but it does not erase the file. This feature allows you to recover a "deleted" file, as discussed in the following section. You may want to recover a "deleted" image or configuration file if the new image or configuration file becomes corrupted.

To delete a file from a specified Flash device, use the following EXEC mode command:

Command	Purpose
delete [*device*:] *filename*	Deletes a file from a Flash memory device.

If you omit the device, the router uses the default device specified by the **cd** command.

The following example deletes the file myconfig from a Flash memory card inserted in slot 0:

```
delete slot0:myconfig
```

Recover Deleted Files on a Flash Device

You can undelete a deleted file. For example, you may want to revert to a previous configuration file because the current one is corrupt.

To undelete a deleted file on a Flash memory device, use the following EXEC mode commands:

Step	Command	Purpose
1	**dir /all** [*filesystem*:]	Determines the index of the deleted file.
2	**undelete** *index* [*filesystem*:]	Undeletes a deleted file on a Flash memory device.

You must undelete a file by its index because you can have multiple deleted files with the same name. For example, the "deleted" list could contain multiple configuration files with the name router-config. You undelete by index to indicate which of the many router-config files from the list to undelete. Use the **dir** command with the **/all** option to learn the index number of the file you want to undelete.

You cannot undelete a file if a valid (undeleted) one with the same name exists. Instead, first delete the existing file and then undelete the file you want. For example, if you had an undeleted version of the router-config file and you wanted to use a previous, deleted version instead, you cannot simply undelete the previous version by index. You must first delete the existing router-config file and then undelete the previous router-config file by index. You can undelete a file as long as the file system has not been permanently erased with the **erase** command. You can delete and undelete a file up to 15 times.

The following example recovers the deleted file whose index number is 1 to the Flash memory card inserted in slot 0:

```
undelete 1 slot0:
```

Erase Flash Memory

In order to reclaim any space taken up by files in Flash memory, you must erase the entire file system using the **erase flash:** or **erase bootflash:** commands. These commands reclaim all of the space in flash memory, erasing all files, deleted or not, in the process. Once erased, these files cannot be recovered. Before erasing Flash memory, save any files you wish to keep in another location (an FTP server, for example). Copy the files back to Flash memory after you have erased the device.

To erase a Flash device, use the following EXEC mode command:

Command	Purpose
erase *filesystem***:**	Erases the Flash file system.

Erase a File System Example

The following example erases all files in the second partition in Flash memory:

```
Router# erase flash:2

System flash directory, partition 2:
File  Length   Name/status
  1   1711088  dirt/gate/c1600-i-mz
[1711152 bytes used, 15066064 available, 16777216 total]

Erase flash device, partition 2? [confirm]
Are you sure? [yes/no]: yes
Erasing device... eeeeeeeeeeeeeeeeeeeeeeeeeeeeeeeeeeeeeeeeeeeeeeeeeeeeeeeeeeeee ...erased
```

Verify Flash

To recompute and verify the checksum of a file in Flash memory on a Class B Flash file system, use the **verify** command.

Class C Flash File Systems

On Class C Flash memory file systems, you can delete individual files with the **delete** command. Files cannot be reclaimed once they have been deleted. Instead, the Flash file system space is reclaimed dynamically. To erase all of the files in Flash, use the **format** command.

Delete Files on a Flash Device

When you no longer need a file on a Flash memory device, you can delete it. When you delete a file on a Class C file system, the file is deleted permanently. The router reclaims the space dynamically.

To delete a file from a specified Flash device, use the following EXEC mode command:

Command	Purpose
delete [*device***:**] *filename*	Deletes a file from a Flash memory device.

If you omit the device, the router uses the default device specified by the **cd** command.

If you attempt to delete the file specified by the CONFIG_FILE or BOOTLDR environment variable, the system prompts you to confirm the deletion. Also, if you attempt to delete the last valid system image specified in the BOOT environment variable, the system prompts you to confirm the deletion.

The following example permanently deletes the *myconfig* file from a Flash memory card inserted in slot 0:

```
delete slot0:myconfig
```

Format Flash

To format a Class C Flash file system, use the following EXEC mode command:

Command	Purpose
format *filesystem*	Formats Flash.

If you format a Flash device, all of the files are erased and cannot be recovered.

Create and Remove Directories

On Class C Flash file systems, you can create a new directory with the **mkdir** command. To remove a directory from a Flash file system, use the **rmdir** command.

On Class C Flash file systems, you can rename a file using the **rename** command.

Check and Verify Flash

On Class C Flash file systems, you can check a file system for damage and repair any problems using the **fsck** command.

Remote File System Management Tasks

On remote file systems (file systems on FTP, rcp, or TFTP servers) you can perform the following tasks:

- View the contents of a file with the **more** command.

- Copy files to or from the router using the **copy** command.

- Show information about a file using the **show file information** command.

NOTE   You cannot delete files on remote systems.

NVRAM File System Management Tasks

On most platforms, NVRAM contains the startup configuration. On Class A Flash file system platforms, the CONFIG_FILE environment variable specifies the location of the startup configuration. However, the file URL nvram:startup-config always specifies the startup configuration, regardless of the CONFIG_FILE environment variable.

You can view the startup-config (with the **more nvram:startup-config** command), replace the startup config with a new configuration file (with the **copy** *source-url* **nvram:startup-config** command), save the startup configuration to another location (with the **copy nvram:startup-config** *destination-url* command), and erase the contents of NVRAM (with the **erase nvram:** command). The **erase nvram:** command also deletes the startup configuration if another location is specified by the CONFIG_FILE variable.

This example displays the startup configuration:

```
nnm3640-2# more nvram:startup-config
Using 2279 out of 129016 bytes
!
! Last configuration change at 10:57:25 PST Wed Apr 22 1998
! NVRAM config last updated at 10:57:27 PST Wed Apr 22 1998
```

```
!
version 11.3
service timestamps log datetime localtime
service linenumber
service udp-small-servers
service pt-vty-logging
...
end
```

The following example displays the contents of the NVRAM file system on a Class A Flash file system platform. The file named startup-config is the current startup configuration file, in physical NVRAM or in Flash memory. If the file is located in a Flash memory file system, this entry is a symbolic link to the actual file. The file named underlying-config is always the NVRAM version of the configuration.

```
Router# dir nvram:
  Directory of nvram:/

    1  -rw-      2703          <no date>  startup-config
    2  ----         5          <no date>  private-config
    3  -rw-      2703          <no date>  underlying-config

  129016 bytes total (126313 bytes free)
```

System File System Management Tasks

The system file system contains the system memory and the current running configuration. You can view the current configuration (with the **more system:running-config** command), save the current configuration to some other location (with the **copy system:running-config** *destination-url* command), or add configuration commands to the current configuration (with the **copy** *source-url* **system:running-config** command).

The following example indicates changes to the system file system, views the contents of the file system, and displays the running configuration:

```
nnm3640-2# cd system:
nnm3640-2# dir
Directory of system:/

    2  dr-x         0          <no date>  memory
    1  -rw-         0          <no date>  running-config

No space information available
nnm3640-2# more system:running-config
!
! No configuration change since last restart
!
version 11.3
service timestamps log datetime localtime
service linenumber
service udp-small-servers
```

```
service pt-vty-logging
!
...
end
```

On some platforms, the system file system contains microcode in its ucode directory.

```
Router# dir system:/ucode
Directory of system:/ucode/

    21  -r--       22900        <no date>  aip20-13
    18  -r--       32724        <no date>  eip20-3
    25  -r--      123130        <no date>  feip20-6
    19  -r--       25610        <no date>  fip20-1
    22  -r--        7742        <no date>  fsip20-7
    23  -r--       17130        <no date>  hip20-1
    24  -r--       36450        <no date>  mip22-2
    29  -r--      154752        <no date>  posip20-0
    28  -r--      704688        <no date>  rsp220-0
    20  -r--       33529        <no date>  trip20-1
    26  -r--      939130        <no date>  vip22-20
    27  -r--     1107862        <no date>  vip222-20

No space information available
```

## CHAPTER 12

Cisco IOS File System Commands

This chapter describes the commands used to configure the Cisco IOS File System (IFS) feature.

cd

To change the default directory or file system, use the **cd** EXEC command.

> **cd** [*filesystem*:]

Syntax	Description
filesystem:	(Optional) URL of the directory or file system followed by a colon.

Default

The initial default file system is **flash:**. For platforms that do not have a physical device named **flash:**, the keyword **flash:** is aliased to the default Flash device.

If you do not specify a directory on a file system, the default is the root directory on that file system.

Command Mode

EXEC

Usage Guidelines

This command first appeared in Cisco IOS Release 11.0.

For all EXEC commands that have an optional *filesystem* argument, the system uses the file system specified by the **cd** command when you omit the optional *filesystem* argument. For example, the **dir** command, which displays a list of files on a file system, contains an optional *filesystem* argument. When you omit this argument, the system lists the files on the file system specified by the **cd** command.

Example

The following example sets the default file system to the Flash memory card inserted in the slot 0:

```
Router# pwd
bootflash:/
```

```
Router# cd slot0:
Router# pwd
slot0:/
```

Related Commands

To locate documentation of related commands, you can search online at www.cisco.com.

copy
delete
dir
pwd
show file systems
undelete

copy verify

The **verify** command replaces the **copy verify** command. Refer to the **verify** command.

copy verify flash

The **verify** command replaces the **copy verify flash** command. Refer to the **verify** command.

delete

To delete a file on a Flash memory device, use the **delete** EXEC command.

> **delete** *flash-url*

Syntax   Description

flash-url   URL of the file to be deleted.

Command Mode
EXEC

Usage Guidelines
This command first appeared in Cisco IOS Release 11.0.

When you delete a file, the software simply marks the file as deleted, but it does not erase the file. This feature allows you to later recover a "deleted" file using the **undelete** command. You can delete and undelete a file up to 15 times. To permanently delete all files marked "deleted" on a Flash memory device, use the **squeeze** command.

If you attempt to delete the configuration file or image specified by the CONFIG_FILE or BOOTLDR environment variable, the system prompts you to confirm the deletion. Also, if you attempt to delete the last valid system image specified in the BOOT environment variable, the system prompts you to confirm the deletion.

Example

The following example deletes the file named test from the Flash card inserted in slot 0:

```
Router# delete slot0:test
Delete slot0:test? [confirm]
```

Related Commands

To locate documentation of related commands, you can search online at www.cisco.com.

cd
dir
show bootvar
show running-config
undelete

dir

To display a list of files on a file system, use the **dir** EXEC command.

dir [**/all**] [*filesystem*: | *file-url*]

Syntax	Description
/all	(Optional) Lists deleted files, undeleted files, and files with errors.
filesystem:	(Optional) File system or directory containing the file(s) to list followed by a colon.
file-url	(Optional) Name of the file(s) to display on a specified device. The files can be of any type. You can use wildcards in the filename. A wildcard character (*) matches all patterns. Strings after a wildcard are ignored.

Default

The default file system is specified by the **cd** command. When you omit the **/all** keyword, the Cisco IOS software displays only undeleted files.

Command Mode

EXEC

Usage Guidelines

This command first appeared in Cisco IOS Release 11.0.

Use the **show (Flash file system)** command to display more detail about the files in a particular file system.

Sample Displays

The following is sample output from the **dir** command:

```
Router# dir slot0:
Directory of slot0:/

   1   -rw-     4720148   Aug 29 1997 17:49:36  hampton/nitro/c7200-j-mz
   2   -rw-     4767328   Oct 01 1997 18:42:53  c7200-js-mz
   5   -rw-         639   Oct 02 1997 12:09:32 rally
   7   -rw-         639   Oct 02 1997 12:37:13  the_time

20578304 bytes total (3104544 bytes free)

Router# dir /all slot0:
Directory of slot0:/

   1   -rw-     4720148   Aug 29 1997 17:49:36  hampton/nitro/c7200-j-mz
   2   -rw-     4767328   Oct 01 1997 18:42:53  c7200-js-mz
   3   -rw-     7982828   Oct 01 1997 18:48:14  [rsp-jsv-mz]
   4   -rw-         639   Oct 02 1997 12:09:17  [the_time]
   5   -rw-         639   Oct 02 1997 12:09:32  rally
   6   -rw-         639   Oct 02 1997 12:37:01  [the_time]
   7   -rw-         639   Oct 02 1997 12:37:13  the_time
```

Table 12-1 describes the fields shown in these displays.

Table 12-1   *dir Field Descriptions*

Field	Description
1	Index number of the file.

Table 12-1 *dir Field Descriptions (Continued)*

Field	Description
-rw-	Permissions. The file can be any or all of the following: • d—directory • r—readable • w—writable • x—executable
4720148	Size of the file.
Aug 29 1997 17:49:36	Last modification date.
hampton/nitro/c7200-j-mz	Filename. Deleted files are indicated by square brackets around the filename.

Related Commands

To locate documentation of related commands, you can search online at www.cisco.com.

cd
delete
undelete

erase

To erase a file system, use the **erase** EXEC command. The **erase nvram:** command replaces the **write erase** command and the **erase startup-config** command.

> **erase** *filesystem***:**

Syntax	Description
*filesystem***:**	File system name followed by a colon.

Command Mode

EXEC

Usage Guidelines

This command first appeared in Cisco IOS Release 11.0.

When a file system is erased, none of the files in the file system can be recovered.

The **erase** command can be used on Class B Flash file systems only. To reclaim space on Flash file systems after deleting files using the **delete** command, you must use the **erase** command. This command erases all of the files in the Flash file system.

Class A Flash file systems cannot be erased. You can delete individual files using the **delete** command and then reclaim the space using the **squeeze** command. You can also use the **format** command to format the Flash file system.

On Class C Flash file systems, space is dynamically reclaimed when you use the **delete** command. You can also use the **format** command to format the Flash file system.

The **erase nvram:** command erases NVRAM. On Class A file system platforms, if the CONFIG_FILE variable specifies a file in Flash memory, the specified file will be marked "deleted."

Examples

The following example erases the NVRAM, including the startup configuration located there:

```
erase nvram:
```

The following example erases all of partition 2 in internal Flash memory:

```
Router# erase flash:2

System flash directory, partition 2:
File  Length   Name/status
  1   1711088  dirt/images/c3600-i-mz
[1711152 bytes used, 15066064 available, 16777216 total]

Erase flash device, partition 2? [confirm]
Are you sure? [yes/no]: yes
Erasing device... eeeeeeeeeeeeeeeeeeeeeeeeeeeeeeeeeeeeeeeeeeeeeeeeeeeeeeeeee ...erased
```

The following example erases Flash memory when Flash is partitioned, but no partition is specified in the command:

```
Router# erase flash:

System flash partition information:
Partition   Size    Used    Free    Bank-Size    State        Copy-Mode
    1       4096K   2048K   2048K   2048K        Read Only    RXBOOT-FLH
    2       4096K   2048K   2048K   2048K        Read/Write   Direct

[Type ?<no> for partition directory; ? for full directory; q to abort]
Which partition? [default = 2]
```

The system will prompt only if there are two or more read/write partitions. If the partition entered is not valid or is the read-only partition, the process terminates. You can enter a partition number, a question mark (**?**) for a directory display of all partitions, or a question mark and a number (**?***number*) for a directory display of a particular partition. The default is the first read/write partition.

```
System flash directory, partition 2:
File  Length   Name/status
   1   3459720  master/igs-bfpx.100-4.3
[3459784 bytes used, 734520 available, 4194304 total]

Erase flash device, partition 2? [confirm] <Return>
```

Part
II

Command Reference

Related Commands

To locate documentation of related commands, you can search online at www.cisco.com.

boot config
delete
more nvram:startup-config
show bootvar
undelete

erase startup-config

The **erase nvram:** command replaces the **erase startup-config** command and the **write erase** command. Refer to the **erase** command in this chapter.

file prompt

To specify the level of prompting, use the **file prompt** global configuration command.

    file prompt {alert | noisy | quiet}

Syntax	Description
alert	(Optional) Prompts only for destructive file operations.
noisy	(Optional) Confirms all file operation parameters.
quiet	(Optional) Seldom prompts for file operations.

Default
alert

Command Mode
Global configuration

Usage Guidelines

This command first appeared in Cisco IOS Release 11.0.

Use this command to change the amount of confirmation needed for different file operations.

This command affects only prompts for confirmation of operations. The router will always prompt for missing information.

Example

The following example configures confirmation prompting for all file operations:

```
file prompt noisy
```

format

To format a Class A or Class C Flash file system, use the **format** EXEC command.

> **format** *filesystem1:* (Class C Flash file systems)
> **format** [**spare** *spare-number*] *filesystem1:* [[*filesystem2:*][*monlib-filename*]] (Class A Flash file system)

CAUTION   Reserve a certain number of memory sectors as spares, in case you must reformat the Flash memory card. If you fail to specify spare sectors, all existing data will be erased.

Syntax	Description
spare	(Optional) Reserves spare sectors as specified by the *spare-number* argument when formatting Flash memory.
spare-number	(Optional) Number of the spare sectors to reserve on formatted Flash memory. Valid values are 0 to 16. The default value is zero.
filesystem1:	Flash memory to format followed by a colon.
filesystem2:	(Optional) File system containing the monlib file to use for formatting *filesystem1 followed by a colon.*

Syntax	Description
monlib-filename	(Optional) Name of the ROM monitor library file (monlib file) to use for formatting *filesystem1*. The default monlib file is the one bundled with the system software.
	When used with HSA and you do not specify the *monlib-filename*, the system takes ROM monitor library file from the slave image bundle. If you specify the *monlib-filename*, the system assumes that the files reside on the slave devices.

Default

The default monlib file is the one bundled with the system software.

Command Mode

EXEC

Usage Guidelines

This command first appeared in Cisco IOS Release 11.0.

Use this command to format Class A or C Flash memory file systems.

In some cases, you might need to insert a new PCMCIA Flash memory card and load images or backup configuration files onto it. Before you can use a new Flash memory card, you must format it.

Sectors in flash memory cards can fail. Reserve certain Flash memory sectors as "spares" by using the **format** command to specify between 0 and 16 sectors as spares. If you reserve a small number of spare sectors for emergencies, you can still use most of the Flash memory card. If you specify 0 spare sectors and some sectors fail, you must reformat the Flash memory card, thereby erasing all existing data.

The monlib file is the ROM monitor library. The ROM monitor uses this file to access files in the Flash file system. The Cisco IOS system software contains a monlib file.

In the command syntax, *filesystem1:* specifies the device to format and *filesystem2:* specifies the optional device containing the monlib file used to format *filesystem1:*. If you omit the optional *filesystem2:* and *monlib-filename* arguments, the system formats *filesystem1:* using the monlib file already bundled with the system software. If you omit only *the optional filesystem2:* argument, the system formats *filesystem1:* using the monlib file from the device you specified with the **cd** command. If you omit only the optional *monlib-filename* argument, the system formats *filesystem1:* using *filesystem2:*'s monlib file. When you specify both arguments—*filesystem2:* and *monlib-filename*—the system formats *filesystem1:* using the monlib file from the specified device. You can specify *filesystem1:*'s own monlib file in this argument. If the system cannot find a monlib file, it terminates its formatting.

CAUTION   You can read from or write to Flash memory cards formatted for Cisco 7000 series Route
Processor (RP) cards in your Cisco 7200 and 7500 series, but you cannot boot the
Cisco 7200 and 7500 series from a Flash memory card formatted for the Cisco 7000
series. Similarly, you can read from or write to Flash memory cards formatted for the
Cisco 7200 and 7500 series in your Cisco 7000 series, but you cannot boot the Cisco 7000
series from a Flash memory card formatted for the Cisco 7200 and 7500 series.

Example

The following example formats a Flash memory card inserted in slot 0:

```
Router# format slot0:
Running config file on this device, proceed? [confirm]y
All sectors will be erased, proceed? [confirm]y
Enter volume id (up to 31 characters): <Return>
Formatting sector 1 (erasing)
Format device slot0 completed
```

When the console returns to the EXEC prompt, the new Flash memory card is successfully formatted
and ready for use.

Related Commands

To locate documentation of related commands, you can search online at www.cisco.com.

cd
copy
delete
show file systems (Flash file system)
show running-config
undelete

fsck

To check a Class C Flash file system for damage and repair any problems, use the **fsck** EXEC command.

  fsck [**/nocrc**] *filesystem:*

Syntax   Description

/nocrc   (Optional) Skips CRC checks.

filesystem: File system to check.

Command Mode

EXEC

Usage Guidelines

This command first appeared in Cisco IOS Release 11.3 AA.

This command is only valid on Class C Flash file systems.

Example

The following example checks the flash: file system:

```
Router# fsck flash:
Fsck operation may take a while. Continue? [confirm]
flashfs[4]: 0 files, 2 directories
flashfs[4]: 0 orphaned files, 0 orphaned directories
flashfs[4]: Total bytes: 8128000
flashfs[4]: Bytes used: 1024
flashfs[4]: Bytes available: 8126976
flashfs[4]: flashfs fsck took 23 seconds.
Fsck of flash: complete
```

kerberos srvtab remote

To retrieve a krb5 SRVTAB file from the specified host, use the **kerberos srvtab remote** global configuration command.

kerberos srvtab remote *file-url*

Syntax	Description
file-url	TFTP URL of the SRVTAB file on the specified host.

Command Mode

Global configuration

Usage Guidelines

This command first appeared in Cisco IOS Release 11.2.

When you use the **kerberos srvtab remote** command to copy the SRVTAB file from the remote host (generally the KDC), it parses the information in this file and stores it in the router's running configuration in the **kerberos srvtab entry** format. The key for each SRVTAB entry is encrypted with the private Data Encryption Standard (DES) key if one is defined on the router. To ensure that the SRVTAB is available (does not need to be acquired from the KDC) when you reboot the router, use the **copy system:running-config nvram:startup-config global** configuration command to save the router's running configuration.

Example

The following example copies the SRVTAB file (scooter.cisco.com-new-srvtab) residing on bucket.cisco.com to the router:

```
kerberos srvtab remote tftp://bucket.cisco.com/scooter.cisco.com-new-srvtab
```

Related Commands

To locate documentation of related commands, you can search online at www.cisco.com.

kerberos srvtab remote
key config-key

mkdir

To create a new directory in a Class C Flash file system, use the **mkdir** EXEC command.

> **mkdir** *directory*

Syntax   Description

directory   Name of the directory to create.

Command Mode

EXEC

Usage Guidelines

This command first appeared in Cisco IOS Release 11.3 AA.

This command is only valid on Class C Flash file systems.

If you do not specify the directory name in the command line, the router prompts you for it.

Example

The following example creates a directory named *newdir*:

```
Router# mkdir newdir
Mkdir file name [newdir]?
Created dir flash:newdir
Router# dir
Directory of flash:

  2  drwx          0  Mar 13 1993 13:16:21  newdir

8128000 bytes total (8126976 bytes free)
```

Related Commands

To locate documentation of related commands, you can search online at www.cisco.com.

dir
rmdir

more

To display a file, use the **more** EXEC command.

more [/ascii | /binary | /ebcdic] *file-url*

Syntax	Description
/ascii	(Optional) Displays a binary file in ASCII format.
/binary	(Optional) Displays a file in hex/text format.
/ebcdic	(Optional) Displays a binary file in EBCDIC format.
file-url	URL of the file to display.

Command Mode

EXEC

Usage Guidelines

This command first appeared in Cisco IOS Release 11.3 AA.

The **more nvram:startup-config** command replaces the **show startup-config** command and the **show configuration** command. The **more system:running-config** command replaces the **show running-config** command and the **write terminal** command.

You can use this command to display configuration files:

- The **more nvram:startup-config** command displays the startup configuration file contained in NVRAM or specified by the CONFIG_FILE environment variable. The Cisco IOS software informs you whether the displayed configuration is a complete configuration or a distilled version. A distilled configuration is one that does not contain access lists.

- The **more system:running-config** command displays the running configuration.

These commands show the version number of the software used when you last changed the configuration file.

You can also display files on remote systems using the **more** command.

Sample Displays

The following partial sample output displays the configuration file named **startup-config** in NVRAM:

```
Router# more nvram:startup-config
!
! No configuration change since last restart
! NVRAM config last updated at 02:03:26 PDT Thu Oct 2 1997
!
version 11.3
service timestamps debug uptime
service timestamps log uptime
service password-encryption
service udp-small-servers
service tcp-small-servers
...
end
```

The following is partial sample output from the **more nvram:startup-config** command when the configuration file has been compressed:

```
Router# more nvram:startup-config

Using 21542 out of 65536 bytes, uncompressed size = 142085 bytes
!
version 11.3
service compress-config
!
hostname rose
!
...
```

The following partial sample output displays the running configuration:

```
Router2# more system:running-config
Building configuration...

Current configuration:
!
```

```
version 11.2
no service udp-small-servers
no service tcp-small-servers
!
hostname Router2
!
...
!
end
```

Related Commands

To locate documentation of related commands, you can search online at www.cisco.com.

boot config
configure terminal
copy system:running-config nvram:startup-config
service compress-config
show bootvar
show system

pwd

To show the current setting of the **cd** command, use the **pwd** EXEC command.

> **pwd**

Syntax Description

This command had no arguments or keywords.

Command Mode

EXEC

Usage Guidelines

This command first appeared in Cisco IOS Release 11.0.

Use the **pwd** command to show what directory or file system is specified as the default by the **cd** command. For all EXEC commands that have an optional *filesystem* argument, the system uses the file system specified by the **cd** command when you omit the optional *filesystem* argument.

For example, the **dir** command contains an optional *filesystem* argument and displays a list of files on a particular file system. When you omit this *filesystem* argument, the system shows a list of the files on the file system specified by the **cd** command.

Examples

The following example shows that the present working file system specified by the **cd** command is slot 0:

```
Router> pwd
slot0:/
```

The following example uses the **cd** command to change the present file system to slot 1: and then uses the **pwd** command to display that present working file system:

```
Router> cd slot1:
Router> pwd
slot1:/
```

Related Commands

To locate documentation of related commands, you can search online at www.cisco.com.

cd
dir

rename

To rename a file in a Class C Flash file system, use the rename EXEC command.

         rename *url1 url2*

Syntax	Description
url1	Original path name.
url2	New path name.

Command Mode

EXEC

Usage Guidelines

This command first appeared in Cisco IOS Release 11.3 AA.

This command is valid only on Class C Flash file systems.

Examples

In the following example, the file named **Karen.1** is renamed **test**:

```
Router# dir
Directory of disk0:/Karen.dir/

    0   -rw-          0   Jan 21 1998 09:51:29   Karen.1
    0   -rw-          0   Jan 21 1998 09:51:29   Karen.2
    0   -rw-          0   Jan 21 1998 09:51:29   Karen.3
    0   -rw-          0   Jan 21 1998 09:51:31   Karen.4
  243   -rw-        165   Jan 21 1998 09:53:17   Karen.cur

340492288 bytes total (328400896 bytes free)

Router# rename disk0:Karen.dir/Karen.1 disk0:Karen.dir/test
Router# dir
Directory of disk0:/Karen.dir/

    0   -rw-          0   Jan 21 1998 09:51:29   Karen.2
    0   -rw-          0   Jan 21 1998 09:51:29   Karen.3
    0   -rw-          0   Jan 21 1998 09:51:31   Karen.4
  243   -rw-        165   Jan 21 1998 09:53:17   Karen.cur
    0   -rw-          0   Apr 24 1998 09:49:19   test

340492288 bytes total (328384512 bytes free)
```

rmdir

To remove an existing directory in a Class C Flash file system, use the **rmdir** EXEC command.

   rmdir *directory*

Syntax   Description

directory   Directory to delete.

Command Mode

EXEC

Usage Guidelines

This command first appeared in Cisco IOS Release 11.3 AA.

This command is valid only on Class C Flash file systems.

Example

The following example deletes the directory named newdir:

```
Router# dir
Directory of flash:

  2  drwx          0   Mar 13 1993 13:16:21  newdir

8128000 bytes total (8126976 bytes free)
Router# rmdir newdir
Rmdir file name [newdir]?
Delete flash:newdir? [confirm]
Removed dir flash:newdir
Router# dir
Directory of flash:

No files in directory

8128000 bytes total (8126976 bytes free)
```

Related Commands

To locate documentation of related commands, you can search online at www.cisco.com.

dir
mkdir

show configuration

The **more nvram:startup-config** command replaces the **show configuration** command. Refer to the **more** command for further details.

show file descriptors

To display a list of open file descriptors, use the **show file descriptors** EXEC command.

> **show file descriptors**

Syntax Description

This command has no arguments or keywords.

Command Mode

EXEC

Usage Guidelines

This command first appeared in Cisco IOS Release 11.3 AA.

File descriptors are the internal representations of open files. You can use this command to see if another user has a file open.

Sample Display

The following is sample output from the **show file descriptors** command:

```
Router# show file descriptors
File Descriptors:

  FD  Position  Open  PID  Path
   0    187392  0001    2  tftp://dirt/hampton/c4000-i-m.a
   1    184320  030A    2  flash:c4000-i-m.a
```

Table 12-2 describes the fields show in this display.

Table 12-2 *show file descriptors Field Descriptions*

Field	Description
FD	File descriptor. The file descriptor is a small integer used to specify the file once it has been opened.
Position	Byte offset from the start of the file.
Open	Flags supplied when opening the file.
PID	Process ID of the process that opened the file.
Path	Location of the file.

show file information

To display information about a file, use the **show file information** EXEC command.

> **show file information** *file-url*

Syntax	Description
file-url	URL of the file to display.

Command Mode

EXEC

Usage Guidelines

This command first appeared in Cisco IOS Release 11.3 AA.

Sample Display

The following is sample output from the **show file information** command:

```
Router# show file information tftp://dirt/hampton/c2500-j-l.a
tftp://dirt/hampton/c2500-j-l.a:
  type is image (a.out) [relocatable, run from flash]
  file size is 8624596 bytes, run size is 9044940 bytes [8512316+112248+420344]
  Foreign image

Router# show file information slot0:c7200-js-mz
slot0:c7200-js-mz:
  type is image (elf) []
  file size is 4770316 bytes, run size is 4935324 bytes
  Runnable image, entry point 0x80008000, run from ram

Router1# show file information nvram:startup-config
nvram:startup-config:
  type is ascii text
```

Table 12-3 describes the possible file types.

Table 12-3   *Possible File Types*

Types	Description
image (a.out)	Runnable image in a.out format.
image (elf)	Runnable image in elf format.
ascii text	Configuration file or other text file.
coff	Runnable image in coff format.
ebcdic	Text generated on an IBM mainframe.
lzw compression	Lzw compressed file.
tar	Text archive file used by the CIP.

show file systems

To list available file systems, use the **show file systems** EXEC command.

show file systems

Syntax Description

This command has no arguments or keywords.

Command Mode

EXEC

Usage Guidelines

This command first appeared in Cisco IOS Release 11.3 AA.

Use this command to learn the names of the file systems your router supports.

Sample Display

The following is sample output from the **show file systems** command:

```
Router# show file systems

File Systems:

       Size(b)        Free(b)    Type     Flags  Prefixes
             -              -     opaque   rw     null:
             -              -     opaque   rw     system:
             -              -     opaque   ro     xmodem:
             -              -     opaque   ro     ymodem:
             -              -     network  rw     tftp:
             -              -     network  rw     rcp:
             -              -     network  rw     ftp:
*      4194304        4190616     flash    rw     flash:
        131066         129185     nvram    rw     nvram:
             -              -     opaque   wo     lex:
```

Table 12-4 describes the fields shown in this display.

Table 12-4 *show file systems Field Descriptions*

Type	Description
Size(b)	Amount of memory in the file system, in bytes.
Free(b)	Amount of free memory in the file system, in bytes.
Type	Type of file system. See Chapter 2, Table 2-3.
Flags	Permissions for file system. See Chapter 2, Table 2-4.
Prefixes	Prefix for file system.

Table 12-5 describes file system types.

Table 12-5 *Possible File System Types*

Type	Description
disk	The file system is for a rotating medium.
flash	The file system is for a Flash memory device.
network	The file system is a network file system (TFTP, rcp, FTP, etc.).
nvram	The file system is for an NVRAM device.
opaque	The file system is a locally generated "pseudo" file system (e.g., the "system") or a download interface, such as brimux.
rom	The file system is for a ROM or EPROM device.
tty	The file system is for a collection of terminal devices.
unknown	The file system is of unknown type.

Table 12-6 describes file system flags.

Table 12-6 *Possible File System Flags*

Flag	Description
ro	The file system is Read Only.
wo	The file system is Write Only.
rw	The file system is Read/Write.

show running-config

The **more system:running-config** command replaces the **show running-config** command. Refer to the **more** command for further details.

show startup-config

The **more nvram:startup-config** command replaces the **show startup-config** command. Refer to the **more** command for further details.

squeeze

To permanently delete Flash files by squeezing a Class A Flash file system, use the **squeeze** EXEC command.

> **squeeze** *filesystem***:**

Syntax	Description
*filesystem***:**	Flash file system followed by a colon.

Command Mode

EXEC

Usage Guidelines

This command first appeared in Cisco IOS Release 11.1.

When Flash memory is full, you might need to rearrange the files so that the space used by the files marked "deleted" can be reclaimed. When you issue the **squeeze** command, the router copies all valid files to the beginning of Flash memory and erases all files marked "deleted." At this point, you cannot recover "deleted" files and you can write to the reclaimed Flash memory space.

In addition to removing deleted files, the **squeeze** command removes any files that the system has marked as error. An error file is created when a file write fails (for example, the device is full). To remove error files, you must use the **squeeze** command.

NOTE   The squeeze operation might take as long as several minutes because it can involve erasing and rewriting almost an entire Flash memory space.

Example

The following example instructs the router to permanently erase the files marked "deleted" from the Flash memory card inserted in slot 1:

```
squeeze slot1:
```

Related Commands

To locate documentation of related commands, you can search online at www.cisco.com.

delete
dir
undelete

tftp-server

To configure a router or a Flash memory device on the router as a TFTP server, use the **tftp-server** global configuration command. To remove a previously defined filename, use the **no** form of this command with the appropriate filename.

> **tftp-server** {*file-url* | **rom**} [**alias** *alt-filename*] [*access-list-number*]
> **no tftp-server** {*file-url* | **rom**}

Syntax	Description
file-url	Location of the file that the TFTP server uses in answering TFTP read requests.
rom	Specifies TFTP service of a file in ROM.
alias	(Optional) Specifies an alternate name for the file that the TFTP server uses in answering TFTP read requests.
alt-filename	(Optional) Alternate name of the file that the TFTP server uses in answering TFTP read requests. A client of the TFTP server can use this alternate name in its read requests.
access-list-number	(Optional) Basic IP access list number. Valid values are 0 to 99.

Default

Disabled

Command Mode

Global configuration

Usage Guidelines

This command first appeared in Cisco IOS Release 11.0.

This command replaces the **tftp-server system** command.

You can specify multiple filenames by repeating the **tftp-server** command. The system sends a copy of the system image contained in ROM, or one of the system images contained in Flash memory, to any client that issues a TFTP read request with this filename. On systems that contain a complete image in ROM, the system sends the ROM image if the requested filename is not found in Flash memory.

Images that run from ROM cannot be loaded over the network. Therefore, it does not make sense to use TFTP to offer the ROMs on these images.

On the Cisco 7000 family, the system sends a copy of the file contained on one of the Flash memory devices to any client that issues a TFTP read request with its filename.

Examples

In the following example, the system uses TFTP to send a copy of the version-10.3 file located in Flash memory in response to a TFTP read request for that file. The requesting host is checked against access list 22.

```
tftp-server flash:version-10.3 22
```

In the following example, the system uses TFTP to send a copy of the ROM image gs3-k.101 in response to a TFTP read request for the gs3-k.101 file:

```
tftp-server rom alias gs3-k.101
```

In the following example, the system uses TFTP to send a copy of the version-11.0 file in response to a TFTP read request for that file. The file is located on the Flash memory card inserted in slot 0.

```
tftp-server slot0:version-11.0
```

The following example enables a router to operate as a TFTP server. The source file c3640-i-mz is in the second partition of internal Flash memory:

```
tftp-server flash:2:dirt/gate/c3640-i-mz
```

Related Commands

To locate documentation of related commands, you can search online at www.cisco.com.

access-list

tftp-server system

The **tftp-server** command replaces the **tftp-server system** command. For further information refer to the **tftp-server** command.

undelete

To recover a file marked "deleted" on a Class A or Class B Flash file system, use the **undelete** EXEC command.

> **undelete** *index* [*filesystem*:]

Syntax	Description
index	Number that indexes the file in the **dir** command output.
filesystem:	(Optional) File system containing the file to undelete.

Default

The default file system is the one specified by the **cd** command.

Command Mode

EXEC

Usage Guidelines

This command first appeared in Cisco IOS Release 11.0.

For Class A and B Flash file systems, when you delete a file, the Cisco IOS software simply marks the file as deleted, but it does not erase the file. This command allows you to recover a "deleted" file on a specified Flash memory device. You must undelete a file by its index because you could have multiple deleted files with the same name. For example, the "deleted" list could contain multiple configuration files with the name router-config. You undelete by index to indicate which of the many router-config files from the list to undelete. Use the **dir** command to learn the index number of the file you want to undelete.

You cannot undelete a file if a valid (undeleted) one with the same name exists. Instead, you first delete the existing file and then undelete the file you want. For example, if you had an undeleted version of the router-config file and you wanted to use a previous, deleted version instead, you could not simply undelete the previous version by index. You would first delete the existing router-config file and then undelete the previous router-config file by index. You can delete and undelete a file up to 15 times.

On Class A Flash file systems, if you try to recover the configuration file pointed to by the CONFIG_FILE environment variable, the system prompts you to confirm recovery of the file. This prompt reminds you that the CONFIG_FILE environment variable points to an undeleted file. To permanently delete all files marked "deleted" on a Flash memory device, use the **squeeze** command.

On Class B Flash file systems, you must use the **erase** command to recover any space taken up by deleted files.

Example

The following example recovers the deleted file whose index number is 1 to the Flash memory card inserted in slot 0:

```
undelete 1 slot0:
```

Related Commands

To locate documentation of related commands, you can search online at www.cisco.com.

delete
dir
squeeze

verify

To verify the checksum of a file on a Flash memory file system, use the **verify** EXEC command.

       verify *file-url*

Syntax	Description
file-url	URL of the file to verify.

Default

The current working device is the default device.

Command Mode

EXEC

Usage Guidelines

This command first appeared in Cisco IOS Release 11.0.

This command replaces the **copy verify** and **copy verify flash** commands.

Use the **verify** command to verify the checksum of a file before using it.

Each software image that is distributed on disk uses a single checksum for the entire image. This checksum is displayed only when the image is copied into Flash memory; it is not displayed when the image file is copied from one disk to another.

The README file, which is included with the image on the disk, lists the name, file size, and checksum of the image. Review the contents of the README file before loading or duplicating the new image so that you can verify the checksum when you copy it into Flash memory or onto a server.

To display the contents of Flash memory, use the **show flash** command. The Flash contents listing does not include the checksum of individual files. To recompute and verify the image checksum after the image has been copied into Flash memory, use the **verify** command.

Examples

The following example verifies that the file named c7200-js-mz is on the Flash memory card inserted in slot 0:

```
Router# dir slot0:
Directory of slot0:/

  1  -rw-     4720148    Aug 29 1997 17:49:36  hampton/nitro/c7200-j-mz
  2  -rw-     4767328    Oct 01 1997 18:42:53  c7200-js-mz
  5  -rw-         639    Oct 02 1997 12:09:32  rally
  7  -rw-         639    Oct 02 1997 12:37:13  the_time

20578304 bytes total (3104544 bytes free)
tw3-7200-1# verify slot0:
Verify filename []? c7200-js-mz
Verified slot0:
```

The following example also verifies that the file named c7200-js-mz is on the Flash memory card inserted in slot 0:

```
Router# verify slot0:?
slot0:c7200-js-mz  slot0:rally slot0:hampton/nitro/c7200-j-mz   slot0:the_time

Router# verify slot0:c7200-js-mz
Verified slot0:c7200-js-mz
```

Related Commands

To locate documentation of related commands, you can search online at www.cisco.com.

cd
copy
dir
pwd
show file systems (Flash file system)

write erase

The **write erase** command has been replaced by the **erase nvam:** command. Refer to the **erase** command in this chapter.

write terminal

The **more system:running-config** command replaces the **write terminal** command. Refer to the **more** command for further details.

## CHAPTER 13

Modifying, Downloading, and Maintaining Configuration Files

This chapter describes how to load and maintain configuration files. Configuration files contain commands entered to customize the function of the Cisco IOS software.

To benefit most from the instructions and organization of this chapter, your router must contain a minimal configuration that allows you to interact with the system software. You can create a basic configuration file using the **setup** command facility.

For a complete description of the configuration file commands in this chapter, refer to Chapter 14, "Configuration File Commands." To locate documentation of other commands that appear in this chapter, you can search online at www.cisco.com.

NOTE   One or more of the commands that previously appeared in this chapter have been replaced by new commands. Table 13-1 maps the old commands to their replacements. The old commands continue to perform their normal functions in the current release, but support for these commands will cease in a future release.

Table 13-1   *Mapping Old Commands to New Commands*

Old Command	New Command
configure network	**copy ftp: system:running-config**
copy rcp running-config	**copy rcp: system:running-config**
copy tftp running-config	**copy tftp: system:running-config**
configure overwrite-network	**copy ftp: nvram:startup-config**
copy rcp startup-config	**copy rcp: nvram:startup-config**
copy tftp startup-config	**copy tftp: nvram:startup-config**
show configuration	**more nvram:startup-config**
show startup-config	
write erase	**erase nvram:**
erase startup-config	

Continues

Table 13-1 *Mapping Old Commands to New Commands (Continued)*

Old Command	New Command
write memory copy running-config startup-config	copy system:running-config nvram:startup-config
write network copy running-config rcp copy running-config tftp	copy system:running-config ftp: copy system:running-config rcp: copy system:running-config tftp:
write terminal show running-config	more system:running-config

Configuration File Task List

To load and maintain configuration files needed for startup, complete any of the tasks in the following sections:

- Display Configuration File Information

- Understand Configuration Files

- Enter Configuration Mode and Select a Configuration Source

- Configure the Cisco IOS Software from the Terminal

- Copy Configuration Files from the Router to a Network Server

- Copy Configuration Files from a Network Server to the Router

- Maintain Configuration Files Larger than NVRAM

- Copy Configuration Files between Different Locations

- Reexecute the Configuration Commands in Startup Configuration

- Clear the Configuration Information

- Specify the Startup Configuration File

NOTE   These tasks assume you have a minimal configuration that you want to modify.

Display Configuration File Information

Use the following commands in EXEC mode to display information about configuration files:

Step	Command	Purpose
1	**show bootvar**	Lists the contents of the BOOT environment variable, the name of the configuration file pointed to by the CONFIG_FILE environment variable, and the contents of the BOOTLDR environment variable.
2	**more** *file-url*	Lists the configuration information stored in a specified file.
3	**more system:running-config**	Lists the configuration information in running memory.
4	**more nvram:startup-config**	Lists the startup configuration information.
		On all platforms except the Class A Flash file system platforms, the startup configuration is usually NVRAM. On the Class A Flash file system platforms, the CONFIG_FILE environment variable points to the startup configuration. The CONFIG_FILE variable defaults to NVRAM.

Understand Configuration Files

Configuration files contain the commands the router uses to customize the function of the Cisco IOS software. The **setup** command facility helps you create a basic configuration file. However, you can manually change the configuration by typing commands in a configuration mode.

Types of Configuration Files

Startup configuration files are used during system startup to configure the software. Running configuration files contain the current configuration of the software. The two configuration files can be different. For example, you may want to change the configuration for a short time period rather than permanently. In this case, you would change the running configuration using the **configure terminal** command but not save the configuration using the **copy system:running-config nvram:startup-config** command.

To change the running configuration, use the **configure terminal** command, as described in the "Configure the Cisco IOS Software from the Terminal" section. To change the startup-config, you can either save the running configuration file to the startup configuration using the **copy system:running-config nvram:startup-config** command (which is also described in the "Configure the Cisco IOS Software from the Terminal" section) or copy commands from a file server to the startup configuration without affecting the running configuration (refer to the "Copy Configuration Files from a Network Server to the Router" section).

Location of Configuration Files

The configuration files are stored in the following places:

- The running configuration is stored in RAM.

- On all platforms except the Class A Flash file system platforms, the startup configuration is stored in nonvolatile random-access memory (NVRAM).

- On Class A Flash file system platforms, the startup configuration is stored in the location specified by the CONFIG_FILE environment variable (refer to the "Specify the CONFIG_FILE Environment Variable (Class A Flash File Systems)" section for details). The CONFIG_FILE variable defaults to NVRAM and can be a file in the following file systems:

    — **nvram:** (NVRAM)

    — **bootflash:** (Internal Flash memory)

    — **slot0:** (First PCMCIA slot)

    — **slot1:** (Second PCMCIA slot)

Enter Configuration Mode and Select a Configuration Source

To enter configuration mode, enter the **configure** command at the privileged EXEC prompt. The Cisco IOS software responds with the following prompt asking you to specify the terminal, memory, or a file stored on a network server (network) as the source of configuration commands:

```
Configuring from terminal, memory, or network [terminal]?
```

Configuring from the terminal allows you to enter configuration commands at the command line. Refer to the "Configure the Cisco IOS Software from the Terminal" section for details. Configuring from memory reexecutes the commands in the startup configuration file. See the "Reexecute the Configuration Commands in Startup Configuration" section for more details. Configuring from the network allows you to load and execute configuration commands over the network. See the "Copy Configuration Files from a Network Server to the Router" section for more details.

Configure the Cisco IOS Software from the Terminal

The Cisco IOS software accepts one configuration command per line. You can enter as many configuration commands as you want.

You can add comments to a configuration file describing the commands you have entered. Precede a comment with an exclamation point (!). Because comments are *not* stored in NVRAM or in the active copy of the configuration file, comments do not appear when you list the active configuration with the **more system:running-config** EXEC command. Also, when the startup configuration is NVRAM, comments do not show up when you list the startup configuration with the **more nvram:startup-config** EXEC command. Comments are stripped out of the configuration file when it is loaded onto the router. However, you can list the comments in configuration files stored on an FTP, rcp, or TFTP server.

When you configure the software from the terminal, the software executes the commands you enter at the system prompts. To configure the software from the terminal, use the following commands:

Step	Command	Purpose
1	**configure terminal**	Enters configuration mode and selects the terminal option.
2	See the appropriate chapter for specific configuration commands.	Enters the necessary configuration commands.
3	**end** or press **Ctrl-Z** (^Z)	Quits configuration mode.
4	**copy system:running-config nvram:startup-config**	Saves the configuration file to your startup configuration. On most platforms, this step saves the configuration to NVRAM. On the Class A Flash file system platforms, this step saves the configuration to the location specified by the CONFIG_FILE environment variable. The CONFIG_FILE variable defaults to NVRAM.

In the following example, the software is configured from the terminal. The comment The following command provides the router host name identifies the purpose of the next command line. The **hostname** command changes the router name from router1 to router2. By pressing **Ctrl-Z** (^Z) or entering the command **end**, the user quits configuration mode. Finally, the **copy system:running-config nvram:startup-config** command saves the current configuration to the startup configuration.

```
Router1# configure terminal
Router1(config)# !The following command provides the router host name.
Router1(config)# hostname router2
Router2(config)# end
Router2# copy system:running-config nvram:startup-config
```

When the startup configuration is NVRAM, it stores the current configuration information in text format as configuration commands, *recording only nondefault settings*. The memory is checksummed to guard against corrupted data.

CAUTION   Some specific commands might not get saved to NVRAM. You will have to enter these commands again if you reboot the machine. These commands are noted in the documentation. We recommend that you keep a listing of these settings so you can quickly reconfigure your router after rebooting.

Copy Configuration Files from the Router to a Network Server

You can copy configuration files from the router to a file server using FTP, rcp, or TFTP. You might do this task to back up a current configuration file to a server before changing its contents, thereby allowing you to restore the original configuration file from the server later. The following sections describe these tasks:

● Copy a Configuration File from the Router to a TFTP Server

● Copy a Configuration File from the Router to an rcp Server

● Copy a Configuration File from the Router to an FTP Server

The protocol you use depends on which type of server you are using. The FTP and rcp transport mechanisms provide faster performance and more reliable delivery of data than TFTP. These improvements are possible because FTP and rcp are built on and use the Transmission Control Protocol/Internet Protocol (TCP/IP) stack, which is connection-oriented.

Copy a Configuration File from the Router to a TFTP Server

In some implementations of TFTP, you must create a dummy file on the TFTP server and give it read, write, and execute permissions before copying a file over it. Refer to your TFTP documentation for more information.

To store configuration information on a TFTP network server, use the following commands in the EXEC mode:

Step	Command	Purpose
1	**copy system:running-config tftp:** [[[*//location*]/*directory*]/*filename*] or **copy nvram:startup-config tftp:** [[[*//location*]/*directory*]/*filename*]	Specifies that the running or startup configuration file be stored on a network server.
2		Replies to any router prompts for additional information or confirmation. The prompting will depend on how much information you provide in the **copy** command and the current setting of the **file prompt** command.

The following example copies a configuration file from a router to a TFTP server:

```
Tokyo# copy system:running-config tftp://172.16.2.155/tokyo-confg
Write file tokyo-confg on host 172.16.2.155? [confirm] y
#
Writing tokyo-confg!!! [OK]
```

Copy a Configuration File from the Router to an rcp Server

You can copy a configuration file from the router to an rcp server. If you copy the configuration file to a personal computer used as a file server, the computer must support rsh.

Understand the rcp Username

The rcp protocol requires a client to send a remote username on each rcp request to a server. When you copy a configuration file from the router to a server using rcp, the Cisco IOS software sends the first valid username in the following list:

1   The username specified in the **copy** command, if a username is specified.

2   The username set by the **ip rcmd remote-username** command, if the command is configured.

3   The remote username associated with the current TTY (terminal) process. For example, if the user is connected to the router through Telnet and was authenticated through the **username** command, the router software sends the Telnet username as the remote username.

4   The router host name.

For the rcp copy request to execute successfully, an account must be defined on the network server for the remote username. If the server has a directory structure, the configuration file or image is written to or copied from the directory associated with the remote username on the server. For example, if the system image resides in the home directory of a user on the server, you can specify that user's name as the remote username.

Use the **ip rcmd remote-username** command to specify a username for all copies. Include the username in the **copy** command if you want to specify a username for that copy operation only.

If you are writing to the server, the rcp server must be properly configured to accept the rcp write request from the user on the router. For UNIX systems, you must add an entry to the .rhosts file for the remote user on the rcp server. For example, suppose the router contains the following configuration lines:

```
hostname Rtr1
ip rcmd remote-username User0
```

If the router's IP address translates to Router1.company.com, then the .rhosts file for User0 on the rcp server should contain the following line:

```
Router1.company.com Rtr1
```

Refer to the documentation for your rcp server for more details.

Copy a Configuration File from the Router to the rcp Server Tasks

To copy a startup configuration file or a running configuration file from the router to an rcp server, use the following commands beginning in privileged EXEC mode:

Step	Command	Purpose
1	**configure terminal**	(Optional) Enters configuration mode from the terminal. This step is required only if you override the default remote username (see Step 2).
2	**ip rcmd remote-username** *username*	(Optional) Changes the default remote username.
3	**end**	(Optional) Exits configuration mode. This step is required only if you override the default remote username (see Step 2).
4	**copy system:running-config rcp:**[[[// [*username*@]*location*]/*directory*]/*filename*] or **copy nvram:startup-config rcp:**[[[// [*username*@]*location*]/*directory*]/*filename*]	Specifies that the router's running configuration or startup configuration file be stored on an rcp server.
5		Replies to any router prompts for additional information or confirmation. The prompting will depend on how much information you provide in the **copy** command and the current setting of the **file prompt** command.

Store a Running Configuration File on a Server Example

The following example copies the running configuration file named rtr2-confg to the netadmin1 directory on the remote host with an IP address of 172.16.101.101:

```
Router# copy system:running-config rcp://netadmin1@172.16.101.101/Rtr2-confg
Write file rtr2-confg on host 172.16.101.101?[confirm]
Building configuration...[OK]
Connected to 172.16.101.101
Router#
```

Store a Startup Configuration File on a Server Example

The following example shows how to store a startup configuration file on a server by using rcp to copy the file:

```
Rtr2# configure terminal
Rtr2(config)# ip rcmd remote-username netadmin2
Rtr2(config)# end
Rtr2# copy nvram:startup-config rcp:
Remote host[]? 172.16.101.101
```

```
Name of configuration file to write [rtr2-confg]?
Write file rtr2-confg on host 172.16.101.101?[confirm]
![OK]
```

Copy a Configuration File from the Router to an FTP Server

You can copy a configuration file from the router to an FTP server.

Understand the FTP Username and Password

The FTP protocol requires a client to send a remote username and password on each FTP request to a server. When you copy a configuration file from the router to a server using FTP, the Cisco IOS software sends the first valid username in the following list:

1 The username specified in the **copy** command, if a username is specified.

2 The username set by the **ip ftp username** command, if the command is configured.

3 Anonymous.

The router sends the first valid password in the following list:

1 The password specified in the **copy** command, if a password is specified.

2 The password set by the **ip ftp password** command, if the command is configured.

3 The router forms a password *username@routername.domain*. The variable *username* is the username associated with the current session, *routername* is the configured host name, and *domain* is the domain of the router.

The username and password must be associated with an account on the FTP server. If you are writing to the server, the FTP server must be properly configured to accept the FTP write request from the user on the router.

If the server has a directory structure, the configuration file or image is written to or copied from the directory associated with the username on the server. For example, if the system image resides in the home directory of a user on the server, specify that user's name as the remote username.

Refer to the documentation for your FTP server for more details.

Use the **ip ftp username** and **ip ftp password** commands to specify a username and password for all copies. Include the username in the **copy** command if you want to specify a username for that copy operation only.

Copy a Configuration File from the Router to the FTP Server Tasks

To copy a startup configuration file or a running configuration file from the router to an FTP server, use the following commands beginning in privileged EXEC mode:

Step	Command	Purpose
1	**configure terminal**	(Optional) Enters configuration mode from the terminal. This step is required only if you override the default remote username or password (see Steps 2 and 3).
2	**ip ftp username** *username*	(Optional) Changes the default remote username.
3	**ip ftp password** *password*	(Optional) Changes the default password.
4	**end**	(Optional) Exits configuration mode. This step is required only if you override the default remote username or password (see Steps 2 and 3).
5	**copy system:running-config ftp:**[[[*//*[*username*[*:password*]*@*]*location*]*/directory*]*/filename*] or **copy nvram:startup-config ftp:**[[[*//*[*username*[*:password*]*@*]*location*]*/directory*]*/filename*]	Specifies that the router's running configuration or startup configuration file be stored on an FTP server.
6		Replies to any router prompts for additional information or confirmation. The prompting will depend on how much information you provide in the **copy** command and the current setting of the **file prompt** command.

Store a Running Configuration File on an FTP Server Example

The following example copies the running configuration file named rtr2-confg to the netadmin1 directory on the remote host with an IP address of 172.16.101.101:

```
Router# copy system:running-config ftp://netadmin1:mypass@172.16.101.101/Rtr2-confg
Write file rtr2-confg on host 172.16.101.101?[confirm]
Building configuration...[OK]
Connected to 172.16.101.101
Router#
```

Store a Startup Configuration File on an FTP Server Example

The following example shows how to store a startup configuration file on a server by using FTP to copy the file:

```
Rtr2# configure terminal
Rtr2(config)# ip ftp username netadmin2
```

```
Rtr2(config)# ip ftp password mypass
Rtr2(config)# end
Rtr2# copy nvram:startup-config rcp:
Remote host[]? 172.16.101.101
Name of configuration file to write [rtr2-confg]?
Write file rtr2-confg on host 172.16.101.101?[confirm]
![OK]
```

Copy Configuration Files from a Network Server to the Router

You can copy configuration files from a TFTP, rcp, or FTP server to the running configuration or startup configuration of the router. You may want to do this for one of the following reasons:

- To restore a backed up configuration file.

- To use the configuration file for another router. For example, you may add another router to your network and want it to have a similar configuration to the original router. By copying the file to the new router, you can change the relevant parts rather than re-create the whole file.

- To load the same configuration commands on to all the routers in your network so that all the routers have similar configurations.

The **copy {ftp: | rcp: | tftp:} system:running-config** command loads the configuration files into the router as if you were typing the commands in at the command line. The router does not erase the existing running configuration before adding the commands. If a command in the copied configuration file replaces a command in the existing configuration file, the existing command will be erased. For example, if the copied configuration file contains a different IP address in a particular command than the existing configuration, the IP address in the copied configuration will be used. However, some commands in the existing configuration may not be replaced or negated. In this case, the resulting configuration file will be a mixture of the existing configuration file and the copied configuration file, with the copied configuration file having precedence.

In order to restore a configuration file to an exact copy of a file stored on a server, you need to copy the configuration file directly to the startup configuration (using the **copy {ftp: | rcp: | tftp:} nvram:startup-config** command) and reload the router.

The following sections describe these tasks:

- Copy a Configuration File from a TFTP Server to the Router

- Copy a Configuration File from an rcp Server to the Router

- Copy a Configuration File from an FTP Server to the Router

The protocol you use depends on which type of server you are using. The FTP and rcp transport mechanisms provide faster performance and more reliable delivery of data than TFTP. These improvements are possible because the FTP and rcp transport mechanisms are built on and use the Transmission Control Protocol/Internet Protocol (TCP/IP) stack, which is connection-oriented.

Copy a Configuration File from a TFTP Server to the Router

To copy a configuration file from a TFTP server to the router, use the following commands in EXEC mode:

Step	Command	Purpose
1	**copy tftp:**[[[*//location*]/*directory*]/*filename*] **system:running-config** or **copy tftp:**[[[*//location*]/*directory*]/*filename*] **nvram:startup-config**	Copies a file from a TFTP server to the router.
2		Replies to any router prompts for additional information or confirmation. The prompting will depend on how much information you provide in the **copy** command and the current setting of the **file prompt** command.

In the following example, the software is configured from the file tokyo-config at IP address 172.16.2.155:

```
Router1# copy tftp://172.16.2.155/tokyo-confg system:running-config
Configure using tokyo-confg from 172.16.2.155? [confirm] y
Booting tokyo-confg from 172.16.2.155:!!! [OK - 874/16000 bytes]
```

Copy a Configuration File from an rcp Server to the Router

You can copy configuration files from an rcp server to the router. If you copy the configuration file to a personal computer used as a file server, the computer must support rsh.

Understand the rcp Username

The rcp protocol requires a client to send a remote username on each rcp request to a server. When you copy a configuration file from the router to a server using rcp, the Cisco IOS software sends the first valid username in the following list:

1   The username specified in the **copy** command, if a username is specified.

2   The username set by the **ip rcmd remote-username** command, if the command is configured.

3   The remote username associated with the current TTY (terminal) process. For example, if the user is connected to the router through Telnet and was authenticated through the **username** command, the router software sends the Telnet username as the remote username.

4   The router host name.

For the rcp copy request to execute successfully, an account must be defined on the network server for the remote username. If the server has a directory structure, the configuration file or image is written to or copied from the directory associated with the remote username on the server. For example, if the system image resides in the home directory of a user on the server, specify that user's name as the remote username.

Copy a Configuration File from an rcp Server to the Router Tasks

To copy a configuration file from an rcp server to the running configuration or startup configuration, use the following commands beginning in privileged EXEC mode:

Step	Command	Purpose
1	**configure terminal**	(Optional) Enters configuration mode from the terminal. This step is required only if you override the default remote username (see Step 2).
2	**ip rcmd remote-username** *username*	(Optional) Specifies the remote username.
3	**end**	(Optional) Exits configuration mode. This step is required only if you override the default remote username (see Step 2).
4	**copy rcp:**[[[*//*[*username@*]*location*]*/ directory*]*/filename*] **system:running-config** or **copy rcp:**[[[*//*[*username@*]*location*]*/ directory*]*/filename*] **nvram:startup-config**	Using rcp, copies the configuration file from a network server to running memory or the startup configuration.
5		Replies to any router prompts for additional information or confirmation. The prompting will depend on how much information you provide in the **copy** command and the current setting of the **file prompt** command.

Copy rcp Running-Config Example

The following example copies a configuration file named host1-confg from the netadmin1 directory on the remote server with an IP address of 172.16.101.101, and loads and runs those commands on the router:

```
Router# copy rcp://netadmin1@172.16.101.101/host1-confg system:running-config
Configure using host1-confg from 172.16.101.101? [confirm]
Connected to 172.16.101.101
Loading 1112 byte file host1-confg:![OK]
Router#
%SYS-5-CONFIG: Configured from host1-config by rcp from 172.16.101.101
```

Copy rcp Startup-Config Example

The following example specifies a remote username of netadmin1. Then it copies the configuration file host2-confg from the netadmin1 directory on the remote server with an IP address of 172.16.101.101 to the startup configuration.

```
Rtr2# configure terminal
Rtr2(config)# ip rcmd remote-username netadmin1
Rtr2(config)# end
Rtr2# copy rcp: nvram:startup-config
Address of remote host [255.255.255.255]? 172.16.101.101
Name of configuration file[rtr2-confg]? host2-confg
Configure using host2-confg from 172.16.101.101?[confirm]
Connected to 172.16.101.101
Loading 1112 byte file host2-confg:![OK]
[OK]
Rtr2#
%SYS-5-CONFIG_NV:Non-volatile store configured from host2-config by rcp from 172.16.101.101
```

Copy a Configuration File from an FTP Server to the Router

You can copy configuration files from an FTP server to the router.

Understand the FTP Username and Password

The FTP protocol requires a client to send a remote username and password on each FTP request to a server. When you copy a configuration file from the router to a server using FTP, the Cisco IOS software sends the first valid username in the following list:

1   The username specified in the **copy** command, if a username is specified.

2   The username set by the **ip ftp username** command, if the command is configured.

3   Anonymous.

The router sends the first valid password in the following list:

1   The password specified in the **copy** command, if a password is specified.

2   The password set by the **ip ftp password** command, if the command is configured.

3   The router forms a password *username@routername.domain*. The variable *username* is the username associated with the current session, *routername* is the configured host name, and *domain* is the domain of the router.

The username and password must be associated with an account on the FTP server. If you are writing to the server, the FTP server must be properly configured to accept the FTP write request from the user on the router.

If the server has a directory structure, the configuration file or image is written to or copied from the directory associated with the username on the server. For example, if the system image resides in the home directory of a user on the server, specify that user's name as the remote username.

Refer to the documentation for your FTP server for more details.

Use the **ip ftp username** and **ip ftp password** commands to specify a username and password for all copies. Include the username in the **copy** command if you want to specify a username for that copy operation only.

Copy a Configuration File from an FTP Server to the Router Tasks

To copy a configuration file from an FTP server to the running configuration or startup configuration, use the following commands beginning in privileged EXEC mode:

Step	Command	Purpose
1	**configure terminal**	(Optional) Enters configuration mode from the terminal. This step is required only if you override the default remote username or password (see Steps 2 and 3).
2	**ip ftp username** *username*	(Optional) Changes the default remote username.
3	**ip ftp password** *password*	(Optional) Changes the default password.
4	**end**	(Optional) Exits configuration mode. This step is required only if you override the default remote username or password (see Steps 2 and 3).
5	**copy ftp:**[[[// [*username*[*:password*]@]*location*] /*directory*]/*filename*] **system:running-config** or **copy ftp:**[[[// [*username*[*:password*]@]*location*] /*directory*]/*filename*] **nvram:startup-config**	Using FTP, copies the configuration file from a network server to running memory or the startup configuration.
6		Replies to any router prompts for additional information or confirmation. The prompting depends on how much information you provide in the **copy** command and the current setting of the **file prompt** command.

Copy FTP Running-Config Example

The following example copies a host configuration file named host1-confg from the netadmin1 directory on the remote server with an IP address of 172.16.101.101, and loads and runs those commands on the router:

```
Router# copy rcp://netadmin1:mypass@172.16.101.101/host1-confg system:running-config
Configure using host1-confg from 172.16.101.101? [confirm]
Connected to 172.16.101.101
Loading 1112 byte file host1-confg:![OK]
Router#
%SYS-5-CONFIG: Configured from host1-config by ftp from 172.16.101.101
```

Copy FTP Startup-Config Example

The following example specifies a remote username of netadmin1. Then it copies the configuration file host2-confg from the netadmin1 directory on the remote server with an IP address of 172.16.101.101 to the startup configuration.

```
Rtr2# configure terminal
Rtr2(config)# ip ftp username netadmin1
Rtr2(config)# ip ftp password mypass
Rtr2(config)# end
Rtr2# copy ftp: nvram:startup-config
Address of remote host [255.255.255.255]? 172.16.101.101
Name of configuration file[rtr2-confg]? host2-confg
Configure using host2-confg from 172.16.101.101?[confirm]
Connected to 172.16.101.101
Loading 1112 byte file host2-confg:![OK]
[OK]
Rtr2#
%SYS-5-CONFIG_NV:Non-volatile store configured from host2-config by ftp from 172.16.101.101
```

Maintain Configuration Files Larger than NVRAM

To maintain a configuration file that exceeds the size of NVRAM, perform one of the tasks in the following sections:

● Compress the Configuration File

● Store the Configuration in Flash Memory (Class A Flash File Systems)

● Load the Configuration Commands from the Network

Compress the Configuration File

The **service compress-config** global configuration command specifies that the configuration file is to be stored compressed in NVRAM. Once the configuration file has been compressed, the router functions normally. When the system is booted, it recognizes that the configuration file is compressed, expands it, and proceeds normally. The **more nvram:startup-config** EXEC command expands the configuration before displaying it.

To compress configuration files, use the following commands beginning in global configuration mode:

Step	Command	Purpose
1	Refer to the appropriate hardware installation and maintenance publication.	Verifies that your system's ROMs support file compression. If not, you can install new ROMs that support file compression.
2	**service compress-config**	Specifies that the configuration file is to be compressed.
3	**end**	Exits global configuration mode.
4	Use FTP, rcp, or TFTP to copy the new configuration. If you try to load a configuration that is more than three times larger than the NVRAM size, the following error message is displayed: "[buffer overflow - *file-size/buffer-size* bytes]." or **configure terminal**	Enters the new configuration.
5	**copy system:running-config nvram:startup-config**	Saves the new configuration when you have finished changing the running-configuration.

The size of the configuration must not exceed three times the NVRAM size. For a 128 KB size NVRAM, the largest expanded configuration file size is 384 KB.

The **service compress-config** command works only if you have Cisco IOS Software Release 10 boot ROMs or later. Installing new ROMs is a one-time operation and is necessary only if you do not already have Cisco IOS Release 10 in ROM. If the boot ROMs do not recognize a compressed configuration, the following message is displayed:

```
Boot ROMs do not support NVRAM compression Config NOT written to NVRAM
```

The example below compresses a 129 KB configuration file to 11 KB.

```
Router# configure terminal
Router(config)# service compress-config
Router(config)# end
Router# copy tftp://172.16.2.15/tokyo-confg system:running-config
Configure using tokyo-confg from 172.16.2.155? [confirm] y
Booting tokyo-confg from 172.16.2.155:!!! [OK - 874/16000 bytes]
Router# copy system:running-config nvram:startup-config
Building configuration...
Compressing configuration from 129648 bytes to 11077 bytes
[OK]
```

Store the Configuration in Flash Memory (Class A Flash File Systems)

On Class A Flash file system routers, you can store the startup configuration in Flash memory by setting the environment variable CONFIG_FILE to a file in internal Flash memory or Flash memory in a PCMCIA slot.

To store the startup configuration in Flash memory, use the following commands beginning in privileged EXEC mode:

Step	Command	Purpose
1	**copy nvram:startup-config** *flash-filesystem:filename*	Copies the current startup configuration to the new location to create the configuration file.
2	**configure terminal**	Enters global configuration mode.
3	**boot buffersize** *bytes*	The buffer that holds the configuration file is usually the size of NVRAM. Larger configurations need larger buffers. Changes the size of the buffer that holds the configuration commands.
4	**boot config** *flash-filesystem:filename*	Specifies that the startup configuration file is to be stored in Flash memory by setting the CONFIG_FILE variable.
5	**end**	Exits global configuration mode.
6	Use FTP, rcp, or TFTP to copy the new configuration. If you try to load a configuration that is more than three times larger than the NVRAM size, the following error message is displayed: "[buffer overflow - *file-size/buffer-size* bytes]." or **configure terminal**	Enters the new configuration.
7	**copy system:running-config nvram:startup-config**	Saves the new configuration when you have finished changing the running-configuration.

Refer to the "Specify the CONFIG_FILE Environment Variable (Class A Flash File Systems)" section for more information.

The following example stores the configuration file in slot 0:

```
Router# copy nvram:startup-config slot0:router-config
Router# configure terminal
Router(config)# boot buffersize 129000
Router(config)# boot config slot0:router-config
Router(config)# end
Router# copy system:running-config nvram:startup-config
```

Care must be taken when editing or changing a large configuration. Flash memory space is used every time a **copy system:running-config nvram:startup-config** is issued. Because file management for Flash memory, such as optimizing free space, is not done automatically, you must pay close attention to available Flash memory. Use the **squeeze** command to reclaim used space. Cisco recommends that you use a large-capacity Flash card of at least 20 MB.

Load the Configuration Commands from the Network

You can also store large configurations on FTP, rcp, or TFTP servers and download them at system startup. To use a network server to store large configurations, use the following commands, beginning in privileged EXEC mode:

Step	Command	Purpose
1	**copy system:running-config {ftp: | rcp: | tftp:}**	Saves the running configuration to an FTP, rcp, or TFTP server.
2	**configure terminal**	Enters global configuration mode.
3	**boot buffersize** *bytes*	The buffer that holds the configuration file is usually the size of NVRAM. Larger configurations need larger buffers. Changes the size of the buffer that holds the configuration commands.
4	**boot network {ftp:[[[//** [*username*[**:***password*]**@**]*location*]*/directory*] */filename*] | **rcp:**[[[//[*username*@]*location*]*/directory*]/ *filename*] | **tftp:**[[[//*location*]*/directory*]*/filename*]}	Specifies that the startup configuration file is to be loaded from the network server at startup.
5	**service config**	Enables the router to download configuration files at system startup.
6	**end**	Exits global configuration mode.
7	**copy system:running-config nvram:startup-config**	Saves the configuration.

Refer to the "Copy Configuration Files from the Router to a Network Server" and "Configure the Router to Download Configuration Files" sections for more information on these commands.

Copy Configuration Files between Different Locations

On many platforms, you can copy configuration files from one Flash memory device, such as internal Flash memory or a Flash memory card in a PCMCIA slot, to other locations. You can also copy configuration files from an FTP, rcp, or TFTP server to Flash memory.

Copy Configuration Files from Flash Memory to the Startup or Running Configuration

To copy a configuration file from Flash memory directly to your startup configuration in NVRAM or your running configuration, enter one of the following commands in EXEC mode:

Command	Purpose
copy *filesystem***:**[*partition-number***:**][*filename*] **nvram:startup-config**	Loads a configuration file directly into NVRAM.
copy *filesystem***:**[*partition-number***:**][*filename*] **system:running-config**	Copies a configuration file to your running configuration.

The following example copies the file ios-upgrade-1 from partition 4 of the Flash memory PC Card in slot 0 to the router's startup configurations.

```
Router# copy slot0:4:ios-upgrade-1 nvram:startup-config

Copy 'ios-upgrade-1' from flash device
  as 'startup-config' ? [yes/no] yes
[OK]
```

Copy Configuration Files between Flash Memory File Systems

On platforms with multiple Flash memory file systems, you can copy files from one Flash memory file system, such as internal Flash memory or a Flash memory card in a PCMCIA slot, to another Flash memory file system. Copying files to different Flash memory file systems lets you create backup copies of working configurations and duplicate configurations for other routers.

To copy a configuration file between Flash memory file systems, use the following commands in EXEC mode:

Step	Command	Purpose
1	**show** *source-filesystem***:**	Displays the layout and contents of Flash memory to verify the file name.
2	**copy** *source-filesystem***:**[*partition-number***:**][*filename*] *dest-filesystem***:**[*partition-number***:**][*filename*]	Copies a configuration file between Flash memory devices.
3	**verify** *dest-filesystem***:**[*partition-number***:**][*filename*]	Verifies the checksum of the file you copied.

NOTE   The source device and the destination device cannot be the same. For example, the command **copy slot1: slot1:** is invalid.

Copy a Configuration File between Local Flash Memory Devices Example

The following example copies the file running-config from partition 1 of internal Flash memory to partition 1 of slot 1 on a Cisco 3600 series router. In this example, the source partition is not specified, so the router prompts for the partition number.

```
Router# copy flash: slot1:

System flash

Partition   Size    Used     Free     Bank-Size  State        Copy Mode
  1         4096K   3070K    1025K    4096K      Read/Write   Direct
  2         16384K  1671K    14712K   8192K      Read/Write   Direct

[Type ?<no> for partition directory; ? for full directory; q to abort]
Which partition? [default = 1]

System flash directory, partition 1:
File  Length    Name/status
  1   3142748   dirt/network/mars-test/c3600-j-mz.latest
  2   850       running-config
[3143728 bytes used, 1050576 available, 4194304 total]

PCMCIA Slot1 flash directory:
File  Length    Name/status
  1   1711088   dirt/gate/c3600-i-mz
  2   850       running-config
[1712068 bytes used, 2482236 available, 4194304 total]

Source file name? running-config

Destination file name [running-config]?
Verifying checksum for 'running-config' (file # 2)...  OK

Erase flash device before writing? [confirm]
Flash contains files. Are you sure you want to erase? [confirm]

Copy 'running-config' from flash: device
  as 'running-config' into slot1: device WITH erase? [yes/no] yes
Erasing device... eeeeeeeeeeeeeeeeeeeeeeeeeeeeeeeeeeeeeeeeeeeeeeeeeeeeeeeeeeeeeeeee
...erased
!
 [OK - 850/4194304 bytes]

Flash device copy took 00:00:30 [hh:mm:ss]
Verifying checksum...  OK (0x16)
```

Copy a Configuration File from a Server to Flash Memory

To copy a configuration file from an FTP server to a Flash memory device, use the following commands in privileged EXEC mode:

Step	Command	Purpose
1	**configure terminal**	(Optional) Enters configuration mode from the terminal. This step is required only if you override the default remote username or password (see Steps 2 and 3).
2	**ip ftp username** *username*	(Optional) Specifies the remote username.
3	**ip ftp password** *password*	(Optional) Specifies the remote password.
4	**end**	(Optional) Exits configuration mode. This step is required only if you override the default remote username (see Steps 2 and 3).
5	**copy ftp:**[[[*//*[*username:password@*]*location*] */directory*]*/filename*] *flash-filesystem***:**[*partition-number***:**][*filename*]	Use FTP, copies the configuration file from a network server to the Flash memory device.
6		Replies to any router prompts for additional information or confirmation. The prompting will depend on how much information you provide in the **copy** command and the current setting of the **file prompt** command.

To copy a configuration file from an rcp server to a Flash memory device, use the following commands in privileged EXEC mode:

Step	Command	Purpose
1	**configure terminal**	(Optional) Enters configuration mode from the terminal. This step is required only if you override the default remote username (see Step 2).
2	**ip rcmd remote-username** *username*	(Optional) Specifies the remote username.
3	**end**	(Optional) Exits configuration mode. This step is required only if you override the default remote username (see Step 2).
4	**copy rcp:**[[[*//*[*username@*]*location*]*/directory*]*/ filename*] *flash-filesystem***:**[*partition-number***:**][*filename*]	Using rcp, copies the configuration file from a network server to the Flash memory device.

Step	Command	Purpose
5		Replies to any router prompts for additional information or confirmation. The prompting will depend on how much information you provide in the **copy** command and the current setting of the **file prompt** command.

To copy a configuration file from a TFTP server to the router, use the following commands from EXEC mode:

Step	Command	Purpose
1	**copy tftp:**[[[*//location*]/*directory*]/*filename*] *flash-filesystem:*[*partition-number:*][*filename*]	Copies the file from a TFTP server to the Flash memory device.
2		Replies to any router prompts for additional information or confirmation. The prompting will depend on how much information you provide in the **copy** command and the current setting of the **file prompt** command.

Copy TFTP example for Cisco 7000 Family

On the Cisco 7000 family, the following example copies the router-config file from a TFTP server to the Flash memory card inserted in slot 0 of the Network Processing Engine (NPE) or Route Switch Processor (RSP) card. The copied file has the name new-config.

```
Router# copy tftp:router-config slot0:new-config
```

Reexecute the Configuration Commands in Startup Configuration

To reexecute the commands located in the startup configuration, use the following command in privileged EXEC mode:

Command	Purpose
configure memory	Reexecutes the configuration commands located in the startup configuration.

Clear the Configuration Information

You can clear the configuration information from the startup configuration. If you reboot the router with no startup configuration, the router will enter the setup facility so that you can configure the router from scratch.

Clear the Startup Configuration

To clear the contents of your startup configuration, use the following command in EXEC mode:

Command	Purpose
erase nvram:	Clears the contents of your startup configuration.

For all platforms except the Class A Flash file system platforms, this command erases NVRAM. The startup configuration file cannot be restored once it has been deleted.

On Class A Flash file system platforms, when you use the **erase startup-config** command, the router erases or deletes the configuration pointed to by CONFIG_FILE environment variable. If this variable points to NVRAM, the router erases NVRAM. If the CONFIG_FILE environment variable specifies a Flash memory device and configuration filename, the router deletes the configuration file. That is, the router marks the file as "deleted," rather than erasing it. This feature allows you to recover a "deleted" file.

Delete a Stored Configuration File

To delete a saved configuration from a specific Flash device, use the following command in EXEC mode:

Command	Purpose
delete *flash-filesystem:filename*	Deletes a specified configuration file on a specified Flash device.

On Class A and B Flash file systems, when you delete a specific file in Flash memory, the system marks the file as deleted, allowing you to later recover a "deleted" file using the **undelete** command. Erased files cannot be recovered. To erase the configuration file permanently, use the **squeeze** command.

On Class C Flash file systems, you cannot recover a file that has been deleted.

If you attempt to erase or delete the configuration file specified by the CONFIG_FILE environment variable, the system prompts you to confirm the deletion.

The following example deletes the myconfig file from a Flash memory card inserted in slot 0:

```
Router# delete slot0:myconfig
```

Specify the Startup Configuration File

Normally, the router uses the startup configuration file in NVRAM or the Flash file system specified by the CONFIG_FILE environment variable (Class A Flash file systems only) at startup. See the "Specify the CONFIG_FILE Environment Variable (Class A Flash File Systems)" section for details on setting the CONFIG_FILE variable.

You can also configure the router to request and receive automatically two configuration files from the network server at startup. See the "Configure the Router to Download Configuration Files" section for details.

Specify the CONFIG_FILE Environment Variable (Class A Flash File Systems)

On Class A Flash file systems, you can configure the Cisco IOS software to load the startup configuration file specified by the CONFIG_FILE environment variable. The CONFIG_FILE variable defaults to NVRAM. To change the CONFIG_FILE variable, use the following commands beginning in EXEC mode:

Step	Command	Purpose
1	**copy** [*flash-url* | *ftp-url* | *rcp-url* | *tftp-url* | **system:running-config** | **nvram:startup-config**] *dest-flash-url*	Copies the configuration file to the Flash file system from which the router will load the file upon restart.
2	**configure terminal**	Enters configuration mode from the terminal.
3	**boot config** *dest-flash-url*	Sets the CONFIG_FILE environment variable. This step modifies the runtime CONFIG_FILE environment variable.
4	**end**	Exits configuration mode.
5	**copy system:running-config nvram:startup-config**	Saves this runtime CONFIG_FILE environment variable to your startup configuration.
6	**show bootvar**	Optionally, verifies the contents of the CONFIG_FILE environment variable.

After you specify a location for the startup configuration file, **nvram:startup-config** is aliased to the new location of the startup configuration file. The **more nvram:startup-config** command will display the startup configuration, regardless of its location. The **erase nvram:startup-config** command will erase the contents of NVRAM and delete the file pointed to by the CONFIG_FILE environment variable.

When you save the configuration using the **copy system:running-config nvram:startup-config** command, the router saves a complete version of the configuration file to the location specified by the CONFIG_FILE environment variable and a distilled version to NVRAM. A distilled version is one that does not contain access list information. If NVRAM contains a complete configuration file, the router prompts you to confirm your overwrite of the complete version with the distilled version. If NVRAM contains a distilled configuration, the router does not prompt you for confirmation and proceeds with overwriting the existing distilled configuration file in NVRAM.

NOTE	If you specify a file in a Flash device as the CONFIG_FILE variable, every time you save your configuration file with the **copy system:running-config nvram:startup-config** command, the old configuration file is marked as deleted, and the new configuration file is saved to that device. Eventually, Flash memory will be full because the old configuration files still take up memory. Use the **squeeze** command to permanently delete the old configuration files and reclaim the space.

The following example copies the running configuration file to the first PCMCIA slot of the RSP card in a Cisco 7500 series. This configuration is then used as the startup configuration when the system is restarted.

```
Router# copy system:running-config slot0:config2
Router# configure terminal
Router(config)# boot config slot0:config2
Router(config)# end
Router# copy system:running-config nvram:startup-config
[ok]
Router# show bootvar
BOOT variable = slot0:rsp-boot-m
CONFIG_FILE variable = nvram:
Current CONFIG_FILE variable = slot0:config2

Configuration register is 0x010F
```

Configure the Router to Download Configuration Files

You can configure the router to load one or two configuration files at system startup. The configuration files are loaded into memory and read in as if you were typing the commands at the command line. Thus, the configuration for the router will be a mixture of the original startup configuration and the one or two downloaded configuration files.

Network Versus Host Configuration Files

For historical reasons, the first file the router downloads is called the *network configuration file*. The second file the router downloads is called the *host configuration file*. Two configuration files can be used when all of the routers on a network use many of the same commands. The network configuration file contains the standard commands used to configure all of the routers. The host configuration files contain the commands specific to one particular host. If you are loading two configuration files, the host configuration file should be the configuration file you want to have precedence over the other file. Both the network and host configuration files must reside on a network server reachable via TFTP, rcp, or FTP, and must be readable.

Understand the rcp Username

The rcp protocol requires a client to send a remote username on each rcp request to a server. When you copy a configuration file from the router to a server using rcp, the Cisco IOS software sends the first valid username in the following list:

1   The username specified in the **boot network** or **boot host** command, if a username is specified.

2   The username set by the **ip rcmd remote-username** command, if the command is configured.

3   The remote username associated with the current TTY (terminal) process. For example, if the user is connected to the router through Telnet and was authenticated through the **username** command, the router software sends the Telnet username as the remote username.

4   The router host name.

For the rcp copy request to execute successfully, an account must be defined on the network server for the remote username. If the server has a directory structure, the configuration file or image is written to or copied from the directory associated with the remote username on the server. For example, if the system image resides in the home directory of a user on the server, specify that user's name as the remote username.

If you copy the configuration file to a personal computer used as a file server, the computer must support rsh.

Understand the FTP Username and Password

The FTP protocol requires a client to send a remote username and password on each FTP request to a server. When you copy a configuration file from the router to a server using FTP, the Cisco IOS software sends the first valid username in the following list:

1   The username specified in the **copy** command, if a username is specified.

2   The username set by the **ip ftp username** command, if the command is configured.

3   Anonymous.

The router sends the first valid password in the following list:

1   The password specified in the **copy** command, if a password is specified.

2   The password set by the **ip ftp password** command, if the command is configured.

3   The router forms a password *username@routername.domain*. The variable *username* is the username associated with the current session, *routername* is the configured host name, and *domain* is the domain of the router.

The username and password must be associated with an account on the FTP server. If you are writing to the server, the FTP server must be properly configured to accept the FTP write request from the user on the router.

If the server has a directory structure, the configuration file or image is written to or copied from the directory associated with the username on the server. For example, if the system image resides in the home directory of a user on the server, specify that user's name as the remote username.

Refer to the documentation for your FTP server for more details.

Use the **ip ftp username** and **ip ftp password** commands to specify a username and password for all copies. Include the username in the **copy** command if you want to specify a username for that copy operation only.

Configure the Router to Download Configuration Files Task List

You can specify an ordered list of network configuration and host configuration filenames. The Cisco IOS software scans this list until it successfully loads the appropriate network or host configuration file.

To configure the router to download configuration files at system startup, perform at least one of the tasks described in the following sections:

● Configure the Router to Download the Network Configuration File

● Configure the Router to Download the Host Configuration File

If the router fails to load a configuration file during startup, it tries again every ten minutes (the default setting) until a host provides the requested files. With each failed attempt, the router displays the following message on the console terminal:

```
Booting host-confg... [timed out]
```

Refer to the *Internetwork Troubleshooting Guide* publication for troubleshooting procedures.

If there are any problems with the startup configuration file, or if the configuration register is set to ignore NVRAM, the router enters the **setup** command facility.

Configure the Router to Download the Network Configuration File

To configure the Cisco IOS software to download a network configuration file from a server at startup, use the following commands:

Step	Command	Purpose
1	**configure terminal**	Enters configuration mode from the terminal.
2	**boot network** {**ftp:**[[[//[*username*[**:***password*]**@**]*location*] /*directory*]/*filename*] | **rcp:**[[[//[*username***@**]*location*]/ *directory*]/*filename*] | **tftp:**[[[//*location*]/*directory*]/*filename*]}	Enters the network configuration filename to download a file using TFTP, rcp, or FTP.
3	**service config**	Enables the router to automatically load the network file upon restart.
4	**end**	Exits configuration mode.
5	**copy system:running-config nvram:startup-config**	Saves the configuration file to your startup configuration.

For Step 2, if you do not specify a network configuration filename, the Cisco IOS software uses the default filename network-confg. If you omit the address, the router uses the broadcast address.

You can specify more than one network configuration file. The software tries them in the order entered until it loads one successfully. This procedure can be useful for keeping files with different configuration information loaded on a network server.

Configure the Router to Download the Host Configuration File

To configure the Cisco IOS software to download a host configuration file from a server at startup, use the following commands in global configuration mode:

Step	Command	Purpose
1	**configure terminal**	Enters configuration mode from the terminal.
2	**boot host** {**ftp:**[[[//[*username*[**:***password*]**@**]*location*] /*directory*]/*filename*] | **rcp:**[[[//[*username***@**]*location*]/ *directory*]/*filename*] | **tftp:**[[[//*location*]/*directory*]/*filename*]}	Enters the host configuration filename to be download using FTP, rcp, or TFTP.
3	**service config**	Enables the device to automatically load the host file upon restart.
4	**end**	Exits configuration mode.
5	**copy system:running-config nvram:startup-config**	Saves the configuration file to your startup configuration.

If you do not specify a host configuration filename, the router uses its own name to form a host configuration filename by converting the name to all lowercase letters, removing all domain information, and appending -confg. If no host name information is available, the software uses the default host configuration filename router-confg. If you omit the address, the router uses the broadcast address.

You can specify more than one host configuration file. The Cisco IOS software tries them in order entered until it loads one successfully. This procedure can be useful for keeping files with different configuration information loaded on a network server.

Configure the Router to Download Configuration Files at System Startup Example

In the following example, a router is configured to download the host configuration file hostfile1 and the network configuration file networkfile1: The router uses TFTP and the broadcast address to obtain the file.

```
Router# configure terminal
Router(config)# boot host tftp:hostfile1
Router(config)# boot network tftp:networkfile1
Router(config)# service config
Router(config)# end
Router# copy system:running-config nvram:startup-config
```

## CHAPTER 14

Configuration File Commands

This chapter provides detailed descriptions of the commands used to load and copy configuration files. Configuration files contain commands entered to customize the function of the Cisco IOS software.

For configuration information and examples, refer to Chapter 13, "Modifying, Downloading, and Maintaining Configuration Files."

Flash Memory File System Types

Cisco platforms use one of three different Flash memory file system types. Some commands are supported on only one or two file system types. This chapter notes commands that are not supported on all file system types.

Refer to Table 14-1 to determine which Flash memory file system type your platform uses.

Table 14-1 *Flash Memory File System Types*

Type	Platforms
Class A	Cisco 7000 family, C12000, LS1010
Class B	Cisco 1003, Cisco 1004, Cisco 1005, Cisco 2500 series, Cisco 3600 series, Cisco 4000 series, Cisco AS5200
Class C	Cisco MC3810, disk0 of SC3640

Replaced Commands

Commands in this chapter that have been replaced by new commands continue to perform their normal functions in the current release but are no longer documented. Support for these commands will cease in a future release.

Table 14-1 maps the old commands with their replacements.

Table 14-1 *Mapping Old Commands to New Commands*

Old Command	New Command
configure network	**copy ftp:**[[[*//*[*username*[**:***password*]**@**]*location*]*/directory*] */filename*] **system:running-config**

Continues

Table 14-1 *Mapping Old Commands to New Commands (Continued)*

Old Command	New Command
configure overwrite-network	**copy ftp:**[[[//[*username*[*:password*]@]*location*]/*directory*] /*filename*] **nvram:startup-config**
copy rcp running-config	**copy rcp:**[[[//[*username*@]*location*]/*directory*]/*filename*] **system:running-config**
copy running-config rcp	**copy system:running-config rcp:**[[[//[*username*@]*location*]/ *directory*]/*filename*]
copy running-config startup-config	**copy system:running-config nvram:startup-config**
copy running-config tftp	**copy system:running-config tftp:**[[[//*location*]/*directory*]/ *filename*]
copy tftp running-config	**copy tftp:**[[[//*location*]/*directory*]/*filename*] **system:running-config**
copy tftp startup-config	**copy tftp:**[[[//*location*]/*directory*]/*filename*] **nvram:startup-config**
erase startup-config	**erase nvram:**
show configuration	**more nvram:startup-config**
show file	**more**
show running-config	**more system:running-config**
write erase	**erase nvram:**
write memory	**copy system:running-config nvram:startup-config**
write network	**copy system:running-config ftp:**[[[//[*username* [*:password*]@]*location*]/*directory*]/*filename*]
write terminal	**more system:running-config**

boot buffersize

To modify the buffer size used to load configuration files, use the **boot buffersize** global configuration command. Use the **no** form of this command to return to the default setting.

> **boot buffersize** *bytes*
> **no boot buffersize**

Syntax   Description

bytes   Specifies the size of the buffer to be used. There is no minimum or maximum size that can be specified.

Default

Buffer size of the NVRAM

Command Mode

Global configuration

Usage Guidelines

This command first appeared in Cisco IOS Release 10.0.

Normally, the Cisco IOS software uses a buffer the size of the system NVRAM to hold configuration commands read from the network. You can increase this size if you have a very complex configuration.

Example

The following example sets the buffer size to 64,000 bytes:

```
boot buffersize 64000
```

boot config

To specify the device and filename of the configuration file from which the router configures itself during initialization (startup), use the **boot config** global configuration command. This command is only available on Class A file system platforms. Use the **no** form of this command to remove the specification.

> **boot config** *file-url*
> **no boot config**

Syntax	Description
file-url	URL of the configuration file. The configuration file must be an ASCII file located in either NVRAM or a Flash file system.

Default

NVRAM (**nvram:**)

Command Mode

Global configuration

Usage Guidelines

This command first appeared in Cisco IOS Release 11.0.

This command is only available on Class A file system platforms.

You set the CONFIG_FILE environment variable in the current running memory when you use the **boot config** command. This variable specifies the configuration file used for initialization (startup).

NOTE   When you use this global configuration command, you affect only the running configuration. You must save the environment variable setting to your startup configuration to place the information under ROM monitor control and to have the environment variable function as expected. Use the **copy system:running-config nvram:startup-config** command to save the environment variable from your running configuration to your startup configuration.

The software displays an error message and does not update the CONFIG_FILE environment variable in the following situations:

● You specify **nvram:** as the file system, and it contains only a distilled version of the configuration. (A distilled configuration is one that does not contain access lists.)

● You specify a configuration file in the *filename* argument that does not exist or is not valid.

The router uses the NVRAM configuration during initialization when the CONFIG_FILE environment variable does not exist or when it is null (such as at first-time startup). If the software detects a problem with NVRAM or the configuration it contains, the device enters **setup** mode.

When you use the **no** form of this command, the router returns to using the NVRAM configuration as the startup configuration.

Examples

In the following example, the first line specifies that the router should use the configuration file *router-config* located in internal Flash memory to configure itself during initialization. The second line copies the specification to the startup configuration, ensuring that this specification will take effect upon the next reload:

```
Router (config)# boot config flash:router-config
Router (config)# end
Router# copy system:running-config nvram:startup-config
```

The following example instructs a Cisco 7500 series router to use the configuration file *router-config* located on the Flash memory card inserted in the second PCMCIA slot of the RSP card during initialization. The second line copies the specification to the startup configuration, ensuring that this specification will take effect upon the next reload:

```
Router (config)# boot config slot1:router-config
Router (config)# end
Router# copy system:running-config nvram:startup-config
```

Related Commands

To locate documentation of related commands, you can search online at www.cisco.com.

copy system:running-config nvram:startup-config
show bootvar

boot host

To change the default name of the host configuration filename from which to load configuration commands, use the **boot host** global configuration command. Use the **no** form of this command to restore the host configuration filename to the default.

> **boot host** *remote-url*
> **no boot host** *remote-url*

Syntax	Description
remote-url	Configures the router to boot the configuration file specified by the FTP, rcp, or TFTP URL:
	• **ftp:**[[[//[*username*[**:***password*]@]*location*]/*directory*]/*filename*]
	• **rcp:**[[[//[*username*@]*location*]/*directory*]/*filename*]
	• **tftp:**[[[//*location*]/*directory*]/*filename*]

Default

The router uses its host name to form a host configuration filename. To form this name, the router converts its name to all lowercase letters, removes all domain information, and appends *-confg*.

Command Mode

Global configuration

Usage Guidelines

This command first appeared in Cisco IOS Release 10.0.

Use the **service config** command to enable the loading of the specified configuration file at reboot time. Without this command, the router ignores the **boot host** command and uses the configuration information in NVRAM. If the configuration information in NVRAM is invalid or missing, the **service config** command is enabled automatically.

The network server will attempt to load two configuration files from remote hosts. The first is the network configuration file containing commands that apply to all network servers on a network. Use the **boot network** command to identify the network configuration file. The second is the host configuration file containing commands that apply to one network server in particular. Use the **boot host** command to identify the host configuration file.

Loading a Configuration File Using rcp

The rcp software requires that a client send the remote username on each rcp request to the network server. If the server has a directory structure (such as UNIX systems), the rcp implementation searches for the configuration files starting in the directory associated with the remote username.

When you load a configuration file from a server using rcp, the Cisco IOS software sends the first valid username in the following list:

1   The username specified in the file-URL if a username is specified.

2   The username set by the **ip rcmd remote-username** command if the command is configured.

3   The router host name.

NOTE   An account for the username must be defined on the destination server. If the network administrator of the destination server did not establish an account for the username, this command will not execute successfully.

Load a Configuration File Using FTP

The FTP protocol requires a client to send a remote username and password on each FTP request to a server. The username and password must be associated with an account on the FTP server. If the server has a directory structure, the configuration file or image copied from the directory associated with the username on the server. Refer to the documentation for your FTP server for more details.

When you load a configuration file from a server using FTP, the Cisco IOS software sends the first valid username in the following list:

1 The username specified in the **boot host** command if a username is specified.

2 The username set by the **ip ftp username** command if the command is configured.

3 Anonymous.

The router send the first valid password in the following list:

1 The password specified in the **boot host** command if a password is specified.

2 The password set by the **ip ftp password** command if the command is configured.

3 The router forms a password *username@routername.domain*. The variable *username* is the username associated with the current session, *routername* is the configured host name, and *domain* is the domain of the router.

Example

The following example sets the host filename to wilma-confg at address 192.168.7.19:

```
boot host tftp://192.168.7.19/usr/local/tftpdir/wilma-confg
service config
```

Related Commands

To locate documentation of related commands, you can search online at www.cisco.com.

boot network
service config

boot network

To change the default name of the network configuration file from which to load configuration commands, use the **boot network** global configuration command. Use the **no** form of this command to restore the network configuration filename to the default.

boot network *remote-url*
no boot network *remote-url*

Syntax	Description
remote-url	Configures the router to boot the configuration file specified by the FTP, rcp, or TFTP URL:

- **ftp:**[[[//[*username*[**:***password*]@]*location*]/*directory*]/*filename*]

- **rcp:**[[[//[*username*@]*location*]/*directory*]/*filename*]

- **tftp:**[[[//*location*]/*directory*]/*filename*]

Default

The default *filename* is network-config.

Command Mode

Global configuration

Usage Guidelines

This command first appeared in Cisco IOS Release 10.0.

When booting from a network server, routers ignore routing information, static IP routes, and bridging information. As a result, intermediate routers are responsible for handling FTP, rcp, or TFTP requests. Before booting from a network server, verify that a server is available by using the **ping** command.

Use the **service config** command to enable the loading of the specified configuration file at reboot time. Without this command, the router ignores the **boot network** command and uses the configuration information in NVRAM. If the configuration information in NVRAM is invalid or missing, the **service config** command is enabled automatically.

The network server will attempt to load two configuration files from remote hosts. The first is the network configuration file containing commands that apply to all network servers on a network. Use the **boot network** command to identify the network configuration file. The second is the host configuration file containing commands that apply to one network server in particular. Use the **boot host** command to identify the host configuration file.

Loading a Configuration File Using rcp

The rcp software requires that a client send the remote username on each rcp request to the network server. If the server has a directory structure (such as UNIX systems), the rcp implementation searches for the configuration files starting in the directory associated with the remote username.

When you load a configuration file from a server using rcp, the Cisco IOS software sends the first valid username in the following list:

1   The username specified in the file-URL if a username is specified.

2   The username set by the **ip rcmd remote-username** command if the command is configured.

3   The router host name.

NOTE	An account for the username must be defined on the destination server. If the network administrator of the destination server did not establish an account for the username, this command will not execute successfully.

Load a Configuration File Using FTP

The FTP protocol requires a client to send a remote username and password on each FTP request to a server. The username and password must be associated with an account on the FTP server. If the server has a directory structure, the configuration file or image copied from the directory associated with the username on the server. Refer to the documentation for your FTP server for more details.

When you load a configuration file from a server using FTP, the Cisco IOS software sends the first valid username in the following list:

1 The username specified in the **boot network** command if a username is specified.

2 The username set by the **ip ftp username** command if the command is configured.

3 Anonymous.

The router send the first valid password in the following list:

1 The password specified in the **boot network** command if a password is specified.

2 The password set by the **ip ftp password** command if the command is configured.

3 The router forms a password *username@routername.domain*. The variable *username* is the username associated with the current session, *routername* is the configured host name, and *domain* is the domain of the router.

Examples

The following example changes the network configuration filename to bridge_9.1 and uses the default broadcast address:

```
boot network tftp:bridge_9.1
service config
```

The following example changes the network configuration filename to bridge_9.1, specifies that rcp is to be used as the transport mechanism, and gives 172.16.1.111 as the IP address of the server on which the network configuration file resides:

```
boot network rcp://172.16.1.111/bridge_9.1
service config
```

Related Commands

To locate documentation of related commands, you can search online at www.cisco.com.

boot host
service config

configure

To enter global configuration mode, use the **configure** privileged EXEC command. You must be in global configuration mode to enter global configuration commands.

> **configure** {**terminal** | **memory**}

Syntax	Description
terminal	Executes configuration commands from the terminal.
memory	For all platforms except Class A Flash file system platforms, executes the commands stored in NVRAM.
	For the Class A Flash file system platforms, executes the configuration specified by the CONFIG_FILE environment variable.

Command Mode

Privileged EXEC

Usage Guidelines

This command first appeared in Cisco IOS Release 10.0.

If you do not specify **terminal** or **memory**, the Cisco IOS software prompts you for the source of configuration commands. If you specify **terminal**, the software executes the commands you enter at the system prompts.

On all platforms except Class A Flash file system platforms, if you specify **memory**, the software executes the commands located in NVRAM.

On Class A Flash file system platforms, if you specify **memory**, the router executes the commands pointed to by the CONFIG_FILE environment variable. The CONFIG_FILE environment variable specifies the location of the configuration file that the router uses to configure itself during initialization. The file can be located in NVRAM or any of the Flash file systems supported by the platform.

When the CONFIG_FILE environment variable specifies NVRAM, the router executes the NVRAM configuration only if it is an entire configuration, not a distilled version. A distilled configuration is one that does not contain access lists.

To view the contents of the CONFIG_FILE environment variable, use the **show bootvar** command. To modify the CONFIG_FILE environment variable, use the **boot config** command and then save your changes by issuing the **copy system:running-config nvram:startup-config** command.

After you enter the **configure** command, the system prompt changes from <router-name># to <router-name>(config)#, indicating that the router is in global configuration mode. To leave global configuration mode and return to the privileged EXEC prompt, type **end** or press **Ctrl-Z**.

Examples

In the following example, a router is configured from the terminal:

```
Router# configure

Configuring from terminal, memory, or network [terminal]?
Enter configuration commands, one per line. End with Cntl-Z.
Router(config)#
```

In the following example, Class A Flash file system router executes the commands pointed to by the CONFIG_FILE environment variable:

```
configure memory
```

Part II

Command Reference

Related Commands

To locate documentation of related commands, you can search online at www.cisco.com.

boot config
copy system:running-config nvram:startup-config
partition system:running-config
partition nvram:startup-config
show bootvar

configure overwrite-network

The **copy** {*ftp-url* | *rcp-url* | *tftp-url*} **nvram:startup-config** command replaces the **configure overwrite-network** command. See the copy command in Chapter 18, "Router Memory Commands," for more information.

erase startup-config

The **erase nvram:** command replaces the **erase startup-config** command. See the erase command in Chapter 18, "Router Memory Commands," for more information.

service compress-config

To compress startup configuration files, use the **service compress-config** global configuration command. To disable compression, use the **no** form of this command.

> **service compress-config**
> **no service compress-config**

Syntax Description

This command has no arguments or keywords.

Default

Disabled

Command Mode

Global configuration

Usage Guidelines

This command first appeared in Cisco IOS Release 10.0.

After you configure the **service compress config** command, the router will compress configuration files every time you save a configuration to the startup configuration. For example, when you enter the **copy system:running-config nvram:startup-config** command, the running configuration will be compressed before storage in NVRAM.

If the file compression completes successfully, the following message is displayed:

```
Compressing configuration from configuration-size to compressed-size
[OK]
```

If the boot ROMs do not recognize a compressed configuration, the following message is displayed:

```
Boot ROMs do not support NVRAM compression Config NOT written to NVRAM
```

If the file compression fails, the following message is displayed:

```
Error trying to compress nvram
```

One way to determine whether a configuration file will compress enough to fit into NVRAM is to use a text editor to enter the configuration; then use the UNIX **compress** command to check the compressed size. To get a closer approximation of the compression ratio, use the UNIX command **compress -b12**.

Once the configuration file has been compressed, the router functions normally. At boot time, the system recognizes that the configuration file is compressed, uncompresses it, and proceeds normally. A **partition nvram:startup-config** command uncompresses the configuration before displaying it.

To disable compression of the configuration file, enter configuration mode and specify the **no service compress-config** command. Then, exit global configuration mode and enter the **copy system:running-config nvram:startup-config** command. The router displays an OK message if it is able to successfully write the uncompressed configuration to NVRAM. Otherwise, the router displays an error message indicating that the configuration is too large to store. If the configuration file is larger than the physical NVRAM, the following message is displayed:

```
##Configuration too large to fit uncompressed in NVRAM Truncate configuration?
[confirm]
```

When the file is truncated, commands at the end of the file are erased. Therefore, you will lose part of your configuration. To truncate and save the configuration, type **Y**. To not truncate and not save the configuration, type **N**.

Example

In the following example, the configuration file is compressed:

```
Router# configure terminal
Enter configuration commands, one per line.  End with Cntl-Z.
Router(config)# service compress-config
Router(config)# end
Router#
%SYS-5-CONFIG_I: Configured from console by console
Router# copy system:running-config nvram:startup-config
Building configuration...
Compressing configuration from 1179 bytes to 674 bytes
[OK]
```

Related Commands

To locate documentation of related commands, you can search online at www.cisco.com.

partition nvram:startup-config

service config

To enable autoloading of configuration files from a network server, use the **service config** global configuration command. Use the **no** form of this command to restore the default.

> **service config**
> **no service config**

Syntax Description

This command has no arguments or keywords.

Default

Disabled, except on systems without NVRAM or with invalid or incomplete information in NVRAM. In these cases, autoloading of configuration files from a network server is enabled automatically.

Command Mode

Global configuration

Usage Guidelines

This command first appeared in Cisco IOS Release 10.0.

Usually, the **service config** command is used in conjunction with the **boot host** or **boot network** command. You must enter the **service config** command to enable the router to automatically configure the system from the file specified by the **boot host** or **boot network** command.

The **service config** command can also be used without the **boot host** or **boot network** command. If you do not specify host or network configuration filenames, the router uses the default configuration files. The default network configuration file is network-confg. The default host configuration file is host-confg; where host is the host name of the router. If the Cisco IOS software cannot resolve its host name, the default host configuration file is router-confg.

Examples

In the following example, a router is configured to autoload the default network and host configuration files. Since no **boot host** or **boot network** commands are specified, the router uses the broadcast address to request the files from a TFTP server.

```
service config
```

The following example changes the network configuration filename to bridge_9.1, specifies that rcp is to be used as the transport mechanism, and gives 172.16.1.111 as the IP address of the server on which the network configuration file resides:

```
boot network rcp://172.16.1.111/bridge_9.1
service config
```

Related Commands

To locate documentation of related commands, you can search online at www.cisco.com.

boot host
boot network

show configuration

The **more nvram:startup-config** command replaces the **show configuration** command. Refer to the description of the **more** command for more information.

show file

The **more** command replaces the **show file** command. Refer to the description of the **more** command for more information.

show running-config

The **more system:running-config** command replaces the **show running-config** command. Refer to the description of the **more** command for more information.

show startup-config

The **more nvram:startup-config** command replaces the **show startup-config** command. Refer to the description of the **more** command for more information.

write erase

The **erase nvram:** command replaces the **write erase** command. Refer to the description of the **erase** command in Chapter 18, "Router Memory Commands," for more information.

write memory

The **copy system:running-config nvram:startup-config** command replaces the **write memory** command. Refer to the description of the **copy** command in Chapter 18, "Router Memory Commands," for more information.

write network

The **copy system:running-config** {*ftp-url* | *rcp-url* | *tftp-url*} command replaces the **write network** command. Refer to the description of the **copy** command in Chapter 18, "Router Memory Commands," for more information.

write terminal

The **more system:running-config** command replaces the **write terminal** command. Refer to the description of the **more** command for more information.

## CHAPTER 15

Loading and Maintaining System Images and Microcode

This chapter describes how to load and maintain system images and microcode. System images contain the system software. Microcode images contain microcode to be downloaded to various hardware devices.

To benefit most from the instructions and organization of this chapter, your router must contain a minimal configuration that allows you to interact with the system software. You can create a basic configuration file using the **setup** command facility. See the user guide for your hardware platform for more information on using **setup** at first-time startup.

For a complete description of the system image and microcode commands mentioned in this chapter, refer to Chapter 16, "System Image and Microcode Commands." To locate documentation of other commands that appear in this chapter, you can search online at www.cisco.com.

NOTE One or more of the commands that previously appeared in this chapter have been replaced by new commands. Table 15-1 maps the old commands to their replacements. The old commands continue to perform their normal functions in the current release, but support for these commands will cease in a future release.

Table 15-1 *Mapping Old Commands to New Commands*

Old Command	New Command
copy erase flash	**erase flash:** (Class B Flash file systems only)
	format (Class A and C Flash file systems only)
copy verify	**verify**
copy verify flash	**verify flash:**
verify flash	
copy verify bootflash	**verify bootflash:**
verify bootflash	

System Images and Microcode Task List

You can perform the tasks involving images described in the following sections:

- Display System Image Information

- Understand Images

- Copy Operation General Output Conventions

- Copy Images from Flash Memory to a Network Server

- Copy Images from a Network Server to Flash Memory

- Copy Images between Local Flash Memory Devices

- Specify the Startup System Image in the Configuration File

- Recovering a System Image Using Xmodem or Ymodem

- Load and Display Microcode Images

NOTE   These tasks assume you have a minimal configuration that you want to modify.

Display System Image Information

Use the following commands in EXEC mode to display information about system software:

Step	Command	Purpose
1	**show bootvar**	Lists the contents of the BOOT environment variable, the name of the configuration file pointed to by the CONFIG_FILE environment variable, and the contents of the BOOTLDR environment variable.
2	**show** *flash-filesystem***: [partition** *number*] **[all	chips	detailed	err	summary]** (Class B Flash file systems) **show** *flash-filesystem***: [all	chips	filesys]** (Class A Flash file systems) **show** *flash-filesystem***:** (Class C Flash file systems)	Lists information about Flash memory.
3	**show microcode**	Displays microcode information.
4	**show version**	Lists the system software release version, configuration register setting, and other information.

Understand Images

System images contain the Cisco IOS software. Your router already has an image on it when you receive it. However, you may want to load a different image onto the router at some point. For example, you may wish to upgrade your software to the latest release or use the same version of the software for all the routers in a network.

Types of Images

The following are two main types of images your router may use:

- System image—The complete Cisco IOS software. This image is loaded when your router boots and is used most of the time.

  On most platforms, the image is located in Flash memory. On platforms with multiple Flash memory file systems (Flash, Bootflash, slot 0, or slot 1), the image can be located in any existing Flash file system. Use the **show file systems** command to determine which file systems your router supports. Refer to your hardware documentation for information about where these images are located by default.

- Boot image—A subset of the Cisco IOS software. This image is used to perform network booting or to load Cisco IOS images onto the router. This image is also used if the router cannot find a valid system image. Depending on your platform, this image may be called xboot image, rxboot image, bootstrap image, or boot loader/helper image.

  On some platforms, the boot image is contained in ROM. In others, the boot image can be stored in Flash memory. On these platforms, you can specify which image should be used as the boot image using the **boot bootldr** command.

  Refer to your hardware documentation for information about the boot image used on your router.

Image Naming Conventions

You can identify the platform, features, and image location by the name of the image. The naming convention for images that are stored on a UNIX system is as follows:

platform-features-type

The *platform* variable indicates which platforms can use this image. Examples of *platform* variables are rsp (Cisco 7000 series with RSP7000 and Cisco 7500 series), c1600 (Cisco 1600 series), and c1005 (Cisco 1005).

The *feature* variable identifies the feature sets supported by the image.

The *type* field can contain the following characters:

- f—The image runs from Flash memory.

- m—The image runs from RAM.

- r—The image runs from ROM.

- l—The image is relocatable.

- z—The image is zip compressed.

- x—The image is mzip compressed.

Copy Operation General Output Conventions

During a copy operation, you may get the following characters:

- A pound sign (#) generally means that a Flash memory device is being cleared and initialized. (Different platforms use different ways of indicating that Flash is being cleared.)

- An exclamation point (!) means that ten packets have been transferred successfully.

- A series of "V" characters means that a checksum verification of the file is occurring after the file is written to Flash memory.

- An "O" means an out-of-order packet.

- A period (.) means a timeout.

The last line in the output indicates whether or not the copy was successful.

To interrupt a copy operation, press **Ctrl-^** or **Ctrl-Shift-6**. The operation terminates, but any partial file copied remains until Flash memory is erased.

Copy Images from Flash Memory to a Network Server

You can copy system images from Flash memory to an FTP, rcp, or TFTP server. You can use this server copy of the system image as a backup copy, or you can use it to verify that the copy in Flash is the same as the original file on disk. The following sections describe these tasks:

- Copy an Image from Flash Memory to a TFTP Server

- Copy an Image from Flash Memory to an rcp Server

- Copy an Image from Flash Memory to an FTP Server

The protocol you use depends on which type of server you are using. The FTP and rcp transport mechanisms provide faster performance and more reliable delivery of data than TFTP. These improvements are possible because the FTP and rcp transport mechanisms are built on and use the Transmission Control Protocol/Internet Protocol (TCP/IP) stack, which is connection-oriented.

To stop the copy process, press **Ctrl-^** or **Ctrl-Shift-6**.

In the output, an exclamation point (!) indicates that the copy process is taking place. Each exclamation point (!) indicates that ten packets have been transferred successfully.

Copy an Image from Flash Memory to a TFTP Server

You can copy a system image to a TFTP network server. In some implementations of TFTP, you must first create a "dummy" file on the TFTP server and give it read, write, and execute permissions before copying a file over it. Refer to your TFTP documentation for more information.

To copy a system image to a TFTP network server, use the following commands in EXEC mode:

Step	Command	Purpose
1	**show** *flash-filesystem***:**	(Optional) Learns the exact spelling of the system image filename in Flash memory.
2	**copy** *flash-url* **tftp:**[[[*//location*]/ *directory*]/*filename*]	Copies the system image from Flash memory to a TFTP server.
3		Replies to any router prompts for additional information or confirmation. The prompting will depend on how much information you provide in the **copy** command and the current setting of the **file prompt** command.

Copy from Flash Memory to a TFTP Server Example

The following example uses the **show flash:** command to learn the name of the system image file and the **copy flash: tftp:** command to copy the system image to a TFTP server.

```
RouterB# show flash:

System flash directory:
File  Length    Name/status
  1   4137888   c3640-c2is-mz.Feb24
[4137952 bytes used, 12639264 available, 16777216 total]
16384K bytes of processor board System flash (Read/Write)\

Router# copy flash: tftp:
IP address of remote host [255.255.255.255]? 172.16.13.110
filename to write on tftp host? c3640-c2is-mz.Feb24
writing c3640-c2is-mz.Feb24 !!!!...
successful tftp write.
```

Copy from Partitioned Flash Memory to a TFTP Server Example

In this example, the file your-ios is copied from partition 1 of the Flash memory PC card in slot 0 to the TFTP server at 172.23.1.129. The file will be saved with the name *your-ios* in the dirt/sysadmin directory relative to the directory of the remote username.

```
Router# copy slot0:1:your-ios tftp://172.23.1.129/dirt/sysadmin/your-ios
Verifying checksum for 'your-ios' (file # 1)...  OK
Copy 'your-ios' from Flash to server
  as 'dirt/sysadmin/ios-2'? [yes/no] yes
!!!!!!!!!!!!!!!!!!!!!!!!!!!!!!!!!!!!!!!!!!!!!!!!!!!!!!!!!!!!!!!!!!!!!!!!!!!!!!!!!!!!!!
!!!!!!!!!!!!!!!!!!!!!!!!!!!!!!!!!!!!!!!!!!!!!!!!!!!!!!!!!!!!!!!!!!!!!!!!!!!!!!!!!!!!!!
!!!!!!!!!!!!!!!!!!!!!!!!!!!!!!!!!!!!!!!!!!!!!!!!!!!!!!!!!!!!!!!!!!!!!!!!!!!!!!!!!!!!!!
!!!!!!!!!!!!!!!!!!!!!!!!!!!!!!!!!!!!!!!!!!!!!!!!!!!!!!!!!!!!!!!!!!!
Upload to server done
Flash device copy took 00:00:23 [hh:mm:ss]
```

Copy an Image from Flash Memory to an rcp Server

You can copy a system image from Flash memory to an rcp network server.

If you copy the configuration file to a personal computer used as a file server, the computer must support rsh.

Understand the rcp Username

The rcp protocol requires a client to send a remote username on each rcp request to a server. When you copy an image from the router to a server using rcp, the Cisco IOS software sends the first valid username in the following list:

1   The remote username specified in the **copy** command if one is specified.

2   The username set by the **ip rcmd remote-username** command if the command is configured.

3   The remote username associated with the current TTY (terminal) process. For example, if the user is connected to the router through Telnet and was authenticated through the **username** command, the router software sends the Telnet username as the remote username.

4   The router host name.

For the rcp copy request to execute successfully, an account must be defined on the network server for the remote username. If the server has a directory structure, the configuration file or image is written or copied relative to the directory associated with the remote username on the server. The path for all files and images to be copied begins at the remote user's home directory. For example, if the system image resides in the home directory of a user on the server, specify that user's name as the remote username.

If you are writing to the server, the rcp server must be properly configured to accept the rcp write request from the user on the router. For UNIX systems, you must add an entry to the .rhosts file for the remote user on the rcp server. For example, suppose the router contains the following configuration lines:

```
hostname Rtr1
ip rcmd remote-username User0
```

If the router's IP address translates to Router1.domain.com, then the .rhosts file for User0 on the rcp server should contain the following line:

```
Router1.domain.com Rtr1
```

Refer to the documentation for your rcp server for more details.

Copy from Flash Memory to an rcp Server Tasks

To copy the system image from Flash memory to a network server, use the following commands:

Step	Command	Purpose
1	**show** *flash-filesystem***:**	Learns the exact spelling of the system image filename in Flash memory.
2	**configure terminal**	(Optional) Enters configuration mode from the terminal. This step is required only if you want to change the default remote username (see Step 3).
3	**ip rcmd remote-username** *username*	(Optional) Configures the remote username.
4	**end**	(Optional) Exits configuration mode. This step is required only if you want to change the default remote username (see Step 3).
5	**copy** *flash-url* **rcp:**[[[//[*username*@]*location*]/ *directory*]/*filename*]	Copies the system image from Flash memory to a network server using rcp.
6		Replies to any router prompts for additional information or confirmation. The prompting will depend on how much information you provide in the **copy** command and the current setting of the **file prompt** command.

Copy from Flash to RCP Server Example

The following example copies the system image c5200-ds-l to the network server at 172.16.1.111 using rcp and a username of netadmin:

```
Router# copy flash:c5200-ds-l rcp:netadmin1@172.16.1.111/c5200-ds-l
Verifying checksum for 'c5200-ds-l' (file # 1)...[OK]
Writing c5200-ds-l -
```

Copy from Slot1 to RCP Server Example

The following example copies a system image file called test from the second PCMCIA slot to a network server using rcp. The remote username is netadmin1. Because the destination address and filename are not specified, the router prompts for this information.

```
Router# configure terminal
Router(config)# ip rcmd remote-username netadmin1
Router(config)# end
Router# copy slot1:test rcp:
```

```
Address or name of remote host [UNKNOWN]? 172.16.1.111
File name to write to? test
Verifying checksum for 'test' (file # 1)...[OK]
Writing test
!!!!!!!!!!!!!!!!!!!!!!!!!!!!!!!!!!!!!!!!!!!!!!!!!!!!!!!!!!!!!!!!!!!!!!!!!!!!!!!!!!!!!!!!!!!!
!!!!!!!!!!!!!!!!!!!!!!!!!!!!!!!!!!!!!!!!!!!!!!!!!!!!!!!!!!!!!!!!!!!!!!!!!!!!!!!!!!!!!!!!!!!!
!!!!!!!!!!!!!!!!!!!!!!!!!!!!!!!!!!!!!!!!!!!!!!!!!!!!!!!!!!!!!!!!!!!!!!!!!!!!!!!!!!!!!!!!!!!!
!!!!!!!!!!!!!!!!!!!!!!!!!!!!!!!!!!!!!!!!!!!!!!!!!!!!!!!!!!!!!!!!!!
Upload to server done
Flash device copy took 00:00:08 [hh:mm:ss]
```

Copy an Image from Flash Memory to an FTP Server

You can copy a system image to an FTP network server.

Understand the FTP Username and Password

The FTP protocol requires a client to send a remote username and password on each FTP request to a server. When you copy a configuration file from the router to a server using FTP, the Cisco IOS software sends the first valid username in the following list:

1   The username specified in the **copy** command if a username is specified.

2   The username set by the **ip ftp username** command if the command is configured.

3   Anonymous.

The router sends the first valid password in the following list:

1   The password specified in the **copy** command if a password is specified.

2   The password set by the **ip ftp password** command if the command is configured.

3   The router forms a password *username@routername.domain*. The variable *username* is the username associated with the current session, *routername* is the configured host name, and *domain* is the domain of the router.

The username and password must be associated with an account on the FTP server. If you are writing to the server, the FTP server must be properly configured to accept the FTP write request from the user on the router.

If the server has a directory structure, the configuration file or image is written to or copied from the directory associated with the username on the server. For example, if the system image resides in the home directory of a user on the server, specify that user's name as the remote username.

Refer to the documentation for your FTP server for more details.

Use the **ip ftp username** and **ip ftp password** commands to specify a username and password for all copies. Include the username in the **copy** command if you want to specify a username for that copy operation only.

Copy from Flash Memory to an FTP Server Tasks

To copy a system image to an FTP network server, use the following commands in EXEC mode:

Step	Command	Purpose
1	**configure terminal**	(Optional) Enters configuration mode from the terminal. This step is required only if you override the default remote username or password (see Steps 2 and 3).
2	**ip ftp username** *username*	(Optional) Changes the default remote username.
3	**ip ftp password** *password*	(Optional) Changes the default password.
4	**end**	(Optional) Exits configuration mode. This step is required only if you override the default remote username or password (see Steps 2 and 3).
5	**show** *flash-filesystem***:**	(Optional) Learns the exact spelling of the system image filename in Flash memory if you do not already know it.
6	**copy** *flash-filesystem***:***filename* **ftp:**[[[//[*username* [**:***password*]**@**]*location*]/ *directory*]/*filename*]	Copies the image to the FTP server.
7		Replies to any router prompts for additional information or confirmation. The prompting will depend on how much information you provide in the **copy** command and the current setting of the **file prompt** command.

Copy from Flash Memory to an FTP Server Example

The following example uses the **show flash:** command to learn the name of the system image file and the **copy flash: tftp:** command to copy the system image (c3640-2is-mz) to a TFTP server. The router uses the default username and password.

```
Router# show flash:

System flash directory:
File  Length    Name/status
  1   4137888   c3640-c2is-mz
[4137952 bytes used, 12639264 available, 16777216 total]
16384K bytes of processor board System flash (Read/Write)\

Router# copy flash: tftp:
```

```
IP address of remote host [255.255.255.255]? 172.16.13.110
filename to write on tftp host? c3600-c2is-mz
writing c3640-c2is-mz !!!!...
successful ftp write.
```

Copy from Slot1 to an FTP Server Example

The following example uses the **show slot1:** command to display the name of the system image file in
the second PCMCIA slot and then copies the file (test) to an FTP server.

```
Router# show slot1:

-#- ED --type-- --crc--- -seek-- nlen -length- -----date/time------ name
1  .. 1      46A11866 2036C   4    746      May 16 1995 16:24:37 test

Router# copy slot1:test ftp://thisuser:thatpass@172.16.13.110/test
writing test!!!!...
successful ftp write.
```

Copy from Partitioned Flash to an FTP Server Example

In this example, the file your-ios is copied from partition 1 of the Flash memory PC card in slot 0 to the
TFTP server at 172.23.1.129. The file will be saved with the name *your-ios* in the dirt/sysadmin
directory relative to the directory of the remote username.

```
Router#show slot0: partition 1

PCMCIA Slot0 flash directory, partition 1:
File  Length   Name/status
  1   1711088 your-ios
[1711152 bytes used, 2483152 available, 4194304 total]

Router# copy slot0:1:your-ios ftp://myuser:mypass@172.23.1.129/dirt/sysadmin/your-ios

Verifying checksum for 'your-ios' (file # 1)...  OK
Copy 'your-ios' from Flash to server
  as 'dirt/sysadmin/ios-2'? [yes/no] yes
!!!!!!!!!!!!!!!!!!!!!!!!!!!!!!!!!!!!!!!!!!!!!!!!!!!!!!!!!!!!!!!!!!!!!!!!!!!!!!!!!!!!!!!!
!!!!!!!!!!!!!!!!!!!!!!!!!!!!!!!!!!!!!!!!!!!!!!!!!!!!!!!!!!!!!!!!!!!!!!!!!!!!!!!!!!!!!!!!
!!!!!!!!!!!!!!!!!!!!!!!!!!!!!!!!!!!!!!!!!!!!!!!!!!!!!!!!!!!!!!!!!!!!!!!!!!!!!!!!!!!!!!!!
!!!!!!!!!!!!!!!!!!!!!!!!!!!!!!!!!!!!!!!!!!!!!!!!!!!!!!!!!!!!!!!!!!!
Upload to server done
Flash device copy took 00:00:23 [hh:mm:ss]
```

Copy Images from a Network Server to Flash Memory

You can copy system images or boot images from a TFTP, rcp, or FTP server to a Flash memory file
system to upgrade or change the Cisco IOS software or boot image on your router.

The protocol you use depends on which type of server you are using. The FTP and rcp transport mechanisms provide faster performance and more reliable delivery of data than TFTP. These improvements are possible because the FTP and rcp transport mechanisms are built on and use the Transmission Control Protocol/Internet Protocol (TCP/IP) stack, which is connection-oriented.

The following sections describe the copying tasks. The first two tasks and the last task are required. If you have a run-from-Flash system, the third section is required. Perform one of the remaining tasks, depending on which file transfer protocol you use.

- Understand Flash Memory Space Considerations

- Output for Image Downloading Process

- Copy to Flash Memory Tasks for Run-from-Flash Systems

- Copy an Image from a TFTP Server to a Flash Memory File System

- Copy an Image from an rcp Server to a Flash Memory File System

- Copy an Image from an FTP Server to a Flash Memory File System

- Verify the Image in Flash Memory

NOTE   When you are upgrading or changing to a different Cisco IOS release, refer to the appropriate release notes for information on system requirements and limitations.

Restrictions on File Naming

Filenames in Flash memory can be up to 63 characters long; they are not case-sensitive and are always converted to lowercase.

NOTE   The destination filename must be an alphanumeric expression. For example, the filename 1 is invalid.

The filename can be in either lowercase or uppercase; the system ignores case. If more than one file of the same name is copied to Flash, regardless of case, the last file copied becomes the valid file.

Understand Flash Memory Space Considerations

Be sure there is enough space available before copying a file to Flash memory. Use the **show** *flash-filesystem***:** command, and compare the size of the file you want to copy to the amount of Flash memory available. If the space available is less than the amount needed, the **copy** command is partially executed, but the entire file is not copied into Flash memory. The failure message "buffer overflow - *xxxx/xxxx*" appears, where *xxxx/xxxx* is the number of bytes read from the source file and the number of bytes available on the destination device.

CAUTION   Do not reboot the router if there is no valid image in Flash memory.

NOTE   For the Cisco 3600 series, if you do not have access to a network server and need to download a system image, you can copy an image from a local or remote computer (such as a PC, UNIX workstation, or Macintosh) using the Xmodem or Ymodem protocols. See the section "Recovering a System Image Using Xmodem or Ymodem" later in this chapter.

On Cisco 2500, Cisco 3000, and Cisco 4000 systems, if the file being downloaded to Flash memory is an uncompressed system image, the **copy** command automatically determines the size of the file being downloaded and validates it with the space available in Flash memory.

On Class B Flash file systems, the router gives you the option of erasing the existing contents of Flash memory before writing to it. If there is no free Flash memory available, or if no files have ever been written to Flash memory, the erase routine is required before new files can be copied. If there is enough free Flash memory, the router gives you the option of erasing the existing Flash memory before writing to it. The system will inform you of these conditions and prompt you for a response.

NOTE   If you enter **n** after the "Erase flash before writing?" prompt, the copy process continues. If you enter **y** and confirm the erasure, the erase routine begins. Be sure to have ample Flash memory space before entering **n** at the erasure prompt.

If you attempt to copy a file into Flash memory that is already there, a prompt informs you that a file with the same name already exists. This file is "deleted" when you copy the new file into Flash.

- On Class A and B Flash file systems, the first copy of the file still resides within Flash memory, but it is rendered unusable in favor of the newest version and is listed with the "deleted" tag when you use the **show** *flash-filesystem***:** command. If you terminate the copy process, the newer file is marked "deleted" because the entire file was not copied and is not valid. In this case, the original file in Flash memory is valid and available to the system.

- On Class C Flash file systems, the first copy of the file is erased.

You can copy normal or compressed images to Flash memory. You can produce a compressed system image on any UNIX platform using the **compress** command. Refer to your UNIX platform's documentation for the exact usage of the **compress** command.

On some platforms, the Flash security jumper must be installed in order to write to Flash memory. In addition, some platforms have a write protect switch that must be set to *unprotected* in order to write to Flash memory.

Output for Image Downloading Process

The output and dialogue may vary depending on the platform.

Output for Partitioned Flash Memory

One of the following prompts displayed after the command indicates how the file can be downloaded:

- None—The file cannot be copied.

- RXBOOT-Manual—You must manually reload to the rxboot image in ROM to copy the image.

- RXBOOT-FLH—The copy is done automatically via the Flash load helper software in boot ROMs.

- Direct—The copy can be done directly.

If the file can be downloaded into more than one partition, you are prompted for the partition number. To obtain help, enter any of the following at the partition number prompt:

- **?**—Display the directory listings of all partitions.

- **?1**—Display the directory of the first partition.

- **?2**—Display the directory of the second partition.

- **q**—Quit the copy command.

Copy to Flash Memory Tasks for Run-from-Flash Systems

You cannot run the system from Flash memory and copy to it at the same time. Therefore, for systems that run from Flash, do *one* of the following before copying to Flash:

- Partition Flash memory or use Flash load helper to allow the system to run from Flash memory while you copy to it.

- Reload the system to use a system image from boot ROMs.

Refer to the "Compare Types of Memory" section in Chapter 17, "Maintaining Router Memory," for more information on run-from-Flash systems.

Refer to the appropriate hardware installation and maintenance publication for information about the jumper settings required for your configuration.

Copy an Image from a TFTP Server to a Flash Memory File System

To copy a system image from a Trivial File Transfer Protocol (TFTP) server to a Flash memory file system, use the following commands in EXEC mode:

Step	Command	Purpose
1	See the instructions in the section "Copy Images from Flash Memory to a Network Server."	Makes a backup copy of the current software image or bootstrap image.
2	**copy tftp:**[[[*//location*]/*directory*]/*filename*] *flash-filesystem*:[*filename*]	Copies a system image or a boot image to Flash memory.
3		Replies to any router prompts for additional information or confirmation. The prompting will depend on how much information you provide in the **copy** command and the current setting of the **file prompt** command.

Copy from a TFTP Server to Flash Memory Example

In the following example, a file is copied from a TFTP server to slot1:

```
Router# copy tftp://theserver/tftpboot/kristen/ken/c7200-js-mz slot1:
Destination filename [c7200-js-mz]?
Accessing tftp://theserver/tftpboot/kristen/ken/c7200-js-mz...Translating
"theserver"...domain server (192.168.2.132) [OK]

Loading tftpboot/kristen/ken/c7200-js-mz from 192.168.2.132 (via Ethernet3/0):
!!!!!!!!!!!!!!!!!!!!!!!!!!!!!!!!!!!!!!!!!!!!!!!!!!!!!!!!!!!!!!!!!!!!!!!!!!!!!!!!!!!!!!!!
!!!!!!!!!!!!!!!!!!!!!!!!!!!!!!!!!!!!!!!!!!!!!!!!!!!!!!!!!!!!!!!!!!!!!!!!!!!!!!!!!!!!!!!!
!!!!!!!!!!!!!!!!!!!!!!!!!!!!!!!!!!!!!!!!!!!!!!!!!!!!!!!!!!!!!!!!!!!!!!!!!!!!!!!!!!!!!!!!
!!!!!!!!!!!!!!!!!!!!!!!!!!!!!!!!!!!!!!!!!!!!!!!!!!!!!!!!!!!!!!!!!!!!!!!!!!!!!!!!!!!!!!!!
!!!!!!!!!!!!!!!!!!!!!!!!!!!!!!!!!!!!!!!!!!!!!!!!!!!!!!!!!!!!!!!!!!!!!!!!!!!!!!!!!!!!!!!!
!!!!!!!!!!!!!!!!!!!!!!!!!!!!!!!!!!!!!!!!!!!!!!!!!!!!!!!!!!!!!!!!!!!!!!!!!!!!!!!!!!!!!!!!
!!!!!!!!!!!!!!!!!!!!!!!!!!!!!!!!!!!!!!!!!!!!!!!!!!!!!!!!!!!!!!!!!!!!!!!!!!!!!!!!!!!!!!!!
!!!!!!!!!!!!!!!!!!!!!!!!!!!!!!!!!!!!!!!!!!!!!!!!!!!!!!!!!!!!!!!!!!!!!!!!!!!!!!!!!!!!!!!!
!!!!!!!!!!!!!!!!!!!!!!!!!!!!!!!!!!!!!!!!!!!!!!!!!!!!!!!!!!!!!!!!!!!!!!!!!!!!!!!!!!!!!!!!
!!!!!!!!!!!!!!!!!!!!!!!!!!!!!!!!!!!!!!!!!!!!!!!!!!!!!!!!!
[OK - 4823492/9646080 bytes]

4823492 bytes copied in 264.312 secs (18270 bytes/sec)
```

The following example copies a system image named igs-p-l from a TFTP server to a Class B Flash file system when Flash memory is too full to copy the file.

```
Router# copy tftp: flash:
IP address or name of remote host [255.255.255.255]? dirt
Translating "DIRT"...domain server (255.255.255.255) [OK]

Name of file to copy? igs-p-l
Copy igs-p-l from 172.16.13.111 into flash memory? [confirm]
Flash is filled to capacity.
Erasure is needed before flash may be written.
Erase flash before writing? [confirm]
Erasing flash EPROMs bank 0

Zeroing bank...zzzzzzzzzzzzzzzz
Verify zeroed...vvvvvvvvvvvvvvvv
Erasing bank...eeeeeeeeeeeeeeee

Erasing flash EPROMs bank 1

Zeroing bank...zzzzzzzzzzzzzzzz
Verify zeroed...vvvvvvvvvvvvvvvv
Erasing bank...eeeeeeeeeeeeeeee

Erasing flash EPROMs bank 2

Zeroing bank...zzzzzzzzzzzzzzzz
Verify zeroed...vvvvvvvvvvvvvvvv
Erasing bank...eeeeeeeeeeeeeeee

Erasing flash EPROMs bank 3

Zeroing bank...zzzzzzzzzzzzzzzz
Verify zeroed...vvvvvvvvvvvvvvvv
Erasing bank...eeeeeeeeeeeeeeee

Loading from 172.16.1.111:!!!!...
 [OK - 1906676/4194240 bytes]
Verifying via checksum...
vvvvvvvvvvvvvvvvvvvvvvvvvvvvvvvvvvvvvvvvvvvvvvvvvvvvvvvvvvvvvvvvvvvvvvvvvvvvvvv
vvvvvvvvvvvvvvvvvvvvvvvvvvvvvvvvvvvvvvvvvvvvvvvvvvvvvvvvvvvvvvvvvvvvvvvvvvvvvvv
vvvvvvvvvvvvvvvvvvvvvvvvvvvvvvvvvvvvvvvvvvvvvvvvvvvvvvvvvvvvvvvvvvvvvvvvvvvvvvv
vvvvvvvvvvvvvvvvvvvvvvvvvvvvvvvvvvvvvvvvvvvvvvvvvvvvvvvvvvvvvvvvvvvvvvvvvvvvvvv
vvvvvvvvvvvvvvvvvvvvvvvvvvvvvvvv
Flash verification successful. Length = 1906676, checksum = 0x12AD
```

Copy from a TFTP Server to Flash Example When File by the Same Name Already Exists

The following example shows how to copy a system image named igs-p-l into the current Flash configuration in which a file named igs-p-l already exists:

```
Router# copy tftp://172.16.13.111/igs-p-l flash:igs-p-l
File igs-p-l already exists; it will be invalidated!
Copy igs-p-l from 172.16.13.111 into flash memory? [confirm]
2287500 bytes available for writing without erasure.
```

```
Erase flash before writing? [confirm]n
Loading from 172.16.1.111:!!!!...
[OK - 1906676/2287500 bytes]
Verifying via checksum...
vvvvvvvvvvvvvvvvvvvvvvvvvvvvvvvvvvvvvvvvvvvvvvvvvvvvvvvvvvvvvvvvvvvvvvvvvvvvvvvvvvvv
vvvvvvvvvvvvvvvvvvvvvvvvvvvvvvvvvvvvvvvvvvvvvvvvvvvvvvvvvvvvvvvvvvvvvvvvvvvvvvvvvvvv
vvvvvvvvvvvvvvvvvvvvvvvvvvvvvvvvvvvvvvvvvvvvvvvvvvvvvvvvvvvvvvvvvvvvvvvvvvvvvvvvvvvv
vvvvvvvvvvvvvvvvvvvvvvvvvvvvvvvvvvvvvvvvvvvvvvvvvvvvvvvvvvvvvvvvvvvvvvvvvvvvvvvvvvvv
vvvvvvvvvvvvvvvvvvvvvvvvvvvvvv
Flash verification successful. Length = 1902192, checksum = 0x12AD
```

Copy from TFTP Server to Flash Example without Security Jumper Installed

In the following example, the Flash security jumper is not installed, so you cannot write files to Flash memory.

```
Router# copy tftp: flash:
Flash: embedded flash security jumper(12V)
        must be strapped to modify flash memory
```

Copy from TFTP Server to Partitioned Flash Example

In the following example, the file c3600-i-mz on the TFTP server at 172.23.1.129 is copied to the first partition of internal Flash Memory.

```
Router# copy tftp://172.23.1.129/c3600-i-mz flash:1:c3600-i-mz/c3600-i-mz
Accessing file 'c3600-i-mz' on 172.23.1.129...
Loading c3600-i-mz from 172.23.1.129 (via Ethernet1/0): ! [OK]
Erase flash device before writing? [confirm]
Flash contains files. Are you sure you want to erase? [confirm]
Copy 'c3600-i-mz' from server
  as 'c3600-i-mz' into Flash WITH erase? [yes/no] yes
Erasing device... eeeeeeeeeeeeeeee ...erased
Loading c3600-i-mz from 172.23.1.129 (via Ethernet1/0):
!!!!!!!!!!!!!!!!!!!!!!!!!!!!!!!!!!!!!!!!!!!!!!!!!!!!!!!!!!!!!!!!!!!!!!!!!!!!!!!!!!!!
!!!!!!!!!!!!!!!!!!!!!!!!!!!!!!!!!!!!!!!!!!!!!!!!!!!!!!!!!!!!!!!!!!!!!!!!!!!!!!!!!!!!
!!!!!!!!!!!!!!!!!!!!!!!!!!!!!!!!!!!!!!!!!!!!!!!!!!!!!!!!!!!!!!!!!!!!!!!!!!!!!!!!!!!!
!!!!!!!!!!!!!!!!!!!!!!!!!!!!!!!!!!!!!!!!!!!!!!!!!!!!!!!!!!!!!!!!
[OK - 1711088/4194304 bytes]

Verifying checksum... OK (0xF89A)
Flash device copy took 00:00:17 [hh:mm:ss]
```

Copy an Image from an rcp Server to a Flash Memory File System

You can copy a system image from an rcp network server to a Flash memory file system.

If you copy the configuration file to a personal computer used as a file server, the computer must support rsh.

Understand the rcp Username

The rcp protocol requires a client to send a remote username on each rcp request to a server. When you copy an image from the router to a server using rcp, the Cisco IOS software sends the first valid username in the following list:

1   The remote username specified in the **copy** command if one is specified.

2   The username set by the **ip rcmd remote-username** command if the command is configured.

3   The remote username associated with the current TTY (terminal) process. For example, if the user is connected to the router through Telnet and was authenticated through the **username** command, the router software sends the Telnet username as the remote username.

4   The router host name.

For the rcp copy request to execute successfully, an account must be defined on the network server for the remote username. If the server has a directory structure, the configuration file or image is written or copied relative to the directory associated with the remote username on the server. The path for all files and images to be copied begins at the remote user's home directory. For example, if the system image resides in the home directory of a user on the server, specify that user's name as the remote username.

Copy from an rcp Server to Flash Memory Tasks

To copy an image from an rcp server to Flash memory, use the following commands, beginning in privileged EXEC mode:

Step	Command	Purpose
1	See the instructions in the section "Copy Images from Flash Memory to a Network Server."	Makes a backup copy of the current system or bootstrap software image.
2	**configure terminal**	(Optional) Enters configuration mode from the terminal. This step is required only if you override the default remote username (see Step 3).
3	**ip rcmd remote-username** *username*	(Optional) Specifies the remote username.
4	**end**	(Optional) Exits configuration mode. This step is required only if you override the default remote username (see Step 3).
5	**copy rcp:**[[[//[*username*@]*location*]/*directory*] /*filename*] *flash-filesystem***:**[*filename*]	Copies the image from an rcp server to a Flash memory file system.
6		Replies to any router prompts for additional information or confirmation. The prompting will depend on how much information you provide in the **copy** command and the current setting of the **file prompt** command.

Copy from an rcp Server to Flash Example

The following example copies a system image named mysysim1 from the netadmin1 directory on the remote server named SERVER1.CISCO.COM with an IP address of 172.16.101.101 to Flash memory. To ensure that enough Flash memory is available to accommodate the system image to be copied, the Cisco IOS software allows you to erase the contents of Flash memory first.

```
Router1# configure terminal
Router1(config)# ip rcmd remote-username netadmin1
Router1(config)# end
Router# copy rcp: flash:

System flash directory:
File name/status
    1 mysysim1
[2076072 bytes used, 21080 bytes available]

Address or name of remote host[UNKNOWN]? 172.16.101.101
Name of file to copy? mysysim1
Copy mysysim1 from SERVER1.CISCO.COM?[confirm]

Checking for file 'mysysim1' on SERVER1.CISCO.COM...[OK]

Erase Flash device before writing?[confirm]
Are you sure?[confirm]
Erasing device...ezeeze...erased.

Connected to 172.16.101.101

Loading 2076007 byte file mysysim1:!!!!...
[OK]

Verifying checksum... (0x87FD)...[OK]
```

Copy from an rcp Server to Partitioned Slot0

In the following example, the file /tftpboot/gate/c3600-i-mz on the rcp server at 172.23.1.129 is copied to partition 3 in slot 0. Because no username is specified, the router uses the default rcp remote username.

```
Router# show slot0: partition 3

PCMCIA Slot0 flash directory, partition 3:
File  Length    Name/status
  1    426       running-config
[492 bytes used, 4193812 available, 4194304 total]

Router# copy rcp://172.23.1.129/tftpboot/gate/c3600-i-mz slot0:3:/tftpboot/gate/c3600-i-mz
Accessing file '/tftpboot/gate/c3600-i-mz' on 172.23.1.129...
Connected to 172.23.1.129
Loading 1711088 byte file c3600-i-mz: ! [OK]

Erase flash device before writing? [confirm]
```

```
Flash contains files. Are you sure you want to erase? [confirm]
Copy '/tftpboot/gate/c3600-i-mz' from server
  as '/tftpboot/gate/c3600-i-mz' into Flash WITH erase? [yes/no] yes
Erasing device... eeeeeeeeeeeeeeeeeeeeeeeeeeeeeeeee ...erased
Connected to 172.23.1.129
Loading 1711088 byte file c3600-i-mz:
!!!!!!!!!!!!!!!!!!!!!!!!!!!!!!!!!!!!!!!!!!!!!!!!!!!!!!!!!!!!!!!!!!!!!!!!!!!!!!!!!!
!!!!!!!!!!!!!!!!!!!!!!!!!!!!!!!!!!!
!!!!!!!!!!!!!!!!!!!!!!!!!!!!!!!!!!!!!!!!!!!!!!!!!!!!!!!!!!!!!!!!!!!!!!!!!!!!!!!!!!
!!!!!!!!!!!!!!!!!!!!!!!!!!!!!!!!!!!!!!!!!!!!!!!!!!!!!!!!!!!!!!!!!!!!!!!!!!!!!!!!!!
!!!!!!!!!!!!!!!!!!!!!!!!!!!!!!!!!!!! [OK]

Verifying checksum...  OK (0xF89A)
Flash device copy took 00:00:16 [hh:mm:ss]
```

Copy an Image from an FTP Server to a Flash Memory File System

You can copy a system image from an FTP server to a Flash memory file system.

Understand the FTP Username and Password

The FTP protocol requires a client to send a remote username and password on each FTP request to a server. When you copy a configuration file from the router to a server using FTP, the Cisco IOS software sends the first valid username in the following list:

1 The username specified in the **copy** command if a username is specified.

2 The username set by the **ip ftp username** command if the command is configured.

3 Anonymous.

The router sends the first valid password in the following list:

1 The password specified in the **copy** command if a password is specified.

2 The password set by the **ip ftp password** command if the command is configured.

3 The router forms a password *username@routername.domain*. The variable *username* is the username associated with the current session, *routername* is the configured host name, and *domain* is the domain of the router.

The username and password must be associated with an account on the FTP server. If you are writing to the server, the FTP server must be properly configured to accept the FTP write request from the user on the router.

If the server has a directory structure, the configuration file or image is written to or copied from the directory associated with the username on the server. For example, if the system image resides in the home directory of a user on the server, specify that user's name as the remote username.

Refer to the documentation for your FTP server for more details.

Use the **ip ftp username** and **ip ftp password** commands to specify a username and password for all copies. Include the username in the **copy** command if you want to specify a username for that copy operation only.

Copy from an FTP Server to Flash Memory Tasks

To copy a system image from an FTP server to a Flash memory file system, use the following commands in EXEC mode:

Step	Command	Purpose
1	See the instructions in the section "Copy Images from Flash Memory to a Network Server."	Makes a backup copy of the current software image or bootstrap image.
2	**configure terminal**	(Optional) Enters configuration mode from the terminal. This step is required only if you override the default remote username or password (see Steps 3 and 4).
3	**ip ftp username** *username*	(Optional) Changes the default remote username.
4	**ip ftp password** *password*	(Optional) Changes the default password.
5	**end**	(Optional) Exits configuration mode. This step is required only if you override the default remote username or password (see Steps 3 and 4).
6	**copy ftp:**[[[*//*[*username*[*:password*]*@*]*location*] */directory*]*/filename*] *flash-filesystem***:**[*filename*]	Using rcp, copies the configuration file from a network server to running memory or the startup configuration.
7		Replies to any router prompts for additional information or confirmation. The prompting will depend on how much information you provide in the **copy** command and the current setting of the **file prompt** command.

Copy from FTP Server to Flash Memory Example

The following example copies the file c7200-js-mz from the FTP server with a username of myuser and a password of mypass:

```
Router# copy ftp://myuser:mypass@theserver/tftpboot/ken/c7200-js-mz slot1:c7200-js-mz
Accessing ftp://theserver/tftpboot/ken/c7200-js-mz...Translating "theserver"...domain
server (192.168.2.132) [OK]

Loading c7200-js-mz from 192.168.2.132 (via Ethernet3/0):
!!!!!!!!!!!!!!!!!!!!!!!!!!!!!!!!!!!!!!!!!!!!!!!!!!!!!!!!!!!!!!!!!!!!!!!!!!!!!!!!!!!!
!!!!!!!!!!!!!!!!!!!!!!!!!!!!!!!!!!!!!!!!!!!!!!!!!!!!!!!!!!!!!!!!!!!!!!!!!!!!!!!!!!!!
!!!!!!!!!!!!!!!!!!!!!!!!!!!!!!!!!!!!!!!!!!!!!!!!!!!!!!!!!!!!!!!!!!!!!!!!!!!!!!!!!!!!
```

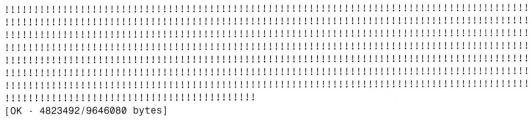

```
!!!!!!!!!!!!!!!!!!!!!!!!!!!!!!!!!!!!!!!!!!!!!!!!!!!!!!!!!!!!!!!!!!!!!!!!!!!!!!!!!!!!!!!!!!!!!
!!!!!!!!!!!!!!!!!!!!!!!!!!!!!!!!!!!!!!!!!!!!!!!!!!!!!!!!!!!!!!!!!!!!!!!!!!!!!!!!!!!!!!!!!!!!!
!!!!!!!!!!!!!!!!!!!!!!!!!!!!!!!!!!!!!!!!!!!!!!!!!!!!!!!!!!!!!!!!!!!!!!!!!!!!!!!!!!!!!!!!!!!!!
!!!!!!!!!!!!!!!!!!!!!!!!!!!!!!!!!!!!!!!!!!!!!!!!!!!!!!!!!!!!!!!!!!!!!!!!!!!!!!!!!!!!!!!!!!!!!
!!!!!!!!!!!!!!!!!!!!!!!!!!!!!!!!!!!!!!!!!!!!!!!!!!!!!!!!!!!!!!!!!!!!!!!!!!!!!!!!!!!!!!!!!!!!!
!!!!!!!!!!!!!!!!!!!!!!!!!!!!!!!!!!!!!!!!!!!!!!!!!!!!!!!!!!!!!!!!!!!!!!!!!!!!!!!!!!!!!!!!!!!!!
!!!!!!!!!!!!!!!!!!!!!!!!!!!!!!!!!!!!!!!!!!!!!!!!!!!!!!!!!!!!!!!!!!!!!!!!!!!!!!!!!!!!!!!!!!!!!
!!!!!!!!!!!!!!!!!!!!!!!!!!!!!!!!!!!!!!!!!!!!!!
[OK - 4823492/9646080 bytes]

4823492 bytes copied in 264.312 secs (18270 bytes/sec)
```

Verify the Image in Flash Memory

Before booting from Flash memory, verify that the checksum of the image in Flash memory matches the checksum listed in the README file that was distributed with the system software image by using the **verify** command. The checksum of the image in Flash memory is displayed at the bottom of the screen when you issue the **copy** command to copy an image. The README file was copied to the network server automatically when you installed the system software image on the server.

CAUTION	If the checksum value does not match the value in the README file, do not reboot the router. Instead, issue the **copy** command and compare the checksums again. If the checksum is repeatedly wrong, copy the original system software image back into Flash memory *before* you reboot the router from Flash memory. If you have a corrupted image in Flash memory and try to boot from Flash, the router will start the system image contained in ROM (assuming that booting from a network server is not configured). If ROM does not contain a fully functional system image, the router will not function and must be reconfigured through a direct console port connection.

The Flash memory content listing does not include the checksum of individual files. To recompute and verify the image checksum after an image is copied into Flash memory or a Flash memory device, use the following EXEC mode command:

Command	Purpose
verify *flash-filesystem***:**[*partition-number***:**][*filename*]	Recomputes and verifies the image checksum after the image is copied into Flash memory.

If you do not provide the filename in the command, the router prompts you. By default, it prompts for the last (most recent) file in Flash. Press **Return** to recompute the default file checksum, or enter the filename of a different file at the prompt. Note that the checksum for microcode images is always 0x0000.

The following example verifies the image c7200-js-mz in slot0:

```
Router# verify slot0:c7200-js-mz
Verified slot0:c7200-js-mz
```

Copy Images between Local Flash Memory Devices

On routers with multiple Flash memory file systems, you can copy images from one Flash memory file system, such as internal Flash memory or a Flash memory card in a PCMCIA slot, to another Flash memory file system, as shown in Figure 15-1. One reason to copy the image to a different flash device is to make a backup copy of it.

Figure 15-1 *Copying Images between Flash Memory File Systems*

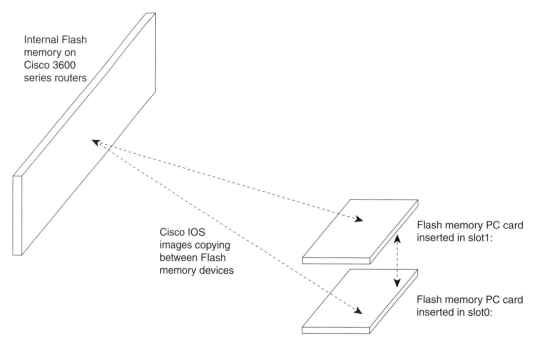

To copy an image between Flash memory file systems, use these commands in EXEC mode:

Step	Command	Purpose
1	**show** *flash-filesystem***:**	Displays the layout and contents of Flash memory.
2	**copy** *source-url destination-url*	Copies an image between Flash memory devices.
3	**verify** *flash-filesystem***:***filename*	Verifies the checksum of the image you copied.

NOTE   The source device and the destination device cannot be the same. For example, the command **copy slot1: slot1:** is invalid.

Copy a File between Local Flash Memory Devices Example

The following example copies the file admin/images/new-ios from partition 1 of internal Flash memory to slot 0:

```
Router# show flash: partition 1

System flash directory, partition 1:
File  Length    Name/status
  1   3142748 admin/images/new-ios
[3142812 bytes used, 1051492 available, 4194304 total]

Router# show slot0:

PCMCIA Slot0 flash directory
File  Length    Name/status
  1   1711088  /tftpboot/gate/c3600-i-mz
[1711152 bytes used, 2483152 available, 4194304 total]

Router# copy flash:1:admin/images/new-ios slot0:admin/images/new-ios
Verifying checksum for 'admin/images/new-ios' (file # 1)...  OK

Erase flash device before writing? [confirm]
Flash contains files. Are you sure you want to erase? [confirm]
Copy 'admin/images/new-ios' from flash: device
  as 'admin/images/new-ios' into slot0: device WITH erase? [yes/no] yes
Erasing device... eeeeeeeeeeeeeeeeeeeeeeeeeeeeeeeeee ...erased
!!!!!!!!!!!!!!!!!!!!!!!!!!!!!!!!!!!!!!!!!!!!!!!!!!!!!!!!!!!!!!!!!!!!!!!!!!!!!!!!!!!!!!!!!
!!!!!!!!!!!!!!!!!!!!!!!!!!!!!!!!!!!!!!!!!!!!!!!!!!!!!!!!!!!!!!!!!!!!!!!!!!!!!!!!!!!!!!!!!
!!!!!!!!!!!!!!!!!!!!!!!!!!!!!!!!!!!!!!!!!!!!!!!!!!!!!!!!!!!!!!!!!!!!!!!!!!!!!!!!!!!!!!!!!
!!!!!!!!!!!!!!!!!!!!!!!!!!!!!!!!!!!!!!!!!!!!!!!!!!!!!!!!!!!!!!!!!!!!!!!!!!!!!!!!!!!!!!!!!
!!!!!!!!!!!!!!!!!!!!!!!!!!!!!!!!!!!!!!!!!!!!!!!!!!!!!!!!!!!!!!!!!!!!!!!!!!!!!!!!!!!!!!!!!
!!!!!!!!!!!!!!!!!!!!!!!!!!!!!!!!!!!!!!!!!!!!!!!!!!!!!!!!!!!!!!!!!!!!!!!!!!!!!!!!!!!!!!!!!
!!!!!!!!!!!!!!!!!!!!!!!!!!!!!!!!!!!!!!!!!!!!!!!!!!!!!!!!!!!!!!!!!!!!!!!!!!!!!!!!!!!!!!!!!
!!!!!!!!!!!!!!!!!!!!!!!!!!!!!!!!!!!!!!!!!!!!!!!!!!!!!!!!!!!!!!!!!!!!!!!!!!!!!!!!!!!!!!!!!
!!!!!!!!!!!!!!!!!!!!!!!!!!!!!!!!!!!!!!!!!!!!!!!!!!!!!!!
 [OK - 3142748/4194304 bytes]

Flash device copy took 00:00:50 [hh:mm:ss]
Verifying checksum...  OK (0xB732)

Router# show slot0:

PCMCIA Slot0 flash directory
File  Length    Name/status
  1   3142748 admin/images/new-ios
[3142812 bytes used, 1051492 available, 4194304 total]
```

Specify the Startup System Image in the Configuration File

You can enter multiple boot commands in the startup configuration file or in the BOOT environment variable to provide backup methods for loading a system image onto the router. The following are three ways to load a system image:

- From Flash memory—Flash memory allows you to copy new system images without changing ROM. Information stored in Flash memory is not vulnerable to network failures that might occur when loading system images from servers.

- From a network server—In case Flash memory becomes corrupted, you can specify that a system image to be loaded from a network server using MOP, TFTP, rcp, or FTP as a backup boot method. For some platforms, you can specify a boot image to be loaded from a network server using TFTP, rcp, or FTP.

- From ROM—In case of both Flash memory corruption and network failure, specifying a system image to be loaded from ROM provides a final backup boot method. System images stored in ROM may not always be as current as those stored in Flash memory or on network servers.

NOTE   Some platforms, such as the Cisco 7000 family, cannot boot from ROM.

You can enter the different types of boot commands in any order in the startup configuration file or in the BOOT environment variable. If you enter multiple boot commands, the Cisco IOS software tries them in the order they are entered.

NOTE   Booting from ROM is faster than booting from Flash memory. However, booting from Flash memory is faster and more reliable than booting from a network server.

Load the System Image from Flash Memory

Use the following sections to configure your router to boot from Flash memory. Flash memory can reduce the effects of network failure by reducing dependency on files that can only be accessed over the network.

Flash Memory Configuration Process

To configure the router to load a system image in Flash memory, perform the following steps:

Step	Task
1	(Optional) Copy a system image or boot image to Flash memory using TFTP, rcp, and FTP. See the "Copy Images from a Network Server to Flash Memory" section at the beginning of this chapter for more information on performing this step.
2	Configure the system to automatically boot from the desired file and location in Flash memory or bootflash memory. See the "Configure the Router to Automatically Boot from an Image in Flash Memory" section.
3	(Optional) Depending on the current configuration register setting, you may need to change the configuration register value. See the "Configure the Router to Automatically Boot from an Image in Flash Memory" section for more information on modifying the configuration register.
4	(Optional) For some platforms, to change the location of the boot image, set the BOOTLDR environment variable.
5	Save your configurations.
6	Power-cycle and reboot your system to ensure that all is working as expected.

Configure the Router to Automatically Boot from an Image in Flash Memory

To configure a router to automatically boot from an image in Flash memory, use the following commands beginning in EXEC mode:

Step	Command	Purpose
1	**configure terminal**	Enters configuration mode from the terminal.
2	**boot system flash** [*flash-filesystem*:] [*partition-number*:] *filename*	Enters the filename of an image stored in Flash memory.
3	**config-register** *value*	Sets the configuration register to enable loading of the system image specified in the configuration file.
4	**end**	Exits configuration mode.
5	**copy system:running-config nvram:startup-config**	Saves the configuration file to your startup configuration.
6	**more nvram:startup-config**	(Optional) Verifies the contents of the startup configuration.
7	**reload**	Power-cycles and reboots the system to ensure that all works as expected.

For routers that are partitioned, if you do not specify a partition, the router boots from the first partition. If you do not specify a filename, the router boots from the first valid image found in the partition.

If you enter more than one image filename, the router tries them in the order entered.

To remove a filename from the configuration file, enter the **no boot system flash** command and specify the file location.

NOTE   The **no boot system** configuration command disables all **boot system** configuration commands regardless of argument. Specifying the **flash** keyword or the *filename* argument with the **no boot system** command disables only the commands specified by these arguments.

The following example shows how to configure the router to automatically boot from an image in Flash memory:

```
Router# configure terminal
Router(config)# boot system flash gsnew-image
Router(config)# config-register 0x010F
Router(config)# end
Router# copy system:running-config nvram:startup-config
[ok]
Router# reload
[confirm]

%SYS-5-RELOAD: Reload requested
System Bootstrap, Version 4.6(0.16), BETA SOFTWARE
Copyright (c) 1986-1995 by Cisco Systems
RP1 processor with 16384 Kbytes of memory
F3: 1871404+45476+167028 at 0x1000

Booting gsnew-image from flash memory RRRRRRRRRRRRRRRRRRRRRRRRRRRR
RRRRRRRRRRRRRRRRRRRRRRRRRRRRRRRRRRRRRRRRRRRRRRRRRRRRRRRRRRRRRRRR
RRRRRRRRRRRRRRRRRRRRRRRRRRRRRRRRRRRRRRRRRRRRRRRRRRRRRRRRRRRRRRRR
RRRRRRRRRRRRRRRRRRRRRRRRRRRRRRRRRRRRRRRRRRRRRRRRRRRRRRRRRRRRRRRR
RRRRRRRRRRRRRRRRRRRRRRRRRRRRRRRRRRRRRRRRRRRRRRRRRRRRRRRRRRRRRRRR
RRRRRRRRRRRRRRRRRRRRRRRRRRRRRRRRRRRRRRRRRRRRRR [OK - 1916912/13767448 bytes]
F3: 1871404+45476+167028 at 0x1000

            Restricted Rights Legend

Use, duplication, or disclosure by the Government is
subject to restrictions as set forth in subparagraph
(c) of the Commercial Computer Software - Restricted
Rights clause at FAR sec. 52.227-19 and subparagraph
(c) (1) (ii) of the Rights in Technical Data and Computer
Software clause at DFARS sec. 252.227-7013.

            Cisco Systems, Inc.
            170 West Tasman Drive
            San Jose, California 95134
```

```
GS Software (GS7), Version 10.2,
Copyright (c) 1986-1995 by Cisco Systems, Inc.
Compiled Thu 05-Nov-94 14:16 by mlw
```

Load the System Image from a Network Server

You can configure the Cisco IOS software to load a system image file from a network server using FTP, TFTP, rcp, or MOP.

If you do not boot from a network server using MOP and you do not specify either FTP, TFTP, or rcp, by default the system image that you specify is booted from a network server via TFTP.

NOTE	If you are using a Sun workstation as a network server and TFTP to transfer the file, set up the workstation to enable verification and generation of User Datagram Protocol (UDP) checksums. See the Sun documentation for details.

For increased performance and reliability, use rcp to boot a system image from a network server. The rcp implementation uses the Transmission Control Protocol (TCP), which ensures reliable delivery of data.

You cannot explicitly specify a remote username when you issue the **boot** command. Instead, the host name of the router is used. If the remote server has a directory structure, as do UNIX systems, and you boot the router from a network server using rcp, the Cisco IOS software searches for the system image on the server relative to the directory of the remote username.

You can also boot from a compressed image on a network server. One reason to use a compressed image is to ensure that there is enough memory available for storage. On routers that do not contain a run-from-ROM image in EPROM, when the router boots software from a network server, the image being booted and the running image both must fit into memory. If the running image is large, there might not be room in memory for the image being booted from the network server.

If there is not enough room in memory to boot a regular image from a network server, you can produce a compressed software image on any UNIX platform using the **compress** command. Refer to your UNIX platform's documentation for the exact usage of the **compress** command.

To specify the loading of a system image from a network server, use the following commands beginning in EXEC mode:

Step	Command	Purpose
1	**configure terminal**	Enters configuration mode from the terminal.
2	**boot system** [**rcp** | **tftp**] *filename* [*ip-address*] **boot system mop** *filename* [*mac-address*] [*interface*]	Specifies the system image file to be booted from a network server using rcp, TFTP, or MOP.
3	**config-register** *value*	Sets the configuration register to enable loading of the image specified in the configuration file.
4	**end**	Exits configuration mode.
5	**copy system:running-config nvram:startup-config**	Saves the configuration file to your startup configuration.

In the following example, a router uses rcp to boot from the testme5.tester system image file on a network server at IP address 172.16.0.1:

```
Router# configure terminal
Router(config)# boot system rcp testme5.tester 172.16.0.1
Router(config)# config-register 0x010F
Router(config)# end
Router# copy system:running-config nvram:startup-config
```

Load the System Image from ROM

To specify the use of the ROM system image as a backup to other boot instructions in the configuration file, use the following commands beginning in EXEC mode:

Step	Command	Purpose
1	**configure terminal**	Enters configuration mode from the terminal.
2	**boot system rom**	Specifies use of the ROM system image as a backup image.
3	**config-register** *value*	Sets the configuration register to enable loading of the system image specified in the configuration file.
4	**end**	Exits configuration mode.
5	**copy system:running-config nvram:startup-config**	Saves the configuration file to your startup configuration.

In the following example, a router is configured to boot from ROM:

```
Router# configure terminal
Router(config)# boot system rom
Router(config)# config-register 0x010F
Router(config)# end
Router# copy system:running-config nvram:startup-config
```

NOTE   The Cisco 7000 family products cannot load from ROM.

Use a Fault-Tolerant Booting Strategy

Occasionally network failures make booting from a network server impossible. To lessen the effects of network failure, consider the following booting strategy. After Flash is installed and configured, you might want to configure the router to boot in the following order:

1   Boot an image from Flash.

2   Boot an image from a network server.

3   Boot from ROM image.

This boot order provides the most fault-tolerant booting strategy. Use the following commands beginning in EXEC mode to allow the router to boot first from Flash, then from a system file from a network server, and finally from ROM:

Step	Command	Purpose
1	**configure terminal**	Enters configuration mode from the terminal.
2	**boot system flash** [*flash-filesystem***:**][*partition-number***:**] *filename*	Configures the router to boot from Flash memory.
3	**boot system** [**rcp** ǀ **tftp**] *filename* [*ip-address*]	Configures the router to boot from a network server.
4	**boot system rom**	Configures the router to boot from ROM.
5	**config-register** *value*	Sets the configuration register to enable loading of the system image specified in the configuration file.
6	**end**	Exits configuration mode.
7	**copy system:running-config nvram:startup-config**	Saves the configuration file to your startup configuration.

In the example, a router is configured to first boot an internal Flash image called *gsxx*. Should that image fail, the router will boot the configuration file *gsxx* from a network server. If that method should fail, then the system will boot from ROM.

```
Router# configure terminal
Router(config)# boot system flash gsxx
Router(config)# boot system gsxx 172.16.101.101
Router(config)# boot system rom
Router(config)# config-register 0x010F
Router(config)# end
Router# copy system:running-config nvram:startup-config
[ok]
```

Using this strategy, a router has three alternative sources from which to boot. These alternative sources help lessen the negative effects of a failure on network or file server.

Recovering a System Image Using Xmodem or Ymodem

If you do not have access to a network server and need to download a system image (to update it, or if all the system images in Flash memory somehow are damaged or erased), you can copy an image from a local or remote computer (such as a PC, UNIX workstation, or Macintosh) using the Xmodem or Ymodem protocols. This functionality primarily serves as a disaster recovery technique and is illustrated in Figure 15-2.

NOTE   Recovering system images using Xmodem or Ymodem is performed on the Cisco 1600 series and Cisco 3600 series routers only.

Xmodem and Ymodem are common protocols used for transferring files and are included in applications such as Windows 3.1 (TERMINAL.EXE), Windows 95 (HyperTerminal), Windows NT 3.5x (TERMINAL.EXE), Windows NT 4.0 (HyperTerminal), and Linux UNIX freeware (minicom).

Cisco 3600 series routers do not support XBOOT functionality, a disaster recovery technique for Cisco IOS software, and do not have a separate boot helper (rxboot) image.

Xmodem and Ymodem downloads are slow, so you should use them only when you do not have access to a network server. You can speed up the transfer by setting the transfer port speed to 115200 bps.

On the Cisco 3600 series, you can perform the file transfer using Cisco IOS software or, if all local system images are damaged or erased, the ROM monitor. When you use Cisco IOS software for an Xmodem or Ymodem file transfer, the transfer can occur on either the AUX port or the console port. The AUX port, which supports hardware flow control, is recommended. File transfers from the ROM monitor must use the console port.

On the Cisco 1600 series, you can only perform the file transfer from the ROM monitor over the console port.

Figure 15-2 *Copying a System Image to a Cisco 3600 Series Router with Xmodem /Ymodem*

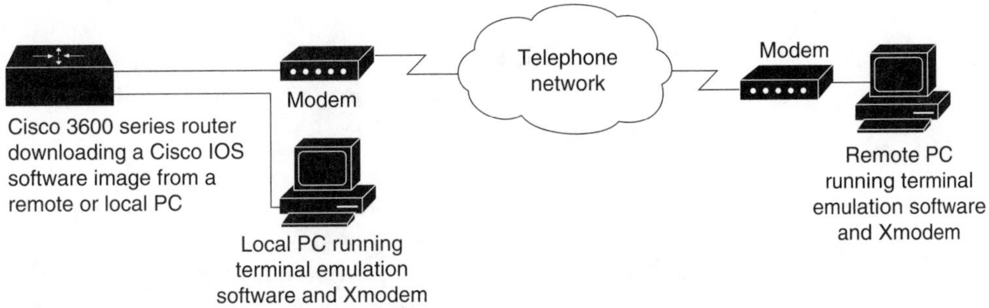

To copy a Cisco IOS image from a computer or workstation to a router using the Xmodem or Ymodem protocol, use one of the following commands:

Command	Purpose
copy xmodem: *flash-filesystem*:[*partition*:][*filename*] or **copy ymodem:** *flash-filesystem*:[*partition*:][*filename*]	For the Cisco 3600 only, copies a system image from a computer to Flash memory using Cisco IOS software in EXEC mode.
xmodem [**-y**] [**-c**] [**-e**] [**-f**] [**-r**] [**-x**] [**-s** *data-rate*][*filename*] (Cisco 1600 series only) **xmodem** [**-c** I **-y** I **-r** I **-x**] [*filename*] (Cisco 3600 series only) The **-c** option provides CRC-16 checksumming; **-y** uses the Ymodem protocol; **-e** erases the first partition in Flash memory; **-f** erases all of Flash memory; **-r** downloads the image to DRAM (the default is Flash memory); **-x** prevents the image from executing after download; and **-s** sets the console port data rate.	Copies a system image from a computer to Flash memory using the ROM monitor.

The computer from which you transfer the Cisco IOS image must be running terminal emulation software and the Xmodem or Ymodem protocol.

For the Cisco 1600 series, if you include the **-r** option (download to DRAM), your router must have enough DRAM to hold the file being transferred. To run from Flash memory, an image must be positioned as the first file in Flash memory. If you are copying a new image to boot from Flash memory, erase all existing files first.

Xmodem Transfer Example Using the Cisco IOS Software (Cisco 3600 series only)

This example shows a file transfer using Cisco IOS software and the Xmodem protocol. The Ymodem protocol follows a similar procedure, using the **copy ymodem:** command.

To transfer a Cisco IOS image from a computer running terminal emulation software and the Xmodem protocol, follow these steps:

Step 1   Place a Cisco IOS software image on the remote computer's hard drive. You can download an image from the Cisco Connection Online.

Step 2   To transfer from a remote computer, connect a modem to the AUX port of your Cisco 3600 series router and to the standard telephone network. The AUX port is set by default to a speed of 9600 bps, 2 stop bits, and no parity. The maximum speed is 115200 bps. Configure the router for both incoming and outgoing calls by entering the **modem inout** command.

Connect a modem to the remote computer and to the telephone network. The remote computer dials through the telephone network and connects to the router.

To transfer from a local computer, connect the router's AUX port to a serial port on the computer, using a null-modem cable. The AUX speed configured on the router must match the transfer speed configured on the local computer.

Step 3   At the EXEC prompt in the terminal emulator window of the computer, enter the **copy xmodem: flash:** command:

```
Router# copy xmodem: flash:
                    **** WARNING ****
x/ymodem is a slow transfer protocol limited to the current
speed
settings of the auxiliary/console ports. The use of the
auxiliary
port for this download is strongly recommended.
During the course of the download no exec input/output will be
available.
                ---- ******* ----
```

Press **Enter** to continue.

Step 4   Specify whether to use cyclic redundancy check (CRC) block checksumming, which verifies that your data has been correctly transferred from the computer to the router. If your computer does not support CRC block checksumming, answer **no** at the prompt:

```
Proceed? [confirm]
Use crc block checksumming? [confirm] no
```

Step 5   Determine how many times the software should try to receive a bad block of data before it declares the copy operation a failure. The default is 10 retries. A higher number may be needed for noisy telephone lines. You can configure an unlimited number of retries.

```
Max Retry Count [10]: 7
```

Step 6   Decide whether you want to check that the file is a valid Cisco 3600 series image:

```
Perform image validation checks? [confirm]
Xmodem download using simple checksumming with image
validation
Continue? [confirm]
```

After the transfer has begun, and if the image is valid, the software checks to see whether enough Flash memory space exists on the router to accommodate the transfer:

```
System flash directory:
File  Length    Name/status
  1   1738244   images/c3600-i-mz
[1738308 bytes used, 2455996 available, 4194304 total]
```

Step 7   Enter the destination filename:

```
Destination file name ? new-ios-image
```

Step 8   If you do not want the contents of internal Flash memory erased before the file transfer, enter **no**:

```
Erase flash device before writing? [confirm] no

Copy '' from server
  as 'new-ios-image' into Flash WITHOUT erase? [yes/no] yes
Ready to receive file..........
```

Step 9   Start an Xmodem or Ymodem send operation with the terminal emulation software on the computer that is sending the system image to the router. See your emulation software application's manual for instructions on how to execute a file transfer. Depending on the application you use, the emulation software may display the progress of the file transfer.

Xmodem Transfer Example Using the ROM Monitor

This example shows a file transfer using the ROM monitor and the Xmodem protocol. To transmit with the Ymodem protocol, use the **xmodem -y** command.

For the Cisco 3600, the router must have enough DRAM to hold the file being transferred, even if you are copying to Flash memory. The image is copied to the first file in internal Flash memory. Any existing files in Flash memory are erased. Copying files to Flash partitions or to the second-file position is not supported.

CAUTION   A modem connection from the telephone network to your console port introduces security issues that you should consider before enabling the connection. For example, remote users can dial into your modem and access the router's configuration settings.

Step 1   Place a Cisco IOS software image on the remote computer's hard drive. You can download an image from Cisco Connection Online or from the Feature Pack (Cisco 1600 series only).

Step 2   To transfer from a remote computer, connect a modem to the console port of your router and to the standard telephone network. The modem and console port must communicate at the same speed, which can be from 9600 to 115200 bps (Cisco 3600 series) or from 1200 to 115200 bps (Cisco 1600 series), depending on the speed supported by your modem. Use the **confreg** ROM monitor command to configure the console port transmission speed for the router. For the Cisco 1600 series, you can also set the transmission speed with the **-s** option.

Connect a modem to the remote computer and to the telephone network. The remote computer dials through the telephone network and connects to the router.

To transfer from a local computer, connect the router's console port to a serial port on the computer, using a null-modem cable. The console port speed configured on the router must match the transfer speed configured on the local computer.

NOTE   If you are transferring from a local computer, you may need to configure the terminal emulation program to ignore RTS/DTR signals.

Step 3   You should see a ROM monitor prompt in the terminal emulation window:

```
rommon >
```

Enter the **xmodem** ROM monitor command, along with any desired copy options and, optionally, the filename of the Cisco IOS image. The image loads into Flash memory by default; to download to DRAM instead, use the **-r** option. The image is normally executed on completion of the file transfer; to prevent execution, use the **-x** option. The **-c** option specifies CRC-16 checksumming, which is more sophisticated and thorough than standard checksumming, if it is supported by the computer:

```
rommon > xmodem -c new-ios-image
Do not start the sending program yet...
        File size            Checksum    File name
   1738244 bytes (0x1a8604)    0xdd25 george-admin/c3600-i-mz

WARNING: All existing data in flash will be lost!
Invoke this application only for disaster recovery.
Do you wish to continue? y/n  [n]: yes
Ready to receive file new-ios-image ...
```

Step 4   Start an Xmodem send operation, which is initiated from the terminal emulation software on the remote computer that is sending the system image to the router. See your emulation software application's manual for instructions on how to execute a Xmodem file transfer.

Step 5   The Cisco IOS image is transferred and executed. If you are transferring from a remote computer, the computer maintains control of your console port even after the new Cisco IOS image is running. To release control to a local terminal, reconfigure the speed of the router's console port to match the speed of the local terminal by entering the **speed** *bps* configuration command from the remote computer at the router prompt:

```
Router# configure terminal
Router(config)# line 0
Router(config-line)# speed 9600
```

The remote connection is broken, and you can disconnect the modem from the console port and reconnect the terminal line.

Load and Display Microcode Images

On the Cisco 7000 series with RSP7000 and Cisco 7500 series, you can also load and display microcode images, as described in the following sections:

- Understand Microcode Images

- Specify the Location of the Microcode Images

- Reload the Microcode Image

- Display Microcode Image Information

Understand Microcode Images

Microcode images contain microcode which runs on various hardware devices. By default, the system loads the microcode bundled with the system software. However, you can configure the router to use microcode stored in Flash.

Cisco 7000 series with a RSP7000 and Cisco 7500 series each have a writable control store (WCS) that stores microcode. You can load updated microcode onto the WCS from bootflash or a Flash memory card inserted in one of the PCMCIA slots of the RSP card.

You can update microcode without having physical access to the router by using the **copy** command to copy microcode to a Flash file system.

Specify the Location of the Microcode Images

By default, the system loads the microcode bundled with the system software. However, you can configure the router to load different microcode.

To specify the location of the microcode to use, use the following commands beginning in EXEC mode:

Step	Command	Purpose
1	**copy tftp: flash:** or **copy tftp:** *file-id*	(Optional) Copies microcode files into Flash. You only need to if you are loading the microcode from Flash. See the section "Copy Images from a Network Server to Flash Memory" for more information about how to copy images to Flash memory.

Step	Command	Purpose
2	**configure terminal**	Enters configuration mode.
3	**microcode** *interface* [*flash-filesystem*:*filename* [*slot*] | **system** [*slot*]]	Configures the router to load microcode into the WCS from Flash memory or the system image. By default, the microcode bundled with the system image is loaded.
4	**end**	Exits configuration mode.
5	**copy system:running-config nvram:startup-config**	Retains new configuration information when the system is rebooted.

If an error occurs when you are attempting to download microcode, the system loads the default system microcode image, which is bundled with the system software.

NOTE   Microcode images cannot be compressed.

Reload the Microcode Image

The configuration commands specifying the microcode are implemented following one of three events:

- The system is booted.

- A card is inserted or removed.

- The configuration command **microcode reload** is issued.

After you have entered a microcode configuration command and one of these events has taken place, all cards are reset, loaded with microcode from the appropriate sources, tested, and enabled for operation.

To signal to the system that all microcode configuration commands have been entered and the processor cards should be reloaded, use the following global configuration mode command:

Command	Purpose
microcode reload	Notifies the system that all microcode configuration commands have been entered and the processor cards should be reloaded.

Immediately after you enter the **microcode reload** command and press **Return**, the system reloads all microcode. Global configuration mode remains enabled. After the reload is complete, enter the **exit** command to return to the EXEC prompt.

If Flash memory is busy because a card is being removed or inserted, or a **microcode reload** command is executed while Flash is locked, the files will not be available and the onboard ROM microcode will be loaded. Issue another **microcode reload** command when Flash memory is available, and the proper microcode will be loaded. The **show flash** command will show if another user or process has locked Flash memory.

NOTE   The **microcode reload** command should not be used while Flash is in use. For example, do not use this command when a **copy** {**ftp:** | **rcp:** | **tftp:**} *flash-filesystem* or **show** *flash-filesystem*: command is active.

The **microcode reload** command is automatically added to your running configuration when you issue a microcode command that changes the system's default behavior of loading all processors from ROM.

In the following example, all controllers are reset, the specified microcode is loaded, and the CxBus complex is reinitialized according to the microcode configuration commands that have been written to memory:

```
Router# configure terminal
Router(config)# microcode reload
Router(config)# end
```

Display Microcode Image Information

To display microcode information, use the following command in EXEC mode:

Command	Purpose
show microcode	Displays microcode information.

Load Cisco IOS Images on the Cisco 12000 GSR

Loading a Cisco IOS image on the GRP on a Cisco 12000 series router is the same as loading images on Cisco 7500 series routers. In addition to the Cisco IOS image that resides on the GRP, each line card on the Cisco 12000 series has a Cisco IOS image. When the router is reloaded, the specified Cisco IOS image is loaded onto the GRP, and that image is automatically dowloaded to all the line cards.

Normally, you want the same Cisco IOS image on the GRP and all line cards. However, if you want to upgrade a line card with a new version of microcode for testing or to fix a defect, you might need to load a Cisco IOS image that is different from the one on the line card. Additionally, you might need to load a new image on the line card to work around a problem that is affecting only one of the line cards.

On the Cisco 12000 series GSR you load the microcode image as described in the following sections:

- Load Image on a Line Card
- Set the LED Message on a Line Card

Load Image on a Line Card

To load a Cisco IOS image on a line card, first use the **copy tftp** command to download the Cisco IOS image to a slot on one of the PCMCIA Flash cards. After you have downloaded the Cisco IOS image on the Flash card, use the following commands beginning in global configuration mode:

Step	Command	Purpose
1	**microcode** {**oc12-atm** | **oc12-pos** | **oc3-pos-4**} **flash** *file_id slot-number*	Specifies the type of line card, location of the Cisco IOS image, and the slot of the line card to download the image. If the slot number is omitted, the image is downloaded to all line cards.
2	**microcode reload** *slot-number*	Reloads the image on the specified line card.
3	**exit**	Exits configuration mode.
4	**execute-on slot** *slot-number* **show version** or **attach** *slot-number* **show version** **exit**	Connects to the line card and verifies that the new Cisco IOS image is on the line card by checking the version number in the display output.

Set the LED Message on a Line Card

You can specify the message that is displayed on the LED on the front panel of one or more line cards. You can also remove the user-specified message that is displayed on the LED on the front panel of one or more line cards and revert to the normal status message for the line card.

To set or clear the LED message, use one of the following commands in privileged EXEC mode:

Command	Purpose
set card-message {**all** | **slot** *number*} [**expire** *seconds*] [**blink** *seconds*] *message* or **clear card-message** {**all** | **slot** *number*}	Sets the message displayed on the LED on the front panel of one or more line cards. Clears the user-specified message that is displayed on the LED on the front panel of one or more line cards and reverts to the normal status message for the line card.

## CHAPTER 16

System Image and Microcode Commands

This chapter provides detailed descriptions of the commands used to load and copy system images and microcode images. System images contain the system software. Microcode images contain microcode to be downloaded to various hardware devices.

For configuration information and examples, refer to Chapter 15, "Loading and Maintaining System Images and Microcode."

Flash Memory File System Types

Cisco platforms use one of three different Flash memory file system types. Some commands are supported on only one or two file system types. This chapter notes commands that are not supported on all file system types.

Refer to Table 16-1 to determine which Flash memory file system type your platform uses.

Table 16-1 *Flash Memory File System Types*

Type	Platforms
Class A	Cisco 7000 family, C12000, LS1010
Class B	Cisco 1003, Cisco 1004, Cisco 1005, Cisco 2500 series, Cisco 3600 series, Cisco 4000 series, Cisco AS5200
Class C	Cisco MC3810, disk0 of SC3640

Replaced Commands

Commands in this chapter that have been replaced by new commands continue to perform their normal functions in the current release but are no longer documented. Support for these commands will cease in a future release.

Table 16-2 maps the old commands with their replacements.

Table 16-2 *Mapping Old Commands to New Commands*

Old Command	New Command
copy erase flash	**erase flash:** or **erase flash** (Class B Flash file systems only)
	format (Class A and C Flash file systems only)
copy verify	**verify**
copy xmodem	**copy xmodem:** or **copy xmodem**
copy ymodem	**copy ymodem:** or **copy ymodem**
copy verify bootflash	**verify bootflash:** or **verify bootflash**
copy verify flash	**verify flash:** or **verify flash**
show flh-log	**more flh: logfile**
verify bootflash	**verify bootflash:** or **verify bootflash**
verify flash	**verify flash:** or **verify flash**

clear card-message

To remove the user-specified message that is displayed on the LED on the front panel of one or more line cards and revert to the normal status message for the line card, use the **clear card-message** privileged EXEC command.

> **clear card-message** {**all** | **slot** *slot-number*}

Syntax	Description
all	Clears the user-specified LED message on all line cards.
slot *slot-number*	Clears the user-specified LED message on a specific line card. Slot numbers range from 0 to 11 for the Cisco 12012 and 0 to 7 for the Cisco 12008.

Command Mode

Privileged EXEC

Usage Guidelines

This command was added in Cisco IOS Release 11.2 GS to support the Cisco 12000 series Gigabit Switch Routers.

To specify the message that is displayed on the LED on the front panel of one or more line cards, use the **set card-message** global configuration command.

Example

The following example clears any user-specified message from all line cards.

```
clear card-message all
```

Related Commands

To locate documentation of related commands, you can search online at www.cisco.com.

set card-message

copy erase flash

The **erase flash:** or **erase flash** command replaces the **copy erase flash** command. Refer to the description of the **erase** command for further details.

copy verify

The **verify** command replaces the **copy verify** command. Refer to the description of the **verify** command for further information.

copy verify bootflash

The **verify bootflash**: or the **verify bootflash** command replaces the **copy verify bootflash** command. Refer to the description of the **verify** command for further information.

copy verify flash

The **verify flash:** or the **verify flash** command replaces the **copy verify flash** command. Refer to the description of the **verify** command for further information.

copy xmodem:

The **copy xmodem:** and **copy xmodem** commands are identical. Refer to the description of the **copy** command for more information.

To copy a Cisco IOS image from a local or remote computer (such as a PC, Macintosh, or UNIX workstation) to Flash memory on a Cisco 3600 series router using the Xmodem protocol, use the **copy xmodem:** EXEC command.

> **copy xmodem:** *flash-filesystem***:**

Syntax	Description
flash-filesystem:	Destination of the copied file.

Command Mode
EXEC

Usage Guidelines
This command first appeared in Cisco IOS Release 11.2 P.

Copying a file using FTP, rcp, or TFTP is much faster than copying a file using Xmodem. Use the **copy xmodem:** command only if you do not have access to an FTP, TFTP, or rcp server.

This copy operation is performed through the console or AUX port. The AUX port, which supports hardware flow control, is recommended.

No output is displayed on the port over which the transfer is occurring. You can use the **logging buffered** command to log all router messages sent to the console port during the file transfer.

Example
The following example initiates a file transfer from a local or remote computer to the router's internal Flash memory using the Xmodem protocol:

```
copy xmodem: flash:
```

Related Commands
To locate documentation of related commands, you can search online at www.cisco.com.

copy
copy ymodem:
xmodem

copy ymodem:

The **copy ymodem:** and **copy ymodem** commands are identical. Refer to the description of the **copy** command for more information.

To copy a Cisco IOS image from a local or remote computer (such as a PC, Macintosh, or UNIX workstation) to Flash memory on a Cisco 3600 series router using the Ymodem protocol, use the **copy ymodem:** EXEC command.

copy ymodem: *flash-filesystem*:

Syntax	Description
flash-filesystem:	Destination of the copied file.

Command Mode
EXEC

Usage Guidelines
This command first appeared in Cisco IOS Release 11.2 P.

Copying a file using FTP, rcp, or TFTP is much faster than copying a file using Ymodem. Use the **copy ymodem:** command only if you do not have access to an FTP, TFTP, or rcp server.

This copy operation is performed through the console or AUX port. The AUX port, which supports hardware flow control, is recommended.

No output is displayed on the port over which the transfer is occurring. You can use the **logging buffered** command to log all router messages sent to the console port during the file transfer.

Example
The following example initiates a file transfer from a local or remote computer to the router's internal Flash memory using the Ymodem protocol:

```
copy ymodem: flash:
```

Related Commands
To locate documentation of related commands, you can search online at www.cisco.com.

copy xmodem:

erase flash:

The **erase flash:** and **erase flash** commands are identical. Refer to the **erase** command for further details.

execute-on

To execute commands remotely on a line card, use the **execute-on slot** privileged EXEC command.

execute-on {**slot** *slot-number* | **all**} *command*

Syntax

Description

slot *slot-number*
Executes the command on the line card in the specified slot. Slot numbers range from 0 to 11 on the Cisco 12012 and 0 to 7 on the Cisco 12008.

all
Executes the command on all line cards.

command
Cisco IOS command to execute on the line card.

Command Mode

Privileged EXEC

Usage Guidelines

This command was added in Cisco IOS Release 11.2 GS to support the Cisco 12000 series Gigabit Switch Routers.

Use this command to execute a command on one or all line cards to monitor and maintain information on one or more line cards.

You can use the **execute-on** privileged EXEC command only from Cisco IOS software running on the GRP card.

NOTE   In Cisco IOS Release 11.2(9)GS, the **execute-on** command does not work properly on commands that require input, the "more" autopaging mechanism does not function, and the line card help is not available.

NOTE   Because not all statistics are maintained on the line cards, the output from some of the **show** commands might not be consistent.

You can also use the **attach** privileged EXEC command, but using the **execute-on slot** command saves you some steps. For example, first you must use the **attach** command to connect you to the Cisco IOS software running on the line card, next you must issue the command, and finally you must disconnect from the line card to return to the Cisco IOS software running on the GRP card. With the **execute-on slot** command, you can perform three steps with one command.

In addition, the **execute-on all** command allows you to perform the same command on all line cards.

Example

The following example executes the **show controllers** command on the line card in slot 4:

```
Router# execute-on slot 4 show controllers
========= Line Card (Slot 4) =======

Interface POS0
Hardware is BFLC POS
lcpos_instance struct   6033A6E0
RX POS ASIC addr space  12000000
TX POS ASIC addr space  12000100
SUNI framer addr space  12000400
SUNI rsop intr status   00
CRC16 enabled, HDLC enc, int clock
no loop

Interface POS1
Hardware is BFLC POS
lcpos_instance struct   6033CEC0
RX POS ASIC addr space  12000000
TX POS ASIC addr space  12000100
SUNI framer addr space  12000600
SUNI rsop intr status   00
CRC32 enabled, HDLC enc, int clock
no loop

Interface POS2
Hardware is BFLC POS
lcpos_instance struct   6033F6A0
RX POS ASIC addr space  12000000
TX POS ASIC addr space  12000100
SUNI framer addr space  12000800
SUNI rsop intr status   00
CRC32 enabled, HDLC enc, int clock
no loop

Interface POS3
Hardware is BFLC POS
lcpos_instance struct   60341E80
RX POS ASIC addr space  12000000
TX POS ASIC addr space  12000100
SUNI framer addr space  12000A00
SUNI rsop intr status   00
CRC32 enabled, HDLC enc, ext clock
no loop
Router#
```

Related Commands

To locate documentation of related commands, you can search online at www.cisco.com.

atm sonet

format

The **format** command replaces the **copy erase flash** command. See the description of the **format** command for further information.

microcode

To specify the location of the microcode that you want to download from Flash memory into the writable control store (WCS) on a Cisco 7000 series with RSP7000 or Cisco 7500 series, use the **microcode** global configuration command. Use the **no** form of this command to load the microcode bundled with the system image.

> **microcode** *interface* [*flash-filesystem*:*filename* [*slot*] | **system** [*slot*]]
> **no microcode** *interface* [*flash-filesystem*:*filename* [*slot*] | **system** [*slot*]]

Syntax	Description
interface	One of the following interface processor names: **aip**, **cip**, **eip**, **feip**, **fip**, **fsip**, **hip**, **mip**, **sip**, **sp**, **ssp**, **trip**, **vip**, or **vip2**.
flash-filesystem:	(Optional) Flash file system. The colon is required. Valid file systems include bootflash, slot0, and slot1. Slave devices such as slaveslot0 are invalid. The slave's file system is not available during microcode reloads.
filename	(Optional) Name of the microcode file.
slot	(Optional) Number of the slot. Range is 0 to 15.
system	(Optional) If **system** is specified, the router loads the microcode from the microcode bundled into the system image you are running for that interface type.

Default

The default is to load from the microcode bundled in the system image.

Command Mode

Global configuration

Usage Guidelines

This command first appeared in Cisco IOS Release 11.0.

When using HSA for simple hardware backup, ensure that the master and slave RSP card contain the same microcode image in the same location when the router is to load the interface processor microcode from a Flash file system. Thus, if the slave RSP becomes the master, it will be able to find the microcode image and download it to the interface processor.

Example

In the following example, all FIP cards will be loaded with the microcode found in Flash memory file fip.v141-7 when the system is booted, when a card is inserted or removed, or when the **microcode reload** global configuration command is issued. The configuration is then written to the startup configuration file.

```
Router(config)# microcode fip slot0:fip.v141-7
Router(config)# end
Router# copy system:running-config nvram:startup-config
```

Related Commands

To locate documentation of related commands, you can search online at www.cisco.com.

more flh:logfile

microcode (Cisco IOS image)

To load a Cisco IOS software image on a line card from Flash memory or the GRP card on a Cisco 12000 series Gigabit Switch Router, use the **microcode** global configuration command. To load the microcode bundled with the GRP system image, use the **no** form of this command.

> **microcode** *interface* {**flash** *file-id* [*slot*] | **system** [*slot*]}
> **no microcode** *interface* [**flash** *file-id* [*slot*] | **system** [*slot*]]

Syntax	Description
interface	One of the following interface names: **oc12-atm**, **oc12-pos**, or **oc3-pos-4**.
flash	Loads the image from the Flash file system.

Syntax	Description
file-id	Specifies the device and filename of the image file to download. A colon (:) must separate the device and filename (for example, slot0:gsr-p-mz). Valid devices are as follows: • **bootflash**—Internal Flash memory. • **slot0**—First PCMCIA slot. • **slot1**—Second PCMCIA slot.
slot	(Optional) Slot number of the line card that you want to copy the software image to. Slot numbers range from 0 to 11 for the Cisco 12012 and 0 to 7 for the Cisco 12008. If you do not specify a slot number, the Cisco IOS software image is downloaded on all line cards.
system	Loads the image from the software image on the GRP card.

Default

The default is to load the image from the GRP card.

Command Mode

Global configuration

Usage Guidelines

This command first appeared in Cisco IOS Release 10.3. This command was modified in Cisco IOS Release 11.2 GS to load the Cisco IOS software image onto a line card in the Cisco 12000 series Gigabit Switch Routers.

You must be in configuration mode to enter this command. Immediately after you enter the **microcode reload** command and press **Return**, the system reloads all microcode. Global configuration mode remains enabled. After the reloading is complete, enter the **exit** command to return to the EXEC system prompt.

In addition to the Cisco IOS image that resides on the GRP card, each line card on a Cisco 12000 series has a Cisco IOS image. When the router is reloaded, the specified image is loaded onto the GRP card and then automatically downloaded to all the line cards.

Normally, you want the same Cisco IOS image on the GRP card and all line cards. However, if you want to upgrade a line card with a new version of microcode for testing or to fix a defect, you might need to load a Cisco IOS image that is different from the one on the line card. Additionally, you might need to load a new image on the line card to work around a problem that is affecting only one of the line cards.

To load a Cisco IOS image on a line card, first use the **copy tftp** command to download the Cisco IOS image to a slot on one of the PCMCIA Flash memory cards. Then use the **microcode** command to download the image to the line card followed by the **microcode reload** command to start the image. To verify that the correct image is running on the line card, use the **execute-on slot** *slot* **show version** command.

Example

In the following example, the Cisco IOS software image in slot 0: is downloaded to the line card in slot 10. This software image is used when the system is booted, a line card is inserted or removed, or the **microcode reload** global configuration command is issued.

To verify that the correct version is loaded, use the **execute-on slot 10 show version** command.

```
Router(config)# microcode oc3-POS-4 flash slot0:fip.v141-7 10
Router(config)# microcode reload 10
Router(config)# exit
Router#
```

Related Commands

To locate documentation of related commands, you can search online at www.cisco.com.

microcode reload

microcode reload

To reload the Cisco IOS image on a line card on the Cisco 7000 series with RSP7000, Cisco 7500 series, or Cisco 12000 series routers after all microcode configuration commands have been entered, use the **microcode reload** global configuration command.

> **microcode reload** [*slot-number*]

Syntax	Description
slot-number	(Optional) Slot number of the line card that you want to reload the Cisco IOS software image on. Slot numbers range from 0 to 11 for the Cisco 12012 and 0 to 7 for the Cisco 12008. If you do not specify a slot number, the Cisco IOS software image is reloaded on all line cards.

Command Mode

Global configuration

Usage Guidelines

This command was modified in Cisco IOS Release 11.2 GS to add the *slot-number* option.

In addition to the Cisco IOS image that resides on the GRP card, each line card on Cisco 12000 series routers has a Cisco IOS image. When the router is reloaded, the specified Cisco IOS image is loaded onto the GRP card and automatically downloaded to all the line cards.

Normally, you want the same Cisco IOS image on the GRP card and all line cards. However, if you want to upgrade a line card with a new version of microcode for testing or to fix a defect, you might need to load a different Cisco IOS image. Additionally, you might need to load a new image on the line card to work around a problem affecting only one of the line cards.

To load a Cisco IOS image on a line card, first use the **copy tftp** command to download the Cisco IOS image to a slot on one of the PCMCIA Flash memory cards. Then use the **microcode** command to download the image to the line card, followed by the **microcode reload** command to start the image. To verify that the correct image is running on the line card, use the **execute-on slot** *slot* **show version** command.

Example

In the following example, the Cisco IOS software is reloaded on the line card in slot 10:

```
Router(config)# microcode reload 10
Router(config)# end
Router#
```

Related Commands

To locate documentation of related commands, you can search online at www.cisco.com.

microcode (Cisco IOS image)
microcode query

more flh:logfile

To view the system console output generated during the Flash load helper operation, use the **more flh:logfile** privileged EXEC command.

more flh:logfile

Syntax Description

This command has no arguments or keywords.

Command Mode

Privileged EXEC

Usage Guidelines

This command first appeared in Cisco IOS Release 11.3 AA.

If you are a remote Telnet user performing the Flash upgrade without a console connection, this command allows you to retrieve console output when your Telnet connection has terminated due to the switch to the ROM image. The output indicates what happened during the download and is particularly useful if the download fails.

This command is a form of the **more** command. Refer to the **more** command for details.

Sample Display

The following is sample output from the **more flh:logfile** command:

```
Router# more flh:logfile

%FLH: abc/igs-kf.914 from 172.16.1.111 to flash...

System flash directory:
File  Length   Name/status
  1   2251320  abc/igs-kf.914

[2251384 bytes used, 1942920 available, 4194304 total]
Accessing file 'abc/igs-kf.914' on 172.16.1.111...
Loading from 172.16.13.111:

Erasing device...... erased
Loading from 172.16.13.111:
- [OK -
2251320/4194304 bytes]

Verifying checksum... OK (0x97FA)
Flash copy took 79292 msecs
%FLH: Re-booting system after download
Loading abc/igs-kf.914 at 0x3000040, size = 2251320 bytes [OK]

F3: 2183364+67924+259584 at 0x3000060


            Restricted Rights Legend

Use, duplication, or disclosure by the Government is
subject to restrictions as set forth in subparagraph
(c) of the Commercial Computer Software - Restricted
Rights clause at FAR sec. 52.227-19 and subparagraph
(c) (1) (ii) of the Rights in Technical Data and Computer
Software clause at DFARS sec. 252.227-7013.
```

```
                    Cisco Systems, Inc.
                    170 West Tasman Drive
                    San Jose, California 95134

Cisco Internetwork Operating System Software
Cisco IOS (tm) GS Software (GS7), Version 11.0
Copyright (c) 1986-1995 by Cisco Systems, Inc.
Compiled Tue 06-Dec-94 14:01 by smith
Image text-base: 0x00001000, data-base: 0x005A9C94

Cisco 2500 (68030) processor (revision 0x00) with 4092K/2048K bytes of
memory.
Processor board serial number 00000000
DDN X.25 software, Version 2.0, NET2 and BFE compliant.
ISDN software, Version 1.0.
Bridging software.
Enterprise software set supported. (0x0)
1 Ethernet/IEEE 802.3 interface.
2 Serial network interfaces.
 --More--

1 ISDN Basic Rate interface.
32K bytes of non-volatile configuration memory.

4096K bytes of processor board System flash (Read ONLY)
```

Related Commands

To locate documentation of related commands, you can search online at www.cisco.com.

more

set card-message

To specify the message that is displayed on the LED on the front panel of one or more line cards, use the **set card-message** privileged EXEC command. To remove the message, use the **clear card-message** global command.

> **set card-message** {**all** | **slot** *slot-number*} [**expire** *seconds*] [**blink** *seconds*] *message*

Syntax	Description
all	Specifies that the LED message is set on all line cards.
slot *slot-number*	Specifies that the LED message is set on a specific line card. Slot numbers range from 0 to 11 for the Cisco 12012 and 0 to 7 for the Cisco 12008.

Syntax	Description
expire *seconds*	(Optional) Specifies how long the message is displayed on the front panel LED. The range is 0 to 31536000 seconds. When you select 0, the message remains on the LED until you clear it by using the **clear card-message** command. When the time expires, the user-specified message is removed, and the LED displays the status message based on the line card's last state.
blink *seconds*	(Optional) Specifies how often the message blinks in seconds. The range is 1 to 10 seconds. If blink is not specified, the message does not blink.
message	Specifies the text to display on the LED on the front panel of one or more line cards. The message can be up to eight alphanumeric characters (four characters per line).

Default

System LED message is displayed.

Command Mode

Privileged EXEC

Usage Guidelines

This command was added in Cisco IOS Release 11.2 GS to support the Cisco 12000 series Gigabit Switch Routers.

The user-specified message is also displayed in the **show diag** command output.

To revert to the normal status message for the line card, use the **clear card-message** global configuration command.

Example

The following example sets the message USER MSG to display on the LED on line card 3. This message blinks every two seconds.

```
Router# set card-message slot 3 blink 2 USER MSG
```

Related Commands

To locate documentation of related commands, you can search online at www.cisco.com.

clear card-message
show diag

show flh-log

The **more flh:logfile** command replaces the **show flh-log** command. Refer to the **more flh:logfile** command for more information.

show microcode

To show the microcode bundled into a Cisco 7000 series with RSP7000 or Cisco 7500 series system, use the **show microcode** EXEC command.

> **show microcode**

Syntax Description

This command has no arguments or keywords.

Command Mode

EXEC

Usage Guidelines

This command first appeared in Cisco IOS Release 10.0.

Sample Display

The following is sample output from the **show microcode** command:

```
Router# show microcode

Microcode bundled in system

Card    Microcode    Target Hardware    Description
Type    Version      Version
----    ---------    ---------------    -----------
SP      2.3              11.x           SP version 2.3
EIP     1.1              1.x            EIP version 1.1
TRIP    1.2              1.x            TRIP version 1.2
```

```
FIP        1.4           2.x        FIP version 1.4
HIP        1.1           1.x        HIP version 1.1
SIP        1.1           1.x        SIP version 1.1
FSIP       1.1           1.x        FSIP version 1.1
```

verify bootflash:

Either of the identical **verify bootflash:** or **verify bootflash** commands replaces the **copy verify bootflash** command. Refer to the **verify** command for more information.

verify flash:

Either of the identical **verify flash:** or **verify flash** commands replaces the **copy verify flash** command. Refer to the **verify** command for more information.

xmodem

To copy a Cisco IOS image to a Cisco 1600 series or Cisco 3600 series router using the ROM monitor and the Xmodem or Ymodem protocol, use the **xmodem** ROM monitor command.

xmodem [**-c**] [**-y**] [**-e**] [**-f**] [**-r**] [**-x**] [**-s** *data-rate*] [*filename*]

Syntax	Description
-c	(Optional) CRC-16 checksumming, which is more sophisticated and thorough than standard checksumming.
-y	(Optional) Uses Ymodem protocol for higher throughput.
-e	(Optional) Erases the first partition in Flash memory before starting the download. This option is only valid for the Cisco 1600.
-f	(Optional) Erases all of Flash memory before starting the download. This option is only valid for the Cisco 1600.
-r	(Optional) Downloads the file to DRAM. The default is Flash memory.
-x	(Optional) Do not execute Cisco IOS image on completion of the download.
-s *data-rate*	(Optional) Sets the console port's data rate during file transfer. Values are 1200, 2400, 4800, 9600, 19200, 38400, and 115200 bps. The default rate is specified in the configuration register. This option is only valid for the Cisco 1600 series.
filename	(Optional) Filename to copy. This argument is ignored when **-r** is specified, because only one file can be copied to DRAM. On the Cisco 1600 series, files are loaded to the ROM for execution.

Default

Xmodem protocol with 8-bit CRC, file downloaded into Flash memory and executed on completion.

Command Mode

ROM monitor

Usage Guidelines

This command first appeared in Cisco IOS Release 11.2 P.

The Cisco 3600 series does not support XBOOT functionality. If your Cisco IOS image is erased or damaged, you cannot load a new image over the network.

Use the **xmodem** ROM monitor command to download a new system image to your router from a local personal computer (such as a PC, Mac, or UNIX workstation), or a remote computer over a modem connection, to the router's console port. The computer must have a terminal emulation application that supports these protocols.

For the Cisco 3600 series, your router must have enough DRAM to hold the file being transferred, even if you are copying to Flash memory. The image is copied to the first file in internal Flash memory. Any existing files in Flash memory are erased. There is no support for partitions or copying as a second file.

For the Cisco 1600 series, if you include the **-r** option, your router must have enough DRAM to hold the file being transferred. To run from Flash, an image must be positioned as the first file in Flash memory. If you are copying a new image to boot from Flash, erase all existing files first.

CAUTION A modem connection from the telephone network to your console port introduces security issues that you should consider before enabling the connection. For example, remote users can dial into your modem and access the router's configuration settings.

NOTE If the file to be downloaded is not a valid router image, the copy operation is automatically terminated.

Example

The following example uses the **xmodem -c** *filename* ROM monitor command to copy the file new-ios-image from a remote or local computer:

```
rommon > xmodem -c new-ios-image
Do not start the sending program yet...
```

```
       File size         Checksum   File name
 1738244 bytes (0x1a8604)   0xdd25 george-admin/c3600-i-mz

WARNING: All existing data in bootflash will be lost!
Invoke this application only for disaster recovery.
Do you wish to continue? y/n  [n]:  yes
Ready to receive file new-ios-image ...
```

Related Commands

To locate documentation of related commands, you can search online at www.cisco.com.

copy xmodem:
copy ymodem:

## CHAPTER 17

Maintaining Router Memory

This chapter describes how to maintain and use the different types of memory on your router.

To benefit most from the instructions and organization of this chapter, your router must contain a minimal configuration that allows you to interact with the system software. You can create a basic configuration file using the **setup** command facility. See the user guide for your hardware platform for more information on using **setup** at first-time startup.

For a complete description of the memory commands mentioned in this chapter, refer to Chapter 18, "Router Memory Commands." To locate documentation of other commands that appear in this chapter, you can search online at www.cisco.com.

| NOTE | One or more of the commands that previously appeared in this chapter have been replaced by new commands. Table 17-1 maps the old commands to their replacements. The old commands continue to perform their normal functions in the current release, but support for these commands will cease in a future release. |

Table 17-1 *Mapping Old Commands to New Commands*

Old Command	New Command
copy erase flash	**erase flash:** (Class B Flash file systems only)
	format (Class A and C Flash file systems only)
copy verify or **copy verify flash**	**verify flash:**
verify flash	**verify**
copy verify bootflash	**verify bootflash:**
verify bootflash	

Maintain Router Memory Task List

You can perform the tasks related to Flash memory in the following sections:

● Display Memory Information

● Compare Types of Memory

● Reallocate DRAM Memory (Cisco 3600 Series Only)

● Partition Flash Memory

- Use Flash Load Helper to Upgrade Software on Run-from-Flash Systems

- Format Flash Memory

Format Flash Memory is a required first task if you are using a new PCMCIA Flash memory card on the Cisco 7000 family.

NOTE   These tasks assume you have a minimal configuration that you want to modify.

Display Memory Information

Use the following commands in EXEC mode to display information about system memory:

Command	Purpose
show *flash-filesystem***:** [**all** | **chips** | **filesys**] (Class A Flash file systems)	Lists information about Flash memory.
show *flash-filesystem***:** [partition *number*] [all | chips | detailed | err | summary] (Class B Flash file systems)	
show *flash-filesystem***:** (Class C Flash file systems)	
show file systems	Lists the names of the file systems currently supported on the router.

Compare Types of Memory

Your router has many different locations where it can store images, configuration files, and microcode. Refer to your hardware documentation for details on the following:

- Which types of memory your router contains

- Where files can be located

- Where images and boot images are located by default

DRAM

Dynamic random-access memory contains two types of memory:

- Primary, main, or processor memory, which is reserved for the CPU to execute Cisco IOS software and to hold the running configuration and routing tables.

- Shared, packet, or I/O memory, which buffers data transmitted or received by the router's network interfaces.

On the Cisco 3600 series routers, you can use the **memory-size iomem** command to configure the proportion of DRAM devoted to main memory and to shared memory.

EPROM

Erasable programmable read-only memory (EPROM). This memory is often referred to simply as ROM. It sometimes contains the following:

- ROM Monitor, which provides a user interface when the router cannot find a valid image.

- The boot loader/helper software (also called the boot image), which helps the router boot when it cannot find a valid Cisco IOS image in Flash memory.

NVRAM

Nonvolatile random-access memory (NVRAM) stores the following information:

- Startup configuration file for every platform except Class A Flash file system platforms.

- For Class A Flash file system platforms, the location of the startup configuration depends on the CONFIG_FILE Environment Variable.

- The software configuration register, which is used to determine which image to use when booting the router.

Flash

Flash memory stores the Cisco IOS software image. On some platforms, it can store configuration files or boot images.

Depending on the hardware platform, Flash memory might be available as EPROMs, single in-line memory modules (SIMMs), or Flash memory cards. Check the appropriate hardware installation and maintenance guide for information about types of Flash memory available on a specific platform.

Depending on the platform, Flash memory is available in the following forms:

- Internal Flash memory

  — Internal Flash memory often contains the system image.

  — Some platforms have two or more banks of Flash memory on one single in-line memory modules (SIMM). If the SIMM has two banks, it is sometimes referred to as *dual-bank Flash memory*. The banks can be partitioned into separate logical devices. See the "Partition Flash Memory" section for information about how to partition Flash memory.

- Bootflash

    — Bootflash often contains the boot image.

    — Bootflash sometimes contains the ROM Monitor.

- Flash memory PC cards or PCMCIA cards

    A Flash memory card that is inserted in to a Personal Computer Memory Card International Association (PCMCIA) slot. This card is used to store system images, boot images, and configuration files.

    The following platforms contains PCMCIA slots:

    — The Cisco 1600 series routers include one PCMCIA slot.

    — The Cisco 3600 series routers include two PCMCIA slots.

    — The Cisco 7200 series Network Processing Engine (NPE) contains two PCMCIA slots.

    — The Cisco 7000 RSP700 card and the Cisco 7500 series Route Switch Processor (RSP) card contain two PCMCIA slots.

    Because the Cisco 3600 series and Cisco 7000 family can boot images and load configuration files from several locations, these systems use special ROM monitor environment variables to specify the location and filename of images and configuration files that the router is to use for various functions.

    Some CiscoFlash MIB variables support the Flash file system on the Cisco 7000 family.

    Note that the internal Flash and the Flash memory card cannot be used as a contiguous bank of Flash memory.

Write Protection

Flash memory provides write protection against accidental erasing or reprogramming.

- Some platforms have a write-protect jumper which can be removed to prevent reprogramming of Flash memory. You must install the jumper when programming is required.

- Some platforms have write protect switched on Flash memory cards that you can use to protect data. You must set the switch to *unprotected* to write data to the Flash memory card.

Refer to your hardware documentation for information on security jumpers and write protect switches.

Run from Flash Systems

Many Cisco routers load the system image from flash storage into RAM in order to run the Cisco IOS. However, some platforms, such as the Cisco 1600 Series and Cisco 2500 Series, execute the Cisco IOS directly in Flash memory. These platforms are run-from-Flash memory systems.

If you want to partition Flash memory, you must use a relocatable image. Relocatable images can be run from any location in Flash and can download images to any location. If you are upgrading from a nonrelocatable image to a relocatable image, you must erase Flash memory during the download so that the image is downloaded as the first file in Flash memory. All images for run-from-Flash platforms from Cisco IOS Release 11.0 and later are relocatable. See the "Image Naming Conventions" section in Chapter 15, "Loading and Maintaining System Images and Microcode" to determine if your images are run-from-Flash images or are relocatable.

Reallocate DRAM Memory (Cisco 3600 Series Only)

DRAM memory in Cisco 3600 series routers is organized as one contiguous address space divided between processor memory and I/O memory. Depending on the type and number of network interfaces you have configured in the router, you may need to reallocate the DRAM memory partitioned to processor memory and I/O memory.

Cisco manufacturing configures most Cisco 3600 series routers to have 25 percent of the address space allocated to I/O memory and 75 percent allocated to processor memory. But for customer orders that require two or more ISDN PRI interfaces, DRAM memory is configured to provide 40 percent of the address space for I/O memory and 60 percent for processor memory. (See Figure 17-1.) Cisco Systems performs these DRAM memory adjustments before it ships each router.

Figure 17-1 *Components and Uses of DRAM Memory for Cisco 3600 Series Routers*

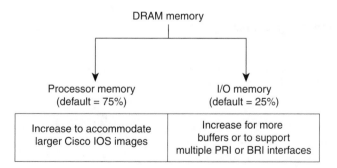

| | NOTE | Routers running two or more ISDN PRI interfaces or 12 or more ISDN BRI interfaces require a DRAM memory configuration of 40 percent I/O memory and 60 percent processor memory. |

However, there are cases where you may have to manually reallocate the DRAM memory split between processor memory and I/O memory after you have received a router from Cisco Systems.

For example, suppose you receive a Cisco 3640 router with the following running configuration:

● 2 Ethernet and 2 WAN interface card

● 8-port ISDN BRI with an NT1 network module

● IP feature set

● 16 MB of DRAM memory (by default, processor memory = 75%, I/O memory = 25%)

● 4 MB of Flash memory

Later, however, you add a 4-port ISDN BRI network module to the router. You now have 12 ISDN BRI interfaces running on the router. At this point, you must use the **memory-size iomem** command to configure 40 percent of the address space for I/O memory and 60 percent for processor memory.

To view your current mix of processor and I/O memory and reassign memory distribution accordingly, use the following commands beginning in privileged EXEC mode:

Step	Command	Purpose
1	**show version**	Views the total amount of memory loaded on the router.
2	**show memory**[1]	Determines the amount of free memory.
3	**configure terminal**	Enters global configuration mode.
4	**memory-size iomem** *I/O-memory-percentage*[2]	Allocates processor memory and I/O memory.
5	**exit**	Exits global configuration mode.
6	**copy system:running-config nvram:startup-config**	Saves the configuration to NVRAM.
7	**reload**	Reloads the router to run the new image.

1. The Free (b) column in the **show memory** command's output shows how much I/O memory is available.
2. The default is 40 percent for I/O memory and 60 percent for processor memory.

Valid I/O memory percentage values are 10, 15, 20, 25, 30, 40 (the default), and 50. I/O memory size is the specified percentage of total memory size, rounded down to the nearest multiple of 1 MB. A minimum of 4 MB of memory is required for I/O memory. The remaining memory is processor memory.

The **memory-size iomem** command does not take effect until you save it to NVRAM using the **copy system:running-config nvram:startup-config** EXEC command and reload the router. However, when you enter the command, the software checks whether the new memory distribution leaves enough processor memory for the currently running Cisco IOS image. If not, the following message appears:

```
Warning: Attempting a memory partition that does not provide enough Processor memory for the
current image. If you write memory now, this version of software may not be able to run.
```

When you enter the **reload** command to run a new image, the software calculates the new processor and I/O memory split. If there is not enough processor memory, it automatically reduces I/O memory to an alternative setting to load the image. If there is still not enough processor memory for the image to run, then you do not have enough DRAM.

Reallocate Processor Memory and I/O Memory Examples

The following example allocates 40 percent of DRAM to I/O memory and the remaining 60 percent to processor memory. The example views the current allocation of memory, changes the allocation, saves the allocation, and reloads the router so the changes can take effect. In the **show memory** command output, the Free (b) column shows how much I/O memory is available:

```
Router# show memory
                  Head     Total(b)     Used(b)     Free(b)   Lowest(b)  Largest(b)
Processor    60913730      3066064      970420     2095644    2090736     2090892
      I/O      C00000      4194304     1382712     2811592    2811592     2805492
--More--

Router# configure terminal
Enter configuration commands, one per line.  End with CNTL/Z.
Router(config)# memory-size iomem 40
Router(config)# exit
Router#
Router# copy system:running-config nvram:startup-config
Building configuration...
[OK]

Router# reload

rommon > boot
program load complete, entry point: 0x80008000, size: 0x32ea24
Self decompressing the image :
###########################################################################
###########################################################################
############################################################ [OK]
```

Partition Flash Memory

On most Class B Flash file systems, you can partition banks of Flash memory into separate, logical devices so that the router can hold and maintain two or more different software images. This partitioning allows you to write software into Flash memory while running software in another bank of Flash memory.

Systems that Support Partitioning

To partition Flash memory, you must have at least two banks of Flash memory; a bank is a set of four chips. This requirement includes systems that support a single SIMM that has two banks of Flash memory. The minimum partition size is the size of a bank.

CiscoFlash MIB variables support partitioned Flash.

Benefits of Partitioning Flash Memory

Partitioning Flash memory provides the following benefits:

- For any system, partitioning—rather than having one logical Flash memory device—provides a cleaner way of managing different files in Flash memory, especially if the Flash memory size is large.

- For systems that execute code out of Flash memory, partitioning allows you to download a new image into the file system in one Flash memory bank while an image is being executed from the file system in the other bank. The download is simple and causes no network disruption or downtime. After the download is complete, you can switch over to the new image at a convenient time.

- One system can hold two different images, one image acting as a backup for the other. Therefore, if a downloaded image fails to boot for some reason, the earlier running, good image is still available. Each bank is treated as a separate device.

Flash Load Helper Versus Dual Flash Bank

Flash load helper is a software option that enables you to upgrade system software on run-from-Flash systems that have a single bank of Flash memory. It is a lower-cost software upgrade solution than dual-bank Flash, which requires two banks of Flash memory on one SIMM. Flash load helper is only available on run-from-Flash platforms, such as the Cisco 2500 series, Cisco 3000, and Cisco 5200.

You might use Flash load helper rather than partitioning Flash into two banks for one of the following reasons:

- If you want to download a new file into the same bank from which the current system image is executing.

- If you want to download a file that is larger than the size of a bank and, hence, want to switch to a single-bank mode.

- If you have only one single-bank Flash SIMM installed. In this case, Flash load helper is the best option for upgrading your software.

See the "Use Flash Load Helper to Upgrade Software on Run-from-Flash Systems" section for information about using Flash load helper.

Partition Flash Memory

To partition Flash memory, use the following command in global configuration mode:

Command	Purpose
partition flash *partitions* [*size1 size2*] **partition** *flash-filesystem*: [*number-of-partitions*][*partition-size*] (Cisco 1600 series and Cisco 3600 series)	Partition Flash memory.

This task will succeed only if the system has at least two banks of Flash and the partitioning does not cause an existing file in Flash memory to be split across the partitions.

For all platforms except the Cisco 1600 series and Cisco 3600 series, Flash memory can only be partitioned into two partitions.

For the Cisco 1600 series and Cisco 3600 series, the number of partitions that you can create in a Flash memory device equals the number of banks in the device. Enter the **show** *flash-filesystem*: **all** command to view the number of banks on the Flash memory device. The number of partition size entries you set must be equal to the number of specified partitions. For example, the **partition slot0: 2 8 8** command configures two partitions to be 8 MB in size each. The first 8 corresponds to the first partition; the second 8 corresponds to the second partition.

Use Flash Load Helper to Upgrade Software on Run-from-Flash Systems

Flash load helper is a software option that enables you to upgrade system software on run-from-Flash systems that have a single bank of Flash memory. It is a lower-cost software upgrade solution than dual-bank Flash, which requires two banks of Flash memory on one SIMM.

The Flash load helper software upgrade process is simple and does not require additional hardware; however, it does require some brief network downtime. A system image running from Flash can use Flash load helper only if the boot ROMs support Flash load helper. Otherwise, you must perform the Flash upgrade manually. See the "Manually Boot from Flash Memory" section.

Flash load helper is an automated procedure that reloads the ROM-based image, downloads the software to Flash memory, and reboots to the system image in Flash memory. Flash load helper performs checks and validations to maximize the success of a Flash upgrade and minimize the chance of leaving Flash memory either in an erased state or with a file that cannot boot.

In run-from-Flash systems, the software image is stored in and executed from the Flash EPROM rather than from RAM. This method reduces memory cost. A run-from-Flash system requires enough Flash EPROM to hold the image and enough main system RAM to hold the routing tables and data structures. The system does not need the same amount of main system RAM as a run-from-RAM system because the full image does not reside in RAM. Run-from-Flash systems include the Cisco 2500 series and some Cisco 3000 series.

Flash Load Helper Features

Flash load helper includes the following features:

- Confirms access to the specified source file on the specified server before erasing Flash memory and reloading to the ROM image for the actual upgrade.

- Warns you if the image being downloaded is not appropriate for the system.

- Prevents reloads to the ROM image for a Flash upgrade if the system is not set up for automatic booting and the user is not on the console terminal. In the event of a catastrophic failure during the upgrade, Flash load helper can bring up the boot ROM image as a last resort rather than forcing the system to wait at the ROM monitor prompt for input from the console terminal.

- Retries Flash downloads up to six times automatically. The retry sequence is as follows:

    — First try

    — Immediate retry

    — Retry after 30 seconds

    — Reload ROM image and retry

    — Immediate retry

    — Retry after 30 seconds

- Allows you to save any configuration changes made before you exit out of the system image.

- Notifies users logged in to the system of the impending switch to the boot ROM image so that they do not lose their connections unexpectedly.

- Logs console output during the Flash load helper operation into a buffer that is preserved through system reloads. You can retrieve the buffer contents from a running image. The output is useful when console access is unavailable or a failure occurs in the download operation.

Flash load helper can also be used on systems with multiple banks of Flash memory that support Flash memory partitioning. Flash load helper enables you to download a new file into the same partition from which the system is executing an image.

For information about how to partition multiple banks of Flash memory so your system can hold two different images, see the "Partition Flash Memory" section.

Flash Load Helper Configuration Task List

Perform the commands in the following sections to use and monitor Flash load helper:

- Download a File Using Flash Load Helper
- Monitor Flash Load Helper

Download a File Using Flash Load Helper

To download a new file to Flash memory using Flash load helper, check to make sure that your boot ROMs support Flash load helper and then use one of the following commands in privileged EXEC mode:

Command	Purpose
copy tftp: flash:	Downloads a new file to Flash memory.
copy rcp: flash:	
copy ftp: flash:	

The following error message displays if you are in a Telnet session and the system is set for manual booting (the boot bits in the configuration register are zero):

```
ERR: Config register boot bits set for manual booting
```

In case of any catastrophic failure in the Flash memory upgrade, this error message helps to minimize the chance of the system going down to ROM monitor mode and being taken out of the remote Telnet user's control.

The system tries to bring up at least the boot ROM image if it cannot boot an image from Flash memory. Before reinitiating the **copy:** command, you must set the configuration register boot field to a nonzero value, using the **config-register** global configuration command.

The **copy** command initiates a series of prompts to which you must provide responses. The dialog is similar to the following:

```
Router# copy tftp: flash:

*************************** NOTICE ******************************
Flash load helper v1.0
This process will accept the TFTP copy options and then terminate
the current system image to use the ROM based image for the copy.
Router functionality will not be available during that time. If
you are logged in via telnet, this connection will terminate. Users
with console access can see the results of the copy operation.
****************************************************************

There are active users logged into the system.
```

```
Proceed? [confirm] y
System flash directory:
File Length  Name/status
1    2251320 abc/igs-kf.914
[2251384 bytes used, 1942920 available, 4194304 total]
Address or name of remote host [255.255.255.255]? 172.16.1.111
Source file name? abc/igs-kf.914
Destination file name [default = source name]? <Return>
Accessing file 'abc/igs-kf.914' on 172.16.1.111....
Loading from 172.16.13.111:
Erase flash device before writing? [confirm] n
File 'abc/igs-kf.914' already exists; it will be invalidated!
Invalidate existing copy of 'abc/igs-kf.914' in flash memory? [confirm] y
Copy 'abc/igs-kf.914' from TFTP server
as 'abc/igs-kf.914' into Flash WITHOUT erase? y

%SYS-5-RELOAD: Reload requested
%FLH: rxboot/igs-kf.914r from 172.16.1.111 to flash...
```

The Flash Load Helper operation verifies the request from the running image by trying to copy a single block from the remote server. Then the Flash load helper is executed, causing the system to reload to the ROM-based system image. If the file does not seem to be a valid image for the system, a warning is displayed and a separate confirmation is sought from you.

If the configuration has been modified but not yet saved, you are prompted to save the configuration:

```
System configuration has been modified. Save? [confirm]
```

Users with open Telnet connections are notified of the system reload, as follows:

```
**System going down for Flash upgrade**
```

If the copy process fails, the copy operation is retried up to three times. If the failure happens in the middle of a copy operation so that only part of the file has been written to Flash memory, the retry does not erase Flash memory unless you specified an erase operation. The partly written file is marked as deleted, and a new file is opened with the same name. If Flash memory runs out of free space in this process, the copy operation is terminated.

After Flash load helper finishes copying (whether the copy operation is successful or not), it automatically attempts an automatic or a manual boot, depending on the value of bit zero of the configuration register boot field according to the following:

● If bit zero equals 0, the system attempts a default boot from Flash memory to load up the first bootable file in Flash memory. This default boot is equivalent to a manual **boot flash** command at the ROM monitor prompt.

● If bit zero equals 1, the system attempts to boot based on the boot configuration commands. If no boot configuration commands exist, the system attempts a default boot from Flash memory; that is, it attempts to load the first bootable file in Flash memory.

Monitor Flash Load Helper

To view the system console output generated during the Flash load helper operation, use the image that has been booted up after the Flash memory upgrade. Use the following command in privileged EXEC mode:

Command	Purpose
more flh:logfile	Views the console output generated during the Flash load helper operation.

If you are a remote Telnet user performing the Flash upgrade without a console connection, this task allows you to retrieve console output when your Telnet connection has terminated due to the switch to the ROM image. The output indicates what happened during the download and is particularly useful if the download fails.

Format Flash Memory

On Class A and Class C Flash file systems, you can format Flash memory. Formatting erases all information in Flash memory.

On the Cisco 7000 family, you must format a new Flash memory card before using it in a PCMCIA slot.

Flash memory cards have sectors that can fail. You can reserve certain Flash memory sectors as "spares" for use when other sectors fail. Use the **format** command to specify between 0 and 16 sectors as spares. If you reserve a small number of spare sectors for emergencies, you do not waste space because you can use most of the Flash memory card. If you specify zero spare sectors and some sectors fail, you must reformat the Flash memory card and thereby erase all existing data.

The format operation requires at least Cisco IOS Release 11.0 system software.

Format Flash Memory Process

CAUTION	The following formatting procedure erases all information in Flash memory. To prevent the loss of important data, proceed carefully.

Use the following procedure to format Flash memory. If you are formatting internal Flash memory, such as bootflash, you can skip the first step. If you are formatting a Flash memory card, complete both steps.

Step 1   Insert the new Flash memory card into a PCMCIA slot. Refer to instructions on maintaining the router and replacing PCMCIA cards in your router's hardware documentation for instructions on performing this step.

Step 2   Format Flash memory.

To format Flash memory, use the following EXEC mode command:

Command	Purpose
format [**spare** *spare-number*] *device1***:** [[*device2***:**][*monlib-filename*]] (Class A Flash file systems)	Formats Flash memory.

The following example shows the **format** command that formats a Flash memory card inserted in slot 0.

```
Router# format slot0:
Running config file on this device, proceed? [confirm]y
All sectors will be erased, proceed? [confirm]y
Enter volume id (up to 31 characters): <Return>
Formatting sector 1 (erasing)
Format device slot0 completed
```

When the router returns you to the EXEC prompt, the new Flash memory card is successfully formatted and ready for use.

Recovering from Locked Blocks

To recover from locked blocks, reformat the Flash memory card. A locked block of Flash memory occurs when power is lost or a Flash memory card is unplugged during a write or erase operation. When a block of Flash memory is locked, it cannot be written to or erased, and the operation will consistently fail at a particular block location. The only way to recover from locked blocks is by reformatting the Flash memory card with the **format** command.

CAUTION   Formatting a Flash memory card to recover from locked blocks will cause existing data to be lost.

CHAPTER 18

Router Memory Commands

This chapter provides detailed descriptions of the commands used to maintain router memory.

For configuration information and examples, refer to Chapter 17, "Maintaining Router Memory."

Flash Memory File System Types

Cisco platforms use one of three different Flash memory file system types. Some commands are supported on only one or two file system types. This chapter notes commands that are not supported on all file system types.

Refer to Table 18-1 to determine which Flash memory file system type your platform uses.

Table 18-1 *Flash Memory File System Types*

Type	Platforms
Class A	Cisco 7000 family, C12000, LS1010
Class B	Cisco 1003, Cisco 1004, Cisco 1005, Cisco 2500 series, Cisco 3600 series, Cisco 4000 series, Cisco AS5200
Class C	Cisco MC3810, disk0 and disk1 of SC3640

Replaced Commands

Commands in this chapter that have been replaced by new commands continue to perform their normal functions in the current release but are no longer documented. Support for these commands will cease in a future release. Table 18-2 maps the old commands with their replacements.

Table 18-2 *Mapping Old Commands to New Commands*

Old Command	New Command
configure network	copy *source-url* system:running-config
configure overwrite-network	copy *source-url* nvram:startup-config
write memory	copy system:running-config nvram:startup-config
write network	copy system:running config *destination-url*

configure network

The **copy** *source-url* **system:running-config** command replaces the **configure network** command. Refer to the description of the **copy** command for further details.

configure overwrite-network

The **copy** *source-url* **nvram: startup-config** command replaces the **configure overwrite-network** command. Refer to the **copy** command for further details.

copy

To copy any file from a source to a destination, use the **copy** EXEC command.

> **copy** [**/erase**] *source-url destination-url*

Syntax	Description
/erase	(Optional) Erases the destination file system before copying.
source-url	The location of the source file or directory to be copied.
destination-url	The destination of the copied file or directory.

The exact format of the source and destination URLs varies according to the file or directory location. You may enter either a keyword for a particular file or a prefix for a file system type (not a file within a type).

Table 18-3 specifies two keyword shortcuts to URLs.

Table 18-3 *Copy Command Keywords*

Keyword	Source or Destination
running-config	(Optional) Keyword shortcut for **system:running-config**, the current running configuration file. This keyword does not work in **more** and **show file** command syntaxes.
startup-config	(Optional) Keyword shortcut for **nvram:startup-config**, the configuration file used for initialization. This file is contained in NVRAM for all platforms except the Cisco 7000 family, which uses the CONFIG_FILE environment variable to specify the startup configuration. The Cisco 4500 series cannot use the **copy running-config startup-config** command. This keyword does not work in **more** and **show file** command syntaxes.

The next tables list prefixes by file system type. If you do not specify a prefix, the router looks for a file in the current directory.

Table 18-4 lists URL prefixes for Special (opaque) file systems. Table 18-5 lists them for network file systems, and Table 18-6 lists them for local writable storage.

Table 18-4 *URL Prefixes for Special File Systems*

Prefix	Source or Destination
flh:	Source URL for flash load helper log files.
modem:	Destination URL for loading modem firmware on Cisco 5200 and 5300 Series routers.
nvram:	Router's NVRAM. You can copy the startup configuration into or from NVRAM. You can also display the size of a private configuration file.
null:	Null destination for copies or files. You can copy a remote file to null to determine its size.
system:	Source or destination URL for system memory, which includes the running configuration.
xmodem:	Source destination for the file from a network machine that uses the Xmodem protocol.
ymodem:	Source destination for the file from a network machine that uses the Xmodem protocol.

Table 18-5 *URL Prefixes for Network File Systems*

Prefix	Source or Destination
ftp:	Source or destination URL for File Transfer Protocol (FTP) network server. The syntax for this prefix is ftp:[[//*username* [:*password*]@] *location*]/*directory*]/*filename*
rcp:	Source or destination URL for a Remote Copy Protocol (rcp) network server. The syntax for this prefix is **rcp:**[[//*username*@]*location*]/*directory*]/*filename*
tftp:	Source or destination URL for a Trivial File Transfer Protocol (TFTP) network server. The syntax for this prefix is **tftp:**[[//*location*]/*directory*]/*filename*

Table 18-6 *URL Prefixes for Local Writable Storage File Systems*

Prefix	Source or Destination
bootflash:	Source or destination URL for Boot Flash memory.
disk0: and disk1:	Source or destination URL of rotating media.
flash:	Source or destination URL for Flash memory. This prefix is available on all platforms. For platforms which lack a flash: device, note that **flash:** is aliased to **slot0:**, allowing you to refer to the main Flash memory storage area on all platforms.

Table 18-6 *URL Prefixes for Local Writable Storage File Systems (Continued)*

Prefix	Source or Destination
slavebootflash:	Source or destination URL for internal Flash memory on the slave RSP card of a router configured for HSA.
slaveram:	NVRAM on a slave RSP card of a router configured for HSA.
slaveslot0:	Source or destination URL of first PCMCIA card on a slave RSP card of a router configured for HSA.
slaveslot1:	Source or destination URL of second PCMCIA slot on a slave RSP card of a router configured for HSA.
slot0:	Source or destination URL of first PCMCIA Flash memory card.
slot1:	Source or destination URL of second PCMCIA Flash memory card.

Command Mode

EXEC

Usage Guidelines

This command first appeared in Cisco IOS Release 11.3 T.

You can enter on the command line all necessary source- and destination- URL information and the username and password to use, or you can enter **copy** and have the router prompt you for any missing information.

If you enter information, choose one of the following three: **running-config**, **startup-config**, or a file system prefix (see tables above). The location of a file system dictates the format of the source or destination URL.

The colon is required after the prefix. However, earlier commands not requiring a colon will remain supported but unavailable in context-sensitive help.

The entire copying process may take several minutes and differs from protocol to protocol and from network to network.

In the prefix syntax for **ftp:**, **rcp:**, and **tftp:** the location is either an IP address or a host name. The filename is specified relative to the directory used for file transfers.

This section contains usage guidelines for the following topics:

● Understanding Invalid Combinations of Source and Destination

● Understanding Character Descriptions

● Understanding Partitions

- Using rcp

- Using FTP

- Storing Images on Servers

- Copying from a Server to Flash Memory

- Verifying Images

- Copying a Configuration File from a Server to the Running Configuration

- Copying a Configuration File from a Server to the Startup Configuration

- Storing the Running or Startup Configuration on a Server

- Saving the Running Configuration to the Startup Configuration

- Using CONFIG_FILE, BOOT, and BOOTLDR Environment Variables

- Understanding High System Availability

Understanding Invalid Combinations of Source and Destination

Some invalid combinations of source and destination exist. Specifically, you cannot copy

- From a running configuration to a running configuration.

- From a startup configuration to a startup configuration.

- From a device to the same device (for example, the **copy flash: flash:** command is invalid).

Understanding Character Descriptions

Table 18-7 describes the characters that you may see during processing of the **copy** command.

Table 18-7 *Character Descriptions in the Copy Command*

Character	Description
!	For net transfers an exclamation point indicates that the copy process is taking place. Each exclamation point indicates the successful transfer of 10 packets (512 bytes each).
.	For net transfers, a period indicates the copy process timed out. Many periods in a row typically mean that the copy process may fail.
O	For net transfers, an uppercase O indicates a packet was received out of order and the copy process may fail.
e	For flash erasures, a lowercase e indicates a device is being erased.
E	An uppercase E indicates an error. The copy process may fail.

Table 18-7 *Character Descriptions in the Copy Command (Continued)*

Character	Description
V	A series of uppercase Vs indicates the progress during the verification of the image checksum.

Understanding Partitions

You cannot copy an image or configuration file to a Flash partition from which you are currently running. For example, if partition 1 is running the current system image, copy the configuration file or image to partition 2. Otherwise, the copy operation will fail.

You can identify the available Flash partitions by entering the **show file system** command.

Using rcp

The rcp protocol requires a client to send a remote username upon each rcp request to a server. When you copy a configuration file or image between the router and a server using rcp, the Cisco IOS software sends the first valid username in the following list:

1   The remote username specified in the **copy** command if one is specified.

2   The username set by the **ip rcmd remote-username** command if the command is configured.

3   The remote username associated with the current tty (terminal) process. For example, if the user is connected to the router through Telnet and was authenticated through the **username** command, the router software sends the Telnet username as the remote username.

4   The router host name.

For the rcp copy request to process successfully, an account must be defined on the network server for the remote username. If the network administrator of the destination server did not establish an account for the remote username, this command will not run successfully. If the server has a directory structure, the configuration file or image is written to or copied from the directory associated with the remote username on the server. For example, if the system image resides in the home directory of a user on the server, specify that user's name as the remote username.

If you are writing to the server, the rcp server must be properly configured to accept the rcp write request from the user on the router. For UNIX systems, add an entry to the .rhosts file for the remote user on the rcp server. Suppose the router contains the following configuration lines:

```
hostname Rtr1
ip rcmd remote-username User0
```

If the router's IP address translates to Router1.company.com, then the *.rhosts* file for User0 on the rcp server should contain the following line:

```
Router1.company.com Rtr1
```

Refer to the documentation for your rcp server for more details.

If you are using a personal computer as a file server, the computer must support rsh.

Using FTP

The FTP protocol requires a client to send a remote username and password upon each FTP request to a server. When you copy a configuration file from the router to a server using FTP, the Cisco IOS software sends the first valid username in the following list:

1   The username specified in the **copy** command if a username is specified.

2   The username set by the **ip ftp username** command if the command is configured.

3   Anonymous.

The router send the first valid password in the following list:

1   The password specified in the **copy** command if a password is specified.

2   The password set by the **ip ftp password** command if the command is configured.

3   The router forms a password *username@routername.domain*. The variable *username* is the username associated with the current session, *routername* is the configured host name, and *domain* is the domain of the router.

The username and password must be associated with an account on the FTP server. If you are writing to the server, the FTP server must be properly configured to accept the FTP write request from the user on the router.

If the server has a directory structure, the configuration file or image is written to or copied from the directory associated with the username on the server. For example, if the system image resides in the home directory of a user on the server, specify that user's name as the remote username.

Refer to the documentation for your FTP server for more details.

Use the **ip ftp username** and **ip ftp password** commands to specify a username and password for all copies. Include the username in the **copy** command if you want to specify a username for that copy operation only.

Storing Images on Servers

Use the **copy** *flash: destination-url* command (for example, **copy flash: tftp:**) to copy a system image or boot image from Flash memory to a network server. Use the copy of the image as a backup copy. Also, use it to verify that the copy in Flash memory is the same as that in the original file.

Copying from a Server to Flash Memory

Use the **copy** *destination-url flash:* command (for example, **copy tftp: flash:**) to copy an image from a server to Flash memory.

On Class B file system platforms, the system provides an option to erase existing Flash memory before writing onto it.

CAUTION   Verify the image in Flash memory before booting the image.

Verifying Images

Before booting from Flash memory, verify that the checksum of the image in Flash memory matches the checksum listed in the README file that was distributed with the image by using the **verify** command. The checksum of the image in Flash memory is displayed when the **copy** command completes. The README file was copied to the server automatically when you installed the image.

CAUTION   If the checksum values do not match, do not reboot the router. Instead, reissue the **copy** command and compare the checksums again. If the checksum is repeatedly wrong, copy the original image back into Flash memory *before* you reboot the router from Flash memory. If you have a corrupted image in Flash memory and try to boot from Flash memory, the router will start the system image contained in ROM (assuming booting from a network server is not configured). If ROM does not contain a fully functional system image, the router might not function and will have to be reconfigured through a direct console port connection.

Copying a Configuration File from a Server to the Running Configuration

Use the **copy** {**ftp:** | **rcp:** | **tftp:**} **system:running-config** command to load a configuration file from a network server to the router's running configuration. The configuration will be added to the running configuration as if the commands were typed in the command line interface. Thus, the resulting configuration will be a combination of the previous running configuration and the loaded configuration file with the loaded configuration file having precedence.

You can copy either a host configuration file or a network configuration file. Accept the default value of *host* to copy and load a host configuration file containing commands that apply to one network server in particular. Enter *network* to copy and load a network configuration file containing commands that apply to all network servers on a network.

Copying a Configuration File from a Server to the Startup Configuration

Use the **copy** {**ftp:** | **rcp:** | **tftp:**} **nvram:startup-config** command to copy a configuration file from a network server to the router's startup configuration. These commands replace the startup configuration file with the copied configuration file.

Storing the Running or Startup Configuration on a Server

Use the **copy system:running-config** {**ftp:** | **rcp:** | **tftp:**} command to copy the current configuration file to a network server using FTP, rcp, or TFTP. Use the **copy nvram:startup-config** {**ftp:** | **rcp:** | **tftp:**} command to copy the startup configuration file to a network server.

The configuration file copy can serve as a backup copy.

Saving the Running Configuration to the Startup Configuration

Use the **copy system:running-config nvram:startup-config** command to copy the running configuration to the startup configuration.

CAUTION   Some specific commands might not get saved to NVRAM. You will have to enter these commands again if you reboot the machine. These commands are noted in the documentation. We recommend that you keep a listing of these settings so you can quickly reconfigure your router after rebooting.

If you issue the **copy system:running-config nvram:startup-config** command from a bootstrap system image, a warning will instruct you to indicate whether you want your previous NVRAM configuration to be overwritten and configuration commands to be lost. This warning does not appear if NVRAM contains an invalid configuration or if the previous configuration in NVRAM was generated by a bootstrap system image.

On all platforms except Class A file system platforms, the **copy system:running-config nvram:startup-config** command copies the currently running configuration to NVRAM.

On the Class A Flash file system platforms, the **copy system:running-config nvram:startup-config** command copies the currently running configuration to the location specified by the CONFIG_FILE environment variable. This variable specifies the device and configuration file used for initialization. When the CONFIG_FILE environment variable points to NVRAM or when this variable does not exist (such as at first-time startup), the software writes the current configuration to NVRAM. If the current configuration is too large for NVRAM, the software displays a message and stops executing the command.

When the CONFIG_FILE environment variable specifies a valid device other than **nvram:** (that is, **flash:**, **bootflash:**, **slot0:**, or **slot1:**), the software writes the current configuration to the specified device and filename and stores a distilled version of the configuration in NVRAM. A distilled version is one that does not contain access list information. If NVRAM already contains a copy of a complete configuration, the router prompts you to confirm the copy.

Using CONFIG_FILE, BOOT, and BOOTLDR Environment Variables

For the Class A Flash file system platforms:

● The CONFIG_FILE environment variable specifies the configuration file used during router initialization.

● The BOOTLDR environment variable specifies the Flash device and filename containing the rxboot image that ROM uses for booting.

● The BOOT environment variable specifies a list of bootable images on various devices.

● Cisco 3600 routers do not use a dedicated boot helper image (rxboot), which many other routers use to help with the boot process. Instead, the BOOTLDR ROM monitor environment variable identifies the Flash memory device and filename that are used as the boot helper; the default is the first system image in Flash memory.

● The BOOT environment variable specifies a list of bootable images on various devices.

To view the contents of environment variables, use the **show bootvar** command. To modify the CONFIG_FILE environment variable, use the **boot config** command. To modify the BOOTLDR environment variable, use the **boot bootldr** command. To modify the BOOT environment variable, use the **boot system** command. To save your modifications, use the **copy system:running-config nvram:startup-config** command.

When the destination of a **copy** command is specified by the CONFIG_FILE or BOOTLDR environment variable, the router prompts you for confirmation before proceeding with the copy. When the destination is the only valid image in the BOOT environment variable, the router also prompts you for confirmation before proceeding with the copy.

Understanding High System Availability

High System Availability (HSA) refers to how quickly your router returns to an operational status after a failure occurs. On the Cisco 7507 and Cisco 7513, you can install two RSP cards in a single router to improve system availability.

On a Cisco 7507 or Cisco 7513 configured for HSA, if you copy a file to **nvram:startup-configuration** with automatic synchronization disabled, the system asks you if you also want to copy the file to the slave's startup configuration. The default answer is **yes**. If automatic synchronization is enabled, the system automatically copies the file to the slave's startup configuration each time you use a **copy** command with **nvram:startup-configuration** as the destination.

Examples

The following examples illustrate uses of the **copy** command. Depending on your platform, the output might be different from that shown in the examples.

- Copy an Image from a Server to Flash Memory Examples

- Save a Copy of an Image on a Server Examples

- Copy from a Server to the Running Configuration Example

- Copy from a Server to the Startup Configuration Example

- Copy the Running Configuration to a Server Example

- Copy the Startup Configuration to a Server Example

- Save the Current Running Configuration Example

- Move Configuration Files to Other Locations Examples

- Copy an Image from the Master RSP Card to the Slave RSP Card Example

Copy an Image from a Server to Flash Memory Examples

The following three examples use a **copy rcp:**, **copy tftp:**, or **copy ftp:** command to copy an image from a server to Flash memory.

- Copy an Image from a Server to Flash Memory

  This example copies a system image named file1 from the remote rcp server with an IP address of 172.16.101.101 to Flash memory. On Class B file system platforms, the Cisco IOS software allows you to erase the contents of Flash memory first to ensure that enough Flash memory is available to accommodate the system image.

```
Router# copy rcp://netadmin@172.16.101.101/file1 flash:file1
Destination file name [file1]?
Accessing file 'file1' on 172.16.101.101...
Loading file1 from 172.16.101.101 (via Ethernet0): ! [OK]

Erase flash device before writing? [confirm]
Flash contains files. Are you sure you want to erase? [confirm]

Copy 'file1' from server
  as 'file1' into Flash WITH erase? [yes/no] yes
Erasing device... eeeeeeeeeeeeeeeeeeeeeeeeeeeeeeee...erased
Loading file1 from 172.16.101.101 (via Ethernet0): !
[OK - 984/8388608 bytes]

Verifying checksum... OK (0x14B3)
Flash copy took 0:00:01 [hh:mm:ss]
```

- Copy from a Server to a Flash Memory Using Flash Load Helper Example

  The following example copies a system image into a partition of Flash memory. The system will prompt for a partition number only if there are two or more read/write partitions or one read-only and one read/write partition and dual Flash bank support in boot ROMs. If the partition entered is not valid, the process terminates. You can enter a partition number, a question mark (**?**) for a directory display of all partitions, or a question mark and a number (**?***number*) for directory display of a particular partition. The default is the first read/write partition. In this case, the partition is read-only and has dual Flash bank support in boot ROM, so the system uses Flash load helper.

```
Router# copy tftp: flash:

System flash partition information:
Partition  Size    Used    Free    Bank-Size  State       Copy-Mode
    1      4096K   2048K   2048K    2048K      Read Only   RXBOOT-FLH
    2      4096K   2048K   2048K    2048K      Read/Write  Direct

[Type ?<no> for partition directory; ? for full directory; q to abort]
Which partition? [default = 2]

                     **** NOTICE ****
Flash load helper v1.0
This process will accept the copy options and then terminate
the current system image to use the ROM based image for the copy.
Routing functionality will not be available during that time.
If you are logged in via telnet, this connection will terminate.
Users with console access can see the results of the copy operation.
                .... ******** ....
Proceed? [confirm]
System flash directory, partition 1:
File  Length    Name/status
  1   3459720   master/igs-bfpx.100-4.3
[3459784 bytes used, 734520 available, 4194304 total]
Address or name of remote host [255.255.255.255]? 172.16.1.1
Source file name? master/igs-bfpx-100.4.3
Destination file name [default = source name]?

Loading master/igs-bfpx.100-4.3 from 172.16.1.111: !
Erase flash device before writing? [confirm]
Flash contains files. Are you sure? [confirm]
Copy 'master/igs-bfpx.100-4.3' from TFTP server
as 'master/igs-bfpx.100-4.3' into Flash WITH erase? [yes/no] yes
```

- Copy an Image from a Server to a Flash Memory Card Partition Example

  The following example copies the file c3600-i-mz from the rcp server at IP address 172.23.1.129 to the Flash memory card in slot 0 of a Cisco 3600 series router, which has only one partition. As the operation progresses, the Cisco IOS software asks you to erase the files on the Flash memory PC card to accommodate the incoming file. This entire operation takes 18 seconds to perform, as indicated at the end of the example.

```
Router# copy rcp: slot0:
PCMCIA Slot0 flash
```

```
Partition   Size    Used     Free    Bank-Size  State       Copy Mode
   1        4096K   3068K    1027K   4096K      Read/Write  Direct
   2        4096K   1671K    2424K   4096K      Read/Write  Direct
   3        4096K      0K    4095K   4096K      Read/Write  Direct
   4        4096K   3825K     270K   4096K      Read/Write  Direct

[Type ?<no> for partition directory; ? for full directory; q to abort]
Which partition? [default = 1]

PCMCIA Slot0 flash directory, partition 1:
File  Length   Name/status
   1  3142288  c3600-j-mz.test
[3142352 bytes used, 1051952 available, 4194304 total]
Address or name of remote host [172.23.1.129]?
Source file name? /tftpboot/images/c3600-i-mz
Destination file name [/tftpboot/images/c3600-i-mz]?
Accessing file '/tftpboot/images/c3600-i-mz' on 172.23.1.129...
Connected to 172.23.1.129
Loading 1711088 byte file c3600-i-mz: ! [OK]

Erase flash device before writing? [confirm]
Flash contains files. Are you sure you want to erase? [confirm]

Copy '/tftpboot/images/c3600-i-mz' from server
  as '/tftpboot/images/c3600-i-mz' into Flash WITH erase? [yes/no] yes
Erasing device... eeeeeeeeeeeeeeeeeeeeeeeeeeeeeeee ...erased
Connected to 172.23.1.129
Loading 1711088 byte file c3600-i-mz:
!!!!!!!!!!!!!!!!!!!!!!!!!!!!!!!!!!!!!!!!!!!!!!!!!!!!!!!!!!!!!!!!!!!!!!!!!!!!!!!!!!
!!!!!!!!!!!!!!!!!!!!!!!!!!!!!!!!!!!!!!!!!!!!!!!!!!!!!!!!!!!!!!!!!!!!!!!!!!!!!!!!!!
!!!!!!!!!!!!!!!!!!!!!!!!!!!!!!!!!!!!!!!!!!!!!!!!!!!!!!!!!!!!!!!!!!!!!!!!!!!!!!!!

Verifying checksum... OK (0xF89A)
Flash device copy took 00:00:18 [hh:mm:ss]
```

Save a Copy of an Image on a Server Examples

The following four examples use **copy** commands to copy images to a server for storage.

● Copy an Image from Flash Memory to an rcp Server Example

The following example copies a system image from Flash Memory to an rcp server using the default remote username. Because the rcp server address and filename are not included in the command, the router prompts for it.

```
Router# copy flash: rcp:
IP address of remote host [255.255.255.255]? 172.16.13.110
Name of file to copy? gsxx
writing gsxx - copy complete
```

- Copy an Image from a Partition of Flash Memory to a Server Example

  The following example copies an image from a particular partition of Flash memory to an rcp server using a remote username of netadmin1.

  The system will prompt if there are two or more partitions. If the partition entered is not valid, the process terminates. You have the option to enter a partition number, a question mark (**?**) for a directory display of all partitions, or a question mark and a number (**?**_number_) for a directory display of a particular partition. The default is the first partition.

```
Router# configure terminal
Router# ip rcmd remote-username netadmin1
Router# end
Router# copy flash: rcp:
System flash partition information:
Partition   Size    Used    Free    Bank-Size   State        Copy-Mode
    1       4096K   2048K   2048K   2048K       Read Only    RXBOOT-FLH
    2       4096K   2048K   2048K   2048K       Read/Write   Direct
[Type ?<number> for partition directory; ? for full directory; q to abort]
Which partition? [1] 2

System flash directory, partition 2:
File  Length   Name/status
  1   3459720  master/igs-bfpx.100-4.3
[3459784 bytes used, 734520 available, 4194304 total]
Address or name of remote host [ABC.CISCO.COM]?
Source file name? master/igs-bfpx.100-4.3
Destination file name [master/igs-bfpx.100-4.3]?
Verifying checksum for 'master/igs-bfpx.100-4.3' (file # 1)... OK
Copy 'master/igs-bfpx.100-4.3' from Flash to server
as 'master/igs-bfpx.100-4.3'? [yes/no] yes
!!!!...
Upload to server done
Flash copy took 0:00:00 [hh:mm:ss]
```

- Copy an Image from a Flash Memory File System to an FTP Server

  The following example copies the file c3600-i-mz from partition 1 of the Flash memory card in slot 0 to an FTP server at IP address 172.23.1.129.

```
Router# show slot0: partition 1

PCMCIA Slot0 flash directory, partition 1:
File  Length   Name/status
  1   1711088  c3600-i-mz
[1711152 bytes used, 2483152 available, 4194304 total]

Router# copy slot0:1:c3600-i-mz ftp://myuser:mypass@172.23.1.129/c3600-i-mz
Verifying checksum for '/tftpboot/cisco_rules/c3600-i-mz' (file # 1)...  OK
Copy '/tftpboot/cisco_rules/c3600-i-mz' from Flash to server
  as 'c3700-i-mz'? [yes/no] yes
!!!!!!!!!!!!!!!!!!!!!!!!!!!!!!!!!!!!!!!!!!!!!!!!!!!!!!!!!!!!!!!!!!!!!!!!!!!!!!!!
!!!!!!!!!!!!!!!!!!!!!!!!!!!!!!!!!!!!!!!!!!!!!!!!!!!!!!!!!!!!!!!!!!!!!!!!!!!!!!!!
!!!!!!!!!!!!!!!!!!!!!!!!!!!!!!!!!!!!!!!!!!!!!!!!!!!!!!!!!!!!!!!!!!!!!!!!!!!!!!!!
!!!!!!!!!!!!!!!!!!!!!!!!!!!!!!!!!!!!!!!!!!!!!!!!!!!!!!!!!!!!!!!
Upload to server done
Flash device copy took 00:00:23 [hh:mm:ss]
```

- Copy an Image from Boot Flash Memory to a TFTP Server

   The following example copies an image from boot Flash memory to a TFTP Server:

```
Router# copy bootflash:file1 tftp://192.168.117.23/file1

Verifying checksum for 'file1' (file # 1)... OK
Copy 'file1' from Flash to server
  as 'file1'? [yes/no]y
!!!!...
Upload to server done
Flash copy took 0:00:00 [hh:mm:ss]
```

Copy from a Server to the Running Configuration Example

The following example copies and runs a configuration filename host1-confg from the netadmin1 directory on the remote server with an IP address of 172.16.101.101.

```
Router# copy rcp://netadmin1@172.16.101.101/host1-confg system:running-config
Configure using host1-confg from 172.16.101.101? [confirm]
Connected to 172.16.101.101
Loading 1112 byte file host1-confg:![OK]
Router#
%SYS-5-CONFIG: Configured from host1-config by rcp from 172.16.101.101
```

Copy from a Server to the Startup Configuration Example

The following example copies a configuration file host2-confg from a remote FTP server to the startup configuration. The IP address is172.16.101.101; the remote username is netadmin1; and the remote password is ftppass.

```
Router# copy ftp://netadmin1:ftppass@172.16.101.101/host2-confg nvram:startup-config
Configure using rtr2-confg from 172.16.101.101?[confirm]
Connected to 172.16.101.101
Loading 1112 byte file rtr2-confg:![OK]
[OK]
Router#
%SYS-5-CONFIG_NV:Non-volatile store configured from rtr2-config by
FTP from 172.16.101.101
```

Copy the Running Configuration to a Server Example

The following example specifies a remote username of netadmin1. Then it copies the running configuration file, named Rtr2-confg, to the netadmin1 directory on the remote host with an IP address of 172.16.101.101.

```
Router# configure terminal
Router(config)# ip rcmd remote-username netadmin1
Router(config)# end
```

```
Router# copy system:running-config rcp:
Remote host[]? 172.16.101.101

Name of configuration file to write [Rtr2-confg]?
Write file rtr2-confg on host 172.16.101.101?[confirm]
Building configuration...[OK]
Connected to 172.16.101.101
```

Copy the Startup Configuration to a Server Example

The following example copies the startup configuration to a TFTP server:

```
Router# copy nvram:startup-config tftp:
Remote host[]? 172.16.101.101

Name of configuration file to write [rtr2-confg]? <cr>
Write file rtr2-confg on host 172.16.101.101?[confirm] <cr>
![OK]
```

Save the Current Running Configuration Example

The following example copies the running configuration to the startup configuration. On a Class A Flash file system platform, this command copies the running configuration to the startup configuration specified by the CONFIG_FILE variable:

```
copy system:running-config nvram:startup-config
```

The following example shows the warning the system provides if you try to save configuration information from bootstrap into the system:

```
Router(boot)# copy system:running-config nvram:startup-config

Warning: Attempting to overwrite an NVRAM configuration written
by a full system image. This bootstrap software does not support
the full configuration command set. If you perform this command now,
some configuration commands may be lost.
Overwrite the previous NVRAM configuration?[confirm]
```

Enter **no** to escape writing the configuration information to memory.

Move Configuration Files to Other Locations Examples

On some routers, you can store copies of configuration files on a Flash memory device. Five examples follow:

- Copy the Startup Configuration to a Flash Memory Device Example

  The following example copies the startup configuration file (specified by the CONFIG_FILE environment variable) to a Flash memory card inserted in slot 0:

```
copy nvram:startup-config slot0:router-confg
```

- Copy the Running Configuration to a Flash Memory Device Example

  The following example copies the running configuration from the router to the Flash memory PC card in slot 0:

```
Router# copy system:running-config slot0:karen2
Building configuration...

5267 bytes copied in 0.720 secs
```

- Copy to the Running Configuration from a Flash Memory Device Example

  The following example copies the file ios-upgrade-1 from the Flash memory card in slot 0 to the running configuration:

```
Router# copy slot0:4:ios-upgrade-1 system:running-config

Copy 'ios-upgrade-1' from flash device
  as 'running-config' ? [yes/no] yes
```

- Copy to the Startup Configuration from a Flash Memory Device Example

  The following example copies the router-image file from the Flash memory to the startup configuration:

```
copy flash:router-image nvram:startup-config
```

- Copy a Configuration File from one Flash Device to Another Example

  This example copies the file running-config from the first partition in internal Flash memory to the Flash memory PC card in slot 1. The file's checksum is verified, and its copying time of 30 seconds is displayed.

```
Router# copy flash: slot1:
System flash

Partition   Size     Used      Free      Bank-Size   State        Copy Mode
   1        4096K    3070K     1025K     4096K       Read/Write   Direct
   2        16384K   1671K     14712K    8192K       Read/Write   Direct

[Type ?<no> for partition directory; ? for full directory; q to abort]
Which partition? [default = 1]

System flash directory, partition 1:
File  Length    Name/status
   1  3142748   dirt/images/mars-test/c3600-j-mz.latest
   2  850       running-config
[3143728 bytes used, 1050576 available, 4194304 total]

PCMCIA Slot1 flash directory:
File  Length    Name/status
   1  1711088   dirt/images/c3600-i-mz
   2  850       running-config
```

```
[1712068 bytes used, 2482236 available, 4194304 total]
Source file name? running-config
Destination file name [running-config]?
Verifying checksum for 'running-config' (file # 2)...  OK
Erase flash device before writing? [confirm]
Flash contains files. Are you sure you want to erase? [confirm]

Copy 'running-config' from flash: device
  as 'running-config' into slot1: device WITH erase? [yes/no] yes
Erasing device... eeeeeeeeeeeeeeeeeeeeeeeeeeeeeeeeeeeeeeeeeeeeeeeeeeeeeeeee ...erased
!
 [OK - 850/4194304 bytes]

Flash device copy took 00:00:30 [hh:mm:ss]
Verifying checksum...  OK (0x16)
```

Copy an Image from the Master RSP Card to the Slave RSP Card Example

The following example copies the router-image file from the Flash memory card inserted in slot 1 of the master RSP card to slot 0 of the slave RSP card in the same router:

```
copy slot1:router-image slaveslot0:
```

Related Commands

To locate documentation of related commands, you can search online at www.cisco.com.

boot config
boot system
cd
copy xmodem: flash:
copy ymodem: flash:
delete
dir
erase
ip rcmd remote-username
reload
show bootvar
show (Flash file system)
slave auto-sync config
verify bootflash:

erase bootflash

The **erase bootflash:** and **erase bootflash** commands have identical function. Refer to the **erase** command for details.

erase flash

The **erase flash:** and **erase flash** commands have identical function. Refer to the **erase** command for details.

memory-size iomem

To reallocate the percentage of DRAM memory to use for I/O memory and processor memory on Cisco 3600 series routers, use the **memory-size iomem** global configuration command. The **no** form of this command reverts to the default allocation of 25 percent I/O memory and 75 percent processor memory.

> **memory-size iomem** *i/o-memory-percentage*
> **no memory-size iomem** *i/o-memory-percentage*

Syntax	Description
i/o-memory-percentage	The percentage of DRAM allocated to I/O memory. The values permitted are **10**, **15**, **20**, **25**, **30**, **40**, and **50** percent. A minimum of 4 MB of memory is required for I/O memory.

Default

The default allocation is 25 percent I/O memory and 75 percent processor memory.

Command Mode

Global configuration

Usage Guidelines

This command first appeared in Cisco IOS Release 11.2 P.

When you specify the percentage of I/O memory in the command line, processor memory automatically acquires the remaining percentage of DRAM memory.

Example

The following example allocates 40 percent of the DRAM memory to I/O memory and the remaining 60 percent to processor memory.

```
Router# configure terminal
Enter configuration commands, one per line.  End with Cntl-Z.
Router(config)# memory-size iomem 40
```

```
Router(config)# exit
Router# copy system:running-config nvram:startup-config
Building configuration...
[OK]

Router# reload

rommon 1 > boot
program load complete, entry point: 0x80008000, size: 0x32ea24
Self decompressing the image :
###########################################################################
###########################################################################
############################################################ [OK]
```

partition

To separate Flash memory into partitions on Class B file system platforms, use the **partition** global configuration command. Use the **no** form of this command to undo partitioning and to restore Flash memory to one partition.

> **partition** *flash-filesystem***:** [*number-of-partitions*][*partition-size*] (Cisco 1600 series and Cisco 3600 series)
> **no partition** *flash-filesystem***:**
>
> **partition flash** *partitions* [*size1 size2*] (all other Class B platforms)
> **no partition flash**

Syntax

Syntax	Description
flash-filesystem	One of the following Flash file systems, which must be followed by a colon (:). The Cisco 1600 series can only use the **flash:** keyword. • **flash:**—Internal Flash memory • **slot0:**—Flash memory card in PCMCIA slot 0 • **slot1:**—Flash memory card in PCMCIA slot 1
number-of-partitions	(Optional) Number of partitions in Flash memory.
partition-size	(Optional) Size of each partition. The number of partition size entries must be equal to the number of specified partitions.
partitions	Number of partitions in Flash memory. Can be one or two.
size1	(Optional) Size of the first partition in megabytes.
size2	(Optional) Size of the second partition in megabytes.

Default

Flash memory consists of one partition.

If the partition size is not specified, partitions of equal size are created.

Command Mode

Global configuration

Usage Guidelines

This command first appeared in Cisco IOS Release 10.3.

For the Cisco 1600 series and Cisco 3600 series, to undo partitioning, use the **partition** *flash-filesystem***:1** or **no partition** *flash-filesystem***:** command. For other Class B platforms, use either the **partition flash 1** or **no partition flash** command. If there are files in a partition other than the first, you must use the command **erase** *flash-filesystem***:***partition-number* to erase the partition before reverting to a single partition.

When creating two partitions, you must not truncate a file or cause a file to spill over into the second partition.

Examples

The following example creates two partitions of 4 MB each in Flash memory:

```
partition flash 2 4 4
```

The following example divides the Flash memory card in slot 0 into two partitions, each 8 MB in size on the Cisco 3600:

```
Router# configure terminal
Enter configuration commands, one per line.  End with Cntl/Z.
Router(config)# partition slot0: 2 8 8
```

The following example creates four partitions of equal size in the card on a Cisco 1600 series:

```
Router# configure terminal
Enter configuration commands, one per line.  End with Cntl/Z.
Router(config)# partition flash: 4
```

Part
II

Command Reference

show (Flash file system)

To display the layout and contents of a Flash memory file system, use the **show** EXEC command:

> **show** *flash-filesystem***:** [**all** | **chips** | **filesys**] (Class A Flash file systems)

> **show** *flash-filesystem***:** [**partition** *number*] [**all** | **chips** | **detailed** | **err** | **summary**] (Class B Flash file systems)

> **show** *flash-filesystem***:** (Class C Flash file systems)

Syntax	Description
flash-filesystem	Flash memory file system (**bootflash:**, **flash:**, **slot0:**, **slot1:**, **slavebootflash:**, **slaveslot0:**, or **slaveslot1:**).
all	(Optional) On Class B Flash file systems, **all** shows complete information about Flash memory, including information about the individual ROM devices in Flash memory and the names and sizes of all system image files stored in Flash memory, including those that are invalid. On Class A Flash file systems, **all** shows the following information: • The information displayed when no keywords are used. • The information displayed by the **filesys** keyword. • The information displayed by the **chips** keyword.
chips	(Optional) Shows information per partition and per chip, including which bank the chip is in plus its code, size, and name.
filesys	(Optional) Shows the Device Info Block, the Status Info, and the Usage Info.
detailed	(Optional) Shows detailed file directory information per partition, including file length, address, name, Flash memory checksum, computer checksum, bytes used, bytes available, total bytes, and bytes of system Flash memory.
err	(Optional) Shows write or erase failures in the form of number of retries.
partition *number*	(Optional) Shows output for the specified partition number. If you do not specify a partition in the command, the router displays output for all partitions. You can use this keyword only when Flash memory has multiple partitions.

Syntax	Description
summary	(Optional) Shows summary information per partition, including the partition size, bank size, state, and method by which files can be copied into a particular partition. You can use this keyword only when Flash memory has multiple partitions.

Command Mode
EXEC

Usage Guidelines
This command first appeared in Cisco IOS Release 11.3 AA.

If Flash memory is partitioned, the command displays the requested output for each partition, unless you use the **partition** keyword.

The command also specifies the location of the current image.

To display the contents of boot Flash memory, use the **show bootflash:** command as follows:

> **show bootflash:** [**all** | **chips** | **filesys**] for Class A Flash file systems

> **show bootflash:** [**partition** *number*] [**all** | **chips** | **detailed** | **err**] for Class B Flash file systems

To display the contents of internal Flash memory, use the **show flash:** command as follows:

> **show flash:** [**all** | **chips** | **filesys**] for Class A Flash file systems

> **show flash:** [**partition** *number*][**all** | **chips** | **detailed** | **err** | **summary**] for Class B Flash file systems

The **show (Flash file system)** command replaces the **show flash devices** command.

Sample Displays
The output of the **show** command depends on the type of Flash file system you select. Types include **flash:**, **bootflash:**, **slot0:**, **slot1:**, **slavebootflash:**, **slaveslot0:**, and **slaveslot1:**.

This section contains examples of output from **show flash:**.

- Class A Flash File System Examples

- Class B Flash File Systems Examples

Although the examples below use **flash:** as the Flash file system, you may also use the other Flash file systems listed above.

Class A Flash File System Examples

The following three examples show sample output for Class A Flash file systems. Table 18-8 describes the fields shown in the output.

Table 18-8   *Show (Class A Flash File System) Field Descriptions*

Field	Description
#	File's index number.
ED	Whether the file contains an error (*E*) or is deleted (*D*).
type	File's *type* (1 = configuration file, 2 = image file). The software displays these values only when the file's type is certain. When the file's type is unknown, the system displays unknown in this field.
crc	File's cyclic redundant check.
seek	Offset into the file system of the next file.
nlen	Length of the file's name.
length	Length of the file itself.
date/time	Date and time the file was created.
name	File's name.

The following is sample output from the **show flash:** command.

```
RouterA# show flash:

-#- ED --type-- --crc--- -seek-- nlen -length- -----date/time------ name
1   .. unknown  317FBA1B 4A0694   24  4720148 Aug 29 1997 17:49:36 hampton/nitro/c7200-j-mz
2   .. unknown  9237F3FF 92C574   11  4767328 Oct 01 1997 18:42:53 c7200-js-mz
3   .D unknown  71AB01F1 10C94E0  10  7982828 Oct 01 1997 18:48:14 rsp-jsv-mz
4   .D unknown  96DACD45 10C97E0   8      639 Oct 02 1997 12:09:17 the_time
5   .. unknown  96DACD45 10C9AE0   3      639 Oct 02 1997 12:09:32 the_time
6   .D unknown  96DACD45 10C9DE0   8      639 Oct 02 1997 12:37:01 the_time
7   .. unknown  96DACD45 10CA0E0   8      639 Oct 02 1997 12:37:13 the_time

3104544 bytes available (17473760 bytes used)
```

The following is sample output from the **show flash: chips** command:

```
RouterA# show flash: chips

******** Intel Series 2+ Status/Register Dump ********

ATTRIBUTE MEMORY REGISTERS:
  Config Option Reg (4000): 2
  Config Status Reg (4002): 0
  Card Status   Reg (4100): 1
  Write Protect Reg (4104): 4
  Voltage Cntrl Reg (410C): 0
  Rdy/Busy Mode Reg (4140): 2
```

```
COMMON MEMORY REGISTERS: Bank 0
  Intelligent ID Code  : 8989A0A0
  Compatible Status Reg: 8080
  Global     Status Reg: B0B0
  Block Status Regs:
     0 :  B0B0  B0B0  B0B0  B0B0  B0B0  B0B0  B0B0  B0B0
     8 :  B0B0  B0B0  B0B0  B0B0  B0B0  B0B0  B0B0  B0B0
    16 :  B0B0  B0B0  B0B0  B0B0  B0B0  B0B0  B0B0  B0B0
    24 :  B0B0  B0B0  B0B0  B0B0  B0B0  B0B0  B0B0  B0B0

COMMON MEMORY REGISTERS: Bank 1
  Intelligent ID Code  : 8989A0A0
  Compatible Status Reg: 8080
  Global     Status Reg: B0B0
  Block Status Regs:
     0 :  B0B0  B0B0  B0B0  B0B0  B0B0  B0B0  B0B0  B0B0
     8 :  B0B0  B0B0  B0B0  B0B0  B0B0  B0B0  B0B0  B0B0
    16 :  B0B0  B0B0  B0B0  B0B0  B0B0  B0B0  B0B0  B0B0
    24 :  B0B0  B0B0  B0B0  B0B0  B0B0  B0B0  B0B0  B0B0

COMMON MEMORY REGISTERS: Bank 2
  Intelligent ID Code  : 8989A0A0
  Compatible Status Reg: 8080
  Global     Status Reg: B0B0
  Block Status Regs:
     0 :  B0B0  B0B0  B0B0  B0B0  B0B0  B0B0  B0B0  B0B0
     8 :  B0B0  B0B0  B0B0  B0B0  B0B0  B0B0  B0B0  B0B0
    16 :  B0B0  B0B0  B0B0  B0B0  B0B0  B0B0  B0B0  B0B0
    24 :  B0B0  B0B0  B0B0  B0B0  B0B0  B0B0  B0B0  B0B0

COMMON MEMORY REGISTERS: Bank 3
  Intelligent ID Code  : 8989A0A0
  Compatible Status Reg: 8080
  Global     Status Reg: B0B0
  Block Status Regs:
     0 :  B0B0  B0B0  B0B0  B0B0  B0B0  B0B0  B0B0  B0B0
     8 :  B0B0  B0B0  B0B0  B0B0  B0B0  B0B0  B0B0  B0B0
    16 :  B0B0  B0B0  B0B0  B0B0  B0B0  B0B0  B0B0  B0B0
    24 :  B0B0  B0B0  B0B0  B0B0  B0B0  B0B0  B0B0  B0B0

COMMON MEMORY REGISTERS: Bank 4
  Intelligent ID Code  : 8989A0A0
  Compatible Status Reg: 8080
  Global     Status Reg: B0B0
  Block Status Regs:
     0 :  B0B0  B0B0  B0B0  B0B0  B0B0  B0B0  B0B0  B0B0
     8 :  B0B0  B0B0  B0B0  B0B0  B0B0  B0B0  B0B0  B0B0
    16 :  B0B0  B0B0  B0B0  B0B0  B0B0  B0B0  B0B0  B0B0
    24 :  B0B0  B0B0  B0B0  B0B0  B0B0  B0B0  B0B0  B0B0
```

The following is sample output from the **show flash: filesys** command:

```
RouterA# show flash: filesys

-------- F I L E   S Y S T E M   S T A T U S --------
```

```
   Device Number = 0
DEVICE INFO BLOCK:
  Magic Number         = 6887635   File System Vers = 10000    (1.0)
  Length               = 1400000   Sector Size      = 20000
  Programming Algorithm = 4        Erased State     = FFFFFFFF
  File System Offset   = 20000     Length = 13A0000
  MONLIB Offset        = 100       Length = C730
  Bad Sector Map Offset = 1FFEC    Length = 14
  Squeeze Log Offset   = 13C0000   Length = 20000
  Squeeze Buffer Offset = 13E0000  Length = 20000
  Num Spare Sectors    = 0
    Spares:
STATUS INFO:
  Writable
  NO File Open for Write
  Complete Stats
  No Unrecovered Errors
  No Squeeze in progress
USAGE INFO:
  Bytes Used     = 10AA0E0  Bytes Available = 2F5F20
  Bad Sectors    = 0        Spared Sectors  = 0
  OK Files       = 4        Bytes = 90C974
  Deleted Files  = 3        Bytes = 79D3EC
  Files w/Errors = 0        Bytes = 0
```

Class B Flash File Systems Examples

Table 18-9 describes fields in the sample output for Class B Flash file systems.

Table 18-9 *Show (Class B Flash File System) All Fields*

Field	Description
addr	Address of the file in Flash memory.
available	Total number of bytes available in Flash memory.
Bank	Bank number.
Bank-Size	Size of bank in bytes.
bytes used	Total number of bytes used in Flash memory.
ccksum	Computed checksum.
Chip	Chip number.
Code	Code number.

Table 18-9 *Show (Class B Flash File System) All Fields (Continued)*

Field	Description
Copy-Mode	Method by which the partition can be copied to: • RXBOOT-MANUAL indicates a user can copy manually by reloading to the boot ROM image. • RXBOOT-FLH indicates user can copy via Flash load helper. • Direct indicates user can copy directly into Flash memory. • None indicates that it is not possible to copy into that partition.
fcksum	Checksum recorded in Flash memory.
File	Number of the system image file. If no filename is specified in the **boot system flash** command, the router boots the system image file with the lowest file number.
Free	Number of bytes free in partition.
Length	Size of the system image file (in bytes).
Name	Name of chip manufacturer and chip type.
Name/status	Filename and status of a system image file. The status [invalidated] appears when a file has been rewritten (recopied) into Flash memory. The first (now invalidated) copy of the file is still present within Flash memory, but it is rendered unusable in favor of the newest version. The [invalidated] status can also indicate an incomplete file that results from the user abnormally terminating the copy process, a network timeout, or a Flash memory overflow.
Partition	Partition number in Flash memory.
Size	Size of partition in bytes or size of chip.
State	State of the partition. It can be one of the following values: • Read-Only indicates the partition that is being executed from. • Read/Write is a partition that can be copied to.
System flash directory	Flash directory and its contents.
total	Total size of Flash memory, in bytes.
Used	Number of bytes used in partition.

The following is sample output from the **show flash:** command:

```
RouterB> show flash:

System flash directory:
File  Length    Name/status
  1   4137888   c3640-c2is-mz.Feb24
[4137952 bytes used, 12639264 available, 16777216 total]
16384K bytes of processor board System flash (Read/Write)\
```

The following example shows detailed information about the second partition in internal Flash memory:

```
RouterB# show flash: partition 2

System flash directory, partition 2:
File  Length   Name/status
  1   1711088  dirt/images/c3600-i-mz
[1711152 bytes used, 15066064 available, 16777216 total]
16384K bytes of processor board System flash (Read/Write)
```

The following is sample output from the **show flash: all** command:

```
RouterB> show flash: all
Partition  Size    Used    Free     Bank-Size  State       Copy Mode
   1       16384K  4040K   12343K   4096K      Read/Write  Direct

System flash directory:
File  Length   Name/status
        addr       fcksum  ccksum
  1   4137888  c3640-c2is-mz.Feb24
        0x40      0xED65  0xED65
[4137952 bytes used, 12639264 available, 16777216 total]
16384K bytes of processor board System flash (Read/Write)

    Chip   Bank   Code    Size     Name
     1      1     01D5    1024KB   AMD   29F080
     2      1     01D5    1024KB   AMD   29F080
     3      1     01D5    1024KB   AMD   29F080
     4      1     01D5    1024KB   AMD   29F080
     1      2     01D5    1024KB   AMD   29F080
     2      2     01D5    1024KB   AMD   29F080
     3      2     01D5    1024KB   AMD   29F080
     4      2     01D5    1024KB   AMD   29F080
     1      3     01D5    1024KB   AMD   29F080
     2      3     01D5    1024KB   AMD   29F080
     3      3     01D5    1024KB   AMD   29F080
     4      3     01D5    1024KB   AMD   29F080
     1      4     01D5    1024KB   AMD   29F080
     2      4     01D5    1024KB   AMD   29F080
     3      4     01D5    1024KB   AMD   29F080
     4      4     01D5    1024KB   AMD   29F080
```

The following is sample output from the **show flash: all** command on a router with Flash memory partitioned:

```
Router# show flash: all

System flash partition information:
Partition  Size    Used    Free     Bank-Size  State       Copy-Mode
   1       4096K   3459K   637K     4096K      Read Only   RXBOOT-FLH
   2       4096K   3224K   872K     4096K      Read/Write  Direct

System flash directory, partition 1:
```

```
File      Length      Name/status
          addr     fcksum      ccksum
  1      3459720       master/igs-bfpx.100-4.3
          0x40     0x3DE1      0x3DE1
[3459784 bytes used, 734520 available, 4194304 total]
4096K bytes of processor board System flash (Read ONLY)

   Chip      Bank      Code      Size      Name
    1         1        89A2     1024KB    INTEL 28F008SA
    2         1        89A2     1024KB    INTEL 28F008SA
    3         1        89A2     1024KB    INTEL 28F008SA
    4         1        89A2     1024KB    INTEL 28F008SA
Executing current image from System flash [partition 1]

 System flash directory, partition2:
File      Length      Name/status
          addr     fcksum      ccksum
  1      3224008       igs-kf.100
          0x40     0xEE91      0xEE91
[3224072 bytes used, 970232 available, 4194304 total]
4096K bytes of processor board System flash (Read/Write)

   Chip      Bank      Code      Size      Name
    1         2        89A2     1024KB    INTEL 28F008SA
    2         2        89A2     1024KB    INTEL 28F008SA
    3         2        89A2     1024KB    INTEL 28F008SA
    4         2        89A2     1024KB    INTEL 28F008SA
```

The following is sample output from the **show flash: chips** command:

```
RouterB> show flash: chips
16384K bytes of processor board System flash (Read/Write)

   Chip      Bank      Code      Size      Name
    1         1        01D5     1024KB    AMD   29F080
    2         1        01D5     1024KB    AMD   29F080
    3         1        01D5     1024KB    AMD   29F080
    4         1        01D5     1024KB    AMD   29F080
    1         2        01D5     1024KB    AMD   29F080
    2         2        01D5     1024KB    AMD   29F080
    3         2        01D5     1024KB    AMD   29F080
    4         2        01D5     1024KB    AMD   29F080
    1         3        01D5     1024KB    AMD   29F080
    2         3        01D5     1024KB    AMD   29F080
    3         3        01D5     1024KB    AMD   29F080
    4         3        01D5     1024KB    AMD   29F080
    1         4        01D5     1024KB    AMD   29F080
    2         4        01D5     1024KB    AMD   29F080
    3         4        01D5     1024KB    AMD   29F080
    4         4        01D5     1024KB    AMD   29F080
```

The following is sample output from the **show flash: detailed** command:

```
RouterB> show flash: detailed

System flash directory:
File  Length   Name/status
        addr      fcksum  ccksum
  1   4137888  c3640-c2is-mz.Feb24
        0x40     0xED65  0xED65
[4137952 bytes used, 12639264 available, 16777216 total]
16384K bytes of processor board System flash (Read/Write)
```

The following is sample output from the **show flash: err** command:

```
RouterB> show flash: err

System flash directory:
File  Length   Name/status
  1   4137888  c3640-c2is-mz.Feb24
[4137952 bytes used, 12639264 available, 16777216 total]
16384K bytes of processor board System flash (Read/Write)
```

```
        Chip   Bank   Code    Size    Name           erase  write
          1     1     01D5   1024KB   AMD  29F080      0      0
          2     1     01D5   1024KB   AMD  29F080      0      0
          3     1     01D5   1024KB   AMD  29F080      0      0
          4     1     01D5   1024KB   AMD  29F080      0      0
          1     2     01D5   1024KB   AMD  29F080      0      0
          2     2     01D5   1024KB   AMD  29F080      0      0
          3     2     01D5   1024KB   AMD  29F080      0      0
          4     2     01D5   1024KB   AMD  29F080      0      0
          1     3     01D5   1024KB   AMD  29F080      0      0
          2     3     01D5   1024KB   AMD  29F080      0      0
          3     3     01D5   1024KB   AMD  29F080      0      0
          4     3     01D5   1024KB   AMD  29F080      0      0
          1     4     01D5   1024KB   AMD  29F080      0      0
          2     4     01D5   1024KB   AMD  29F080      0      0
          3     4     01D5   1024KB   AMD  29F080      0      0
          4     4     01D5   1024KB   AMD  29F080      0      0
```

Refer to Table 18-9 for a description of the fields. The **show flash: err** command also displays two extra fields: erase and write. The erase field indications the number of erase errors. The write field indicates the number of write errors.

The following is sample output from the **show flash summary** command on a router with Flash memory partitioned. The partition in the Read Only state is the partition from which the Cisco IOS image is being executed.

```
Router# show flash summary

System flash partition information:
Partition   Size    Used    Free    Bank-Size   State        Copy-Mode
    1       4096K   2048K   2048K   2048K       Read Only    RXBOOT-FLH
    2       4096K   2048K   2048K   2048K       Read/Write   Direct
```

Related Commands

show flash
show flash ?
show flash all
show flash chips
show flash filesys

write memory

The **copy system:running-config nvram: startup-config** command replaces the **write memory** command. Refer to the **copy** command for further details.

write network

The **copy system:running-config** *destination-url* command replaces the **write network** command. Refer to the **copy** command for further details.

## CHAPTER 19

Rebooting a Router

This chapter describes the basic procedure a router follows when it reboots, how to alter the procedure, and how to use the ROM Monitor.

For a complete description of the booting commands mentioned in this chapter, refer to Chapter 20, "Booting Commands." To locate documentation of other commands that appear in this chapter, you can search online at www.cisco.com.

Reboot a Router Task List

You can perform the tasks related to rebooting discussed in the following sections:

- Display Booting Information
- Rebooting Procedures
- Modify the Configuration Register Boot Field
- Set Environment Variables
- Schedule a Reload of the System Image
- Configure High System Availability Operation (Cisco 7500 Series)
- Stop Booting and Enter ROM Monitor Mode
- Manually Load a System Image from ROM Monitor

Display Booting Information

Use the following commands in EXEC mode to display information about system software, system image files, and configuration files:

Step	Command	Purpose
1	show bootvar	Lists the contents of the BOOT environment variable, the name of the configuration file pointed to by the CONFIG_FILE environment variable, and the contents of the BOOTLDR environment variable.
2	more nvram:startup-config	Lists the startup configuration information. On all platforms except the Class A Flash file systems, the startup configuration is usually in NVRAM. On Class A Flash file systems, the CONFIG_FILE environment variable points to the startup configuration, defaulting to NVRAM.
3	show version	Lists the system software release version, configuration register setting, and other information.

You can also use the **o** command (the **confreg** command for some platforms) in ROM monitor mode to list the configuration register settings on some models.

Rebooting Procedures

The following sections describe what happens when the router reboots:

- What Configuration File Does the Router Use upon Startup?

- What Image Does the Router Use upon Startup?

What Configuration File Does the Router Use upon Startup?

On all platforms except Class A Flash file system platforms:

- If the configuration register is set to ignore NVRAM, the router enters setup mode.

- If the configuration register is not set to ignore NVRAM,

    — The startup software checks for configuration information in NVRAM.

    — If NVRAM holds valid configuration commands, the Cisco IOS software executes the commands automatically at startup.

    — If the software detects a problem with NVRAM or the configuration it contains (a CRC checksum error), it enters **setup** mode and prompts for configuration.

On Class A Flash file system platforms:

- If the configuration register is set to ignore NVRAM, the router enters setup mode.

- If the configuration register is not set to ignore NVRAM,

    — The startup software uses the configuration pointed to by the CONFIG_FILE environment variable.

    — When the CONFIG_FILE environment variable does not exist or is null (such as at first-time startup), the router uses NVRAM as the default startup device.

    — When the router uses NVRAM to start up and the system detects a problem with NVRAM or the configuration it contains, the router enters **setup** mode.

Problems can include a bad checksum for the information in NVRAM or an empty NVRAM with no configuration information. For more information on environment variables, refer to the "Set Environment Variables" section later in this chapter.

What Image Does the Router Use upon Startup?

When a router is powered on or rebooted, the following events happen:

- The ROM Monitor initializes.

- The ROM Monitor checks the configuration register boot field (the lowest four bits in the register).

  — If the boot field is 0x0, the system does not boot an IOS image and waits for user intervention at the ROM Monitor prompt.

  — If the boot field is 0x1, the ROM Monitor boots the boot helper image. (On some platforms, the boot helper image is specified by the BOOTLDR environment variable.)

  — If the boot field is 0x2 through 0xF, the ROM Monitor boots the first valid image specified in the configuration file or specified by the BOOT environment variable.

When the boot field is 0x2 through 0xF, the router goes through each **boot system** command in order until it boots a valid image. If bit 13 in the configuration register is set, each command will be tried once. If bit 13 is not set, the **boot system** commands specifying a network server will be tried up to five more times. The timeouts between each consecutive attempt are 2, 4, 16, 256, and 300 seconds.

If the router cannot find a valid image, the following events happen:

- If all boot commands in the system configuration file specify booting from a network server and all commands fail, the system attempts to boot the first valid file in Flash memory.

- If the "boot-default-ROM-software" option in the configuration register is set, the router will start the boot image (the image contained in boot ROM or specified by the BOORLDR environment variable).

- If the "boot-default-ROM-software" option in the configuration register is not set, the system waits for user intervention at the ROM Monitor prompt. You must boot the router manually.

- If a fully functional system image is not found, the router will not function and must be reconfigured through a direct console port connection.

NOTE   Refer to your platform documentation for information on the default location of the boot image.

When looking for a bootable file in Flash memory:

- The system searches for the filename in Flash memory. If a filename is not specified, the software searches through the entire Flash directory for a bootable file instead of picking only the first file.

- The system attempts to recognize the file in Flash memory. If the file is recognized, the software decides whether it is bootable by performing the following checks:

  — For run-from-Flash images, the software determines whether it is loaded at the correct execution address.

— For run-from-RAM images, the software determines whether the system has enough RAM to execute the image.

Figure 19-1 illustrates the basic booting decision process.

Figure 19-1 *Booting Process*

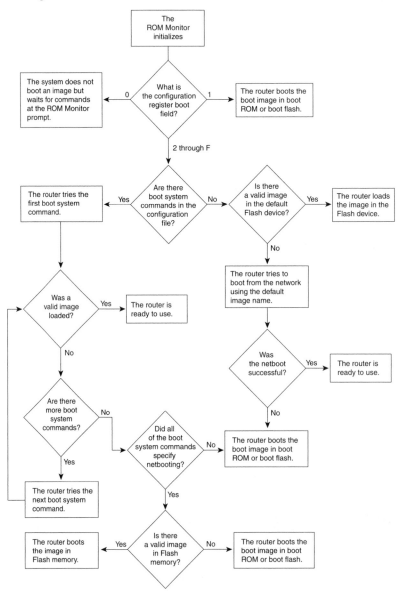

Modify the Configuration Register Boot Field

The configuration register boot field determines whether the router loads an operating system image, and if so, where it obtains this system image. This section contains the following topics:

- How the Router Uses the Boot Field
- Hardware Versus Software Configuration Register Boot Fields
- Modify the Software Configuration Register Boot Field

Refer to the documentation for your platform for more information on the configuration register.

How the Router Uses the Boot Field

The lowest 4 bits of the 16-bit configuration register (bits 3, 2, 1, and 0) form the boot field. The following boot field values determine if the router loads an operating system and where it obtains the system image:

- When the entire boot field equals 0-0-0-0 (0x0), the router does not load a system image. Instead, it enters ROM monitor or "maintenance" mode from which you can enter ROM monitor commands to manually load a system image. Refer to the "Manually Load a System Image from ROM Monitor" section for details on ROM monitor mode.
- When the entire boot field equals 0-0-0-1 (0x1), the router loads the boot helper or rxboot image.
- When the entire boot field equals a value between 0-0-1-0 (0x2) and 1-1-1-1 (0xF), the router loads the system image specified by **boot system** commands in the startup configuration file. When the startup configuration file does not contain **boot system** commands, the router tries to load a default system image stored on a network server.

  When loading a default system image from a network server, the router uses the configuration register settings to determine the default system image filename for booting from a network server. The router forms the default boot filename by starting with the word "cisco" and then appending the octal equivalent of the boot field number in the configuration register, followed by a hyphen (-) and the processor type name (cisco*nn-cpu*). See the appropriate hardware installation guide for details on the configuration register and the default filename.

Hardware Versus Software Configuration Register Boot Fields

You modify the boot field from either the hardware configuration register or the software configuration register, depending on the platform.

Most platforms use a software configuration register. Refer to your hardware documentation for information on the configuration register for your platform.

The hardware configuration register can be changed only on the processor card with dual in-line package (DIP) switches located at the back of the router. For information on modifying the hardware configuration register, refer to the appropriate hardware installation guide.

Modify the Software Configuration Register Boot Field

To modify the software configuration register boot field, use the following commands:

Step	Command	Purpose
1	**show version**	Obtains the current configuration register setting. The configuration register is listed as a hexadecimal value.
2	**configure terminal**	Enters configuration mode, selecting the terminal option.
3	**config-register** *value*	Modifies the existing configuration register setting to reflect the way in which you want to load a system image. The configuration register value is in hexadecimal form with a leading "0x."
4	**end**	Exits configuration mode.
5	**show version**	Verifies that the configuration register setting is correct. Repeat Steps 2 through 5 again if the setting is not correct.
6	**reload**	Reboots the router to make your changes take effect.

In ROM monitor mode, use the **o** command or the **confreg** command on some platforms to list the value of the configuration register boot field.

Modify the current configuration register setting to reflect the way in which you want to load a system image. To do so, change the least significant hexadecimal digit to one of the following:

- 0 to load the system image manually using the **boot** command in ROM monitor mode.

- 1 to load the system image from boot ROMs. On the Cisco 7200 series and Cisco 7500 series, this setting configures the system to automatically load the system image from bootflash.

- 2–F to load the system image from **boot system** commands in the startup configuration file or from a default system image stored on a network server.

For example, if the current configuration register setting is 0x101 and you want to load a system image from **boot system** commands in the startup configuration file, you would change the configuration register setting to 0x102.

Modify the Software Configuration Register Boot Field Example

In the following example, the **show version** command indicates that the current configuration register is set so that the router does not automatically load an operating system image. Instead, it enters ROM monitor mode and waits for user-entered ROM monitor commands. The new setting instructs the router to a load a system image from commands in the startup configuration file or from a default system image stored on a network server.

```
Router1# show version

Cisco Internetwork Operating System Software
IOS (tm) 4500 Software (C4500-J-M), Version 11.1(10.4), MAINTENANCE INTERIM SOFTWARE
Copyright (c) 1986-1997 by cisco Systems, Inc.
Compiled Mon 07-Apr-97 19:51 by dschwart
Image text-base: 0x600088A0, data-base: 0x60718000

ROM: System Bootstrap, Version 5.1(1) [daveu 1], RELEASE SOFTWARE (fc1)
FLASH: 4500-XBOOT Bootstrap Software, Version 10.1(1), RELEASE SOFTWARE (fc1)

Router1 uptime is 6 weeks, 5 days, 2 hours, 22 minutes
System restarted by error - a SegV exception, PC 0x6070F7AC
System image file is "c4500-j-mz.111-current", booted via flash

cisco 4500 (R4K) processor (revision 0x00) with 32768K/4096K bytes of memory.
Processor board ID 01242622
R4600 processor, Implementation 32, Revision 1.0
G.703/E1 software, Version 1.0.
Bridging software.
SuperLAT software copyright 1990 by Meridian Technology Corp).
X.25 software, Version 2.0, NET2, BFE and GOSIP compliant.
TN3270 Emulation software (copyright 1994 by TGV Inc).
Basic Rate ISDN software, Version 1.0.
2 Ethernet/IEEE 802.3 interfaces.
2 Token Ring/IEEE 802.5 interfaces.
4 ISDN Basic Rate interfaces.
128K bytes of non-volatile configuration memory.
8192K bytes of processor board System flash (Read/Write)
4096K bytes of processor board Boot flash (Read/Write)

Configuration register is 0x2100

Router1# configure terminal
Router1(config)# config-register 0x210F
Router1(config)# end
Router1# reload
```

Set Environment Variables

Because many platforms can boot images from several locations, these systems use special ROM monitor environment variables to specify the location and filename of images that the router is to use. In addition, Class A Flash file systems can load configuration files from several locations and use an environment variable to specify startup configurations.

These special environment variables are as follows:

- BOOT Environment Variable
- BOOTLDR Environment Variable
- CONFIG_FILE Environment Variable

BOOT Environment Variable

The BOOT environment variable specifies a list of bootable system images on various file systems. Refer to the "Specify the Startup System Image in the Configuration File" section in Chapter 15, "Loading and Maintaining System Images and Microcode." After you save the BOOT environment variable to your startup configuration, the router checks the variable upon startup to determine the device and filename of the image to boot.

The router tries to boot the first image in the BOOT environment variable list. If the router is unsuccessful at booting that image, it tries to boot the next image specified in the list. The router tries each image in the list until it successfully boots. If the router cannot boot any image in the BOOT environment variable list, the router attempts to boot the boot image.

If an entry in the BOOT environment variable list does not specify a device, the router assumes the device is **tftp**. If an entry in the BOOT environment variable list specifies an invalid device, the router skips that entry.

BOOTLDR Environment Variable

The BOOTLDR environment specifies the Flash file system and filename containing the boot image that the ROM monitor uses if it cannot find a valid system image. In addition, a boot image is required to boot the router with an image from a network server.

You can change the BOOTLDR environment variable on platforms that use a software boot image rather than boot ROMs. On these platforms, the boot image can be changed without having to replace the boot ROM.

This environment variable allows you to have several boot images. After you save the BOOTLDR environment variable to your startup configuration, the router checks the variable upon startup to determine which boot image to use if the system cannot be loaded.

NOTE	Refer to your platform documentation for information on the default location of the boot image.

CONFIG_FILE Environment Variable

For Class A Flash file systems, the CONFIG_FILE environment variable specifies the file system and filename of the configuration file to use for initialization (startup). Valid file systems can include **nvram:**, **bootflash:**, **slot0:**, and **slot1:**. Refer to the "Location of Configuration Files" section in Chapter 13, "Modifying, Downloading, and Maintaining Configuration Files." After you save the CONFIG_FILE environment variable to your startup configuration, the router checks the variable upon startup to determine the location and filename of the configuration file to use for initialization.

The router uses the NVRAM configuration during initialization when the CONFIG_FILE environment variable does not exist or when it is null (such as at first-time startup). If the router detects a problem with NVRAM or a checksum error, the router enters **setup** mode.

Controlling Environment Variables

Although the ROM Monitor controls environment variables, you can create, modify, or view them with certain commands. To create or modify the BOOT, BOOTLDR, and CONFIG_FILE environment variables, use the **boot system**, **boot bootldr**, and **boot config** global configuration commands, respectively.

Refer to the "Specify the Startup System Image in the Configuration File" section in Chapter 15, "Loading and Maintaining System Images and Microcode" for details on setting the BOOT environment variable. Refer to the "Specify the Startup Configuration File" section in Chapter 13, "Modifying, Downloading, and Maintaining Configuration Files" for details on setting the CONFIG_FILE variable.

NOTE   When you use these three global configuration commands, you affect only the running configuration. You must save the environment variable settings to your startup configuration to place the information under ROM monitor control and for the environment variables to function as expected. Use the **copy system:running-config nvram:startup-config** command to save the environment variables from your running configuration to your startup configuration.

You can view the contents of the BOOT, BOOTLDR, and the CONFIG_FILE environment variables by issuing the **show bootvar** command. This command displays the settings for these variables as they exist in the startup configuration as well as in the running configuration if a running configuration setting differs from a startup configuration setting.

Use the **more nvram:startup-config** command to display the contents of the configuration file pointed to by the CONFIG_FILE environment variable.

Set the BOOTLDR Environment Variable

To set the BOOTLDR environment variable, use the following commands, beginning in privileged EXEC mode:

Step	Command	Purpose
1	**dir** [*flash-filesystem*:]	Verifies that internal Flash or bootflash contains the boot helper image.
2	**configure terminal**	Enters the configuration mode from the terminal.
3	**boot bootldr** *file-url*	Sets the BOOTLDR environment variable to specify the Flash device and filename of the boot helper image. This step modifies the runtime BOOTLDR environment variable.
4	**end**	Exits configuration mode.
5	**copy system:running-config nvram:startup-config**	Saves this runtime BOOTLDR environment variable to your startup configuration.
6	**show bootvar**	Optionally, verifies the contents of the BOOTLDR environment variable.

The following example sets the BOOTLDR environment to change the location of the boot helper image from internal Flash to slot 0.

```
Router# dir bootflash:
-#- -length- -----date/time------ name
1   620       May 04 1995 26:22:04 rsp-boot-m
2   620       May 24 1995 21:38:14 config2

7993896 bytes available (1496 bytes used)
Router# configure terminal
Router (config)# boot bootldr slot0:rsp-boot-m
Router (config)# end
Router# copy system:running-config nvram:startup-config
[ok]
Router# show bootvar
BOOT variable = slot0:rsp-boot-m
CONFIG_FILE variable = nvram:
Current CONFIG_FILE variable = slot0:router-config

Configuration register is 0x0
```

Schedule a Reload of the System Image

You may want to schedule a reload of the system image to occur on the router at a later time (for example, late at night or during the weekend when the router is used less), or you may want to synchronize a reload network-wide (for example, to perform a software upgrade on all routers in the network).

NOTE   A scheduled reload must take place within approximately 24 days.

Configure a Scheduled Reload

To configure the router to reload the Cisco IOS software at a later time, use one of the following commands in privileged EXEC command mode:

Command	Purpose
reload in [*hh*:]*mm* [*text*]	Schedules a reload of the software to take effect in the specified minutes or hours and minutes.
reload at *hh*:*mm* [*month day* | *day month*] [*text*]	Schedules a reload of the software to take place at the specified time (using a 24-hour clock).

If you specify the month and day, the reload is scheduled to take place at the specified time and date. If you do not specify the month and day, the reload takes place at the specified time on the current day (if the specified time is later than the current time), or on the next day (if the specified time is earlier than the current time). Specifying 00:00 schedules the reload for midnight.

NOTE   The **at** keyword can only be used if the system clock has been set on the router (either through NTP, the hardware calendar, or manually). The time is relative to the configured time zone on the router. To schedule reloads across several routers to occur simultaneously, the time on each router must be synchronized with NTP.

The following example illustrates how to use the **reload** command to reload the software on the router on the current day at 7:30 p.m.:

```
Router# reload at 19:30
Reload scheduled for 19:30:00 UTC Wed Jun 5 1996 (in 2 hours and 25 minutes)
Proceed with reload? [confirm]
```

The following example illustrates how to use the **reload** command to reload the software on the router at a future time:

```
Router# reload at 02:00 jun 20
Reload scheduled for 02:00:00 UTC Thu Jun 20 1996 (in 344 hours and 53 minutes)
Proceed with reload? [confirm]
```

Display Information about a Scheduled Reload

To display information about a previously scheduled reload or to determine if a reload has been scheduled on the router, use the following command in EXEC command mode:

Command	Purpose
show reload	Displays reload information including the time the reload is scheduled to occur and the reason for the reload if it was specified when the reload was scheduled.

Cancel a Scheduled Reload

To cancel a previously scheduled reload, use the following command in privileged EXEC command mode:

Command	Purpose
reload cancel	Cancels a previously scheduled reload of the software.

The following example illustrates how to use the **reload cancel** command to stop a scheduled reload:

```
Router# reload cancel
Router#
***
*** --- SHUTDOWN ABORTED ---
***
```

Configure High System Availability Operation (Cisco 7500 Series)

High system availability (HSA) refers to how quickly your router returns to an operational status after a failure occurs. On the Cisco 7507 and Cisco 7513, you can install two RSP cards in a single router to improve system availability.

Two RSP cards in a router provide the most basic level of increased system availability through a "cold restart" feature. A "cold restart" means that when one RSP card fails, the other RSP card reboots the router. In this way, your router is never in a failed state for very long, thereby increasing system availability.

When one RSP card takes over operation from another, system operation is interrupted. This change is similar to issuing the **reload** command. The following events occur when one RSP card fails and the other takes over:

- The router stops passing traffic.

- Route information is lost.

- All connections are lost.

- The backup or "slave" RSP card becomes the active or "master" RSP card that reboots and runs the router. Thus, the slave has its own image and configuration file so that it can act as a single processor.

NOTE   HSA does not impact performance in terms of packets per second or overall bandwidth. Additionally, HSA does not provide fault-tolerance or redundancy.

Understand Master and Slave Operation

A router configured for HSA operation has one RSP card that is the master and one that is the slave. The master RSP card functions as if it were a single processor, controlling all functions of the router. The slave RSP card does nothing but actively monitor the master for failure.

A system crash can cause the master RSP to fail or go into a nonfunctional state. When the slave RSP detects a nonfunctional master, the slave resets itself and takes part in *master-slave arbitration*. Master-slave arbitration is a ROM Monitor process that determines which RSP card is the master and which is the slave upon startup (or reboot).

If a system crash causes the master RSP to fail, the slave RSP becomes the new master RSP and uses its own system image and configuration file to reboot the router. The failed RSP card now becomes the slave. The failure state of the slave (formerly the master) can be accessed from the console via the **show stacks** command.

With HSA operation, the following items are important to note:

- An RSP card that acts as the slave runs a different software version than it does when it acts as the master. The slave mode software is a subset of the master mode software.

- The two RSP cards do not have to run the same master software image and configuration file. When the slave reboots the system and becomes the new master, it uses its own system image and configuration file to reboot the router.

- When enabled, automatic synchronization mode automatically ensures that the master and slave RSP card have the same configuration file.

- Both hardware and software failures can cause the master RSP to enter a nonfunctional state; but, the system does not indicate the type of failure.

- The console is always connected to master. A Y cable is shipped with your Cisco 7507 or Cisco 7513. The "top" of the Y cable plugs into the console port on each RSP card, while the "bottom" of the Y cable plugs into a terminal or terminal server. The master RSP card has ownership of the Y cable in that the slave Universal Asynchronous Receiver Transmitter (UART) drivers are disabled. Thus, no matter which RSP card has mastership of the system, your view of the internetwork environment is always from the master's perspective. Refer to your product's hardware installation and maintenance publication for information on properly installing the Y cable.

Understand Implementation Methods

There are two common ways to use HSA. You can use HSA for:

- Simple hardware backup

  Use this method to protect against an RSP card failure. With this method, you configure both RSP cards with the same software image and configuration information. Also, you configure the router to automatically synchronize configuration information on both cards when changes occur.

- Software error protection

  Use this method to protect against critical Cisco IOS software errors in a particular release. With this method, you configure the RSP cards with different software images, but with the same configuration information. If you are using new or experimental Cisco IOS software, consider using the software error protection method.

You can also use HSA for advanced implementations. For example, you can configure the RSP cards with the following:

- Similar software versions, but different configuration files

- Different software images *and* different configuration files

- Widely varied configuration files (for example, various features or interfaces can be turned off and on per card)

NOTE   While other uses are possible, the configuration information in this guide describes commands for only the two common methods—simple hardware backup and software error protection.

Understand System Requirements

To configure HSA operation, you must have a Cisco 7507 or Cisco 7513 containing two RSP processor cards and Cisco IOS Release 11.1 or later.

Configure HSA Operation Task List

When configuring HSA operation, complete the tasks in the following sections. The first two and last two tasks are required for both implementations. The third and fourth tasks relate to simple hardware backup. The fifth task relates to software error protection only.

- Specify the Default Slave RSP (both implementations)

- Ensure That Both RSP Cards Contain the Same Configuration File (both implementations)

- Ensure That Both RSP Cards Contain the Same System Image (simple hardware backup only)

- Ensure That Both RSP Cards Contain the Same Microcode Image (simple hardware backup only)

- Specify Different Startup Images for the Master and Slave RSP (software error protection only)

- Set Environment Variables on the Master and Slave RSP (both implementations)

- Monitor and Maintain HSA Operation (both implementations)

Specify the Default Slave RSP

Because your view of the environment is always from the master RSP perspective, you define a default slave RSP. The router uses the default slave information when booting as follows:

- If a system boot is due to powering up the router or using the **reload** command, then the specified default slave will be the slave RSP.

- If a system boot is due to a system crash or hardware failure, then the system ignores the default slave designation and makes the crashed or faulty RSP the slave RSP.

To define the default slave RSP, use the following command, beginning in privileged EXEC mode:

Step	Command	Purpose
1	**configure terminal**	Enters the configuration mode from the terminal.
2	**slave default-slot** *processor-slot-number*	Defines the default slave RSP.
3	**end**	Exits configuration mode.
4	**copy system:running-config nvram:startup-config**	Saves this information to your startup configuration.

Upon the next system reboot, the above changes take effect (if both RSP cards are operational). Thus, the specified default slave becomes the slave RSP card. The other RSP card takes over mastership of the system and controls all functions of the router.

If you do not specifically define the default slave RSP, the RSP card located in the higher number processor slot is the default slave. On the Cisco 7507, processor slot 3 contains the default slave RSP. On the Cisco 7513, processor slot 7 contains the default slave RSP.

The following example sets the default slave RSP to processor slot 2 on a Cisco 7507:

```
Router# configure terminal
Router (config)# slave default-slot 2
Router (config)# end
Router# copy system:running-config nvram:startup-config
```

Ensure That Both RSP Cards Contain the Same Configuration File

With both the simple hardware backup and software error protection implementation methods, you always want your master and slave configuration files to match. To ensure that they match, turn on automatic synchronization. In automatic synchronization mode, the master copies its startup configuration to the slave's startup configuration when you issue a **copy** command that specifies the master's startup configuration (**nvram:startup-config**) as the target.

Automatic synchronization mode is on by default; however, to turn it on manually, use the following commands, beginning in privileged EXEC mode:

Step	Command	Purpose
1	**configure terminal**	Enters the configuration mode from the terminal.
2	**slave auto-sync config**	Turns on automatic synchronization mode.
3	**end**	Exits configuration mode.
4	**copy system:running-config nvram:startup-config**	Saves this information to your startup configuration and copies the configuration to the slave's startup configuration.

The following example turns on automatic configuration file synchronization:

```
Router# configure terminal
Router (config)# slave auto-sync config
Router (config)# end
Router# copy system:running-config nvram:startup-config
```

Ensure That Both RSP Cards Contain the Same System Image

For simple hardware backup, ensure that both RSP cards have the same system image.

To ensure that both RSP cards have the same system image, use the following commands in EXEC mode:

Step	Command	Purpose
1	**show bootvar**	Displays the contents of the BOOT environment variable to learn the current booting parameters for the master and slave RSP.

Step	Command	Purpose
2	**dir** {**bootflash:** | **slot0:** | **slot1:**}	Verifies the location and version of the master RSP software image.
3	**dir** {**slavebootflash:** | **slaveslot0:** | **slaveslot1:**}	Determines if the slave RSP contains the same software image in the same location.
4	**copy** {**bootflash:**[*filename*] | **slot0:**[*filename*] | **slot1:**[*filename*]} {**slavebootflash:**[*filename*] | **slaveslot0:**[*filename*] | **slaveslot1:**[*filename*]} Note that you might also have to use the **delete** and/or **squeeze** command in conjunction with the **copy** command to accomplish this step.	Copies the master's system image to the appropriate slave location if the slave RSP does not contain the same system image in the same location.

The following example ensures that both RSP cards have the same system image. Note that because no environment variables are set, the default environment variables are in effect for both the master and slave RSP. Therefore, the router will boot the image in slot 0.

```
Router# show bootvar

BOOT variable =
CONFIG_FILE variable =
Current CONFIG_FILE variable =
BOOTLDR variable does not exist

Configuration register is 0x0

current slave is in slot 7
BOOT variable =
CONFIG_FILE variable =
BOOTLDR variable does not exist

Configuration register is 0x0

Router# dir slot0:
-#- -length- -----date/time------ name
1    3482498  May 4 1993 21:38:04 rsp-k-mz11.2

7993896 bytes available (1496 bytes used)

Router# dir slaveslot0:
-#- -length- -----date/time------ name
1    3482498  May 4 1993 21:38:04 rsp-k-mz11.1

7993896 bytes available (1496 bytes used)

Router# delete slaveslot0:rsp-k-mz11.1
Router# copy slot0:rsp-k-mz11.2 slaveslot0:rsp-k-mz11.2
```

Ensure That Both RSP Cards Contain the Same Microcode Image

To ensure that interface processors will load the same microcode, regardless of which RSP is used, use the following commands beginning in privileged EXEC mode:

Step	Command	Purpose
1	**show controller cbus**	Determines the microcode images used on the interface processors. If all interface processors are running from the bundled system microcode, no further action is required.
2	**dir** {**bootflash:**	**slot0:**	**slot1:**}	If any interface processors are running from the Flash file system, verifies the location and version of the master RSP's supplementary microcode.
3	**dir** {**slavebootflash:**	**slaveslot0:**	**slaveslot1:**}	Determines if the slave RSP contains the same microcode image in the same location.
4	**copy** {**bootflash:**[*filename*]	**slot0:**[*filename*]	**slot1:**[*filename*]} {**slavebootflash:**[*filename*]	**slaveslot0:**[*filename*]	**slaveslot1:**[*filename*]} Note that you might also have to use the **delete** and/or **squeeze** command in conjunction with the **copy** command to accomplish this step.	If the slave RSP does not contain the same microcode image in the same location, copies the master's microcode image to the appropriate slave location.

The following example ensures that both RSP cards have the same microcode image. Notice that slots 0, 1, 4, 9, and 10 load microcode from the bundled software, as noted by the statement "software loaded from system." Slot 11, the FSIP (Fast Serial Interface Processor) processor, does not use the microcode bundled with the system. Instead, it loads the microcode from slot0:pond/bath/rsp_fsip20-1. Thus, you must ensure that the slave RSP has a copy of the same FSIP microcode in the same location.

```
Router# show controller cbus

MEMD at 40000000, 2097152 bytes (unused 416, recarves 3, lost 0)
  RawQ 48000100, ReturnQ 48000108, EventQ 48000110
  BufhdrQ 48000128 (2948 items), LovltrQ 48000140 (5 items, 1632 bytes)
  IpcbufQ 48000148 (16 items, 4096 bytes)
  3571 buffer headers (48002000 - 4800FF20)
  pool0: 28 buffers, 256 bytes, queue 48000130
  pool1: 237 buffers, 1536 bytes, queue 48000138
  pool2: 333 buffers, 4544 bytes, queue 48000150
  pool3: 4 buffers, 4576 bytes, queue 48000158
  slot0: EIP, hw 1.5, sw 20.00, ccb 5800FF30, cmdq 48000080, vps 4096
    software loaded from system
    Ethernet0/0, addr 0000.0ca3.cc00 (bia 0000.0ca3.cc00)
      gfreeq 48000138, lfreeq 48000160 (1536 bytes), throttled 0
      rxlo 4, rxhi 42, rxcurr 0, maxrxcurr 2
      txq 48000168, txacc 48000082 (value 27), txlimit 27
                .........
  slot1: FIP, hw 2.9, sw 20.02, ccb 5800FF40, cmdq 48000088, vps 4096
```

```
        software loaded from system
    Fddi1/0, addr 0000.0ca3.cc20 (bia 0000.0ca3.cc20)
        gfreeq 48000150, lfreeq 480001C0 (4544 bytes), throttled 0
        rxlo 4, rxhi 165, rxcurr 0, maxrxcurr 0
        txq 480001C8, txacc 480000B2 (value 0), txlimit 95
  slot4: AIP, hw 1.3, sw 20.02, ccb 5800FF70, cmdq 480000A0, vps 8192
      software loaded from system
    ATM4/0, applique is SONET (155Mbps)
        gfreeq 48000150, lfreeq 480001D0 (4544 bytes), throttled 0
        rxlo 4, rxhi 165, rxcurr 0, maxrxcurr 0
        txq 480001D8, txacc 480000BA (value 0), txlimit 95
  slot9: MIP, hw 1.0, sw 20.02, ccb 5800FFC0, cmdq 480000C8, vps 8192
      software loaded from system
    T1 9/0, applique is Channelized T1
        gfreeq 48000138, lfreeq 480001E0 (1536 bytes), throttled 0
        rxlo 4, rxhi 42, rxcurr 0, maxrxcurr 0
        txq 480001E8, txacc 480000C2 (value 27), txlimit 27
                .......

  slot10: TRIP, hw 1.1, sw 20.00, ccb 5800FFD0, cmdq 480000D0, vps 4096
      software loaded from system
    TokenRing10/0, addr 0000.0ca3.cd40 (bia 0000.0ca3.cd40)
        gfreeq 48000150, lfreeq 48000200 (4544 bytes), throttled 0
        rxlo 4, rxhi 165, rxcurr 1, maxrxcurr 1
        txq 48000208, txacc 480000D2 (value 95), txlimit 95
                .........

  slot11: FSIP, hw 1.1, sw 20.01, ccb 5800FFE0, cmdq 480000D8, vps 8192
      software loaded from flash slot0:pond/bath/rsp_fsip20-1
    Serial11/0, applique is Universal (cable unattached)
        gfreeq 48000138, lfreeq 48000240 (1536 bytes), throttled 0
        rxlo 4, rxhi 42, rxcurr 0, maxrxcurr 0
        txq 48000248, txacc 480000F2 (value 5), txlimit 27
                ..........

Router# dir slot0:pond/bath/rsp_fsip20-1
-#- -length- -----date/time------ name
3    10242    Jan 01 1995 03:46:31 pond/bath/rsp_fsip20-1

Router# dir slaveslot0:pond/bath/rsp_fsip20-1
No such file

4079832 bytes available (3915560 bytes used)

Router# copy slot0:pond/bath/rsp_fsip20-1 slaveslot0:
4079704 bytes available on device slaveslot0, proceed? [confirm]

Router# dir slaveslot0:pond/bath/rsp_fsip20-1
-#- -length- -----date/time------ name
3    10242    Mar 01 1993 02:35:04 pond/bath/rsp_fsip20-1

4069460 bytes available (3925932 bytes used)
```

Specify Different Startup Images for the Master and Slave RSP

For software error protection, the RSP cards should have different system images.

When the factory sends you a new Cisco 7507 or Cisco 7513 with two RSPs, you receive the same system image on both RSP cards. For the software error protection method, you need two different software images on the RSP cards. Thus, you copy a desired image to the master RSP card and modify the **boot system** commands to reflect booting two different system images. Each RSP card uses its own image to boot the router when it becomes the master.

To specify different startup images for the master and slave RSP, use the following commands beginning in EXEC mode:

Step	Command	Purpose
1	**dir** {**bootflash:**	**slot0:**	**slot1:**}	Verifies the location and version of the master RSP software image.
2	**dir** {**slavebootflash:**	**slaveslot0:**	**slaveslot1:**}	Determines if the slave RSP contains the same software image in the same location.
3	**copy** *source-url* {**bootflash:**	**slot0:**	**slot1:**}	Copies a different system image to the master RSP.
4	**configure terminal**	Enters configuration mode from the terminal.
5	**boot system flash bootflash:**[*filename*] **boot system flash slot0:**[*filename*] **boot system flash slot1:**[*filename*]	From global configuration mode, configures the master RSP to boot the new image from the appropriate location.
6	**boot system flash bootflash:**[*filename*] **boot system flash slot0:**[*filename*] **boot system flash slot1:**[*filename*]	Adds a **boot system** command that specifies the slave's boot image and location. This is the boot image that the slave uses when it becomes the master RSP and boots the system. Note that because the slave will boot this image when the slave is actually the new master RSP, the command syntax does not use a **slave** prefix.
7	**boot system** {**rcp**	**tftp**	**ftp**} [*filename*] [*ip-address*]	(Optional) Configures the master RSP to boot from a network server.
8	**config-register** *value*[1]	Sets the configuration register to enable the system to load the system image from a network server or from Flash.
9	**end**	Exits configuration mode.

Step	Command	Purpose
10	**copy system:running-config nvram:startup-config**	Saves the configuration file to the master's startup configuration. Because automatic synchronization is turned on, this step saves the **boot system** commands to the master and slave startup configuration.
11	**reload**	Resets the router with the new configuration information.

1.Refer to the "Modify the Configuration Register Boot Field" section for more information on systems that can use this command to modify the software configuration register.

HSA: Upgrading to a New Software Version Example

In this example, assume the following:

● The master RSP is in processor slot 6 and the slave RSP is in processor slot 7 of a Cisco 7513.

● The system has the same image rsp-k-mz11.1 in PCMCIA slot 0 of both the master and slave RSP card.

● You want to upgrade to Cisco IOS Release 12.0, but you want to guard against software failures. So, you configure HSA operation for software error protection.

Figure 19-2 illustrates the software error protection configuration for this example. The configuration commands for this configuration follow the figure.

Figure 19-2 *Software Error Protection: Upgrading to a New Software Version*

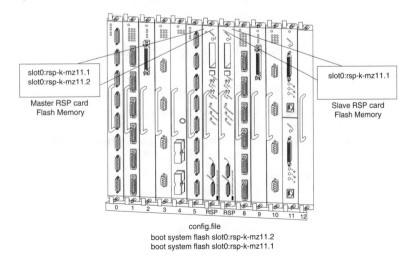

```
config.file
boot system flash slot0:rsp-k-mz11.2
boot system flash slot0:rsp-k-mz11.1
```

Because you always view the environment from the master RSP perspective, in the following command you view the master's slot 0 to verify the location and version of the master's software image:

```
Router# dir slot0:
-#- -length- -----date/time------ name
1    3482496  May 4 1993 21:38:04 rsp-k-mz11.1

7993896 bytes available (1496 bytes used)
```

Now view the slave's software image location and version:

```
Router# dir slaveslot0:
-#- -length- -----date/time------ name
1    3482496  May 4 1993 21:38:04 rsp-k-mz11.1

7993896 bytes available (1496 bytes used)
```

Because you want to run the Release 12.0 system image on one RSP card and the Release 11.1 system image on the other RSP card, copy the Release 12.0 system image to the master's slot 0:

```
Router# copy tftp: slot0:rsp-k-mz12.0
```

Enter global configuration mode and configure the system to boot first from a Release 12.0 system image and then from a Release 11.1 system image.

```
Router# configure terminal
Router (config)# boot system flash slot0:rsp-k-mz12.0
Router (config)# boot system flash slot0:rsp-k-mz11.1
```

With this configuration, when the slot 6 RSP card is master, it looks first in its PCMCIA slot 0 for the system image file rsp-k-mz11.2 to boot. Finding this file, the router boots from that system image. When the slot 7 RSP card is master, it also looks first in its slot 0 for the system image file rsp-k-mz12.0 to boot. Because that image does not exist in that location, the slot 7 RSP card looks for the system image file rsp-k-mz11.1 in slot 0 to boot. Finding this file in its PCMCIA slot 0, the router boots from that system image. In this way, each RSP card can reboot the system using its own system image when it becomes the master RSP card.

Configure the system further with a fault-tolerant booting strategy:

```
Router (config)# boot system tftp rsp-k-mz11.1 192.168.1.25
```

Set the configuration register to enable loading of the system image from a network server or from Flash and save the changes to the master and slave startup configuration file:

```
Router (config)# config-register 0x010F
Router (config)# end
Router# copy system:running-config nvram:startup-config
```

Reload the system so that the master RSP uses the new Release 12.0 system image:

```
Router# reload
```

HSA: Backing Up with an Older Software Version Example

In the following example, assume the following:

- The master RSP is in processor slot 6 and the slave RSP is in processor slot 7 of a Cisco 7513.

- The system has the same image rsp-k-mz11.2 in PCMCIA slot 0 of both the master and slave RSP card.

- You want to use to Cisco IOS Release 11.1 as backup to guard against software failures. So, you configure HSA operation for software error protection.

In this scenario, you begin with the configuration shown in Figure 19-3.

Figure 19-3 *Software Error Protection: Backing Up with an Older Software Version, Part I*

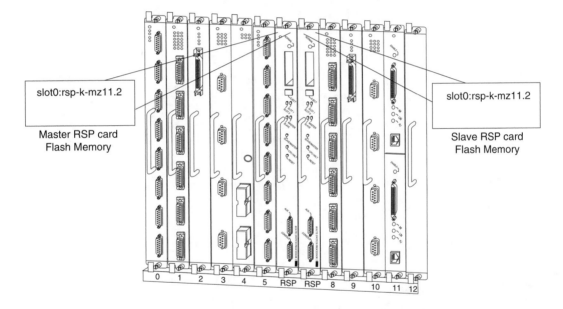

First, copy the rsp-k-mz11.1 image to the master and slave RSP card, as shown in Figure 19-4.

Figure 19-4 *Software Error Protection: Backing Up with an Older Software Version, Part II*

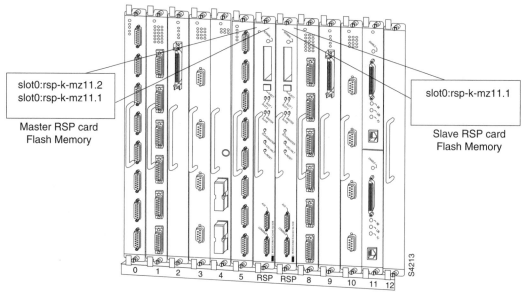

slot0:rsp-k-mz11.2
slot0:rsp-k-mz11.1

Master RSP card
Flash Memory

slot0:rsp-k-mz11.2
slot0:rsp-k-mz11.1

Slave RSP card
Flash Memory

Next, you delete the rsp-k-mz11.2 image from the slave RSP card. The final configuration is shown in Figure 19-5.

Figure 19-5 *Software Error Protection: Backing Up with an Older Software Version, Part III*

slot0:rsp-k-mz11.2
slot0:rsp-k-mz11.1

Master RSP card
Flash Memory

slot0:rsp-k-mz11.1

Slave RSP card
Flash Memory

The following commands configure software error protection for this example scenario.

View the master and slave slot 0 to verify the location and version of their software images:

```
Router# dir slot0:
-#- -length- -----date/time------ name
1    3482498  May 4 1993 21:38:04 rsp-k-mz11.2

7993896 bytes available (1496 bytes used)

Router# dir slaveslot0:
-#- -length- -----date/time------ name
1    3482498  May 4 1993 21:38:04 rsp-k-mz11.2

7993896 bytes available (1496 bytes used)
```

Copy the Release 11.1 system image to the master and slave slot 0:

```
Router# copy tftp: slot0:rsp-k-mz11.1
Router# copy tftp: slaveslot0:rsp-k-mz11.1
```

Delete the rsp-k-mz11.2 image from the slave RSP card:

```
Router# delete slaveslot0:rsp-k-mz11.2
```

Configure the system to boot first from a Release 11.2 system image and then from a Release 11.1 system image:

```
Router# configure terminal
Router (config)# boot system flash slot0:rsp-k-mz11.2
Router (config)# boot system flash slot0:rsp-k-mz11.1
```

Configure the system further with a fault-tolerant booting strategy:

```
Router (config)# boot system tftp rsp-k-mz11.1 192.168.1.25
```

Set the configuration register to enable loading of the system image from a network server or from Flash and save the changes to the master and slave startup configuration file:

```
Router (config)# config-register 0x010F
Router (config)# end
Router# copy system:running-config nvram:startup-config
```

NOTE   You do not need to reload the router in this example, because the router is currently running the Release 11.2 image.

Set Environment Variables on the Master and Slave RSP

You can optionally set environment variables on both RSP cards in a Cisco 7507 and Cisco 7513. For more information on environment variables, refer to the "Set Environment Variables" section.

NOTE   When configuring HSA operation, Cisco recommends that you use the default environment variables. If you change the variables, Cisco recommends setting the same device for equivalent environment variables on each RSP card. For example, if you set one RSP card's CONFIG_FILE environment variable device to NVRAM, set the other RSP card's CONFIG_FILE environment variable device to NVRAM also.

You set environment variables on the master RSP just as you would if it were the only RSP card in the system. Refer to the following sections for more information on these steps:

● Controlling Environment Variables

● Specify the Startup System Image in the Configuration File (in Chapter 15, "Loading and Maintaining System Images and Microcode")

● Set the BOOTLDR Environment Variable

● Specify the CONFIG_FILE Environment Variable (Class A Flash File Systems) (in Chapter 13, "Modifying, Downloading, and Maintaining Configuration Files")

You can set the same environment variables on the slave RSP card, manually or automatically. The following sections describe these two methods:

● Automatically Set Environment Variables on the Slave RSP

● Manually Set Environment Variables on the Slave RSP

Automatically Set Environment Variables on the Slave RSP

With automatic synchronization turned on, the system automatically saves the same environment variables to the slave's startup configuration when you set the master's environment variables and save them.

NOTE   Automatic synchronization mode is on by default. To turn off automatic synchronization, use the **no slave auto-sync config** global configuration command.

To set environment variables on the slave RSP when automatic synchronization is on, use the following commands beginning in global configuration mode:

Step	Command	Purpose
1		Sets the master's environment variables as described in the "Controlling Environment Variables," "Set the BOOTLDR Environment Variable," and "Specify the CONFIG_FILE Environment Variable (Class A Flash File Systems)" sections.
2	**copy system:running-config nvram:startup-config**	Saves the settings to the startup configuration. This also puts the information under that RSP card's ROM monitor control.
3	**show bootvar**	Verifies the environment variable settings.

Manually Set Environment Variables on the Slave RSP

If you disable automatic synchronization of configuration files, you must manually synchronize the slave's configuration file to the master's configuration file to store environment variables on the slave RSP.

Once you set the master's environment variables, you can manually set the same environment variables on the slave RSP card using the **slave sync config** command.

To manually set environment variables on the slave RSP, use the following commands beginning in global configuration mode:

Step	Command	Purpose
1		Sets the master's environment variables as described in the "Controlling Environment Variables," "Set the BOOTLDR Environment Variable," and "Specify the CONFIG_FILE Environment Variable (Class A Flash File Systems)" sections.
2	**end**	Exits global configuration mode.
3	**copy system:running-config nvram:startup-config**	Saves the settings to the startup configuration. This also puts the information under that RSP card's ROM monitor control.
4	**slave sync config**	Saves the same environment variables to the slave RSP by manually synchronizing their configuration files.
5	**show bootvar**	Verifies the environment variable settings.

Monitor and Maintain HSA Operation

To monitor and maintain HSA operation, complete the following tasks in the following sections:

- Override the Slave Image Bundled with the Master Image
- Manually Synchronize Configuration Files

- Troubleshoot a Failed RSP Card

- Disable Access to Slave Console

- Display Information about Master and Slave RSP Cards

Override the Slave Image Bundled with the Master Image

You can override the slave image that is bundled with the master image. To do so, use the following command in global configuration mode:

Command	Purpose
slave image {**system** | *file-url*}	Specifies which image the slave runs.

Manually Synchronize Configuration Files

You can manually synchronize configuration files and ROM Monitor environment variables on the master and slave RSP card. To do so, use the following command in privileged EXEC mode:

Command	Purpose
slave sync config	Manually synchronizes master and slave configuration files.

CAUTION   When you install a second RSP card for the first time, you *must* immediately configure it using the **slave sync config** command. This ensures that the new slave is configured consistently with the master. Failure to do so can result in an unconfigured slave RSP card taking over mastership of the router when the master fails, rendering the network inoperable.

The **slave sync config** command is also a useful tool for more advanced implementation methods not discussed in this chapter.

Troubleshoot a Failed RSP Card

When a new master RSP card takes over mastership of the router, it automatically reboots the failed RSP card as the slave RSP card. You can access the state of the failed RSP card in the form of a stack trace from the master console using the **show stacks** command.

You can also manually reload a failed, inactive RSP card from the master console. This task returns the card to the active slave state. If the master RSP fails, the slave will be able to become the master. To manually reload the inactive RSP card, use the following command in global configuration mode:

Command	Purpose
slave reload	Reloads the inactive slave RSP card.

Disable Access to Slave Console

The slave console does not have enable password protection. Thus, an individual connected to the slave console port can enter privileged EXEC mode and view or erase the configuration of the router. Use the **no slave terminal** command to disable slave console access and prevent security problems. When the slave console is disabled, users cannot enter commands.

If slave console access is disabled, the following message appears periodically on the slave console:

```
%%Slave terminal access is disabled. Use "slave terminal" command in master RSP configuration
mode to enable it.
```

Display Information about Master and Slave RSP Cards

You can also display information about both the master and slave RSP cards. To do so, use any of the following commands in EXEC mode:

Command	Purpose
show bootvar	Displays the environment variable settings and configuration register settings for both the master and slave RSP cards.
show file systems	Shows a list of flash devices currently supported on the router.
show version	Displays the software version running on the master and slave RSP card.
show stacks	Displays the stack trace and version information of the master and slave RSP cards.

Stop Booting and Enter ROM Monitor Mode

During the first 60 seconds of startup, you can force the router to stop booting. The router will enter ROM Monitor mode, where you can change the configuration register value or boot the router manually.

To stop booting and enter ROM monitor mode, use the following commands in EXEC mode:

Step	Command	Purpose
1	**reload** Press the Break[1] key during the first 60 seconds while the system is booting.	Enters ROM monitor mode from privileged EXEC mode.
2	**?**	Lists the ROM monitor commands.

1. This key will not work on the Cisco 7000 unless it has at least Cisco IOS Release 10 boot ROMs.

The ROM monitor prompt is the angle bracket (>):

```
> ?
$ state      Toggle cache state (? for help)
B [filename] [TFTP Server IP address ¦ TFTP Server Name]
             Load and execute system image from ROM or from TFTP server
C [address]  Continue execution [optional address]
D /S M L V   Deposit value V of size S into location L with modifier M
E /S M L     Examine location L with size S with modifier M
G [address]  Begin execution
H            Help for commands
I            Initialize
K            Stack trace
L [filename] [TFTP Server IP address ¦ TFTP Server Name]
             Load system image from ROM or from TFTP server, but do not
             begin execution
O            Show configuration register option settings
P            Set the break point
S            Single step next instruction
T function   Test device (? for help)
Deposit and Examine sizes may be B (byte), L (long) or S (short).
Modifiers may be R (register) or S (byte swap).
Register names are: D0-D7, A0-A6, SS, US, SR, and PC
```

To return to user EXEC mode, type **continue**. To initialize the router or access server, enter the **i** command. The **i** command causes the bootstrap program to reinitialize the hardware, clear the contents of memory, and boot the system. (It is best to issue the **i** command before you run any tests or boot software.) To boot the system image file, use the **b** command. For details on ROM monitor mode commands, refer to the appropriate hardware installation guide.

Manually Load a System Image from ROM Monitor

If your router does not find a valid system image, or if its configuration file is corrupted at startup, and the configuration register is set to enter ROM Monitor mode, the system enters ROM Monitor mode. From this mode, you can manually load a system image from the following locations:

- Internal Flash memory or a Flash memory PC card

- A network server file

- ROM

- A local or remote computer, using the Xmodem or Ymodem protocol (Cisco 1600 series and Cisco 3600 series only)

You may only boot from a location if the router can store an image there. Therefore, not all platforms can manually load from these locations.

You can also enter ROM Monitor mode by restarting the router and then pressing the **Break** key or issuing a "send break" command from a Telnet session during the first 60 seconds of startup.

Manually Boot from Flash Memory

To manually boot from Flash memory, use the following command in ROM Monitor mode:

Command	Purpose
boot flash [*filename*] **boot flash** *partition-number*:[*filename*] **boot flash flash:**[*partition-number*:] [*filename*] **boot** [*flash-fs*:][*partition-number*:][*filename*] (Cisco 1600 series and Cisco 3600 series) **boot** *device*:[*filename*] (Cisco 7000 family)	Manually boots the router from Flash. Refer to your hardware documentation for the correct form of this command to use.

If the filename is not specified, the first bootable file found in the device and partition is used.

In the following example, a router is manually booted from Flash memory. Because the optional *filename* argument is absent, the first valid file in Flash memory is loaded.

```
> boot flash
F3: 1858656+45204+166896 at 0x1000

Booting gs7-k from flash memory RRRRRRRRRRRRRRRRRRRRRRRRRRRRRRRRRRRRRRRR
RRRRRRRRRRRRRRRRRRRRRRRRRRRRRRRRRRRRRRRRRRRRRRRRRRRRRRRRRRRRRRRRRRRRRRRRRRRRRR
RRRRRRRRRRRRRRRRRRRRRRRRRRRRRRRRRRRRRRRRRRRRRRRRRRRRRRRRRRRRRRRRRRRRRRRRRRRRRR
RRRRRRRRRRRRRRRRRRRRRRRRRRRRRRRRRRRRRRRRRRRRRRRRRRRRRRRRRRRRRRRRRRRRRRRRRRRRRR
RRRRRRRRRRRRRRRRRRRRRRRRRRRRRRRRRRRRRRRRRRRRRRRRRRRRRRRRRRRRRRRRRRRRRRR [OK -
1903912/13765276 bytes]
F3: 1858676+45204+166896 at 0x1000

          Restricted Rights Legend

Use, duplication, or disclosure by the Government is
subject to restrictions as set forth in subparagraph
(c) of the Commercial Computer Software - Restricted
```

In the following example, the **boot flash** command is used with the filename gs7-k—the name of the file that is loaded:

```
> boot flash gs7-k
F3: 1858656+45204+166896 at 0x1000

Booting gs7-k from flash memory RRRRRRRRRRRRRRRRRRRRRRRRRRRRRRRRRRRRRRRRRR
RRRRRRRRRRRRRRRRRRRRRRRRRRRRRRRRRRRRRRRRRRRRRRRRRRRRRRRRRRRRRRRRRRRRRRRRRRRRRR
RRRRRRRRRRRRRRRRRRRRRRRRRRRRRRRRRRRRRRRRRRRRRRRRRRRRRRRRRRRRRRRRRRRRRRRRRRRRRR
RRRRRRRRRRRRRRRRRRRRRRRRRRRRRRRRRRRRRRRRRRRRRRRRRRRRRRRRRRRRRRRRRRRRRRRRRRRRRR
RRRRRRRRRRRRRRRRRRRRRRRRRRRRRRRRRRRRRRRRRRRRRRRRRRRRRRRRRRRRRRRRRRRRRRRRRRRRRR
RRRRRRRRRRRRRR [OK - 1903912/13765276 bytes]
F3: 1858676+45204+166896 at 0x1000

             Restricted Rights Legend

Use, duplication, or disclosure by the Government is
subject to restrictions as set forth in subparagraph
(c) of the Commercial Computer Software - Restricted
System Bootstrap, Version 4.6(1012) [mlw 99], INTERIM SOFTWARE
Copyright (c) 1986-1992 by cisco Systems
RP1 processor with 16384 Kbytes of memory
```

The following command instructs the ROM Monitor to boot the first file in the first partition of internal Flash memory:

```
> boot flash:
```

This command instructs the ROM Monitor to boot the first file in the second partition of the Flash memory card in slot 0:

```
> boot slot0:2:
```

In this example, the ROM Monitor boots the file named imagename from the third partition of the Flash memory card in slot 0:

```
> boot slot0:3:imagename
```

The following command fails to specify a valid device type (**flash:**, **slot0:**, or **slot1:**), so the ROM monitor invokes the boot helper to boot a system image.

```
> boot flash
```

Manually Boot from a Network File

To manually boot from a network file, use the following command in ROM Monitor mode:

Command	Purpose
boot *filename* [*ip-address*]	Manually boots the router from a network file.

In the following example, a router is manually booted from the network file *network1*:

```
>boot network1
```

Manually Boot from ROM

To manually boot the router from ROM, use the following command in ROM Monitor mode:

Command	Purpose
boot	Manually boots the router from ROM.

On the Cisco 7200 series and Cisco 7500 series, the **boot** command loads the first bootable image located in bootflash.

In the following example, a router is manually booted from ROM:

```
>boot
```

Manually Boot Using MOP

You can interactively boot system software using MOP. Typically, you do this to verify that system software has been properly installed on the MOP boot server before configuring the router to automatically boot the system software image.

To manually boot the router using MOP, use the following command in ROM Monitor mode:

Command	Purpose
boot mop *filename* [*mac-address*] [*interface*]	Manually boots the router using MOP.

The Cisco 7200 series and Cisco 7500 series do not support the **boot mop** command.

In the following example, a router is manually booted from a MOP server:

```
>boot mop network1
```

Use the System Image Instead of Reloading

To return to EXEC mode from the ROM Monitor to use the system image instead of reloading, use the following command in ROM Monitor mode:

Command	Purpose
continue	Returns to EXEC mode to use the system image.

## CHAPTER 20

Booting Commands

This chapter provides detailed descriptions of the commands used to modify the rebooting procedures of the router.

For configuration information and examples, refer to Chapter 19, "Rebooting a Router."

NOTE	Commands in this chapter replaced by new commands continue to perform their normal functions in the current release, but they are no longer documented. Support for these commands will cease in a future release. Table 20-1 maps the old command to its replacement.

Table 20-1 *Mapping Old Commands to New Commands*

Old Command	New Command
show boot	show bootvar

Flash Memory File System Types

Cisco platforms use one of three different Flash memory file system types. Some commands are supported on only one or two file system types. This chapter notes commands that are not supported on all file system types.

Refer to Table 20-2 to determine which Flash memory file system type your platform uses.

Table 20-2 *Flash Memory File System Types*

Type	Platforms
Class A	Cisco 7000 family, C12000, LS1010
Class B	Cisco 1003, Cisco 1004, Cisco 1005, Cisco 2500 series, Cisco 3600 series, Cisco 4000 series, Cisco AS5200
Class C	Cisco MC3810, disk0 of SC3640

boot

To boot the router manually, use the **boot** ROM monitor command. The syntax of this command varies according to the platform and ROM Monitor version. Refer to the documentation for your platform to determine which command to use.

> **boot**
> **boot** *file-url*
> **boot** *filename* [*ip-address*]
> **boot flash** [*filename*]
> **boot flash** [*partition-number*:][*filename*]
> **boot** *flash-fs*:[*filename*] (Cisco 7000 family)
> **boot** [*flash-fs*:][*partition-number*:][*filename*] (Cisco 1600 and Cisco 3600 series)

Syntax	Description
file-url	URL of the image to boot. This option is only available with later ROM Monitor releases.
filename	When used in conjunction with the *ip-address* argument, the *filename* argument is the name of the system image file to boot from a network server. The filename is case sensitive.
	When used in conjunction with the **flash** keyword, the *filename* argument is the name of the system image file to boot from Flash memory.
	On all platforms except the Cisco 1600 series, Cisco 3600 series, and Cisco 7000 family, the system obtains the image file from internal Flash memory.
	On the Cisco 1600 series, Cisco 3600 series and Cisco 7000 family, the *flash-fs*: argument specifies the Flash memory device from which to obtain the system image. See the *flash-fs*: argument later in this table for valid device values. The filename is case sensitive. Without *filename*, the first valid file in Flash memory is loaded.
ip-address	(Optional) IP address of the TFTP server on which the system image resides. If omitted, this value defaults to the IP broadcast address of 255.255.255.255.
flash	(Optional) Boots the router from Flash memory.

Syntax	Description
flash-fs:	Only newer ROM monitors support the flash-fs:filename format. Specifying the Flash file system is optional for all platforms except the Cisco 7500 series. Possible file systems are:
	• **flash:**—Internal Flash memory on the Cisco 1600 series and Cisco 3600 series. This is the only valid Flash file system for the Cisco 1600 series.
	• **bootflash:**—Internal Flash memory on the Cisco 7000 family.
	• **slot0:**—Flash memory card in first PCMCIA slot on the Cisco 7000 family and Cisco 3600 series.
	• **slot1:**—Flash memory card in second PCMCIA slot on the Cisco 7000 family and Cisco 3600 series.
partition-number:	(Optional) Boots the router from Flash memory with the optional filename of the image you want loaded from the specified Flash partition. If you do not specify a filename, the first valid file in the specified partition of Flash memory is loaded. This option is relevant to platforms such as the Cisco 2500 where Flash memory may be partitioned.

Part
II

Command Reference

Default

For most platforms, if you enter the **boot** command and press Return, the router boots from ROM by default. However, for some platforms, such as the Cisco 3600 series, if you enter the **boot** command and press **Enter**, the router boots the first image in Flash memory. Refer to the documentation for your platform for information about the default image.

If you enter the **boot flash** command without a *filename*, the first valid file in Flash memory is loaded.

For other defaults, see the "Syntax Description" section.

Command Mode

ROM monitor

Usage Guidelines

This command first appeared in Cisco IOS Release 10.3.

Use this command only when your router cannot find the boot configuration information needed in nonvolatile random-access memory (NVRAM). To get into ROM monitor mode, use one of the following methods:

- Enter the **reload** EXEC command, then press the **Break** key during the first 60 seconds of startup.

- Set configuration register bits 0 to 3 to zero (manual booting) and enter the **reload** command.

The ROM monitor prompt is either ">" or for newer platforms "rommon *x*>". Enter only lowercase commands.

These commands work only if there is a valid image to boot. Also, from the ROM monitor prompt, issuing a prior reset command is necessary for the boot to be always successful.

Refer to your hardware documentation for information on correct jumper settings for your platform.

Examples

In the following example, a router is manually booted from ROM (except the Cisco 3600 series):

```
> boot
F3:
(ROM Monitor copyrights)
```

In the following example, a router boots the file routertest from a network server with the IP address 172.16.15.112:

```
> boot routertest 172.16.15.112
F3:
(ROM Monitor copyrights)
```

In the following example, a router boots the file routertest from a network server with the IP address 172.16.15.112 using the new *file-url* syntax:

```
> boot tftp://172.16.15.112/routertest
F3
(ROM Monitor copyrights)
```

The following example shows the **boot flash** command without the *filename* argument. The first valid file in Flash memory is loaded.

```
> boot flash
F3: 1858656+45204+166896 at 0x1000
Booting gs7-k from flash memory RRRRRRRRRRRRRRRRRRRRRRRRRRRRRRRRRRRRRRRR
RRRRRRRRRRRRRRRRRRRRRRRRRRRRRRRRRRRRRRRRRRRRRRRRRRRRRRRRRRRRRRRRRRRRRRRRRRRR
RRRRRRRRRRRRRRRRRRRRRRRRRRRRRRRRRRRRRRRRRRRRRRRRRRRRRRRRRRRRRRRRRRRRRRRRRRRR
RRRRRRRRRRRRRRRRRRRRRRRRRRRRRRRRRRRRRRRRRRRRRRRRRRRRRRRRRRRRRRRRRRRRRRRRRRRR
RRRRRRRRRRRRRRRRRRRRRRRRRRRRRRRRRRRRRRRRRRRRRRRRRRRRRRRRRRRRRRRRRRRRRRRRRRRR
RRRRRRRRRRRRRRRRRRRRRRRRRRRRRRRRRRRR [OK - 1903912/13765276 bytes]
F3: 1858676+45204+166896 at 0x1000
(ROM Monitor copyrights)
```

The following example boots from Flash memory using the file gs7-k.

```
> boot flash gs7-k
F3: 1858656+45204+166896 at 0x1000
```

```
Booting gs7-k from flash memory RRRRRRRRRRRRRRRRRRRRRRRRRRRRRRRRRRRRRRRRRR
RRRRRRRRRRRRRRRRRRRRRRRRRRRRRRRRRRRRRRRRRRRRRRRRRRRRRRRRRRRRRRRRRRRRRRRRRRR
RRRRRRRRRRRRRRRRRRRRRRRRRRRRRRRRRRRRRRRRRRRRRRRRRRRRRRRRRRRRRRRRRRRRRRRRRRR
RRRRRRRRRRRRRRRRRRRRRRRRRRRRRRRRRRRRRRRRRRRRRRRRRRRRRRRRRRRRRRRRRRRRRRRRRRR
RRRRRRRRRRRRRRRRRRRRRRRRRRRRRRRRRRRRRRRRRRRRRRRRRRRRRRRRRRRRRRRRRRRRRRRRRRR
RRRRRRRRRRRRRR [OK - 1903912/13765276 bytes]
F3: 1858676+45204+166896 at 0x1000

(ROM Monitor copyrights)
```

In the following example, the **boot flash flash:** command boots the relocatable image file igs-bpx-l from partition 2 in Flash memory:

```
> boot flash flash:2:igs-bpx-l
F3: 3562264+98228+303632 at 0x30000B4

(ROM Monitor copyrights)
```

Use the following example if the boot image has been inadvertently erased. (The IOS is directly launched from the ROM monitor without the intermediate boot stage. This startup requires less system memory.)

```
> boot flash:c4500-j-mz.103-7
```

In the following example, the Cisco 7000 family accepts the **flash** keyword for compatibility but ignores it and boots from slot 0:

```
> boot flash slot0:gs7-k-mz.103-9
F3: 8468+3980384+165008 at 0x1000
```

In the following example, the new rommon requires new syntax.

```
rommon 8 > b flash flash:c4500-j-mz.103-12
boot of "flash flash:c4500-j-mz.103-12" using boot helper "bootflash:c4500-xboot.101-1"
failed
```

In the following example, the command did not function because it must be entered in lowercase.

```
rommon 10 > BOOT
command "BOOT" not found
```

The following example shows the ROM monitor booting the first file in the first partition of internal Flash memory of a Cisco 3600 series:

```
> boot flash:
```

This example boots the first image file in the first partition of the Flash memory card in slot 0 of a Cisco 3600 series:

```
> boot slot0:
```

The following example shows the ROM monitor booting the first file in the first Flash memory partition on a Cisco 1600 series:

```
> boot flash:
```

Related Commands

To locate documentation of related commands, you can search online at www.cisco.com.

continue

boot bootldr

To specify the location of the boot image that ROM uses for booting, use the **boot bootldr** global configuration command. Use the **no** form of this command to remove this boot image specification.

> **boot bootldr** *file-url*
> **no boot bootldr**

Syntax	Description
file-url	URL of the boot image on a Flash file system.

Default

Refer to your platform documentation for the location of the default boot image.

Command Mode

Global configuration

Usage Guidelines

This command first appeared in Cisco IOS Release 11.0.

The **boot bootldr** command sets the BOOTLDR environment variable in the current running configuration. You must specify both the Flash file system and the filename.

NOTE When you use this global configuration command, you affect only the running configuration. You must save the environment variable setting to your startup configuration to place the information under ROM monitor control and to have the environment variable function as expected. Use the **copy system:running-config nvram:startup-config** command to save the environment variable from your running configuration to your startup configuration.

The **no** form of the command sets the BOOTLDR environment variable to a null string. On the Cisco 7000 family, a null string causes the first image file in bootflash to be used as the boot image that ROM uses for booting.

Use the **show boot** command to display the current value for the BOOTLDR environment variable.

Examples

In the following example, the internal Flash memory contains the boot image:

```
boot bootldr bootflash:boot-image
```

The following example specifies that the Flash memory card inserted in slot 0 contains the boot image:

```
boot bootldr slot0:boot-image
```

Related Commands

To locate documentation of related commands, you can search online at www.cisco.com.

copy system:running-config nvram:startup-config
show bootvar
show (Flash file system)

boot bootstrap

To configure the filename that is used to boot a secondary bootstrap image, use the **boot bootstrap** global configuration command. Use the **no** form of this command to disable booting from a secondary bootstrap image.

> **boot bootstrap** *file-url*
> **no boot bootstrap** *file-url*

> **boot bootstrap flash** [*filename*]
> **no boot bootstrap flash** [*filename*]

> **boot bootstrap** [**tftp**] *filename* [*ip-address*]
> **no boot bootstrap** [**tftp**] *filename* [*ip-address*]

Syntax	Description
file-url	URL of the bootstrap image.
flash	Boots the router from Flash memory.

Syntax	Description
filename	(Optional with **flash**) Name of the system image to boot from a network server or from Flash memory. If you omit the filename when booting from Flash memory, the router uses the first system image stored in Flash memory.
tftp	(Optional) Boots the router from a system image stored on a TFTP server.
ip-address	(Optional) IP address of the TFTP server on which the system image resides. If omitted, this value defaults to the IP broadcast address of 255.255.255.255.

Default

No secondary bootstrap

Command Mode

Global configuration

Usage Guidelines

This command first appeared in Cisco IOS Release 10.0.

The **boot bootstrap** command causes the router to load a secondary bootstrap image over the network. The secondary bootstrap image then loads the specified system image file. See the appropriate hardware installation guide for details on the configuration register and secondary bootstrap filename.

Use this command when you have attempted to load a system image but have run out of memory even after compressing the system image. Secondary bootstrap allows you to load a larger system image through a smaller secondary image.

Example

In the following example, the system image file sysimage-2 will be loaded by using a secondary bootstrap image:

```
boot bootstrap bootflash:sysimage-2
```

boot system

To specify the system image that the router loads at startup, use one of the following **boot system** global configuration commands. Use a **no** form of this command to remove the startup system image specification.

boot system *file-url*
no boot system *file-url*

boot system flash [*flash-fs***:**][*partition-number***:**][*filename*]
no boot system flash [*flash-fs***:**][*partition-number***:**][*filename*]

boot system rom
no boot system rom

boot system {**rcp** | **tftp** | **ftp**} *filename* [*ip-address*]
no boot system {**rcp** | **tftp** | **ftp**} *filename* [*ip-address*]

no boot system

Syntax	Description
file-url	URL of the system image to load at system startup.
flash	On all platforms except the Cisco 1600 series, Cisco 3600 series, and Cisco 7000 family, this keyword boots the router from internal Flash memory. If you omit all arguments that follow this keyword, the system searches internal Flash for the first bootable image.
	On the Cisco 1600 series, Cisco 3600 series, and Cisco 7000 family, this keyword boots the router from a Flash device, as specified by the *device:* argument. On the Cisco 1600 series and Cisco 3600 series, if you omit all optional arguments, the router searches internal Flash memory for the first bootable image. On the Cisco 7000 family, when you omit all arguments that follow this keyword, the system searches the PCMCIA slot 0 for the first bootable image.
*flash-fs***:**	(Optional) Flash file system containing the system image to load at startup. The colon (:) is required. Valid file systems are as follows:

- **flash:**—Internal Flash memory on the Cisco 1600 series and Cisco 3600 series. For the Cisco 1600 series and Cisco 3600 series, this file system is the default if you do not specify a file system. This is the only valid file system for the Cisco 1600 series.
- **bootflash**—Internal Flash memory in the Cisco 7000 family.
- **slot0**—First PCMCIA slot on the Cisco 3600 series and Cisco 7000 family. For the Cisco 7000 family, this file system is the default if you do not specify a file system.
- **slot1**—Flash memory card in the second PCMCIA slot on the Cisco 3600 series and Cisco 7000 family.

Syntax	Description
partition-number:	(Optional) Number of the Flash memory partition that contains the system image to boot, specified by the optional *filename* argument. If you do not specify a filename, the router loads the first valid file in the specified partition of Flash memory. This argument is only valid on routers which can be partitioned.
filename	(Optional when used with **boot system flash**) Name of the system image to load at startup. It is case sensitive. If you do not specify a filename, the router loads the first valid file in the specified Flash file system, the specified partition of Flash memory, or the default Flash file system if you also omit the *flash-fs*: argument.
rom	Boots the router from ROM. Do not use this keyword with the Cisco 3600 series or the Cisco 7000 family.
rcp	Boots the router from a system image stored on a network server using rcp.
tftp	Boots the router from a system image stored on a TFTP server.
ftp	Boots the router from a system image stored on an FTP server.
ip-address	(Optional) IP address of the server containing the system image file. If omitted, this value defaults to the IP broadcast address of 255.255.255.255.

Default

If you configure the router to boot from a network server but do not specify a system image file with the **boot system** command, the router uses the configuration register settings to determine the default system image filename. The router forms the default boot filename by starting with the word *cisco* and then appending the octal equivalent of the boot field number in the configuration register, followed by a hyphen (-) and the processor type name (cisco*nn-cpu*). See the appropriate hardware installation guide for details on the configuration register and default filename. See also the **config-register** or **confreg** command. See also the table preceding this section.

Command Mode

Global configuration

Usage Guidelines

This command first appeared in Cisco IOS Release 10.0.

For this command to work, the **config-register** command must be set properly.

Enter several **boot system** commands to provide a fail-safe method for booting your router. The router stores and executes the **boot system** commands in the order in which you enter them in the configuration file. If you enter multiple boot commands of the same type—for example, if you enter two commands that instruct the router to boot from different network servers—the router tries them in the order in which they appear in the configuration file. If a **boot system** command entry in the list specifies an invalid device, the router skips that entry. Use the **boot system rom** command to specify use of the ROM system image as a backup to other **boot** commands in the configuration.

For some platforms, the boot image must be loaded before the system image is loaded. However, on many platforms, the boot image is loaded only if the router is booting from a network server or if the flash file system is not specified. If the file system is specified, the router will boot faster because it does not have to load the boot image first.

This section contains the following usage guideline sections:

- Change the List of Boot System Commands

- Boot Compressed Images

- Understand the rcp Protocol

- Stop Booting and Enter ROM Monitor Mode

- Cisco 1600 Series, Cisco 3600 Series, and Cisco 7000 Family Notes

Change the List of Boot System Commands

To remove a single entry from the bootable image list, use the **no** form of the command with an argument. For example, to remove the entry that specifies a bootable image on a Flash memory card inserted in the second slot, use the **no boot system flash slot1:**[*filename*] command. All other entries in the list remain.

To eliminate all entries in the bootable image list, use the **no boot system** command. At this point, you can redefine the list of bootable images using the previous **boot system** commands. Remember to save your changes to your startup configuration by issuing the **copy system:running-config nvram:startup-config** command.

Each time you write a new software image to Flash memory, you must delete the existing filename in the configuration file with the **no boot system flash** *filename* command. Then add a new line in the configuration file with the **boot system flash** *filename* command.

NOTE   If you want to rearrange the order of the entries in the configuration file, you must first issue the **no boot system** command and then redefine the list.

Boot Compressed Images

You can boot the router from a compressed image on a network server. When a network server boots software, both the image being booted and the running image must fit into memory. Use compressed images to ensure that enough memory is available to boot the router. You can compress a software image on any UNIX platform using the **compress** command. Refer to your UNIX platform's documentation for the exact usage of the **compress** command. (You can also uncompress data with the UNIX **uncompress** command.)

Understand the rcp Protocol

The rcp protocol requires a client to send the remote username in an rcp request to a server. When the router executes the **boot system rcp** command, the Cisco IOS software sends the host name as both the remote and local usernames by default. For the rcp protocol to execute properly, an account must be defined on the network server for the remote username configured on the router.

If the server has a directory structure, the rcp software searches for the system image to boot from the remote server relative to the directory of the remote username.

By default, the router software sends the host name as the remote username. You can override the default remote username by using the **ip rcmd remote-username** command. For example, if the system image resides in the home directory of a user on the server, you can specify that user's name as the remote username.

Understand TFTP

You need a TFTP server running in order to fetch the router image from the host.

Understand FTP

You need an FTP server running in order to fetch the router image from the host. You also need an account on the server or anonymous file access to the server.

Stop Booting and Enter ROM Monitor Mode

During the first 60 seconds of startup, you can force the router to stop booting by pressing the Break key. The router will enter ROM Monitor mode, where you can change the configuration register value or boot the router manually.

Cisco 1600 Series, Cisco 3600 Series, and Cisco 7000 Family Notes

For the Cisco 3600 series and Cisco 7000 family, the **boot system** command modifies the BOOT environment variable in the running configuration. The BOOT environment variable specifies a list of bootable images on various devices.

NOTE	When you use the **boot system** global configuration command on the Cisco 1600 series, Cisco 3600 series, and Cisco 7000 family, you affect only the running configuration. You must save the BOOT environment variable settings to your startup configuration to place the information under ROM monitor control and to have the environment variable function as expected. Use the **copy system:running-config nvram:startup-config** command to save the environment variable from your running configuration to your startup configuration.

To view the contents of the BOOT environment variable, use the **show bootenv** command.

Examples

The following example illustrates a list specifying two possible internetwork locations for a system image, with the ROM software being used as a backup:

```
boot system tftp://192.168.7.24/cs3-rx.90-1
boot system tftp://192.168.7.19/cs3-rx.83-2
boot system rom
```

The following example boots the system boot relocatable image file igs-bpx-l from partition 2 of the Flash device:

```
boot system flash:2:igs-bpx-l
```

The following example instructs the router to boot from an image located on the Flash memory card inserted in slot 0 of the Cisco 7000 RSP7000 card, Cisco 7200 NPE card, or Cisco 7500 series RSP card:

```
boot system slot0:new-config
```

This example specifies the file new-ios-image as the system image for a Cisco 3600 series router to load at startup. This file is located in the fourth partition of the Flash memory card in slot 0:

```
Router# configure terminal
Enter configuration commands, one per line.  End with Ctrl-Z.
Router(config)# boot system slot0:4:dirt/images/new-ios-image
```

This example boots from the image file c1600-y-l in partition 2 of Flash memory of a Cisco 1600 series:

```
Router# configure terminal
Enter configuration commands, one per line.  End with Ctrl-Z.
Router(config)# boot system flash:2:c1600-y-l
```

Related Commands

To locate documentation of related commands, you can search online at www.cisco.com.

config-register
copy

copy system:running-config nvram:startup-config
ip rcmd remote username
show bootvar

config-register

To change the configuration register settings, use the **config-register** global configuration command.

config-register *value*

Syntax

Description

value

Hexadecimal or decimal value that represents the 16-bit configuration register value that you want to use the next time the router is restarted. The value range is from 0x0 to 0xFFFF (0 to 65535 in decimal).

Default

Refer to the documentation for your platform for the default configuration register value. For many newer platforms, the default is 0x2102, which causes the router to boot from Flash memory and the Break key to be ignored.

Command Mode

Global configuration

Usage Guidelines

This command first appeared in Cisco IOS Release 10.0.

This command applies only to platforms which use a software configuration register.

The lowest four bits of the configuration register (bits 3, 2, 1, and 0) form the boot field. The boot field determines if the router boots manually, from ROM, from Flash or the network.

To change the boot field value and leave all other bits set to their default values, follow these guidelines:

- If you set the configuration register boot field value to 0x0, you must boot the operating system manually with the **boot** command.

- If you set the configuration register boot field value to 0x1, the router boots using the default ROM software.

- If you set the configuration register boot field to any value from 0x2 to 0xF, the router uses the boot field value to form a default boot filename for booting from a network server.

For more information about the configuration register bit settings and default filenames, see the appropriate router hardware installation guide.

Example

In the following example, the configuration register is set to boot the system image from Flash memory:

```
config-register 0x2102
```

Related Commands

To locate documentation of related commands, you can search online at www.cisco.com.

boot system
confreg
o
show version

confreg

To change the configuration register settings while in ROM Monitor mode, use the **confreg** ROM Monitor command.

confreg [*value*]

Syntax   Description

value   (Optional) Hexadecimal value that represents the 16-bit configuration register value that you want to use the next time the router is restarted. The value range is from 0x0 to 0xFFFF.

Default

Refer to your platform documentation for the default configuration register value.

Command Mode

ROM Monitor

Usage Guidelines

This command first appeared in Cisco IOS Release 10.0.

Not all versions in the ROM Monitor support this command. Refer to your platform documentation for more information on ROM Monitor mode.

If you use this command without specifying the configuration register value, the router prompts for each bit of the configuration register.

The lowest four bits of the configuration register (bits 3, 2, 1, and 0) form the boot field. The boot field determines if the router boots manually, from ROM, from Flash, or from the network.

To change the boot field value and leave all other bits set to their default values, follow these guidelines:

- If you set the configuration register boot field value to 0x0, you must boot the operating system manually with the **boot** command.

- If you set the configuration register boot field value to 0x1, the router boots using the default ROM software.

- If you set the configuration register boot field to any value from 0x2 to 0xF, the router uses the boot field value to form a default boot filename for booting from a network server.

For more information about the configuration register bit settings and default filenames, see the appropriate router hardware installation guide.

Examples

In the following example, the configuration register is set to boot the system image from Flash memory:

```
confreg 0x210F
```

In the following example, no configuration value is entered, so the system prompt for each bit in the register:

```
rommon 7 > confreg

    Configuration Summary
enabled are:
console baud: 9600
boot: the ROM Monitor

do you wish to change the configuration? y/n  [n]:  y
enable  "diagnostic mode"? y/n  [n]:  y
enable  "use net in IP bcast address"? y/n  [n]:

enable  "load rom after netboot fails"? y/n  [n]:
enable  "use all zero broadcast"? y/n  [n]:
enable  "break/abort has effect"? y/n  [n]:
enable  "ignore system config info"? y/n  [n]:
change console baud rate? y/n  [n]:  y
enter rate: 0 = 9600, 1 = 4800, 2 = 1200, 3 = 2400  [0]:  0
change the boot characteristics? y/n  [n]:  y
enter to boot:
 0 = ROM Monitor
 1 = the boot helper image
```

```
   2-15 = boot system
     [0]:  0

      Configuration Summary
enabled are:
diagnostic mode
console baud: 9600
boot: the ROM Monitor

do you wish to change the configuration? y/n  [n]:

You must reset or power cycle for new config to take effect.
rommon 8>
```

continue

To return to the EXEC mode from ROM monitor mode, use the **continue** ROM monitor command.

> **continue**

Syntax Description

This command has no arguments or keywords.

Command Mode

ROM monitor

Usage Guidelines

This command first appeared in Cisco IOS Release 11.0.

Use this command to return to EXEC mode from ROM monitor mode, to use the system image instead of reloading. On older platforms, the angle bracket (>) indicates the router is in ROM monitor mode. On newer platforms, "rommon *number*>" is the default ROM monitor prompt. Typically, the router is in ROM monitor mode when you manually load a system image or perform diagnostic tests. Otherwise, the router will most likely never be in this mode.

CAUTION	While in ROM monitor mode, the Cisco IOS system software is suspended until you issue either a reset or the **continue** command.

Example

In the following example, the **continue** command switches the router from ROM monitor to EXEC mode:

```
> continue
Router#
```

Related Commands

To locate documentation of related commands, you can search online at www.cisco.com.

boot

o

To list the value of the boot field (bits 0-3) in the configuration register, use the ROM monitor **o** command. To reset the value of the boot field so that the router boots from ROM, use the ROM monitor **o/r** command.

> **o**
> **o/r**

Syntax Description

This command has no arguments or keywords.

Default

Refer to the appropriate hardware installation guide for default values.

Command Mode

ROM monitor

Usage Guidelines

This command first appeared in Cisco IOS Release 10.0.

Not all platforms support the **o** command.

To get to the ROM monitor prompt, use the **reload** EXEC command if the configuration register has a boot value of 0. (For systems with a software configuration register, a value can be included on the **o/r** command line.) Use the **i** command in conjunction with the **o/r** command to initialize the router. (The **i** command is documented in the hardware installation and maintenance publication for your product.)

The **o/r** command resets the configuration register to 0x141, which disables the Break key, ignores the NVRAM configuration, and boots the default system image from ROM.

Examples

The following is a sample display from the **o** command:

```
> o
Bit#    Configuration register option settings:
15      Diagnostic mode disabled
14      IP broadcasts do not have network numbers
13      Do not boot default ROM software if network boot fails
12-11   Console speed is 9600 baud
10      IP broadcasts with ones
09      Do not use secondary bootstrap
08      Break enabled
07      OEM disabled
06      Ignore configuration disabled
03-00   Boot to ROM monitor
>
```

The following is an example of the **o/r** and **i** commands used to reset and boot the default system image from ROM:

```
> o/r
> i
```

Related Commands

To locate documentation of related commands, you can search online at www.cisco.com.

config-register
confreg

reload

To reload the operating system, use the **reload** EXEC command.

> **reload** [*text* | **in** [*hh*:]*mm* [*text*] | **at** *hh*:*mm* [*month day* | *day month*] [*text*] | **cancel**]

Syntax   Description

text	(Optional) Reason for the reload, 1 to 255 characters long.
in [*hh*:]*mm*	(Optional) Schedule a reload of the software to take effect in the specified minutes or hours and minutes. The reload must take place within approximately 24 days.

Syntax	Description
at *hh:mm*	(Optional) Schedule a reload of the software to take place at the specified time (using a 24-hour clock). If you specify the month and day, the reload is scheduled to take place at the specified time and date. If you do not specify the month and day, the reload takes place at the specified time on the current day (if the specified time is later than the current time), or on the next day (if the specified time is earlier than the current time). Specifying 00:00 schedules the reload for midnight. The reload must take place within approximately 24 days.
month	(Optional) Name of the month, any number of characters in a unique string.
day	(Optional) Number of the day in the range 1 to 31.
cancel	(Optional) Cancel a scheduled reload.

Command Mode

EXEC

Usage Guidelines

This command first appeared in Cisco IOS Release 10.0.

The **reload** command halts the system. If the system is set to restart on error, it reboots itself. Use the **reload** command after configuration information is entered into a file and saved to the startup configuration.

You cannot reload from a virtual terminal if the system is not set up for automatic booting. This prevents the system from dropping to the ROM monitor and thereby taking the system out of the remote user's control.

If you modify your configuration file, the system prompts you to save the configuration. During a save operation, the system asks you if you want to proceed with the save if the CONFIG_FILE environment variable points to a startup configuration file that no longer exists. If you say "yes" in this situation, the system goes to **setup** mode upon reload.

When you schedule a reload to occur at a later time, it must take place within approximately 24 days.

The **at** keyword can only be used if the system clock has be set on the router (either through NTP, the hardware calendar, or manually). The time is relative to the configured time zone on the router. To schedule reloads across several routers to occur simultaneously, the time on each router must be synchronized with NTP.

To display information about a scheduled reload, use the **show reload** command.

Examples

The following example immediately reloads the software on the router:

```
Router# reload
```

The following example reloads the software on the router in 10 minutes:

```
Router# reload in 10
Router# Reload scheduled for 11:57:08 PDT Fri Apr 21 1996 (in 10 minutes)
Proceed with reload? [confirm]
Router#
```

The following example reloads the software on the router at 1:00 p.m. today:

```
Router# reload at 13:00
Router# Reload scheduled for 13:00:00 PDT Fri Apr 21 1996 (in 1 hour and 2 minutes)
Proceed with reload? [confirm]
Router#
```

The following example reloads the software on the router on April 20 at 2:00 a.m.:

```
Router# reload at 02:00 apr 20
Router# Reload scheduled for 02:00:00 PDT Sat Apr 20 1996 (in 38 hours and 9 minutes)
Proceed with reload? [confirm]
Router#
```

The following example cancels a pending reload:

```
Router# reload cancel
%Reload cancelled.
```

Related Commands

To locate documentation of related commands, you can search online at www.cisco.com.

copy system:running-config nvram:startup-config
show reload

show boot

The **show bootvar** command replaces the **show boot** command. See the **show bootvar** command for more information.

show bootvar

To display the contents of the BOOT environment variable, the name of the configuration file pointed to by the CONFIG_FILE environment variable, the contents of the BOOTLDR environment variable, and the configuration register setting, use the **show bootvar** EXEC command.

show bootvar

Part II Command Reference

Syntax Description

This command has no arguments or keywords.

Command Mode

EXEC

Usage Guidelines

This command first appeared in Cisco IOS Release 11.3 AA.

The **show bootvar** command replaces the **show boot** command.

The **show bootvar** command allows you to view the current settings for the following environment variables:

● BOOT

● CONFIG_FILE

● BOOTLDR

The BOOT environment variable specifies a list of bootable images on various devices. The CONFIG_FILE environment variable specifies the configuration file used during system initialization. The BOOTLDR environment variable specifies the Flash device and filename containing the rxboot image that ROM uses for booting. You set these environment variables with the **boot system**, **boot config**, and **boot bootldr** commands, respectively.

When you use this command on a Cisco 7507 or Cisco 7513 configured for High System Availability (HSA), this command also shows you the environment variable settings for both the master and slave RSP card.

HSA refers to how quickly your router returns to an operational status after a failure occurs. On the Cisco 7507 and Cisco 7513, you can install two RSP cards in a single router to improve system availability.

Sample Displays

The following is sample output from the **show bootvar** command:

```
Router# show bootvar

BOOT variable =
CONFIG_FILE variable = nvram:
Current CONFIG_FILE variable = slot0:router-config
BOOTLDR variable not exist

Configuration register is 0x0

Router#
```

In the sample output, the BOOT environment variable contains a null string. That is, a list of bootable images is not specified.

The CONFIG_FILE environment variable points to the configuration file in NVRAM as the startup (initialization) configuration. The run-time value for the CONFIG_FILE environment variable points to the router-config file on the Flash memory card inserted in the first slot of the RSP card. That is, during the run-time configuration, you have modified the CONFIG_FILE environment variable using the **boot config** command, but you have not saved the run-time configuration to the startup configuration. To save your run-time configuration to the startup configuration, use the **copy system:running-config nvram:startup-config** command. If you do not save the run-time configuration to the startup configuration, then the system reverts back to the saved CONFIG_FILE environment variable setting for initialization information upon reload. In this sample, the system reverts back to NVRAM for the startup configuration file.

The BOOTLDR environment variable does not yet exist. That is, you have not created the BOOTLDR environment variable using the **boot bootldr** command.

The following example is output from the **show bootvar** command for a Cisco 7513 configured for HSA:

```
Router# show bootvar

BOOT variable =
CONFIG_FILE variable =
Current CONFIG_FILE variable =
BOOTLDR variable does not exist

Configuration register is 0x0

current slave is in slot 7
BOOT variable =
CONFIG_FILE variable =
BOOTLDR variable does not exist

Configuration register is 0x0

Router#
```

Related Commands

To locate documentation of related commands, you can search online at www.cisco.com.

boot bootstrap
boot config
boot system
show version

show reload

To display the reload status on the router, use the **show reload** EXEC command.

> **show reload**

Syntax Description

This command has no arguments or keywords.

Command Mode

EXEC

Usage Guidelines

This command first appeared in Cisco IOS Release 11.2.

You can use the **show reload** command to display a pending software reload. To cancel the reload, use the **reload cancel** privileged EXEC command.

Sample Display

The following sample output from the **show reload** command shows that a reload is schedule for 12:00 a.m. (midnight) on Saturday, April 20:

```
Router# show reload
Reload scheduled for 00:00:00 PDT Sat April 20 1996 (in 12 hours and 12 minutes)
Router#
```

Related Commands

To locate documentation of related commands, you can search online at www.cisco.com.

reload

show version

To display the configuration of the system hardware, the software version, the names and sources of configuration files, and the boot images, use the **show version** EXEC command.

> **show version**

Syntax Description

This command has no arguments or keywords.

Command Mode

EXEC

Usage Guidelines

This command first appeared in Cisco IOS Release 10.0.

You can also use this command with a Cisco 7507 or Cisco 7513 configured with High System Availability (HSA). HSA refers to how quickly your router returns to an operational status after a failure occurs. On the Cisco 7507 and Cisco 7513, you can install two RSP cards in a single router to improve system availability.

When used with HSA, this command also displays the currently running slave RSP card and the Cisco IOS release that it is running.

Sample Displays

The following is sample output from the **show version** command:

```
Router1> show version

Cisco Internetwork Operating System Software
IOS (tm) 7200 Software (C7200-J-M), Experimental Version 11.3(19970915:164752)
[hampton-nitro-baseline 249]
Copyright (c) 1986-1997 by cisco Systems, Inc.
Compiled Wed 08-Oct-97 06:39 by hampton
Image text-base: 0x60008900, data-base: 0x60B98000

ROM: System Bootstrap, Version 11.1(11855) [beta 2], INTERIM SOFTWARE
BOOTFLASH: 7200 Software (C7200-BOOT-M), Version 11.1(472), RELEASE SOFTWARE (fc 1)

Router1 uptime is 23 hours, 33 minutes
System restarted by abort at PC 0x6022322C at 10:50:55 PDT Tue Oct 21 1997
System image file is "tftp://171.69.1.129/hampton/nitro/c7200-j-mz"

cisco 7206 (NPE150) processor with 57344K/8192K bytes of memory.
R4700 processor, Implementation 33, Revision 1.0 (512KB Level 2 Cache)
Last reset from power-on
Bridging software.
X.25 software, Version 3.0.0.
(SuperLAT software copyright 1990 by Meridian Technology Corp).
TN3270 Emulation software.
8 Ethernet/IEEE 802.3 interface(s)
2 FastEthernet/IEEE 802.3 interface(s)
```

```
4 Token Ring/IEEE 802.5 interface(s)
4 Serial network interface(s)
1 FDDI network interface(s)
125K bytes of non-volatile configuration memory.
1024K bytes of packet SRAM memory.

20480K bytes of Flash PCMCIA card at slot 0 (Sector size 128K).
20480K bytes of Flash PCMCIA card at slot 1 (Sector size 128K).
4096K bytes of Flash internal SIMM (Sector size 256K).
Configuration register is 0x0
```

Table 20-3 describes significant fields shown in these displays.

Table 20-3 *Show Version Field Descriptions*

Field	Description
IOS (tm) 7200 Software (C7200-J-M), Experimental Version 11.3	Always specify the complete version number when reporting a possible software problem. In the example output, the version number is 11.3.
ROM: System Bootstrap, Version 11.1(11855) [beta 2], INTERIM SOFTWARE	Bootstrap version string.
BOOTFLASH: 7200 Software (C7200-BOOT-M), Version 11.1(472), RELEASE SOFTWARE	Boot version string.
Router1 uptime is...	The amount of time the system has been up and running.
System restarted by...	Also displayed is a log of how the system was last booted, both as a result of normal system startup and of system error. For example, information can be displayed to indicate a bus error that is generally the result of an attempt to access a nonexistent address, as follows: System restarted by bus error at PC 0xC4CA, address 0x210C0C0
System image file is...	If the software was booted over the network, the Internet address of the boot host is shown. If the software was loaded from onboard ROM, this line reads "running default software."
cisco 7206 (NPE150) processor	The remaining output in each display shows the hardware configuration and any nonstandard software options.
Configuration register is...	The configuration register contents, displayed in hexadecimal notation.

The output of the **show version** EXEC command can also provide certain messages, such as bus error messages. If such error messages appear, report the complete text of this message to your technical support specialist.

The following is sample output from the **show version** command on a Cisco 7500 series router with an RSP2 and three VIP2s with a variety of interfaces:

```
Router# show version

Cisco Internetwork Operating System Software
IOS (tm) GS Software (RSP-JV-M), Experimental Version 11.1(12816)
[getchell 108]
Copyright (c) 1986-1996 by cisco Systems, Inc.
Compiled Mon 03-Jun-96 11:39 by getchell
Image text-base: 0x600108A0, data-base: 0x60910000

ROM: System Bootstrap, Version 5.3(16645) [szhang 571], INTERIM SOFTWARE

Router uptime is 4 minutes
System restarted by reload
System image file is "slot0:dirt/vip2/master/rsp-jv-mz.960603", booted via tftp from
172.18.2.3

cisco RSP2 (R4600) processor with 24576K bytes of memory.
R4600 processor, Implementation 32, Revision 2.0
Last reset from power-on
G.703/E1 software, Version 1.0.
SuperLAT software copyright 1990 by Meridian Technology Corp).
Bridging software.
X.25 software, Version 2.0, NET2, BFE and GOSIP compliant.
TN3270 Emulation software (copyright 1994 by TGV Inc).
Primary Rate ISDN software, Version 1.0.
Chassis Interface.
1 CIP controller (3 IBM Channels).
1 CIP2 controller (3 IBM Channels).
1 EIP controller (6 Ethernet).
1 HIP controller (1 HSSI).
1 FSIP controller (8 Serial).
1 AIP controller (1 ATM).
1 TRIP controller (4 Token Ring).
1 FIP controller (1 FDDI).
1 MIP controller (2 T1).
3 VIP2 controllers (1 FastEthernet)(13 Ethernet)(4 Serial)(4 Token Ring)(1 Fddi).
1 FEIP controller (1 FastEthernet).
19 Ethernet/IEEE 802.3 interfaces.
2 FastEthernet/IEEE 802.3 interfaces.
8 Token Ring/IEEE 802.5 interfaces.
12 Serial network interfaces.
1 HSSI network interface.
2 FDDI network interfaces.
1 ATM network interface.
2 Channelized T1/PRI ports.
125K bytes of non-volatile configuration memory.

8192K bytes of Flash PCMCIA card at slot 0 (Sector size 128K).
8192K bytes of Flash PCMCIA card at slot 1 (Sector size 128K).
8192K bytes of Flash internal SIMM (Sector size 256K).
No slave installed in slot 7.
Configuration register is 0x0
```

Table 20-4 describes the fields in this display for Cisco 7500 series routers with an RSP2 route switch processor.

Table 20-4 *Show Version Field Descriptions on Cisco 7500 Series Routers*

Field	Description
IOS (tm) GS Software, Version 11.1	Always specify the complete version number when reporting a possible software problem. In the example output, the version number is 11.1.
ROM: System Bootstrap, Version 5.3(16645) [szhang 571], INTERIM SOFTWARE	Bootstrap version string.
Router uptime is... System restarted by... System image file is...	The amount of time the system has been up and running, how the system was restarted, and the name of the system image file.
System last reset by...	Also displayed is a log of how the system was last booted, both as a result of normal system startup and of system error. For example, information can be displayed to indicate a bus error that is generally the result of an attempt to access a nonexistent address, as follows: System restarted by bus error at PC 0xC4CA, address 0x210C0C0
Cisco RSP2 (R4600) processor...	The remaining output in each display shows the software currently running, hardware configuration, and any nonstandard software options. The configuration register contents are displayed in hexadecimal notation.

The following is sample output of the **show version** command from a Cisco 7513. In this example, the current slave is processor slot 7.

```
Router# show version

Cisco Internetwork Operating System Software
IOS (tm) GS Software (RSP-P-M), Experimental Version 11.1(5479) [dbath 119]
Copyright (c) 1986-1995 by Cisco Systems, Inc.
Compiled Wed 08-Nov-95 17:51 by dbath
Image text-base: 0x600088A0, data-base: 0x603B6000

ROM: System Bootstrap, Version 5.3(18168) [mansonw 63], INTERIM SOFTWARE

Router uptime is 4 days, 31 minutes
System restarted by reload
System image file is "slot0:dirt/dbath/rsp-p-mz-ark-1", booted via tftp from 172.31.7.19


Cisco RSP2 (R4600) processor with 16384K bytes of memory.
R4600 processor, Implementation 32, Revision 2.0
Last reset from power-on
G.703/E1 software, Version 1.0.
Primary Rate ISDN software, Version 1.0.
Chassis Interface.
```

```
1 CIP controller (3 IBM Channels).
1 CIP2 controller (3 IBM Channels).
1 EIP controller (6 Ethernet).
1 FSIP controller (8 Serial).
1 AIP controller (1 ATM).
1 TRIP controller (4 Token Ring).
1 FIP controller (1 FDDI).
1 MIP controller (2 T1).
6 Ethernet/IEEE 802.3 interfaces.
4 Token Ring/IEEE 802.5 interfaces.
8 Serial network interfaces.
1 FDDI network interface.
1 ATM network interface.
2 Channelized T1/PRI ports.
125K bytes of non-volatile configuration memory.

8192K bytes of Flash PCMCIA card at slot 0 (Sector size 128K).
8192K bytes of Flash internal SIMM (Sector size 256K).

Slave in slot 7 is running Cisco Internetwork Operating System Software
IOS (tm) GS Software (RSP-DW-M), Experimental Version 11.1(5479) [dbath 118]
Copyright (c) 1986-1995 by Cisco Systems, Inc.
Compiled Wed 08-Nov-95 16:57 by dbath

Configuration register is 0x0
```

Related Commands

To locate documentation of related commands, you can search online at www.cisco.com.

reload

slave auto-sync config

To turn on automatic synchronization of configuration files for a Cisco 7507 or Cisco 7513 that is configured for High System Availability (HSA), use the **slave auto-sync config** global configuration command. To turn off automatic synchronization, use the **no** form of the command.

> **slave auto-sync config**
> **no slave auto-sync config**

Syntax Description

This command has no arguments or keywords.

Default

Enabled

Command Mode

Global configuration

Usage Guidelines

This command first appeared in Cisco IOS Release 11.1.

Use this command for a Cisco 7507 or Cisco 7513 that is configured for High System Availability (HSA). HSA refers to how quickly your router returns to an operational status after a failure occurs. On the Cisco 7507 and Cisco 7513, you can install two RSP cards in a single router to improve system availability.

In automatic synchronization mode, when you issue a **copy** EXEC command that specifies the master's startup configuration (**nvram:startup-config**) as the target, the master also copies the same file to the slave's startup configuration (**slavenvram:startup-config**). Use this command when implementing HSA for simple hardware backup or for software error protection to ensure that the master and slave RSP contain the same configuration files.

Example

The following example turns on automatic configuration file synchronization. When the **copy system:running-config nvram:startup-config** command is issued, the running configuration is saved to the startup configurations of both the master RSP and the slave RSP.

```
Router(config)# slave auto-sync config
Router(config)# end
Router# copy system:running-config nvram:startup-config
```

Related Commands

To locate documentation of related commands, you can search online at www.cisco.com.

slave sync config

slave default-slot

To specify the default slave RSP card on a Cisco 7507 or Cisco 7513, use the **slave default-slot** global configuration command.

> **slave default-slot** *processor-slot-number*

Syntax	Description
processor-slot-number	Number of processor slot that contains the default slave RSP. On the Cisco 7507, valid values are 2 or 3. On the Cisco 7513, valid values are 6 or 7. The default is the higher number processor slot.

Default

The default slave is the RSP card located in the higher number processor slot. On the Cisco 7507, processor slot 3 contains the default slave RSP. On the Cisco 7513, processor slot 7 contains the default slave RSP.

Command Mode

Global configuration

Usage Guidelines

This command first appeared in Cisco IOS Release 11.1.

Use this command for a Cisco 7507 or Cisco 7513 that is configured for High System Availability (HSA). HSA refers to how quickly your router returns to an operational status after a failure occurs. On the Cisco 7507 and Cisco 7513, you can install two RSP cards in a single router to improve system availability.

The router uses the default slave information when booting:

- If a system boot is due to powering up the router or using the **reload** command, then the specified default slave will be the slave RSP.

- If a system boot is due to a system crash or hardware failure, then the system ignores the default slave designation, and makes the crashed or faulty RSP card the slave RSP.

Example

The following example sets the default slave RSP to processor slot 2 on a Cisco 7507:

```
slave default-slot 2
```

Related Commands

To locate documentation of related commands, you can search online at www.cisco.com.

reload

slave image

To specify the image that the slave RSP runs on a Cisco 7507 or Cisco 7513, use the **slave image** global configuration command.

> **slave image** {**system** | *file-url*}

Syntax	Description
system	Loads the slave image that is bundled with the master system image. This is the default.
file-url	Loads the slave image from the specified file in a Flash file system. If you do not specify a filename, the first file on the specified Flash file system is the default file.

Default

The default is to load the image from the system bundle.

Command Mode

Global configuration

Usage Guidelines

This command first appeared in Cisco IOS Release 11.1.

Use this command for a Cisco 7507 or Cisco 7513 that is configured for High System Availability (HSA). HSA refers to how quickly your router returns to an operational status after a failure occurs. On the Cisco 7507 and Cisco 7513, you can install two RSP cards in a single router to improve system availability.

Use the **slave image** command to override the slave image that is bundled with the master image.

When using HSA for simple hardware backup, ensure that the slave image is in the same location on the master and the slave RSP card. Thus, if the slave RSP card becomes the master, it will be able to find the slave image and download it to the new slave.

Example

The following example specifies that the slave RSP run the rsp-dw-mz.ucode.111-3.2 image from slot 0.

```
slave image slot0:rsp-dw-mz.ucode.111-3.2
```

Related Commands

To locate documentation of related commands, you can search online at www.cisco.com.

slave reload

slave reload

To force a reload of the image that the slave RSP card is running on a Cisco 7507 or Cisco 7513, use the **slave reload** global configuration command.

> **slave reload**

Syntax Description

This command has no arguments or keywords.

Command Mode

Global configuration

Usage Guidelines

This command first appeared in Cisco IOS Release 11.1.

Use this command for a Cisco 7507 or Cisco 7513 that is configured for High System Availability (HSA). HSA refers to how quickly your router returns to an operational status after a failure occurs. On the Cisco 7507 and Cisco 7513, you can install two RSP cards in a single router to improve system availability.

After using the **slave image** global configuration command to specify the image that the slave RSP runs on a Cisco 7507 or Cisco 7513, use the **slave reload** command to reload the slave with the new image. The **slave reload** command can also be used to force the slave to reboot its existing image.

Example

The following example reloads an inactive slave RSP card. If the slave successfully reloads, it will return to an active slave state. If the master RSP fails, the slave RSP will become the master.

```
slave reload
```

Related Commands

To locate documentation of related commands, you can search online at www.cisco.com.

slave image

slave sync config

To manually synchronize configuration files on the master and slave RSP cards of a Cisco 7507 or Cisco 7513, use the **slave sync config** privileged EXEC command.

> **slave sync config**

Syntax Description

This command has no arguments or keywords.

Default

Automatic synchronization is turned on.

Command Mode

Privileged EXEC

Usage Guidelines

This command first appeared in Cisco IOS Release 11.1.

Use this command for a Cisco 7507 or Cisco 7513 that is configured for High System Availability (HSA). HSA refers to how quickly your router returns to an operational status after a failure occurs. On the Cisco 7507 and Cisco 7513, you can install two RSP cards in a single router to improve system availability.

This command allows you to synchronize the configuration files of the master and slave RSP cards on a case-by-case basis when you do not have automatic synchronization turned on. This command copies the master's configuration file to the slave RSP card.

NOTE   You *must* use this command when you insert a new slave RSP card into a Cisco 7507 or Cisco 7513 for the first time to ensure the new slave is configured consistently with the master.

Example

The following example synchronizes the configuration files on the master and slave RSP card:

```
slave sync config
```

Related Commands

To locate documentation of related commands, you can search online at www.cisco.com.

slave auto-sync config

slave terminal

To enable access to the slave RSP console, use the **slave terminal** global configuration command. The **no** form of this command disables access to the slave RSP console.

> **slave terminal**
> **no slave terminal**

Syntax Description

This command has no arguments or keywords.

Default

Enabled

Command Mode

Global configuration

Usage Guidelines

This command first appeared in Cisco IOS Release 11.1.

The slave console does not have enable password protection. Thus, an individual connected to the slave console port can enter privileged EXEC mode and view or erase the configuration of the router. Use the **no slave terminal** command to disable slave console access and prevent security problems. When the slave console is disabled, users cannot enter commands.

If slave console access is disabled, the following message appears periodically on the slave console:

```
%%Slave terminal access is disabled. Use "slave terminal" command in master RSP configuration
mode to enable it.
```

Example

The following example disables console access to the slave RSP:

```
no slave terminal
```

## CHAPTER 21

Configuring Additional File Transfer Functions

This chapter describes how to configure a router as a server, change MOP parameters, configure the router to forward extended BOOTP requests over asynchronous interfaces, configure rcp, rsh, and FTP.

For a complete description of the file transfer function commands mentioned in this chapter, see Chapter 22, "Additional File Transfer Function Commands." To locate documentation of other commands that appear in this chapter, you can search online at www.cisco.com.

Additional Functions Task List

To configure additional file transfer functions, perform any of the tasks in the following sections:

- Configure a Router as a Server
- Change MOP Request Parameters
- Specify Asynchronous Interface Extended BOOTP Requests
- Configure a Router to Use rsh and rcp
- Configure a Router to Use FTP Connections

Configure a Router as a Server

It is too costly and inefficient to have a machine which only acts as server on every network segment. However, when you do not have a server on every segment, your network operations can incur enormous time delays across network segments. You can configure a router to serve as a Reverse Address Resolution Protocol (RARP) or Trivial File Transfer Protocol (TFTP) server to reduce costs and time delays in your network while allowing you to use your router for its regular functions.

Typically, a router that is configured as a server provides other routers with operating system images from its Flash memory. You can also configure the router to respond to other types of service requests, such as RARP requests.

To configure the router as a server, perform any of the tasks in the following sections. The tasks are not mutually exclusive.

- Configure a Router as a TFTP Server
- Configure a Router as a RARP Server

In addition, you can configure the Cisco IOS software to forward extended BOOTP requests over asynchronous interfaces.

Configure a Router as a TFTP Server

As a TFTP server host, the router responds to TFTP Read Request messages by sending a copy of the system image contained in ROM or one of the system images contained in Flash memory to the requesting host. The TFTP Read Request message must use one of the filenames that are specified in the configuration.

NOTE   For the Cisco 7000 family, the filename used must represent a software image that is present in Flash memory. If no image resides in Flash memory, the client router will boot the server's ROM image as a default.

Flash memory can be used as a TFTP file server for other routers on the network. This feature allows you to boot a remote router with an image that resides in the Flash server memory.

With Cisco IOS Release 11.0, the Cisco 7000 family allow you to specify one of the different Flash memory devices (**bootflash:**, **slot0:**, **slot1:**, **slavebootflash:**, **slaveslot0:**, or **slaveslot1:**) as the TFTP server.

In the description that follows, one Cisco 7000 router is referred to as the *Flash server*, and all other routers are referred to as *client routers*. Example configurations for the Flash server and client routers include commands as necessary.

Configure a Router as a TFTP Server Task List

To configure a router as a TFTP server, perform the tasks in the following sections:

● Perform Prerequisite Tasks

● Configure the Server

● Configure the Client Router

Perform Prerequisite Tasks

The server and client router must be able to reach each other before the TFTP function can be implemented. Verify this connection by pinging between the server and client router (in either direction) with the **ping** command.

An example use of the **ping** command is as follows:

```
Router# ping 172.16.101.101
```

In this example, the Internet Protocol (IP) address of 172.16.101.101 belongs to the client router. Connectivity is indicated by a series of exclamation points (!), while a series of periods (.) plus *[timed out]* or *[failed]* indicates no connection. If the connection fails, reconfigure the interface, check the physical connection between the Flash server and client router, and ping again.

After you verify the connection, ensure that a TFTP-bootable image is present on the server. This is the system software image the client router will boot. Note the name of this software image so you can verify it after the first client boot.

CAUTION	For full functionality, the software image sent to the client must be the same type as the ROM software installed on the client router. For example, if the server has X.25 software, and the client does not have X.25 software in ROM, the client will not have X.25 capabilities after booting from the server's image in Flash memory.

Configure the Server

To specify TFTP server operation, use the following commands in configuration mode:

Step	Command	Purpose
1	**configure terminal**	Enters configuration mode from the terminal.
2	**tftp-server flash** [*partition-number***:**] *filename1* [**alias** *filename2*] [*access-list-number*]	Specifies the system image to send in response to Read Requests. You can enter multiple lines to specify multiple images.
	tftp-server flash *device***:***filename* (Cisco 7000 family only)	
	tftp-server flash [*device***:**] [*partition-number***:**]*filename* (Cisco 1600 series and Cisco 3600 series only)	
	tftp-server rom alias *filename1* [*access-list-number*]	
3	**end**	Exits configuration mode.
4	**copy running-config startup-config**	Saves the configuration file to your startup configuration.

The TFTP session can sometimes fail. TFTP generates the following special characters to help you determine why a TFTP session fails:

- An "E" character indicates that the TFTP server received an erroneous packet.

- An "O" character indicates that the TFTP server received an out-of-sequence packet.

- A period (.) indicates a timeout.

For diagnosing any undue delay in the transfer, the output is useful.

In the following example, the system can use TFTP to send copies of the Flash memory file *version-10.3* in response to a TFTP Read Request for that file. The requesting host is checked against access list 22.

```
tftp-server flash version-10.3 22
```

In the following example, the system can use TFTP to send a copy of the ROM image *gs3-k.101* in response to a TFTP Read Request for the *gs3-k.101* file:

```
tftp-server rom alias gs3-k.101
```

In the following example, a router sends a copy of the file *gs7-k.9.17* in Flash memory in response to a TFTP Read Request. The client router must reside on a network specified by access list 1. Thus, in the example, the any clients on network 172.16.101.0 are permitted access to the file.

```
Server# configure terminal
Enter configuration commands, one per line. End with Ctrl-Z
Server(config)# tftp-server flash gs7-k.9.17 1
Server(config)# access-list 1 permit 172.16.101.0 0.0.0.255
Server(config)# end
Server# copy running-config startup-config
[ok]
Server#
```

Configure the Client Router

Configure the client router to first load a system image from the server. As a backup, configure the client router to then load its own ROM image if the load from the server fails. To configure the client router, use the following commands beginning in privileged EXEC mode:

Step	Command	Purpose
1	**configure terminal**	Enters configuration mode from the terminal.
2	**no boot system**	Removes all previous **boot system** statements from the configuration file.
3	**boot system [tftp]** *filename* [*ip-address*]	Specifies that the client router load a system image from the server.
4	**boot system rom**	As a backup, specifies that the client router loads its own ROM image.
5	**config-register** *value*	Sets the configuration register to enable the client router to load a system image from a network server.
6	**end**	Exits configuration mode.
7	**copy running-config startup-config**	Saves the configuration file to your startup configuration.
8	**reload**	Reloads the router to make your changes take effect.
9	**show version**	After the router reboots, verifies that the client router booted the correct image from the TFTP server.

CAUTION   Using the **no boot system** command, as in the following example, will invalidate *all* other boot system commands currently in the client router system configuration. Before proceeding, determine whether the system configuration stored in the client router should first be saved (uploaded) to a TFTP file server so you have a backup copy.

The following example shows how to configure a router to use a TFTP server:

```
Client# configure terminal
Enter configuration commands, one per line. End with Ctrl-Z
Client(config)# no boot system
Client(config)# boot system gs7-k.9.17 172.31.111.111
Client(config)# boot system rom
Client(config)# config-register 0x010F
Client(config)# end
Client# copy running-config startup-config
[ok]
Client# reload
```

In this example, the **no boot system** command invalidates all other **boot system** commands currently in the configuration memory, and any **boot system** commands entered after this command will be executed first. The second command, **boot system** *filename address*, tells the client router to look for the file *gs7-k.9.17* on the TFTP server with an IP address of 172.31.111.111. Failing this, the client router will boot from its system ROM in response to the **boot system rom** command, which is included as a backup in case of a network problem. The **copy running-config startup-config** command copies the configuration to the startup configuration, and the **reload** command boots the system.

CAUTION   The system software (*gs7-k.9.17* in the example) to be booted from the server (172.31.111.111 in the example) must reside in Flash memory on the server. If it is not in Flash memory, the client router will boot the server's system ROM.

The following example shows sample output of the **show version** command after the router has rebooted:

```
Client> show version
GS Software (GS7), Version 9.1.17
Copyright (c) 1986-1992 by cisco Systems, Inc.
Compiled Wed 21-Oct-92 22:49

System Bootstrap, Version 4.6(0.15)

Current date and time is Thu 10-22-1992 13:15:03
Boot date and time is Thu 10-22-1992 13:06:55
env-chassis uptime is 9 minutes
System restarted by power-on
System image file is "gs7-k.9.17", booted via tftp from 172.31.111.111
```

```
RP1 (68040) processor with 16384K bytes of memory.
X.25 software.
Bridging software.
1 Switch Processor.
1 EIP controller (6 Ethernet).
6 Ethernet/IEEE 802.3 interface.
128K bytes of non-volatile configuration memory.
4096K bytes of flash memory on embedded flash (in RP1).
Configuration register is 0x010F
```

The important information in this example is contained in the first line "GS Software..." and in the line that begins "System image file...." The "GS Software..." line shows the version of the operating system in the client router's RAM. The "System image file...." line shows the filename of the system image loaded from the TFTP server.

Configure a Router as a RARP Server

You can configure the router as a RARP server. This feature enables the Cisco IOS software to answer RARP requests, making diskless booting of various systems possible (for example, Sun workstations or PCs on networks where the client and server are on separate subnets).

To configure the router as a RARP server, use the following command in interface configuration mode:

Command	Purpose
ip rarp-server *ip-address*	Configures the router as a RARP server.

Figure 21-1 illustrates a network configuration in which a router is configured to act as a RARP server.

Figure 21-1 *Configuring a Router as a RARP Server*

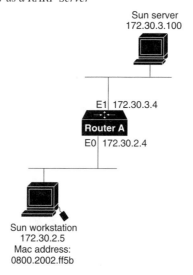

Router A's configuration:

```
! Allow the router to forward broadcast portmapper requests
ip forward-protocol udp 111
! Provide the router with the IP address of the diskless sun
arp 172.30.2.5 0800.2002.ff5b arpa
interface ethernet 0
! Configure the router to act as a RARP server, using the Sun Server's IP
! address in the RARP response packet.
ip rarp-server 172.30.3.100
! Portmapper broadcasts from this interface are sent to the Sun Server.
ip helper-address 172.30.3.100
```

The Sun client and server's IP addresses must use the same major network number because of a limitation with the current SunOS *rpc.bootparamd* daemon.

Figure 21-2 illustrates a similar configuration with an access server.

Figure 21-2 *Configuring an Access Server as a RARP Server*

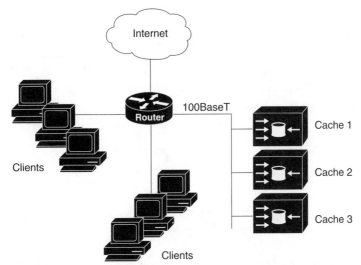

In the following example, the access server is configured to act as a RARP server. Figure 21-2 illustrates the network configuration.

```
! Allow the access server to forward broadcast portmapper requests
 ip forward-protocol udp 111
! Provide the access server with the IP address of the diskless sun
 arp 172.30.2.5 0800.2002.ff5b arpa
 interface ethernet 0
! Configure the access server to act as a RARP server, using the Sun Server's
! IP address in the RARP response packet.
 ip rarp-server 172.30.3.100
! Portmapper broadcasts from this interface are sent to the Sun Server.
 ip helper-address 172.30.3.100
```

The Sun client and server's IP addresses must use the same major network number because of a limitation with the current SunOS *rpc.bootparamd* daemon.

Change MOP Request Parameters

By default, when the software transmits a request that requires a response from a MOP boot server and the server does not respond, the message will be retransmitted after 4 seconds. The message will be retransmitted a maximum of eight times. The MOP device code is set to the Cisco device code by default.

If the MOP boot server and router are separated by a slow serial link, it may take longer than 4 seconds for the router to receive a response to its message. Therefore, you might want to configure the software to wait longer than 4 seconds before retransmitting the message if you are using such a link. You may also want to change the maximum number of retires for the MOP request or the MOP device code.

To change the Cisco IOS software parameters for transmitting boot requests to a MOP server, use the following commands starting in privileged EXEC mode:

Step	Command	Purpose
1	**configure terminal**	Enters configuration mode from the terminal.
2	**mop device-code {cisco	ds200}** **mop retransmit-timer** *seconds* **mop retries** *count*	Changes MOP server parameters.
3	**end**	Exits configuration mode.
4	**copy running-config startup-config**	Saves the configuration file to your startup configuration.

In the following example, if the MOP boot server does not respond within 10 seconds after the router sends a message, the software will retransmit the message:

```
Router# configure terminal
Router (config)# mop retransmit-timer 10
Router (config)# end
Router# copy running-config startup-config
```

Specify Asynchronous Interface Extended BOOTP Requests

The Boot Protocol (BOOTP) server for asynchronous interfaces supports the extended BOOTP requests specified in RFC 1084. The following command is useful in conjunction with using the auxiliary port as an asynchronous interface.

To configure extended BOOTP requests for asynchronous interfaces, use the following command in global configuration mode:

Command	Purpose
async-bootp *tag* [*:hostname*] *data*	Configures extended BOOTP requests for asynchronous interfaces.

You can display the extended BOOTP requests by using the following command in EXEC mode:

Command	Purpose
show async-bootp	Shows parameters for BOOTP requests.

Configure a Router to Use rsh and rcp

Remote shell (rsh) gives users the ability to execute commands remotely. Remote copy (rcp) allows users to copy files to and from a file system residing on a remote host or server on the network. Cisco's implementation of rsh and rcp interoperates with standard implementations.

This section is divided into the following sections:

- Configure a Router to Use rsh
- Configure a Router to Use rcp
- Configure a Router to Use FTP Connections (Optional)

Configure a Router to Use rsh

You can use rsh to execute commands on remote systems to which you have access. When you issue the rsh command, a shell is started on the remote system. The shell allows you to execute commands on the remote system without having to log in to the target host.

You do not need to connect to the system, router, or access server and then disconnect after you execute a command if you use rsh. For example, you can use rsh to remotely look at the status of other devices *without* connecting to the target device, executing the command, and then disconnecting. This capability is useful for looking at statistics on many different routers.

Maintaining rsh Security

To gain access to a remote system running rsh, such as a UNIX host, an entry must exist in the system's *.rhosts* file or its equivalent identifying you as a user who is authorized to execute commands remotely on the system. On UNIX systems, the *.rhosts* file identifies users who can remotely execute commands on the system.

You can enable rsh support on a router to allow users on remote systems to execute commands. However, our implementation of rsh does not support an *.rhosts* file. Instead, you must configure a local authentication database to control access to the router by users attempting to execute commands remotely using rsh. A local authentication database is similar to a UNIX *.rhosts* file. Each entry that you configure in the authentication database identifies the local user, the remote host, and the remote user.

Configure the Router to Allow Remote Users to Execute Commands Using rsh

To configure the router as an rsh server, use the following commands in global configuration mode:

Step	Command	Purpose
1	**ip rcmd remote-host** *local-username* {*ip-address* | *host*} *remote-username* [**enable** [*level*]]	Creates an entry in the local authentication database for each remote user who is allowed to execute rsh commands.
2	**ip rcmd rsh-enable**	Enables the software to support incoming rsh commands.

To disable the software from supporting incoming rsh commands, use the **no ip rcmd rsh-enable** command.

NOTE   When support of incoming rsh commands is disabled, you can still issue an rsh command to be executed on other routers that support the remote shell protocol and on UNIX hosts on the network.

The following example shows how to add two entries for remote users to the authentication database, and enable a router to support rsh commands from remote users:

```
ip rcmd remote-host Router1 172.16.101.101 rmtnetad1
ip rcmd remote-host Router1 172.16.101.101 netadmin4 enable
ip rcmd rsh-enable
```

The users, named *rmtnetad1* and *netadmin4*, are both on the remote host at IP address 172.16.101.101. Although both users are on the same remote host, you must include a unique entry for each user. Both users are allowed to connect to the router and remotely execute rsh commands on it after the router is enabled for rsh. The user named *netadmin4* is allowed to execute privileged EXEC mode commands on the router. Both authentication database entries give the router's host name *Router1* as the local username. The last command enables the router to support rsh commands issued by remote users.

Remotely Execute Commands Using rsh

You can use rsh to execute commands remotely on network servers that support the remote shell protocol. To use this command, the *.rhosts* files (or equivalent files) on the network server must include an entry that permits you to remotely execute commands on that host.

If the remote server has a directory structure, as do UNIX systems, the rsh command that you issue is remotely executed from the directory of the account for the remote user that you specify through the **/user** *username* keyword and argument pair.

If you do not specify the **/user** keyword and argument, the Cisco IOS software sends a default remote username. As the default value of the remote username, the software sends the remote username associated with the current TTY process, if that name is valid. If the TTY remote username is invalid, the software uses the router host name as the both the remote and local usernames.

To execute a command remotely on a network server using rsh, use the following commands in privileged EXEC mode:

Step	Command	Purpose
1	**enable** [*password*]	Enters privileged EXEC mode.
2	**rsh** {*ip-address*	*host*} [**/user** *username*] *remote-command*	Enters the rsh command to be executed remotely.

The following example executes the **ls** -a command in the home directory of the user **sharon** on **mysys.cisco.com** using **rsh**:

```
Router# enable
Router# rsh mysys.cisco.com /user sharon ls -a
.
..
.alias
.cshrc
.emacs
.exrc
.history
.login
.mailrc
.newsrc
.oldnewsrc
.rhosts
.twmrc
.xsession
jazz
Router#
```

Configure a Router to Use rcp

The rcp copy commands rely on the rsh server (or daemon) on the remote system. To copy files using rcp, you do not need to create a server for file distribution, as you do with TFTP. You need only to have access to a server that supports the remote shell (rsh). (Most UNIX systems support rsh.) Because you are copying a file from one place to another, you must have read permission on the source file and write permission on the destination file. If the destination file does not exist, rcp creates it for you.

Although our rcp implementation emulates the functions of the UNIX rcp implementation—copying files among systems on the network—our command syntax differs from the UNIX rcp command syntax. Our rcp support offers a set of copy commands that use rcp as the transport mechanism. These rcp copy commands are similar in style to our TFTP copy commands, but they offer an alternative that provides faster performance and reliable delivery of data. These improvements are possible because the rcp transport mechanism is built on and uses the Transmission Control Protocol/Internet Protocol (TCP/IP) stack, which is connection-oriented. You can use rcp commands to copy system images and configuration files from the router to a network server and vice versa.

You can also enable rcp support to allow users on remote systems to copy files to and from the router.

Configure the Router to Accept rcp Requests from Remote Users

To configure the Cisco IOS software to support incoming rcp requests, use the following commands in global configuration mode:

Step	Command	Purpose
1	**ip rcmd remote-host** *local-username* {*ip-address* | *host*} *remote-username* [**enable** [*level*]]	Creates an entry in the local authentication database for each remote user who is allowed to execute rcp commands.
2	**ip rcmd rcp-enable**	Enables the software to support incoming rcp requests.

To disable the software from supporting incoming rcp requests, use the **no ip rcmd rcp-enable** command.

NOTE	When support for incoming rcp requests is disabled, you can still use the rcp commands to copy images from remote servers. The support for incoming rcp requests is distinct from its ability to handle outgoing rcp requests.

The following example shows how to add two entries for remote users to the authentication database and then enable the software to support remote copy requests from remote users. The users, named *netadmin1* on the remote host at IP address 172.16.15.55 and *netadmin3* on the remote host at IP address 172.16.101.101, are both allowed to connect to the router and remotely execute rcp commands on it after the router is enabled to support rcp. Both authentication database entries give the host name *Router1* as the local username. The last command enables the router to support for rcp requests from remote users.

```
ip rcmd remote-host Router1 172.16.15.55 netadmin1
ip rcmd remote-host Router1 172.16.101.101 netadmin3
ip rcmd rcp-enable
```

Configure the Remote to Send rcp Requests

The rcp protocol requires a client to send a remote username on each rcp request to a server. When you copy a configuration file from a server to the router using rcp, the Cisco IOS software sends the first valid username in the following list:

1   The username set by the **ip rcmd remote-username** command, if the command is configured.

2   The remote username associated with the current TTY (terminal) process. For example, if the user is connected to the router through Telnet and was authenticated through the **username** command, the router software sends the Telnet username as the remote username.

NOTE	For Cisco, TTYs are commonly used in access servers. The concept of TTY originated with UNIX. For UNIX systems, each physical device is represented in the file system. Terminals are called *TTY devices*, which stands for *teletype*, the original UNIX terminal.

3   The router host name.

For **boot** commands using rcp, the software sends the router host name; you cannot explicitly configure the remote username.

For the rcp copy request to execute successfully, an account must be defined on the network server for the remote username.

If you are writing to the server, the rcp server must be properly configured to accept the rcp write request from the user on the router. For UNIX systems, you must add an entry to the *.rhosts* file for the remote user on the rcp server. For example, if the router contains the following configuration lines

```
hostname Rtr1
ip rcmd remote-username User0
```

and the router's IP address translates to Router1.company.com, then the *.rhosts* file for User0 on the rcp server should contain the following line:

```
Router1.company.com Rtr1
```

Refer to the documentation for your rcp server for more details.

If the server has a directory structure, the configuration file or image is written or copied relative to the directory associated with the remote username on the server. Use the **ip rcmd remote-username** command to specify which directory on the server to use. For example, if the system image resides in the home directory of a user on the server, you can specify that user's name as the remote username.

If you copy the configuration file to a personal computer used as a file server, the computer must support rsh.

To override the default remote username sent on rcp requests, use the following commands starting in privileged EXEC mode:

Step	Command	Purpose
1	**configure terminal**	Enters configuration mode from the terminal.
2	**ip rcmd remote-username** *username*	Specifies the remote username.

To remove the remote username and return to the default value, use the **no ip rcmd remote-username** command.

Configure a Router to Use FTP Connections

You configure a router to transfer files between systems on the network using the Internet File Transfer Protocol (FTP). With the Cisco IOS implementation of FTP, you can set the following features:

- Passive-mode FTP

- Username

- Password

- IP address

FTP Configuration Task List

Use the instructions in the section "Configure FTP Connections" to configure FTP on a router.

Configure FTP Connections

To configure FTP connections on a router, use the following commands in global configuration mode:

Command	Purpose
ip ftp username *string*	Specifies the username to be used for the FTP connection.
ip ftp password [*type*] *password*	Specifies the password to be used for the FTP connection.

Command	Purpose
ip ftp passive or **no ip ftp passive**	Configures the router to only use passive-mode FTP connections. Allows all types of FTP connections (default).
ip ftp source-interface *interface*	Specifies the source IP address for FTP connections.

The following example demonstrates how to capture a core dump using the Cisco IOS FTP feature. The router accesses a server at IP address 192.168.10.3 with login name **zorro** and password **sword**. The default passive-mode FTP is used, and the server is accessed using Token Ring interface to1 on the router where the core dump will occur:

```
ip ftp username zorro
ip ftp password sword
ip ftp passive
ip ftp source-interface to1
exception protocol ftp
! This command allows the core-dump code to use FTP rather than TFTP or RCP
exception dump 192.168.10.3
! This command creates the core dump in the event the system at IP
  address 192.168.10.3 crashes
```

## CHAPTER 22

Additional File Transfer Function Commands

This chapter provides detailed descriptions of commands used to configure the router for additional file transfer functions.

NOTE   Commands in this chapter that have been replaced by new commands continue to perform their normal functions in the current release, but are no longer documented. Support for these commands will cease in a future release. Table 22-1 maps the old command with its replacement.

Table 22-1   *Mapping Old Commands to New Commands*

Old Command	New Command
tftp-server system	tftp-server

For configuration information and examples, see Chapter 21, "Configuring Additional File Transfer Functions."

async-bootp

To configure extended BOOTP requests for asynchronous interfaces as defined in RFC 1084, use the **async-bootp** global configuration command. Use the **no** form of this command to restore the default.

async-bootp *tag* [**:***hostname*] *data*
no async-bootp

Syntax	Description
tag	Item being requested; expressed as filename, integer, or IP dotted-decimal address. See Table 22-2 for possible keywords.
:*hostname*	(Optional) This entry applies only to the host specified. The argument **:***hostname* accepts both an IP address and a logical host name.
data	List of IP addresses entered in dotted-decimal notation or as logical host names, a number, or a quoted string.

Table 22-2 *async-bootp* *Tag Keywords*

Keyword	Description
bootfile	Specifies use of a server boot file from which to download the boot program. Use the optional *:hostname* and *data* arguments to specify the filename.
subnet-mask *mask*	Dotted-decimal address specifying the network and local subnetwork mask (as defined by RFC 950).
time-offset *offset*	Signed 32-bit integer specifying the time offset of the local subnetwork in seconds from Universal Coordinated Time (UTC).
gateway *address*	Dotted-decimal address specifying the IP addresses of gateways for this subnetwork. A preferred gateway should be listed first.
time-server *address*	Dotted-decimal address specifying the IP address of time servers (as defined by RFC 868).
IEN116-server *address*	Dotted-decimal address specifying the IP address of name servers (as defined by IEN 116).
nbns-server *address*	Dotted decimal address specifying the IP address of Windows NT servers.
DNS-server *address*	Dotted-decimal address specifying the IP address of domain name servers (as defined by RFC 1034).
log-server *address*	Dotted-decimal address specifying the IP address of an MIT-LCS UDP log server.
quote-server *address*	Dotted-decimal address specifying the IP address of Quote of the Day servers (as defined in RFC 865).
lpr-server *address*	Dotted-decimal address specifying the IP address of Berkeley UNIX Version 4 BSD servers.
impress-server *address*	Dotted-decimal address specifying the IP address of Impress network image servers.
rlp-server *address*	Dotted-decimal address specifying the IP address of Resource Location Protocol (RLP) servers (as defined in RFC 887).
hostname *name*	The name of the client, which may or may not be domain qualified, depending upon the site.
bootfile-size *value*	A two-octet value specifying the number of 512-octet (byte) blocks in the default boot file.

Default

If no extended BOOTP commands are entered, the Cisco IOS software generates a gateway and subnet mask appropriate for the local network.

Command Mode

Global configuration

Usage Guidelines

This command first appeared in Cisco IOS Release 10.0.

Use the EXEC command **show async-bootp** to list the configured parameters. Use the **no async-bootp** command to clear the list.

Examples

The following example illustrates how to specify different boot files: one for a PC, and one for a Macintosh. With this configuration, a BOOTP request from the host on 172.30.1.1 results in a reply listing the boot filename as *pcboot*. A BOOTP request from the host named *mac* results in a reply listing the boot filename as *macboot*.

```
async-bootp bootfile :172.30.1.1 "pcboot"
async-bootp bootfile :mac "macboot"
```

The following example specifies a subnet mask of 255.255.0.0:

```
async-bootp subnet-mask 255.255.0.0
```

The following example specifies a negative time offset of the local subnetwork of -3600 seconds:

```
async-bootp time-offset -3600
```

The following example specifies the IP address of a time server:

```
async-bootp time-server 128.128.1.1
```

Related Commands

To locate documentation of related commands, you can search online at www.cisco.com.

show async-bootp

ip ftp passive

To configure the router to use only passive FTP connections, use the **ip ftp passive** global configuration command. To allow all types of FTP connections, use the **no** form of this command.

> **ip ftp passive**
> **no ip ftp passive**

Syntax Description

This command has no arguments or keywords.

Default

All types of FTP connections are allowed.

Command Mode

Global configuration

Usage Guidelines

This command first appeared in Cisco IOS Release 10.3.

Example

The following example configures the router to use only passive FTP connections:

```
ip ftp passive
```

Related Commands

To locate documentation of related commands, you can search online at www.cisco.com.

ip ftp password
ip ftp source-interface
ip ftp username

ip ftp password

To specify the password to be used for FTP connections, use the **ip ftp password** global configuration command. Use the **no** form of this command to return the password to its default.

ip ftp password [*type*] *password*
no ip ftp password

Syntax

Description

type

(Optional) Type of encryption to use on the password. A value of 0 disables encryption. A value of 7 indicates proprietary encryption.

password

Password to use for FTP connections.

Default

The router forms a password *username@routername.domain*. The variable *username* is the username associated with the current session, *routername* is the configured host name, and *domain* is the domain of the router.

Command Mode

Global configuration

Usage Guidelines

This command first appeared in Cisco IOS Release 10.3.

Example

The following example configures the router to use the username *red* and the password *blue* for FTP connections:

```
ip ftp username red
ip ftp password blue
```

Related Commands

To locate documentation of related commands, you can search online at www.cisco.com.

ip ftp password
ip ftp source-interface
ip ftp username

ip ftp source-interface

To specify the source IP address for FTP connections, use the **ip ftp source-interface** global configuration command. Use the **no** form of this command to use the address of the interface where the connection is made.

> **ip ftp source-interface** *interface*
> **no ip ftp source-interface**

Syntax

interface	The interface type and number to use to obtain the source address for FTP connections.

Default

The FTP source address is the IP address of the interface the FTP packets use to leave the router.

Command Mode

Global configuration

Usage Guidelines

This command first appeared in Cisco IOS Release 10.3.

Use this command to set the same source address for all FTP connections.

Example

The following example configures the router to use the IP address associated with the Ethernet 0 interface as the source address on all FTP packets, regardless of which interface is actually used to transmit the packet:

```
ip ftp source-interface ethernet 0
```

Related Commands

To locate documentation of related commands, you can search online at www.cisco.com.

ip ftp passive
ip ftp password
ip ftp username

ip ftp username

To configure the username for FTP connections, use the **ip ftp username** global configuration command. To configure the router to attempt anonymous FTP, use the **no** form of this command.

> **ip ftp username** *username*
> **no ip ftp username**

Syntax	Description
username	Username for FTP connections.

Default

The Cisco IOS software attempts an anonymous FTP.

Command Mode

Global configuration

Usage Guidelines

This command first appeared in Cisco IOS Release 10.3.

The remote username must be associated with an account on the destination server.

Example

The following example configures the router to use the username *red* and the password *blue* for FTP connections:

```
ip ftp username red
ip ftp password blue
```

Related Commands

To locate documentation of related commands, you can search online at www.cisco.com.

ip ftp passive
ip ftp password
ip ftp source-interface

ip rarp-server

Use the **ip rarp-server** interface configuration command to enable the router to act as a Reverse Address Resolution Protocol (RARP) server. Use the **no** form of this command to restore the interface to the default of no RARP server support.

> **ip rarp-server** *ip-address*
> **no ip rarp-server** *ip-address*

Syntax   Description

ip-address   IP address that is to be provided in the source protocol address field of the RARP response packet. Normally, this is set to whatever address you configure as the primary address for the interface.

Default
Disabled

Command Mode
Interface configuration

Usage Guidelines
This command first appeared in Cisco IOS Release 10.0.

This feature makes diskless booting of clients possible between network subnets where the client and server are on separate subnets.

RARP server support is configurable on a per interface basis, so that the router does not interfere with RARP traffic on subnets that do not need RARP assistance.

The Cisco IOS software answers incoming RARP requests only if both of the following two conditions are met:

- The **ip rarp-server** command has been configured for the interface on which the request was received.

- There is a static entry found in the IP ARP table that maps the MAC address contained in the RARP request to an IP address.

Use the **show ip arp** EXEC command to display the contents of the IP ARP cache.

Sun Microsystems, Inc. makes use of RARP and UDP-based network services to facilitate network-based booting of SunOS on their workstations. By bridging RARP packets and using both the **ip helper-address** interface configuration command and the **ip forward-protocol** global configuration command, the Cisco IOS software should be able to perform the necessary packet switching to enable booting of Sun workstations across subnets. Unfortunately, some Sun workstations assume that the sender of the RARP response, in this case the router, is the host that the client can contact to TFTP load the bootstrap image. This causes the workstations to fail to boot.

By using the **ip rarp-server** feature, the Cisco IOS software can be configured to answer these RARP requests, and the client machine should be able to reach its server by having its TFTP requests forwarded through the router that acts as the RARP server.

In the case of RARP responses to Sun workstations attempting to diskless boot, the IP address specified in the **ip rarp-server** interface configuration command should be the IP address of the TFTP server. In addition to configuring RARP service, the Cisco IOS software must also be configured to forward UDP-based Sun portmapper requests to completely support diskless booting of Sun workstations. This can be accomplished using configuration commands of the form:

```
ip forward-protocol udp 111
interface interface name
ip helper-address target-address
```

RFC 903 documents the Reverse Address Resolution Protocol.

Examples

The following partial example configures a router to act as a RARP server. The router is configured to use the primary address of the specified interface in its RARP responses.

```
arp 172.30.2.5 0800.2002.ff5b arpa
interface ethernet 0
ip address 172.30.3.100 255.255.255.0
ip rarp-server 172.30.3.100
```

In the following example, a router is configured to act as a RARP server, with TFTP and portmapper requests forwarded to the Sun server:

```
! Allow the router to forward broadcast portmapper requests
ip forward-protocol udp 111
! Provide the router with the IP address of the diskless sun
arp 172.30.2.5 0800.2002.ff5b arpa
interface ethernet 0
! Configure the router to act as a RARP server, using the Sun Server's IP
! address in the RARP response packet.
ip rarp-server 172.30.3.100
! Portmapper broadcasts from this interface are sent to the Sun Server.
ip helper-address 172.30.3.100
```

Related Commands

To locate documentation of related commands, you can search online at www.cisco.com.

ip forward-protocol
ip helper-address

ip rcmd domain-lookup

Use the **ip rcmd domain-lookup** global configuration command to enable Domain Name System (DNS) security for rcp and rsh. To bypass DNS security for rcp and rsh, use the **no** form of this command.

> **ip rcmd domain-lookup**
> **no ip rcmd domain-lookup**

Syntax Description

This command has no arguments or keywords.

Default

Enabled

Command Mode

Global configuration

Usage Guidelines

This command first appeared in Cisco IOS Release 10.3.

If you do not want to use DNS for rcmd queries, but DNS has been enabled with the **ip domain-lookup** command, use the **no ip rcmd domain-lookup** command.

This command will turn off DNS lookups for rsh and rcp only. The **no ip domain-lookup** command takes precedence over the **ip rcmd domain-lookup** command. If **ip domain-lookup** is disabled with the **no ip domain-lookup** command, DNS will be bypassed for rcp and rsh, even if **ip rcmd domain-lookup** is enabled.

NOTE Cisco IOS Release 10.3 added the **ip** keyword to **rcmd** commands. If you are upgrading from Release 10.2 to Release 10.3 or later, this keyword is automatically added to any **rcmd** commands you have in your Release 10.2 configuration files.

Example

The following example enables DNS security is for rcp and rsh:

```
ip rcmd domain-lookup
```

Related Commands

To locate documentation of related commands, you can search online at www.cisco.com.

ip domain-lookup

ip rcmd rcp-enable

To configure the Cisco IOS software to allow remote users to copy files to and from the router, use the **ip rcmd rcp-enable** global configuration command. Use the **no** form of this command to disable a router that is enabled for rcp.

> **ip rcmd rcp-enable**
> **no ip rcmd rcp-enable**

Syntax Description

This command has no arguments or keywords.

Default

To ensure security, the router is not enabled for rcp by default.

Command Mode

Global configuration

Usage Guidelines

This command first appeared in Cisco IOS Release 10.3.

To allow a remote user to execute rcp commands on the router, you must also create an entry for the remote user in the local authentication database.

The **no ip rcmd rcp-enable** command does not prohibit a local user from using rcp to copy system images and configuration files to and from the router.

To protect against unauthorized users copying the system image or configuration files, the router is not enabled for rcp by default.

NOTE	Cisco IOS Release 10.3 added the **ip** keyword to **rcmd** commands. If you are upgrading from Release 10.2 to Release 10.3 or later, this keyword is automatically added to any **rcmd** commands you have in your Release 10.2 configuration files.

Example

The following example shows how to enable the router for rcp:

```
rcp-enable
```

Related Commands

To locate documentation of related commands, you can search online at www.cisco.com.

ip rcmd remote-host

ip rcmd remote-host

To create an entry for the remote user in a local authentication database so that remote users can execute commands on the router using rsh or rcp, use the **ip rcmd remote-host** global configuration command. Use the **no** form of this command to remove an entry for a remote user from the local authentication database.

> **ip rcmd remote-host** *local-username* {*ip-address* | *host*} *remote-username*
> [**enable** [*level*]]
> **no ip rcmd remote-host** *local-username* {*ip-address* | *host*} *remote-username*
> [**enable** [*level*]]

Syntax	Description
local-username	Name of the user on the local router. You can specify the router host name as the username. This name needs to be communicated to the network administrator or the user on the remote system. To be allowed to remotely execute commands on the router, the remote user must specify this value correctly.
ip-address	IP address of the remote host from which the local router will accept remotely executed commands. Either the IP address or the host name is required.
host	Name of the remote host from which the local router will accept remotely executed commands. Either the host name or the IP address is required.

Syntax	Description
remote-username	Name of the user on the remote host from which the router will accept remotely executed commands.
enable *level*	(Optional) Enables the remote user to execute privileged EXEC commands using rsh or to copy files to the router using rcp. The range is 1 to 15. The default is 15.

Default

There are no entries in the local authentication database.

Command Mode

Global configuration

Usage Guidelines

This command first appeared in Cisco IOS Release 10.3.

A TCP connection to a router is established using an IP address. Using the host name is valid only when you are initiating an rcp or rsh command from a local router. The host name is converted to an IP address using DNS or host-name aliasing.

To allow a remote user to execute rcp or rsh commands on a local router, you must create an entry for the remote user in the local authentication database. You must also enable the router to act as an rsh or rcp server.

To enable the router to act as an rsh server, issue the **ip rcmd rsh-enable** command. To enable the router to act as an rcp server, issue the **ip rcmd rcp-enable** command. The router cannot act as a server for either of these protocols unless you explicitly enable the capacity.

A local authentication database, which is similar to a UNIX *.rhosts* file, is used to enforce security on the router through access control. Each entry that you configure in the authentication database identifies the local user, the remote host, and the remote user. To permit a remote user of rsh to execute commands in privileged EXEC mode or to permit a remote user of rcp to copy files to the router, specify the **enable** keyword and level.

An entry that you configure in the authentication database differs from an entry in a UNIX *.rhost* file in the following aspect. Because the *.rhosts* file on a UNIX system resides in the home directory of a local user account, an entry in a UNIX *.rhosts* file does not need to include the local username; the local username is determined from the user account. To provide equivalent support on a router, specify the local username along with the remote host and remote username in each authentication database entry that you configure.

For a remote user to be able to execute commands on the router in its capacity as a server, the local username, host address or name, and remote username sent with the remote client request must match values configured in an entry in the local authentication file.

A remote client host should be registered with DNS. The Cisco IOS software uses DNS to authenticate the remote host's name and address. Because DNS can return several valid IP addresses for a host name, the Cisco IOS software checks the address of the requesting client against all of the IP addresses for the named host returned by DNS. If the address sent by the requester is considered invalid, that is, it does not match any address listed with DNS for the host name, then the software will reject the remote-command execution request.

Note that if no DNS servers are configured for the router, then that device cannot authenticate the host in this manner. In this case, the Cisco IOS software sends a broadcast request to attempt to gain access to DNS services on another server. If DNS services are not available, you must use the **no ip domain-lookup** command to disable the attempt to access a DNS server by sending a broadcast request.

If DNS services are not available and, therefore, you bypass the DNS security check, the software will accept the request to remotely execute a command *only if* all three values sent with the request match exactly the values configured for an entry in the local authentication file.

NOTE   Cisco IOS Release 10.3 added the **ip** keyword to **rcmd** commands. If you are upgrading from Release 10.2 to Release 10.3 or later, this keyword is automatically added to any **rcmd** commands you have in your Release 10.2 configuration files.

Example

The following example allows the remote user *netadmin3* on a remote host with the IP address 172.16.101.101 to execute commands on *router1* using the rsh or rcp protocol. User *netadmin3* is allowed to execute commands in privileged EXEC mode.

```
ip rcmd remote-host router1 172.16.101.101 netadmin3 enable
```

Related Commands

To locate documentation of related commands, you can search online at www.cisco.com.

ip rcmd rcp-enable
ip rcmd rsh-enable
no ip domain-lookup

ip rcmd remote-username

To configure the remote username to be used when requesting a remote copy using rcp, use the **ip rcmd remote-username** global configuration command. To remove from the configuration the remote username, use the **no** form of this command.

> **ip rcmd remote-username** *username*
> **no ip rcmd remote-username** *username*

CAUTION   The remote username must be associated with an account on the destination server.

Syntax

Description

Syntax	Description
username	Name of the remote user on the server. This name is used for rcp copy requests. All files and images to be copied are searched for or written relative to the directory of the remote user's account, if the server has a directory structure, for example, as do UNIX systems.

Default

If you do not issue this command, the Cisco IOS software sends the remote username associated with the current TTY process, if that name is valid, for rcp copy commands. For example, if the user is connected to the router through Telnet and the user was authenticated through the **username** command, then the software sends that username as the remote username.

If the username for the current TTY process is not valid, the Cisco IOS software sends the host name as the remote username. For rcp boot commands, the Cisco IOS software sends the access server host name by default.

NOTE   For Cisco, TTY lines are commonly used for access services. The concept of TTYs originated with UNIX. For UNIX systems, each physical device is represented in the file system. Terminals are called TTY devices (which stands for teletype, the original UNIX terminal).

Command Mode

Global configuration

Usage Guidelines

This command first appeared in Cisco IOS Release 10.3.

The rcp protocol requires that a client send the remote username on an rcp request to the server. Use this command to specify the remote username to be sent to the server for an rcp copy request. If the server has a directory structure, as do UNIX systems, all files and images to be copied are searched for or written relative to the directory of the remote user's account.

NOTE	Cisco IOS Release 10.3 added the **ip** keyword to **rcmd** commands. If you are upgrading from Release 10.2 to Release 10.3 or later, this keyword is automatically added to any **rcmd** commands you have in your Release 10.2 configuration files.

Example

The following example configures the remote username to *netadmin1*:

```
ip rcmd remote-username netadmin1
```

Related Commands

To locate documentation of related commands, you can search online at www.cisco.com.

boot network rcp
boot system rcp
copy

ip rcmd rsh-enable

To configure the router to allow remote users to execute commands on it using rsh, use the **ip rcmd rsh-enable** global configuration command. Use the **no** form of this command to disable a router that is enabled for rsh.

> **ip rcmd rsh-enable**
> **no ip rcmd rsh-enable**

Syntax Description

This command has no arguments or keywords.

Default

To ensure security, the router is not enabled for rsh by default.

Command Mode

Global configuration

Usage Guidelines

This command first appeared in Cisco IOS Release 10.3.

Use this command to enable the router to receive rsh requests from remote users. In addition to issuing this command, you must create an entry for the remote user in the local authentication database to allow a remote user to execute rsh commands on the router.

The **no ip rcmd rsh-enable** command does not prohibit a local user of the router from executing a command on other routers and UNIX hosts on the network using rsh. It disables a router that is enabled for rsh.

NOTE   Cisco IOS Release 10.3 added the **ip** keyword to **rcmd** commands. If you are upgrading from Release 10.2 to Release 10.3 or later, this keyword is automatically added to any **rcmd** commands you have in your Release 10.2 configuration files.

Example

The following example enables a router as an rsh server:

```
ip rcmd rsh-enable
```

Related Commands

To locate documentation of related commands, you can search online at www.cisco.com.

ip rcmd remote-host

mop device-code

To identify the type of device sending MOP sysid messages and request program messages, use the **mop device-code** global configuration command. Use the **no** form of this command to set the identity to the default value.

> **mop device-code** {**cisco** | **ds200**}
> **no mop device-code** {**cisco** | **ds200**}

Syntax	Description
cisco	Denotes a Cisco device code.
ds200	Denotes a DECserver 200 device code.

Default
Cisco device code

Command Mode
Global configuration

Usage Guidelines
This command first appeared in Cisco IOS Release 10.0.

The sysid messages and request program messages use the identity information indicated by this command.

Example
The following example identifies a DECserver 200 device as sending MOP sysid and request program messages:

```
mop device-code ds200
```

Related Commands
To locate documentation of related commands, you can search online at www.cisco.com.

mop sysid

mop retransmit-timer

To configure the length of time that the Cisco IOS software waits before retransmitting boot requests to a MOP server, use the **mop retransmit-timer** global configuration command. Use the **no** form of this command to reinstate the default value.

> **mop retransmit-timer** *seconds*
> **no mop retransmit-timer**

Syntax	Description
seconds	Sets the length of time, in seconds, that the software waits before retransmitting a message. The value is a number from 1 to 20.

Default

4 seconds

Command Mode

Global configuration

Part
II

Command Reference

Usage Guidelines

This command first appeared in Cisco IOS Release 10.0.

By default, when the software transmits a request that requires a response from a MOP boot server and the server does not respond, the message is retransmitted after 4 seconds. If the MOP boot server and router are separated by a slow serial link, it might take longer than 4 seconds for the software to receive a response to its message. Therefore, you might want to configure the software to wait longer than 4 seconds before retransmitting the message if you are using such a link.

Example

In the following example, if the MOP boot server does not respond within 10 seconds after the router sends a message, the server will retransmit the message:

```
mop retransmit-timer 10
```

Related Commands

To locate documentation of related commands, you can search online at www.cisco.com.

mop device-code
mop enabled

mop retries

To configure the number of times the Cisco IOS software will retransmit boot requests to a MOP server, use the **mop retries** global configuration command. Use the **no** form of this command to reinstate the default value.

mop retries *count*
no mop retries

Syntax	Description
count	Indicates the number of times the software will retransmit a MOP boot request. The value is a number from 3 to 24.

Default

Eight times

Command Mode

Global configuration

Usage Guidelines

This command first appeared in Cisco IOS Release 10.0.

Example

In the following example, the software will attempt to retransmit a message to an unresponsive host 11 times before declaring a failure:

```
mop retries 11
```

Related Commands

To locate documentation of related commands, you can search online at www.cisco.com.

mop device-code
mop enabled
mop retransmit-timer

rsh

To execute a command on a remote rsh host, use the **rsh** privileged EXEC command.

rsh {*ip-address* | *host*} [**/user** *username*] *remote-command*

Syntax	Description
ip-address	IP address of the remote host on which to execute the rsh command. Either the IP address or the host name is required.
host	Name of the remote host on which to execute the command. Either the host name or the IP address is required.
/user *username*	(Optional) Remote username.
remote-command	Command to be executed remotely. This is a required parameter.

Default

If you do not specify the **/user** keyword and argument, the Cisco IOS software sends a default remote username. As the default value of the remote username, the software sends the username associated with the current TTY process, if that name is valid. For example, if the user is connected to the router through Telnet and the user was authenticated through the **username** command, then the software sends that username as the remote username. If the TTY username is invalid, the software uses the host name as the both the remote and local usernames.

NOTE For Cisco, TTY lines are commonly used for access services. The concept of TTY originated with UNIX. For UNIX systems, each physical device is represented in the file system. Terminals are called *TTY devices*, which stands for *teletype*, the original UNIX terminal.

Command Mode

Privileged EXEC

Usage Guidelines

This command first appeared in Cisco IOS Release 10.0.

Use the **rsh** command to execute commands remotely. The host on which you remotely execute the command must support the rsh protocol, and the *.rhosts* files on the rsh host must include an entry that permits you to remotely execute commands on that host.

For security reasons, the software does not default to a remote login if no command is specified, as does UNIX. Instead, the router provides Telnet and connect services that you can use rather than rsh.

Example

The following command specifies that user *sharon* attempts to remotely execute the UNIX **ls** command with the *-a* argument on the remote host *mysys.cisco.com*. The command output resulting from the remote execution follows the command example:

```
Router1# rsh mysys.cisco.com /user sharon ls -a
.
..
.alias
.cshrc
.emacs
.exrc
.history
.login
.mailrc
.newsrc
.oldnewsrc
.rhosts
.twmrc
.xsession
jazz
```

show async-bootp

To display the extended BOOTP request parameters that have been configured for asynchronous interfaces, use the **show async-bootp** privileged EXEC command.

   show async-bootp

Syntax Description

This command has no arguments or keywords.

Command Mode

Privileged EXEC

Usage Guidelines

This command first appeared in Cisco IOS Release 10.0.

Sample Display

The following is sample output from the **show async-bootp** command:

```
Router# show async-bootp
```

The following extended data will be sent in BOOTP responses:

```
bootfile (for address 192.168.1.1) "pcboot"
bootfile (for address 172.16.1.111) "dirtboot"
subnet-mask 255.255.0.0
time-offset -3600
time-server 192.168.1.1
```

Table 22-3 describes significant fields shown in the display.

Table 22-3   *show async-bootp Field Descriptions*

Field	Description
bootfile... "pcboot"	Boot file for address 192.168.1.1 is named pcboot.
subnet-mask 255.255.0.0	Subnet mask.
time-offset -3600	Local time is one hour (3600 seconds) earlier than UTC time.
time-server 192.168.1.1	Address of the time server for the network.

Related Commands

To locate documentation of related commands, you can search online at www.cisco.com.

async-bootp

tftp-server

To configure a router or a Flash memory device on the router as a TFTP server, use one of the following **tftp-server** global configuration commands. This command replaces the **tftp-server system** command. To remove a previously defined filename, use the **no tftp-server** command with the appropriate filename.

tftp-server flash [*partition-number***:**]*filename1* [**alias** *filename2*] [*access-list-number*] (all others)

tftp-server rom alias *filename1* [*access-list-number*] (all others)

no tftp-server {**flash** [*partition-number***:**]*filename1* | **rom alias** *filename2*} (all others)

tftp-server flash [*device***:**][*partition-number***:**]*filename* (Cisco 1600 series and Cisco 3600 series)
no tftp-server flash [*device***:**][*partition-number***:**]*filename* (Cisco 1600 series and Cisco 3600 series)

tftp-server flash *device***:**filename* (Cisco 7000 family)
no tftp-server flash *device***:**filename*

Syntax	Description
flash	Specifies TFTP service of a file in Flash memory.
rom	Specifies TFTP service of a file in ROM.
filename1	Name of a file in Flash or in ROM that the TFTP server uses in answering TFTP Read Requests.
alias	Specifies an alternate name for the file that the TFTP server uses in answering TFTP Read Requests.
filename2	Alternate name of the file that the TFTP server uses in answering TFTP Read Requests. A client of the TFTP server can use this alternate name in its Read Requests.
access-list-number	(Optional) Basic IP access-list number. Valid values are 0 to 99.
partition-number:	(Optional) Specifies TFTP service of a file in the specified partition of Flash memory. If the partition number is not specified, the file in the first partition is used.
	For the Cisco 1600 series and Cisco 3600 series, you must enter a colon (:) after the partition number if a filename follows it.
device:	Specifies TFTP service of a file on a Flash memory device in the Cisco 1600 series, Cisco 3600 series and Cisco 7000 family. The colon (:) is required. Valid devices are as follows:
	• **flash**—Internal Flash memory on the Cisco 1600 series and Cisco 3600 series. This is the only valid device for the Cisco 1600.
	• **bootflash**—Internal Flash memory in the Cisco 7000 family.
	• **slot0**—First PCMCIA slot on the Cisco 3600 series and Cisco 7000 family.
	• **slot1**—Second PCMCIA slot on the Cisco 3600 series and Cisco 7000 family.
	• **slavebootflash**—Internal Flash memory on the slave RSP card of a Cisco 7507 or Cisco 7513 configured for HSA.
	• **slaveslot0**—First PCMCIA slot of the slave RSP card on a Cisco 7507 or Cisco 7513 configured for HSA.
	• **slaveslot1**—Second PCMCIA slot of the slave RSP card on a Cisco 7507 or Cisco 7513 configured for HSA.
filename	Name of the file on a Flash memory device that the TFTP server uses in answering a TFTP Read Request. Use this argument only with the Cisco 1600 series, Cisco 3600 series, Cisco 7000 series or Cisco 7500 series.

Default
Disabled

Command Mode
Global configuration

Usage Guidelines
This command first appeared in Cisco IOS Release 11.0.

You can specify multiple filenames by repeating the **tftp-server** command. The system sends a copy of the system image contained in ROM or one of the system images contained in Flash memory to any client that issues a TFTP Read Request with this filename.

If the specified *filename1* or *filename2* exists in Flash memory, a copy of the Flash image is sent. On systems that contain a complete image in ROM, the system sends the ROM image if the specified *filename1* or *filename2* is not found in Flash memory.

Images that run from ROM cannot be loaded over the network. Therefore, it does not make sense to use TFTP to offer the ROMs on these images.

On the Cisco 7000 family, the system sends a copy of the file contained on one of the Flash memory devices to any client that issues a TFTP Read Request with its filename.

Examples
In the following example, the system uses TFTP to send a copy of the *version-10.3* file located in Flash memory in response to a TFTP Read Request for that file. The requesting host is checked against access list 22.

```
tftp-server flash version-10.3 22
```

In the following example, the system uses TFTP to send a copy of the ROM image *gs3-k.101* in response to a TFTP Read Request for the *gs3-k.101* file:

```
tftp-server rom alias gs3-k.101
```

In the following example, the system uses TFTP to send a copy of the *version-11.0* file in response to a TFTP Read Request for that file. The file is located on the Flash memory card inserted in slot 0.

```
tftp-server flash slot0:version-11.0
```

The following example enables a Cisco 3600 series router to operate as a TFTP server. The source file *c3640-i-mz* is in the second partition of internal Flash memory:

```
Router# configure terminal
Enter configuration commands, one per line.  End with Ctrl-Z.
router(config)# tftp-server flash flash:2:dirt/gate/c3640-i-mz
```

In the next example, the source file is in the second partition of the Flash memory PC card in slot 0 on a Cisco 3600 series:

```
Router# configure terminal
Enter configuration commands, one per line.  End with Ctrl-Z.
router(config)# tftp-server flash slot0:2:dirt/gate/c3640-j-mz
```

The following example enables a Cisco 1600 series router to operate as a TFTP server. The source file *c1600-i-mz* is in the second partition of Flash memory:

```
router# configure terminal
Enter configuration commands, one per line.  End with Ctrl-Z.
router(config)# tftp-server flash flash:2:dirt/gate/c1600-i-mz
```

Related Commands

To locate documentation of related commands, you can search online at www.cisco.com.

access-list

tftp-server system

The **tftp-server system** command has been replaced by the **tftp-server** command. See the **tftp-server** command for further details.

System Management

## CHAPTER 23

Monitoring the Router and Network

This chapter describes the tasks that you can perform to monitor the router and network.

For a complete description of the router monitoring commands mentioned in this chapter, refer to Chapter 24, "Router and Network Monitoring Commands." To locate documentation of other commands that appear in this chapter, you can search online at www.cisco.com.

Monitoring the Router and Network Task List

This chapter describes the tasks you can perform to manage the router and its performance on the network. Perform any of the tasks in the following sections:

- Configure SNMP Support
- Configure RMON Support
- Configure the Cisco Discovery Protocol
- Configure Response Time Reporter

Configure SNMP Support

The Simple Network Management Protocol (SNMP) system consists of the following three parts:

- An SNMP manager
- An SNMP agent
- A Management Information Base (MIB)

SNMP is an application-layer protocol that provides a message format for communication between SNMP managers and agents.

The SNMP manager can be part of a Network Management System (NMS), such as CiscoWorks. The agent and MIB reside on the router. To configure SNMP on the router, you define the relationship between the manager and the agent.

The SNMP agent contains MIB variables whose values the SNMP manager can request or change. A manager can get a value from an agent or store a value into that agent. The agent gathers data from the MIB, the repository for information about device parameters and network data. The agent can also respond to a manager's requests to get or set data.

An agent can send unsolicited traps to the manager. Traps are messages alerting the SNMP manager to a condition on the network. Traps can indicate improper user authentication, restarts, link status (up or down), closing of a TCP connection, loss of connection to a neighbor router, or other significant events.

Figure 23-1 illustrates the communications relationship between the SNMP manager and agent. A manager can send the agent requests to get and set MIB values. The agent can respond to these requests. Independent of this interaction, the agent can send unsolicited traps to the manager to notify the manager of network conditions.

Figure 23-1 *Communication between an SNMP Agent and Manager*

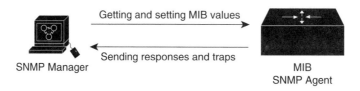

SNMP Notifications

The SNMP Inform Requests feature allows routers to send inform requests to SNMP managers.

Routers can send notifications to SNMP managers when particular events occur. For example, an agent router might send a message to a manager when the agent router experiences an error condition.

SNMP notifications can be sent as traps or inform requests. Traps are unreliable because the receiver does not send any acknowledgment when it receives a trap. The sender cannot determine if the trap was received. However, an SNMP manager that receives an inform request acknowledges the message with an SNMP response PDU. If the manager does not receive an inform request, it does not send a response. If the sender never receives a response, the inform request can be sent again. Thus, informs are more likely to reach their intended destination.

Because they are more reliable, informs consume more resources in the router and in the network. Unlike a trap, which is discarded as soon as it is sent, an inform request must be held in memory until a response is received or the request times out. Also, traps are sent only once, while an inform may be retried several times. The retries increase traffic and contribute to a higher overhead on the network. Thus, traps and inform requests provide a trade-off between reliability and resources. If it is important that the SNMP manager receives every notification, use inform requests. On the other hand, if you are concerned about traffic on your network or memory in the router and you do not need to receive every notification, use traps.

Figure 23-2 through Figure 23-5 illustrate the differences between traps and inform requests.

Figure 23-2, the agent router successfully sends a trap to the SNMP manager. Although the manager receives the trap, it does not send any acknowledgment to the agent. The agent has no way of knowing that the trap reached its destination.

Figure 23-2 *Trap Sent to SNMP Manager Successfully*

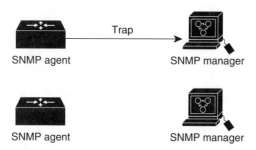

Figure 23-3, the agent router successfully sends an inform request to the manager. When the manager receives the inform request, it sends a response back to the agent. Thus, the agent knows that the inform request successfully reached its destination. Notice that, in this example, twice as much traffic is generated as in Figure 23-2; however, the agent is sure that the manager received the notification.

Figure 23-3 *Inform Request Sent to SNMP Manager Successfully*

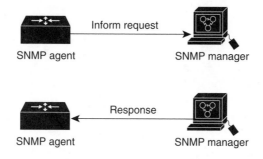

In Figure 23-4, the agent sends a trap to the manager, but the trap does not reach the manager. Since the agent has no way of knowing that the trap did not reach its destination, the trap is not sent again. The manager never receives the trap.

Figure 23-4 *Trap Unsuccessfully Sent to SNMP Manager*

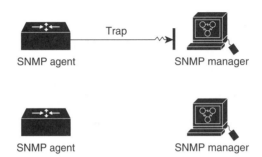

In Figure 23-5, the agent sends an inform request to the manager, but the inform request does not reach the manager. Since the manager did not receive the inform request, it does not send a response. After a period of time, the agent will resend the inform request. The second time, the manager receives the inform request and replies with a response. In this example, there is more traffic than in Figure 23-4; however, the notification reaches the SNMP manager.

Figure 23-5 *Inform Request Unsuccessfully Sent to SNMP Manager*

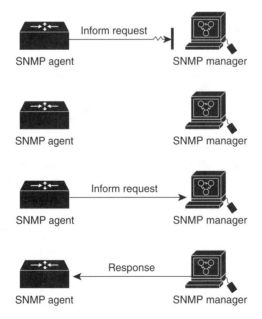

Versions of SNMP

Cisco IOS Release 12.0 software supports the following versions of SNMP:

- **SNMPv1**—The Simple Network Management Protocol, a Full Internet Standard, defined in RFC 1157.

- **SNMPv2C**, which consists of the following:

    - **SNMPv2**—Version 2 of the Simple Network Management Protocol, a Draft Internet Standard, defined in RFCs 1902 through 1907.

    - **SNMPv2C**—The Community-based Administrative Framework for SNMPv2, an Experimental Internet Protocol defined in RFC 1901.

Cisco IOS Release 11.3 removed support for the following version of SNMP:

- **SNMPv2Classic**—IETF Proposed Internet Standard of Version 2 of the Simple Network Management Protocol, defined in RFCs 1441 through 1451.

SNMPv2C replaces the Party-based Administrative and Security Framework of SNMPv2Classic with the Community-based Administrative Framework of SNMPv2C while retaining the bulk retrieval and improved error handling of SNMPv2Classic.

Both SNMPv1 and SNMPv2C use a community-based form of security. The community of managers able to access the agent's MIB is defined by an IP address access control list and password.

SNMPv2C support includes a bulk retrieval mechanism and more detailed error message reporting to management stations. The bulk retrieval mechanism supports the retrieval of tables and large quantities of information, minimizing the number of round-trips required. The SNMPv2C improved error handling support includes expanded error codes that distinguish different kinds of error conditions; these conditions are reported through a single error code in SNMPv1. Error return codes now report the error type. Three kinds of exceptions are also reported: no such object exceptions, no such instance exceptions, and end of MIB view exceptions.

You must configure the SNMP agent to use the version of SNMP supported by the management station. An agent can communicate with multiple managers; for this reason, you can configure the Cisco IOS software to support communications with one management station using the SNMPv1 protocol and another using the SNMPv2 protocol.

Supported MIBs

Cisco's implementation of SNMP supports all MIB II variables (as described in RFC 1213) and SNMP traps (as described in RFC 1215).

Cisco no longer supports RFC 1447, "SNMPv2 Party MIB" (April 1993) or RFC 1450, "SNMPv2 MIB" (April 1993).

Cisco provides its own private MIB extensions with every system. One of the set of MIB objects provided is the Cisco Chassis MIB that enables the SNMP manager to gather data on system card descriptions, serial numbers, hardware and software revision levels, and slot locations. Another set is the Entity MIB (RFC 2037), which describes the logical resources, physical resources, and logical-to-physical mappings of devices managed by a single SNMP agent. The Entity MIB also records the time of the last modification to any object in the Entity MIB and sends out a trap when any object is modified.

SNMP Configuration Task List

There is no specific command that you use to enable SNMP. The first **snmp-server** command that you enter enables both versions of SNMP.

To configure SNMP support, perform any of the tasks in the following sections. The second task is required; all other tasks are optional.

- Create or Modify an SNMP View Record

- Create or Modify Access Control for an SNMP Community

- Enable the SNMP Agent Shutdown Mechanism

- Establish the Contact, Location, and Serial Number of the SNMP Agent

- Define the Maximum SNMP Agent Packet Size

- Limit TFTP Servers Used Via SNMP

- Monitor SNMP Status

- Disable the SNMP Agent

- Configure SNMP Traps

- Configure SNMP Informs

- Configure the Router as an SNMP Manager

Create or Modify an SNMP View Record

You can assign views to community strings to limit which MIB objects an SNMP manager can access. You can use a predefined view, or create your own view. If you are using a predefined view or no view at all, skip this task.

To create or modify an SNMP view record, use the following command in global configuration mode:

Command	Purpose
snmp-server view *view-name oid-tree* {**included** | **excluded**}	Creates or modifies a view record.

To remove a view record, use the **no snmp-server view** command.

You can enter this command multiple times for the same view record. Later lines take precedence when an object identifier is included in two or more lines.

Create or Modify Access Control for an SNMP Community

Use an SNMP community string to define the relationship between the SNMP manager and the agent. The community string acts like a password to permit access to the agent on the router. Optionally, you can specify one or more of the following characteristics associated with the string:

- An access list of IP addresses of the SNMP managers that are permitted to use the community string to gain access to the agent.

- A MIB view, which defines the subset of all MIB objects accessible to the given community.

- Read and write or read-only permission for the MIB objects accessible to the community.

To configure a community string, use the following command in global configuration mode:

Command	Purpose
snmp-server community *string* [**view** *view-name*] [**ro** | **rw**] [*number*]	Defines the community access string.

You can configure one or more community strings. To remove a specific community string, use the **no snmp-server community** command.

For an example of configuring a community string, see the section "SNMP Examples" at the end of this chapter.

Enable the SNMP Agent Shutdown Mechanism

Using SNMP packets, a network management tool can send messages to users on virtual terminals and the console. This facility operates in a similar fashion to the EXEC **send** command; however, the SNMP request that causes the message to be issued to the users also specifies the action to be taken after the message is delivered. One possible action is a shutdown request. After a system is shut down, typically it is reloaded. Because the ability to cause a reload from the network is a powerful feature, it is protected by the **snmp-server system-shutdown** global configuration command. If you do not issue this command, the shutdown mechanism is not enabled. To enable the SNMP agent shutdown mechanism, use the following command in global configuration mode:

Command	Purpose
snmp-server system-shutdown	Uses the SNMP message reload feature and request a system shutdown message.

To understand how to use this feature with SNMP requests, read the document OLD-CISCO-SYSTEM-MIB.my, available on Cisco Connection Online.

Establish the Contact, Location, and Serial Number of the SNMP Agent

You can set the system contact, location, and serial number of the SNMP agent so that these descriptions can be accessed through the configuration file. To do so, use one or more of the following commands in global configuration mode:

Command	Purpose
snmp-server contact *text*	Sets the system contact string.
snmp-server location *text*	Sets the system location string.
snmp-server chassis-id *number*	Sets the system serial number.

Define the Maximum SNMP Agent Packet Size

You can set the maximum packet size permitted when the SNMP agent is receiving a request or generating a reply. To do so, use the following command in global configuration mode:

Command	Purpose
snmp-server packetsize *byte-count*	Establishes the maximum packet size.

Limit TFTP Servers Used Via SNMP

You can limit the TFTP servers used for saving and loading configuration files via SNMP to the servers specified in an access list. To do so, use the following command in global configuration mode:

Command	Purpose
snmp-server tftp-server-list *number*	Limits TFTP servers used for configuration file copies via SNMP to the servers in an access list.

Monitor SNMP Status

To monitor SNMP input and output statistics, including the number of illegal community string entries, errors, and requested variables, use the following command in EXEC mode:

Command	Purpose
show snmp	Monitors SNMP status.

Disable the SNMP Agent

To disable both versions of SNMP (SNMPv1 and SNMPv2C), use the following command in global configuration mode:

Command	Purpose
no snmp-server	Disables SNMP agent operation.

Configure SNMP Traps

To configure the router to send SNMP traps, use the following commands. The second task is optional.

- Configure the Router to Send Traps
- Change Trap Operation Values

Configure the Router to Send Traps

To configure the router to send traps to a host, use the following commands in global configuration mode:

Step	Command	Purpose
1	**snmp-server host** *host* [**version** {**1** | **2c**}] *community-string* [**udp-port** *port*] [*notification-type*]	Specifies the recipient of the trap message.
2	**snmp-server enable traps** [*notification-type*] [*notification-option*]	Specifies the types of traps sent. This command also specifies which types of informs are enabled.

The **snmp-server host** command specifies which hosts will receive traps. The **snmp-server enable traps** command globally enables the trap production mechanism for the specified traps.

Some traps are not controlled by the **snmp-server enable traps** command. These traps are either enabled by default or controlled through other commands. For example, by default, SNMP link traps are sent when an interface goes up or down. For interfaces expected to go up and down during normal usage, such as ISDN interfaces, the output generated by these traps may not be useful. Use the **no snmp trap link-status** interface configuration command to disable these traps.

In order for a host to receive a trap, an **snmp-server host** command must be configured for that host, and the trap must be enabled globally through the **snmp-server enable traps** command, through a different command, such as **snmp trap link-status**, or by default.

Change Trap Operation Values

Optionally, you can specify a value other than the default for the source interface, message (packet) queue length for each host, or retransmission interval.

To change trap operation values, use any of the following optional commands in global configuration mode:

Command	Purpose
snmp-server trap-source *interface*	Specifies the source interface (and hence IP address) of the trap message. This command also sets the source IP address for informs.
snmp-server queue-length *length*	Establishes the message queue length for each trap host.
snmp-server trap-timeout *seconds*	Defines how often to resend trap messages on the retransmission queue.

Configure SNMP Informs

To configure the router to send SNMP informs, use the following commands. The second task is optional.

● Configure the Router to Send Informs

● Change Inform Operation Values

Configure the Router to Send Informs

To configure the router to send informs to a host, use the following commands in global configuration mode:

Command	Purpose
snmp-server host *host* **informs** [**version 2c**] *community-string* [**udp-port** *port*] [*notification-type*]	Specifies the recipient of the inform message.
snmp-server enable traps [*notification-type*] [*notification-option*]	Specifies the types of inform requests sent. This command also specifies which types of traps are enabled.

The **snmp-server host** command specifies which hosts will receive informs. The **snmp-server enable traps** command globally enables the production mechanism for the specified notifications (traps and informs).

Some informs are not controlled by the **snmp-server enable traps** command. These informs are either enabled by default or controlled through other commands. For example, by default, SNMP link notifications are sent when an interface goes up or down. For interfaces expected to go up and down during normal usage, such as ISDN interfaces, the output generated by these notifications may not be useful. Use the **no snmp trap link-status** interface configuration command to disable these notifications.

In order for a host to receive an inform, an **snmp-server host informs** command must be configured for that host, and the inform must be enabled globally through the **snmp-server enable traps** command, through a different command, such as **snmp trap link-status**, or by default.

Change Inform Operation Values

Optionally, you can specify a value other than the default for number of retries, the retransmission interval, the maximum number of pending requests, or the source IP address.

To change inform operation values, use the following optional command in global configuration mode:

Step	Command	Purpose
1	**snmp-server informs** [**retries** *retries*] [**timeout** *seconds*] [**pending** *pending*]	Sets options related to resending unacknowledged inform requests.
2	**snmp-server trap-source** *interface*	Specifies the source interface (and hence IP address) of the inform request. This command also changes the source interface for traps.

Configure the Router as an SNMP Manager

The SNMP Manager feature allows a router to serve as an SNMP manager. As an SNMP manager, the router can send SNMP requests to agents and receive SNMP responses and notifications from agents. When the SNMP manager process is enabled, the router can query other SNMP agents and process incoming SNMP traps.

Security Considerations

Most network security policies assume that routers will be accepting SNMP requests, sending SNMP responses, and sending SNMP notifications.

With the SNMP manager functionality enabled, the router may also be sending SNMP requests, receiving SNMP responses, and receiving SNMP notifications. Your security policy implementation may need to be updated prior to enabling this feature.

SNMP requests are typically sent to UDP port 161. SNMP responses are typically sent from UDP port 161. SNMP notifications are typically sent to UDP port 162.

SNMP Sessions

Sessions are created when the SNMP manager in the router sends SNMP requests (such as inform requests) to a host or receives SNMP notifications from a host. One session is created for each destination host. If there is no further communication between the router and host within the session timeout period, the session will be deleted.

The router tracks statistics, such as the average round-trip time required to reach the host, for each session. Using the statistics for a session, the SNMP manager in the router can set reasonable timeout periods for future requests, such as informs, for that host. If the session is deleted, all statistics are lost. If another session with the same host is later created, the request timeout value for replies will return to the default value.

Sessions consume memory. A reasonable session timeout value should be large enough that regularly used sessions are not prematurely deleted, yet small enough such that irregularly used, or one-shot sessions, are purged expeditiously.

Configuration Tasks

To configure the router to act as an SNMP manager, use the tasks in the following sections:

● Enable the SNMP Manager

● Monitor the SNMP Manager

Enable the SNMP Manager

To enable the SNMP manager process and optionally set the session timeout value, use the following commands in global configuration mode:

Step	Command	Purpose
1	**snmp-server manager**	Enables the SNMP Manager.
2	**snmp-server manager session-timeout** *seconds*	(Optional) Changes the session timeout value.

Monitor the SNMP Manager

To monitor the SNMP manager process, use any one of the following commands in EXEC mode:

Step	Command	Purpose
1	**show snmp**	Displays global SNMP information.
2	**show snmp sessions [brief]**	Displays information about current sessions.
3	**show snmp pending**	Displays information about current pending requests.

Configure RMON Support

The Remote Monitoring (RMON) option provides visibility of individual nodal activity and allows you to monitor all nodes and their interaction on a LAN segment. RMON, used in conjunction with the SNMP agent in the router, allows you to view both traffic that flows through the router and segment traffic not necessarily destined for the router. Combining RMON alarms and events with existing MIBs allows you to choose where proactive monitoring will occur.

Full RMON packet analysis as described in RFC 1757 is available only on an Ethernet interface of the Cisco 2500 series and Cisco AS5200 series routers. RMON requires that SNMP be configured. A generic RMON console application is recommended in order to take advantage of RMON's network management capabilities.

RMON can be very data and processor intensive. Users should measure usage effects to ensure that router performance is not degraded and to minimize excessive management traffic overhead. Native mode is less intensive than promiscuous mode.

All Cisco IOS software images ordered without the explicit RMON option include limited RMON support (RMON alarms and event groups only). Images ordered with the RMON option include support for all nine groups (statistics, history, alarms, hosts, hostTopN, matrix, filter, capture, and event). As a security precaution, support for the packet capture group allows capture of packet header information only; data payloads are not captured.

To enable RMON on an Ethernet interface, use the following command in interface configuration mode:

Command	Purpose
rmon {native | promiscuous}	Enables RMON.

In native mode, RMON monitors only the packets normally received by the interface. In promiscuous mode, RMON monitors all packets on the LAN segment.

The default size of the queue that holds packets for analysis by the RMON process is 64 packets. To change the size of the queue, use the following command in global configuration mode:

Command	Purpose
rmon queuesize *size*	Changes the size of the RMON queue.

To set an RMON alarm or event, use one of the following commands in global configuration mode:

Command	Purpose
rmon alarm *number variable interval* {**delta** | **absolute**} **rising-threshold** *value* [*event-number*] **falling-threshold** *value* [*event-number*] [**owner** *string*]	Sets an alarm on a MIB object.
rmon event *number* [**log**] [**trap** *community*] [**description** *string*] [**owner** *string*]	Adds or removes an event in the RMON event table.

You can set an alarm on any MIB object in the access server. To disable an alarm, you must enable the **no** form of this command on each alarm you configure. You cannot disable all the alarms you configure at once. Refer to RFC 1757 to learn more about alarms and events and how they interact with each other.

To display the current RMON status, use one or more of the following commands in EXEC mode:

Command	Purpose
show rmon or **show rmon task**	Displays general RMON statistics.
show rmon alarms	Displays the RMON alarm table.
show rmon capture	Displays the RMON buffer capture table. Available on Cisco 2500 series and Cisco AS5200 only.
show rmon events	Displays the RMON event table.
show rmon filter	Displays the RMON filter table. Available on Cisco 2500 series and Cisco AS5200 only.
show rmon history	Displays the RMON history table. Available on Cisco 2500 series and Cisco AS5200 only.
show rmon hosts	Displays the RMON hosts table. Available on Cisco 2500 series and Cisco AS5200 only.
show rmon matrix	Displays the RMON matrix table. Available on Cisco 2500 series and Cisco AS5200 only.

Command	Purpose
show rmon statistics	Displays the RMON statistics table. Available on Cisco 2500 series and Cisco AS5200 only.
show rmon topn	Displays the RMON top-n hosts table. Available on Cisco 2500 series and Cisco AS5200 only.

For an example of configuring RMON alarms and events, see the section "RMON Alarm and Event Examples" at the end of this chapter.

Configure the Cisco Discovery Protocol

The Cisco Discovery Protocol (CDP) is media- and protocol-independent, and runs on all Cisco-manufactured equipment including routers, bridges, access servers, and switches. With CDP, network management applications can learn the device type and the SNMP agent address of neighboring devices. This enables applications to send SNMP queries to neighboring devices.

CDP runs on all media that support Subnetwork Access Protocol (SNAP), including local-area network (LAN), Frame Relay, and Asynchronous Transfer Mode (ATM) media. CDP runs over the data link layer only. Therefore, two systems that support different network-layer protocols can learn about each other.

Each device configured for CDP sends periodic messages to a multicast address. Each device advertises at least one address at which it can receive SNMP messages. The advertisements also contain time-to-live, or holdtime, information, which indicates the length of time a receiving device should hold CDP information before discarding it.

There is a CDP MIB for the management of CDP on Cisco devices.

CDP Configuration Task List

To configure CDP, perform the tasks in the following sections:

- Set the CDP Transmission Timer and Hold Time
- Enable CDP
- Enable CDP on an Interface
- Monitor and Maintain CDP

NOTE   The **cdp enable**, **cdp timer**, and **cdp run** commands affect the operation of the IP on demand routing feature (that is, the **router odr** global configuration command).

Set the CDP Transmission Timer and Hold Time

To set the frequency of CDP transmissions and the hold time for CDP packets, use the following commands in global configuration mode:

Step	Command	Purpose
1	**cdp timer** *seconds*	Specifies frequency of transmission of CDP updates.
2	**cdp holdtime** *seconds*	Specifies the amount of time a receiving device should hold the information sent by your device before discarding it.

Enable CDP

CDP is enabled by default. If you prefer not to use the CDP device discovery capability, you can disable it with the **no cdp run** command.

To re-enable CDP after disabling it, use the following command in global configuration mode:

Command	Purpose
cdp run	Enables CDP.

Enable CDP on an Interface

CDP is enabled by default on all supported interfaces to send and receive CDP information. However, some interfaces, such as ATM interfaces, do not support CDP. You can disable CDP on an interface which supports CDP with the **no cdp enable** command.

To re-enable CDP on an interface after disabling it, use the following command in interface configuration mode:

Command	Purpose
cdp enable	Enables CDP on an interface.

Monitor and Maintain CDP

To monitor and maintain CDP on your device, use one or more of the following commands in privileged EXEC mode:

Command	Purpose
clear cdp counters	Resets the traffic counters to zero.
clear cdp table	Deletes the CDP table of information about neighbors.

Command	Purpose
show cdp	Displays global information such as frequency of transmissions and the holdtime for packets being transmitted.
show cdp entry *entry-name* [**protocol** | **version**]	Displays information about a specific neighbor. Display can be limited to protocol or version information.
show cdp interface [*type number*]	Displays information about interfaces on which CDP is enabled.
show cdp neighbors [*type number*] [**detail**]	Displays information about neighbors. The display can be limited to neighbors on a specific interface and expanded to provide more detailed information.
show cdp traffic	Displays CDP counters, including the number of packets sent and received and checksum errors.
show debugging	Displays information about the types of debugging that are enabled for your router. See the *Debug Command Reference* for more information about CDP **debug** commands.

Configure Response Time Reporter

The response time reporter feature allows you to monitor network performance, network resources, and applications by measuring response times and availability. With this feature you can perform troubleshooting, problem notifications, and pre-problem analysis using response time reporter statistics as a baseline.

The response time reporter feature is currently available only with the IBM feature set of the Cisco IOS software. A CiscoWorks Blue network management application will be available to support the response time reporter feature. Both the CiscoWorks Blue network management application and the router use the Cisco Round Trip Time Monitor (RTTMON) MIB.

You can use the response time reporter feature to troubleshoot problems by checking the time delays between devices (such as a router and an MVS host) and the time delays on the path from the source device to the destination device at the protocol level.

You can also use this feature to send any combination of SNMP traps and SNA Alerts/Resolutions when one of the following has occurred: a user-configured threshold is exceeded, a connection is lost and reestablished, or when a timeout occurs. Thresholds can also be used to trigger additional collection of time delay statistics.

You can use this feature to perform pre-problem analysis by scheduling the response time reporter and collecting the results as history and accumulated statistics. You can then use the statistics to model and predict future network topologies.

Response Time Reporter Configuration Task List

To configure the response time reporter feature, complete the tasks in the following sections. Configuring the probe and scheduling the probe are required tasks; the remaining tasks are optional.

- Configure the Probe
- Capture Statistics and Collect Error Information
- Collect History
- Set Reaction Conditions
- Schedule the Probe
- Reset the Probe
- Monitor the Response Time Reporter Feature

See the end of this chapter for "Response Time Reporter Examples."

Configure the Probe

Response time and availability information is collected by *probes* (devices specifically placed in a network to collect data about the network) that you configure on the router. To configure a new response time reporter probe, use the following commands starting in global configuration mode:

Step	Command	Purpose
1	**rtr** *probe*	Enters response time reporter configuration mode.
2	**type** {**echo** | **pathecho**} **protocol** *type type-target*	Specifies the type of probe.

You must configure the probe's type before you can configure any of the other characteristics.

| NOTE | When the probe type is **pathEcho**, statistics are recorded for each hop along the path that the probe takes to reach its destination. |

To configure optional characteristics, use the following commands in response time reporter configuration mode:

Step	Command	Purpose
1	**frequency** *seconds*	Sets the rate at which the probe starts a response time reporter operation.
2	**owner** *text*	Configures the SNMP owner of the probe.
3	**threshold** *milliseconds*	Sets the rising threshold (hysteresis) that generates a reaction event and stores history information for the probe.
4	**timeout** *milliseconds*	Sets the amount of time the probe waits for a response from its request packet.
5	**request-data-size** *bytes*	Sets the protocol data size in the payload of the probe's request packet.
6	**response-data-size** *bytes*	Sets the protocol data size in the payload of the probe's response packet.
7	**tag** *text*	Logically links probes together in a group.
8	**verify-data**	Checks each probe response for corruption.

Capture Statistics and Collect Error Information

The main purpose of the probe is to capture statistics and collect error information. By default, the following information is captured and collected:

- Minimum and maximum response times
- Number of completions
- Sum of completion times
- Sum of the squares of completion times
- Accumulation of errors for noncompletions
- Total attempts (errors plus number of completions)
- Statistical distributions of response times

In most situations, you do not need to change the statistical distribution interval or size. Only change the size when distributions are needed (for example, when performing statistical modeling of your network).

To control how much and what type of statistics are stored on the router, use the following optional commands in response time reporter configuration mode:

Command	Purpose
statistics-distribution-interval *milliseconds*	Sets the time interval for each statistical distribution kept.
distributions-of-statistics-kept *size*	Sets number of statistical distributions kept per hop during the probe's lifetime.
hops-of-statistics-kept *size*	Sets the number of hops for which statistics are maintained per path for the probe.
paths-of-statistics-kept *size*	Sets the number of paths for which statistics are maintained per hour for the probe.
hours-of-statistics-kept *hours*	Sets the number of hours for which statistics are maintained for the probe.

NOTE   When using a distribution size of 1 (the default), you do not need to set the **statistics-distribution-interval** response time reporter configuration command because it has no effect on the statistics kept. For more information, refer to the command in Chapter 24, "Router and Network Monitoring Commands."

Collect History

A probe can collect history and capture statistics. By default, history is not collected. When a problem arises where history is useful (for example, a large number of timeouts are occurring), you can configure the probe to collect history.

NOTE   Collecting history increases the RAM usage. Only collect history when you think there is a problem. For general network response time information, use statistics.

To control how much and what type of history is stored on the router, use the following commands in response time reporter configuration mode. The first command is required; the remainder are optional.

Step	Command	Purpose
1	**samples-of-history-kept** *samples*	Sets the number of entries kept in the history table per bucket.

Step	Command	Purpose
2	**buckets-of-history-kept** *size*	Sets the number of history buckets that are kept per lives-of-history-kept.
3	**lives-of-history-kept** *lives*	Enables history collection and set the number of lives maintained in the history table for the probe.
4	**filter-for-history** {**none** I **all** I **overthreshold** I **failures**}	Defines the type of information kept in the history table for the probe.

To disable history collection, use the default value (0 lives) for the **lives-of-history-kept** command rather than the **filter-for-history none** response time reporter configuration command. The **lives-of-history-kept** command disables history collection before the probe's operation is attempted, and the **filter-for-history** command with the **none** keyword checks for history inclusion after the probe's operation attempt is made.

Set Reaction Conditions

You can configure the probe to send threshold notifications and use those notifications to trigger additional collection of time delay statistics. You can also configure the probe to send notifications when the probe loses connection, reestablishes connections, times out, and first succeeds after a timeout.

To configure the probe's reaction conditions, use the following optional commands in global configuration mode:

Step	Command	Purpose
1	**rtr reaction-configuration** *probe* [**connection-loss-enable**] [**timeout-enable**] [**threshold-falling** *milliseconds*] [**threshold-type** *option*] [**action-type** *option*]	Configures certain actions to occur based on events under the control of the response time reporter.
2	**rtr reaction-trigger** *probe target-probe*	Defines the target probe to make the transition from a "pending" state to an "active" state when one of the trigger action-type options is defined for the probe.

Schedule the Probe

After you have configured the probe, you must schedule the probe to begin capturing statistics and collecting error information. To do so, use the following command in global configuration mode:

Command	Purpose
rtr schedule *probe* [**life** *seconds*] [**start-time** {**pending** | **now** | *hh*:*mm* [*month day* | *day month*]}] [**ageout** *seconds*]	Schedules the probe by configuring the time parameters.

NOTE	After you schedule the probe with the **rtr schedule** command, you cannot change the probe's configuration with the **rtr** global configuration command. To change the configuration of a probe that has been scheduled, use the **no** form of the **rtr** command. The **no** form removes all the probe's configuration information including the probe's schedule, reaction configuration, and reaction triggers. You can now create a new configuration for the probe.

If the probe is in a pending state (the default), you can define the conditions under which the probe makes the transition from pending to active with the **rtr reaction-trigger** global configuration command. When the probe is in an active state it immediately begins collecting information.

Reset the Probe

To perform a shutdown and restart of the response time reporter, use the following command in global configuration mode:

Command	Purpose
rtr reset	Stops all probes and clears the response time reporter configuration information.

CAUTION	Use the **rtr reset** command only in extreme situations such as the incorrect configuration of a number of probes.

In addition to stopping all probes and clearing the response time reporter configuration information, the **rtr reset** command returns the response time reporter feature to the startup condition. This command does not reread the configuration stored in NVRAM. You must retype the response time reporter's configuration or use the **config memory** command (this has the side effect of reconfiguring the router to its startup configuration).

Monitor the Response Time Reporter Feature

To display information about the status and configuration of the response time reporter feature, use the following commands in EXEC mode. You can display information in a tabular or full format. Tabular format displays information in a column reducing the number of screens required to display the information. Full format displays all information using identifiers next to each displayed value.

Command	Purpose
show rtr application [**tabular** | **full**]	Displays global information about the response time reporter feature.
show rtr collection-statistics [*probe*] [**tabular** | **full**]	Displays error totals collected for all probes or the specified probe.
show rtr configuration [*probe*] [**tabular** | **full**]	Displays configuration values including all defaults for all probes or the specified probe.
show rtr distribution-statistics [*probe*] [**tabular** | **full**]	Displays statistical distribution information (captured response times) for all probes or the specified probe.
show rtr history [*probe*] [**tabular** | **full**]	Displays history collected for all probes or the specified probe.
show rtr operational-state [*probe*] [**tabular** | **full**]	Displays the operational state of all probes or the specified probe.
show rtr reaction-trigger [*probe*] [**tabular** | **full**]	Displays the reaction trigger information for all probes or the specified probe.
show rtr totals-statistics [*probe*] [**tabular** | **full**]	Displays the total statistic values (accumulation of error counts and completions) for all probes or the specified probe.

Monitor the Router and Network Configuration Examples

The following sections provide system management examples:

- SNMP Examples
- RMON Alarm and Event Examples
- Response Time Reporter Examples

SNMP Examples

The following example enables SNMPv1 and SNMPv2C. The configuration permits any SNMP manager to access all objects with read-only permissions using the community string public. This configuration does not cause the router to send any traps.

```
snmp-server community public
```

The following example permits any SNMP to access all objects with read-only permission using the community string public. The router will also send ISDN traps to the hosts 192.180.1.111 and 192.180.1.33 using SNMPv1 and to the host 192.180.1.27 using SNMPv2C. The community string public is sent with the traps.

```
snmp-server community public
snmp-server enable traps isdn
snmp-server host 192.180.1.27 version 2c public
snmp-server host 192.180.1.111 version 1 public
snmp-server host 192.180.1.33 public
```

The following example allows read-only access for all objects to members of access list 4 that specify the comaccess community string. No other SNMP managers have access to any objects. SNMP Authentication Failure traps are sent by SNMPv2C to the host cisco.com using the community string public.

```
snmp-server community comaccess ro 4
snmp-server enable traps snmp authentication
snmp-server host cisco.com version 2c public
```

The following example sends Entity MIB traps to the host cisco.com. The community string is restricted. The first line enables the router to send Entity MIB traps in addition to any traps previously enabled. The second line specifies the destination of these traps and overwrites any previous **snmp-server host** commands for the host cisco.com.

```
snmp-server enable traps entity
snmp-server host cisco.com restricted entity
```

The following example sends the SNMP and Cisco environmental monitor enterprise-specific traps to address 172.30.2.160:

```
snmp-server enable traps
snmp-server host 172.30.2.160 public snmp envmon
```

The following example enables the router to send all traps to the host myhost.cisco.com using the community string public:

```
snmp-server enable traps
snmp-server host myhost.cisco.com public
```

The following example will not send traps to any host. The BGP traps are enabled for all hosts, but only the ISDN traps are enabled to be sent to a host.

```
snmp-server enable traps bgp
snmp-server host bob public isdn
```

The following example enables the router to send all inform requests to the host myhost.cisco.com using the community string public:

```
snmp-server enable traps
snmp-server host myhost.cisco.com informs version 2c public
```

SNMP Manager Example

The following example enables the SNMP manager and sets the session timeout to a larger value than the default:

```
snmp-server manager
snmp-server manager session-timeout 1000
```

RMON Alarm and Event Examples

The following example enables the **rmon event** command:

```
rmon event 1 log trap eventtrap description "High ifOutErrors" owner sdurham
```

This example creates RMON event number 1, which is defined as *High ifOutErrors*, and generates a log entry when the event is triggered by an alarm. The user *sdurham* owns the row that is created in the event table by this command. This example also generates a Simple Network Management Protocol (SNMP) trap when the event is triggered.

The following example configures an RMON alarm using the **rmon alarm** command:

```
rmon alarm 10 ifEntry.20.1 20 delta rising-threshold 15 1 falling-threshold 0 owner jjohnson
```

This example configures RMON alarm number 10. The alarm monitors the MIB variable *ifEntry.20.1* once every 20 seconds until the alarm is disabled, and checks the change in the variable's rise or fall. If the *ifEntry.20.1* value shows a MIB counter increase of 15 or more, such as from 100000 to 100015, the alarm is triggered. The alarm in turn triggers event number 1, which is configured with the **rmon event** command. Possible events include a log entry or an SNMP trap. If the *ifEntry.20.1* value changes by 0, the alarm is reset and can be triggered again.

Response Time Reporter Examples

The following sections contain examples of setting up probes on the router to monitor network performance and send notifications:

- Perform Normative Analysis for SNA LU2
- Perform Troubleshooting for IP/ICMP
- Configure a Trigger for Connection Loss

Perform Normative Analysis for SNA LU2

In the example shown in Figure 23-6, probe 1 is configured from router A to host 2, and probe 2 is configured from router B to host 2 to perform a normative analysis of the network to determine a baseline from which triggers (and reactions in general) are then configured. Also, two SNA Physical Units (PUs) are assumed to be configured: CWBC0A and CWBC0B.

Figure 23-6 *Configure Probes for Normative Analysis—SNA LU2*

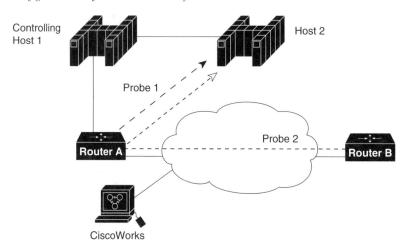

Router A's Configuration:

```
RouterA(config)# rtr 1
RouterA(config-rtr)# type echo protocol snaLU2EchoAppl CWBC0A
RouterA(config-rtr)# exit
RouterA(config)# rtr schedule 1 start-time now
RouterA(config)# exit
```

Router B's Configuration:

```
RouterB(config)# rtr 2
RouterB(config-rtr)# type echo protocol snaLU2EchoAppl CWBC0B
RouterB(config-rtr)# exit
RouterB(config)# rtr schedule 1 start-time now
RouterB(config)# exit
```

Configuration Files for Router A and Router B

After you save the configurations (using the **copy running-config startup-config** command), the following information is stored in the configuration files. Note the addition of the "kept" commands in the configuration file. They are automatically included because they differ depending on the **type** you specify for the probe.

```
!Router A Configuration File
! Router A's PU Configuration
sna host CWBC0A xid-snd 05dcc00a rmac 4001.3745.1088 rsap 4 lsap 12 focalpoint
rtr 1
 type echo protocol snaLU2EchoAppl CWBC0A
 paths-of-statistics-kept 1
 hops-of-statistics-kept 1
 samples-of-history-kept 1
rtr schedule 1 start-time now

!Router B Configuration File
!Router B's PU Configuration from the Configuration File:
sna host CWBC0B xid-snd 05dcc00b rmac 4001.3745.1088 rsap 4 lsap 12 focalpoint
rtr 2
 type echo protocol snaLU2EchoAppl CWBC0B
 paths-of-statistics-kept 1
 hops-of-statistics-kept 1
 samples-of-history-kept 1
rtr schedule 2 start-time now
```

Perform Troubleshooting for IP/ICMP

In the example shown in Figure 23-7, probe 3 is configured from router B to router A to perform troubleshooting of the network to determine a network problem from which triggers (and reactions in general) are then configured.

Figure 23-7 *Configure a Probe for Troubleshooting—IP/ICMP*

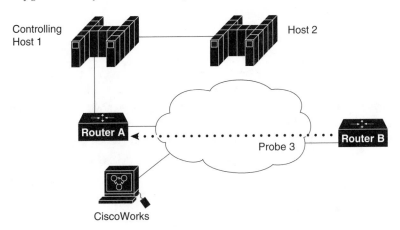

This example sets up a **pathEcho** (with history) pending entry from router B to router A via IP/ICMP. It will attempt to execute three times in 25 seconds (first attempt starts at 0 seconds) and will keep those three times with three buckets. It can be started five times before wrapping over stored history (lives 5). Because this configuration keeps history, it uses more RAM on the router.

Router B's Configuration:

```
RouterB(config)# rtr 3
RouterB(config-rtr)# type pathEcho protocol ipIcmpEcho RouterA
RouterB(config-rtr)# frequency 10
RouterB(config-rtr)# lives-of-history-kept 5
RouterB(config-rtr)# buckets-of-history-kept 3
RouterB(config-rtr)# filter-for-history all
RouterB(config-rtr)# exit
RouterB(config)# rtr schedule 3 life 25
RouterB(config)# exit
```

Configuration File for Router B

After you save the configuration (using the **copy running-config startup-config** command), the following information is stored in the configuration file. Note the addition of commands in the configuration file. They are automatically included because they differ depending on the **type** you specify for the probe.

```
rtr 3
 type pathEcho protocol ipIcmpEcho 172.28.161.21
 frequency 10
 response-data-size 1
 lives-of-history-kept 5
 buckets-of-history-kept 3
 filter-for-history all
rtr schedule 3 life 25 start-time pending
```

Configure a Trigger for Connection Loss

Figure 23-8 shows probes 1, 2, and 3 in the network. This example shows how to configure a trigger if probe 2 encounters a connection loss from router B to host 2. If a connection loss occurs between router B and host 2, a trap is issued, an SNA NMVT Alert is issued, and probe 3's state is changed to "active."

Figure 23-8 *Configure a Trigger for Connection Loss*

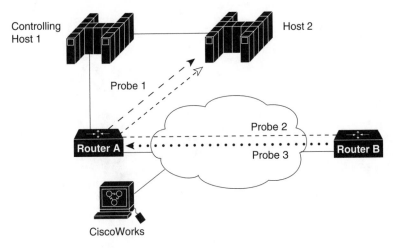

Router B's Configuration:

```
RouterB(config)# rtr reaction-configuration 2 connection-loss-enable
                 action-type trapNmvtAndTrigger
RouterB(config)# rtr reaction-trigger 2 3
```

NOTE	The probe numbers need only be unique within one router. The examples shown use three different probe numbers for clarity.

## CHAPTER 24

Router and Network Monitoring Commands

This chapter describes the commands used to monitor the router and network.

For system management configuration tasks and examples, refer to Chapter 23, "Monitoring the Router and Network."

buckets-of-history-kept

To set the number of history buckets that are kept during the response time reporter probe's lifetime, use the **buckets-of-history-kept** response time reporter configuration command. Use the **no** form of this command to return to the default value.

> **buckets-of-history-kept** *size*
> **no buckets-of-history-kept**

Syntax	Description
size	Number of history buckets kept during the response time reporter probe's lifetime.

Default

50 buckets

Command Mode

Response time reporter configuration

Usage Guidelines

This command first appeared in Cisco IOS Release 11.2.

A response time reporter probe can collect history and capture statistics. By default, history is not collected. When a problem arises where history is useful (for example, a large number of timeouts are occurring), you can configure the **lives-of-history-kept** response time reporter configuration command to collect history. You can optionally adjust the **buckets-of-history-kept**, **filter-for-history**, and **samples-of-history-kept** response time reporter configuration commands.

When the number of buckets reaches the size specified, no further history for this life is stored.

NOTE   Collecting history increases the RAM usage. Only collect history when you think there is a problem. For general network response time information, use statistics.

If history is collected, each bucket contains one or more history entries from the probe. When the probe type is **pathEcho**, an entry is created for each hop along the path that the probe takes to reach its destination. The type of entry stored in the history table is controlled by the **filter-for-history** response time reporter configuration command. The total number of entries stored in the history table is controlled by the combination of **samples-of-history-kept**, **buckets-of-history-kept**, and **lives-of-history-kept** response time reporter configuration commands.

Each time the probe starts a response time reporter operation, a new bucket is created until the number of history buckets matches the specified size or the probe's lifetime expires. History buckets do not wrap. The probe's lifetime is defined by the **rtr schedule** global configuration command. The probe starts a response time reporter operation based on the seconds specified by the **frequency** response time reporter configuration command.

Example

The following example configures probe 1 to keep 25 history buckets during the probe's lifetime:

```
rtr 1
 type echo protocol ipIcmpEcho 172.16.161.21
 buckets-of-history-kept 25
 lives-of-history-kept 1
```

Related Commands

To locate documentation of related commands, you can search online at www.cisco.com.

filter-for-history
lives-of-history-kept
rtr
rtr schedule
samples-of-history-kept

cdp enable

To enable Cisco Discovery Protocol (CDP) on an interface, use the **cdp enable** interface configuration command. Use the **no** form of this command to disable CDP on an interface.

cdp enable
no cdp enable

Syntax Description

This command has no arguments or keywords.

Default

Enabled at the global level and on all supported interfaces.

Command Mode

Interface configuration

Usage Guidelines

This command first appeared in Cisco IOS Release 10.3.

CDP is enabled by default at the global level and on each supported interface in order to send or receive CDP information. However, some interfaces, such as ATM interfaces, do not support CDP.

NOTE   The **cdp enable**, **cdp timer**, and **cdp run** commands affect the operation of the IP on demand routing feature (that is, the **router odr** global configuration command).

Example

The following example enables CDP on Ethernet interface 0:

```
interface ethernet 0
 cdp enable
```

Related Commands

To locate documentation of related commands, you can search online at www.cisco.com.

cdp run

cdp holdtime

To specify the amount of time the receiving device should hold a CDP packet from your router before discarding it, use the **cdp holdtime** global configuration command. Use the **no** form of this command to revert to the default setting.

> **cdp holdtime** *seconds*
> **no cdp holdtime**

Syntax

Syntax	Description
seconds	Specifies the hold time to be sent in the CDP update packets.

Default

180 seconds

Command Mode

Global configuration

Usage Guidelines

This command first appeared in Cisco IOS Release 10.3.

CDP packets are sent with time-to-live, or hold time, that is nonzero after an interface is enabled and a hold time of 0 immediately before an interface is idled down.

The CDP hold time must be set to a higher number of seconds than the time between CDP transmissions, which is set using the **cdp timer** command.

Example

In the following example, the CDP packets being sent from your router should be held by the receiving device for 60 seconds before being discarded. You might want to set the hold time lower than the default setting of 180 seconds if information about your router changes often and you want the receiving devices to purge this information more quickly.

```
cdp holdtime 60
```

Related Commands

To locate documentation of related commands, you can search online at www.cisco.com.

cdp timer
show cdp

cdp run

To enable CDP, use the **cdp run** global configuration command. Use the **no** form of this command to disable CDP.

> **cdp run**
> **no cdp run**

Syntax Description

This command has no arguments or keywords.

Default

Enabled

Command Mode

Global configuration

Usage Guidelines

This command first appeared in Cisco IOS Release 10.3.

CDP is enabled on your router by default, which means the Cisco IOS software will receive CDP information. CDP also is enabled on supported interfaces by default. To disable CDP on an interface, use the **no cdp enable** interface configuration command.

NOTE   The **cdp enable**, **cdp timer**, and **cdp run** commands affect the operation of the IP on demand routing feature (that is, the **router odr** global configuration command).

Example

The following example disables CDP:

```
no cdp run
```

Related Commands

To locate documentation of related commands, you can search online at www.cisco.com.

cdp enable

cdp timer

To specify how often the Cisco IOS software sends CDP updates, use the **cdp timer** global configuration command. Use the **no** form of this command to revert to the default setting.

> **cdp timer** *seconds*
> **no cdp timer**

Syntax	Description
seconds	Specifies how often the Cisco IOS software sends CDP updates.

Default

60 seconds

Command Mode

Global configuration

Usage Guidelines

This command first appeared in Cisco IOS Release 10.3.

The trade-off with sending more frequent transmissions is providing up-to-date information versus using bandwidth more often.

NOTE   The **cdp enable**, **cdp timer**, and **cdp run** commands affect the operation of the IP on demand routing feature (that is, the **router odr** global configuration command).

Example

In the following example, CDP updates are sent every 80 seconds, which is less frequently than the default setting of 60 seconds. You might want to make this change if you are concerned about preserving bandwidth.

```
cdp timer 80
```

Related Commands

To locate documentation of related commands, you can search online at www.cisco.com.

cdp holdtime
show cdp

clear cdp counters

To reset CDP traffic counters to zero (0), use the **clear cdp counters** privileged EXEC command.

    clear cdp counters

Syntax Description

This command has no arguments or keywords.

Command Mode

Privileged EXEC

Usage Guidelines

This command first appeared in Cisco IOS Release 10.3.

Example

The following example clears the CDP counters. The **show cdp traffic** output shows that all of the traffic counters have been reset to zero (0).

```
Router# clear cdp counters
Router# show cdp traffic

CDP counters:
        Packets output: 0, Input: 0
        Hdr syntax: 0, Chksum error: 0, Encaps failed: 0
        No memory: 0, Invalid packet: 0, Fragmented: 0
```

Related Commands

To locate documentation of related commands, you can search online at www.cisco.com.

clear cdp table
show cdp traffic

clear cdp table

To clear the table that contains CDP information about neighbors, use the **clear cdp table** privileged EXEC command.

clear cdp table

Syntax Description

This command has no arguments or keywords.

Command Mode

Privileged EXEC

Usage Guidelines

This command first appeared in Cisco IOS Release 10.3.

Example

The following example clears the CDP table. The output of the **show cdp neighbors** command shows that all information has been deleted from the table.

```
Router# clear cdp table

CDP-AD: Deleted table entry for neon.cisco.com, interface Ethernet0
CDP-AD: Deleted table entry for neon.cisco.com, interface Serial0
Router# show cdp neighbors

Capability Codes: R - Router, T - Trans Bridge, B - Source Route Bridge
                  S - Switch, H - Host, I - IGMP

Device ID       Local Intrfce    Holdtme   Capability  Platform  Port ID
```

Related Commands

To locate documentation of related commands, you can search online at www.cisco.com.

clear cdp counter
show cdp neighbors

distributions-of-statistics-kept

To set the number of statistic distributions kept per hop during the response time reporter probe's lifetime, use the **distributions-of-statistics-kept** response time reporter configuration command. Use the **no** form of this command to return to the default value.

> **distributions-of-statistics-kept** *size*
> **no distributions-of-statistics-kept**

Syntax	Description
size	Number of statistic distributions kept per hop.

Default

1 distribution

Command Mode

Response time reporter configuration

Usage Guidelines

This command first appeared in Cisco IOS Release 11.2.

In most situations, you do not need to change the statistic distribution size for the response time reporter. Only change the size when distributions are needed (for example, when performing statistical modeling of your network).

NOTE	Increasing the distributions also increases the RAM usage. The total number of statistics distributions captured will be the value of **distributions-of-statistics-kept** times the value of **hops-of-statistics-kept** times the value of **paths-of-statistics-kept** times the value of **hours-of-statistics-kept**.

When the number of distributions reaches the size specified, no further distribution information is stored.

Example

The following example sets the distribution to 5 and the distribution interval to 10 ms. This means that the first distribution will contain statistics from 0 to 9 ms, the second distribution will contain statistics from 10 to 19 ms, the third distribution will contain statistics from 20 to 29 ms, the fourth distribution

Part
III

Command Reference

will contain statistics from 30 to 39 ms, and the fifth distribution will contain statistics from 40 ms to infinity.

```
rtr 1
 type echo protocol ipIcmpEcho 172.16.161.21
 distributions-of-statistics-kept 5
 statistics-distribution-interval 10
```

Related Commands

To locate documentation of related commands, you can search online at www.cisco.com.

hops-of-statistics-kept
hours-of-statistics-kept
paths-of-statistics-kept
rtr
statistics-distribution-interval

filter-for-history

To define the type of information kept in the history table for the response time reporter probe, use the **filter-for-history** response time reporter configuration command. Use the **no** form of this command to return to the default value.

filter-for-history {**none** | **all** | **overThreshold** | **failures**}
no filter-for-history {**none** | **all** | **overThreshold** | **failures**}

Syntax	Description
none	No history kept.
all	All probe operations attempted are kept in the history table.
overThreshold	Only packets that are over the threshold are kept in the history table.
failures	Only packets that fail for any reason are kept in the history table.

Default
none

Command Mode
Response time reporter configuration

Usage Guidelines

This command first appeared in Cisco IOS Release 11.2.

Use the **filter-for-history** command to control what gets stored in the history table for the response time reporter. To control how much history gets saved in the history table, use the **lives-of-history-kept**, **buckets-of-history-kept**, and the **samples-of-history-kept** response time reporter configuration commands.

A probe can collect history and capture statistics. By default, history is not collected. When a problem arises where history is useful (for example, a large number of timeouts are occurring), you can configure the **lives-of-history-kept** command to collect history.

NOTE   Collecting history increases the RAM usage. Only collect history when you think there is a problem. For general network response time information, use statistics.

Example

In the following example, only probe packets that fail are kept in the history table:

```
rtr 1
 type echo protocol ipIcmpEcho 172.16.161.21
 lives-of-history-kept 1
 filter-for-history failures
```

Related Commands

To locate documentation of related commands, you can search online at www.cisco.com.

buckets-of-history-kept
lives-of-history-kept
rtr
samples-of-history-kept

frequency

To set the rate at which the response time reporter probe starts a response time operation, use the **frequency** response time reporter configuration command. Use the **no** form of this command to return to the default value.

frequency *second*
no frequency

Syntax

Description

second   Number of seconds between the probe's response time reporter
                    operations.

Default

60 seconds

Command Mode

Response time reporter configuration

Usage Guidelines

This command first appeared in Cisco IOS Release 11.2.

CAUTION   For normal operation, do not set the frequency value to less than 60 seconds for the
              following reasons: It is not needed when keeping statistics (the default), and it can slow
              down the WAN because of the potential overhead that numerous probes can cause.

If the probe takes longer to execute the current response time reporter operation than the specified
frequency value, a statistics counter called *busy* is incremented in lieu of starting a second operation.

The value specified for the **frequency** command cannot be less than the value specified for the **timeout**
response time reporter configuration command.

Example

The following example configures the probe to execute a response time reporter operation every 90
seconds:

```
rtr 1
 type echo protocol ipIcmpEcho 172.16.1.176
 frequency 90
```

Related Commands

To locate documentation of related commands, you can search online at www.cisco.com.

rtr
timeout

hops-of-statistics-kept

To set the number of hops for which statistics are maintained per path for the response time reporter probe, use the **hops-of-statistics-kept** response time reporter configuration command. Use the **no** form of this command to return to the default value.

> **hops-of-statistics-kept** *size*
> **no hops-of-statistics-kept**

Syntax

Syntax	Description
size	Number of hops for which statistics are maintained per path.

Default

16 hops for type **pathEcho**

1 hop for type **echo**

Command Mode

Response time reporter configuration

Usage Guidelines

This command first appeared in Cisco IOS Release 11.2.

One hop is the passage of a timed packet from this router to another network device. The other network device (is assumed to) be a device along the path to the destination (including the destination) when the probe type is **pathEcho**, or just the destination when the type is **echo**.

When the number of hops reaches the size specified, no further hop information is stored.

Example

The following example monitors probe 2's statistics for only 10 hops:

```
rtr 2
 type pathecho protocol ipIcmpEcho 172.16.1.177
 hops-of-statistics-kept 10
```

Related Commands

To locate documentation of related commands, you can search online at www.cisco.com.

distributions-of-statistics-kept
hours-of-statistics-kept
paths-of-statistics-kept
rtr
statistics-distribution-interval

hours-of-statistics-kept

To set the number of hours for which statistics are maintained for the response time reporter probe, use the **hours-of-statistics-kept** response time reporter configuration command. Use the **no** form of this command to return to the default value.

> **hours-of-statistics-kept** *hours*
> **no hours-of-statistics-kept**

Syntax   Description

hours   Number of hours that the router maintains statistics.

Default

2 hours

Command Mode

Response time reporter configuration

Usage Guidelines

This command first appeared in Cisco IOS Release 11.2.

When the number of hours exceeds the specified value, the statistics table wraps (that is, the oldest information is replaced by newer information).

Example

The following example maintains probe 2's statistics for 3 hours:

```
rtr 2
 type pathecho protocol ipIcmpEcho 172.16.1.177
 hours-of-statistics-kept 3
```

Related Commands

To locate documentation of related commands, you can search online at www.cisco.com.

distributions-of-statistics-kept
hops-of-statistics-kept
paths-of-statistics-kept
rtr
statistics-distribution-interval

lives-of-history-kept

To set the number of lives maintained in the history table for the response time reporter probe, use the **lives-of-history-kept** response time reporter configuration command. Use the **no** form of this command to return to the default value.

> **lives-of-history-kept** *lives*
> **no lives-of-history-kept**

Syntax Description

lives	Number of lives maintained in the history table for the probe.

Default

0 lives

Command Mode

Response time reporter configuration

Usage Guidelines

This command first appeared in Cisco IOS Release 11.2.

The default value (0 lives) means that history is not collected for the probe. To disable history collection, use the default value for the **lives-of-history-kept** command rather than the **filter-for-history none** response time reporter configuration command. The **lives-of-history-kept** command disables history collection before the probe's operation is attempted, and the **filter-for-history** command checks for history inclusion after the probe's operation attempt is made.

When the number of lives exceeds the specified value, the history table wraps (that is, the oldest information is replaced by newer information).

When a probe makes a transition from pending to active, a life starts. When a probe's life ends, the probe makes a transition from active to pending.

Example

The following example maintains probe 1's history for 5 lives:

```
rtr 1
 type echo protocol ipIcmpEcho 172.16.1.176
 lives-of-history-kept 5
```

Related Commands

To locate documentation of related commands, you can search online at www.cisco.com.

buckets-of-history-kept
filter-for-history
rtr
samples-of-history-kept

owner

To configure the SNMP owner of the response time reporter probe, use the **owner** response time reporter configuration command. Use the **no** form of this command to return to the default value.

> **owner** *text*
> **no owner**

Syntax   Description

text   Name of the SNMP owner from 0 to 255 ASCII characters. The default is none.

Default

No owner is specified.

Command Mode

Response time reporter configuration

Usage Guidelines

This command first appeared in Cisco IOS Release 11.2.

The owner name contains one or more of the following: ASCII form of the network management station's transport address, network management station name (that is, the domain name), and network management personnel's name, location, or phone number. In some cases, the agent itself will be the owner of the probe. In these cases, the name can begin with "agent."

Example

The following example sets probe 1's owner is set:

```
rtr 1
 type echo protocol ipIcmpEcho 172.16.1.176
 owner 172.16.1.189 cwb.cisco.com John Doe RTP 555-1212
```

Related Commands

To locate documentation of related commands, you can search online at www.cisco.com.

rtr

paths-of-statistics-kept

To set the number of paths for which statistics are maintained per hour for the response time reporter probe, use the **paths-of-statistics-kept** response time reporter configuration command. Use the **no** form of this command to return to the default value.

paths-of-statistics-kept *size*
no paths-of-statistics-kept

Syntax   Description

size   Number of paths for which statistics are maintained per hour. The default
                 is 5 paths for type **pathEcho** and 1 path for type **echo**.

Default

5 paths for type **pathEcho**

1 path for type **echo**

Command Mode

Response time reporter configuration

Usage Guidelines

This command first appeared in Cisco IOS Release 11.2.

A path is the route the probe's request packet takes through the network to get to its destination. The probe may take a different path to reach its destination for each response time reporter operation.

When the number of paths reaches the size specified, no further path information is stored.

Example

The following example maintains probe 2's statistics for only 3 paths:

```
rtr 2
 type pathEcho protocol ipIcmpEcho 172.16.1.177
 paths-of-statistics-kept 3
```

Related Commands

To locate documentation of related commands, you can search online at www.cisco.com.

distributions-of-statistics-kept
hops-of-statistics-kept
hours-of-statistics-kept
rtr
statistics-distribution-interval

request-data-size

To set the protocol data size in the payload of the response time reporter probe's request packet, use the **request-data-size** response time reporter configuration command. Use the **no** form of this command to return to the default value.

> **request-data-size** *byte*
> **no request-data-size**

Syntax   Description

byte   Size of the protocol data in the payload of the probe's request packet.
                Range is 0 to the protocol's maximum.

Default

1 byte

Command Mode

Response time reporter configuration

Usage Guidelines

This command first appeared in Cisco IOS Release 11.2.

When the protocol name has the suffix "appl," the packet uses both a request and respond data size (see the **response-data-size** response time reporter configuration command), and the data size is 12 bytes smaller than the normal payload size (this 12 bytes is the ARR Header used to control send and data response sizes).

Example

The following example sets probe 3's request packet size to 40 bytes:

```
rtr 3
 type echo protocol snalu0echoappl cwbc0a
 request-data-size 40
```

Related Commands

To locate documentation of related commands, you can search online at www.cisco.com.

response-data-size
rtr

response-data-size

To set the protocol data size in the payload of the response time reporter probe's response packet, use the **response-data-size** response time reporter configuration command. Use the **no** form of this command to return to the default value.

> **response-data-size** *byte*
> **no response-data-size**

Syntax	Description
byte	Size of the protocol data in the payload in the probe's response packet.

Part
III

Command Reference

Default

For "appl" protocols, 0 bytes

For all others, the same value as the **request-data-size**

Command Mode

Response time reporter configuration

Usage Guidelines

This command first appeared in Cisco IOS Release 11.2.

The **response-data-size** command is only applicable for protocols defined with the **type** command that end in "appl" (for example, **snalu0echoappl**). When the protocol ends in "appl," the response data size is 12 bytes smaller than normal payload size.

Example

The following example sets probe 3's response packet size to 1,440 bytes:

```
rtr 3
 type echo protocol snalu0echoappl cwbc0a
 response-data-size 1440
```

Related Commands

To locate documentation of related commands, you can search online at www.cisco.com.

request-data-size
rtr

rmon

To enable Remote Network Monitoring (RMON) on an Ethernet interface, use the **rmon** interface configuration command. Use the **no** form of this command to disable RMON on the interface.

>   **rmon {native | promiscuous}**
>   **no rmon**

Syntax	Description
native	Enables RMON on the Ethernet interface. In native mode, the router processes only packets destined for this interface.

Syntax	Description
promiscuous	Enables RMON on the Ethernet interface. In promiscuous mode, the router examines every packet.

Default

RMON is disabled on the interface.

Command Mode

Interface configuration

Usage Guidelines

This command first appeared in Cisco IOS Release 11.1.

This command enables RMON on Ethernet interfaces of Cisco 2500 series and Cisco AS5200 series routers only. A generic RMON console application is recommended in order to use the RMON network management capabilities. SNMP must also be configured. RMON provides visibility of individual nodal activity and allows you to monitor all nodes and their interaction on a LAN segment. When the **rmon** command is issued, the router automatically installs an Ethernet statistics study for the associated interface.

Part
III

Command Reference

NOTE	RMON can be very data and processor intensive. Users should measure usage effects to ensure that router performance is not degraded and to minimize excessive management traffic overhead. Native mode is less intensive than promiscuous mode.

All Cisco IOS software Release 11.3 feature sets support RMON alarm and event groups. Additional RMON groups are supported in certain feature sets. Refer to the Release Notes for feature set descriptions. As a security precaution, support for the packet capture group allows capture of packet header information only; data payloads are not captured.

The RMON MIB is described in RFC 1757.

Example

The following example enables RMON on Ethernet interface 0 and allows the router to examine only packets destined for the interface:

```
interface ethernet 0
  rmon native
```

Related Commands

To locate documentation of related commands, you can search online at www.cisco.com.

rmon alarm
rmon event
rmon queuesize
show rmon

rmon alarm

To set an alarm on any MIB object, use the **rmon alarm** global configuration command. Use the **no** form of this command to disable the alarm.

> **rmon alarm** *number variable interval* {**delta** | **absolute**} **rising-threshold** *value*
> [*event-number*]
> **falling-threshold** *value* [*event-number*] [**owner** *string*]
> **no rmon alarm** *number*

Syntax	Description
number	Alarm number, which is identical to the *alarmIndex* in the alarmTable in the RMON (Remote Monitoring) MIB.
variable	MIB object to monitor, which translates into the *alarmVariable* used in the alarmTable of the RMON MIB.
interval	Time in seconds the alarm monitors the MIB variable, which is identical to the *alarmInterval* used in the alarmTable of the RMON MIB.
delta	Tests the change between MIB variables, which affects the *alarmSampleType* in the alarmTable of the RMON MIB.
absolute	Tests each MIB variable directly, which affects the *alarmSampleType* in the alarmTable of the RMON MIB.
rising-threshold *value*	Value at which the alarm is triggered.
event-number	(Optional) Event number to trigger when the rising or falling threshold exceeds its limit. This value is identical to the alarmRisingEventIndex or the alarmFallingEventIndex in the alarmTable of the RMON MIB.
falling-threshold *value*	Value at which the alarm is reset.
owner *string*	(Optional) Specifies an owner for the alarm, which is identical to the *alarmOwner* in the alarmTable of the RMON MIB.

Default

No alarms configured

Command Mode

Global configuration

Usage Guidelines

This command first appeared in Cisco IOS Release 11.2.

The MIB object must be specified as a dotted decimal value after the entry sequence (for example, ifEntry.10.1). You cannot specify the variable name and the instance (for example, ifInOctets.1) or the entire dotted decimal notation. The variable must be of the form *entry.integer.instance*.

To disable the RMON alarms, you must use the **no** form of the command on each configured alarm. For example, enter **no rmon alarm 1**, where the 1 identifies which alarm is to be removed.

See RFC 1757 for more information about the RMON alarm group.

Part
III

Command Reference

Example

The following example configures an RMON alarm using the **rmon alarm** command:

```
rmon alarm 10 ifEntry.20.1 20 delta rising-threshold 15 1 falling-threshold 0
    owner jjohnson
```

This example configures RMON alarm number 10. The alarm monitors the MIB variable *ifEntry.20.1* once every 20 seconds until the alarm is disabled, and checks the change in the variable's rise or fall. If the *ifEntry.20.1* value shows a MIB counter increase of 15 or more, such as from 100000 to 100015, the alarm is triggered. The alarm in turn triggers event number 1, which is configured with the **rmon event** command. Possible events include a log entry or a SNMP trap. If the *ifEntry.20.1* value changes by 0 (falling-threshold 0), the alarm is reset and can be triggered again.

Related Commands

To locate documentation of related commands, you can search online at www.cisco.com.

rmon
rmon event
show rmon

rmon event

To add or remove an event in the RMON event table that is associated with an RMON event number, use the **rmon event** global configuration command. Use the **no** form of this command to disable RMON on the interface.

rmon event *number* [**log**] [**trap** *community*] [**description** *string*] [**owner** *string*]
no rmon event *number*

Syntax	Description
number	Assigned event number, which is identical to the *eventIndex* in the eventTable in the RMON MIB.
log	(Optional) Generates an RMON log entry when the event is triggered and sets the *eventType* in the RMON MIB to *log* or *log-and-trap*.
trap *community*	(Optional) SNMP community string used for this trap. Configures the setting of the *eventType* in the RMON MIB for this row as either *snmp-trap* or *log-and-trap*. This value is identical to the *eventCommunityValue* in the eventTable in the RMON MIB.
description *string*	(Optional) Specifies a description of the event, which is identical to the event description in the eventTable of the RMON MIB.
owner *string*	(Optional) Owner of this event, which is identical to the *eventOwner* in the eventTable of the RMON MIB.

Default

No events configured

Command Mode

Global configuration

Usage Guidelines

This command first appeared in Cisco IOS Release 11.2.

This command applies only to the Cisco 2500 series and Cisco AS5200 series.

See RFC 1757 for more information about the RMON MIB.

Example

The following example enables the **rmon event** command:

```
rmon event 1 log trap eventtrap description "High ifOutErrors" owner sdurham
```

This example configuration creates RMON event number 1, which is defined as High *ifOutErrors*, and generates a log entry when the event is triggered by an alarm. The user *sdurham* owns the row that is created in the event table by this command. This configuration also generates a Simple Network Management Protocol (SNMP) trap when the event is triggered.

Related Commands

To locate documentation of related commands, you can search online at www.cisco.com.

rmon
show rmon

rmon queuesize

To change the size of the queue that holds packets for analysis by the Remote Network Monitoring (RMON) process, use the **rmon queuesize** global configuration command. Use the **no** form of this command to restore the default value.

rmon queuesize *size*
no rmon queuesize

Syntax   Description

size   Number of packets allowed in the queue awaiting RMON analysis.

Default

64 packets

Command Mode

Global configuration

Usage Guidelines

This command first appeared in Cisco IOS Release 11.1.

This command applies to the RMON function, which is available on Ethernet interfaces of Cisco 2500 series and Cisco AS5200 series routers only.

You might want to increase the queue size if the RMON function indicates it is dropping packets. You can determine this from the output of the **show rmon** command or from the etherStatsDropEvents object in the etherStats table. A feasible maximum queue size depends on the amount of memory available in the router and the configuration of the buffer pool.

Example

The following example configures the RMON queue size to be 128 packets:

```
rmon queuesize 128
```

Related Commands

To locate documentation of related commands, you can search online at www.cisco.com.

rmon
show rmon

rtr

To configure a response time reporter probe, use the **rtr** global configuration command. Use the **no** form of this command to remove all configuration information for a probe including the probe's schedule, reaction configuration, and reaction triggers.

> **rtr** *probe*
> **no rtr** *probe*

Syntax   Description

probe   Number of the response time reporter probe (instance) to configure.

Default

None

Command Mode

Global configuration

Usage Guidelines

This command first appeared in Cisco IOS Release 11.2.

A probe is used for the purpose of collecting response time information.

Each platform has a limit on the number of probes that can be configured. In general this limit is less than 20.

Debugging is supported only on the first 32 probe numbers.

The response time reporter feature allows customers to monitor the performance of their network, network resources, and applications by measuring response times and availability. With this feature, a customer can perform troubleshooting, problem notification, and preproblem analysis. The response time reporter feature is currently available only with the IBM feature set of the Cisco IOS software. For more information, refer to Chapter 23, "Monitoring the Router and Network."

This command places you in response time reporter configuration mode.

NOTE	After you schedule a probe with the **rtr schedule** global configuration command, you cannot modify the probe's configuration. To modify the probe's configuration after it is scheduled, use the **no rtr** command. You can now reenter the probe's configuration with the **rtr** command.

Use the following response time reporter configuration commands (config-rtr) to configure the probe's characteristics:

- **buckets-of-history-kept**
- **distributions-of-statistics-kept**
- **filter-for-history**
- **frequency**
- **hops-of-statistics-kept**
- **hours-of-statistics-kept**
- **lives-of-history-kept**
- **owner**
- **paths-of-statistics-kept**
- **request-data-size**
- **response-data-size**
- **samples-of-history-kept**

- **statistics-distribution-interval**

- **tag**

- **threshold**

- **type**

- **timeout**

- **verify-data**

After you configure a probe, you must schedule the probe. For information on scheduling a probe, refer to the **rtr schedule** global configuration command. You can also optionally set reaction triggers for the probe. For information on reaction triggers, refer to the **rtr reaction-configuration** and **rtr reaction-trigger** global configuration commands.

To display the probe's current configuration settings, use the **show rtr configuration** EXEC command.

Example

In the following example, probe 1 is configured to perform end-to-end response time operations using an SNA LU Type 0 connection with the host name *cwbc0a*. Only the **type** response time reporter configuration command is required; all others are optional.

```
rtr 1
 type echo protocol snalu0echoappl cwbc0a
 request-data-size 40
 response-data-size 1440
```

NOTE	If probe 1 already existed and it has not been scheduled, you are placed into response time reporter configuration command mode. If the probe already exists and has been scheduled, this command will fail.

Related Commands

To locate documentation of related commands, you can search online at www.cisco.com.

rtr reaction-configuration
rtr reaction-trigger
rtr reset
rtr schedule

rtr reaction-configuration

To configure certain actions to occur based on events under the control of the response time reporter, use the **rtr reaction-configuration** global configuration command. Use the **no** form of this command to return to the probe's default values.

> **rtr reaction-configuration** *probe* [**connection-loss-enable**] [**timeout-enable**]
> [**threshold-falling** *milliseconds*] [**threshold-type** *option*] [**action-type** *option*]
> **no rtr reaction-configuration** *probe*

Syntax	Description
probe	Number of the response time reporter probe to configure.
connection-loss-enable	(Optional) Enable checking for connection loss in connection-oriented protocols. The default is disabled.
timeout-enable	(Optional) Enable checking for response time reporting operation timeouts based on the timeout value configured for the probe with the **timeout** response time reporter configuration command. The default is disabled.
threshold-falling *milliseconds*	(Optional) Set the falling threshold (standard RMON-type hysteresis mechanism) in milliseconds. When the falling threshold is met, generate a resolution reaction event. The probe's rising over threshold is set with the **threshold** response time reporter configuration command. The default value is 3000 ms.
threshold-type *option*	(Optional) Specify the algorithm used by the response time reporter to calculate over and falling threshold violations. Option can be one of the following keywords:
	• **never**—Do not calculate threshold violations (the default).
	• **immediate**—When the response time exceeds the rising over threshold or drops below the falling threshold, immediately perform the action defined by **action-type**.
	• **consecutive** [*occurrences*]—When the response time exceeds the rising threshold consecutively five times or drops below the falling threshold consecutively five times, perform the action defined by **action-type**. Optionally specify the number of consecutive occurrences. The default is five.
	• **xofy** [*x-value y-value*]—When the response time exceeds the rising threshold five out of the last five times or drops below the falling threshold five out of the last five times, perform the action defined by **action-type**. Optionally specify the number of violations that must occur and the number that must occur within a specified number. The default is five for both x-value and y-value.

Part III

Command Reference

Syntax	Description
	• **average** [*attempts*]—When the average of the last five response times exceeds the rising threshold or when the average of the last five response times drops below the falling threshold, perform the action defined by **action-type**. Optionally specify the number of operations to average. The default is the average of the last five response time operations. For example: if the probe's threshold is 5000 ms and the probe's last three attempts results are 6000, 6000, and 5000 ms, the average would be 6000+6000+5000=17000/3>5000, thus violating the 5000-ms threshold.
action-type *option*	(Optional) Specify what action or combination of actions the probe performs when you configure **connection-loss-enable** or **timeout-enable**, or threshold events occur. For the **action-type** to occur for threshold events, the **threshold-type** must be defined to anything other than **never**. Option can be one of the following keywords:

- **none**—No action is taken.
- **trapOnly**—Send an SNMP trap on both over and falling threshold violations.
- **nmvtOnly**—Send an SNA NMVT Alert on over threshold violation and an SNA NMVT Resolution on falling threshold violations.
- **triggerOnly**—Have one or more target probe's operational state make the transition from "pending" to "active" on over (and falling) threshold violations. The target probes are defined with the **rtr reaction-trigger** command. A target probe will continue until its life expires as specified by the target probe's life value configured with the **rtr schedule** global configuration command. A triggered target probe must finish its life before it can be triggered again.
- **trapAndNmvt**—Send a combination of **trapOnly** and **nmvtOnly**.
- **trapAndTrigger**—Send a combination of **trapOnly** and **triggerOnly**.
- **nmvtAndTrigger**—Send a combination of **nmvtOnly** and **triggerOnly**.
- **trapNmvtAndTrigger**—Send a combination of **trapOnly**, **nmvtOnly**, and **triggerOnly**.

Default

No reactions are generated.

Command Mode

Global configuration

Usage Guidelines

This command first appeared in Cisco IOS Release 11.2.

Triggers are used for diagnostics purposes and are not used in normal operation.

You can use triggers to assist you in determining where delays are happening in the network when excessive delays are being seen on an end-to-end basis.

The reaction applies only to attempts to the target (that is, attempts to any hops along the path in **pathEcho** do not generate reactions).

NOTE   Keywords are not case sensitive and are shown in mixed case for readability only.

Example

In the following example, probe 19 sends an SNMP trap when there is an over or falling threshold violation:

```
rtr reaction-configuration 19 threshold-type immediate action-type trapOnly
```

Figure 24-1 shows that an alert (rising trap) would be issued immediately when the response time exceeds the rising threshold and a resolution (falling trap) would be issued immediately when the response time drops below the falling threshold.

Figure 24-1 *Example of Rising and Falling Thresholds*

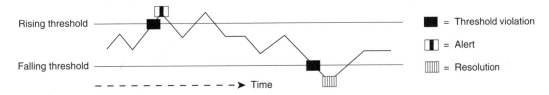

Related Commands

To locate documentation of related commands, you can search online at www.cisco.com.

rtr
rtr reaction-trigger
threshold
timeout

rtr reaction-trigger

To define a second response time reporter probe to make the transition from a "pending" state to an "active" state when one of the trigger action-type options are defined with the **rtr reaction-configuration** global configuration command, use the **rtr reaction-trigger** global configuration command. Use the **no** form of this command to remove the trigger combination.

> **rtr reaction-trigger** *probe target-probe*
> **no rtr reaction-trigger** *probe*

Syntax	Description
probe	Number of the probe in the "active" state that has the **action-type** set with the **rtr reaction-configuration** global configuration command.
target-probe	Number of the probe in the "pending" state that is waiting to be triggered with the **rtr** global configuration command.

Default

No trigger combination is defined.

Command Mode

Global configuration

Usage Guidelines

This command first appeared in Cisco IOS Release 11.2.

Triggers are usually used for diagnostics purposes and are not used in normal operation.

Example

In the following example, probe 1's state is changed from pending state to active state when probe 2's **action-type** occurs:

```
rtr reaction-trigger 2 1
```

Related Commands

To locate documentation of related commands, you can search online at www.cisco.com.

rtr
rtr reaction-configuration
rtr schedule

rtr reset

To perform a shutdown and restart of the response time reporter, use the **rtr reset** global configuration command.

> **rtr reset**

Syntax Description

This command has no arguments or keywords.

Command Mode

Global configuration

Usage Guidelines

This command first appeared in Cisco IOS Release 11.2.

CAUTION   Use the **rtr reset** command only in extreme situations such as the incorrect configuration of a number of probes.

The **rtr reset** command stops all probes, clears response time reporter configuration information, and returns the response time reporter feature to the startup condition. This command does not reread the response time reporter configuration stored in startup-config in NVRAM. You must retype the configuration or perform a **config memory** command.

Example

The following example resets the response time reporter feature:

```
rtr reset
```

Related Commands

To locate documentation of related commands, you can search online at www.cisco.com.

rtr

rtr schedule

To configure the time parameters for a response time reporter probe, use the **rtr schedule** global configuration command. Use the **no** form of this command to stop the probe and restart it with the default parameters (that is, pending).

> **rtr schedule** *probe* [**life** *seconds*] [**start-time** {**pending** | **now** | *hh:mm* [*month day* | *day month*]}] [**ageout** *seconds*]
> **no rtr schedule** *probe*

Syntax	Description
probe	Number of the response time reporter probe to schedule.
life *seconds*	(Optional) Number of seconds the probe actively collects information. The default is 3,600 seconds (one hour).
start-time	(Optional) Time when the probe starts collecting information. If the **start-time** is not specified, no information is collected until the **start-time** is configured or a trigger occurs that performs a **start-time now**.
pending	No information is collected. This is the default value.
now	Information is immediately collected.
hh:mm	Information is collected at the specified time (use a 24-hour clock). The time is the current day if you do not specify the month and day.
month	(Optional) Name of the month. If month is not specified, the current month is used. This requires a day.
day	Number of the day in the range 1 to 31. If day is not specified, the current day is used. This requires a month.
ageout *seconds*	(Optional) Number of seconds to keep the probe when it is not actively collecting information. The default is 0 seconds (never ages out).

Default

Place the probe in a pending state (that is, the probe is started but not actively collecting information).

Command Mode

Global configuration

Usage Guidelines

This command first appeared in Cisco IOS Release 11.2.

After you schedule the probe with the **rtr schedule** command, you cannot change the probe's configuration (with the **rtr** global configuration command). To change the probe's configuration, use the **no** form of the **rtr** global command and reenter the configuration information.

If the probe is in a pending state, you can define the conditions under which the probe makes the transition from pending to active with the **rtr reaction-trigger** and **rtr reaction-configuration** global configuration commands. When the probe is in an active state, it immediately begins collecting information.

The following time line shows the probe's age-out process:

```
W---------------------X---------------------Y---------------------Z
```

- W is the time the probe was configured with the **rtr** global configuration command.
- X is the probe's start time or start of life (that is, when the probe became "active").
- Y is the end of life as configured with the **rtr schedule** global configuration command (life seconds have counted down to zero).
- Z is the probe's age out.

Age out starts counting down at W and Y, is suspended between X and Y, and is reset to its configured size at Y.

It is possible for the probe to age out before it executes (that is, Z can occur before X). To ensure that this does not happen, the difference between the probe's configuration time and start time (X and W) must be less than the age-out seconds.

NOTE The total RAM required to hold the history and statistics tables is allocated at this time. This is to prevent router memory problems when the router gets heavily loaded and to lower the amount of overhead the feature causes on a router when it is active.

Example

In the following example, probe 25 begins actively collecting data at 3:00 p.m. on April 5. This probe will age out after 12 hours of inactivity, which can be before it starts or after it has finished with its life.

When this probe ages out, all configuration information for the probe is removed (that is, the configuration information is no longer in the running-config in RAM.)

```
rtr schedule 25 life 43200 start-time 15:00 apr 5 ageout 43200
```

Related Commands

To locate documentation of related commands, you can search online at www.cisco.com.

rtr
rtr reaction-configuration
rtr reaction-trigger

samples-of-history-kept

To set the number of entries kept in the history table per bucket for the response time reporter probe, use the **samples-of-history-kept** response time reporter configuration command. Use the **no** form of this command to return to the default value.

> **samples-of-history-kept** *samples*
> **no samples-of-history-kept**

Syntax   Description

samples   Number of entries kept in the history table per bucket.

Default

16 entries for type **pathEcho**

1 entry for type **echo**

Command Mode

Response time reporter configuration

Usage Guidelines

This command first appeared in Cisco IOS Release 11.2.

Use the **samples-of-history-kept** command to control how many entries are saved in the history table. To control the type of information that gets saved in the history table, use the **filter-for-history** command. To set how many buckets get created in the history table, use the **buckets-of-history-kept** command.

A probe can collect history and capture statistics. By default, history is not collected. When a problem arises where history is useful (for example, a large number of timeouts are occurring), you can configure the **lives-of-history-kept** response time reporter configuration command to collect history.

NOTE   Collecting history increases the usage of RAM. Only collect history when you think there is a problem. For general network response time information, use statistics.

Example

In the following example, 10 entries are kept in the history table for each of the of probe's three lives:

```
rtr 1
 type pathecho protocol ipIcmpEcho 172.16.1.176
 lives-of-history-kept 3
 samples-of-history-kept 10
```

Related Commands

To locate documentation of related commands, you can search online at www.cisco.com.

buckets-of-history-kept
filter-for-history
lives-of-history-kept
rtr

show cdp

To display global CDP information, including timer and hold-time information, use the **show cdp** privileged EXEC command.

> **show cdp**

Syntax Description

This command has no arguments or keywords.

Command Mode

Privileged EXEC

Usage Guidelines

This command first appeared in Cisco IOS Release 10.3.

Sample Display

The following is sample output from the **show cdp** command. Global CDP timer and hold-time parameters are set to the defaults of 60 and 180 seconds, respectively.

```
Router# show cdp

Global CDP information:
        Sending CDP packets every 60 seconds
        Sending a holdtime value of 180 seconds
```

Related Commands

To locate documentation of related commands, you can search online at www.cisco.com.

cdp holdtime
cdp timer
show cdp entry
show cdp interface
show cdp neighbors
show cdp traffic

show cdp entry

To display information about a neighbor device listed in the CDP table, use the **show cdp entry** privileged EXEC command.

> **show cdp entry** {* | *entry-name* [**protocol** | **version**]}

Syntax	Description
*	Shows all of the CDP neighbors.
entry-name	Name of neighbor about which you want information.
	You can enter an asterisk (*) at the end of an *entry-name*, such as show cdp entry dev*, which would show information about the neighbor, device.cisco.com.
protocol	(Optional) Limits the display to information about the protocols enabled on a router.
version	(Optional) Limits the display to information about the version of software running on the router.

Command Mode
Privileged EXEC

Usage Guidelines
This command first appeared in Cisco IOS Release 10.3.

Sample Displays
The following is sample output from the **show cdp** entry command with no limits. Information about the neighbor *device.cisco.com* is displayed, including device ID, address and protocol, platform, interface, hold time, and version.

```
Router# show cdp entry device.cisco.com

-----------------------
Device ID: device.cisco.com
Entry address(es):
  IP address: 192.168.68.18
  CLNS address: 490001.1111.1111.1111.00
  DECnet address: 10.1
Platform: cisco 4500,  Capabilities: Router
Interface: Ethernet0/1,  Port ID (outgoing port): Ethernet0
Holdtime : 125 sec

Version :
Cisco Internetwork Operating System Software
IOS (tm) 4500 Software (C4500-J-M), Version 11.1(10.4), MAINTENANCE INTERIM SOFTWARE
Copyright (c) 1986-1997 by cisco Systems, Inc.
Compiled Mon 07-Apr-97 19:51 by dschwart
```

The following is sample output from the **show cdp entry protocol** command. Only information about the protocols enabled on *device.cisco.com* is displayed.

```
Router# show cdp entry device.cisco.com protocol

Protocol information for device.cisco.com:
  IP address: 192.168.68.18
  CLNS address: 490001.1111.1111.1111.00
  DECnet address: 10.1
```

The following is sample output from the **show cdp entry version** command. Only information about the version of software running on *device.cisco.com* is displayed.

```
Router# show cdp entry device.cisco.com version

Version information for device.cisco.com:
  Cisco Internetwork Operating System Software
IOS (tm) 4500 Software (C4500-J-M), Version 11.1(10.4), MAINTENANCE INTERIM SOFTWARE
Copyright (c) 1986-1997 by cisco Systems, Inc.
Compiled Mon 07-Apr-97 19:51 by dschwart
```

Related Commands

To locate documentation of related commands, you can search online at www.cisco.com.

show cdp
show cdp interface
show cdp neighbors
show cdp traffic

show cdp interface

To display information about the interfaces on which CDP is enabled, use the **show cdp interface** privileged EXEC command.

show cdp interface [type number]

Syntax Description

Syntax	Description
type	(Optional) Type of interface about which you want information.
number	(Optional) Number of the interface about which you want information.

Command Mode

Privileged EXEC

Usage Guidelines

This command first appeared in Cisco IOS Release 10.3.

Sample Displays

The following sample output form the **show cdp interface** command. Status information and information about CDP timer and hold time settings is displayed for all interfaces on which CDP is enabled.

```
Router# show cdp interface

Serial0 is up, line protocol is up, encapsulation is SMDS
  Sending CDP packets every 60 seconds
  Holdtime is 180 seconds
Ethernet0 is up, line protocol is up, encapsulation is ARPA
  Sending CDP packets every 60 seconds
  Holdtime is 180 seconds
```

The following is sample output from the **show cdp interface** command with an interface specified. Status information and information about CDP timer and holdtime settings is displayed for Ethernet interface 0 only.

```
Router# show cdp interface ethernet 0

Ethernet0 is up, line protocol is up, encapsulation is ARPA
  Sending CDP packets every 60 seconds
  Holdtime is 180 seconds
```

Related Commands

To locate documentation of related commands, you can search online at www.cisco.com.

show cdp
show cdp entry
show cdp neighbors
show cdp traffic

show cdp neighbors

To display information about neighbors, use the **show cdp neighbors** privileged EXEC command.

show cdp neighbors [*type number*] [**detail**]

Syntax	Description
type	(Optional) Type of the interface connected to the neighbors about which you want information.
number	(Optional) Number of the interface connected to the neighbors about which you want information.
detail	(Optional) Displays detailed information about a neighbor (or neighbors) including network address, enabled protocols, hold time, and software version.

Command Mode

Privileged EXEC

Usage Guidelines

This command first appeared in Cisco IOS Release 10.3.

Sample Displays

The following is sample output from the **show cdp neighbors** command. Device ID, interface type and number, holdtime settings, capabilities, platform, and port ID information about neighbors is displayed.

```
Router# show cdp neighbors

Capability Codes: R - Router, T - Trans Bridge, B - Source Route Bridge
                  S - Switch, H - Host, I - IGMP, r - Repeater

Device ID          Local Intrfce    Holdtme     Capability  Platform  Port ID
device1.cisco.com   Eth 0/1          122          T S        WS-C2900  2/11
device2.cisco.com   Eth 0/1          179          R          4500      Eth 0
device3.cisco.com   Eth 0/1          155          R          2500      Eth 0
device4.cisco.com   Eth 0/1          155          R          2509      Eth 0
```

The following is sample output for one neighbor from the **show cdp neighbors detail** command. Additional detail is shown about neighbors, including network address, enabled protocols, and software version:

```
Router# show cdp neighbors detail

- - - - - - - - - - - - - - - - - - - - - -
Device ID: device2.cisco.com
Entry address(es):
  IP address: 171.68.162.134
Platform: cisco 4500,  Capabilities: Router
Interface: Ethernet0/1,  Port ID (outgoing port): Ethernet0
Holdtime : 156 sec

Version :
Cisco Internetwork Operating System Software
IOS (tm) 4500 Software (C4500-J-M), Version 11.1(10.4), MAINTENANCE INTERIM SOFTWARE
Copyright (c) 1986-1997 by Cisco Systems, Inc.
Compiled Mon 07-Apr-97 19:51 by dschwart
```

Related Commands

To locate documentation of related commands, you can search online at www.cisco.com.

show cdp
show cdp entry
show cdp interface
show cdp traffic

show cdp traffic

To display traffic information from the CDP table, use the **show cdp traffic** privileged EXEC command.

       show cdp traffic

Syntax Description

This command has no arguments or keywords.

Command Mode

Privileged EXEC

Usage Guidelines

This command first appeared in Cisco IOS Release 10.3.

Sample Display

The following is sample output from the **show cdp traffic** command:

```
Router# show cdp traffic

CDP counters:
        Packets output: 94, Input: 75
        Hdr syntax: 0, Chksum error: 0, Encaps failed: 0
        No memory: 0, Invalid packet: 0, Fragmented: 0
```

In this example, traffic information is displayed including the numbers of packets sent, the number of packets received, header syntax, checksum errors, failed encapsulations, memory problems, and invalid and fragmented packets is displayed. Header syntax indicates the number of packets CDP receives with that have an invalid header format.

Related Commands

To locate documentation of related commands, you can search online at www.cisco.com.

show cdp
show cdp entry
show cdp interface
show cdp neighbors

show rmon

Use the **show rmon** EXEC command to display the current RMON agent status on the router.

> **show rmon [alarms | capture | events | filter | history | hosts | matrix | statistics | task | topn]**

Syntax	Description
alarms	(Optional) Displays the RMON alarm table.
capture	(Optional) Displays the RMON buffer capture table. Available on Cisco 2500 series and Cisco AS5200 series only.
events	(Optional) Displays the RMON event table.
filter	(Optional) Displays the RMON filter table. Available on Cisco 2500 series and Cisco AS5200 series only.
history	(Optional) Displays the RMON history table. Available on Cisco 2500 series and Cisco AS5200 series only.
hosts	(Optional) Displays the RMON hosts table. Available on Cisco 2500 series and Cisco AS5200 series only.
matrix	(Optional) Displays the RMON matrix table. Available on Cisco 2500 series and Cisco AS5200 series only.
statistics	(Optional) Displays the RMON statistics table. Available on Cisco 2500 series and Cisco AS5200 series only.
task	(Optional) Displays general RMON statistics. This is the default.
topn	(Optional) Displays the RMON top-n hosts table. Available on Cisco 2500 series and Cisco AS5200 series only.

Default

If no option is specified, the **task** option is displayed.

Command Mode

EXEC

Usage Guidelines

This command first appeared in Cisco IOS Release 11.1.

Refer to the specific **show rmon** command for an example and description of the fields.

For additional information, refer to the RMON MIB described in RFC 1757.

Sample Display

The following is sample output from the **show rmon** command. All counters are from the time the router was initialized.

```
Router# show rmon

145678 packets input (34562 promiscuous), 0 drops
145678 packets processed, 0 on queue, queue utilization 15/64
```

Table 24-1 describes the fields shown in the display.

Table 24-1 *Show RMON Field Descriptions*

Field	Description
x packets input	Number of packets received on RMON-enabled interfaces.
x promiscuous	Number of input packets that were seen by the router only because RMON placed the interface in promiscuous mode.
x drops	Number of input packets that could not be processed because the RMON queue overflowed.
x packets processed	Number of input packets actually processed by the RMON task.
x on queue	Number of input packets that are sitting on the RMON queue, waiting to be processed.
queue utilization *x/y*	*y* is the maximum size of the RMON queue; *x* is the largest number of packets that were ever on the queue at a particular time.

Related Commands

To locate documentation of related commands, you can search online at www.cisco.com.

rmon
rmon alarm
rmon event
rmon queuesize
show rmon alarms
show rmon capture
show rmon events
show rmon filter
show rmon history
show rmon hosts
show rmon matrix
show rmon statistics
show rmon topn

show rmon alarms

Use the **show rmon alarms** EXEC command to display the contents of the router's RMON alarm table.

show rmon alarms

Syntax Description

This command has no arguments or keywords.

Command Mode

EXEC

Usage Guidelines

This command first appeared in Cisco IOS Release 11.2.

For additional information, refer to the RMON MIB described in RFC 1757.

You must have first enabled RMON on the interface, and configured RMON alarms to display alarm information with the **show rmon alarms** command.

Sample Display

The following is sample output from the **show rmon alarms** command:

```
Router# show rmon alarms

Alarm 2 is active, owned by manager1
 Monitors ifEntry.1.1 every 30 seconds
 Taking delta samples, last value was 0
 Rising threshold is 15, assigned to event 12
 Falling threshold is 0, assigned to event 0
 On startup enable rising or falling alarm
```

Table 24-2 describes the fields shown in the display.

Table 24-2 *Show RMON Alarms Field Descriptions*

Field	Description
Alarm 2 is active, owned by manager1	Unique index into the alarmTable, showing the alarm status is active, and the owner of this row, as defined in the alarmTable of RMON.
Monitors ifEntry.1.1	Object identifier of the particular variable to be sampled. Equivalent to alarmVariable in RMON.
Every 30 seconds	Interval in seconds over which the data is sampled and compared with the rising and falling thresholds. Equivalent to alarmInterval in RMON.

Table 24-2 *Show RMON Alarms Field Descriptions (Continued)*

Field	Description
Taking delta samples	Method of sampling the selected variable and calculating the value to be compared against the thresholds. Equivalent to alarmSampleType in RMON.
Last value was	Value of the statistic during the last sampling period. Equivalent to alarmValue in RMON.
Rising threshold is	Threshold for the sampled statistic. Equivalent to alarmRisingThreshold in RMON.
Assigned to event	Index of the eventEntry that is used when a rising threshold is crossed. Equivalent to alarmRisingEventIndex in RMON.
Falling threshold is	Threshold for the sampled statistic. Equivalent to alarmFallingThreshold in RMON.
Assigned to event	Index of the eventEntry that is used when a falling threshold is crossed. Equivalent to alarmFallingEventIndex in RMON.
On startup enable rising or falling alarm	Alarm that may be sent when this entry is first set to valid. Equivalent to alarmStartupAlarm in RMON.

Related Commands

To locate documentation of related commands, you can search online at www.cisco.com.

rmon
rmon alarm
show rmon

show rmon capture

Use the **show rmon capture** EXEC command to display the contents of the router's RMON capture table.

> **show rmon capture**

Syntax Description

This command has no arguments or keywords.

Command Mode

EXEC

Part
III

Command Reference

Usage Guidelines

This command first appeared in Cisco IOS Release 11.2.

For additional information, refer to the RMON MIB described in RFC 1757.

You must have first enabled RMON on the interface, and configured RMON alarms and events to display alarm information with the **show rmon capture** command.

This command is available on the Cisco 2500 series and Cisco AS5200 series only.

Sample Display

The following is sample output from the **show rmon capture** command:

```
Router# show rmon capture

Buffer 4096 is active, owned by manager1
 Captured data is from channel 4096
 Slice size is 128, download size is 128
 Download offset is 0
 Full Status is spaceAvailable, full action is lockWhenFull
 Granted 65536 octets out of 65536 requested
 Buffer has been on since 00:01:16, and has captured 1 packets
  Current capture buffer entries:
   Packet 1 was captured 416 ms since buffer was turned on
   Its length is 326 octets and has a status type of 0
   Packet ID is 634, and contains the following data:
00 00 0c 03 12 ce 00 00 0c 08 9d 4e 08 00 45 00
01 34 01 42 00 00 1d 11 e3 01 ab 45 30 15 ac 15
31 06 05 98 00 a1 01 20 9f a8 00 00 00 00 00 00
00 00 00 00 00 00 00 00 00 00 00 00 00 00 00 00
00 00 00 00 00 00 00 00 00 00 00 00 00 00 00 00
00 00 00 00 00 00 00 00 00 00 00 00 00 00 00 00
00 00 00 00
```

Table 24-3 describes the fields shown in the display.

Table 24-3 *Show RMON Capture Field Descriptions*

Field	Description
Buffer 4096 is active	Equates to bufferControlIndex in the bufferControlTable of RMON. Uniquely identifies a valid (active) row in this table.
Owned by manager1	Denotes the owner of this row. Equates to bufferControlOwner in the bufferControlTable of RMON.
Captured data is from channel	Equates to the bufferControlChannelIndex and identifies which RMON channel is the source of these packets.
Slice size is	Identifies the maximum number of octets of each packet that will be saved in this capture buffer. Equates to bufferControlCaptureSliceSize of RMON.

Table 24-3 *Show RMON Capture Field Descriptions (Continued)*

Field	Description
Download size is	Identifies the maximum number of octets of each packet in this capture buffer that will be returned in an SNMP retrieval of that packet. Equates to bufferControlDownloadSliceSize in RMON.
Download offset is	Offset of the first octet of each packet in this capture buffer that will be returned in an SNMP retrieval of that packet. Equates to bufferControlDownloadOffset in RMON.
Full Status is spaceAvailable	Shows whether the buffer is full or has room to accept new packets. Equates to bufferControlFullStatus in RMON.
Full action is lockWhenFull	Controls the action of the buffer when it reaches full status. Equates to bufferControlFullAction in RMON.
Granted 65536 octets	Actual maximum number of octets that can be saved in this capture buffer. Equates to bufferControlMaxOctetsGranted in RMON.
Out of 65536 requested	Requested maximum number of octets to be saved in this capture buffer. Equates to bufferControlMaxOctetsRequested in RMON.
Buffer has been on since	Indicates how long the buffer has been available.
And has captured 1 packets	Number of packets captured since buffer was turned on. Equates to bufferControlCapturedPackets in RMON.
Current capture buffer entries:	Lists each packet captured.
Packet 1 was captured 416 ms since buffer was turned on Its length is 326 octets and has a status type of 0	Zero indicates the error status of this packet. Equates to captureBufferPacketStatus in RMON, where its value options are documented.
Packet ID is	Index that describes the order of packets received on a particular interface. Equates to captureBufferPacketID in RMON.
And contains the following data:	Data inside the packet, starting at the beginning of the packet.

Related Commands

To locate documentation of related commands, you can search online at www.cisco.com.

rmon
rmon alarm
rmon event
show rmon

show rmon events

Use the **show rmon events** EXEC command to display the contents of the router's RMON event table.

>   **show rmon events**

Syntax Description

This command has no arguments or keywords.

Command Mode

EXEC

Usage Guidelines

This command first appeared in Cisco IOS Release 11.2.

For additional information, refer to the RMON MIB described in RFC 1757.

You must have first enabled RMON on the interface, and configured RMON events to display alarm information with the **show rmon events** command.

Sample Display

The following is sample output from the **show rmon events** command:

```
Router# show rmon events

Event 12 is active, owned by manager1
 Description is interface-errors
 Event firing causes log and trap to community rmonTrap, last fired 00:00:00
```

Table 24-4 describes the fields shown in the display.

Table 24-4   *Show RMON Events Field Descriptions*

Field	Description
Event 12 is active, owned by manager1	Unique index into the eventTable, showing the event status is active, and the owner of this row, as defined in the eventTable of RMON.
Description is interface-errors	Type of event, in this case an interface error.
Event firing causes log and trap	Type of notification that the router will make about this event. Equivalent to eventType in RMON.
Community rmonTrap	If an SNMP trap is to be sent, it will be sent to the SNMP community specified by this octet string. Equivalent to eventCommunity in RMON.
Last fired	Last time the event was generated.

Related Commands

To locate documentation of related commands, you can search online at www.cisco.com.

rmon
rmon event
show rmon

show rmon filter

Use the **show rmon filter** EXEC command to display the contents of the router's RMON filter table.

> **show rmon filter**

Syntax Description

This command has no arguments or keywords.

Command Mode

EXEC

Usage Guidelines

This command first appeared in Cisco IOS Release 11.2.

For additional information, refer to the RMON MIB described in RFC 1757.

You must have first enabled RMON on the interface, and configured RMON alarms and events to display alarm information with the **show rmon filter** command.

This command is available on the Cisco 2500 series and Cisco AS5200 series only.

Sample Display

The following is sample output from the **show rmon filter** command:

```
Router# show rmon filter

Filter 4096 is active, and owned by manager1
 Data offset is 12, with
 Data of  08 00 00 00 00 00 00 00 00 00 00 00 00 00 ab 45 30 15 ac 15 31 06
 Data Mask is ff ff 00 00 00 00 00 00 00 00 00 00 00 00 ff ff ff ff ff ff ff ff
 Data Not Mask is 0
 Pkt status is 0, status mask is 0, not mask is 0
 Associated channel 4096 is active, and owned by manager1
 Type of channel is acceptFailed, data control is off
 Generate event index 0
```

```
Event status is eventFired, # of matches is 1482
Turn on event index is 0, turn off event index is 0
Description:
```

Table 24-5 describes the fields shown in the display.

Table 24-5 *Show RMON Filter Field Descriptions*

Field	Description
Filter 4096 is active, and owned by manager1	Unique index of the filter, its current state, and the owner, as defined in the filterTable of RMON.
Data offset is	Offset from the beginning of each packet where a match of packet data will be attempted. Equivalent to filterPktDataOffset in RMON.
Data of	Data that is to be matched with the input packet. Equivalent to filterPktData in RMON.
Data Mask is	Mask that is applied to the match process. Equivalent to filterPktDataMask in RMON.
Data Not Mask is	Inversion mask that is applied to the match process. Equivalent to filterPktDataNotMask in RMON.
Pkt status is	Status that is to be matched with the input packet. Equivalent to filterPktStatus in RMON.
Status mask is	Mask that is applied to the status match process. Equivalent to filterPktStatusMask in RMON.
Not mask is	Inversion mask that is applied to the status match process. Equivalent to filterPktStatusNotMask in RMON.
Associated channel 4096 is active, and owned by manager1	Unique index of the channel, its current state, and the owner, as defined in the channelTable of RMON.
Type of channel is acceptFailed	This object controls the action of the filters associated with this channel. Equivalent to channelAcceptType of RMON.
Data control is off	This object controls the flow of data through this channel. Equivalent to channelDataControl in RMON.
Generate event index 0	Value of this object identifies the event that is configured to be generated when the associated channelDataControl is on and a packet is matched. Equivalent to channelEventIndex in RMON.
Event status is eventFired	When the channel is configured to generate events when packets are matched, this message indicates the means of controlling the flow of those events. Equivalent to channelEventStatus in RMON.
# of matches is	Number of times this channel has matched a packet. Equivalent to channelMatches in RMON.

Table 24-5 *Show RMON Filter Field Descriptions (Continued)*

Field	Description
Turn on event index is	Value of this object identifies the event that is configured to turn the associated channelDataControl from off to on when the event is generated. Equivalent to channelTurnOnEventIndex in RMON.
Turn off event index is	Value of this object identifies the event that is configured to turn the associated channelDataControl from on to off when the event is generated. Equivalent to channelTurnOffEventIndex in RMON.
Description:	Comment describing this channel.

Related Commands

To locate documentation of related commands, you can search online at www.cisco.com.

rmon
rmon alarm
rmon event
show rmon

show rmon history

Use the **show rmon history** EXEC command to display the contents of the router's RMON history table.

>   **show rmon history**

Syntax Description

This command has no arguments or keywords.

Command Mode

EXEC

Usage Guidelines

This command first appeared in Cisco IOS Release 11.2.

For additional information, refer to the RMON MIB described in RFC 1757.

You must have first enabled RMON on the interface, and configured RMON alarms and events to display alarm information with the **show rmon history** command.

This command is available on the Cisco 2500 series and Cisco AS5200 series only.

Sample Display

The following is sample output from the **show rmon history** command:

```
Router# show rmon history

Entry 1 is active, and owned by manager1
 Monitors ifEntry.1.1 every 30 seconds
 Requested # of time intervals, ie buckets, is 5
 Granted # of time intervals, ie buckets, is 5
  Sample # 14 began measuring at 00:11:00
   Received 38346 octets, 216 packets,
   0 broadcast and 80 multicast packets,
   0 undersized and 0 oversized packets,
   0 fragments and 0 jabbers,
   0 CRC alignment errors and 0 collisions.
   # of dropped packet events is 0
   Network utilization is estimated at 10
```

Table 24-6 describes the fields shown in the display.

Table 24-6 *Show RMON History Field Descriptions*

Field	Description
Entry 1 is active, and owned by manager1	Unique index of the history entry, its current state, and the owner as defined in the historyControlTable of RMON.
Monitors ifEntry.1.1	This object identifies the source of the data for which historical data was collected and placed in a media-specific table. Equivalent to historyControlDataSource in RMON.
Every 30 seconds	Interval in seconds over which the data is sampled for each bucket in the part of the media-specific table associated with this historyControlEntry. Equivalent to historyControlInterval in RMON.
Requested # of time intervals, ie buckets, is	Requested number of discrete time intervals over which data is to be saved in the part of the media-specific table associated with this historyControlEntry. Equivalent to historyControlBucketsRequested in RMON.
Granted # of time intervals, ie buckets, is	Actual number of discrete time intervals over which data is to be saved in the part of the media-specific table associated with this historyControlEntry. Equivalent to historyControlBucketsGranted in RMON.
Sample # 14 began measuring at	Time at the start of the interval over which this sample was measured.
Received 38346 octets	Total number of octets of data (including those in bad packets) received on the network (excluding framing bits but including FCS octets). Equivalent to etherHistoryOctets in RMON.

Table 24-6 *Show RMON History Field Descriptions (Continued)*

Field	Description
x packets	Number of packets (including bad packets) received during this sampling interval. Equivalent to etherHistoryPkts in RMON.
x broadcast	Number of good packets received during this sampling interval that were directed to the broadcast address. Equivalent to etherHistoryBroadcastPkts in RMON.
x multicast packets	Number of good packets received during this sampling interval that were directed to a multicast address. Equivalent to etherHistoryMulticastPkts in RMON.
x undersized	Number of packets received during this sampling interval that were fewer than 64 octets long (excluding framing bits but including FCS octets) and were otherwise well formed. Equivalent to etherHistoryUndersizedPkts in RMON.
x oversized packets	Number of packets received during this sampling interval that were longer than 1,518 octets (excluding framing bits but including FCS octets) but were otherwise well formed. Equivalent to etherHistoryOversizePkts in RMON.
x fragments	Total number of packets received during this sampling interval that were fewer than 64 octets in length (excluding framing bits but including FCS octets), and had either a bad Frame Check Sequence (FCS) with an integral number of octets (FCS Error) or a bad FCS with a nonintegral number of octets (Alignment Error). Equivalent to etherHistoryFragments in RMON.
x jabbers	Number of packets received during this sampling interval that were longer than 1,518 octets (excluding framing bits but including FCS octets), and had either a bad Frame Check Sequence (FCS) with an integral number of octets (FCS Error) or a bad FCS with a nonintegral number of octets (Alignment Error). Note that this definition of jabber is different than the definition in IEEE-802.3 section 8.2.1.5 (10BASE5) and section 10.3.1.4 (10BASE2). Equivalent to etherHistoryJabbers in RMON.
x CRC alignment errors	Number of packets received during this sampling interval that had a length (excluding framing bits but including FCS octets) from 64 to 1,518 octets, inclusive, but had either a bad Frame Check Sequence (FCS) with an integral number of octets (FCS Error) or a bad FCS with a nonintegral number of octets (Alignment Error). Equivalent to etherHistoryCRCAlignErrors in RMON.
x collisions	Best estimate of the total number of collisions on this Ethernet segment during this sampling interval. Equivalent to etherHistoryCollisions in RMON.
# of dropped packet events is	Total number of events in which packets were dropped by the probe because of resources during this sampling interval. Note that this number is not necessarily the number of packets dropped, it is just the number of times this condition has been detected. Equivalent to etherHistoryDropEvents in RMON.
Network utilization is estimated at	Best estimate of the mean physical-layer network usage on this interface during this sampling interval, in hundredths of a percent. Equivalent to etherHistoryUtilization in RMON.

Part
III

Command Reference

Related Commands

To locate documentation of related commands, you can search online at www.cisco.com.

rmon
rmon alarm
rmon event
show rmon

show rmon hosts

Use the **show rmon hosts** EXEC command to display the contents of the router's RMON hosts table.

show rmon hosts

Syntax Description

This command has no arguments or keywords.

Command Mode

EXEC

Usage Guidelines

This command first appeared in Cisco IOS Release 11.2.

For additional information, refer to the RMON MIB described in RFC 1757.

You must have first enabled RMON on the interface, and configured RMON alarms and events to display alarm information with the **show rmon hosts** command.

This command is available on the Cisco 2500 series and Cisco AS5200 series only.

Sample Display

The following is sample output from the **show rmon hosts** command:

```
Router# show rmon hosts

Host Control Entry 1 is active, and owned by manager1
 Monitors host ifEntry.1.1
 Table size is 51, last time an entry was deleted was 00:00:00
  Creation Order number is 1
   Physical address is 0000.0c02.5808
   Packets: rcvd 6963, transmitted 7041
   Octets: rcvd 784062, transmitted 858530
   # of packets transmitted: broadcast 28, multicast 48
   # of bad packets transmitted is 0
```

Table 24-7 describes the fields shown in the display.

Table 24-7 *Show RMON Hosts Field Descriptions*

Field	Description
Host Control Entry 1 is active, and owned by manager1	Unique index of the host entry, its current state, and the owner as defined in the hostControlTable of RMON.
Monitors host ifEntry.1.1	This object identifies the source of the data for this instance of the host function. Equivalent to hostControlDataSource in RMON.
Table size is	Number of hostEntries in the hostTable and the hostTimeTable associated with this hostControlEntry. Equivalent to hostControlTableSize in RMON.
Last time an entry was deleted was	Time when the last entry was deleted from the hostTable.
Creation Order number is	Index that defines the relative ordering of the creation time of hosts captured for a particular hostControlEntry. Equivalent to hostCreationOrder in RMON.
Physical address is	Physical address of this host. Equivalent to hostAddress in RMON.
Packets: rcvd	Number of good packets transmitted to this address. Equivalent to hostInPkts in RMON.
Transmitted	Number of packets, including bad packets transmitted by this address. Equivalent to hostOutPkts in RMON.
Octets: rcvd	Number of octets transmitted to this address since it was added to the hostTable (excluding framing bits but including FCS octets), except for those octets in bad packets. Equivalent to hostInOctets in RMON.
Transmitted	Number of octets transmitted by this address since it was added to the hostTable (excluding framing bits but including FCS octets), including those octets in bad packets. Equivalent to hostOutOctets in RMON.
# of packets transmitted:	Number of good packets transmitted by this address that were broadcast or multicast.
# of bad packets transmitted is	Number of bad packets transmitted by this address.

Related Commands

To locate documentation of related commands, you can search online at www.cisco.com.

rmon
rmon alarm
rmon event
show rmon

show rmon matrix

Use the **show rmon matrix** EXEC command to display the contents of the router's RMON matrix table.

show rmon matrix

Syntax Description

This command has no arguments or keywords.

Command Mode

EXEC

Usage Guidelines

This command first appeared in Cisco IOS Release 11.2.

For additional information, refer to the RMON MIB described in RFC 1757.

You must have first enabled RMON on the interface, and configured RMON alarms and events to display alarm information with the **show rmon matrix** command.

This command is available on the Cisco 2500 series and Cisco AS5200 series only.

Sample Display

The following is sample output from the **show rmon matrix** command:

```
Router# show rmon matrix

Matrix 1 is active, and owned by manager1
 Monitors ifEntry.1.1
 Table size is 451, last time an entry was deleted was at 00:00:00
```

Table 24-8 describes the fields shown in the display.

Table 24-8 *Show RMON Matrix Field Descriptions*

Field	Description
Matrix 1 is active, and owned by manager1	Unique index of the matrix entry, its current state, and the owner as defined in the matrixControlTable of RMON.
Monitors ifEntry.1.1	This object identifies the source of the data for this instance of the matrix function. Equivalent to matrixControlDataSource in RMON.
Table size is 451, last time an entry was deleted was at	Size of the matrix table and the time that the last entry was deleted.

Related Commands

To locate documentation of related commands, you can search online at www.cisco.com.

rmon
rmon alarm
rmon event
show rmon

show rmon statistics

Use the **show rmon statistics** EXEC command to display the contents of the router's RMON statistics table.

       show rmon statistics

Syntax Description

This command has no arguments or keywords.

Command Mode

EXEC

Usage Guidelines

This command first appeared in Cisco IOS Release 11.2.

For additional information, refer to the RMON MIB described in RFC 1757.

You must have first enabled RMON on the interface, and configured RMON alarms and events to display alarm information with the **show rmon statistics** command.

This command is available on the Cisco 2500 series and Cisco AS5200 series only.

Sample Display

The following is sample output from the **show rmon statistics** command:

```
Router# show rmon statistics

Interface 1 is active, and owned by config
 Monitors ifEntry.1.1 which has
 Received 60739740 octets, 201157 packets,
 1721 broadcast and 9185 multicast packets,
 0 undersized and 0 oversized packets,
 0 fragments and 0 jabbers,
```

```
0 CRC alignment errors and 32 collisions.
# of dropped packet events (due to lack of resources): 511
# of packets received of length (in octets):
 64: 92955, 65-127: 14204, 128-255: 1116,
 256-511: 4479, 512-1023: 85856, 1024-1518:2547
```

Table 24-9 describes the fields shown in the display.

Table 24-9 *Show RMON Statistics Field Descriptions*

Field	Description
Interface 1 is active, and owned by config	Unique index of the statistics entry, its current state, and the owner as defined in the etherStatsTable of RMON.
Monitors ifEntry.1.1	This object identifies the source of the data that this etherStats entry is configured to analyze. Equivalent to etherStatsDataSource in RMON.
Received 60,739,740 octets	Total number of octets of data (including those in bad packets) received on the network (excluding framing bits but including FCS octets). Equivalent to etherStatsOctets in RMON.
x packets	Number of packets (including bad packets) received. Equivalent to etherStatsPkts in RMON.
x broadcast	Number of good packets received that were directed to the broadcast address. Equivalent to etherStatsBroadcastPkts in RMON.
x multicast packets	Number of good packets received that were directed to a multicast address. Equivalent to etherStatsMulticastPkts in RMON.
x undersized	Number of packets received that were fewer than 64 octets long (excluding framing bits but including FCS octets) and were otherwise well formed. Equivalent to etherStatsUndersizedPkts in RMON.
x oversized packets	Number of packets received that were longer than 1,518 octets (excluding framing bits but including FCS octets) but were otherwise well formed. Equivalent to etherStatsOversizePkts in RMON.
x fragments	Total number of packets received that were fewer than 64 octets in length (excluding framing bits but including FCS octets), and had either a bad Frame Check Sequence (FCS) with an integral number of octets (FCS Error) or a bad FCS with a nonintegral number of octets (Alignment Error). Equivalent to etherStatsFragments in RMON.
x jabbers	Number of packets received that were longer than 1,518 octets (excluding framing bits but including FCS octets), and had either a bad Frame Check Sequence (FCS) with an integral number of octets (FCS Error) or a bad FCS with a nonintegral number of octets (Alignment Error). Note that this definition of jabber is different than the definition in IEEE-802.3 section 8.2.1.5 (10BASE5) and section 10.3.1.4 (10BASE2). Equivalent to etherStatsJabbers in RMON.

Table 24-9 *Show RMON Statistics Field Descriptions (Continued)*

Field	Description
x CRC alignment errors	Number of packets received that had a length (excluding framing bits but including FCS octets) from 64 to 1,518 octets, inclusive, but had either a bad Frame Check Sequence (FCS) with an integral number of octets (FCS Error) or a bad FCS with a nonintegral number of octets (Alignment Error). Equivalent to etherStatsCRCAlignErrors in RMON.
x collisions	Best estimate of the total number of collisions on this Ethernet segment. Equivalent to etherHistoryCollisions in RMON.
# of dropped packet events (due to lack of resources):	Total number of events in which packets were dropped by the probe because of a lack of resources. Note that this number is not necessarily the number of packets dropped, it is just the number of times this condition has been detected. Equivalent to etherStatsDropEvents in RMON.
# of packets received of length (in octets):	Separates the received packets (good and bad) by packet size in the given ranges (64, 65 to 127,128 to 255, 256 to 511, 512 to 1023, and 1024 to 1516).

Related Commands

To locate documentation of related commands, you can search online at www.cisco.com.

rmon
rmon alarm
rmon event
show rmon

show rmon topn

Use the **show rmon topn** EXEC command to display the contents of the router's RMON Top-N host table.

show rmon topn

Syntax Description

This command has no arguments or keywords.

Command Mode

EXEC

Usage Guidelines

This command first appeared in Cisco IOS Release 11.2.

For additional information, refer to the RMON MIB described in RFC 1757.

You must have first enabled RMON on the interface, and configured RMON events to display alarm information with the **show rmon events** command.

This command is available on the Cisco 2500 series and Cisco AS5200 series only.

Sample Display

The following is sample output from the **show rmon topn** command:

```
Router# show rmon topn

Host Entry 1 of report 1 is active, owned by manager1
 The rate of change is based on hostTopNInPkts
 This report was last started at 00:00:00
 Time remaining in this report is 0 out of 0
 Hosts physical address is 00ad.beef.002b
 Requested # of hosts: 10, # of hosts granted: 10
Report # 1 of Top N hosts entry 1 is recording
Host 0000.0c02.5808 at a rate of 12
```

Table 24-10 describes the fields shown in the display.

Table 24-10 *Show RMON Top-N Field Descriptions*

Field	Description
Host Entry 1 of report 1 is active, owned by manager1	Unique index of the hostTopN entry, its current state, and the owner as defined in the hostTopNControlTable of RMON.
The rate of change is based on hostTopNInPkts	Variable for each host that the hostTopNRate variable is based on.
This report was last started at	Time the report was started.
Time remaining in this report is	Number of seconds left in the report currently being collected. Equivalent to hostTopNTimeRemaining in RMON.
Out of	Number of seconds that this report has collected during the last sampling interval, or if this report is currently being collected, the number of seconds that this report is being collected during this sampling interval. Equivalent to hostTopNDuration in RMON.
Hosts physical address is	Host address.
Requested # of hosts:	Maximum number of hosts requested for the Top-N table. Equivalent to hostTopNRequestedSize in RMON.
# of hosts granted:	Maximum number of hosts granted for the Top-N table. Eqivalent to hostTopNGrantedSiz in RMON.

Table 24-10 *Show RMON Top-N Field Descriptions (Continued)*

Field	Description
Report # 1 of Top N hosts entry 1 is recording	Report number and entry.
Host 0000.0c02.5808 at a rate of	Physical address of the host, and the amount of change in the selected variable during this sampling interval. Equivalent to hostTopNAddress and hostTopNRate in RMON.

Related Commands

To locate documentation of related commands, you can search online at www.cisco.com.

rmon
rmon alarm
rmon event
show rmon

show rtr application

Use the **show rtr application** EXEC command to display global information about the response time reporter feature.

show rtr application [tabular | full]

Syntax	Description
tabular	(Optional) Display information in a column format reducing the number of screens required to display the information.
full	(Optional) Display all information using identifiers next to each displayed value. This is the default.

Default

Full format

Command Mode

EXEC

Usage Guidelines

This command first appeared in Cisco IOS Release 11.2.

Use the **show rtr application** command to display information such as supported operation types and supported protocols.

Sample Display

The following is sample output from the **show rtr application** command in full format:

```
Router# show rtr application

        Response Time Reporter
Version: 1.0.0 Initial Round Trip Time MIB
Max Packet Data Size (ARR and Data): 16384
Time of Last Change in Whole RTR: *16:49:53.000 UTC Thu May 16 1996
System Max Number of Entries: 20

        Supported Operation Types
Type of Operation to Perform: echo
Type of Operation to Perform: pathEcho

        Supported Protocols
Protocol Type: ipIcmpEcho
Protocol Type: snaRUEcho
Protocol Type: snaLU0EchoAppl
Protocol Type: snaLU2EchoAppl
```

Related Commands

To locate documentation of related commands, you can search online at www.cisco.com.

show rtr configuration

show rtr collection-statistics

Use the **show rtr collection-statistics** EXEC command to display statistical errors for all response time reporter probes or the specified probe.

show rtr collection-statistics [*probe*] [**tabular** | **full**]

Syntax	Description
probe	(Optional) Number of the response time reporter probe to display.
tabular	(Optional) Display information in a column format reducing the number of screens required to display the information.

Syntax	Description
full	(Optional) Display all information using identifiers next to each displayed value. This is the default.

Default

Full format for all probes

Command Mode

EXEC

Usage Guidelines

This command first appeared in Cisco IOS Release 11.2.

Use the **show rtr collection-statistics** command to display information such as the number of failed operations and the failure reason. You can also use the **show rtr distribution-statistics** and **show rtr totals-statistics** commands to display additional statistical information.

Sample Display

The following is sample output from the **show rtr collection-statistics** command in full format.

```
Router# show rtr collection-statistics 1

        Collected Statistics
Entry Number: 1
Start Time Index: *17:15:41.000 UTC Thu May 16 1996
Path Index: 1
Hop in Path Index: 1
Number of Failed Operations due to a Disconnect: 0
Number of Failed Operations due to a Timeout: 0
Number of Failed Operations due to a Busy: 0
Number of Failed Operations due to a No Connection: 0
Number of Failed Operations due to an Internal Error: 0
Number of Failed Operations due to a Sequence Error: 0
Number of Failed Operations due to a Verify Error: 0
Target Address: 172.16.1.176
```

Part
III

Command Reference

Related Commands

To locate documentation of related commands, you can search online at www.cisco.com.

show rtr configuration
show rtr distributions-statistics
show rtr totals-statistics

show rtr configuration

Use the **show rtr configuration** EXEC command to display configuration values including all defaults for all response time reporter probes or the specified probe.

show rtr configuration [*probe*] [**tabular** | **full**]

Syntax	Description
probe	(Optional) Number of the response time reporter probe to display.
tabular	(Optional) Display information in a column format reducing the number of screens required to display the information.
full	(Optional) Display all information using identifiers next to each displayed value. This is the default.

Default

Full format for all probes

Command Mode

EXEC

Usage Guidelines

This command first appeared in Cisco IOS Release 11.2.

Sample Display

The following is sample output from the **show rtr configuration** command in full format:

```
Router# show rtr configuration 1

        Complete Configuration Table (includes defaults)
Entry Number: 1
Owner: "Sample Owner"
```

```
Tag: "Sample Tag Group"
Type of Operation to Perform: echo
Reaction and History Threshold (milliseconds): 5000
Operation Frequency (seconds): 60
Operation Timeout (milliseconds): 5000
Verify Data: FALSE
Status of Entry (SNMP RowStatus): active
Protocol Type: ipIcmpEcho
Target Address: 172.16.1.176
Request Size (ARR data portion): 1
Response Size (ARR data portion): 1
Life (seconds): 3600
Next Start Time: Start Time already passed
Entry Ageout (seconds): 3600
Connection Loss Reaction Enabled: FALSE
Timeout Reaction Enabled: FALSE
Threshold Reaction Type: never
Threshold Falling (milliseconds): 3000
Threshold Count: 5
Threshold Count2: 5
Reaction Type: none
Number of Statistic Hours kept: 2
Number of Statistic Paths kept: 1
Number of Statistic Hops kept: 1
Number of Statistic Distribution Buckets kept: 1
Number of Statistic Distribution Intervals (milliseconds): 20
Number of History Lives kept: 0
Number of History Buckets kept: 50
Number of History Samples kept: 1
History Filter Type: none
```

Related Commands

To locate documentation of related commands, you can search online at www.cisco.com.

show rtr application
show rtr collection-statistics
show rtr distributions-statistics
show rtr history
show rtr operational-state
show rtr reaction-trigger
show rtr totals-statistics

show rtr distributions-statistics

Use the **show rtr distributions-statistics** EXEC command to display statistic distribution information (captured response times) for all response time reporter probes or the specified probe.

show rtr distributions-statistics [*probe*] [**tabular** | **full**]

Syntax	Description
probe	(Optional) Number of the response time reporter probe to display.
tabular	(Optional) Display information in a column format reducing the number of screens required to display the information. This is the default.
full	(Optional) Display all information using identifiers next to each displayed value.

Default

Tabular format for all probes

Command Mode

EXEC

Usage Guidelines

This command first appeared in Cisco IOS Release 11.2.

The distributions statistics consist of:

● The sum of completion times (used to calculate the mean)

● The sum of the completions times squared (used to calculate standard deviation)

● The maximum and minimum completion time

● The number of completed attempts

You can also use the **show rtr collection-statistics** and **show rtr totals-statistics** commands to display additional statistical information.

Sample Display

The following is sample output from the **show rtr distributions-statistics** command in tabular format:

```
Router# show rtr distributions-statistics

        Captured Statistics
        Multiple Lines per Entry
Line 1
Entry   = Entry Number
StartT  = Start Time of Entry (hundredths of seconds)
Pth     = Path Index
Hop     = Hop in Path Index
Dst     = Time Distribution Index
```

```
Comps     = Operations Completed
OvrTh     = Operations Completed Over Thresholds
SumCmp    = Sum of Completion Times (milliseconds)
Line 2
SumCmp2L = Sum of Completion Times Squared Low 32 Bits (milliseconds)
SumCmp2H = Sum of Completion Times Squared High 32 Bits (milliseconds)
TMax      = Completion Time Maximum (milliseconds)
TMin      = Completion Time Minimum (milliseconds)
Entry StartT       Pth Hop Dst Comps        OvrTh        SumCmp
  SumCmp2L   SumCmp2H   TMax        TMin
1     17417068   1   1   1   2            0            128
   8192       0          64          64
```

Related Commands

To locate documentation of related commands, you can search online at www.cisco.com.

show rtr collection-statistics
show rtr configuration
show rtr totals-statistics

show rtr history

Use the **show rtr history** EXEC command to display history collected for all response time reporter probes or the specified probe.

show rtr history [*probe*] [**tabular** | **full**]

Syntax	Description
probe	(Optional) Number of the response time reporter probe to display.
tabular	(Optional) Display information in a column format reducing the number of screens required to display the information. This is the default.
full	(Optional) Display all information using identifiers next to each displayed value.

Default

Tabular format for all probes

Command Mode

EXEC

Usage Guidelines

This command first appeared in Cisco IOS Release 11.2.

The response return codes are listed in Table 24-11.

Table 24-11   *Response Return Codes*

Code	Meaning
1	Okay
2	Disconnected
3	Over threshold
4	Timeout
5	Busy
6	Not connected
7	Dropped
8	Sequence error
9	Verify error
10	Application specific

Sample Display

The following is sample output from the **show rtr history** command in tabular format:

```
Router# show rtr history

        Point by point History
          Multiple Lines per Entry
Line 1
Entry    = Entry Number
LifeI    = Life Index
BucketI  = Bucket Index
SampleI  = Sample Index
SampleT  = Sample Start Time
CompT    = Completion Time (milliseconds)
Sense    = Response Return Code
Line 2 has the Target Address
Entry LifeI     BucketI    SampleI    SampleT    CompT    Sense
2     1         1          1          17436548   16       1
  AB 45 A0 16
2     1         2          1          17436551   4        1
  AC 12 7   29
2     1         2          2          17436551   1        1
  AC 12 5   22
2     1         2          3          17436552   4        1
  AB 45 A7 22
2     1         2          4          17436552   4        1
  AB 45 A0 16
```

Related Commands

To locate documentation of related commands, you can search online at www.cisco.com.

show rtr configuration

show rtr operational-state

Use the **show rtr operational-state** EXEC command to display the operational state of all response time reporter probes or the specified probe.

> **show rtr operational-state** [*probe*] [**tabular** | **full**]

Syntax	Description
probe	(Optional) Number of the response time reporter probe to display.
tabular	(Optional) Display information in a column format reducing the number of screens required to display the information.
full	(Optional) Display all information using identifiers next to each displayed value. This is the default.

Default

Full format for all probes

Command Mode

EXEC

Usage Guidelines

This command first appeared in Cisco IOS Release 11.2.

Use the **show rtr operational-state** command to determine whether a connection loss, timeout, and over threshold occurred; how much life the probe has left; whether the probe is active; and the completion time. It also displays the results of the latest operation attempt.

Sample Display

The following is sample output from the **show rtr operational-state** command in full format:

```
Router# show rtr operational-state 1
      Current Operational State
```

Part
III

Command Reference

```
Entry Number: 1
Modification Time: *17:15:41.000 UTC Thu May 16 1996
Diagnostics Text:
Last Time this Entry was Reset: Never
Number of Octets in use by this Entry: 2438
Connection Loss Occurred: FALSE
Timeout Occurred: FALSE
Over Thresholds Occurred: FALSE
Number of Operations Attempted: 6
Current Seconds Left in Life: 3336
Operational State of Entry: active
Latest Completion Time (milliseconds): 60
Latest Operation Return Code: ok
Latest Operation Start Time: *17:19:41.000 UTC Thu May 16 1996
Latest Target Address: 172.16.1.176
```

Related Commands

To locate documentation of related commands, you can search online at www.cisco.com.

show rtr configuration

show rtr reaction-trigger

Use the **show rtr reaction-trigger** EXEC command to display the reaction trigger information for all response time reporter probes or the specified probe.

show rtr reaction-trigger [*probe*] [**tabular** | **full**]

Syntax	Description
probe	(Optional) Number of the response time reporter probe to display.
tabular	(Optional) Display information in a column format reducing the number of screens required to display the information.
full	(Optional) Display all information using identifiers next to each displayed value. This is the default.

Default

Full format for all probes

Command Mode

EXEC

Usage Guidelines

This command first appeared in Cisco IOS Release 11.2.

Use the **show rtr reaction-trigger** command to display the configuration status and operational state of target probes that will be triggered as defined with the **rtr reaction-configuration** global command.

Sample Display

The following is sample output from the **show rtr reaction-trigger** command in full format:

```
Router# show rtr reaction-trigger 1

        Reaction Table
Entry Number: 1
Target Entry Number: 2
Status of Entry (SNMP RowStatus): active
Operational State: pending
```

Related Commands

To locate documentation of related commands, you can search online at www.cisco.com.

show rtr configuration

show rtr totals-statistics

Use the **show rtr totals-statistics** EXEC command to display the total statistical values (accumulation of error counts and completions) for all response time reporter probes or the specified probe.

show rtr totals-statistics [*probe*] [**tabular** | **full**]

Syntax	Description
probe	(Optional) Number of the response time reporter probe to display.
tabular	(Optional) Display information in a column format reducing the number of screens required to display the information.
full	(Optional) Display all information using identifiers next to each displayed value. This is the default.

Default

Full format for all probes

Part III

Command Reference

Command Mode

EXEC

Usage Guidelines

This command first appeared in Cisco IOS Release 11.2.

The total statistics consist of the following items:

● The probe number

● The start time of the current hour of statistics

● The age of the current hour of statistics

● The number of attempted operations

You can also use the **show rtr distributions-statistics** and **show rtr collection-statistics** commands to display additional statistical information.

Sample Display

The following is sample output from the **show rtr totals-statistics** command in full format:

```
Router# show rtr totals-statistics

        Statistic Totals
Entry Number: 1
Start Time Index: *17:15:41.000 UTC Thu May 16 1996
Age of Statistics Entry (hundredths of seconds): 48252
Number of Initiations: 10
```

Related Commands

To locate documentation of related commands, you can search online at www.cisco.com.

show rtr collection-statistics
show rtr configuration
show rtr distributions-statistics

show snmp

To check the status of SNMP communications, use the **show snmp** EXEC command.

show snmp

Syntax Description

This command has no arguments or keywords.

Command Mode

EXEC

Usage Guidelines

This command first appeared in Cisco IOS Release 10.0.

This command provides counter information for SNMP operations. It also displays the chassis ID string defined with the **snmp-server chassis-id** command.

Sample Display

The following is sample output from the **show snmp** command:

```
Router# show snmp

Chassis: 01506199
37 SNMP packets input
    0 Bad SNMP version errors
    4 Unknown community name
    0 Illegal operation for community name supplied
    0 Encoding errors
    24 Number of requested variables
    0 Number of altered variables
    0 Get-request PDUs
    28 Get-next PDUs
    0 Set-request PDUs
78 SNMP packets output
    0 Too big errors (Maximum packet size 1500)
    0 No such name errors
    0 Bad values errors
    0 General errors
    24 Response PDUs
    13 Trap PDUs

SNMP logging: enabled
    Logging to 171.69.58.33.162, 0/10, 13 sent, 0 dropped.

SNMP Manager-role output packets
    4 Get-request PDUs
    4 Get-next PDUs
    6 Get-bulk PDUs
    4 Set-request PDUs
    23 Inform-request PDUs
    30 Timeouts
```

```
    0 Drops
SNMP Manager-role input packets
    0 Inform response PDUs
    2 Trap PDUs
    7 Response PDUs
    1 Responses with errors

SNMP informs: enabled
    Informs in flight 0/25 (current/max)
    Logging to 171.69.217.141.162
        4 sent, 0 in-flight, 1 retries, 0 failed, 0 dropped
    Logging to 171.69.58.33.162
        0 sent, 0 in-flight, 0 retries, 0 failed, 0 dropped
```

Table 24-12 describes the fields shown in the display.

Table 24-12 *Show SNMP Field Descriptions*

Field	Description
Chassis	Chassis ID string.
SNMP packets input	Total number of SNMP packets input.
Bad SNMP version errors	Number of packets with an invalid SNMP version.
Unknown community name	Number of SNMP packets with an unknown community name.
Illegal operation for community name supplied	Number of packets requesting an operation not allowed for that community.
Encoding errors	Number of SNMP packets that were improperly encoded.
Number of requested variables	Number of variables requested by SNMP managers.
Number of altered variables	Number of variables altered by SNMP managers.
Get-request PDUs	Number of get requests received.
Get-next PDUs	Number of get-next requests received.
Set-request PDUs	Number of set requests received.
SNMP packets output	Total number of SNMP packets sent by the router.
Too big errors	Number of SNMP packets which were larger than the maximum packet size.
Maximum packet size	Maximum size of SNMP packets.
No such name errors	Number of SNMP requests that specified a MIB object which does not exist.
Bad values errors	Number of SNMP set requests that specified an invalid value for a MIB object.
General errors	Number of SNMP set requests that failed due to some other error. (It was not a noSuchName error, badValue error, or any of the other specific errors.)
Response PDUs	Number of responses sent in reply to requests.
Trap PDUs	Number of SNMP traps sent.

Table 24-12 *Show SNMP Field Descriptions (Continued)*

Field	Description
SNMP logging	Indicates whether logging is enabled or disabled.
Sent	Number of traps sent.
Dropped	Number of traps dropped. Traps are dropped when the trap queue for a destination exceeds the maximum length of the queue, as set by the **snmp-server queue-length** command.
SNMP Manager-role output packets	Information related to packets sent by the router as an SNMP manager.
Get-request PDUs	Number of get requests sent.
Get-next PDUs	Number of get-next requests sent.
Get-bulk PDUs	Number of get-bulk requests sent.
Set-request PDUs	Number of set requests sent.
Inform-request PDUs	Number of inform requests sent.
Timeouts	Number of request timeouts.
Drops	Number of requests dropped. Reasons for drops include no memory, a bad destination address, or an unreasonable destination address.
SNMP Manager-role input packets	Information related to packets received by the router as an SNMP manager.
Inform response PDUs	Number of inform request responses received.
Trap PDUs	Number of SNMP traps received.
Response PDUs	Number of responses received.
Responses with errors	Number of responses containing errors.
SNMP informs	Indicates whether SNMP informs are enabled.
Informs in flight	Current and maximum possible number of informs waiting to be acknowledged.
Logging to	Destination of the following informs.
Sent	Number of informs sent to this host.
In-flight	Number of informs currently waiting to be acknowledged.
Retries	Number of inform retries sent.
Failed	Number of informs that were never acknowledged.
Dropped	Number of unacknowledged informs that were discarded to make room for new informs.

Related Commands

To locate documentation of related commands, you can search online at www.cisco.com.

show snmp pending
show snmp sessions
snmp-server chassis-id
snmp-server manager
snmp-server manager session-timeout
snmp-server queue-length

show snmp pending

To display the current set of pending SNMP requests, use the **show snmp pending** EXEC command.

>   **show snmp pending**

Syntax Description

This command has no arguments or keywords.

Command Mode

EXEC

Usage Guidelines

This command first appeared in Cisco IOS Release 11.3 T.

After the SNMP manager sends a request, the request is "pending" until the manager receives a response or the request timeout expires.

Sample Display

The following is sample output from the **show snmp pending** command:

```
Router# show snmp pending

req id: 47, dest: 171.69.58.33.161, V2C community: public, Expires in 5 secs
req id: 49, dest: 171.69.58.33.161, V2C community: public, Expires in 6 secs
req id: 51, dest: 171.69.58.33.161, V2C community: public, Expires in 6 secs
req id: 53, dest: 171.69.58.33.161, V2C community: public, Expires in 8 secs
```

Table 24-13 describes the fields shown in the display.

Table 24-13 *Show SNMP Pending Field Descriptions*

Field	Description
req id	ID number of the pending request.
dest	IP address of the intended receiver of the request.
V2C Community	SNMP version 2C community string sent with the request.
Expires in	Remaining time before request timeout expires.

Related Commands

To locate documentation of related commands, you can search online at www.cisco.com.

show snmp
show snmp sessions
snmp-server manager
snmp-server manager session-timeout

show snmp sessions

To display the current SNMP sessions, use the **show snmp sessions** EXEC command.

> **show snmp sessions [brief]**

Syntax	Description
brief	(Optional) Displays a list of sessions only. Does not display session statistics.

Command Mode

EXEC

Usage Guidelines

This command first appeared in Cisco IOS Release 11.3 T.

Sessions are created when the SNMP manager in the router sends SNMP requests, such as inform requests, to a host or receives SNMP notifications from a host. One session is created for each destination host. If there is no further communication between the router and host within the session timeout period, the corresponding session will be deleted.

Sample Display

The following is sample output from the **show snmp sessions** command:

```
Router# show snmp sessions

Destination: 171.69.58.33.162, V2C community: public
  Round-trip-times: 0/0/0 (min/max/last)
  packets output
    0 Gets, 0 GetNexts, 0 GetBulks, 0 Sets, 4 Informs
    0 Timeouts, 0 Drops
  packets input
    0 Traps, 0 Informs, 0 Responses (0 errors)
Destination: 171.69.217.141.162, V2C community: public, Expires in 575 secs
  Round-trip-times: 1/1/1 (min/max/last)
  packets output
    0 Gets, 0 GetNexts, 0 GetBulks, 0 Sets, 4 Informs
    0 Timeouts, 0 Drops
  packets input
    0 Traps, 0 Informs, 4 Responses (0 errors)
```

The following is sample output from the **show snmp sessions brief** command:

```
Router# show snmp sessions brief

Destination: 171.69.58.33.161, V2C community: public, Expires in 55 secs
```

Table 24-14 describes the fields shown in these displays.

Table 24-14   *Show SNMP Sessions Field Descriptions*

Field	Description
Destination	IP address of the remote agent.
V2C community	SNMP version 2C community string used to communicate with the remote agent.
Expires in	Remaining time before the session timeout expires.
Round-trip-times	Minimum, maximum, and the last round-trip time to the agent.
Packets output	Packets sent by the router.
Gets	Number of get requests sent.
GetNexts	Number of get-next requests sent.
GetBulks	Number of get-bulk requests sent.
Sets	Number of set requests sent.
Informs	Number of inform requests sent.
Timeouts	Number of request timeouts.
Drops	Number of packets that could not be sent.
Packets input	Packets received by the router.

Table 24-14 *Show SNMP Sessions Field Descriptions (Continued)*

Field	Description
Traps	Number of traps received.
Informs	Number of inform responses received.
Responses	Number of request responses received.
Errors	Number of responses that contained an SNMP error code.

Related Commands

To locate documentation of related commands, you can search online at www.cisco.com.

show snmp
show snmp pending
snmp-server manager
snmp-server manager session-timeout

snmp-server access-policy

This command is no longer valid. The functionality provided by this command has been removed from the Cisco IOS software.

snmp-server chassis-id

To provide a message line identifying the SNMP server serial number, use the **snmp-server chassis-id** global configuration command. Use the **no** form of this command to restore the default value, if any.

> **snmp-server chassis-id** *text*
> **no snmp-server chassis-id**

Syntax

text Message you want to enter to identify the chassis serial number.

Default

On hardware platforms where the serial number can be machine read, the default is the serial number. For example, a Cisco 7000 has a default value of its serial number.

Command Mode

Global configuration

Usage Guidelines

This command first appeared in Cisco IOS Release 10.0.

The Cisco MIB provides a chassis MIB variable that enables the SNMP manager to gather data on system card descriptions, chassis type, chassis hardware version, chassis ID string, software version of ROM monitor, software version of system image in ROM, bytes of processor RAM installed, bytes of NVRAM installed, bytes of NVRAM in use, current configuration register setting, and the value of the configuration register at the next reload. The following installed card information is provided: type of card, serial number, hardware version, software version, and chassis slot number.

The chassis ID message can be seen with the **show snmp** command.

Example

In the following example, the chassis serial number specified is 1234456:

```
snmp-server chassis-id 1234456
```

Related Commands

To locate documentation of related commands, you can search online at www.cisco.com.

show snmp

snmp-server community

To set up the community access string to permit access to the SNMP protocol, use the **snmp-server community** global configuration command. The **no** form of this command removes the specified community string.

>**snmp-server community** *string* [**view** *view-name*] [**ro** | **rw**] [*number*]
>**no snmp-server community** *string*

Syntax	Description
string	Community string that acts like a password and permits access to the SNMP protocol.
view view-name	(Optional) Name of a previously defined view. The view defines the objects available to the community.

Syntax	Description
ro	(Optional) Specifies read-only access. Authorized management stations are only able to retrieve MIB objects.
rw	(Optional) Specifies read-write access. Authorized management stations are able to both retrieve and modify MIB objects.
number	(Optional) Integer from 1 to 99 that specifies an access list of IP addresses that are allowed to use the community string to gain access to the SNMP agent.

Default

By default, an SNMP community string permits read-only access to all objects.

Command Mode

Global configuration

Usage Guidelines

This command first appeared in Cisco IOS Release 10.0.

The **no snmp-server** command disables both versions of SNMP (SNMPv1 and SNMPv2C).

The first **snmp-server** command that you enter enables both versions of SNMP.

Examples

The following example assigns the string comaccess to SNMP allowing read-only access and specifies that IP access list 4 can use the community string:

```
snmp-server community comaccess ro 4
```

The following example assigns the string mgr to SNMP allowing read-write access to the objects in the restricted view:

```
snmp-server community mgr view restricted rw
```

The following example removes the community comaccess:

```
no snmp-server community comaccess
```

The following example disables both versions of SNMP:

```
no snmp-server
```

Related Commands

To locate documentation of related commands, you can search online at www.cisco.com.

access-list
snmp-server view

snmp-server contact

To set the system contact (sysContact) string, use the **snmp-server contact** global configuration command. Use the **no** form to remove the system contact information.

> **snmp-server contact** *text*
> **no snmp-server contact**

Syntax   Description

text   String that describes the system contact information.

Default

No system contact string is set.

Command Mode

Global configuration

Usage Guidelines

This command first appeared in Cisco IOS Release 10.0.

Example

The following is an example of a system contact string:

```
snmp-server contact Dial System Operator at beeper # 27345
```

Related Commands

To locate documentation of related commands, you can search online at www.cisco.com.

snmp-server location

snmp-server context

This command is no longer valid. The functionality provided by this command has been removed from the Cisco IOS software.

snmp-server enable traps

To enable the router to send SNMP traps and informs, use the **snmp-server enable traps** global configuration command. Use the **no** form of this command to disable SNMP notifications.

> **snmp-server enable traps** [*notification-type*] [*notification-option*]
> **no snmp-server enable traps** [*notification-type*] [*notification-option*]

Syntax	Description
notification-type	(Optional) Type of notification to enable. If no type is specified, all notifications are sent (including the **envmon** and **repeater** notifications). The notification type can be one of the following keywords:

- **bgp**—Sends Border Gateway Protocol (BGP) state change notifications.
- **config**—Sends configuration notifications.
- **entity**—Sends Entity MIB modification notifications.
- **envmon**—Sends Cisco enterprise-specific environmental monitor notifications when an environmental threshold is exceeded. When the **envmon** keyword is used, you can specify a *notification-option* value.
- **frame-relay**—Sends Frame Relay notifications.
- **isdn**—Sends Integrated Services Digital Network (ISDN) notifications. When the **isdn** keyword is used on Cisco 1600 series routers, you can specify a *notification-option* value.
- **repeater**—Sends Ethernet hub repeater notifications. When the **repeater** keyword is selected, you can specify a *notification-option* value.
- **rtr**—Sends response time reporter (RTR) notifications.
- **snmp**—Sends Simple Network Management Protocol (SNMP) notifications. When the **snmp** keyword is used, you can specify a *notification-option* value.
- **syslog**—Sends error message notifications (Cisco Syslog MIB). Specify the level of messages to be sent with the **logging history level** command.

Part
III

Command Reference

Syntax	Description
notification-option	(Optional) When the **envmon** keyword is used, you can enable a specific environmental notification type, or accept all notification types from the environmental monitor system. If no option is specified, all environmental notifications are enabled. The option can be one or more of the following keywords: **voltage**, **shutdown**, **supply**, **fan**, and **temperature**.
	When the **isdn** keyword is used, you can specify the **call-information** keyword to enable an SNMP ISDN call information notification for the ISDN MIB subsystem, or you can specify the **isdnu-interface** keyword to enable an SNMP ISDN U interface notification for the ISDN U interface MIB subsystem.
	When the **repeater** keyword is used, you can specify the repeater option. If no option is specified, all repeater notifications are enabled. The option can be one or more of the following keywords:
	• **health**—Enables IETF Repeater Hub MIB (RFC 1516) health notification.
	• **reset**—Enables IETF Repeater Hub MIB (RFC 1516) reset notification.
	When the **snmp** keyword is used, you can specify the **authentication** option to enable SNMP Authentication Failure notifications. (The **snmp-sever enable traps snmp authentication** command replaces the **snmp-server trap-authentication** command.) If no option is specified, all SNMP notifications are enabled.

Defaults

This command is disabled by default. Most notification types are disabled. However, some notification types cannot be controlled with this command. For example, some notification types are always enabled. Other notification types are enabled by a different command. For example, the linkUpDown notifications are controlled by the **snmp trap link-status** command.

If you enter this command with no *notification-type* keywords, the default is to enable all notification types controlled by this command.

Command Mode

Global configuration

Usage Guidelines

This command first appeared in Cisco IOS Release 11.1.

This command is useful for disabling notifications that are generating a large amount of uninteresting or useless noise.

SNMP notifications can be sent as traps or inform requests. This command enables both traps and inform requests for the specified notification types.

If you do not enter an **snmp-server enable traps** command, no notifications controlled by this command are sent. In order to configure the router to send these SNMP notifications, you must enter at least one **snmp-server enable traps** command. If you enter the command with no keywords, all notification types are enabled. If you enter the command with a keyword, only the notification type related to that keyword is enabled. In order to enable multiple types of notifications, you must issue a separate **snmp-server enable traps** command for each notification type and notification option.

The **snmp-server enable traps** command is used in conjunction with the **snmp-server host** command. Use the **snmp-server host** command to specify which host or hosts receive SNMP notifications. In order to send notifications, you must configure at least one **snmp-server host** command.

For a host to receive a notification controlled by this command, both the **snmp-server enable traps** command and the **snmp-server host** command for that host must be enabled. If the notification type is not controlled by this command, just the appropriate **snmp-server host** command must be enabled.

The notification types used in this command all have an associated MIB object that allows them to be globally enabled or disabled. Not all of the notification types available in the **snmp-server host** command have notificationEnable MIB objects, so some of these cannot be controlled using the **snmp-server enable** command.

Examples

The following example enables the router to send all traps to the host myhost.cisco.com using the community string public:

```
snmp-server enable traps
snmp-server host myhost.cisco.com public
```

The following example enables the router to send Frame Relay and environmental monitor traps to the host myhost.cisco.com using the community string public:

```
snmp-server enable traps frame-relay
snmp-server enable traps envmon temperature
snmp-server host myhost.cisco.com public
```

The following example will not send traps to any host. The BGP traps are enabled for all hosts, but the only traps enabled to be sent to a host are ISDN traps.

```
snmp-server enable traps bgp
snmp-server host bob public isdn
```

The following example enables the router to send all inform requests to the host myhost.cisco.com using the community string public:

```
snmp-server enable traps
snmp-server host myhost.cisco.com informs version 2c public
```

Related Commands

To locate documentation of related commands, you can search online at www.cisco.com.

snmp-server host
snmp-server informs
snmp-server trap-source
snmp trap illegal-address

snmp-server host

To specify the recipient of an SNMP notification operation, use the **snmp-server host** global configuration command. Use the **no** form of this command to remove the specified host.

> **snmp-server host** *host* [**traps** | **informs**] [**version** {**1** | **2c**}] *community-string*
> [**udp-port** *port*] [*notification-type*]
> **no snmp-server host** *host* [**traps** | **informs**]

Syntax	Description
host	Name or Internet address of the host.
traps	(Optional) Send SNMP traps to this host. This is the default.
informs	(Optional) Send SNMP informs to this host.
version	(Optional) Version of the Simple Network Management Protocol (SNMP) used to send the traps.
	• **1**—SNMPv1. This option is not available with informs.
	• **2c** —SNMPv2C.
community-string	Password-like community string sent with the notification operation.
udp-port *port*	UDP port of the host to use. The default is 162.

Part
III

Command Reference

Syntax	Description
notification-type	(Optional) Type of notification to be sent to the host. If no type is specified, all notifications are sent. The notification type can be one or more of the following keywords:

- **bgp**—Sends Border Gateway Protocol (BGP) state change notifications.
- **config**—Sends configuration notifications.
- **dspu**—Sends downstream physical unit (DSPU) notifications.
- **entity**—Sends Entity MIB modification notifications.
- **envmon**—Sends Cisco enterprise-specific environmental monitor notifications when an environmental threshold is exceeded.
- **frame-relay**—Sends Frame Relay notifications.
- **isdn**—Sends Integrated Services Digital Network (ISDN) notifications.
- **llc2**—Sends Logical Link Control, type 2 (LLC2) notifications.
- **rptr**—Sends standard repeater (hub) notifications.
- **rsrb**—Sends remote source-route bridging (RSRB) notifications.
- **rtr**—Sends response time reporter (RTR) notifications.
- **sdlc**—Sends Synchronous Data Link Control (SDLC) notifications.
- **sdllc**—Sends SDLLC notifications.
- **snmp**—Sends Simple Network Management Protocol (SNMP) notifications defined in RFC 1157.
- **stun**—Sends serial tunnel (STUN) notifications.
- **syslog**—Sends error message notifications (Cisco Syslog MIB). Specify the level of messages to be sent with the **logging history level** command.
- **tty**—Sends Cisco enterprise-specific notifications when a Transmission Control Protocol (TCP) connection closes.
- **x25**—Sends X.25 event notifications.

Defaults

This command is disabled by default. No notifications are sent.

If you enter this command with no keywords, the default is to send all trap types to the host. No informs will be sent to this host.

If no **version** keyword is present, the default is version 1. If no **traps** or **informs** keyword is present, traps are enabled.

The **no snmp-server host** command with no keywords will disable traps, but not informs, to the host. In order to disable informs, use the **no snmp-server host informs** command.

Command Mode

Global configuration

Usage Guidelines

This command first appeared in Cisco IOS Release 10.0.

SNMP notifications can be sent as traps or inform requests. Traps are unreliable because the receiver does not send acknowledgments when it receives traps. The sender cannot determine if the traps were received. However, an SNMP entity that receives an inform request acknowledges the message with an SNMP response PDU. If the sender never receives the response, the inform request can be sent again. Thus, informs are more likely to reach their intended destination.

However, informs consume more resources in the agent and in the network. Unlike a trap, which is discarded as soon as it is sent, an inform request must be held in memory until a response is received or the request times out. Also, traps are sent only once, while an inform may be retried several times. The retries increase traffic and contribute to a higher overhead on the network.

If you do not enter an **snmp-server host** command, no notifications are sent. In order to configure the router to send SNMP notifications, you must enter at least one **snmp-server host** command. If you enter the command with no keywords, all trap types are enabled for the host. In order to enable multiple hosts, you must issue a separate **snmp-server host** command for each host. You can specify multiple notification types in the command for each host.

When multiple **snmp-server host** commands are given for the same host and kind of notification (trap or inform), each succeeding command overwrites the previous command. Only the last **snmp-server host** command will be in effect. For example, if you enter an **snmp-server host inform** command for a host and then enter another **snmp-server host inform** command for the same host, the second command will replace the first.

The **snmp-server host** command is used in conjunction with the **snmp-server enable** command. Use the **snmp-server enable** command to specify which SNMP notifications are sent globally. For a host to receive most notifications, at least one **snmp-server enable** command and the **snmp-server host** command for that host must be enabled.

However, some notification types cannot be controlled with the **snmp-server enable** command. For example, some notification types are always enabled. Other notification types are enabled by a different command. For example, the linkUpDown notifications are controlled by the **snmp trap link-status** command. These notification types do not require an **snmp-server enable** command.

A notification-type option's availability depends on the router type and Cisco IOS software features supported on the router. For example, the **envmon** notification-type is available only if the environmental monitor is part of the system.

Examples

The following example sends the SNMP traps defined in RFC 1157 to the host specified by the name myhost.cisco.com. The community string is defined as comaccess.

```
snmp-server enable traps
snmp-server host myhost.cisco.com comaccess snmp
```

The following example sends the SNMP and Cisco environmental monitor enterprise-specific traps to address 172.30.2.160:

```
snmp-server enable traps
snmp-server host 172.30.2.160 public snmp envmon
```

The following example enables the router to send all traps to the host myhost.cisco.com using the community string public:

```
snmp-server enable traps
snmp-server host myhost.cisco.com public
```

The following example will not send traps to any host. The BGP traps are enabled for all hosts, but only the ISDN traps are enabled to be sent to a host.

```
snmp-server enable traps bgp
snmp-server host bob public isdn
```

The following example enables the router to send all inform requests to the host myhost.cisco.com using the community string public:

```
snmp-server enable traps
snmp-server host myhost.cisco.com informs version 2c public
```

Related Commands

To locate documentation of related commands, you can search online at www.cisco.com.

snmp-server host
snmp-server informs
snmp-server trap-source
snmp-server trap-timeout

snmp-server informs

To specify inform request options, use the **snmp-server informs** global configuration command. The **no** form of this command returns the settings to the defaults.

> **snmp-server informs** [**retries** *retries*] [**timeout** *seconds*] [**pending** *pending*]
> **no snmp-server informs** [**retries** *retries*] [**timeout** *seconds*] [**pending** *pending*]

Syntax	Description
retries *retries*	(Optional) Maximum number of times to resend an inform request. The default is 3.
timeout *second*	(Optional) Number of seconds to wait for an acknowledgment before resending. The default is 30 seconds.
pending *pending*	(Optional) Maximum number of informs waiting for acknowledgments at any one time. When the maximum is reached, older pending informs are discarded. The default is 25.

Default

Inform requests are resent three times. Informs are resent after 30 seconds if no response is received. The maximum number of informs waiting for acknowledgments at any one time is 25.

Command Mode

Global configuration

Usage Guidelines

This command first appeared in Cisco IOS Release 11.3 T.

Examples

If you are seeing a large number of inform drops, you may want to increase the pending queue size.

```
snmp-server informs pending 50
```

If you are sending informs over slow network links, you may want to increase the default timeout. Since informs will be sitting in the queue for a longer period of time, you may also need to increase the pending queue size.

```
snmp-server informs timeout 60 pending 40
```

If you are sending informs over very fast links, you may want to decrease the default timeout.

```
snmp-server informs timeout 5
```

If you are sending informs over unreliable links, it may be desirable to increase the retry count. Since informs will be sitting in the queue for a longer period of time, you may need to increase the pending queue size.

```
snmp-server informs retries 10 pending 45
```

Related Commands

To locate documentation of related commands, you can search online at www.cisco.com.

snmp-server enable traps

snmp-server location

To set the system location string, use the **snmp-server location** global configuration command. Use the **no** form of this command to remove the location string.

> **snmp-server location** *text*
> **no snmp-server location**

Syntax	Description
text	String that describes the system location information.

Default

No system location string is set.

Command Mode

Global configuration

Usage Guidelines

This command first appeared in Cisco IOS Release 10.0.

Example

The following example illustrates a system location string:

```
snmp-server location Building 3/Room 214
```

Related Commands

To locate documentation of related commands, you can search online at www.cisco.com.

snmp-server contact

snmp-server manager

To start the SNMP manager process, use the **snmp-server manager** global configuration command. The **no** form of this command stops the SNMP manager process.

> **snmp-server manager**
> **no snmp-server manager**

Syntax Description

This command has no arguments or keywords.

Default

Disabled

Command Mode

Global configuration

Usage Guidelines

This command first appeared in Cisco IOS Release 11.3 T.

The SNMP manager process sends SNMP requests to agents and receives SNMP responses and notifications from agents. When the SNMP manager process is enabled, the router can query other SNMP agents and process incoming SNMP traps.

Most network security policies assume that routers will be accepting SNMP requests, sending SNMP responses, and sending SNMP notifications. With the SNMP manager functionality enabled, the router may also be sending SNMP requests, receiving SNMP responses, and receiving SNMP notifications. The security policy implementation may need to be updated prior to enabling this functionality.

SNMP requests are typically sent to UDP port 161. SNMP responses are typically sent from UDP port 161. SNMP notifications are typically sent to UDP port 162.

Example

The following example enables the SNMP manager process:

```
snmp-server manager
```

Related Commands

To locate documentation of related commands, you can search online at www.cisco.com.

show snmp
show snmp pending
show snmp sessions
snmp-server manager session-timeout

snmp-server manager session-timeout

To set the amount of time before a non-active session is destroyed, use the **snmp-server manager session-timeout** global configuration command. The **no** form of this command returns the value to its default.

> **snmp-server manager session-timeout** *seconds*
> **no snmp-server manager session-timeout**

Syntax	Description
seconds	Number of seconds before an idle session is timed out.

Default

Idle sessions time out after 600 seconds (10 minutes).

Command Mode

Global configuration

Usage Guidelines

This command first appeared in Cisco IOS Release 11.3 T.

Sessions are created when the SNMP manager in the router sends SNMP requests, such as inform requests, to a host or receives SNMP notifications from a host. One session is created for each destination host. If there is no further communication between the router and host within the session timeout period, the session will be deleted.

The router tracks statistics, such as the average round-trip time required to reach the host, for each session. Using the statistics for a session, the SNMP manager in the router can set reasonable timeout periods for future requests, such as informs, for that host. If the session is deleted, all statistics are lost. If another session with the same host is later created, the request timeout value for replies will return to the default value.

However, sessions consume memory. A reasonable session timeout value should be large enough such that regularly used sessions are not prematurely deleted, yet small enough such that irregularly used, or one-shot sessions, are purged expeditiously.

Example

The following example sets the session timeout to a larger value than the default:

```
snmp-server manager
snmp-server manager session-timeout 1000
```

Related Commands

To locate documentation of related commands, you can search online at www.cisco.com.

show snmp pending
show snmp sessions
snmp-server manager

snmp-server packetsize

To establish control over the largest SNMP packet size permitted when the SNMP server is receiving a request or generating a reply, use the **snmp-server packetsize** global configuration command. Use the **no** form of this command to restore the default value.

> **snmp-server packetsize** *byte-count*
> **no snmp-server packetsize**

Syntax	Description
byte-count	Integer byte count from 484 to 8,192.

Default

1,500 bytes

Command Mode

Global configuration

Usage Guidelines

This command first appeared in Cisco IOS Release 10.0.

Example

The following example establishes a packet filtering of a maximum size of 1,024 bytes:

```
snmp-server packetsize 1024
```

Related Commands

To locate documentation of related commands, you can search online at www.cisco.com.

snmp-server queue-length

snmp-server party

This command is no longer valid. The functionality provided by this command has been removed from the Cisco IOS software.

snmp-server queue-length

To establish the message queue length for each trap host, use the **snmp-server queue-length** global configuration command.

        snmp-server queue-length *length*

Syntax	Description
length	Integer that specifies the number of trap events that can be held before the queue must be emptied.

Default

10 events

Command Mode

Global configuration

Usage Guidelines

This command first appeared in Cisco IOS Release 10.0.

This command defines the length of the message queue for each trap host. Once a trap message is successfully transmitted, software will continue to empty the queue, but never faster than at a rate of four trap messages per second.

Example

The following example establishes a message queue that traps four events before it must be emptied:

```
snmp-server queue-length 4
```

Part
III

Command Reference

Related Commands

To locate documentation of related commands, you can search online at www.cisco.com.

snmp-server packetsize

snmp-server system-shutdown

To use the SNMP message reload feature, the router configuration must include the **snmp-server system-shutdown** global configuration command. The **no** form of this command prevents an SNMP system-shutdown request (from an SNMP manager) from resetting the Cisco agent.

> **snmp-server system-shutdown**
> **no snmp-server system-shutdown**

Syntax Description

This command has no arguments or keywords.

Default

This command is not included in the configuration file.

Command Mode

Global configuration

Usage Guidelines

This command first appeared in Cisco IOS Release 10.0.

Example

The following example enables the SNMP message reload feature:

```
snmp-server system-shutdown
```

snmp-server tftp-server-list

To limit the TFTP servers used via SNMP-controlled TFTP operations (saving and loading configuration files) to the servers specified in an access list, use the **snmp-server tftp-server-list** global configuration command. To disable this feature, use the **no** form of this command.

snmp-server tftp-server-list *number*
no snmp-server tftp-server-list

Syntax   Description

number	Standard IP access list number from 1 to 99.

Default
Disabled

Command Mode
Global configuration

Usage Guidelines
This command first appeared in Cisco IOS Release 10.2.

Example
The following example limits the TFTP servers that can be used for configuration file copies via SNMP to the servers in access list 44:

```
snmp-server tftp-server-list 44
```

snmp-server trap-authentication

The **snmp-server enable traps snmp authentication** command replaces this command. Refer to the description of **snmp-server host** for more information.

snmp-server trap-source

To specify the interface (and hence the corresponding IP address) that an SNMP trap should originate from, use the **snmp-server trap-source** global configuration command. Use the **no** form of the command to remove the source designation.

snmp-server trap-source *interface*
no snmp-server trap-source

Syntax	Description
interface	Interface from which the SNMP trap originates. The argument includes the interface type and number in platform-specific syntax.

Default

No interface is specified.

Command Mode

Global configuration

Usage Guidelines

This command first appeared in Cisco IOS Release 10.0.

When an SNMP trap is sent from a Cisco SNMP server, it has a trap address of whatever interface it happened to go out of at that time. Use this command if you want to use the trap address to trace particular needs.

Examples

The following example specifies that the IP address for interface Ethernet 0 is the source for all traps:

```
snmp-server trap-source ethernet 0
```

The following example specifies that the IP address for interface Ethernet 2/1 on a Cisco 7000 is the source for all traps:

```
snmp-server trap-source ethernet 2/1
```

Related Commands

To locate documentation of related commands, you can search online at www.cisco.com.

snmp-server enable traps
snmp-server host

snmp-server trap-timeout

To define how often to try resending trap messages on the retransmission queue, use the **snmp-server trap-timeout** global configuration command.

        snmp-server trap-timeout *seconds*

Syntax	Description
seconds	Integer that sets the interval, in seconds, for resending the messages.

Default

30 seconds

Command Mode

Global configuration

Usage Guidelines

This command first appeared in Cisco IOS Release 10.0.

Before the Cisco IOS software tries to send a trap, it looks for a route to the destination address. If there is no known route, the trap is saved in a retransmission queue. The **server trap-timeout** command determines the number of seconds between retransmission attempts.

Example

The following example sets an interval of 20 seconds to try resending trap messages on the retransmission queue:

```
snmp-server trap-timeout 20
```

Related Commands

To locate documentation of related commands, you can search online at www.cisco.com.

snmp-server host
snmp-server queue-length

snmp-server view

To create or update a view entry, use the **snmp-server view** global configuration command. To remove the specified SNMP server view entry, use the **no** form of this command.

> **snmp-server view** *view-name oid-tree* {**included** | **excluded**}
> **no snmp-server view** *view-name*

Syntax	Description
view-name	Label for the view record that you are updating or creating. The name is used to reference the record.
oid-tree	Object identifier of the ASN.1 subtree to be included or excluded from the view. To identify the subtree, specify a text string consisting of numbers, such as *1.3.6.2.4*, or a word, such as *system*. Replace a single subidentifier with the asterisk (*) wildcard to specify a subtree family; for example 1.3.*.4.
included | excluded	Type of view. You must specify either **included** or **excluded**.

Default

No view entry exists.

Command Mode

Global configuration

Usage Guidelines

This command first appeared in Cisco IOS Release 10.0.

Other SNMP commands require a view as an argument. You use this command to create a view to be used as arguments for other commands that create records including a view.

Two standard predefined views can be used when a view is required, instead of defining a view. One is *everything*, which indicates that the user can see all objects. The other is *restricted,* which indicates that the user can see three groups: system, snmpStats, and snmpParties. The predefined views are described in RFC 1447.

The first **snmp-server** command that you enter enables both versions of SNMP.

Examples

The following example creates a view that includes all objects in the MIB-II subtree:

```
snmp-server view mib2 mib-2 included
```

The following example creates a view that includes all objects in the MIB-II system group and all objects in the Cisco enterprise MIB:

```
snmp-server view phred system included
snmp-server view phred cisco included
```

The following example creates a view that includes all objects in the MIB-II system group except for sysServices (System 7) and all objects for interface 1 in the MIB-II interfaces group:

```
snmp-server view agon system included
snmp-server view agon system.7 excluded
snmp-server view agon ifEntry.*.1 included
```

Related Commands

To locate documentation of related commands, you can search online at www.cisco.com.

snmp-server community

snmp trap link-status

To enable SNMP link trap generation, use the **snmp trap link-status** interface configuration command. To disable SNMP link traps, use the **no** form of this command.

> **snmp trap link-status**
> **no snmp trap link-status**

Syntax Description

This command has no arguments or keywords.

Default

SNMP link traps are sent when an interface goes up or down.

Command Mode

Interface configuration

Usage Guidelines

This command appeared before Cisco IOS Release 10.0.

By default, SNMP link traps are sent when an interface goes up or down. For interfaces expected to go up and down during normal usage, such as ISDN interfaces, the output generated by these traps may not be useful. The **no** form of this command disables these traps.

Example

This example disables the sending of SNMP link traps related to the ISDN BRI 0 interface.

```
interface bri 0
 no snmp trap link-status
```

statistics-distribution-interval

To set the time interval for each statistics distribution kept for the response time reporter, use the **statistics-distribution-interval** response time reporter configuration command. Use the **no** form of this command to return to the default value.

> **statistics-distribution-interval** *milliseconds*
> **no statistics-distribution-interval**

Syntax	Description
milliseconds	Number of milliseconds used for each statistics distribution kept.

Default

20 ms

Command Mode

Response time reporter configuration

Usage Guidelines

This command first appeared in Cisco IOS Release 11.2.

In most situations, you do not need to change the statistical distribution interval or size. Only change the interval or size when distributions are needed, for example, when performing statistical modeling of your network. To set the statistical distributions size, use the **distributions-of-statistics-kept** response time reporter configuration command.

Example

In the following example, the distribution is set to five and the distribution interval is set to 10 ms. This means that the first distribution will contain statistics from 0 to 9 ms, the second distribution will contain statistics from 10 to 19 ms, the third distribution will contain statistics from 20 to 29 ms, the fourth distribution will contain statistics from 30 to 39 ms, and the fifth distribution will contain statistics from 40 ms to infinity.

```
rtr 1
 type echo protocol ipIcmpEcho 172.28.161.21
 distribution-of-statistics-kept 5
 statistics-distribution-interval 10
```

Related Commands

To locate documentation of related commands, you can search online at www.cisco.com.

distributions-of-statistics-kept
hops-of-statistics-kept
hours-of-statistics-kept
paths-of-statistics-kept
rtr

tag

To create a user-specified identifier for a response time reporter probe, use the **tag** response time reporter configuration command. It is normally used to logically link probes in a group. Use the **no** form of this command to remove a tag from a probe.

> **tag** *text*
> **no tag**

Part
III

Command Reference

Syntax	Description
text	Name of a group that this probe belongs to. From 0 to 16 ASCII characters.

Default

No probes are tagged.

Command Mode

Response time reporter configuration

Usage Guidelines

This command first appeared in Cisco IOS Release 11.2.

Tags can be used to support automation (for example, by using the same tag for two different probes on two different routers echoing the same target).

Example

In the following example, probe 1 is tagged with the label *bluebell*:

```
rtr 1
 type echo protocol ipIcmpEcho 172.16.1.176
 tag bluebell
```

Related Commands

To locate documentation of related commands, you can search online at www.cisco.com.

rtr

threshold

To set the rising threshold (hysteresis) that generates a reaction event and stores history information for the response time reporter probe, use the **threshold** response time reporter configuration command. Use the **no** form of this command to return to the default value.

> **threshold** *millisecond*
> **no threshold**

Syntax   Description

millisecond   Number of milliseconds required for a rising threshold to be declared.

Default

5000 ms

Command Mode

Response time reporter configuration

Usage Guidelines

This command first appeared in Cisco IOS Release 11.2.

The value specified for the **threshold** command must not exceed the value specified for the **timeout** response time reporter configuration command.

The threshold value is used by the **rtr reaction-configuration** and **filter-for-history** commands.

Example

In the following example, probe 1's threshold is set to 2500 ms:

```
rtr 1
 type echo protocol ipIcmpEcho 172.16.1.176
 threshold 2500
```

Related Commands

To locate documentation of related commands, you can search online at www.cisco.com.

filter-for-history
rtr
rtr reaction-configuration

timeout

To set the amount of time the response time reporter probe waits for a response from its request packet, use the **timeout** response time reporter configuration command. Use the **no** form of this command to return to the default value.

>   **timeout** *millisecond*
>   **no timeout**

Syntax   Description

millisecond   Number of milliseconds the probe waits to receive a response from its request packet.

Default

5000 ms

Command Mode

Response time reporter configuration

Usage Guidelines

This command first appeared in Cisco IOS Release 11.2.

Use the **timeout** command to set how long the probe waits to receive a response, and use the **frequency** command to set the rate at which the probe starts a response time report operation.

The value specified for the **timeout** command cannot be greater than the value specified for the **frequency** response time reporter configuration command.

Example

In the following example, the timeout is set for 2500 ms:

```
rtr 1
 type echo protocol ipIcmpEcho 172.16.1.176
 timeout 2500
```

Related Commands

To locate documentation of related commands, you can search online at www.cisco.com.

frequency
rtr

type

To configure the type of response time reporter probe, use the **type** response time reporter configuration command. You must configure the probe's type before you can configure any of the other characteristics of the probe. Use the **no** form of this command to remove the type configuration for the probe.

> **type** {**echo** | **pathEcho**} **protocol** *type type-target*
> **no type** {**echo** | **pathEcho**} **protocol** *type type-target*

Syntax	Description
echo	Perform end-to-end response time reporter operations only.
pathEcho	Perform response time reporter operations by using a route discovery algorithm to find a path to the destination and echo each device on the path.

Syntax

protocol *type*
type-target

Description

Protocol used by the probe. Type can be one of the following keywords (whether the keyword is available depends on the Cisco IOS software features installed on your router) followed by the required type parameter:

- **ipIcmpEcho** {*ip-address* | *ip-host-name*}—IP/ICMP Echo that requires a destination IP address or IP host name.

- **snaRUEcho** *sna-host-name*—SNA's SSCP Native Echo that requires the host name defined for the SNA's Physical Unit connection to VTAM.

- **snaLU0EchoAppl** *sna-host-name* [*sna-application*] [*sna-mode*]—An SNA LU Type 0 connection to Cisco's NSPECHO host application that requires the host name defined for the SNA's Physical Unit connection to VTAM. Optionally specify the host application name (the default is NSPECHO) and SNA mode to access the application.

- **snaLU2EchoAppl** *sna-host-name* [*sna-application*] [*sna-mode*]—An SNA LU Type 2 connection to Cisco's NSPECHO host application that requires the host name defined for the SNA's Physical Unit connection to VTAM. Optionally specify the host application name (the default is NSPECHO), and SNA mode to access the application.

Default

No probe types are configured.

Command Mode

Response time reporter configuration

Usage Guidelines

This command first appeared in Cisco IOS Release 11.2.

Support of echo to a protocol and pathEcho to a protocol is dependent on the protocol type and implementation. In general, most protocols support echo and few protocols support pathEcho.

| NOTE | Keywords are not case sensitive and are shown in mixed case for readability only. |

Example

In the following example, probe 10 is created and configured as echo using the IP/ICMP Echo protocol and the destination IP address 172.16.1.175:

```
rtr 10
 type echo protocol ipIcmpEcho 172.16.1.175
```

Related Commands

To locate documentation of related commands, you can search online at www.cisco.com.

rtr

verify-data

To cause the response time reporter probe to check each response for corruption, use the **verify-data** response time reporter configuration command. Use the **no** form of this command to return to the default value.

> **verify-data**
> **no verify-data**

Syntax Description

This command has no arguments or keywords.

Default

Disabled

Command Mode

Response time reporter configuration

Usage Guidelines

This command first appeared in Cisco IOS Release 11.2.

Only use the **verify-data** command when corruption may be an issue.

CAUTION   Do not enable this feature during normal operation because it causes unnecessary overhead.

Example

In the following example, probe 5 is configured to verify the data for each response:

```
rtr 5
 type echo protocol ipIcmpEcho 172.16.1.174
 response-data-size 2
 verify-data
```

Related Commands

To locate documentation of related commands, you can search online at www.cisco.com.

rtr

Troubleshooting the Router

This chapter describes basic tasks that you can perform to troubleshoot your router and network. For a complete description of the troubleshooting commands in this chapter, refer to Chapter 26, "Troubleshooting Commands." To locate documentation of other commands that appear in this chapter, you can search online at www.cisco.com.

Understanding Fault Management

To manage network faults, you need to discover, isolate, and fix the problems. You can discover problems with the system's monitoring commands, isolate problems with the system's test commands, and resolve problems with other commands, including **debug** commands.

To perform general fault management, use the commands in the following sections:

- Display System Information Using Show Commands
- Receiving Automatic Warning Messages
- Receiving the Automatic Shutdown Message
- Test Network Connectivity
- Test Memory and Interfaces
- Log System Error Messages
- Use Field Diagnostics
- Store Line Card Crash Information
- Enable Debug Operations
- Enable Conditionally Triggered Debugging

In addition, some chapters in the Cisco IOS software configuration guides include fault management tasks in a monitoring and maintaining section.

Display System Information Using Show Commands

To provide information about system processes, the Cisco IOS software includes an extensive list of EXEC commands that begin with the word **show**, which, when executed, display detailed tables of system information. Following is a list of the more common system management **show** commands. Use these commands in EXEC mode to display the information described:

Command	Purpose
show c2600	Displays information about the Cisco 2600 platform, including interrupts, IOS Priority Masks, and IDMA status, for troubleshooting.
show c7200	Displays information about the CPU and midplane for the Cisco 7200 series routers.
show context	Displays information stored in NVRAM when the router crashes. This command is only useful to your technical support representative. This command is supported on the Cisco 2600 and 7000 series routers.
show controllers (GRP image)	Displays information that is specific to the Cisco 12000 series Gigabit Switch Router hardware options listed with this command.
show controllers (line card image)	Displays information specific to the hardware on a line card installed in the Cisco 12000 series Gigabit Switch Router.
show controllers logging	Displays logging information about a VIP card.
show controllers tech-support	Displays general information about a VIP card when reporting a problem.
show diag	Displays hardware information including DRAM and SRAM on the line cards.
**show environment [all	last	table]**	Displays a message indicating whether an environmental warning condition currently exists, the temperature and voltage information, the last measured value from each of the six test points stored in nonvolatile memory, or the environmental specifications. This command is supported on the Cisco 7000 series routers.
show gsr	Displays hardware information on the Cisco 12000 series Gigabit Switch Router.
show gt64010	Displays all GT64010 internal registers and interrupt status on the Cisco 7200 series routers.
show memory [*type*] [**free**] [**summary**]	Displays memory pool statistics including summary information about the activities of the system memory allocator and a block-by-block listing of memory use.
**show pci {hardware	bridge** [*register*]}	Displays information about the peripheral component interconnect (PCI) hardware registers or bridge registers for the Cisco 2600 and 7000 series routers.
show processes [cpu]	Displays information about all active processes.
show processes memory	Displays information about memory usage.
show protocols	Displays the configured protocols.

Command	Purpose
show stacks	Displays stack usage of processes and interrupt routines, including the reason for the last system reboot. This command is only useful to your technical support representative.
show subsys [**class** *class* | **name** *name*]	Displays subsystem information.
show tcp [*line-number*]	Displays the status of TCP connections.
show tcp brief [**all**]	Displays a concise description of TCP connection endpoints.
show tdm [**connections** | **data**] [**motherboard** | **slot** *number*]	Displays a snapshot of the time-division multiplexing (TDM) bus connection or data memory in a Cisco AS5200 access server.
show tech-support [**page**] [**password**] **show controllers vip** *slot-number* **tech-support**	Displays general information about the router or VIP card when reporting a problem.

Receiving Automatic Warning Messages

Some routers have an environmental monitor which monitors the physical condition of the router. If a measurement exceeds acceptable margins, a warning message is printed to the system console. The system software collects measurements once every 60 seconds, but warnings for a given test point are printed at most once every four hours. If the temperature measurements are out of specification more than the shutdown margin, the software shuts the router down but the fan will stay on. The router has to be manually turned off and on after such a shutdown. You can query the environmental monitor using the **show environment** command at any time to determine whether a measurement is out of tolerance.

Receiving the Automatic Shutdown Message

On routers with an environmental monitor, if the software detects that any of its temperature test points have exceeded maximum margins, it performs the following steps in this order:

1   Saves the last measured values from each of the six test points to internal nonvolatile memory.

2   Interrupts the system software and causes a shutdown message to be printed on the system console.

3   Shuts off the power supplies after a few milliseconds of delay.

The following is the message the system displays if temperatures exceed maximum margins, along with a message indicating the reason for the shutdown:

```
Router#
%ENVM-1-SHUTDOWN: Environmental Monitor initiated shutdown
%ENVM-2-TEMP: Inlet temperature has reached SHUTDOWN level at 64(C)
```

Refer to the hardware installation and maintenance publication for your router for more information about environmental specifications.

Using Field Diagnostics

Each line card on the Cisco 12000 series can perform field diagnostic testing to isolate faulty hardware without disrupting normal operation of the system. However, performing field diagnostic testing on a line card does halt all activity on the line card for the duration of the testing. After successful completion of the field diagnostic testing, the Cisco IOS software is automatically reloaded on the line card.

NOTE	The field diagnostic **diag** command must be executed from the GRP main console port.

To perform field diagnostic testing on a line card, use the following commands in privileged EXEC mode:

Step	Command	Purpose
1	**diag** *slot-number* [**previous** | **post** | **verbose** | **wait**]	Specifies the line card that you want to perform diagnostic testing on.
		Optionally, specifies that previous test results are displayed, that only extended power-on self-tests (POST) be performed, that the maximum messages are displayed, or that the Cisco IOS software not be reloaded on the line card after successful completion of the tests. The following prompt is displayed.
		``` Running Diags will halt ALL activity on the requested slot. [confirm] ```
		At the prompt, press **Return** to confirm that you want to perform field diagnostic testing on the specified line card, or type **no** to stop the testing.

To stop field diagnostic testing on a line card, use the following commands in privileged EXEC mode:

Command	Purpose
diag *slot-number* **halt** or **no diag** *slot-number*	Specifies the line card that you want to stop perform diagnostic testing on.

NOTE	When you stop the field diagnostic test, the line card remains down (that is, in an unbooted state). In most cases, you stopped the testing because you need to remove the line card or replace the line card. If that is not the case and you want to bring the line card back up (that is, on-line), you must use the **microcode reload** global configuration command or power cycle the line card.

Storing Line Card Crash Information

This section explains how to enable storing of crash information for a line card and optionally specify the type and amount of information stored. Technical support representatives need to be able to look at the crash information from the line card to troubleshoot serious problems on the line card. The crash information contains all the line card memory information including the main memory and transmit and receive buffer information.

CAUTION	Use the **exception linecard** global configuration command only when directed by a technical support representative and only enable options that the technical support representative requests you to enable.

To enable and configure the crash information options for a line card, use the following command in global configuration mode:

Command	Purpose
exception linecard {**all**	**slot** *number*} [**corefile** *filename*	**main-memory** *size* [**k**	**m**]	**queue-ram** *size* [**k**	**m**]	**rx-buffer** *size* [**k**	**m**]	**sqe-register-rx**	**sqe-register-tx**	**tx-buffer** *size* [**k**	**m**]]	Specifies the line card that you want crash information for when a line card resets. Optionally, specifies the type and amount of memory to be stored.

Test Network Connectivity

Use the commands in the following sections to test basic network connectivity:

● Set Up the TCP Keepalive Packet Service

● Test Connections with the Ping Command

● Trace Packet Routes

Set Up the TCP Keepalive Packet Service

The TCP keepalive capability allows a router to detect when the host with which it is communicating experiences a system failure, even if data stops being transmitted (in either direction). This is most useful on incoming connections. For example, if a host failure occurs while talking to a printer, the router might never notice, because the printer does not generate any traffic in the opposite direction. If keepalives are enabled, they are sent once every minute on otherwise idle connections. If five minutes pass and no keepalives are detected, the connection is closed. The connection is also closed if the host replies to a keepalive packet with a reset packet. This will happen if the host crashes and comes back up again.

To set up the TCP keepalive packet service, use the following command in global configuration mode:

Command	Purpose
service {**tcp-keepalives-in** | **tcp-keepalives-out**}	Generates TCP keepalive packets on idle network connections—either incoming connections initiated by a remote host or outgoing connections initiated by a user.

Test Connections with the Ping Command

As an aid to diagnosing basic network connectivity, many network protocols support an echo protocol. The protocol involves sending a special datagram to the destination host, then waiting for a reply datagram from that host. Results from this echo protocol can help in evaluating the path-to-host reliability, delays over the path, and whether the host can be reached or is functioning.

To use the echo protocol, use the following command in either user or privileged EXEC mode:

Command	Purpose
ping [*protocol*] {*host* | *address*}	Invokes a diagnostic tool for testing connectivity.

Look for specific **ping** commands in the tables of configuration commands found throughout the chapters in Cisco IOS software configuration guides.

Trace Packet Routes

To discover the routes that packets will actually take when traveling to their destinations, use the following command in either user or privileged EXEC mode:

Command	Purpose
trace [*protocol*] [*destination*]	Traces packet routes through the network (privileged level).

Test Memory and Interfaces

You can test the status of the following items:

- Flash memory
- System memory
- Interfaces

CAUTION	We do not recommend using these test commands; they are intended to aid manufacturing personnel in checking system functionality.

Test Flash Memory

To test the status of Flash memory, use the following command in privileged EXEC mode:

Command	Purpose
test flash	Tests Flash memory on MCI and envm Flash EPROM interfaces.

Test System Memory

To test the status of system memory, use the following command in privileged EXEC mode:

Command	Purpose
test memory	Diagnoses Multibus memory, including nonvolatile memory.

Test Interfaces

CAUTION	Do not use this test to diagnose problems with an operational server.

To test the status of the interfaces, use the following command on a nonoperational server in privileged EXEC mode:

Command	Purpose
test interfaces	Checks network interfaces.

Log System Error Messages

By default, routers send the output from the **debug** EXEC command and system error messages to a logging process. The logging process controls the distribution of logging messages to the various destinations, such as the logging buffer, terminal lines, or a UNIX syslog server, depending on your configuration. The process also sends messages to the console. When the logging process is on, the messages are displayed on the console after the process that generated them has finished.

NOTE   The syslog format is compatible with 4.3 BSD UNIX.

When the logging process is disabled, messages are sent only to the console. The messages are sent as they are generated, so error and debug output will be interspersed with prompts or output from the command.

You can set the severity level of the messages to control the type of messages displayed for the console and each of the destinations. You can timestamp log messages or set the syslog source address to enhance real-time debugging and management.

Enable Message Logging

Message logging is enabled by default. It must be enabled in order to send messages to any destination other than the console.

To disable message logging, use the **no logging on** command. Disabling the logging process can slow down the router because a process must wait until the messages are written to the console before continuing.

To re-enable message logging after it has been disabled, use the following command in global configuration mode:

Command	Purpose
logging on	Enables message logging.

Enable Message Logging for a Slave Card

To enable slave Versatile Interface Processor (VIP) cards to log important messages to the console, use the following command in global configuration mode:

Command	Purpose
service slave-log	Enables slave message logging.

Set the Error Message Display Device

If message logging is enabled, you can send messages to specified locations, in addition to the console.

To specify the locations that receive messages, use one or more of the following commands in global configuration mode:

Command	Purpose
logging buffered [*size*]	Logs messages to an internal buffer.
terminal monitor	Logs messages to a nonconsole terminal.
logging *host*	Logs messages to a UNIX syslog server host.

The **logging buffered** command copies logging messages to an internal buffer. The buffer is circular, so newer messages overwrite older messages after the buffer is full. To display the messages that are logged in the buffer, use the **show logging** EXEC command. The first message displayed is the oldest message in the buffer. To clear the current contents of the buffer, use the **clear logging** privileged EXEC command.

The EXEC command **terminal monitor** locally accomplishes the task of displaying the system error messages to a nonconsole terminal.

The **logging** command identifies a syslog server host to receive logging messages. The argument *host* is the name or Internet address of the host. By issuing this command more than once, you build a list of syslog servers that receive logging messages. The **no logging** command deletes the syslog server with the specified address from the list of syslogs.

Configure Synchronization of Logging Messages

You can configure the system to synchronize unsolicited messages and **debug** command output with solicited device output and prompts for a specific line. You can identify the types of messages to be output asynchronously based on the level of severity. You can also determine the maximum number of buffers for storing asynchronous messages for the terminal after which messages are dropped.

When synchronous logging of unsolicited messages and **debug** command output is turned on, unsolicited device output is displayed on the console or printed after solicited device output is displayed or printed. Unsolicited messages and **debug** command output is displayed on the console after the prompt for user input is returned. Therefore, unsolicited messages and **debug** command output are not interspersed with solicited device output and prompts. After the unsolicited messages are displayed, the console displays the user prompt again.

To configure for synchronous logging of unsolicited messages and **debug** command output with solicited device output and prompts, use the following commands beginning in global configuration mode:

Step	Command	Purpose
1	**line** [**aux** | **console** | **vty**] *line-number* [*ending-line-number*]	Specifies the line to be configured for synchronous logging of messages.
2	**logging synchronous** [**level** *severity-level* | **all**] [**limit** *number-of-buffers*]	Enables synchronous logging of messages.

Enable Timestamps on Log Messages

By default, log messages are not timestamped. You can enable timestamping of log messages by using the following command in global configuration mode:

Command	Purpose
service timestamps log uptime	Enables log timestamps.
or	
service timestamps log datetime [**msec**] [**localtime**] [**show-timezone**]	

Define the Error Message Severity Level and Facilities

You can limit messages displayed to the selected device by specifying the severity level of the error message. To do so, use one of the following commands in global configuration mode:

Command	Purpose
logging console *level*	Limits messages logged to the console.
logging monitor *level*	Limits messages logged to the terminal lines.
logging trap *level*	Limits messages logged to the syslog servers.

If you have enabled syslog message traps to be sent to an SNMP network management station with the **snmp-server enable trap** command, you can also change the level of messages sent and stored in a history table on the router. You can also change the number of messages that get stored in the history table.

Messages are stored in the history table because SNMP traps are not guaranteed to reach their destination. By default, one message of the level warning and above (see Table 25-1) is stored in the history table even if syslog traps are not enabled.

To change the level and table size defaults, use the following commands in global configuration mode:

Step	Command	Purpose
1	**logging history** *level*	Changes the default level of syslog messages stored in the history file and sent to the SNMP server.
2	**logging history size** *number*	Changes the number of syslog messages that can be stored in the history table.

NOTE   Table 25-1 lists the level keywords and severity level. For SNMP usage, the severity level values use +1. For example, **emergency** equals 1, not 0, and **critical** equals 3, not 2.

The **logging console** command limits the logging messages displayed on the console terminal to messages with a level number at or below the specified severity level, which is specified by the *level* argument. Table 25-1 lists the error message *level* keywords and corresponding UNIX syslog definitions in order from the most severe level to the least severe level.

The **no logging console** command disables logging to the console terminal.

Table 25-1   *Error Message Logging Keywords*

Level Keyword	Level	Description	Syslog Definition
emergencies	0	System unusable	LOG_EMERG
alerts	1	Immediate action needed	LOG_ALERT
critical	2	Critical conditions	LOG_CRIT
errors	3	Error conditions	LOG_ERR
warnings	4	Warning conditions	LOG_WARNING
notifications	5	Normal but significant condition	LOG_NOTICE
informational	6	Informational messages only	LOG_INFO
debugging	7	Debugging messages	LOG_DEBUG

The default is to log messages to the console at the **debugging** level and those level numbers that are lower, which means all levels. The **logging monitor** command defaults to **debugging** also. The **logging trap** command defaults to **informational**.

To display logging messages on a terminal, use the **terminal monitor** EXEC command.

Current software generates four categories of error messages:

● Error messages about software or hardware malfunctions, displayed at levels **warnings** through **emergencies**

● Output from the **debug** commands, displayed at the **debugging** level

● Interface up/down transitions and system restart messages, displayed at the **notifications** level

● Reload requests and low-process stack messages, displayed at the **informational** level

Define the UNIX System Logging Facility

You can log messages produced by UNIX system utilities. To do this, enable this type of logging and define the UNIX system facility from which you want to log messages. Table 25-2 lists the UNIX system facilities supported by the Cisco IOS software. Consult the operators manual for your UNIX operating system for more information about these UNIX system facilities.

Define UNIX system facility message logging by using the following command in global configuration mode:

Command	Purpose
logging facility *facility-type*	Configures system log facilities.

Table 25-2 *Logging Facility Type Keywords*

Facility Type Keyword	Description
auth	Indicates the authorization system.
cron	Indicates the cron facility.
daemon	Indicates the system daemon.
kern	Indicates the Kernel.
local0–7	Reserved for locally defined messages.
lpr	Indicates line printer system.
mail	Indicates mail system.
news	Indicates USENET news.
sys9	Indicates system use.
sys10	Indicates system use.
sys11	Indicates system use.
sys12	Indicates system use.

Table 25-2 *Logging Facility Type Keywords (Continued)*

Facility Type Keyword	Description
sys13	Indicates system use.
sys14	Indicates system use.
syslog	Indicates the system log.
user	Indicates user process.
uucp	Indicates UNIX-to-UNIX copy system.

Refer also to your syslog manual pages.

Display Logging Information

To display logging information, use the following command in EXEC mode:

Step	Command	Purpose
1	**show logging** **show controllers vip** *slot-number* logging	Displays the state of syslog error and event logging, including host addresses, whether console logging is enabled, and other logging statistics.
2	**show logging history**	Displays information in the syslog history table such as the table size, the status of messages, and the text of the messages stored in the table.

Log Errors to a UNIX Syslog Daemon

To set up the syslog daemon on a 4.3 BSD UNIX system, include a line such as the following in the /etc/syslog.conf file:

```
local7.debugging /usr/adm/logs/cisco.log
```

The **debugging** keyword specifies the syslog level; see Table 25-1 for a general description of other keywords. The **local7** keyword specifies the logging facility to be used; see Table 25-2 for a general description of other keywords.

The syslog daemon sends messages at this level or at a more severe level to the file specified in the next field. The file must already exist, and the syslog daemon must have permission to write to it.

Set the Syslog Source Address

By default, a syslog message contains the IP address of the interface it uses to leave the router. To require that all syslog messages contain the same IP address, regardless of which interface they use, use the following command in global configuration mode:

Command	Purpose
logging source-interface *type number*	Sets the syslog source address.

Use Field Diagnostics

Each line card on the Cisco 12000 series can perform field diagnostic testing to isolate faulty hardware without disrupting normal operation of the system. However, performing field diagnostic testing on a line card does halt all activity on the line card for the duration of the testing. After successful completion of the field diagnostic testing, the Cisco IOS software is automatically reloaded on the line card.

NOTE   The field diagnostic **diag** command must be executed from the GRP main console port.

To perform field diagnostic testing on a line card, perform the following commands in privileged EXEC mode:

Step	Command	Purpose
1	**diag** *slot-number* [**previous** | **post** | **verbose** | **wait**]	Specifies the line card that you want to perform diagnostic testing on.
		Optionally, specifies that previous test results are displayed, that only extended power-on self-tests (POST) be performed, that the maximum messages are displayed, or that the Cisco IOS software not be reloaded on the line card after successful completion of the tests. The following prompt is displayed.
		``` Running Diags will halt ALL activity on the requested slot. [confirm] ```
		At the prompt, press **Return** to confirm that you want to perform field diagnostic testing on the specified line card, or type **no** to stop the testing.

To stop field diagnostic testing on a line card, use the following commands in privileged EXEC mode:

Command	Purpose
diag *slot-number* **halt** or **no diag** *slot-number*	Specifies the line card that you want to stop perform diagnostic testing on.

NOTE	When you stop the field diagnostic test, the line card remains down (that is, in an unbooted state). In most cases, you stopped the testing because you need to remove the line card or replace the line card. If that is not the case and you want to bring the line card back up (that is, on-line), you must use the **microcode reload** global configuration command or power cycle the line card.

Store Line Card Crash Information

This section explains how to enable storing of crash information for a line card and optionally specify the type and amount of information stored. Technical support representatives need to be able to look at the crash information from the line card to troubleshoot serious problems on the line card. The crash information contains all the line card memory information including the main memory and transmit and receive buffer information.

CAUTION	Use the **exception linecard** global configuration command only when directed by a technical support representative and only enable options that the technical support representative requests you to enable.

To enable and configure the crash information options for a line card, use the following command in global configuration mode:

Command	Purpose
exception linecard {**all** | **slot** *number*} [**corefile** *filename* | **main-memory** *size* [**k** | **m**] | **queue-ram** *size* [**k** | **m**] | **rx-buffer** *size* [**k** | **m**] | **sqe-register-rx** | **sqe-register-tx** | **tx-buffer** *size* [**k** | **m**]]	Specifies the line card that you want crash information for when a line card resets. Optionally, specifies the type and amount of memory to be stored.

Enable Debug Operations

Your router includes hardware and software to aid in tracking down internal problems and problems with other hosts on the network. The privileged **debug** EXEC commands start the console display of several classes of network events. The following commands describe in general the system debug message feature.

Command	Purpose
show debugging	Displays the state of each debugging option.
debug ?	Displays a list and brief description of all the **debug** command options.
debug *command*	Begins message logging for the specified **debug** command.
no debug *command*	Turns message logging off for the specified **debug** command.

CAUTION   The system gives high priority to debugging output. For this reason, debugging commands should be turned on only for troubleshooting specific problems or during troubleshooting sessions with technical support personnel. Excessive debugging output can render the system inoperable.

You can configure timestamping of system debug messages. Timestamping enhances real-time debugging by providing the relative timing of logged events. This information is especially useful when customers send debugging output to your technical support personnel for assistance. To enable timestamping of system debug messages, use the following command in global configuration mode:

Command	Purpose
service timestamps debug uptime or **service timestamps debug datetime [msec]** **[localtime] [show-timezone]**	Enables timestamping of system debug messages.

Normally, the messages are displayed only on the console terminal. See the section "Set the Error Message Display Device" earlier in this chapter to change the output device.

Enable Conditionally Triggered Debugging

When the Conditionally Triggered Debugging feature is enabled, the router generates debugging messages for packets entering or leaving the router on a specified interface; the router will not generate debugging output for packets entering or leaving through a different interface. You can specify the interfaces explicitly. For example, you may only want to see debugging messages for one interface or subinterface. You can also turn on debugging for all interfaces that meet specified condition. This feature is useful on dial access servers, which have a large number of ports.

Normally, the router will generate debugging messages for every interface, resulting in a large number of messages. The large number of messages consumes system resources, and can make it difficult to find the specific information you need. By limiting the debugging messages, you can receive messages related to only the ports you wish to troubleshoot.

Conditionally Triggered Debugging controls the output from the following protocol-specific **debug** commands:

- **debug aaa** {**accounting** I **authorization** I **authentication**}
- **debug dialer** {**events** I **packets**}
- **debug isdn** {**q921** I **q931**}
- **debug modem** {**oob** I **trace**}
- **debug ppp** {**all** I **authentication** I **chap** I **error** I **negotiation** I **multilink events** I **packet**}

While this feature limits the output of the above commands, it does not automatically enable the generation of debugging output from these commands. Debugging messages are generated only when the protocol-specific **debug** command is enabled. **Debug** command output is controlled through two processes:

- The protocol-specific **debug** commands specify which protocols are being debugged. For example, the **debug dialer events** command generates debugging output related to dialer events.
- The **debug condition** commands limit these debugging messages to those related to a particular interface. For example, the **debug condition username bob** command generates debugging output only for interfaces with packets that specify a username of bob.

To configure Conditionally Triggered Debugging, perform the following tasks:

- Enable Protocol-Specific Debug Commands
- Enable Conditional Debugging Commands
- Specify Multiple Conditions

Enable Protocol-Specific Debug Commands

In order to generate any debugging output, the protocol-specific **debug** command for the desired output must be enabled. Use the **show debugging** command to determine which types of debugging are enabled. Use the following commands in privileged EXEC mode to enable the desired protocol-specific **debug** commands:

Command	Purpose
show debugging	Determines which types of debugging are enabled.
debug *protocol*	Enables the desired debugging commands.
no debug *protocol*	Disables the debugging commands that are not desired.

If you wish to have no output, disable all the protocol-specific **debug** commands.

Enable Conditional Debugging Commands

If no **debug condition** commands are enabled, all debugging output, regardless of the interface, will be displayed for the enabled protocol-specific **debug** commands.

The first **debug condition** command you enter enables conditional debugging. The router will only display messages for interfaces that meet one of the specified conditions. If multiple conditions are specified, the interface must meet at least one of the conditions in order for messages to be displayed.

You can enable messages for interfaces specified explicitly or for interfaces that meet certain conditions, as described in the following sections:

● Display Messages for One Interface

● Display Messages for Multiple Interfaces

● Limit Messages Based on Conditions

Display Messages for One Interface

To disable debugging messages for all interfaces except one, use the following command in privileged EXEC mode:

Command	Purpose
debug condition interface *interface*	Disables debugging messages for all interfaces except one.

If you enter the **debug condition interface** command, the debugging output will be turned off for all interfaces except the specified interface. To reenable debugging output for all interfaces, use the **no debug interface command**.

Display Messages for Multiple Interfaces

To enable debugging messages for multiple interfaces, use the following commands in privileged EXEC mode:

Command	Purpose
debug condition interface *interface*	Disables debugging messages for all interfaces except one.
debug condition interface *interface*	Enables debugging messages for additional interfaces. Repeats this task until debugging messages are enabled for all desired interfaces.

If you specify more than one interface by entering this command multiple times, debugging output will be displayed for all of the specified interfaces. To turn off debugging on a particular interface, use the **no debug interface** command. If you use the **no debug interface all** command or remove the last **debug interface** command, debugging output will be reenabled for all interfaces.

Limit Messages Based on Conditions

The router can monitor interfaces to see if any packets contain the specified value for one of the following conditions:

- username
- calling party number
- called party number

If you enter a condition, such as calling number, debug output will be stopped for all interfaces. The router will then monitor every interface to see if a packet with the specified calling party number is sent or received on any interfaces. If the condition is met on an interface or subinterface, **debug** command output will be displayed for that interface. The debugging output for an interface is "triggered" when the condition has been met. The debugging output continues to be disabled for the other interfaces. If, at some later time, the condition is met for another interface, the debug output will become enabled for that interface as well.

Once debugging output has been triggered on an interface, the output will continue until the interface goes down. However, the session for that interface might change, resulting in a new username, called party number, or calling party number. Use the **no debug interface** command to reset the debug trigger mechanism for a particular interface. The debugging output for that interface will be disabled until the interface meets one of the specified conditions.

To limit debugging messages based on a specified condition, use the following command in privileged EXEC mode:

Command	Purpose
debug condition {**username** *username* | **called** *dial-string* | **caller** *dial-string*}	Enables conditional debugging. The router will only display messages for interfaces that meet this condition.

To reenable the debugging output for all interfaces, enter the **no debug condition all** command.

Specify Multiple Conditions

To limit debugging messages based on more than one condition, use the following commands in privileged EXEC mode:

Command	Purpose
debug condition {**username** *username* | **called** *dial-string* | **caller** *dial-string*}	Enables conditional debugging and specify the first condition.
debug condition {**username** *username* | **called** *dial-string* | **caller** *dial-string*}	Specifies the second condition. Repeat this task until all conditions are specified.

If you enter multiple **debug condition** commands, debugging output will be generated if an interface meets at least one of the conditions. If you remove one of the conditions, using the **no debug condition** command, interfaces that meet only that condition will no longer produce debugging output. However, interfaces that meet a condition other than the removed condition will continue to generate output. Only if no active conditions are met for an interface will the output for that interface be disabled.

Conditionally Triggered Debugging Configuration Examples

In this example, four conditions have been set by the following commands:

- **debug condition interface serial 0**
- **debug condition interface serial 1**
- **debug condition interface virtual-template 1**
- **debug condition username fred**

The first three conditions have been met by one interface. The fourth condition has not yet been met.

```
Router# show debug condition

Condition 1: interface Se0 (1 flags triggered)
        Flags: Se0
```

```
Condition 2: interface Se1 (1 flags triggered)
        Flags: Se1
Condition 3: interface Vt1 (1 flags triggered)
        Flags: Vt1
Condition 4: username fred (0 flags triggered)
```

When any **debug condition** command is entered, debugging messages for conditional debugging are enabled. The following debugging messages show conditions being met on different interfaces as the serial 0 and serial 1 interfaces come up. For example, the second line of output indicates that serial interface 0 meets the username fred condition.

```
*Mar  1 00:04:41.647: %LINK-3-UPDOWN: Interface Serial0, changed state to up
*Mar  1 00:04:41.715: Se0 Debug: Condition 4, username fred triggered, count 2
*Mar  1 00:04:42.963: %LINEPROTO-5-UPDOWN: Line protocol on Interface Serial0, changed state
to up
*Mar  1 00:04:43.271: Vi1 Debug: Condition 3, interface Vt1 triggered, count 1
*Mar  1 00:04:43.271: %LINK-3-UPDOWN: Interface Virtual-Access1, changed state to up
*Mar  1 00:04:43.279: Vi1 Debug: Condition 4, username fred triggered, count 2
*Mar  1 00:04:43.283: Vi1 Debug: Condition 1, interface Se0 triggered, count 3
*Mar  1 00:04:44.039: %IP-4-DUPADDR: Duplicate address 172.27.32.114 on Ethernet 0, sourced
by 00e0.1e3e.2d41
*Mar  1 00:04:44.283: %LINEPROTO-5-UPDOWN: Line protocol on Interface Virtual-Access1,
changed state to up
*Mar  1 00:04:54.667: %LINK-3-UPDOWN: Interface Serial1, changed state to up
*Mar  1 00:04:54.731: Se1 Debug: Condition 4, username fred triggered, count 2
*Mar  1 00:04:54.735: Vi1 Debug: Condition 2, interface Se1 triggered, count 4
*Mar  1 00:04:55.735: %LINEPROTO-5-UPDOWN: Line protocol on Interface Serial1, changed state
to up
```

After a period of time, the **show debug condition** command displays the revised list of conditions.

```
Router# show debug condition
```

```
Condition 1: interface Se0 (2 flags triggered)
        Flags: Se0 Vi1
Condition 2: interface Se1 (2 flags triggered)
        Flags: Se1 Vi1
Condition 3: interface Vt1 (2 flags triggered)
        Flags: Vt1 Vi1
Condition 4: username fred (3 flags triggered)
        Flags: Se0 Vi1 Se1
```

Next, the serial 1 and serial 0 interfaces go down. When an interface goes down, conditions for that interface are cleared.

```
*Mar  1 00:05:51.443: %LINK-3-UPDOWN: Interface Serial1, changed state to down
*Mar  1 00:05:51.471: Se1 Debug: Condition 4, username fred cleared, count 1
*Mar  1 00:05:51.479: Vi1 Debug: Condition 2, interface Se1 cleared, count 3
*Mar  1 00:05:52.443: %LINEPROTO-5-UPDOWN: Line protocol on Interface Serial1, changed state
to down
*Mar  1 00:05:56.859: %LINK-3-UPDOWN: Interface Serial0, changed state to down
*Mar  1 00:05:56.887: Se0 Debug: Condition 4, username fred cleared, count 1
*Mar  1 00:05:56.895: Vi1 Debug: Condition 1, interface Se0 cleared, count 2
*Mar  1 00:05:56.899: Vi1 Debug: Condition 3, interface Vt1 cleared, count 1
```

```
*Mar  1 00:05:56.899: Vi1 Debug: Condition 4, username fred cleared, count 0
*Mar  1 00:05:56.903: %LINK-3-UPDOWN: Interface Virtual-Access1, changed state to down
*Mar  1 00:05:57.907: %LINEPROTO-5-UPDOWN: Line protocol on Interface Serial0, changed state
to down
*Mar  1 00:05:57.907: %LINEPROTO-5-UPDOWN: Line protocol on Interface Virtual-Access1,
changed state to down
```

The final **show debug condition** output is the same as the output before the interfaces came up.

```
Router# show debug condition

Condition 1: interface Se0 (1 flags triggered)
        Flags: Se0
Condition 2: interface Se1 (1 flags triggered)
        Flags: Se1
Condition 3: interface Vt1 (1 flags triggered)
        Flags: Vt1
Condition 4: username fred (0 flags triggered)
```

## CHAPTER 26

Troubleshooting Commands

This chapter describes the commands used to troubleshoot your router. To troubleshoot, you need to discover, isolate, and fix the problems. You can discover problems with the system's monitoring commands, isolate problems with the system's test commands, and resolve problems with other commands, including **debug**.

This chapter describes general fault management commands.

For troubleshooting tasks and examples, refer to Chapter 25, "Troubleshooting the Router."

attach

To access the Cisco IOS software image on a line card to monitor and maintain information on the line card, use the **attach** privileged EXEC command. To exit from the Cisco IOS software image on the line card and return to the Cisco IOS image on the GRP card, use the **exit** command.

> **attach** *slot-number*

Syntax   Description

slot-number   Slot number of the line card you want to connect to. Slot numbers range from 0 to 11 for the Cisco 12012 and 0 to 7 for the Cisco 12008. If the slot number is omitted, you are prompted for the slot number.

Default
Access to the Cisco IOS software image running on the GRP card.

Command Mode
Privileged EXEC

Usage Guidelines
This command was added in Cisco IOS Release 11.2 GS to support the Cisco 12000 series Gigabit Switch Routers.

Use the **attach** EXEC command to get specific information about a line card.

After you connect to the Cisco IOS image on the line card using the **attach** command, the prompt changes to "LC-Slot*x*#," where *x* is the slot number of the line card.

You can also use the **execute-on slot** privileged EXEC command to execute commands on one or all line cards.

NOTE   Do not execute the **config** command from the Cisco IOS software image on the line card.

NOTE   Because not all statistics are maintained on the line cards, the output from some of the
show commands might not be consistent.

Example

The following example connects to the Cisco IOS image running on the line card in slot 9, gets a list of valid **show** commands, and returns the Cisco IOS image running on the GRP:

```
Router# attach 9
Entering Console for 4 Port Packet Over SONET OC-3c/STM-1 in Slot: 9
Type exit to end this session

Press RETURN to get started!

LC-Slot9# show ?
  cef       Cisco Express Forwarding
  clock     Display the system clock
  context   Show context information about recent crash(s)
  history   Display the session command history
  hosts     IP domain-name, lookup style, nameservers, and host table
  ipc       Interprocess communications commands
  location  Display the system location
  sessions  Information about Telnet connections
  terminal  Display terminal configuration parameters
  users     Display information about terminal lines
  version   System hardware and software status

LC-Slot9# exit

Disconnecting from slot 9.
Connection Duration: 00:01:04
Router#
```

Related Commands

To locate documentation of related commands, you can search online at www.cisco.com.

execute-on slot

clear logging

To clear messages from the logging buffer, use the **clear logging** privileged EXEC command.

> **clear logging**

Syntax Description

This command has no arguments or keywords.

Command Mode

Privileged EXEC

Usage Guidelines

This command first appeared in Cisco IOS Release 11.2.

Example

The following example clears the logging buffer:

```
Router# clear logging

Clear logging buffer [confirm]
Router#
```

Related Commands

To locate documentation of related commands, you can search online at www.cisco.com.

logging buffered
show logging

diag

To perform field diagnostics on a line card, on the Gigabit Route Processor (GRP), on the Switch Fabric Cards (SFC), and on the Clock Scheduler Card (CSC) in the Cisco 12000 series Gigabit Switch Routers, use the **diag** privileged EXEC command. To disable field diagnostics on a line card, use the **no** form of this command.

> **diag** *slot-number* [**halt** | **previous** | **post** | **verbose** [**wait**] | **wait**]
> **no diag** *slot-number*

Syntax	Description
slot-number	Slot number of the line card you want to test. Slot numbers range from 0 to 11 for the Cisco 12012 and 0 to 7 for the Cisco 12008. Slot numbers for the CSC are 16 and 17 and for the FSC are18, 19, and 20.
halt	(Optional) Stops the field diagnostic testing on the line card.
previous	(Optional) Displays previous test results (if any) for the line card.
post	(Optional) Initiates a EPROM-based extended power-on self-test (EPOST) only. The EPOST test suite is not as comprehensive as the field diagnostics, and a pass/fail message is the only message displayed on the console.
verbose [**wait**]	(Optional) Enables the maximum status messages to be displayed on the console. By default, only the minimum status messages are displayed on the console. If you specify the optional **wait** keyword, the Cisco IOS software is not be automatically reloaded on the line card after the test completes successfully.
wait	(Optional) Stops the automatic reloading of the Cisco IOS software on the line card after the successful completion of the field diagnostic testing. If you use this keyword, you must use the **microcode reload** *slot* global configuration command, or manually remove and insert the line card (to power it up) in the slot so that the GRP will recognize the line card and download the Cisco IOS software image to the line card.

Default
No field diagnostics tests are performed on the line card.

Command Mode
Privileged EXEC

Usage Guidelines
This command was added in Cisco IOS Release 11.2 GS to support the Cisco 12000 series Gigabit Switch Routers.

NOTE   The **diag** command must be executed from the GRP main console port.

Perform diagnostics on the CSC only if a redundant CSC is in the router.

Diagnostics will stop and ask you for confirmation before altering the router's configuration. For example, running diagnostics on a SFC or CSC will cause the fabric to go from full bandwidth to one quarter bandwidth. Bandwidth is not affected by GRP or line card diagnostics.

The field diagnostic software image is bundled with the Cisco IOS software and is downloaded automatically from the GRP to the target line card prior to testing.

CAUTION   Performing field diagnostics on a line card stops all activity on the line card. Before the **diag** EXEC command begins running diagnostics, you are prompted to confirm the request to perform field diagnostics on the line card.

In normal mode, if a test fails, the title of the failed test is displayed on the console. However, not all tests that are performed are displayed. To view all the tests that are performed, use the **verbose** keyword.

After all diagnostic tests are completed on the line card, a PASSED or TEST FAILURE message is displayed. If the line card sends a PASSED message, the Cisco IOS software image on the line card is automatically reloaded unless the **wait** keyword is specified. If the line card sends a TEST FAILURE message, the Cisco IOS software image on the line card is not automatically reloaded.

If you want to reload the line card after it fails diagnostic testing, use the **microcode reload** *slot* global configuration command.

NOTE   When you stop the field diagnostic test, the line card remains down (that is, in an unbooted state). In most cases, you stopped the testing because you need to remove the line card or replace the line card. If that is not the case, and you want to bring the line card back up (that is, online), you must use the **microcode reload** global configuration command or power cycle the line card.

If the line card fails the test, the line card is defective and should be replaced. In future releases this might not be the case because DRAM and SDRAM SIMM modules might be field replaceable units. For example, if the DRAM test failed you might only need to replace the DRAM on the line card.

For more information, refer to the Cisco 12000 series installation and configuration guides.

Examples

The following example shows the output when field diagnostics are performed on the line card in slot 3. After the line card passes all field diagnostic tests, the Cisco IOS software is automatically reloaded on the card. Before starting the diagnostic tests, you must confirm the request to perform these tests on the line card because all activity on the line card is halted. The total/indiv. timeout set to 600/220 sec. message indicates that 600 seconds are allowed to perform all field diagnostics tests, and that no single test should exceed 220 seconds to complete.

```
Router# diag 3
Running Diags will halt ALL activity on the requested slot. [confirm]
Router#
Launching a Field Diagnostic for slot 3
Running DIAG config check
RUNNING DIAG download to slot 3 (timeout set to 400 sec.)
sending cmd FDIAG-DO ALL to fdiag in slot 3
(total/indiv. timeout set to 600/220 sec.)
Field Diagnostic ****PASSED**** for slot 3
Field Diag eeprom values: run 159 fial mode 0 (PASS) slot 3
   last test failed was 0, error code 0
sending SHUTDOWN FDIAG_QUIT to fdiag in slot 3

Board will reload
...
Router#
```

The following example shows the output when field diagnostics are performed on the line card in slot 3 in verbose mode:

```
Router# diag 3 verbose
Running Diags will halt ALL activity on the requested slot. [confirm]
Router#
Launching a Field Diagnostic for slot 3
Running DIAG config check
RUNNING DIAG download to slot 3 (timeout set to 400 sec.)
sending cmd FDIAG-DO ALL to fdiag in slot 3
(total/indiv. timeout set to 600/220 sec.)
FDIAG_STAT_IN_PROGRESS: test #1 R5K Internal Cache
FDIAG_STAT_PASS test_num 1
FDIAG_STAT_IN_PROGRESS: test #2 Sunblock Ordering
FDIAG_STAT_PASS test_num 2
FDIAG_STAT_IN_PROGRESS: test #3 Dram Datapins
FDIAG_STAT_PASS test_num 3
...
Field Diags: FDIAG_STAT_DONE
Field Diagnostic ****PASSED**** for slot 3
Field Diag eeprom values: run 159 fial mode 0 (PASS) slot 3
   last test failed was 0, error code 0
sending SHUTDOWN FDIAG_QUIT to fdiag in slot 3

Board will reload
...
Router#
```

Related Commands

To locate documentation of related commands, you can search online at www.cisco.com.

microcode reload

exception core-file

To specify the name of the core dump file, use the **exception core-file** global configuration command. To return to the default core filename, use the **no** form of this command.

> **exception core-file** *name*
> **no exception core-file**

Syntax	Description
name	Name of the core dump file saved on the server.

Default

The core file is named *hostname*-core, where *hostname* is the name of the router.

Command Mode

Global configuration

Usage Guidelines

This command first appeared in Cisco IOS Release 10.

CAUTION   Use the **exception** commands only under the direction of a technical support representative. Creating a core dump while the router is functioning in a network can disrupt network operation. The resulting binary file, which is very large, must be transferred to a TFTP, FTP, or rcp server and subsequently interpreted by technical personnel who have access to source code and detailed memory maps.

If you use TFTP to dump the core file to a server, the router will only dump the first 16MB of the core file. If the router's memory is larger than 16MB, the whole core file will not be copied to the server. Therefore, use rcp or FTP to dump the core file.

Part
III

Command Reference

Example

The following example configures a router to use FTP to dump a core file named *dumpfile* to the FTP server at 172.17.92.2 when it crashes:

```
ip ftp username red
ip ftp password blue
exception protocol ftp
exception dump 172.17.92.2
exception core-file dumpfile
```

Related Commands

To locate documentation of related commands, you can search online at www.cisco.com.

exception dump
exception memory
exception protocol
ip ftp password
ip ftp username

exception dump

To configure the router to dump a core file to a particular server when the router crashes, use the **exception dump** global configuration command. To disable core dumps, use the **no** form of this command.

> **exception dump** *ip-address*
> **no exception dump**

Syntax	Description
ip-address	IP address of the server that stores the core dump file.

Default

Disabled

Command Mode

Global configuration

Usage Guidelines

This command first appeared in Cisco IOS Release 10.3.

CAUTION   Use the **exception** commands only under the direction of a technical support
representative. Creating a core dump while the router is functioning in a network can
disrupt network operation. The resulting binary file, which is very large, must be
transferred to a TFTP, FTP, or rcp server and subsequently interpreted by technical
personnel who have access to source code and detailed memory maps.

If you use TFTP to dump the core file to a server, the router will only dump the first 16MB of the core
file. If the router's memory is larger than 16MB, the whole core file will not be copied to the server.
Therefore, use rcp or FTP to dump the core file.

The core dump is written to a file named *hostname*-core on your server, where *hostname* is the name of
the router. You can change the name of the core file by configuring the **exception core-file** command.

This procedure can fail for certain types of system crashes. However, if successful, the core dump file
will be the size of the memory available on the processor (for example, 16MB for a CSC/4).

Example

The following example configures a router to use FTP to dump a core file to the FTP server at
172.17.92.2 when it crashes:

```
ip ftp username red
ip ftp password blue
exception protocol ftp
exception dump 172.17.92.2
```

Related Commands

To locate documentation of related commands, you can search online at www.cisco.com.

exception core-file
exception memory
exception protocol
ip ftp password
ip ftp username
ip rcmd remote-username

exception linecard

To enable storing of crash information for a line card and optionally specify the type and amount of
information stored, use the **exception linecard** global configuration command. To disable the storing
of crash information for the line card, use the **no** form of this command.

> **exception linecard** {**all** | **slot** *slot-number*} [**corefile** *filename* | **main-memory** *size*
> [**k** | **m**] |
> **queue-ram** *size* [**k** | **m**] | **rx-buffer** *size* [**k** | **m**] | **sqe-register-rx** |
> **sqe-register-tx** |
> **tx-buffer** *size* [**k** | **m**]]
> **no exception linecard**

Syntax	Description
all	Stores crash information for all line cards.
slot *slot- number*	Stores crash information for the line card in the specified slot. Slot numbers range from 0 to 11 for the Cisco 12012 and 0 to 7 for the Cisco 12008.
corefile *filename*	(Optional) Stores the crash information in the specified file in NVRAM. The default file name is *hostname*-**core**-*slot-number* (for example, c12012-core-8).
main-memory *size*	(Optional) Stores the crash information for the main memory on the line card and specify the size of the crash information. Size of the memory to store is 0 to 268,435,456.
queue-ram *size*	(Optional) Stores the crash information for the queue RAM memory on the line card and specify the size of the crash information. Size of the memory to store can be from 0 to 1,048,576.
rx-buffer *size* **tx-buffer** *size*	(Optional) Stores the crash information for the receive and transmit buffer on the line card and specify the size of the crash information. Size of the memory to store can be from 0 to 67,108,864.
sqe-register-rx **sqe-register-tx**	(Optional) Stores crash information for the receive or transmit silicon queueing engine registers on the line card.
k **m**	(Optional) The **k** option multiplies the specified *size* by 1K (1024), and the **m** option multiplies the specified *size* by 1M (1024*1024).

Default

No crash information is stored for the line card.

If enabled with no options, the default is to store 256MB of main memory.

Command Mode

Global configuration

Usage Guidelines

This command was added in Cisco IOS Release 11.2 GS to support the Cisco 12000 series Gigabit Switch Routers.

Use the **exception linecard** global configuration command only when directed by a technical support representative and only enable options that the technical support representative requests you to enable. Technical support representatives need to be able to look at the crash information from the line card to troubleshoot serious problems on the line card. The crash information contains all the line card memory information including the main memory and transmit and receive buffer information.

CAUTION   Use caution when enabling the **exception linecard** global configuration command. Enabling all options could cause a large amount (150 to 250MB) of crash information to be sent to the server.

Example

The following example enables the storing of crash information for line card 8. By default, 256 MB of main memory is stored.

```
exception linecard slot 8
end
```

exception memory

To cause the router to create a core dump and reboot when certain memory size parameters are violated, use the **exception memory** global configuration command. To disable the rebooting and core dump, use the **no** form of this command.

> **exception memory** {**fragment** *size* | **minimum** *size*}
> **no exception memory** {**fragment** | **minimum**}

Syntax	Description
fragment *size*	The minimum contiguous block of memory in the free pool, in bytes.
minimum *size*	The minimum size of the free memory pool, in bytes.

Default

Disabled

Command Mode

Global configuration

Usage Guidelines

This command first appeared in Cisco IOS Release 10.3.

CAUTION   Use the **exception** commands only under the direction of a technical support
representative. Creating a core dump while the router is functioning in a network can
disrupt network operation. The resulting binary file, which is very large, must be
transferred to a TFTP, FTP, or rcp server and subsequently interpreted by technical
personnel who have access to source code and detailed memory maps.

This command is useful to troubleshoot memory leaks.

The size is checked every 60 seconds. If you enter a size that is greater than the free memory, a core
dump and router reload is generated after 60 seconds.

The **exception dump** command must be configured in order to generate a core file. If the
exception dump command is not configured, the router reloads without generating a core dump.

Example

The following example configures the router to monitor the free memory. If the amount of free memory
falls below 250,000 bewitches router will dump the core file and reload.

```
exception dump 131.108.92.2
exception core-file memory.overrun
exception memory minimum 250000
```

Related Commands

To locate documentation of related commands, you can search online at www.cisco.com.

exception core-file
exception dump
exception protocol
ip ftp password
ip ftp username

exception protocol

To configure the protocol used for core dumps, use the **exception protocol** global configuration command. To configure the router to use the default protocol, use the **no** form of this command.

> **exception protocol** {**ftp** | **rcp** | **tftp**}
> **no exception protocol**

Syntax	Description
ftp	Use FTP for core dumps.
rcp	Use rcp for core dumps.
tftp	Use TFTP for core dumps.

Default

tftp

Command Mode

Global configuration

Usage Guidelines

This command first appeared in Cisco IOS Release 10.3.

CAUTION   Use the **exception** commands only under the direction of a technical support representative. Creating a core dump while the router is functioning in a network can disrupt network operation. The resulting binary file, which is very large, must be transferred to a TFTP, FTP, or rcp server and subsequently interpreted by technical personnel who have access to source code and detailed memory maps.

If you use TFTP to dump the core file to a server, the router will only dump the first 16MB of the core file. If the router's memory is larger than 16MB, the whole core file will not be copied to the server. Therefore, use rcp or FTP to dump the core file.

Example

The following example configures a router to use FTP to dump a core file to the FTP server at 172.17.92.2 when it crashes:

```
ip ftp username red
ip ftp password blue
exception protocol ftp
exception dump 172.17.92.2
```

Related Commands

To locate documentation of related commands, you can search online at www.cisco.com.

exception core-file
exception dump
exception memory
ip ftp password
ip ftp username

logging

To log messages to a syslog server host, use the **logging** global configuration command. The **no** form of this command deletes the syslog server with the specified address from the list of syslogs.

> **logging** *host*
> **no logging** *host*

Syntax   Description

host   Name or IP address of the host to be used as a syslog server.

Default

No messages are logged to a syslog server host.

Command Mode

Global configuration

Usage Guidelines

This command first appeared in Cisco IOS Release 10.0.

This command identifies a syslog server host to receive logging messages. By issuing this command more than once, you build a list of syslog servers that receive logging messages.

Example

The following example logs messages to a host named *johnson*:

```
logging johnson
```

Related Commands

To locate documentation of related commands, you can search online at www.cisco.com.

logging trap
service timestamps

logging buffered

To log messages to an internal buffer, use the **logging buffered** global configuration command. The **no** form of this command cancels the use of the buffer. The **default** form of this command returns the buffer size to the default size.

> **logging buffered** [*size*]
> **no logging buffered**
> **default logging buffered**

Syntax   Description

size   (Optional) Size of the buffer from 4096 to 4,294,967,295 bytes. The default size varies by platform.

Default

For most platforms, the Cisco IOS software logs messages to the internal buffer.

Command Mode

Global configuration

Usage Guidelines

This command first appeared in Cisco IOS Release 10.0.

This command copies logging messages to an internal buffer. The buffer is circular in nature, so newer messages overwrite older messages after the buffer is filled.

To display the messages that are logged in the buffer, use the EXEC command **show logging**. The first message displayed is the oldest message in the buffer.

Do not make the buffer size too large because the router could run out of memory for other tasks. You can use the **show memory** EXEC command to view the free processor memory on the router; however, this is the maximum available and should not be approached. The command **default logging buffered** resets the buffer size to the default for the platform.

Example

The following example enables logging to an internal buffer:

```
logging buffered
```

Related Commands

To locate documentation of related commands, you can search online at www.cisco.com.

clear logging
show logging

logging console

To limit messages logged to the console based on severity, use the **logging console** global configuration command. The **no** form of this command disables logging to the console terminal.

> **logging console** *level*
> **no logging console**

Syntax   Description

level   Limits the logging of messages displayed on the console terminal to a specified level. See Chapter 24, Table 24-12 for a list of the *level* keywords.

Default
debugging

Command Mode
Global configuration

Usage Guidelines

This command first appeared in Cisco IOS Release 10.0.

Specifying a *level* causes messages at that level and numerically lower levels to be displayed at the console terminal.

The EXEC command **show logging** displays the addresses and levels associated with the current logging setup, as well as any other logging statistics. See Table 26-1.

Table 26-1   *Error Message Logging Priorities*

Level Keyword	Level	Description	Syslog Definition
emergencies	0	System unusable	LOG_EMERG
alerts	1	Immediate action needed	LOG_ALERT
critical	2	Critical conditions	LOG_CRIT
errors	3	Error conditions	LOG_ERR
warnings	4	Warning conditions	LOG_WARNING
notifications	5	Normal but significant condition	LOG_NOTICE
informational	6	Informational messages only	LOG_INFO
debugging	7	Debugging messages	LOG_DEBUG

The effect of the **log** keyword with the IP **access list (extended)** command depends on the setting of the **logging console** command. The **log** keyword takes effect only if the logging console level is set to 6 or 7. If you change the default to a level lower than 6 and specify the **log** keyword with the IP **access list (extended)** command, no information is logged or displayed.

Example

The following example changes the level of messages displayed to the console terminal to **alerts**, which means alerts and emergencies are displayed:

```
logging console alerts
```

Related Commands

To locate documentation of related commands, you can search online at www.cisco.com.

logging facility
access-list (extended)

logging facility

To configure the syslog facility in which error messages are sent, use the **logging facility** global configuration command. To revert to the default of **local7**, use the **no** form of this command.

logging facility *facility-type*
no logging facility

Syntax   Description

facility-type   Syslog facility. See Chapter 24, Table 24-13 for the *facility-type* keywords.

Default
local7

Command Mode
Global configuration

Usage Guidelines
This command first appeared in Cisco IOS Release 10.0.

Table 26-2 describes the acceptable options for the *facility-type* keyword.

Table 26-2 *Logging Facility-Type Keywords*

Keyword	Description
auth	Authorization system
cron	Cron facility
daemon	System daemon
kern	Kernel
local0–7	Reserved for locally defined messages
lpr	Line printer system
mail	Mail system
news	USENET news
sys9	System use
sys10	System use
sys11	System use

Table 26-2 *Logging Facility-Type Keywords (Continued)*

Keyword	Description
sys12	System use
sys13	System use
sys14	System use
syslog	System log
user	User process
uucp	UNIX-to-UNIX copy system

Example

The following example configures the syslog facility to the kernel facility type:

```
logging facility kern
```

Related Commands

To locate documentation of related commands, you can search online at www.cisco.com.

logging console

logging history

To limit syslog messages sent to the router's history table and the SNMP network management station based on severity, use the **logging history** global configuration command. The **no** form of this command returns the logging of syslog messages to the default level.

> **logging history** *level*
> **no logging history**

Syntax   Description

level   Limits the messages saved in the history table and sent to the SNMP
                 network management station to the specified set of levels. See Chapter 24,
                 Table 24-14 for a list of the *level* keywords.

Default

warnings, **errors**, **critical**, **alerts**, and **emergencies** messages

Command Mode

Global configuration

Usage Guidelines

This command first appeared in Cisco IOS Release 11.2.

Sending syslog messages to the SNMP network management station occurs when you enable syslog traps with the **snmp-server enable trap** global configuration command. Because SNMP traps are inherently unreliable and much too important to lose, at least one syslog message, the most recent message, is stored in a history table on the router. The number of messages stored in the table is governed by the **logging history size** command.

Specifying a *level* causes messages at that severity level and numerically lower levels to be stored in the router's history table and sent to the SNMP network management station. Severity levels are numbered 1 to 8 with 1 being the most important message and 8 being the least important message (that is, the lower the number, the more critical the message). For example, specifying the level **critical** causes critical (3), alerts (2), and emergencies (1) messages to be stored to the history table and sent to the SNMP network management station. See Table 26-3 for a list of severity levels.

As shown in Table 26-3, the EXEC command **show logging history** displays information about the history table such as the table size, the status of messages, and text of the messages stored in the table.

Table 26-3 *Error Message Logging Priorities for Histry Table and SNMP Server*

Level Keyword	Severity Level	Description	Syslog Definition
emergencies	1	System unusable	LOG_EMERG
alerts	2	Immediate action needed	LOG_ALERT
critical	3	Critical conditions	LOG_CRIT
errors	4	Error conditions	LOG_ERR
warnings	5	Warning conditions	LOG_WARNING
notifications	6	Normal but significant condition	LOG_NOTICE
informational	7	Informational messages only	LOG_INFO
debugging	8	Debugging messages	LOG_DEBUG

Example

The following example changes the level of messages sent to the history table and to the SNMP server to **alerts**, which means alerts (2) and emergencies (1) are sent:

```
logging history alerts
```

Related Commands

To locate documentation of related commands, you can search online at www.cisco.com.

logging history size
show logging
snmp-server host

logging history size

To change the number of syslog messages stored in the router's history table, use the **logging history size** global configuration command. The **no** form of this command returns the number of messages to the default value.

> **logging history size** *number*
> **no logging history size**

Syntax	Description
number	Number from 1 to 500 that indicates the maximum number of messages stored in the history table.

Default

One message

Command Mode

Global configuration

Usage Guidelines

This command first appeared in Cisco IOS Release 11.2.

When the history table is full (that is, it contains the maximum number of message entries specified with the **logging history size** command), the oldest message entry is deleted from the table to allow the new message entry to be stored.

Example

The following example sets the number of messages stored in the history table to 20:

```
logging history size 20
```

Related Commands

To locate documentation of related commands, you can search online at www.cisco.com.

logging history
show logging

logging linecard

To log messages to an internal buffer on a line card, use the **logging linecard** global configuration command. To cancel the use of the internal buffer on the line cards, use the **no** form of this command.

> **logging linecard** [*size* | *message-level*]
> **no logging linecard**

Syntax	Description
size	(Optional) Size of the buffer used for each line card. The range is 4,096 to 65,536 bytes. The default is 8KB.
message-level	(Optional) Limits the logging of messages displayed on the console terminal to a specified level. The message level can be:

- **alerts**—Immediate action needed
- **critical**—Critical conditions
- **debugging**—Debugging messages
- **emergencies**—System is unusable
- **errors**—Error conditions
- **informational**—Informational messages
- **notifications**—Normal but significant conditions
- **warnings**—Warning conditions

Default

The Cisco IOS software logs messages to the internal buffer on the GRP card.

Command Mode

Global configuration

Usage Guidelines

This command was added in Cisco IOS Release 11.2 GS to support the Cisco 12000 series Gigabit Switch Routers.

Specifying a message level causes messages at that level and numerically lower levels to be stored in the internal buffer on the line cards.

Table 26-4 lists the message levels and associated numerical level. For example, if you specify a message level of critical, all critical, alert, and emergency messages will be logged.

Table 26-4 *Message Levels*

Level Keyword	Level
emergencies	0
alerts	1
critical	2
errors	3
warnings	4
notifications	5
informational	6
debugging	7

To display the messages that are logged in the buffer, use the EXEC command **show logging slot**. The first message displayed is the oldest message in the buffer.

Do not make the buffer size too large because the router could run out of memory for other tasks. You can use the **show memory** EXEC command to view the free processor memory on the router; however, this is the maximum available and should not be approached.

Example

The following example enables logging to an internal buffer on the line cards using the default buffer size and logging warning, error, critical, alert, and emergency messages:

```
logging linecard warnings
end
```

Related Commands

clear logging
show logging

Part
III

Command Reference

logging monitor

To limit messages logged to the terminal lines (monitors) based on severity, use the **logging monitor** global configuration command. This command limits the logging messages displayed on terminal lines other than the console line to messages with a level at or above *level*. The **no** form of this command disables logging to terminal lines other than the console line.

> **logging monitor** *level*
> **no logging monitor**

Syntax

Description

level   One of the *level* keywords listed in Table 26-2.

Default

debugging

Command Mode

Global configuration

Usage Guidelines

This command first appeared in Cisco IOS Release 10.0.

Specifying a level causes messages at that level and numerically lower levels to be displayed to the monitor.

Example

The following example specifies that only messages of the levels **errors**, **critical**, **alerts**, and **emergencies** be displayed on terminals:

```
logging monitor errors
```

Related Commands

To locate documentation of related commands, you can search online at www.cisco.com.

terminal monitor

logging on

To control logging of error messages, use the **logging on** global configuration command. This command sends debug or error messages to a logging process, which logs messages to designated locations asynchronously to the processes that generated the messages. The **no** form of this command disables the logging process.

> **logging on**
> **no logging on**

Syntax Description

This command has no arguments or keywords.

Default

The Cisco IOS software sends messages to the asynchronous logging process.

Command Mode

Global configuration

Usage Guidelines

This command first appeared in Cisco IOS Release 10.0.

The logging process controls the distribution of logging messages to the various destinations, such as the logging buffer, terminal lines, or syslog server. You can turn logging on and off for these destinations individually using the **logging buffered**, **logging monitor**, and **logging** commands. However, if the **logging on** command is disabled, no messages will be sent to these destinations. Only the console will receive messages.

Additionally, the logging process logs messages to the console and the various destinations after the processes that generated them have completed. When the logging process is disabled, messages are displayed on the console as soon as they are produced, often appearing in the middle of command output.

CAUTION   Disabling the **logging on** command will significantly slow down the router. Any process generating debug or error messages will wait until the messages have been displayed on the console before continuing.

Part III

Command Reference

The **logging synchronous** command also affects the displaying of messages to the console. When the **logging synchronous** command is enabled, messages will only appear after the user types a carriage return.

Examples

The following example shows command output and message output when logging is enabled. The ping process finishes before any of the logging information is printed to the console (or any other destination).

```
Router(config)# logging on
Router(config)# end
Router#
%SYS-5-CONFIG_I: Configured from console by console
Router# ping dirt

Type escape sequence to abort.
Sending 5, 100-byte ICMP Echos to 172.16.1.129, timeout is 2 seconds:
!!!!!
Success rate is 100 percent (5/5), round-trip min/avg/max = 4/5/8 ms
Router#
IP: s=172.21.96.41 (local), d=172.16.1.129 (Ethernet1/0), len 100, sending
IP: s=171.69.1.129 (Ethernet1/0), d=172.21.96.41, len 114, rcvd 1
IP: s=172.21.96.41 (local), d=172.16.1.129 (Ethernet1/0), len 100, sending
IP: s=171.69.1.129 (Ethernet1/0), d=172.21.96.41, len 114, rcvd 1
IP: s=172.21.96.41 (local), d=172.16.1.129 (Ethernet1/0), len 100, sending
IP: s=171.69.1.129 (Ethernet1/0), d=172.21.96.41, len 114, rcvd 1
IP: s=172.21.96.41 (local), d=172.16.1.129 (Ethernet1/0), len 100, sending
IP: s=171.69.1.129 (Ethernet1/0), d=172.21.96.41, len 114, rcvd 1
IP: s=172.21.96.41 (local), d=172.16.1.129 (Ethernet1/0), len 100, sending
IP: s=171.69.1.129 (Ethernet1/0), d=172.21.96.41, len 114, rcvd 1
```

In the next example, logging is disabled. The message output is displayed as messages are generated, causing the debug messages to be interspersed with the message "Type escape sequence to abort."

```
Router(config)# no logging on
Router(config)# end

%SYS-5-CONFIG_I: Configured from console by console
Router#
Router# ping dirt

IP: s=172.21.96.41 (local), d=172.16.1.129 (Ethernet1/0), len 100, sendingTyp
IP: s=171.69.1.129 (Ethernet1/0), d=172.21.96.41, len 114, rcvd 1e
IP: s=172.21.96.41 (local), d=172.16.1.129 (Ethernet1/0), len 100, sending esc
IP: s=171.69.1.129 (Ethernet1/0), d=172.21.96.41, len 114, rcvd 1
IP: s=172.21.96.41 (local), d=172.16.1.129 (Ethernet1/0), len 100, sendingape
IP: s=171.69.1.129 (Ethernet1/0), d=172.21.96.41, len 114, rcvd 1
IP: s=172.21.96.41 (local), d=172.16.1.129 (Ethernet1/0), len 100, sendingse
IP: s=171.69.1.129 (Ethernet1/0), d=172.21.96.41, len 114, rcvd 1
IP: s=172.21.96.41 (local), d=172.16.1.129 (Ethernet1/0), len 100, sendingquen
IP: s=171.69.1.129 (Ethernet1/0), d=172.21.96.41, len 114, rcvd 1ce to abort.
```

```
Sending 5, 100-byte ICMP Echos to 172.16.1.129, timeout is 2 seconds:
!!!!!
Success rate is 100 percent (5/5), round-trip min/avg/max = 152/152/156 ms
Router#
```

Related Commands

To locate documentation of related commands, you can search online at www.cisco.com.

logging
logging buffered
logging monitor
logging synchronous

logging source-interface

To specify the source IP address of syslog packets, use the **logging source-interface** global configuration command. Use the **no** form of this command to remove the source designation.

> **logging source-interface** *type number*
> **no logging source-interface**

Syntax

Description

type

Interface type

number

Interface number

Default

No interface is specified.

Command Mode

Global configuration

Usage Guidelines

This command first appeared in Cisco IOS Release 11.2.

Normally, a syslog message contains the IP address of the interface it uses to leave the router. The **logging source-interface** command specifies that syslog packets contain the IP address of a particular interface, regardless of which interface the packet uses to exit the router.

Examples

The following example specifies that the IP address for Ethernet interface 0 is the source IP address for all syslog messages:

```
logging source-interface ethernet 0
```

The following example specifies that the IP address for Ethernet interface 2/1 on a Cisco 7000 series router is the source IP address for all syslog messages:

```
logging source-interface ethernet 2/1
```

Related Commands

To locate documentation of related commands, you can search online at www.cisco.com.

logging

logging synchronous

To synchronize unsolicited messages and debug output with solicited Cisco IOS software output and prompts for a specific console port line, auxiliary port line, or virtual terminal line, use the **logging synchronous** line configuration command. Use the **no** form of this command to disable synchronization of unsolicited messages and debug output.

> **logging synchronous** [**level** *severity-level* | **all**] [**limit** *number-of-buffers*]
> **no logging synchronous** [**level** *severity-level* | **all**] [**limit** *number-of-buffers*]

Syntax	Description
level *severity-level*	(Optional) Specifies the message severity level. Messages with a severity level equal to or higher than this value are printed asynchronously. Low numbers indicate greater severity and high numbers indicate lesser severity. The default value is 2.
all	(Optional) Specifies that all messages are printed asynchronously, regardless of the severity level.
limit *number-of-buffers*	(Optional) Specifies the number of buffers to be queued for the terminal after which new messages are dropped. The default value is 20.

Defaults

This feature is turned off by default.

If you do not specify a severity level, the default value of 2 is assumed.

If you do not specify the maximum number of buffers to be queued, the default value of 20 is assumed.

Command Mode

Line configuration

Usage Guidelines

This command first appeared in Cisco IOS Release 10.0.

When synchronous logging of unsolicited messages and debug output is turned on, unsolicited Cisco IOS software output is displayed on the console or printed after solicited Cisco IOS software output is displayed or printed. Unsolicited messages and debug output is displayed on the console after the prompt for user input is returned. This is to keep unsolicited messages and debug output from being interspersed with solicited software output and prompts. After the unsolicited messages are displayed, the console displays the user prompt again.

When specifying a severity level number, consider that for the logging system, low numbers indicate greater severity and high numbers indicate lesser severity.

When a terminal line's message-queue limit is reached, new messages are dropped from the line, although these messages might be displayed on other lines. If messages are dropped, the notice "%SYS-3-MSGLOST *number-of-messages* due to overflow" follows any messages that are displayed. This notice is displayed only on the terminal that lost the messages. It is not sent to any other lines, any logging servers, or the logging buffer.

CAUTION   By configuring abnormally large message-queue limits and setting the terminal to "terminal monitor" on a terminal that is accessible to intruders, you expose yourself to "denial of service" attacks. An intruder could carry out the attack by putting the terminal in synchronous output mode, making a Telnet connection to a remote host, and leaving the connection idle. This could cause large numbers of messages to be generated and queued, and these messages would consume all available RAM. Although unlikely to occur, you should guard against this type of attack through proper configuration.

Example

The following example identifies line 4 and enables synchronous logging for line 4 with a severity level of 6. Then the example identifies another line, line 2, and enables synchronous logging for line 2 with a severity level of 7 and specifies a maximum number of buffers to be 70,000:

```
line 4
logging synchronous level 6
line 2
logging synchronous level 7 limit 70000
```

Related Commands

To locate documentation of related commands, you can search online at www.cisco.com.

line
logging on

logging trap

To limit messages logged to the syslog servers based on severity, use the **logging trap** global configuration command. The command limits the logging of error messages sent to syslog servers to only those messages at the specified level. Use the **no** form of this command to disable logging to syslog servers.

> **logging trap** *level*
> **no logging trap**

Syntax	Description
level	One of the *level* keywords listed in Table 26-2.

Default

Informational

Command Mode

Global configuration

Usage Guidelines

This command first appeared in Cisco IOS Release 10.0.

The EXEC command **show logging** displays the addresses and levels associated with the current logging setup. The command output also includes ancillary statistics.

Table I-1 in the Introduction lists the syslog definitions that correspond to the debugging message levels. Additionally, there are four categories of messages generated by the software, as follows:

- Error messages about software or hardware malfunctions at the LOG_ERR level.

- Output for the debug commands at the LOG_WARNING level.

- Interface up/down transitions and system restarts at the LOG_NOTICE level.

- Reload requests and low process stacks are at the LOG_INFO level.

Use the **logging** and **logging trap** commands to send messages to a UNIX syslog server.

Example

The following example logs messages to a host named *johnson*:

```
logging johnson
logging trap notifications
```

Related Commands

To locate documentation of related commands, you can search online at www.cisco.com.

logging

ping (privileged)

Use the **ping** (packet internet groper) privileged EXEC command to diagnose basic network connectivity on Apollo, AppleTalk, Connectionless Network Service (CLNS), DECnet, IP, Novell IPX, VINES, or XNS networks.

ping [*protocol*] {*host* | *address*}

Syntax   Description

Syntax	Description
protocol	(Optional) Protocol keyword, one of **apollo**, **appletalk**, **clns**, **decnet**, **ip**, **ipx**, **vines**, or **xns**.
host	Host name of system to ping.
address	Address of system to ping.

Command Mode

Privileged EXEC

Usage Guidelines

This command first appeared in Cisco IOS Release 10.0.

The ping program sends an echo request packet to an address, then awaits a reply. Ping output can help you evaluate path-to-host reliability, delays over the path, and whether the host can be reached or is functioning.

To abnormally terminate a ping session, type the escape sequence—by default, **Ctrl-^ X**. You type the default by simultaneously pressing and releasing the **Ctrl**, **Shift**, and **6** keys, and then pressing the **X** key.

Part III

Command Reference

Table 26-5 describes the test characters that the ping facility sends.

Table 26-5   *Ping Test Characters*

Char	Meaning
!	Each exclamation point indicates receipt of a reply.
.	Each period indicates the network server timed out while waiting for a reply.
U	A destination unreachable error PDU was received.
C	A congestion experienced packet was received.
I	User interrupted test.
?	Unknown packet type.
&	Packet lifetime exceeded.

NOTE   Not all protocols require hosts to support pings. For some protocols, the pings are Cisco-defined and are only answered by another Cisco router.

Example

After you enter the **ping** command in privileged mode, the system prompts for one of the following keywords: **appletalk**, **clns**, **ip**, **novell**, **apollo**, **vines**, **decnet**, or **xns**. The default protocol is IP.

If you enter a host name or address on the same line as the **ping** command, the default action is taken as appropriate for the protocol type of that name or address.

While the precise dialog varies somewhat from protocol to protocol, all are similar to the ping session using default values shown in the following display.

```
Router# ping
Protocol [ip]:
Target IP address: 192.168.7.27
Repeat count [5]:
Datagram size [100]:
Timeout in seconds [2]:
Extended commands [n]:
Sweep range of sizes [n]:
Type escape sequence to abort.
Sending 5, 100-byte ICMP Echos to 192.168.7.27, timeout is 2 seconds:
!!!!!
Success rate is 100 percent, round-trip min/avg/max = 1/2/4 ms
```

Table 26-6 describes the default **ping** fields shown in the display.

Table 26-6   *Ping Field Descriptions*

Field	Description
Protocol [ip]:	Prompts for a supported protocol. Enter **appletalk, clns, ip, novell, apollo, vines, decnet,** or **xns**. Default: **ip**.
Target IP address:	Prompts for the IP address or host name of the destination node you plan to ping. If you have specified a supported protocol other than IP, enter an appropriate address for that protocol here. Default: none.
Repeat count [5]:	Number of ping packets that will be sent to the destination address. Default: 5.
Datagram size [100]:	Size of the ping packet (in bytes). Default: 100 bytes.
Timeout in seconds [2]:	Timeout interval. Default: 2 (seconds).
Extended commands [n]:	Specifies whether or not a series of additional commands appears. Many of the following displays and tables show and describe these commands.
Sweep range of sizes [n]:	Allows you to vary the sizes of the echo packets being sent. This capability is useful for determining the minimum sizes of the MTUs configured on the nodes along the path to the destination address. Packet fragmentation contributing to performance problems can then be reduced.
!!!!!	Each exclamation point (!) indicates receipt of a reply. A period (.) indicates the network server timed out while waiting for a reply. Other characters may appear in the ping output display, depending on the protocol type.
Success rate is 100 percent	Percentage of packets successfully echoed back to the router. Anything less than 80 percent is usually considered problematic.
round-trip min/avg/max = 1/2/4 ms	Round-trip travel time intervals for the protocol echo packets, including minimum/average/maximum (in milliseconds).

Related Commands

To locate documentation of related commands, you can search online at www.cisco.com.

ping (user)

ping (user)

Use the **ping** (packet internet groper) user EXEC command to diagnose basic network connectivity on AppleTalk, CLNS, IP, Novell, Apollo, VINES, DECnet, or XNS networks.

> **ping** [*protocol*] {*host* | *address*}

Syntax	Description
protocol	(Optional) Protocol keyword, one of **apollo**, **appletalk**, **clns**, **decnet**, **ip**, **ipx**, **vines**, or **xns**.
host	Host name of system to ping.
address	Address of system to ping.

Command Mode

EXEC

Usage Guidelines

This command first appeared in Cisco IOS Release 10.0.

The user-level ping feature provides a basic ping facility for users who do not have system privileges. This feature allows the Cisco IOS software to perform the simple default ping functionality for a number of protocols. Only the terse form of the **ping** command is supported for user-level pings.

If the system cannot map an address for a host name, it returns an "%Unrecognized host or address" error message.

To abnormally terminate a ping session, type the escape sequence—by default, **Ctrl-^ X**. You type the default by simultaneously pressing and releasing the **Ctrl**, **Shift**, and **6** keys and then pressing the **X** key.

Table 26-7 describes the test characters that the ping facility sends.

Table 26-7   *Ping Test Characters*

Char	Meaning
!	Each exclamation point indicates receipt of a reply.
.	Each period indicates the network server timed out while waiting for a reply.
U	A destination unreachable error PDU was received.
C	A congestion experienced packet was received.
I	User interrupted test.
?	Unknown packet type.
&	Packet lifetime exceeded.

Example

The following display shows sample ping output when you ping the IP host named *donald*:

```
Router> ping donald
Type escape sequence to abort.
Sending 5, 100-byte ICMP Echos to 192.168.7.27, timeout is 2 seconds:
!!!!!
Success rate is 100 percent, round-trip min/avg/max = 1/3/4 ms
```

Related Commands

To locate documentation of related commands, you can search online at www.cisco.com.

ping (privileged)

service slave-log

To allow slave Versatile Interface Processor (VIP) cards to log important error messages to the console, use the **service slave-log** global configuration command. Use the **no** form of this command to disable slave logging.

> **service slave-log**
> **no service slave-log**

Syntax Description

This command has no arguments or keywords.

Default

This command is enabled by default.

Command Mode

Global configuration

Usage Guidelines

This command first appeared in Cisco IOS Release 11.1.

This command allows slave slots to log error messages of level 2 or higher (critical, alerts, and emergencies).

Part
III

Command Reference

Examples

The following example logs important messages from the slave cards to the console:

```
service slave-log
```

The following example illustrates sample output when this command is enabled:

```
%IPC-5-SLAVELOG: VIP-SLOT2:
 IPC-2-NOMEM: No memory available for IPC system initialization
```

The first line indicates which slot sent the message. The second line contains the error message.

service tcp-keepalives-in

To generate keepalive packets on idle incoming network connections (initiated by the remote host), use the **service tcp-keepalives-in** global configuration command. The **no** form of this command with the appropriate keyword disables the keepalives.

> **service tcp-keepalives-in**
> **no service tcp-keepalives-in**

Syntax Description

This command has no arguments or keywords.

Default

Disabled

Command Mode

Global configuration

Usage Guidelines

This command first appeared in Cisco IOS Release 10.0.

Example

The following example generates keepalives on incoming TCP connections:

```
service tcp-keepalives-in
```

Related Commands

To locate documentation of related commands, you can search online at www.cisco.com.

service tcp-keepalives-out

service tcp-keepalives-out

To generate keepalive packets on idle outgoing network connections (initiated by a user), use the **service tcp-keepalives-out** global configuration command. The **no** form of this command with the appropriate keyword disables the keepalives.

> **service tcp-keepalives-out**
> **no service tcp-keepalives-out**

Syntax Description

This command has no arguments or keywords.

Default

Disabled

Command Mode

Global configuration

Usage Guidelines

This command first appeared in Cisco IOS Release 10.0.

Example

The following example generates keepalives on outgoing TCP connections:

```
service tcp-keepalives-out
```

Related Commands

To locate documentation of related commands, you can search online at www.cisco.com.

service tcp-keepalives-in

service timestamps

To configure the system to timestamp debugging or logging messages, use one of the **service timestamps** global configuration commands. Use the **no** form of this command to disable this service.

> **service timestamps** *type* [**uptime**]
> **service timestamps** *type* **datetime** [**msec**] [**localtime**] [**show-timezone**]
> **no service timestamps** *type*

Syntax	Description
type	Type of message to timestamp: **debug** or **log**.
uptime	(Optional) Timestamp with time since the system was rebooted.
datetime	Timestamp with the date and time.
msec	(Optional) Include milliseconds in the date and timestamp.
localtime	(Optional) Timestamp relative to the local time zone.
show-timezone	(Optional) Include the time zone name in the timestamp.

Default

No timestamping.

If **service timestamps** is specified with no arguments or keywords, default is **service timestamps debug uptime**.

The default for **service timestamps** *type* **datetime** is to format the time in UTC, with no milliseconds and no time zone name.

The command **no service timestamps** by itself disables timestamps for both debug and log messages.

Command Mode

Global configuration

Usage Guidelines

This command first appeared in Cisco IOS Release 10.0.

Timestamps can be added to either debugging or logging messages independently. The **uptime** form of the command adds timestamps in the format HHHH:MM:SS, indicating the time since the system was rebooted. The **datetime** form of the command adds timestamps in the format MMM DD HH:MM:SS, indicating the date and time according to the system clock. If the system clock has not been set, the date and time are preceded by an asterisk (*) to indicate that the date and time are probably not correct.

Examples

The following example enables timestamps on debugging messages, showing the time since reboot:

```
service timestamps debug uptime
```

The following example enables timestamps on logging messages, showing the current time and date relative to the local time zone, with the time zone name included:

```
service timestamps log datetime localtime show-timezone
```

Related Commands

To locate documentation of related commands, you can search online at www.cisco.com.

clock set
debug
ntp

show c2600 (for the Cisco 2600 Series)

To display information for troubleshooting the Cisco 2600 Series router, enter the **show c2600** EXEC command.

Command Mode

EXEC and Privileged EXEC

Usage Guidelines

This command first appeared in Cisco IOS Release 11.3 XA.

The **show c2600** command provides complex troubleshooting information that pertains to the platform's shared references rather than to a specific interface.

Sample Display

The following example shows sample display output for the **show c2600** EXEC command. See Table 26-8 for a description of the output display fields.

```
router# show c2600
C2600 Platform Information:
Interrupts:

 Assigned Handlers...
  Vect  Handler    # of Ints   Name
   00  801F224C   00000000    Xilinx bridge error interrupt
```

```
01  801DE768  0D3EE155  MPC860 TIMER INTERRUPT
02  801E94E0  0000119E  16552 Con/Aux Interrupt
04  801F0D94  00000000  PA Network Management Int Handler
05  801E6C34  00000000  Timebase Reference Interrupt
06  801F0DE4  00002C1A  PA Network IO Int Handler
07  801F0EA0  0000015D  MPC860 CPM INTERRUPT
14  801F224C  00000000  Xilinx bridge error interrupt

IOS Priority Masks...
 Level 00 = [ EF020000 ]
 Level 01 = [ EC020000 ]
 Level 02 = [ E8020000 ]
 Level 03 = [ E0020000 ]
 Level 04 = [ E0020000 ]
 Level 05 = [ E0020000 ]
 Level 06 = [ C0020000 ]
 Level 07 = [ 00000000 ]

SIU_IRQ_MASK = FFFFFFFF  SIEN  = EF02xxxx  Current Level = 00
Spurious IRQs = 00000000  SIPEND = 0000xxxx

Interrupt Throttling:
 Throttle Count = 00000000  Timer Count     = 00000000
 Netint usec    = 00000000  Netint Mask usec = 000003E8
 Active         =        0  Configured      =        0
 Longest IRQ    = 00000000

IDMA Status:
Requests = 00000349     Drops               = 00000000
Complete = 00000349     Post Coalesce Frames = 00000349
Giant    = 00000000
Available Blocks = 256/256

ISP Status:
 Version string burned in chip: "A986122997"
 New version after next program operation: "B018020998"
 ISP family type: "2096"
 ISP chip ID: 0x0013
 Device is  programmable
```

Table 26-8 *Show c2600 Field Descriptions*

Field	Description
Interrupts	Denotes that the next section describes the status of the interrupt services.
Assigned Handlers	Denotes a subsection of the Interrupt section which displays data about the interrupt handlers.
Vect	The processor vector number.
Handler	The execution address of the handler assigned to this vector.
# of Ints	The number of times this handler has been called.

Table 26-8 *Show c2600 Field Descriptions (Continued)*

Field	Description
Name	The name of the handler assigned to this vector.
IOS Priority Masks	Denotes the subsection of the Interrupt section which displays internal IOS priorities. Each item in this subsection indicates an IOS interrupt level and the bit mask used to mask out interrupt sources when that IOS level is being processed. Used exclusively for debugging.
SIU_IRQ_MASK	For engineering level debug only.
Spurious IRQs	For engineering level debug only.
Interrupt Throttling:	This subsection describes the behavior of the Interrupt Throttling mechanism on the platform.
Throttle Count	Number of times throttle has become active.
Timer Count	Number of times throttle has deactivated because the maximum masked out time for network interrupt level has been reached.
Netint usec	Maximum time network level is allowed to run, in microseconds.
Netint Mask usec	Maximum time network level interrupt is masked out to allow process level code to run, in mirocseconds
Active	Indicates that the network level interrupt is masked or the router is in interrupt throttle state.
Configured	Indicates throttling is enabled or configured when set to 1.
Longest IRQ	Duration of longest network level interrupt, in microseconds.
IDMA Status	Monitors the activity of the Internal Direct Memory Access (IDMA) hardware and software. Used to coalesce packets (turn particalized packets into non-particalized packets) for transfer to the process level switching mechanism.
Requests	Number of times the IDMA engine is asked to coalesce a packet.
Drops	Number of times the coalescing operation was aborted.
Complete	Number of times the operation was successful.
Post Coalesce Frames	Number of Frames completed post-coalesce processing.
Giant	Number of packets too large to coalesce.
Available Blocks	Indicates the status of the request queue, in the format N/M where N is the number of empty slots in queue and M is the total number of slots; for example, 2/256 indicates that the queue has 256 entries and can accept two more requests before it is full.
ISP Status	Provides status of In-System-Programmable hardware.

continues

Part
III

Command Reference

Table 26-8 *Show c2600 Field Descriptions (Continued)*

Field	Description
Version string burned in chip	Current version of ISP hardware.
New version after next program operation	Version of ISP hardware after next ISP programming operation.
ISP family type	Device family number of ISP hardware.
ISP chip ID	Internal ID of ISP hardware as designated by chip manufacturer.
Device is programmable	"Yes" or "No." Indicates if an ISP operation is possible on this board.

Related Commands

To locate documentation of related commands, you can search online at www.cisco.com.

show context

show c7200 (for the Cisco 7200 Series Routers)

Use the **show c7200** EXEC command to display information about the CPU and midplane for Cisco 7200 series routers.

       show c7200

Syntax Description

This command has no arguments or keywords.

Command Mode

EXEC

Usage Guidelines

This command first appeared in Cisco IOS Release 11.2.

You can use the output of this command to determine whether the hardware version level and upgrade is current. The information is generally useful for diagnostic tasks performed by technical support only.

Sample Display

The following is sample output from the **show c7200** command:

```
Router# show c7200

C7200 Network IO Interrupt Throttling:
 throttle count=0, timer count=0
 active=0, configured=0
 netint usec=3999, netint mask usec=200

C7200 Midplane EEPROM:
        Hardware revision 1.2          Board revision A0
        Serial number    2863311530    Part number    170-43690-170
        Test history     0xAA          RMA number     170-170-170
        MAC=0060.3e28.ee00, MAC Size=1024
        EEPROM format version 1, Model=0x6
        EEPROM contents (hex):
          0x20: 01 06 01 02 AA AA AA AA AA AA AA AA 00 60 3E 28
          0x30: EE 00 04 00 AA AA AA AA AA AA AA 50 AA AA AA AA

C7200 CPU EEPROM:
        Hardware revision 2.0          Board revision A0
        Serial number    3509953       Part number    73-1536-02
        Test history     0x0           RMA number     00-00-00
        EEPROM format version 1
        EEPROM contents (hex):
          0x20: 01 15 02 00 00 35 8E C1 49 06 00 02 00 00 00 00
          0x30: 50 00 00 00 FF FF FF FF FF FF FF FF FF FF FF FF
```

show context (for Cisco 2600 Series Routers)

Use the **show context** EXEC command to display information stored in NVRAM when an exception occurs.

show context

Syntax Description

This command has no arguments or keywords.

Command Mode

EXEC and Privileged EXEC

Usage Guidelines

This command first appeared in Cisco IOS Release 10.3.

Context information is specific to processors and architectures, whereas software version and uptime information are not specific to architectures. Context information for the Cisco 2600 Series router differs from that for other router types because the Cisco 2600 runs with an M860 processor. The display from the **show context** command includes the following information:

- Reason for the system reboot

- Stack trace

- Software version

- The signal number, code, and router uptime information

- All the register contents at the time of the crash

This information is useful only to your technical support representative for analyzing crashes in the field. Use this information when you read the displayed statistics to an engineer over the phone.

Sample Display

The following displays sample output from the **show context** command following a system failure on a Cisco 2600 series router. See Table 26-9 for a description of the fields in this output.

```
router# show context
S/W Version: Cisco Internetwork Operating System Software
IOS (tm) c2600 Software (c2600-JS-M), Released Version 11.3(19980115:184921]
Copyright (c) 1986-1998 by cisco Systems, Inc.
Compiled Thu 15-Jan-98 13:49 by mmagno
Exception occurred at: 00:02:26 UTC Mon Mar 1 1993
Exception type: Data TLB Miss (0x1200)
CPU Register Context:
PC  = 0x80109964  MSR = 0x00009030  CR  = 0x55FFFD35  LR    = 0x80109958
CTR = 0x800154E4  XER = 0xC000BB6F  DAR = 0x00000088  DSISR = 0x00000249
DEC = 0x7FFFDFCA  TBU = 0x00000000  TBL = 0x15433FCF  IMMR  = 0x68010020
R0  = 0x80000000  R1  = 0x80E80BD0  R2  = 0x80000000  R3    = 0x00000000
R4  = 0x80E80BC0  R5  = 0x40800000  R6  = 0x00000001  R7    = 0x68010000
R8  = 0x00000000  R9  = 0x00000060  R10 = 0x00001030  R11   = 0xFFFFFFFF
R12 = 0x00007CE6  R13 = 0xFFF379E8  R14 = 0x80D50000  R15   = 0x00000000
R16 = 0x00000000  R17 = 0x00000000  R18 = 0x00000000  R19   = 0x00000000
R20 = 0x00000000  R21 = 0x00000001  R22 = 0x00000010  R23   = 0x00000000
R24 = 0x00000000  R25 = 0x80E91348  R26 = 0x01936010  R27   = 0x80E92A80
R28 = 0x00000001  R29 = 0x019BA920  R30 = 0x00000000  R31   = 0x00000018
Stack trace:
Frame 00: SP = 0x80E80BD0    PC = 0x80109958
Frame 01: SP = 0x80E80C28    PC = 0x8010A720
Frame 02: SP = 0x80E80C40    PC = 0x80271010
Frame 03: SP = 0x80E80C50    PC = 0x8025EE64
Frame 04: SP = 0x80DEE548    PC = 0x8026702C
Frame 05: SP = 0x80DEE558    PC = 0x8026702C
```

Table 26-9 *Show Context Field Descriptions*

Field	Description
S/W Version	Standard IOS version string as displayed.
Exception occurred at	Router real time when exception occurred. The router must have the clock time properly configured for this to be accurate.
Exception type	Technical reason for exception. For engineering analysis.
CPU Register Context	Technical processor state information. For engineering analysis.
Stack trace	Technical processor state information. For engineering analysis.

Related Commands

To locate documentation of related commands, you can search online at www.cisco.com.

show processes
show stacks

show context

To display information stored in NVRAM when the router crashes, use the **show context** EXEC command.

> **show context summary**
> **show context** {**all** | **slot** *slot-number* [*crash-index*] [**all**] [**debug**]}

Syntax	Description
summary	Displays a summary of all the crashes recorded.
all	Displays all crashes for all the slots. When optionally used with the **slot** keyword, displays crash information for the specified slot.
slot *slot-number* [*crash-index*]	Displays information for a particular line card. Slot numbers range from 0 to 11 for the Cisco 12012 and 0 to 7 for the Cisco 12008. The index number allows you to look at previous crash contexts. Contexts from the last 24 line card crashes are saved on the GRP card. If the GRP reloads, the last 24 line card crash contexts are lost. For example, **show context slot 3 2** shows the second most recent crash for line card in slot 3. Index numbers are displayed by the **show context summary** command
debug	(Optional) Displays crash information as hex record dump in addition to one of the options listed above.

Command Mode

EXEC

Usage Guidelines

This command was modified in Cisco IOS Release 11.2 GS to add the **all**, **debug**, **slot**, and **summary** keywords.

The display from the **show context** command includes the following information:

- Reason for the system reboot

- Stack trace

- Software version

- The signal number, code, and router uptime information

- All the register contents at the time of the crash

NOTE   This information is of use only to technical support representatives in analyzing crashes in the field. It is included here in case you need to read the displayed statistics to an engineer over the phone.

Sample Display

The following is sample output from the **show context** command following a system failure:

```
Router> show context

System was restarted by error - a Software forced crash, PC 0x60189354
GS Software (RSP-PV-M), Experimental Version 11.1(2033) [ganesh 111]
Compiled Mon 31-Mar-97 13:21 by ganesh
Image text-base: 0x60010900, data-base: 0x6073E000
Stack trace from system failure:
FP: 0x60AEA798, RA: 0x60189354
FP: 0x60AEA798, RA: 0x601853CC
FP: 0x60AEA7C0, RA: 0x6015E98C
FP: 0x60AEA7F8, RA: 0x6011AB3C
FP: 0x60AEA828, RA: 0x601706CC
FP: 0x60AEA878, RA: 0x60116340
FP: 0x60AEA890, RA: 0x6011632C
Fault History Buffer:
GS Software (RSP-PV-M), Experimental Version 11.1(2033) [ganesh 111]
Compiled Mon 31-Mar-97 13:21 by ganesh
Signal = 23, Code = 0x24, Uptime 00:04:19
$0 : 00000000, AT : 60930120, v0 : 00000032, v1 : 00000120
a0 : 60170110, a1 : 6097F22C, a2 : 00000000, a3 : 00000000
```

```
t0 : 60AE02A0, t1 : 8000FD80, t2 : 34008F00, t3 : FFFF00FF
t4 : 00000083, t5 : 3E840024, t6 : 00000000, t7 : 11010132
s0 : 00000006, s1 : 607A25F8, s2 : 00000001, s3 : 00000000
s4 : 00000000, s5 : 00000000, s6 : 00000000, s7 : 6097F755
t8 : 600FABBC, t9 : 00000000, k0 : 30408401, k1 : 30410000
gp : 608B9860, sp : 60AEA798, s8 : 00000000, ra : 601853CC
EPC : 60189354, SREG : 3400EF03, Cause : 00000024
Router>
```

The following is sample output from the **show context summary** command on a Cisco 12012 router. The **show context summary** command displays a summary of all the crashes recorded.

```
Router# show context summary
CRASH INFO SUMMARY
  Slot 0 : 0 crashes
  Slot 1 : 0 crashes
  Slot 2 : 0 crashes
  Slot 3 : 0 crashes
  Slot 4 : 0 crashes
  Slot 5 : 0 crashes
  Slot 6 : 0 crashes
  Slot 7 : 2 crashes
    1 - crash at 18:06:41 UTC Tue Nov 5 1996
    2 - crash at 12:14:55 UTC Mon Nov 4 1996
  Slot 8 : 0 crashes
  Slot 9 : 0 crashes
  Slot 10: 0 crashes
  Slot 11: 0 crashes
Router#
```

Related Commands

To locate documentation of related commands, you can search online at www.cisco.com.

show processes
show stacks

show controllers (GRP image)

To display information that is specific to the hardware, use the **show controllers** privileged EXEC command.

show controllers [atm *number* **| clock | csar [register] | csc-fpga | dp83800 | fab-clk |**
fia [register] | pos *[number]* **[details] | queues** *[slot-number]* **| sca | xbar]**

Syntax	Description
atm *number*	(Optional) Displays the ATM controllers. Number is slot-number/ port-number (for example, 4/0). Slot numbers range from 0 to 11 for the Cisco 12012 and 0 to 7 for the Cisco 12008.
clock	(Optional) Displays the clock card configuration.
csar [register]	(Optional) Displays the Cisco Cell Segmentation and Reassembly (CSAR) information. CSAR is the name of the chip on the card that handles traffic between the GRP and the switch fabric interface ASICs.
csc-fpga	(Optional) Displays the clock and scheduler card register information in the field programmable gate array (FPGA).
dp83800	(Optional) Displays the Ethernet information on the GRP card.
fab-clk	(Optional) Display the switch fabric clock register information. The switch fabric clock FPGA is a chip that monitors the incoming fabric clock generated by the switch fabric. This clock is needed by each card connecting to the switch fabric to properly communicate with it. There are two switch fabric clocks arriving at each card; only one can be used. The FPGA monitors both clocks and selects which one to use if only one of them is running.
fia [register]	(Optional) Displays the fabric interface ASIC information and optionally display the register information.
pos *[number]* **[details]**	(Optional) Displays the POS framer state and optionally displays all the details for the interface. Number is slot-number/ port-number (for example, 4/0). Slot numbers range from 0 to 11 for the Cisco 12012 and 0 to 7 for the Cisco 12008.
queues *[slot-number]*	(Optional) Displays the SDRAM buffer carve information and optionally displays the information for a specific line card. The SDRAM buffer carve information displayed is suggested carve information from the GRP card to the line card. Line cards might change the shown percentages based on SDRAM available. Slot numbers range from 0 to 11 for the Cisco 12012 and 0 to 7 for the Cisco 12008.
sca	(Optional) Displays the SCA register information. The SCA is an ASIC that arbitrates among the line cards requests to use the switch fabric.
xbar	(Optional) Displays the crossbar register information. The XBAR is an ASIC that switches the data as it passes through the switch fabric.

Command Mode
Privileged EXEC

Usage Guidelines
This command was added in Cisco IOS Release 11.2 GS to support the Cisco 12000 series Gigabit Switch Routers.

NOTE	This information is of use only to technical support representatives in analyzing system failures in the field. It is included here in case you need to read the displayed statistics to an engineer over the phone.

Sample Display
The following is sample output from the **show controllers pos** command for a Cisco 12012:

```
Router# show controllers pos 7/0
POS7/0
SECTION
  LOF = 2          LOS = 0                          BIP(B1) = 5889
  Active Alarms: None
LINE
  AIS = 2          RDI = 2        FEBE = 146        BIP(B2) = 2106453
  Active Alarms: None
PATH
  AIS = 2          RDI = 4        FEBE = 63         BIP(B3) = 3216
  LOP = 0          PSE = 8        NSE = 3           NEWPTR = 2
  Active Alarms: None
APS
  COAPS = 3        PSBF = 2
  State: PSBF_state = False
  Rx(K1/K2): F0/15  Tx(K1/K2): 00/00
  S1S0 = 00, C2 = 64
PATH TRACE BUFFER : STABLE
  Remote hostname : GSR-C
  Remote interface: POS10/0
  Remote IP addr  : 10.201.101.2
  Remote Rx(K1/K2): F0/15  Tx(K1/K2): 00/00
Router#
```

Related Commands
To locate documentation of related commands, you can search online at www.cisco.com.

clear controllers
show controllers (line card image)

show controllers (line card image)

To display information that is specific to the hardware on a line card, use the **attach** privileged EXEC command to connect to the line card and then use the **show controllers** privileged EXEC command or the **execute-on** privileged EXEC command.

> **show controllers atm** [[*port-number*] [**all** | **sar** | **summary**]]
> **show controllers fia** [**register**]
> **show controllers** {**frfab** | **tofab**} {**bma** {**microcode** | **ms-inst** | **register**} |
>   **qelem** *start-queue-element* [*end-queue-element*] |
>   **qnum** *start-queue-number* [*end-queue-number*] |
>   **queues** | **statistics**}
> **show controllers io**
> **show controllers l3**
> **show controllers pos** {**framers** | **queues** | **registers** |
>   **rxsram** *port-number queue-start-address* [*queue-length*] |
>   **txsram** *port-number queue-start-address* [*queue-length*]}

Syntax	Description
atm	Displays the ATM controller information.
port-number	(Optional)Displays request for the physical interface on the ATM card. The range of choices is 0 to 3.
all	(Optional) Lists all details.
sar	(Optional) Lists SAR interactive command.
summary	(Optional) Lists SAR status summary.
fia	Displays the fabric interface ASIC information.
register	(Optional) Displays the register information.
frfab	(Optional) Displays the from fabric (transmit).
tofab	(Optional) Displays the to fabric (receive) information.
bma	For the **frfab** or **tofab** keywords, displays microcode, micro-sequencer, or register information for the silicon queuing engine (SQE), also known as the buffer management ASIC (BMA).
microcode	Displays silicon queuing engine (SQE) information for the microcode bundled in the line card and currently running version.
mis-inst	Displays silicon queuing engine (SQE) information for the micro sequencer instruction.
register	Displays silicon queuing engine (SQE) information for the register.

Syntax	Description
qelem	For the **frfab** or **tofab** keywords, displays the SDRAM buffer pool queue element summary information.
start-queue-element	Specifies the start queue element number (0 to 65,535).
end-queue-element	(Optional) Specifies the end queue element number (0 to 65,535).
qnum	For the **frfab** or **tofab** keywords, displays the SDRAM buffer pool queue detail information.
start-queue-number	Specifies the start free queue number (0 to 127).
end-queue-number	(Optional) Specifies the end free queue number (0 to 127).
queues	For the **frfab** or **tofab** keywords, displays the SDRAM buffer pool information.
statistics	For the **frfab** or **tofab** keywords, displays the BMA counters.
io	Displays input/output registers.
l3	Displays Layer 3 ASIC information.
pos	Displays packet-over-sonic (POS) information for framer registers, framer queues, and ASIC registers.
framers	Displays the POS framer registers.
queues	Displays the POS framer queue information.
registers	Displays the ASIC registers.
rxsram	Displays the receive queue SRAM.
port-number	Specifies a port number (valid range is 0 to 3).
queue-start-address	Specifies the queue SRAM logica starting address.
queue-length	(Optional) Specifies the queue SRAM length.
txsram	Displays the transmit queue SRAM.

Command Mode
Privileged EXEC

Usage Guidelines
This command was added in Cisco IOS Release 11.2 GS to support the Cisco 12000 series Gigabit Switch Routers.

Part
III

Command Reference

NOTE   This information is of use only to technical support representatives in analyzing crashes in the field. It is included here in case you need to read the displayed statistics to an engineer over the phone.

Sample Displays

Because you are executing this command on the line card, you must use the **execute-on** command to perform the **show** command, or you must connect to the card using the **attach** command. All examples in this section use the **execute-on** command.

The following is partial sample output from the **show controllers atm** command:

```
Router# execute-on slot 4 show controllers atm 0
TX SAR (Beta 1.0.0) is Operational;
RX SAR (Beta 1.0.0) is Operational;

Interface Configuration Mode:
      STS-12c

Active Maker Channels: total # 6
VCID  ChnnlID  Type  OutputInfo  InPkts   InOAMs  MacString
   1    0888   UBR   0C010010         0        0  08882000AAAA030000000800
   2    0988   VBR   04010020         0        0  09882000
   3    8BC8   UBR   0C010030         0        0  8BC82000AAAA030000000800
   4    0E08   UBR   0C010040         0        0  0E082000AAAA030000000800
  10    1288   VBR   040100A0         0        0  12882000
  11    8BE8   VBR   0C0100B0         0        0  8BE82000AAAA030000000800

SAR Total Counters:
total_tx_idle_cells 215267  total_tx_paks 0  total_tx_abort_paks 0
total_rx_paks 0  total_rx_drop_paks 0  total_rx_discard_cells 15

Switching Code Counters:
total_rx_crc_err_paks 0  total_rx_giant_paks 0
total_rx_abort_paks 0  total_rx_crc10_cells 0
total_rx_tmout_paks 0  total_rx_unknown_paks 0
total_rx_out_buf_paks 0  total_rx_unknown_vc_paks 0
BATMAN Asic Register Values:
hi_addr_reg 0x8000, lo_addr_reg 0x000C, boot_msk_addr 0x0780,
rmcell_msk_addr 0x0724, rmcnt__msk_addr 0x07C2, txbuf_msk_addr 0x070C,
...
CM622 SAR Boot Configuration:
txind_q_addr 0x14000 txcmd_q_addr 0x20000
...
SUNI-622 Framer Register Values:
Master Rst and Ident/Load Meters Reg (#0x0): 0x10
Master Configuration Reg (#0x1): 0x1F
Master Interrupt Status Reg (#0x2): 0x00
PISO Interrupt Reg (#0x3): 0x04
Master Auto Alarm Reg (#0x4): 0x03
Master Auto Alarm Reg (#0x5): 0x07
Parallel Output Port Reg (#0x6): 0x02
```

```
...
BERM Line BIP Threshold LSB Reg (#0x74): 0x00
BERM Line BIP Threshold MSB Reg (#0x75): 0x00
Router#
```

The following is partial sample output from the **show controllers** command:

```
Router# execute-on slot 6 show controllers
Interface POS0
Hardware is BFLC POS
lcpos_instance struct    60311B40
RX POS ASIC addr space   12000000
TX POS ASIC addr space   12000100
SUNI framer addr space   12000400
SUNI rsop intr status    00
CRC32 enabled, HDLC enc, int clock
no loop

Interface POS1
Hardware is BFLC POS
lcpos_instance struct    603142E0
RX POS ASIC addr space   12000000
TX POS ASIC addr space   12000100
SUNI framer addr space   12000600
SUNI rsop intr status    00
CRC32 enabled, HDLC enc, int clock
no loop
...
Router#
```

The following is partial sample output from the **show controllers pos framers** command:

```
Router# execute-on slot 6 show controllers pos framers
Framer 0, addr=0x12000400:
master reset           C0
master config          1F        rrate sts3c trate sts3c fixptr
master control         00
clock rcv cntrl        D0
RACP control           84
RACP gfc control       0F
TACP control status    04        hcsadd
RACP intr enable       04
RSOP cntrl intr enable 00
RSOP intr status       00
TPOP path sig lbl (c2) 13
SPTB control           04        tnull
SPTB status            00

Framer 1, addr=0x12000600:
master reset           C0
master config          1F        rrate sts3c trate sts3c fixptr
master control         00
clock rcv cntrl        D0
RACP control           84
RACP gfc control       0F
TACP control status    04        hcsadd
```

```
RACP intr enable        04
RSOP cntrl intr enable  00
RSOP intr status        00
TPOP path sig lbl (c2)  13
SPTB control            04          tnull
SPTB status             00

Framer 2, addr=0x12000800:
master reset            C0
master config           1F          rrate sts3c trate sts3c fixptr
master control          00
clock rcv cntrl         D0
RACP control            84
RACP gfc control        0F
TACP control status     04          hcsadd
RACP intr enable        04
RSOP cntrl intr enable  00
RSOP intr status        00
TPOP path sig lbl (c2)  13
SPTB control            04          tnull
SPTB status             00
...
Router#
```

The following is partial sample output from the **show controllers fia** command:

```
Router# execute-on slot 7 show controllers fia
========= Line Card (Slot 7) =======

Fabric configuration: Full bandwidth redundant
Master Scheduler: Slot 17

From Fabric FIA Errors
-------------------------
redund fifo parity 0       redund overflow 0          cell drops 0
crc32 lkup parity  0       cell parity     0          crc32       0
            0        1         2         3         4
        -------- -------- -------- -------- --------
los     0        0         0         0         0
crc16   0        0         0         0         0

To Fabric FIA Errors
------------------------
sca not pres 0       req error       0       uni fifo overflow 0
grant parity 0       multi req       0       uni fifo undrflow 0
cntrl parity 0       uni req         0       crc32 lkup parity 0
multi fifo   0       empty dst req 0         handshake error   0
```

Related Commands

You can use the master indexes or search online to find documentation of a related command.

clear controllers
show controllers (GRP image)

show controllers logging

To display logging information about a VIP card, use the **show controllers logging** privileged EXEC command.

show controllers vip *slot-number* **logging**

Syntax

vip *slot-number*

Description

VIP slot number.

Command Mode

Privileged EXEC

Usage Guidelines

This command first appeared in Cisco IOS Release 11.2.

This command displays the state of syslog error and event logging, including host addresses, and whether console logging is enabled.

Sample Display

The following is sample output from the **show controllers logging** command:

```
Router# show controllers vip 4 logging

Syslog logging: enabled
    Console logging: disabled
    Monitor logging: level debugging, 266 messages logged.
    Trap logging: level informational, 266 messages logged.
    Logging to 192.180.2.238
```

Table 26-10 describes significant fields shown in the display.

Table 26-10 *Show Controllers Logging Field Descriptions*

Field	Description
Syslog logging	When enabled, system logging messages are sent to a UNIX host that acts as a syslog server; that is, it captures and saves the messages.
Console logging	If enabled, states the level; otherwise, this field displays disabled.

continues

Table 26-10   *Show Controllers Logging Field Descriptions (Continued)*

Field	Description
Monitor logging	Minimum level of severity required for a log message to be sent to a monitor terminal (not the console).
Trap logging	Minimum level of severity required for a log message to be sent to a syslog server.

Related Commands

To locate documentation of related commands, you can search online at www.cisco.com.

show logging

show controllers tech-support

To display general information about a VIP card when reporting a problem, use the **show controllers tech-support** privileged EXEC command.

show controllers vip *slot-number* **tech-support**

Syntax	Description
vip *slot-number*	VIP slot number.

Command Mode

Privileged EXEC

Usage Guidelines

This command first appeared in Cisco IOS Release 11.2.

Use this command to help collect general information about a VIP card when you are reporting a problem. This command displays the equivalent of the following **show** commands for the VIP card:

- **show version**
- **more system:running-config**
- **show controllers**
- **show stacks**
- **show interfaces**
- **show buffers**

- **show processes memory**

- **show processes cpu**

For a sample display of the **show controllers tech-support** command output, refer to these **show** commands.

Related Commands

To locate documentation of related commands, you can search online at www.cisco.com.

more system:running-config
show buffers
show controllers
show interfaces
show processes
show processes memory
show stacks
show tech-support
show version

show debugging

To display information about the types of debugging that are enabled for your router, use the **show debugging** privileged EXEC command.

> **show debugging**

Syntax Description

This command has no arguments or keywords.

Command Mode

Privileged EXEC

Usage Guidelines

This command first appeared in Cisco IOS Release 11.1.

Sample Display

The following is sample output from the **show debugging** command. In this example, three types of CDP debugging are enabled.

```
Router# show debugging

CDP:
  CDP packet info debugging is on
  CDP events debugging is on
  CDP neighbor info debugging is on
```

Related Commands

To locate documentation of related commands, you can search online at www.cisco.com.

debug

show diag

To display hardware information including DRAM and SRAM on the line cards, use the **show diag** privileged EXEC command.

show diag [slot-number] [details] [summary]

Syntax	Description
slot-number	(Optional) Slot number of the interface.
details	(Optional) Displays more details than the normal **show diag** output.
summary	(Optional) Displays a summary (one line per slot) of the chassis.

Command Mode

Privileged EXEC

Usage Guidelines

This command was modified in Cisco IOS Release 11.2 GS to include sample output from the Cisco 12000 series Gigabit Switch Routers.

Use this command to determine the type of hardware installed in your router.

Sample Display

The following is sample output from the **show diag** command:

```
Router# show diag 3
SLOT 3  (RP/LC 3 ): 4 Port Packet Over SONET OC-3c/STM-1 Multi Mode
  MAIN: type 33,  00-0000-00 rev 70 dev 0
```

```
          HW config: 0x01    SW key: 00-00-00
  PCA:    73-2147-02 rev 94 ver 2
          HW version 1.0  S/N 04499695
  MBUS:   MBUS Agent (1)   73-2146-05 rev 73 dev 0
          HW version 1.1  S/N 04494882
          Test hist: 0x00    RMA#: 00-00-00    RMA hist: 0x00
  DIAG: Test count: 0x05000001    Test results: 0x00000000
  MBUS Agent Software version 01.27 (RAM) using CAN Bus A
  ROM Monitor version 00.0D
  Fabric Downloader version used 00.0D (ROM version is 00.0D)
  Board is analyzed
  Board State is Line Card Enabled (IOS  RUN )
  Insertion time: 00:00:10 (00:04:51 ago)
  DRAM size: 33554432 bytes
  FrFab SDRAM size: 67108864 bytes
  ToFab SDRAM size: 16777216 bytes
Router#
```

The following is sample output from the **show diag summary** command:

```
Router# show diag summary
SLOT 0  (RP/LC 0 ): Route Processor
SLOT 2  (RP/LC 2 ): 4 Port Packet Over SONET OC-3c/STM-1 Single Mode
SLOT 4  (RP/LC 4 ): 4 Port Packet Over SONET OC-3c/STM-1 Single Mode
SLOT 7  (RP/LC 7 ): 4 Port Packet Over SONET OC-3c/STM-1 Single Mode
SLOT 9  (RP/LC 9 ): 4 Port Packet Over SONET OC-3c/STM-1 Single Mode
SLOT 11 (RP/LC 11): 4 Port Packet Over SONET OC-3c/STM-1 Single Mode
SLOT 16 (CSC 0   ): Clock Scheduler Card
SLOT 17 (CSC 1   ): Clock Scheduler Card
SLOT 18 (SFC 0   ): Switch Fabric Card
SLOT 19 (SFC 1   ): Switch Fabric Card
SLOT 20 (SFC 2   ): Switch Fabric Card
SLOT 24 (PS A1   ): AC Power Supply
SLOT 26 (PS B1   ): AC Power Supply
SLOT 28 (TOP FAN ): Blower Module
SLOT 29 (BOT FAN ): Blower Module
Router#
```

The following is sample output from the **show diag details** command:

```
Router# show diag 4 details
SLOT 4  (RP/LC 4): 4 Port Packet Over SONET OC-3c/STM-1 Single Mode
  MAIN: type 33,  800-2389-01 rev 71 dev 16777215
          HW config: 0x00    SW key: FF-FF-FF
  PCA:    73-2275-03 rev 75 ver 3
          HW version 1.1  S/N 04529465
  MBUS: MBUS Agent (1)   73-2146-06 rev 73 dev 0
          HW version 1.1  S/N 04541395
          Test hist: 0xFF    RMA#: FF-FF-FF    RMA hist: 0xFF
  DIAG: Test count: 0x05000001    Test results: 0x00000000
  EEPROM contents (hex):
  00: 01 00 01 00   49 00 08 62   06 03 00 00   00 FF FF FF
  10: 30 34 35 34   31 33 39 35   FF FF FF FF   FF FF FF FF
  20: 01 01 00 00   00 00 00 FF   FF FF FF FF   FF FF FF FF
  30: A5 FF A5 A5   A5 A5 FF A5   A5 A5 A5 A5   A5 A5 A5 A5
```

```
40: 00 21 01 01  00 49 00 08  E3 03 05 03  00 01 FF FF
50: 03 20 00 09  55 01 01 FF  FF FF 00 FF  FF FF FF FF
60: 30 34 35 32  39 34 36 35  FF FF FF FF  FF FF FF FF
70: FF FF FF FF  FF FF FF FF  05 00 00 01  00 00 00 00
MBUS Agent Software version 01.24 (RAM)
Fabric Downloader version 00.0D
Board is analyzed
Flags: 0x4
Board State is Line Card Enabled (IOS  RUN)
Insertion time: 00:00:10 (00:04:51 ago)
DRAM size: 33554432 bytes
FrFab SDRAM size: 67108864 bytes
ToFab SDRAM size: 16777216 bytes
Router#
```

show environment

To display temperature, voltage, and blower information on the Cisco 7000 series, Cisco 7200 series, Cisco 7500 series routers, and Cisco 12000 series Gigabit Switch Router, use the **show environment** privileged EXEC command.

> **show environment [alarms | all | fans | hardware | last | leds | power-supply | table | temperatures | voltages]**

Syntax	Description
alarms	(Optional) Displays the alarm contact information.
all	(Optional) Displays a detailed listing of the power supplies, temperature readings, voltage readings, and blower speeds.
fans	(Optional) Displays blower and fan information.
hardware	(Optional) Displays hardware-specific information.
last	(Optional) Displays information on the last measurement made.
leds	(Optional) Displays the status of the MBus LEDs on the clock and scheduler cards and switch fabric cards.
power-supply	(Optional) Displays power supply voltage and current information.
table	(Optional) Displays the temperature, voltage, and blower thresholds.
temperature	(Optional) Displays temperature information.
voltages	(Optional) Displays voltage information.

Default

If no options are specified, the current environmental parameters are displayed.

Command Mode

Privileged EXEC

Usage Guidelines

This command first appeared in Cisco IOS Release 10.0 and was modified in Cisco IOS Release 11.2 GS to include the **alarms**, **fans**, **hardware**, **leds**, **power-supply**, **temperature**, and **voltages** keywords and to provide sample output for the Cisco 12000 series Gigabit Switch Routers.

Once a minute, a routine is run that gets environmental measurements from sensors and stores the output into a buffer. This buffer is displayed on the console when **show environment** is invoked.

If a measurement exceeds desired margins, but has not exceeded fatal margins, a warning message is printed to the system console. The system software queries the sensors for measurements once a minute, but warnings for a given test point are printed at most once every hour for sensor readings in the warning range and once every 5 minutes for sensor readings in the critical range. If a measurement is out of line within these time segments, an automatic warning message appears on the console. As noted, you can query the environmental status with the **show environment** command at any time to determine whether a measurement is at the warning or critical tolerance.

If a shutdown occurs because of detection of fatal environmental margins, the last measured value from each sensor is stored in internal nonvolatile memory.

For environmental specifications, refer to the hardware installation and configuration publication for your individual chassis.

If the Cisco 12000 series exceeds environmental conditions, a message similar to the one below is displayed on the console:

```
%GSR_ENV-2-WARNING: Slot 3 Hot Sensor Temperature exceeds 40 deg C;
Check cooling systems
```

NOTE   Blower temperatures that exceed environmental conditions do not generate a warning message.

Sample Displays

The following example shows the typical **show environment** display when there are no warning conditions in the system for the Cisco 7000 series and Cisco 7200 series. This information may vary slightly depending on the platform you are using. The date and time of the query are displayed, along with the data refresh information and a message indicating that there are no warning conditions.

```
Router> show environment

Environmental Statistics
```

```
Environmental status as of 13:17:39 UTC Thu Jun 6 1996
Data is 7 second(s) old, refresh in 53 second(s)

All Environmental Measurements are within specifications
```

Table 26-11 describes the fields shown in the display.

Table 26-11   *Show Environment Field Descriptions*

Field	Description
Environmental status as of...	Current date and time.
Data is..., refresh in...	Environmental measurements are output into a buffer every 60 seconds, unless other higher-priority processes are running.
Status message	If environmental measurements are not within specification, warning messages are displayed.

Sample Displays for the Cisco 7000 Series

The following are examples of messages that display on the system console when a measurement has exceeded an acceptable margin:

```
ENVIRONMENTAL WARNING: Air flow appears marginal.
ENVIRONMENTAL WARNING: Internal temperature measured 41.3(C)
ENVIRONMENTAL WARNING: +5 volt testpoint measured 5.310(V)
```

The system displays the following message if voltage or temperature exceed maximum margins:

```
SHUTDOWN: air flow problem
```

In the following example, there have been two intermittent power failures since a router was turned on, and the lower power supply is not functioning. The last intermittent power failure occurred on Monday, June 10, 1996, at 11:07 p.m.

```
7000# show environment all

Environmental Statistics
  Environmental status as of 23:19:47 UTC Wed Jun 12 1996
  Data is 6 second(s) old, refresh in 54 second(s)

  WARNING: Lower Power Supply is NON-OPERATIONAL

  Lower Power Supply:700W, OFF     Upper Power Supply: 700W, ON

  Intermittent Powerfail(s): 2     Last on 23:07:05 UTC Mon Jun 10 1996

  +12 volts measured at  12.05(V)
   +5 volts measured at   4.96(V)
  -12 volts measured at -12.05(V)
  +24 volts measured at  23.80(V)

  Airflow temperature measured at 38(C)
  Inlet temperature measured at 25(C)
```

Table 26-12 describes the fields shown in the display.

Table 26-12 *Show Environment All Field Descriptions for the Cisco 7000*

Field	Description
Environmental status as of...	Date and time of last query.
Data is..., refresh in...	Environmental measurements are output into a buffer every 60 seconds, unless other higher-priority processes are running.
WARNING:	If environmental measurements are not within specification, warning messages are displayed.
Lower Power Supply	Type of power supply installed and its status (On or Off).
Upper Power Supply	Type of power supply installed and its status (On or Off).
Intermittent Powerfail(s)	Number of power hits (not resulting in shutdown) since the system was last booted.
Voltage specifications	System voltage measurements.
Airflow and inlet temperature	Temperature of air coming in and going out.

The following example is for the Cisco 7000 series router. The router retrieves the environmental statistics at the time of the last shutdown. In this example, the last shutdown was Friday, May 19, 1995, at 12:40 p.m., so the environmental statistics at that time are displayed:

```
Router# show environment last

Environmental Statistics
   Environmental status as of 14:47:00 UTC Sun May 21 1995
   Data is 6 second(s) old, refresh in 54 second(s)

   WARNING: Upper Power Supply is NON-OPERATIONAL

LAST Environmental Statistics
   Environmental status as of 12:40:00 UTC Fri May 19 1995
   Lower Power Supply: 700W, ON     Upper Power Supply: 700W, OFF

   No Intermittent Powerfails

   +12 volts measured at  12.05(V)
    +5 volts measured at   4.98(V)
   -12 volts measured at -12.00(V)
   +24 volts measured at  23.80(V)

   Airflow temperature measured at 30(C)
   Inlet   temperature measured at 23(C)
```

Table 26-13 describes the fields shown in the display.

Table 26-13   *Show Environment Last Field Descriptions for the Cisco 7000*

Field	Description
Environmental status as of...	Current date and time.
Data is..., refresh in...	Environmental measurements are output into a buffer every 60 seconds, unless other higher-priority processes are running.
WARNING:	If environmental measurements are not within specification, warning messages are displayed.
LAST Environmental Statistics	Displays test point values at time of the last environmental shutdown.
Lower Power Supply:	For the Cisco 7000, indicates the status of the two 700W power supplies.
Upper Power Supply:	For the Cisco 7010, indicates the status of the single 600W power supply.

The following sample output shows the current environmental status in tables that list voltage and temperature parameters. There are three warning messages: one each about the lower power supply, the airflow temperature, and the inlet temperature. In this example, voltage parameters are shown to be in the normal range, airflow temperature is at a critical level, and inlet temperature is at the warning level:

```
Router> show environment table

Environmental Statistics
  Environmental status as of Mon 11-2-1992 17:43:36
  Data is 52 second(s) old, refresh in 8 second(s)

  WARNING: Lower Power Supply is NON-OPERATIONAL
  WARNING: Airflow temperature has reached CRITICAL level at 73(C)
  WARNING: Inlet temperature has reached WARNING level at 41(C)

Voltage Parameters:

  SENSE       CRITICAL              NORMAL              CRITICAL
  -------|--------------------|------------------------|--------------------

  +12(V)                10.20     12.05(V)      13.80
   +5(V)                 4.74      4.98(V)       5.26
  -12(V)               -10.20    -12.05(V)     -13.80
  +24(V)                20.00     24.00(V)      28.00

Temperature Parameters:

  SENSE     WARNING    NORMAL     WARNING    CRITICAL    SHUTDOWN
  -------|------------|----------|----------|----------|---------

  Airflow           10         60         70   73(C)        88
  Inlet             10         39   41(C)   46                64
```

Table 26-14 describes the fields shown in the display.

Table 26-14 *Show Environment Field Descriptions for the Cisco 7000*

Field	Description
SENSE (Voltage Parameters)	Voltage specification for DC line.
SENSE (Temperature Parameters)	Air being measured. Inlet measures the air coming in, and Airflow measures the temperature of the air inside the chassis.
WARNING	System is approaching an out-of-tolerance condition.
NORMAL	All monitored conditions meet normal requirements.
CRITICAL	Out-of-tolerance condition exists.
SHUTDOWN	Processor has detected condition that could cause physical damage to the system.

Sample Displays for the Cisco 7200 Series

The system displays the following message if the voltage or temperature enters the "Warning" range:

```
%ENVM-4-ENVWARN: Chassis outlet 3 measured at 55C/131F
```

The system displays the following message if the voltage or temperature enters the "Critical" range:

```
%ENVM-2-ENVCRIT: +3.45 V measured at +3.65 V
```

The system displays the following message if the voltage or temperature exceeds the maximum margins:

```
%ENVM-0-SHUTDOWN: Environmental Monitor initiated shutdown
```

The following message is sent to the console if a power supply has been inserted or removed from the system. This message relates only to systems that have two power supplies:

```
%ENVM-6-PSCHANGE: Power Supply 1 changed from Zytek AC Power Supply to removed
```

The following message is sent to the console if a power supply has been powered on or off. In the case of the power supply being shut off, this message can be due to the user shutting off the power supply or to a failed power supply. This message relates only to systems that have two power supplies:

```
%ENVM-6-PSLEV: Power Supply 1 state changed from normal to shutdown
```

The following is sample output from the **show environment all** command on the Cisco 7200 series router when there is a voltage warning condition in the system:

```
7200# show environment all

Power Supplies:
        Power supply 1 is unknown. Unit is off.
        Power supply 2 is Zytek AC Power Supply. Unit is on.
```

```
Temperature readings:
        chassis inlet     measured at 25C/77F
        chassis outlet 1 measured at 29C/84F
        chassis outlet 2 measured at 36C/96F
        chassis outlet 3 measured at 44C/111F
Voltage readings:
        +3.45 V measured at +3.83 V:Voltage in Warning range!
        +5.15 V measured at +5.09 V
        +12.15  measured at +12.42 V
        -11.95  measured at -12.10 V
```

Table 26-15 describes the fields shown in the display.

Table 26-15 *Show Environment All Field Descriptions for the Cisco 7200*

Field	Description
Power Supplies:	Current condition of the power supplies including the type and whether the power supply is on or off.
Temperature readings:	Current measurements of the chassis temperature at the inlet and outlet locations.
Voltage readings:	Current measurement of the power supply test points.

The following example is for the Cisco 7200 series router. This example shows the measurements immediately before the last shutdown and the reason for the last shutdown (if appropriate).

```
7200# show environment last

    chassis inlet     previously measured at 27C/80F
    chassis outlet 1 previously measured at 31C/87F
    chassis outlet 2 previously measured at 37C/98F
    chassis outlet 3 previously measured at 45C/113F
    +3.3 V            previously measured at 4.02
    +5.0 V            previously measured at 4.92
    +12.0 V           previously measured at 12.65
    -12.0 V           previously measured at 11.71

last shutdown reason - power supply shutdown
```

Table 26-16 describes the fields shown in the display.

Table 26-16 *Show Environment Last Field Descriptions for the Cisco 7200*

Field	Description
chassis inlet	Temperature measurements at the inlet area of the chassis.
chassis outlet	Temperature measurements at the outlet areas of the chassis.
voltages	Power supply test point measurements.
last shutdown reason	Possible shutdown reasons are power supply shutdown, critical temperature, and critical voltage.

The following example is for the Cisco 7200 series router. This information lists the temperature and voltage shutdown thresholds for each sensor.

```
7200# show environment table

Sample Point     LowCritical   LowWarning   HighWarning   HighCritical
chassis inlet                                40C/104F      50C/122F
chassis outlet 1                             43C/109F      53C/127F
chassis outlet 2                             75C/167F      75C/167F
chassis outlet 3                             55C/131F      65C/149F
+3.45 V          +2.76         +3.10         +3.80         +4.14
+5.15 V          +4.10         +4.61         +5.67         +6.17
+12.15 V         +9.72         +10.91        +13.37        +14.60
-11.95 V         -8.37         -9.57         -14.34        -15.53
Shutdown system at 70C/158F
```

Table 26-17 describes the fields shown in the display.

Table 26-17 *Show Environment Table Field Descriptions for the Cisco 7200*

Field	Description
Sample Point	Area for which measurements are taken.
LowCritical	Level at which a critical message is issued for an out-of-tolerance voltage condition. The system continues to operate; however, the system is approaching shutdown.
LowWarning	Level at which a warning message is issued for an out-of-tolerance voltage condition. The system continues to operate, but operator action is recommended to bring the system back to a normal state.
HighWarning	Level at which a warning message is issued. The system continues to operate, but operator action is recommended to bring the system back to a normal state.
HighCritical	Level at which a critical message is issued. For the chassis, the router is shut down. For the power supply, the power supply is shut down.
Shutdown system at	The system is shut down if the specified temperature is met.

Sample Displays for the Cisco 7500 Series

The sample output for the Cisco 7500 series routers may vary depending on the specific model (for example, the Cisco 7513). The following is sample output from the **show environment all** command on the Cisco 7500 series router:

```
7500# show environment all

Arbiter type 1, backplane type 7513 (id 2)
Power supply #1 is 1200W AC (id 1), power supply #2 is removed (id 7)
Active fault conditions: none
Fan transfer point: 100%
Active trip points: Restart_Inhibit
15 of 15 soft shutdowns remaining before hard shutdown
```

```
                        1
              0123456789012
Dbus slots:   X    XX    X

card        inlet      hotpoint     exhaust
RSP(6)      35C/95F    47C/116F     40C/104F
RSP(7)      35C/95F    43C/109F     39C/102F

Shutdown temperature source is 'hotpoint' on RSP(6), requested RSP(6)

+12V measured at 12.31
+5V measured at 5.21
-12V measured at -12.07
+24V measured at 22.08
+2.5 reference is 2.49

PS1 +5V Current       measured at 59.61 A (capacity 200 A)
PS1 +12V Current      measured at 5.08 A (capacity 35 A)
PS1 -12V Current      measured at 0.42 A (capacity 3 A)
PS1 output is 378 W
```

Table 26-18 describes the fields shown in the display.

Table 26-18 *Show Environment All Field Descriptions for the Cisco 7500*

Field	Description
Arbiter type 1	Numbers indicating the arbiter type and backplane type.
Power supply	Number and type of power supply installed in the chassis.
Active fault conditions:	If any fault conditions exist (such as power supply failure, fan failure, and temperature too high), they are listed here.
Fan transfer point:	Software controlled fan speed. If the router is operating below its automatic restart temperature, the transfer point is reduced by 10 percent of the full range each minute. If the router is at or above its automatic restart temperature, the transfer point is increased in the same way.
Active trip points:	Temperature sensor is compared against the values displayed at the bottom of the **show environment table** command output.
15 of 15 soft shutdowns remaining	When the temperature increases above the "board shutdown" level, a soft shutdown occurs (that is, the cards are shut down, and the power supplies, fans, and CI continue to operate). When the system cools to the restart level, the system restarts. The system counts the number of times this occurs and keeps the up/down cycle from continuing forever. When the counter reaches zero, the system performs a hard shutdown, which requires a power cycle to recover. The soft shutdown counter is reset to its maximum value after the system has been up for 6 hours.
Dbus slots:	Indicates which chassis slots are occupied.

Table 26-18 *Show Environment All Field Descriptions for the Cisco 7500 (Continued)*

Field	Description
card, inlet, hotpoint, exhaust	Temperature measurements at the inlet, hotpoint, and exhaust areas of the card. The (6) and (7) indicate the slot numbers. Dual-RSP chassis can show two RSPs.
Shutdown temperature source	Indicates which of the three temperature sources is selected for comparison against the "shutdown" levels listed with the **show environment table** command.
Voltages (+12V, +5V, -12V, +24V, +2.5)	Voltages measured on the backplane.
Power supply current (PS1)	Current measured on the power supply.

The following example is for the Cisco 7500 series router. This example shows the measurements immediately before the last shutdown.

```
7500# show environment last

RSP(4) Inlet      previously measured at 37C/98F
RSP(4) Hotpoint   previously measured at 46C/114F
RSP(4) Exhaust    previously measured at 52C/125F
+12 Voltage       previously measured at 12.26
+5 Voltage        previously measured at 5.17
-12 Voltage       previously measured at -12.03
+24 Voltage       previously measured at 23.78
```

Table 26-19 describes the fields shown in the display.

Table 26-19 *Show Environment Last Field Descriptions for the Cisco 7500*

Field	Description
RSP(4) Inlet, Hotpoint, Exhaust	Temperature measurements at the inlet, hotpoint, and exhaust areas of the card.
Voltages	Voltages measured on the backplane.

The following example is for the Cisco 7500 series router. This information lists the temperature and voltage thresholds for each sensor. These thresholds indicate when error messages occur. There are two level of messages: warning and critical.

```
7500# show environment table

Sample Point    LowCritical    LowWarning    HighWarning    HighCritical
RSP(4) Inlet                                  44C/111F       50C/122F
RSP(4) Hotpoint                               54C/129F       60C/140F
RSP(4) Exhaust
+12 Voltage     10.90          11.61          12.82          13.38
+5 Voltage      4.61           4.94           5.46           5.70
-12 Voltage     -10.15         -10.76         -13.25         -13.86
```

Part III

Command Reference

```
+24 Voltage          20.38          21.51          26.42          27.65
2.5 Reference                        2.43           2.51
Shutdown boards at                   70C/158F
Shutdown power supplies at           76C/168F
Restart after shutdown below 40C/104F
```

Table 26-20 describes the fields shown in the display.

Table 26-20 *Show Environment Table Field Descriptions for the Cisco 7500*

Field	Description
Sample Point	Area for which measurements are taken.
LowCritical	Level at which a critical message is issued for an out-of-tolerance voltage condition. The system continues to operate; however, the system is approaching shutdown.
LowWarning	Level at which a warning message is issued for an out-of-tolerance voltage condition. The system continues to operate, but operator action is recommended to bring the system back to a normal state.
HighWarning	Level at which a warning message is issued. The system continues to operate, but operator action is recommended to bring the system back to a normal state.
HighCritical	Level at which a critical message is issued. For the chassis, the router is shut down. For the power supply, the power supply is shut down.
Shutdown boards at	The card is shut down if the specified temperature is met.
Shutdown power supplies at	The system is shut down if the specified temperature is met.
Restart after shutdown	The system will restart when the specified temperature is met.

Sample Displays for the Cisco 12000 Series GSR

The following examples are for the Cisco 12000 series Gigabit Switch Routers.

The following is sample output from the **show environment** command for a Cisco 12012. Slots 0 through 11 are the line cards, slots 16 and 17 are the clock and scheduler cards, slots 18 through 20 are the switch fabric cards, slots 24 through 26 are the power supplies, and slots 28 and 29 are the blowers. An "NA" in the table means that no values was returned. In some cases, it is because the equipment is not supported for that environmental parameter (for example, the power supply and blowers in slots 24, 26, 28, and 29 do not have a 3V power supply so an NA is displayed).

```
Router# show environment
Slot #   3V      5V      MBUS 5V Hot Sensor    Inlet Sensor
         (mv)    (mv)    (mv)    (deg C)         (deg C)
0        3300    4992    5040      42.0           37.0
2        3296    4976    5136      40.0           33.0
4        3280    4992    5120      38.5           31.5
7        3280    4984    5136      42.0           32.0
9        3292    4968    5160      39.5           31.5
```

```
11      3288    4992    5152    40.0        30.5
16      3308    NA      5056    42.5        38.0
17      3292    NA      5056    40.5        36.5
18      3304    NA      5176    36.5        35.0
19      3300    NA      5184    37.5        33.5
20      3304    NA      5168    36.5        34.0
24      NA      5536    5120    NA          31.5
26      NA      5544    5128    NA          31.5
28      NA      NA      5128    NA          NA
29      NA      NA      5104    NA          NA

Slot #  48V     AMP_48
        (Volt)  (Amp)
24      46      12
26      46      19

Slot #  Fan 0   Fan 1   Fan 2
        (RPM)   (RPM)   (RPM)
28      2160    2190    2160
29      2130    2190    2070
Router#
```

Table 26-21 describes the fields shown above and lists the equipment supported by each environmental parameter. "NA" indicates the reading could not be obtained. Try the command again.

Table 26-21 *Show Environment Field Descriptions*

Field	Description
Slot #	Slot number of the equipment. On the Cisco 12012, slots 0 through 11 are the line cards, slots 16 and 17 are the clock and scheduler cards, slots 18 through 20 are the switch fabric cards, slots 24 through 27 are the power supplies, and slots 28 and 29 are the blowers.
3V (mv)	Measures the 3-volt power supply on the card. The 3-volt power supply is on the line cards, GRP card, clock and scheduler cards, and switch fabric cards.
5V (mv)	Measures the 5-volt power supply on the card. The 5-volt power supply is on the line cards, GRP card, and power supplies.
MBUS 5V (mv)	Measures the 5-volt MBus on the card. The 5-volt MBus is on all equipment.
Hot Sensor (deg C)	Measures the temperature at the hot sensor on the card. The hot sensor is on the line cards, GRP card, clock and scheduler cards, switch fabric cards, and blowers.
Inlet Sensor (deg C)	Measures the current inlet temperature on the card. The inlet sensor is on the line cards, GRP card, clock and scheduler cards, switch fabric cards, and power supplies.
48V (Volt)	Measures the DC power supplies.
AMP_48 (Amp)	Measures the AC power supplies.
Fan 0, Fan 1, Fan 2	Measures the fan speed in rotations per minute.

The following is sample output from the **show environment all** command for the Cisco 12008. Slots 0 through 7 are the line cards, slots 16 and 17 are the clock scheduler cards (the clock scheduler cards control the fans), slots 18 through 20 are the switch fabric cards, and slots 24 and 26 are the power supplies. The Cisco 12008 does not support slots 25, 27, 28, and 29. An "NA" in the table means that no values were returned. In some cases, it is because the equipment is not supported for that environmental parameter (for example, the power supplies in slots 24 and 26 do not have a hot sensor, so an NA is displayed).

```
Router# show environment all
Slot #  Hot Sensor       Inlet Sensor
        (deg C)          (deg C)
2          31.0             22.0
5          33.5             26.5
16         25.5             21.5
18         22.0             21.0
19         22.5             21.0
24         NA               29.5
26         NA               24.5

Slot #  3V      5V       MBUS 5V
        (mv)    (mv)     (mv)
2       3292    5008     5136
5       3292    5000     5128
16      3272    NA       5128
18      3300    NA       5128
19      3316    NA       5128

Slot #  5V      MBUS 5V  48V      AMP_48
        (mv)    (mv)     (Volt)   (Amp)
24      0       5096     3        0
26      5544    5144     47       3

Slot #  Fan Information
16      Voltage 16V Speed slow: Main Fans Ok Power Supply fans Ok

Alarm Indicators
No alarms

Slot #  Card Specific Leds
16      Mbus OK SFCs Failed
18      Mbus OK
19      Mbus OK
24      Input Failed
26      Input Ok
```

The following is sample output from the **show environment table** command for a Cisco 12012. The **show environment table** command lists the warning, critical, and shutdown limits on your system and includes the GRP card and line cards (slots 0-15), clock and scheduler cards (slots 16-17), switch fabric cards (slots 18-20), and blowers.

```
Router# show environment table

Hot Sensor Temperature Limits (deg C):
                        Warning Critical Shutdown
GRP/GLC (Slots 0-15)       40      46      57
CSC     (Slots 16-17)      46      51      65
SFC     (Slots 18-20)      41      46      60

Inlet Sensor Temperature Limits (deg C):
                        Warning Critical Shutdown
GRP/GLC (Slots 0-15)       35      40      52
CSC     (Slots 16-17)      40      45      59
SFC     (Slots 18-20)      37      42      54

3V Ranges (mv):
                        Warning        Critical       Shutdown
                     Below  Above    Below  Above    Below  Above
GRP/GLC (Slots 0-15)  3200   3400     3100   3500     3050   3550
CSC     (Slots 16-17) 3200   3400     3100   3500     3050   3550
SFC     (Slots 18-20) 3200   3400     3100   3500     3050   3550

5V Ranges (mv):
                        Warning        Critical       Shutdown
                     Below  Above    Below  Above    Below  Above
GRP/GLC (Slots 0-15)  4850   5150     4750   5250     4680   5320

MBUS_5V Ranges (mv):
                        Warning        Critical       Shutdown
                     Below  Above    Below  Above    Below  Above
GRP/GLC (Slots 0-15)  5000   5250     4900   5350     4750   5450
CSC     (Slots 16-17) 4820   5150     4720   5250     4750   5450
SFC     (Slots 17-20) 5000   5250     4900   5350     4750   5450

Blower Operational Range (RPM):

Top Blower:
             Warning    Critical
             Below      Below
Fan 0        1000       750
Fan 1        1000       750
Fan 2        1000       750

Bottom Blower:
             Warning    Critical
             Below      Below
Fan 0        1000       750
Fan 1        1000       750
Fan 2        1000       750
```

The following is sample output from the **show environment leds** command for a Cisco 12012. The **show environment leds** command lists the status of the MBus LEDs on the clock, scheduler, and the switch fabric cards.

```
Router# show environment leds
16 leds Mbus OK
18 leds Mbus OK
19 leds Mbus OK
20 leds Mbus OK
```

show gsr

To display hardware information on the Cisco 12000 series Gigabit Switch Routers (GSR), use the **show gsr** EXEC command.

show gsr [**chassis-info** [**details**]]

Syntax   Description

chassis-info   (Optional) Displays backplane NVRAM information.

details   (Optional) In addition to the information displayed, this option includes hexadecimal output of the backplane NVRAM information.

Command Mode
EXEC

Usage Guidelines

This command was added in Cisco IOS Release 11.2 GS to support the Cisco 12000 series Gigabit Switch Routers.

Use this command to determine the type of hardware installed in your router.

Sample Displays

The following is sample output from the **show gsr** command for a Cisco 12012. This command shows the type and state of the card installed in the slot.

```
Router# show gsr
Slot 0  type  = Route Processor
        state = IOS Running  MASTER
Slot 7  type  = 1 Port Packet Over SONET OC-12c/STM-4c
        state = Card Powered
Slot 16 type  = Clock Scheduler Card
        state = Card Powered  PRIMARY CLOCK
```

The following is sample output from the **show gsr chassis-info** command for a Cisco 12012:

```
Router# show gsr chassis-info
Backplane NVRAM [version 0x20] Contents -
```

```
Chassis: type 12012 Fab Ver: 1
  Chassis S/N: ZQ24CS3WT86MGVHL
PCA: 800-3015-1  rev: A0  dev: 257  HW ver: 1.0
  Backplane S/N: A109EXPR75FUNYJK
MAC Addr: base 0000.EAB2.34FF  block size: 1024
RMA Number: 0x5F-0x2D-0x44  code: 0x01  hist: 0x1A
```

show gt64010 (for the Cisco 7200 Series)

Use the **show gt64010** EXEC command to display all GT64010 internal registers and interrupt status on the Cisco 7200 series routers.

show gt64010

Syntax Description

This command has no arguments or keywords.

Command Mode

EXEC

Usage Guidelines

This command first appeared in Cisco IOS Release 11.2.

This command displays information about the CPU interface, DRAM/device address space, device parameters, DMA channels, timers and counters, and PCI internal registers. The information is generally useful for diagnostic tasks performed by technical support only.

Sample Display

The following is a partial sample output for the **show gt64010** command:

```
Router# show gt64010

GT64010 Channel 0 DMA:
 dma_list=0x6088C3EC, dma_ring=0x4B018480, dma_entries=256
 dma_free=0x6088CECC, dma_reqt=0x6088CECC, dma_done=0x6088CECC
 thread=0x6088CEAC, thread_end=0x6088CEAC
 backup_thread=0x0, backup_thread_end=0x0
 dma_working=0, dma_complete=6231, post_coalesce_frames=6231
 exhausted_dma_entries=0, post_coalesce_callback=6231

GT64010 Register Dump: Registers at 0xB4000000

CPU Interface:
 cpu_interface_conf   : 0x80030000 (b/s 0x00000380)
```

Part
III

Command Reference

```
addr_decode_err     : 0xFFFFFFFF (b/s 0xFFFFFFFF)
Processor Address Space :
  ras10_low         : 0x00000000 (b/s 0x00000000)
  ras10_high        : 0x07000000 (b/s 0x00000007)
  ras32_low         : 0x08000000 (b/s 0x00000008)
  ras32_high        : 0x0F000000 (b/s 0x0000000F)
  cs20_low          : 0xD0000000 (b/s 0x000000D0)
  cs20_high         : 0x74000000 (b/s 0x00000074)
  cs3_boot_low      : 0xF8000000 (b/s 0x000000F8)
  cs3_boot_high     : 0x7E000000 (b/s 0x0000007E)
  pci_io_low        : 0x00080000 (b/s 0x00000800)
  pci_io_high       : 0x00000000 (b/s 0x00000000)
  pci_mem_low       : 0x00020000 (b/s 0x00000200)
  pci_mem_high      : 0x7F000000 (b/s 0x0000007F)
  internal_spc_decode : 0xA0000000 (b/s 0x000000A0)
  bus_err_low       : 0x00000000 (b/s 0x00000000)
  bus_err_high      : 0x00000000 (b/s 0x00000000)
...
```

show logging

To display the state of logging (syslog), use the **show logging** privileged EXEC command.

show logging [**history** | **slot** *slot-number* | **summary**]

Syntax

Description

history	(Optional) Displays information in the syslog history table only.
slot *slot-number*	(Optional) Displays information in the syslog history table for a specific line card. Slot numbers range from 0 to 11 for the Cisco 12012 and 0 to 7 for the Cisco 12008.
summary	(Optional) Displays counts of messages by type for each line card.

Command Mode

Privileged EXEC

Usage Guidelines

This command first appeared in Cisco IOS Release 10.0 and was modified in Cisco IOS Release 11.2 GS to add the **slot** and **summary** keywords.

This command displays the state of syslog error and event logging, including host addresses, and whether console logging is enabled. This command also displays Simple Network Management Protocol (SNMP) configuration parameters and protocol activity.

When you use the optional **history** keyword, information about the syslog history table is displayed such as the table size, the status of messages, and text of messages stored in the table. Messages stored in the table are governed by the **logging history** global configuration command.

Sample Displays

The following is sample output from the **show logging** command:

```
Router# show logging

Syslog logging: enabled
    Console logging: disabled
    Monitor logging: level debugging, 266 messages logged.
    Trap logging: level informational, 266 messages logged.
    Logging to 192.180.2.238

SNMP logging: disabled, retransmission after 30 seconds
    0 messages logged
Router#
```

Table 26-22 describes significant fields shown in the display.

Table 26-22 *Fields and Descriptions in show logging Command*

Field	Description
Syslog logging	When enabled, system logging messages are sent to a UNIX host that acts as a syslog server; that is, it captures and saves the messages.
Console logging	If enabled, states the level; otherwise, this field displays disabled.
Monitor logging	Minimum level of severity required for a log message to be sent to a monitor terminal (not the console).
Trap logging	Minimum level of severity required for a log message to be sent to a syslog server.
SNMP logging	Shows whether SNMP logging is enabled and the number of messages logged, and the retransmission interval.

The following is sample output from the **show logging history** command:

```
Router# show logging history

Syslog History Table: 1 maximum table entry, saving level notifications or higher
0 messages ignored, 0 dropped, 15 table entries flushed,
SNMP notifications not enabled
  entry number 16: SYS-5-CONFIG_I
  Configured from console by console
  timestamp: 1110
Router#
```

Table 26-23 describes the significant fields shown in the display.

Table 26-23   *Show Logging History Field Descriptions*

Field	Description
maximum table entry	Number of messages that can be stored in the history table. Set with the **logging history size** command.
saving level notifications or higher	Level of messages that are stored in the history table and sent to the SNMP server (if SNMP notification is enabled). Set with the **logging history** command.
messages ignored	Number of messages not stored in the history table because the severity level is greater than that specified with the **logging history** command.
dropped	Number of messages that could not be processed due to lack of system resources. Dropped messages do not appear in the history table and are not sent to the SNMP server.
table entries flushed	Number of messages that have been removed from the history table to make room for newer messages.
SNMP notifications	Whether syslog traps of the appropriate level are sent to the SNMP server. Syslog traps are either enabled or not enabled through the **snmp-server enable** command.
entry number	Number of the message entry in the history table.
SYS-5-CONFIG_I Configured from console by console	Cisco IOS syslog message consisting of the facility name (SYS) which indicates where the message came from, the severity level (5), the message name (CONFIG_I), and the message text.
timestamp	Time, based on the router's up time, that the message was generated.

The following is sample output from the **show logging summary** command for the Cisco 12012. A number in the column indicates that the syslog contains that many messages for the line card. For example, line card in slot 9 has 1 error message, 4 warning messages, and 47 notification messages.

```
Router# show logging summary
+-----+-------+-------+-------+-------+-------+-------+-------+-------+
| SLOT | EMERG | ALERT | CRIT  | ERROR |WARNING| NOTICE| INFO  | DEBUG |
+-----+-------+-------+-------+-------+-------+-------+-------+-------+
|* 0* |   .   |   .   |   .   |   .   |   .   |   .   |   .   |   .   |
|  1  |       |       |       |       |       |       |       |       |
|  2  |       |       |       |   1   |   4   |   45  |       |       |
|  3  |       |       |       |       |       |       |       |       |
|  4  |       |       |       |   5   |   4   |   54  |       |       |
|  5  |       |       |       |       |       |       |       |       |
|  6  |       |       |       |       |       |       |       |       |
|  7  |       |       |       |  17   |   4   |   48  |       |       |
|  8  |       |       |       |       |       |       |       |       |
|  9  |       |       |       |   1   |   4   |   47  |       |       |
```

```
| 10 |       |       |       |      |      |      |       |      |
| 11 |       |       |       |   12 |   4  |  65  |       |      |
+----+-------+-------+-------+------+------+------+-------+------+
Router#
```

Table 26-24 describes the logging level fields shown in the display.

Table 26-24 *Show Logging Summary Field Descriptions*

Field	Description
SLOT	Indicates the slot number of the line card. An asterisk next to the slot number indicates the GRP card whose error message counts are not displayed. For information on the GRP card, use the **show logging** command.
EMERG	Indicates the system is unusable.
ALERT	Indicates immediate action is needed.
CRIT	Indicates a critical condition.
ERROR	Indicates an error condition.
WARNING	Indicates a warning condition.
NOTIFICE	Indicates a normal but significant condition.
INFO	Indicates an informational message only.
DEBUG	Indicates a debugging message.

Related Commands

To locate documentation of related commands, you can search online at www.cisco.com.

clear logging
logging history size
logging linecard

show memory

Use the **show memory** EXEC command to show statistics about memory, including memory-free pool statistics.

show memory [*memory-type*] [**free**] [**summary**]

Syntax	Description
memory-type	(Optional) Memory type to display (**processor**, **multibus**, **io**, **sram**). If *type* is not specified, statistics for all memory types present are displayed.
free	(Optional) Displays free memory statistics.
summary	(Optional) Displays a summary of memory usage including the size and number of blocks allocated for each address of the system call that allocated the block.

Command Mode

EXEC

Usage Guidelines

This command first appeared in Cisco IOS Release 10.0.

The **show memory** command displays information about memory available after the system image decompresses and loads.

Sample Displays

The following is sample output from the **show memory** command:

```
Router# show memory

              Head    Total(b)    Used(b)    Free(b)   Lowest(b)  Largest(b)
Processor    B0EE38    5181896    2210036    2971860    2692456    2845368

              Processor memory
Address    Bytes Prev.    Next      Ref  PrevF  NextF   Alloc PC  What
B0EE38     1056 0         B0F280     1                  18F132    List Elements
B0F280     2656 B0EE38    B0FD08     1                  18F132    List Headers
B0FD08     2520 B0F280    B10708     1                  141384    TTY data
B10708     2000 B0FD08    B10F00     1                  14353C    TTY Input Buf
B10F00      512 B10708    B11128     1                  14356C    TTY Output Buf
B11128     2000 B10F00    B11920     1                  1A110E    Interrupt Stack
B11920       44 B11128    B11974     1                  970DE8    *Init*
B11974     1056 B11920    B11DBC     1                  18F132    messages
B11DBC       84 B11974    B11E38     1                  19ABCE    Watched Boolean
B11E38       84 B11DBC    B11EB4     1                  19ABCE    Watched Boolean
B11EB4       84 B11E38    B11F30     1                  19ABCE    Watched Boolean
B11F30       84 B11EB4    B11FAC     1                  19ABCE    Watched Boolean
Router#
```

The following is sample output from the **show memory free** command:

```
Router# show memory free

            Head    Total(b)   Used(b)    Free(b)   Lowest(b)  Largest(b)
Processor   B0EE38  5181896    2210076    2971820   2692456    2845368

            Processor memory
Address  Bytes Prev.    Next     Ref  PrevF    NextF    Alloc PC  What
         24    Free list 1
CEB844   32    CEB7A4   CEB88C   0    0        0        96B894    SSE Manager
         52    Free list 2
         72    Free list 3
         76    Free list 4
         80    Free list 5
D35ED4   80    D35E30   D35F4C   0    0        D27AE8   96B894    SSE Manager
D27AE8   80    D27A48   D27B60   0    D35ED4   0        22585E    SSE Manager
         88    Free list 6
         100   Free list 7
D0A8F4   100   D0A8B0   D0A980   0    0        0        2258DA    SSE Manager
         104   Free list 8
B59EF0   108   B59E8C   B59F84   0    0        0        2258DA    (fragment)
```

The display of **show memory free** contains the same types of information as the **show memory** display, except that only free memory is displayed, and the information is displayed in order for each free list.

The first section of the display includes summary statistics about the activities of the system memory allocator. Table 26-25 describes significant fields shown in the first section of the display.

Table 26-25 *Show Memory Field Descriptions—First Section*

Field	Description
Head	Hexadecimal address of the head of the memory allocation chain.
Total(b)	Sum of used bytes plus free bytes.
Used(b)	Amount of memory in use.
Free(b)	Amount of memory not in use.
Lowest(b)	Smallest amount of free memory since last boot.
Largest(b)	Size of largest available free block.

The second section of the display is a block-by-block listing of memory use. Table 26-26 describes significant fields shown in the second section of the display.

Table 26-26 *Characteristics of each Block of Memory—Second Section*

Field	Description
Address	Hexadecimal address of block.

continues

Table 26-26 *Characteristics of each Block of Memory—Second Section (Continued)*

Field	Description
Bytes	Size of block in bytes.
Prev.	Address of previous block (should match Address on previous line).
Next	Address of next block (should match address on next line).
Ref	Reference count for that memory block, indicating how many different processes are using that block of memory.
PrevF	Address of previous free block (if free).
NextF	Address of next free block (if free).
Alloc PC	Address of the system call that allocated the block.
What	Name of process that owns the block, or "fragment" if the block is a fragment, or "coalesced" if the block was coalesced from adjacent free blocks.

The **show memory io** command displays the free I/O memory blocks. On the Cisco 4000, this command quickly shows how much unused I/O memory is available.

The following is sample output from the **show memory io** command:

```
Router# show memory io

Address  Bytes   Prev.     Next      Ref  PrevF    NextF     Alloc PC  What
6132DA0  59264   6132664   6141520   0    0        600DDEC   3FCF0     *Packet Buffer*
600DDEC  500     600DA4C   600DFE0   0    6132DA0  600FE68   0
600FE68  376     600FAC8   600FFE0   0    600DDEC  6011D54   0
6011D54  652     60119B4   6011FE0   0    600FE68  6013D54   0
614FCA0  832     614F564   614FFE0   0    601FD54  6177640   0
6177640  2657056 6172E90   0         0    614FCA0  0         0
Total: 2723244
```

The **show memory sram** command displays the free SRAM memory blocks. For the Cisco 4000, this command supports the high-speed static RAM memory pool to make it easier to debug or diagnose problems with allocation or freeing of such memory.

The following is sample output from the **show memory sram** command:

```
Router# show memory sram

Address  Bytes  Prev.  Next  Ref  PrevF  NextF  Alloc PC  What
7AE0     38178  72F0   0     0    0      0      0
Total    38178
```

The **show memory** command on the Cisco 4000 includes information about SRAM memory and I/O memory, and appears as follows:

```
Router# show memory

             Head    Total(b)   Used(b)    Free(b)  Lowest(b) Largest(b)
Processor   49C724   28719324   1510864   27208460   26511644  15513908
      I/O   6000000    4194304   1297088    2897216    2869248   2896812
     SRAM      1000      65536     63400       2136       2136      2136

Address  Bytes Prev.   Next    Ref   PrevF   NextF   Alloc PC  What
1000     2032 0        17F0     1                     3E73E    *Init*
17F0     2032 1000     1FE0     1                     3E73E    *Init*
1FE0      544 17F0     2200     1                     3276A    *Init*
2200       52 1FE0     2234     1                     31D68    *Init*
2234       52 2200     2268     1                     31DAA    *Init*
2268       52 2234     229C     1                     31DF2    *Init*
72F0     2032 6E5C     7AE0     1                     3E73E     Init
7AE0    38178 72F0        0     0     0       0           0
```

The **show memory summary** command displays a summary of all memory pools as well as memory usage per Alloc PC (address of the system call that allocated the block).

The following is a partial sample output from the **show memory summary** command. This command shows the size, blocks, and bytes allocated. Bytes equal the size multiplied by the blocks. For a description of the other fields, see Table 20 and Table 21.

```
Router# show memory summary

Head     Total(b)     Used(b)     Free(b)   Lowest(b) Largest(b)
Processor   B0EE38     5181896     2210216    2971680    2692456     2845368

           Processor memory
Alloc PC        Size      Blocks      Bytes     What
0x2AB2           192          1         192     IDB: Serial Info
0x70EC            92          2         184     Init
0xC916           128         50        6400     RIF Cache
0x76ADE         4500          1        4500     XDI data
0x76E84         4464          1        4464     XDI data
0x76EAC          692          1         692     XDI data
0x77764          408          1         408     Init
0x77776          116          1         116     Init
0x777A2          408          1         408     Init
0x777B2          116          1         116     Init
0xA4600           24          3          72     List
0xD9B5C           52          1          52     SSE Manager
....................
0x0                0       3413     2072576     Pool Summary
0x0                0         28     2971680     Pool Summary (Free Blocks)
0x0               40       3441      137640     Pool Summary(All Block Headers)
0x0                0       3413     2072576     Memory Summary
0x0                0         28     2971680     Memory Summary (Free Blocks)
```

Related Commands

To locate documentation of related commands, you can search online at www.cisco.com.

show processes memory

show pci

Use the **show pci** EXEC command to display information about the peripheral component interconnect (PCI) hardware registers or bridge registers for the Cisco 7200 series routers.

show pci {**hardware** | **bridge** [*register*]}

Syntax	Description
hardware	Displays PCI hardware registers.
bridge	Displays PCI bridge registers.
register	(Optional) Number of a specific bridge register in the range 0 to 7. If not specified, this command displays information about all registers.

Command Mode

EXEC

Usage Guidelines

This command first appeared in Cisco IOS Release 11.2.

The output of this command is generally useful for diagnostic tasks performed by technical support only.

NOTE   The **show pci hardware** command displays a significant amount of information.

Sample Displays

The following is sample output for the PCI bridge register 1 on a Cisco 7200 series router:

```
Router# show pci bridge 1

Bridge 4, Port Adaptor 1, Handle=1
DEC21050 bridge chip, config=0x0
(0x00): cfid   = 0x00011011
(0x04): cfcs   = 0x02800147
(0x08): cfccid = 0x06040002
(0x0C): cfpmlt = 0x00010010

(0x18): cfsmlt = 0x18050504
(0x1C): cfsis  = 0x22805050
(0x20): cfmla  = 0x48F04880
(0x24): cfpmla = 0x00004880
```

```
(0x3C): cfbc   = 0x00000000
(0x40): cfseed = 0x00100000
(0x44): cfstwt = 0x00008020
```

The following is partial sample output for the PCI hardware register, which also includes information on all the PCI bridge registers on a Cisco 7200 series router:

```
Router# show pci hardware

GT64010 External PCI Configuration registers:
  Vendor / Device ID  : 0xAB114601 (b/s 0x014611AB)
  Status / Command    : 0x17018002 (b/s 0x02800117)
  Class / Revision    : 0x00000006 (b/s 0x06000000)
  Latency             : 0x0F000000 (b/s 0x0000000F)
  RAS[1:0] Base       : 0x00000000 (b/s 0x00000000)
  RAS[3:2] Base       : 0x00000001 (b/s 0x01000000)
  CS[2:0] Base        : 0x00000000 (b/s 0x00000000)
  CS[3] Base          : 0x00000000 (b/s 0x00000000)
  Mem Map Base        : 0x00000014 (b/s 0x14000000)
  IO Map Base         : 0x01000014 (b/s 0x14000001)
  Int Pin / Line      : 0x00010000 (b/s 0x00000100)

Bridge 0, Downstream MB0 to MB1, Handle=0
DEC21050 bridge chip, config=0x0
(0x00): cfid   = 0x00011011
(0x04): cfcs   = 0x02800143
(0x08): cfccid = 0x06040002
(0x0C): cfpmlt = 0x00011810

(0x18): cfsmlt = 0x18000100
(0x1C): cfsis  = 0x02809050
(0x20): cfmla  = 0x4AF04880
(0x24): cfpmla = 0x4BF04B00

(0x3C): cfbc   = 0x00000000
(0x40): cfseed = 0x00100000
(0x44): cfstwt = 0x00008020
...
```

show pci hardware

Use the **show pci hardware** EXEC command to display information about the Host-PCI bridge.

show pci hardware

Syntax Description

This command has no arguments or keywords.

Command Mode

EXEC

Usage Guidelines

This command first appeared in Cisco IOS Release 11.2.

The output of this command is generally useful for diagnostic tasks performed by technical support only.

```
router#show pci hardware
hardware PCI hardware registers

Each device on the PCI bus is assigned a PCI device number.  For the
C2600, device numbers are as follows:

Device    Device number
0         First LAN device
1         Second LAN device
2         AIM device (if present)
3         Not presently used
4         Port module - first PCI device
5         Port module - second PCI device
6         Port module - third PCI device
7         Port module - fourth PCI device
8-14      Not presently used
15        Xilinx PCI bridge
```

Sample Display

The following is partial sample output for the PCI hardware register, which also includes information on all the PCI bridge registers. See Table 26-27 for a description of the output display fields.

```
router# show pci hardware

XILINX Host-PCI Bridge Registers:
Vendor / Device ID: 0x401310EE
Status / Command: 0x040001C6
PCI Slave Base Reg 0: 0x00000000
PCI Slave Base Reg 1: 0x04000000
```

Table 26-27 *Show PCI Hardware Field Descriptions*

Field	Description
Device/Vendor ID	Identifies the PCI vendor and device. The value 0x401310EE identifies the device as the Xilinx-based Host-PCI bridge for the Cisco 2600 router.
Status/Command	Provides status of the Host-PCI bridge. Refer to the PCI Specification for more information.

Table 26-27 *Show PCI Hardware Field Descriptions (Continued)*

Field	Description
PCI Slave Base Reg 0	The base address of PCI Target Region 0 for the Host-PCI bridge. This region is used for Big-Endian transfers between PCI devices and memory.
PCI Slave Base Reg 1	The base address of PCI Target Region 1 for the Host-PCI bridge. This region is used for Little-Endian transfers between PCI devices and memory.

show processes

Use the **show processes** EXEC command to display information about the active processes.

> **show processes [cpu]**

Syntax   Description

cpu   (Optional) Displays detailed CPU utilization statistics.

Command Mode

EXEC

Usage Guidelines

This command first appeared in Cisco IOS Release 10.0.

Sample Displays

The following is sample output from the **show processes** command:

```
Router# show processes

CPU utilization for five seconds: 21%/0%; one minute: 2%; five minutes: 2%
PID QTy       PC Runtime (ms)    Invoked   uSecs    Stacks      TTY Process
  1 Mwe    2FEA4E        1808        464    3896   1796/3000      0 IP-EIGRP Router
  2 Lst    11682        10236        109   93908   1828/2000      0 Check heaps
  3 Mst     3AE9C           0        280       0   1768/2000      0 Timers
  4 Lwe     74AD2           0         12       0   1492/2000      0 ARP Input
  5.ME      912E4           0          2       0   1892/2000      0 IPC Zone Manager
  6.ME      91264           0          1       0   1936/2000      0 IPC Realm Manager
  7.ME      91066           0         30       0   1784/2000      0 IPC Seat Manager
  8.ME     133368           0          1       0   1928/2000      0 CXBus hot stall
  9.ME     1462EE           0          1       0   1940/2000      0 Microcode load
 10 Msi   127538           4         76      52   1608/2000      0 Env Mon
 11.ME    160CF4           0          1       0   1932/2000      0 MIP Mailbox
 12 Mwe   125D7C           4        280      14   1588/2000      0 SMT input
```

```
13 Lwe AFD0E            0         1        0    1772/2000    0 Probe Input
14 Mwe AF662            0         1        0    1784/2000    0 RARP Input
15 Hwe A1F9A          228       549      415    3240/4000    0 IP Input
16 Msa C86A0            0       114        0    1864/2000    0 TCP Timer
17 Lwe CA700            0         1        0    1756/2000    0 TCP Protocols
18.ME  CCE7C            0         1        0    1940/2000    0 TCP Listener
19 Mwe AC49E            0         1        0    1592/2000    0 BOOTP Server
20 Mwe 10CD84          24        77      311    1652/2000    0 CDP Protocol
21 Mwe 27BF82           0         2        0    1776/2000    0 ATMSIG Input
```

The following is sample output from the **show processes cpu** command:

```
Router# show processes cpu

CPU utilization for five seconds: 5%/2%; one minute: 3%; five minutes: 2%
  PID  Runtime (ms)    Invoked   uSecs   5Sec   1Min   5Min   TTY Process
    1          1736         58   29931     0%     0%     0%   Check heaps
    2            68        585     116  1.00%  1.00%     0%   IP Input
    3             0        744       0     0%     0%     0%   TCP Timer
    4             0          2       0     0%     0%     0%   TCP Protocols
    5             0          1       0     0%     0%     0%   BOOTP Server
    6            16        130     123     0%     0%     0%   ARP Input
    7             0          1       0     0%     0%     0%   Probe Input
    8             0          7       0     0%     0%     0%   MOP Protocols
    9             0          2       0     0%     0%     0%   Timers
   10           692         64   10812     0%     0%     0%   Net Background
   11             0          5       0     0%     0%     0%   Logger
   12             0         38       0     0%     0%     0%   BGP Open
   13             0          1       0     0%     0%     0%   Net Input
   14           540       3466     155     0%     0%     0%   TTY Background
   15             0          1       0     0%     0%     0%   BGP I/O
   16          5100       1367    3730     0%     0%     0%   IGRP Router
   17            88       4232      20  0.20%  1.00%     0%   BGP Router
   18           152      14650      10     0%     0%     0%   BGP Scanner
   19           224         99    2262     0%     0%  1.00%   Exec
```

Table 26-28 describes significant fields shown in the two displays.

Table 26-28   *Show Processes Field Descriptions*

Field	Description
CPU utilization for five seconds	CPU utilization for the last 5 seconds. The second number indicates the percent of CPU time spent at the interrupt level.
one minute	CPU utilization for the last minute.
five minutes	CPU utilization for the last 5 minutes.
PID	Process ID.
Q	Process queue priority. Possible values: H (high), M (medium), L (low).

Table 26-28 *Show Processes Field Descriptions (Continued)*

Field	Description
Ty	Scheduler test. Possible values: * (currently running), E (waiting for an event), S (ready to run, voluntarily relinquished processor), rd (ready to run, wakeup conditions have occurred), we (waiting for an event), sa (sleeping until an absolute time), si (sleeping for a time interval), sp (sleeping for a time interval (alternate call), st (sleeping until a timer expires), hg (hung; the process will never execute again), xx (dead. The process has terminated, but not yet been deleted.).
PC	Current program counter.
Runtime (ms)	CPU time the process has used, in milliseconds.
Invoked	Number of times the process has been invoked.
uSecs	Microseconds of CPU time for each process invocation.
Stacks	Low water mark/Total stack space available, shown in bytes.
TTY	Terminal that controls the process.
Process	Name of process.
5Sec	CPU utilization by task in the last 5 seconds.
1Min	CPU utilization by task in the last minute.
5Min	CPU utilization by task in the last 5 minutes.

NOTE   Because the network server has a 4-millisecond clock resolution, run times are considered reliable only after a large number of invocations or a reasonable, measured run time.

Related Commands

To locate documentation of related commands, you can search online at www.cisco.com.

show processes memory

show processes memory

Use the **show processes memory** EXEC command to show memory used.

> **show processes memory**

Syntax Description

This command has no arguments or keywords.

Command Mode

EXEC

Usage Guidelines

This command first appeared in Cisco IOS Release 10.0.

Sample Display

The following is sample output from the **show processes memory** command:

```
Router# show processes memory

Total: 5611448, Used: 2307548, Free: 3303900
 PID  TTY  Allocated    Freed       Holding    Getbufs     Retbufs  Process
   0    0     199592       1236      1907220          0           0  *Init*
   0    0        400      76928          400          0           0  *Sched*
   0    0    5431176    3340052       140760     349780           0  *Dead*
   1    0        256        256         1724          0           0  Load Meter
   2    0        264          0         5032          0           0  Exec
   3    0          0          0         2724          0           0  Check heaps
   4    0      97932          0         2852      32760           0  Pool Manager
   5    0        256        256         2724          0           0  Timers
   6    0         92          0         2816          0           0  CXBus hot stall
   7    0          0          0         2724          0           0  IPC Zone Manager
   8    0          0          0         2724          0           0  IPC Realm Manager
   9    0          0          0         2724          0           0  IPC Seat Manager
  10    0        892        476         3256          0           0  ARP Input
  11    0         92          0         2816          0           0  SERIAL A'detect
  12    0        216          0         2940          0           0  Microcode Loader
  13    0          0          0         2724          0           0  RFSS watchdog
  14    0   15659136   15658584         3276          0           0  Env Mon
...
  77    0        116          0         2844          0           0  IPX-EIGRP Hello
                                     2307224 Total
```

Table 26-29 describes significant fields shown in the display.

Table 26-29 *Show Processes Memory Field Descriptions*

Field	Description
Total	Total amount of memory held.
Used	Total amount of used memory.
Free	Total amount of free memory.
PID	Process ID.
TTY	Terminal that controls the process.
Allocated	Bytes of memory allocated by the process.

Table 26-29 *Show Processes Memory Field Descriptions (Continued)*

Field	Description
Freed	Bytes of memory freed by the process, regardless of who originally allocated it.
Holding	Amount of memory currently allocated to the process.
Getbufs	Number of times the process has requested a packet buffer.
Retbufs	Number of times the process has relinquished a packet buffer.
Process	Process name.
Init	System initialization.
Sched	The scheduler.
Dead	Processes as a group that are now dead.
Total	Total amount of memory held by all processes.

Related Commands

To locate documentation of related commands, you can search online at www.cisco.com.

show memory
show processes

show protocols

Use the **show protocols** EXEC command to display the configured protocols.

This command shows the global and interface-specific status of any configured Level 3 protocol; for example, IP, DECnet, IPX, AppleTalk, and so forth.

> **show protocols**

Syntax Description

This command has no arguments or keywords.

Command Mode

EXEC

Usage Guidelines

This command first appeared in Cisco IOS Release 10.0.

Sample Display

The following is sample output from the **show protocols** command:

```
Router# show protocols

Global values:
  Internet Protocol routing is enabled
  DECNET routing is enabled
  XNS routing is enabled
  Appletalk routing is enabled
  X.25 routing is enabled
Ethernet 0 is up, line protocol is up
  Internet address is 192.168.1.1, subnet mask is 255.255.255.0
  Decnet cost is 5
  XNS address is 2001.AA00.0400.06CC
  AppleTalk address is 4.129, zone Twilight
Serial 0 is up, line protocol is up
  Internet address is 192.168.7.49, subnet mask is 255.255.255.240
Ethernet 1 is up, line protocol is up
  Internet address is 192.168.2.1, subnet mask is 255.255.255.0
  Decnet cost is 5
  XNS address is 2002.AA00.0400.06CC
  AppleTalk address is 254.132, zone Twilight
Serial 1 is down, line protocol is down
  Internet address is 192.168.7.177, subnet mask is 255.255.255.240
  AppleTalk address is 999.1, zone Magnolia Estates
```

show stacks

Use the **show stacks** EXEC command to monitor the stack usage of processes and interrupt routines.

> **show stacks**

Syntax Description

This command has no arguments or keywords.

Command Mode

EXEC

Usage Guidelines

This command first appeared in Cisco IOS Release 10.0.

The display from this command includes the reason for the last system reboot. If the system was reloaded because of a system failure, a saved system stack trace is displayed. This information is of use only to your technical support representative in analyzing crashes in the field. It is included here in case you need to read the displayed statistics to an engineer over the phone.

Sample Display

The following is sample output from the **show stacks** command following a system failure:

```
Router# show stacks

Minimum process stacks:
Free/Size  Name
 652/1000  Router Init
 726/1000  Init
 744/1000  BGP Open
 686/1200  Virtual Exec

Interrupt level stacks:
Level    Called Free/Size  Name
  1           0 1000/1000  env-flash
  3         738  900/1000  Multiport Communications Interfaces
  5         178  970/1000  Console UART
System was restarted by bus error at PC 0xAD1F4, address 0xD0D0D1A
GS Software (GS3), Version 9.1(0.16), BETA TEST SOFTWARE
Compiled Tue 11-Aug-92 13:27 by jthomas
Stack trace from system failure:
FP: 0x29C158, RA: 0xACFD4
FP: 0x29C184, RA: 0xAD20C
FP: 0x29C1B0, RA: 0xACFD4
FP: 0x29C1DC, RA: 0xAD304
FP: 0x29C1F8, RA: 0xAF774
FP: 0x29C214, RA: 0xAF83E
FP: 0x29C228, RA: 0x3E0CA
FP: 0x29C244, RA: 0x3BD3C
```

Related Commands

To locate documentation of related commands, you can search online at www.cisco.com.

show processes

show subsys

To display the subsystem information, use the **show subsys** privileged EXEC command.

> **show subsys** [**class** *class* | **name** *name*]

Syntax	Description
class *class*	(Optional) Shows the subsystems of the specified class. Valid classes are **driver**, **kernel**, **library**, **management**, **protocol**, and **registry**.
name *name*	(Optional) Shows the specified subsystem. Use the asterisk character (*) as a wildcard at the end of the name to list all subsystems starting with the specified characters.

Command Mode

Privileged EXEC

Usage Guidelines

This command first appeared in Cisco IOS Release 11.1.

Use the **show subsys** command to confirm that all required features are in the running image.

Sample Display

The following example shows partial sample output from the **show subsys** command:

```
Router# show subsys

                    Class       Version
static_map          Kernel      1.000.001
arp                 Kernel      1.000.001
ether               Kernel      1.000.001
compress            Kernel      1.000.001
alignment           Kernel      1.000.002
monvar              Kernel      1.000.001
slot                Kernel      1.000.001
oir                 Kernel      1.000.001
atm                 Kernel      1.000.001
ip_addrpool_sys     Library     1.000.001
chat                Library     1.000.001
dialer              Library     1.000.001
flash_services      Library     1.000.001
ip_localpool_sys    Library     1.000.001
nvram_common        Driver      1.000.001
ASP                 Driver      1.000.001
sonict              Driver      1.000.001
oc3suni             Driver      1.000.001
oc12suni            Driver      1.000.001
ds3suni             Driver      1.000.001
...
```

Table 26-30 describes the fields shown in this display.

Table 26-30   *Show Subsys Field Descriptions*

Field	Description
static_map	Name of the subsystem.
Class	Class of the subsystem. Possible classes include Kernel, Library, Driver, Protocol, Management, Registry, and SystemInit.
Version	Version of the subsystem.

show tcp

Use the **show tcp** EXEC command to display the status of TCP connections.

> **show tcp** [*line-number*]

Syntax	Description
line-number	(Optional) Absolute line number of the line for which you want to display Telnet connection status.

Command Mode

EXEC

Usage Guidelines

This command first appeared in Cisco IOS Release 10.0.

Sample Display

The following is sample output from the **show tcp** command:

```
Router# show tcp

tty0, connection 1 to host cider
Connection state is ESTAB, I/O status: 1, unread input bytes: 0
Local host: 172.31.232.17, Local port: 11184
Foreign host: 172.31.1.137, Foreign port: 23

Enqueued packets for retransmit: 0, input: 0, saved: 0

Event Timers (current time is 67341276):
Timer:        Retrans   TimeWait    AckHold    SendWnd  KeepAlive
Starts:           30          0         32          0          0
Wakeups:           1          0         14          0          0
Next:              0          0          0          0          0

iss:    67317172  snduna:   67317228  sndnxt:   67317228     sndwnd:    4096
irs: 1064896000   rcvnxt: 1064897597  rcvwnd:        2144  delrcvwnd:       0

SRTT: 317 ms, RTTO: 900 ms, RTV: 133 ms, KRTT: 0 ms
minRTT: 4 ms, maxRTT: 300 ms, ACK hold: 300 ms
Flags: higher precedence, idle user, retransmission timeout

Datagrams (max data segment is 536 bytes):
Rcvd: 41 (out of order: 0), with data: 34, total data bytes: 1596
Sent: 57 (retransmit: 1), with data: 35, total data bytes: 55
```

Table 26-31 describes the first five lines of output shown in the display.

Table 26-31 *Show TCP Field Descriptions—First Section of Output*

Field	Description
tty0	Identifying number of the line.
connection 1	Number identifying the TCP connection.
to host xxx	Name of the remote host to which the connection has been made.
Connection state is ESTAB	A connection progresses through a series of states during its lifetime. These states follow in the order in which a connection progresses through them. • LISTEN—Waiting for a connection request from any remote TCP and port. • SYNSENT—Waiting for a matching connection request after having sent a connection request. • SYNRCVD—Waiting for a confirming connection request acknowledgment after having both received and sent a connection request. • ESTAB—Indicates an open connection; data received can be delivered to the user. This is the normal state for the data transfer phase of the connection. • FINWAIT1—Waiting for a connection termination request from the remote TCP or an acknowledgment of the connection termination request previously sent. • FINWAIT2—Waiting for a connection termination request from the remote TCP host. • CLOSEWAIT—Waiting for a connection termination request from the local user. • CLOSING—Waiting for a connection termination request acknowledgment from the remote TCP host. • LASTACK—Waiting for an acknowledgment of the connection termination request previously sent to the remote TCP host. • TIMEWAIT—Waiting for enough time to pass to be sure the remote TCP host has received the acknowledgment of its connection termination request. • CLOSED—Indicates no connection state at all. For more information, see RFC 793, *Transmission Control Protocol Functional Specification.*
I/O status:	Number describing the current internal status of the connection.
unread input bytes:	Number of bytes that the lower-level TCP processes have read, but the higher level TCP processes have not yet processed.
Local host:	IP address of the network server.
Local port:	Local port number, as derived from the following equation: *line-number* + (512 * *random-number*). (The line number uses the lower nine bits; the other bits are random.)
Foreign host:	IP address of the remote host to which the TCP connection has been made.

continues

Table 26-31 *Show TCP Field Descriptions—First Section of Output (Continued)*

Field	Description
Foreign port:	Destination port for the remote host.
Enqueued packets for retransmit:	Number of packets waiting on the retransmit queue. These are packets on this TCP connection that have been sent but have not yet been acknowledged by the remote TCP host.
input:	Number of packets that are waiting on the input queue to be read by the user.
saved:	Number of received out-of-order packets that are waiting for all packets comprising the message to be received before they enter the input queue. For example, if packets 1, 2, 4, 5, and 6 have been received, packets 1 and 2 would enter the input queue, and packets 4, 5, and 6 would enter the saved queue.

The following line of output shows the current time according to the system clock of the local host:

```
Event Timers (current time is 67341276):
```

The time shown is the number of milliseconds since the system started.

The following lines of output display the number of times that various local TCP timeout values were reached during this connection. In this example, the local host retransmitted 30 times because it received no response from the remote host, and it transmitted an acknowledgment many more times because there was no data on which to piggyback.

```
Timer:      Retrans   TimeWait    AckHold   SendWnd   KeepAlive
Starts:          30          0         32         0           0
Wakeups:          1          0         14         0           0
Next:             0          0          0         0           0
```

Table 26-32 describes the fields in the preceding lines of output.

Table 26-32 *Show TCP Field Descriptions—Second Section of Output*

Field	Description
Timer:	The names of the timers in the display.
Starts:	The number of times the timer has been started during this connection.
Wakeups:	Number of keepalives transmitted without receiving any response. (This field is reset to zero when a response is received.)
Next:	The system clock setting that will trigger the next time this timer will go off.
Retrans	The Retransmission timer is used to time TCP packets that have not been acknowledged and are waiting for retransmission.
TimeWait	The TimeWait timer is used to ensure that the remote system receive a request to disconnect a session.

Table 26-32 *Show TCP Field Descriptions—Second Section of Output (Continued)*

Field	Description
AckHold	The Acknowledgment timer is used to delay the sending of acknowledgments to the remote TCP in an attempt to reduce network use.
SendWnd	The Send Window is used to ensure that there is no closed window due to a lost TCP acknowledgment.
KeepAlive	The KeepAlive timer is used to control the transmission of test messages to the remote TCP to ensure that the link has not been broken without the local TCP's knowledge.

The following lines of output display the sequence numbers that TCP uses to ensure sequenced, reliable transport of data. The local host and remote host each use these sequence numbers for flow control and to acknowledge receipt of datagrams. Table 26-33 describes the specific fields in these lines of output:

```
iss:   67317172  snduna:   67317228  sndnxt:   67317228    sndwnd:    4096
irs: 1064896000  rcvnxt: 1064897597  rcvwnd:       2144  delrcvwnd:       0
```

Table 26-33 *Show TCP Field Descriptions—Sequence Number*

Field	Description
iss:	Initial send sequence number.
snduna:	Last send sequence number the local host sent but has not received an acknowledgment for.
sndnxt:	Sequence number the local host will send next.
sndwnd:	TCP window size of the remote host.
irs:	Initial receive sequence number.
rcvnxt:	Last receive sequence number the local host has acknowledged.
rcvwnd:	Local host's TCP window size.
delrcvwnd:	Delayed receive window—data the local host has read from the connection, but has not yet subtracted from the receive window the host has advertised to the remote host. The value in this field gradually increases until it is larger than a full-sized packet, at which point it is applied to the rcvwnd field.

The following lines of output display values that the local host uses to keep track of transmission times so that TCP can adjust to the network it is using.

Table 26-34 describes the fields in the following line of output:

```
SRTT: 317 ms, RTTO: 900 ms, RTV: 133 ms, KRTT: 0 ms
minRTT: 4 ms, maxRTT: 300 ms, ACK hold: 300 ms
Flags: higher precedence, idle user, retransmission timeout
```

Table 26-34 *Show TCP Field Descriptions—Line Beginning with SRTT*

Field	Description
SRTT:	A calculated smoothed round-trip timeout.
RTTO:	Round-trip timeout.
RTV:	Variance of the round-trip time.
KRTT:	New round-trip timeout (using the Karn algorithm). This field separately tracks the round-trip time of packets that have been retransmitted.
minRTT:	Smallest recorded round-trip timeout (hard wire value used for calculation).
maxRTT:	Largest recorded round-trip timeout.
ACK hold:	Time the local host will delay an acknowledgment in order to piggyback data on it.
Flags:	Properties of the connection.

For more information on these fields, refer to "Round Trip Time Estimation," P. Karn & C. Partridge, ACM SIGCOMM-87, August 1987.

Table 26-35 describes the fields in the following lines of output:

```
Datagrams (max data segment is 536 bytes):
Rcvd: 41 (out of order: 0), with data: 34, total data bytes: 1596
Sent: 57 (retransmit: 1), with data: 35, total data bytes: 55
```

Table 26-35 *Show TCP Field Descriptions—Last Section of Output*

Field	Description
Rcvd:	Number of datagrams the local host has received during this connection (and the number of these datagrams that were out of order).
with data:	Number of these datagrams that contained data.
total data bytes:	Total number of bytes of data in these datagrams.
Sent:	Number of datagrams the local host sent during this connection (and the number of these datagrams that had to be retransmitted).
with data:	Number of these datagrams that contained data.
total data bytes:	Total number of bytes of data in these datagrams.

Related Commands

To locate documentation of related commands, you can search online at www.cisco.com.

show tcp brief

show tcp brief

To display a concise description of TCP connection endpoints, use the **show tcp brief** EXEC command.

> **show tcp brief [all]**

Syntax	Description
all	(Optional) Displays status for all endpoints. Without this keyword, endpoints in the LISTEN state are not shown.

Command Mode

EXEC

Usage Guidelines

This command first appeared in Cisco IOS Release 11.2.

Sample Display

The following is sample output from the **show tcp brief** command while a user has connected into the system via Telnet:

```
Router> show tcp brief

TCB       Local Address       Foreign Address       (state)
609789AC  Router.cisco.com.23  cider.cisco.com.3733  ESTAB
```

Table 26-36 describes the fields shown in the display.

Table 26-36 *Show TCP Brief Field Descriptions*

Field	Description
TCB	An internal identifier for the endpoint.
Local Address	The local IP address and port.
Foreign Address	The foreign IP address and port (at the opposite end of the connection).
(state)	The state of the connection. States are described in syntax description of the **show tcp** command.

Related Commands

To locate documentation of related commands, you can search online at www.cisco.com.

show tcp

show tdm connections

To display a snapshot of the time-division multiplexing (TDM) bus connection memory in a Cisco AS5200 access server, use the **show tdm connections** EXEC command.

show tdm connections [**motherboard** | **slot** *number*]

Syntax	Description
motherboard	(Optional) Motherboard in the Cisco AS5200 access server.
slot *number*	(Optional) Slot number.

Command Mode

EXEC

Usage Guidelines

This command first appeared in Cisco IOS Release 11.2.

The **show tdm connections** command shows the connection memory for all TDM bus connections in the access server if you do not limit the display to the motherboard or a slot.

Sample Display

The following example shows source stream 3 (ST3) channel 2 switched out of stream 6 (ST6) channel 2:

```
AS5200# show tdm connections motherboard

MT8980 motherboard unit 0, Control Register = 0x1F, ODE Register = 0x06
Connection Memory for ST6:
Ch0:   0x62, Ch1:   0x00, Ch2:   0x00, Ch3:   0x00
Ch4:   0x00, Ch5:   0x00, Ch6:   0x00, Ch7:   0x00
Ch8:   0x00, Ch9:   0x00, Ch10:  0x00, Ch11:  0x00
Ch12:  0x00, Ch13:  0x00, Ch14:  0x00, Ch15:  0x00
Ch16:  0x00, Ch17:  0x00, Ch18:  0x00, Ch19:  0x00
Ch20:  0x00, Ch21:  0x00, Ch22:  0x00, Ch23:  0x00
Ch24:  0x00, Ch25:  0x00, Ch26:  0x00, Ch27:  0x00
Ch28:  0x00, Ch29:  0x00, Ch30:  0x00, Ch31:  0x00
```

To interpret the hexadecimal number 0x62 into meaningful information, you must translate it into binary code. These two hexadecimal numbers represent a connection from any stream and a channel on any stream. The number 6 translates into the binary code 0110, which represents the third-source stream. The number 2 translates into the binary code 0010, which represents the second-source channel.

Stream 6 (ST6) channel 0 is the destination for source stream 3 (ST3) channel 2 in this example.

Related Commands

To locate documentation of related commands, you can search online at www.cisco.com.

show tdm data

show tdm data

To display a snapshot of the time-division multiplexing (TDM) bus data memory in a Cisco AS5200 access server, use the **show tdm data** EXEC command.

show tdm data [motherboard | slot *number*]

Syntax	Description
motherboard	(Optional) Motherboard in the Cisco AS5200 access server.
slot *number*	(Optional) Slot number.

Command Mode

EXEC

Usage Guidelines

This command first appeared in Cisco IOS Release 11.2.

The data memory for all TDM bus connections in the access server is displayed if you do not specify a motherboard or slot.

Sample Display

The following example shows a snapshot of TDM memory where the normal ISDN idle pattern (0x7E) is present on all channels of the TDM device resident on the motherboard:

```
AS5200# show tdm data motherboard
MT8980 motherboard unit 0, Control Register = 0x1F, ODE Register = 0x06
Data Memory for ST0:
Ch0:  0x7E, Ch1:  0x7E, Ch2:  0x7E, Ch3:  0x7E
Ch4:  0x7E, Ch5:  0x7E, Ch6:  0x7E, Ch7:  0x7E
Ch8:  0x7E, Ch9:  0x7E, Ch10: 0x7E, Ch11: 0x7E
Ch12: 0x7E, Ch13: 0x7E, Ch14: 0x7E, Ch15: 0x7E
Ch16: 0x7E, Ch17: 0x7E, Ch18: 0x7E, Ch19: 0x7E
Ch20: 0x7E, Ch21: 0x7E, Ch22: 0x7E, Ch23: 0x7E
Ch24: 0x7E, Ch25: 0x7E, Ch26: 0x7E, Ch27: 0x7E
Ch28: 0x7E, Ch29: 0x7E, Ch30: 0x7E, Ch31: 0x7E
Data Memory for ST1:
Ch0:  0x7E, Ch1:  0x7E, Ch2:  0x7E, Ch3:  0x7E
```

```
Ch4:  0x7E, Ch5:  0x7E, Ch6:  0x7E, Ch7:  0x7E
Ch8:  0x7E, Ch9:  0x7E, Ch10: 0x7E, Ch11: 0x7E
Ch12: 0x7E, Ch13: 0x7E, Ch14: 0x7E, Ch15: 0x7E
Ch16: 0x7E, Ch17: 0x7E, Ch18: 0x7E, Ch19: 0x7E
Ch20: 0x7E, Ch21: 0x7E, Ch22: 0x7E, Ch23: 0x7E
Ch24: 0x7E, Ch25: 0x7E, Ch26: 0x7E, Ch27: 0x7E
Ch28: 0x7E, Ch29: 0x7E, Ch30: 0x7E, Ch31: 0x7E
```

Related Commands

To locate documentation of related commands, you can search online at www.cisco.com.

show tdm connections

show tech-support

To display general information about the router when reporting a problem, use the **show tech-support** privileged EXEC command.

> **show tech-support** [**page**] [**password**]

Part
III

Command Reference

Syntax	Description
page	(Optional) Causes the output to display a page of information at a time. Use the return key to display the next line of output or use the space bar to display the next page of information. If not used, the output scrolls (that is, does not stop for page breaks).
password	(Optional) Leaves passwords and other security information in the output. If not used, passwords and other security-sensitive information in the output are replaced with the label "<removed>" (this is the default).

Default

Display output without page breaks and remove passwords and other security information.

Command Mode

Privileged EXEC

Usage Guidelines

This command first appeared in Cisco IOS Release 11.2.

Use this command to help collect general information about the router when you are reporting a problem. This command displays the equivalent of the following **show** commands:

- **show buffers**
- **show controllers**
- **show interfaces**
- **show running-config**
- **show processes cpu**
- **show processes memory**
- **show stacks**
- **show version**

For a sample display of the output of the **show tech-support** command, refer to these **show** commands.

Related Commands

To locate documentation of related commands, you can search online at www.cisco.com.

show buffers
show controllers
show controllers tech-support
show interfaces
show processes cpu
show processes memory
show running-config
show stacks
show version

test flash

To test Flash memory on MCI and envm Flash EPROM interfaces, use the **test flash** EXEC command.

        test flash

Syntax Description

This command has no arguments or keywords.

Command Mode

EXEC

Usage Guidelines

This command first appeared in Cisco IOS Release 10.0.

Example

The following example tests the Flash memory:

```
test flash
```

Related Commands

To locate documentation of related commands, you can search online at www.cisco.com.

test interfaces
test memory

test interfaces

To test the system interfaces on the modular router, use the **test interfaces** EXEC command.

test interfaces

Syntax Description

This command has no arguments or keywords.

Command Mode

EXEC

Usage Guidelines

This command first appeared in Cisco IOS Release 10.0.

The **test interfaces** EXEC command is intended for the factory checkout of network interfaces. It is not intended for diagnosing problems with an operational router. The **test interfaces** output does not report correct results if the router is attached to a "live" network. For each network interface that has an IP address that can be tested in loopback (MCI and ciscoBus Ethernet and all serial interfaces), the **test**

interfaces command sends a series of ICMP echoes. Error counters are examined to determine the operational status of the interface.

Example

The following example tests the system interfaces:

```
test interfaces
```

Related Commands

To locate documentation of related commands, you can search online at www.cisco.com.

test flash
test memory

test memory

To perform a test of Multibus memory (including nonvolatile memory) on the modular router, use the **test memory** EXEC command. The memory test overwrites memory.

       test memory

Syntax Description

This command has no arguments or keywords.

Command Mode

EXEC

Usage Guidelines

This command first appeared in Cisco IOS Release 10.0.

CAUTION   The memory test overwrites memory. If you use the **test memory** command, you will need to rewrite nonvolatile memory. For example, if you test Multibus memory, which is the memory used by the CSC-R 4-Mbps Token Ring interfaces, you will need to reload the system before the network interfaces will operate properly. The **test memory** command is intended primarily for use by Cisco personnel.

The following example tests memory:

```
test memory
```

Related Commands

To locate documentation of related commands, you can search online at www.cisco.com.

test flash
test interfaces

trace (privileged)

Use the **trace** privileged EXEC command to discover the routes that packets will actually take when traveling to their destination.

> **trace** [*protocol*] [*destination*]

Syntax   Description

protocol   (Optional) Protocols that can be used are **appletalk**, **clns**, **ip** and **vines**.

destination   (Optional) Destination address or host name on the command line. The default parameters for the appropriate protocol are assumed and the tracing action begins.

Default

The *protocol* argument is based on the Cisco IOS software's examination of the format of *destination*. For example, if the software finds a *destination* argument in IP format, the *protocol* value defaults to **ip**.

Command Mode

Privileged EXEC

Usage Guidelines

This command first appeared in Cisco IOS Release 10.0.

The **trace** command works by taking advantage of the error messages generated by routers when a datagram exceeds its time-to-live (TTL) value.

The **trace** command starts by sending probe datagrams with a TTL value of one. This causes the first router to discard the probe datagram and send back an error message. The **trace** command sends several probes at each TTL level and displays the round-trip time for each.

The **trace** command sends out one probe at a time. Each outgoing packet may result in one or two error messages. A "time exceeded" error message indicates that an intermediate router has seen and discarded the probe. A "destination unreachable" error message indicates that the destination node has received the probe and discarded it because it could not deliver the packet. If the timer goes off before a response comes in, **trace** prints an asterisk (*).

The **trace** command terminates when the destination responds, when the maximum TTL is exceeded, or when the user interrupts the trace with the escape sequence. By default, to invoke the escape sequence, type **Ctrl-^ X**—by simultaneously pressing and releasing the **Ctrl**, **Shift**, and **6** keys, and then pressing the **X** key.

To use nondefault parameters and invoke an extended **trace** test, enter the command without a *destination* argument. You will be stepped through a dialog to select the desired parameters.

Common Trace Problems

Due to bugs in the IP implementation of various hosts and routers, the IP **trace** command may behave in odd ways.

Not all destinations will respond correctly to a probe message by sending back an "ICMP port unreachable" message. A long sequence of TTL levels with only asterisks, terminating only when the maximum TTL has been reached, may indicate this problem.

There is a known problem with the way some hosts handle an "ICMP TTL exceeded" message. Some hosts generate an "ICMP" message but they reuse the TTL of the incoming packet. Since this is zero, the ICMP packets do not make it back. When you trace the path to such a host, you may see a set of TTL values with asterisks (*). Eventually the TTL gets high enough that the *ICMP* message can get back. For example, if the host is six hops away, **trace** will time out on responses 6 through 11.

Sample Display Showing Trace IP Routes

The following display shows sample IP **trace** output when a destination host name has been specified:

```
Router# trace ABA.NYC.mil

Type escape sequence to abort.
Tracing the route to ABA.NYC.mil (26.0.0.73)
        1 DEBRIS.CISCO.COM (192.180.1.6) 1000 msec 8 msec 4 msec
        2 BARRNET-GW.CISCO.COM (192.180.16.2) 8 msec 8 msec 8 msec
        3 EXTERNAL-A-GATEWAY.STANFORD.EDU (192.42.110.225) 8 msec 4 msec 4 msec
        4 BB2.SU.BARRNET.NET (192.200.254.6) 8 msec 8 msec 8 msec
        5 SU.ARC.BARRNET.NET (192.200.3.8) 12 msec 12 msec 8 msec
        6 MOFFETT-FLD-MB.in.MIL (192.52.195.1) 216 msec 120 msec 132 msec
        7 ABA.NYC.mil (26.0.0.73) 412 msec 628 msec 664 msec
```

Table 26-37 describes the fields shown in the display.

Table 26-37   *Trace Field Descriptions*

Field	Description
1	Indicates the sequence number of the router in the path to the host.
DEBRIS.CISCO.COM	Host name of this router.
192.180.1.61	Internet address of this router.
1000 msec 8 msec 4 msec	Round-trip time for each of the three probes that are sent.

Sample Display Showing Extended IP Trace Dialog

The following display shows a sample **trace** session involving the extended dialog of the **trace** command.

```
Router# trace

Protocol [ip]:
Target IP address: mit.edu
Source address:
Numeric display [n]:
Timeout in seconds [3]:
Probe count [3]:
Minimum Time to Live [1]:
Maximum Time to Live [30]:
Port Number [33434]:
Loose, Strict, Record, Timestamp, Verbose[none]:
Type escape sequence to abort.
Tracing the route to MIT.EDU (18.72.2.1)
  1 ICM-DC-2-V1.ICP.NET (192.108.209.17) 72 msec 72 msec 88 msec
  2 ICM-FIX-E-H0-T3.ICP.NET (192.157.65.122) 80 msec 128 msec 80 msec
  3 192.203.229.246 540 msec 88 msec 84 msec
  4 T3-2.WASHINGTON-DC-CNSS58.T3.ANS.NET (140.222.58.3) 84 msec 116 msec 88 msec
  5 T3-3.WASHINGTON-DC-CNSS56.T3.ANS.NET (140.222.56.4) 80 msec 132 msec 88 msec
  6 T3-0.NEW-YORK-CNSS32.T3.ANS.NET (140.222.32.1) 92 msec 132 msec 88 msec
  7 T3-0.HARTFORD-CNSS48.T3.ANS.NET (140.222.48.1) 88 msec 88 msec 88 msec
  8 T3-0.HARTFORD-CNSS49.T3.ANS.NET (140.222.49.1) 96 msec 104 msec 96 msec
  9 T3-0.ENSS134.T3.ANS.NET (140.222.134.1) 92 msec 128 msec 92 msec
 10 W91-CISCO-EXTERNAL-FDDI.MIT.EDU (192.233.33.1) 92 msec 92 msec 112 msec
 11 E40-RTR-FDDI.MIT.EDU (18.168.0.2) 92 msec 120 msec 96 msec
 12 MIT.EDU (18.72.2.1) 96 msec 92 msec 96 msec
```

Table 26-38 describes the fields that are unique to the extended trace sequence, as shown in the display.

Table 26-38   *Trace Field Descriptions*

Field	Description
Target IP address	You must enter a host name or an IP address. There is no default.

Table 26-38   *Trace Field Descriptions (Continued)*

Field	Description
Source address	One of the interface addresses of the router to use as a source address for the probes. The router will normally pick what it feels is the best source address to use.
Numeric display	The default is to have both a symbolic and numeric display; however, you can suppress the symbolic display.
Timeout in seconds	The number of seconds to wait for a response to a probe packet. The default is 3 seconds.
Probe count	The number of probes to be sent at each TTL level. The default count is 3.
Minimum Time to Live [1]	The TTL value for the first probes. The default is 1, but it can be set to a higher value to suppress the display of known hops.
Maximum Time to Live [30]	The largest TTL value that can be used. The default is 30. The **trace** command terminates when the destination is reached or when this value is reached.
Port Number	The destination port used by the UDP probe messages. The default is 33,434.
Loose, Strict, Record, Timestamp, Verbose	IP header options. You can specify any combination. The **trace** command issues prompts for the required fields. Note that **trace** will place the requested options in each probe; however, there is no guarantee that all routers (or end nodes) will process the options.
Loose	Allows you to specify a list of nodes that must be traversed when going to the destination.
Strict	Allows you to specify a list of nodes that must be the only nodes traversed when going to the destination.
Record	Allows you to specify the number of hops to leave room for.
Timestamp	Allows you to specify the number of time stamps to leave room for.
Verbose	If you select any option, the verbose mode is automatically selected and **trace** prints the contents of the option field in any incoming packets. You can prevent verbose mode by selecting it again, toggling its current setting.

Table 26-39 describes the characters that can appear in **trace** command output.

Table 26-39   *IP Trace Text Characters*

Char	Description
nn msec	For each node, the round-trip time in milliseconds for the specified number of probes.
*	The probe timed out.

continues

Table 26-39 *IP Trace Text Characters (Continued)*

Char	Description
?	Unknown packet type.
A	Administratively unreachable. Usually, this output indicates that an access list is blocking traffic.
H	Host unreachable.
N	Network unreachable.
P	Protocol unreachable.
Q	Source quench.
U	Port unreachable.

Related Commands

To locate documentation of related commands, you can search online at www.cisco.com.

trace (user)

trace (user)

Use the **trace** EXEC command to discover the IP routes that packets will actually take when traveling to their destination.

> **trace** [*protocol*] [*destination*]

Syntax	Description
protocol	(Optional) Protocols that can be used are **appletalk**, **clns**, **ip** and **vines**.
destination	(Optional) Destination address or host name on the command line. The default parameters for the appropriate protocol are assumed and the tracing action begins.

Default

The *protocol* argument is based on the Cisco IOS software examination of the format of the *destination* argument. For example, if the software finds a *destination* in IP format, the *protocol* defaults to **ip**.

Command Mode

EXEC

Usage Guidelines

This command first appeared in Cisco IOS Release 10.0.

The **trace** command works by taking advantage of the error messages generated by routers when a datagram exceeds its time-to-live (TTL) value.

The **trace** command starts by sending probe datagrams with a TTL value of one. This causes the first router to discard the probe datagram and send back an error message. The **trace** command sends several probes at each TTL level and displays the round-trip time for each.

The **trace** command sends out one probe at a time. Each outgoing packet may result in one or two error messages. A "time exceeded" error message indicates that an intermediate router has seen and discarded the probe. A "destination unreachable" error message indicates that the destination node has received the probe and discarded it because it could not deliver the packet. If the timer goes off before a response comes in, **trace** prints an asterisk (*).

The **trace** command terminates when the destination responds, when the maximum TTL is exceeded, or when the user interrupts the trace with the escape sequence. By default, to invoke the escape sequence, type **Ctrl-^ X** by simultaneously pressing and releasing the **Ctrl**, **Shift**, and **6** keys, and then pressing the **X** key.

Common Trace Problems

Due to bugs in the IP implementation of various hosts and routers, the IP **trace** command may behave in odd ways.

Not all destinations will respond correctly to a probe message by sending back an "ICMP port unreachable" message. A long sequence of TTL levels with only asterisks, terminating only when the maximum TTL has been reached, may indicate this problem.

There is a known problem with the way some hosts handle an "ICMP TTL exceeded" message. Some hosts generate an *ICMP* message but they reuse the TTL of the incoming packet. Since this is zero, the ICMP packets do not make it back. When you trace the path to such a host, you may see a set of TTL values with asterisks (*). Eventually, the TTL gets high enough that the "ICMP" message can get back. For example, if the host is six hops away, **trace** will time out on responses 6 through 11.

Sample Display Showing Trace IP Routes

The following display shows sample IP **trace** output when a destination host name has been specified:

```
Router# trace ip ABA.NYC.mil

Type escape sequence to abort.
Tracing the route to ABA.NYC.mil (26.0.0.73)
  1 DEBRIS.CISCO.COM (192.180.1.6) 1000 msec 8 msec 4 msec
  2 BARRNET-GW.CISCO.COM (192.180.16.2) 8 msec 8 msec 8 msec
  3 EXTERNAL-A-GATEWAY.STANFORD.EDU (192.42.110.225) 8 msec 4 msec 4 msec
  4 BB2.SU.BARRNET.NET (192.200.254.6) 8 msec 8 msec 8 msec
```

```
5 SU.ARC.BARRNET.NET (192.200.3.8) 12 msec 12 msec 8 msec
6 MOFFETT-FLD-MB.in.MIL (192.52.195.1) 216 msec 120 msec 132 msec
7 ABA.NYC.mil (26.0.0.73) 412 msec 628 msec 664 msec
```

Table 26-40 describes the fields shown in the display.

Table 26-40   *Trace Field Descriptions*

Field	Description
1	Indicates the sequence number of the router in the path to the host.
DEBRIS.CISCO.COM	Host name of this router.
192.180.1.61	Internet address of this router.
1000 msec 8 msec 4 msec	Round-trip time for each of the three probes that are sent.

Table 26-41 describes the characters that can appear in **trace** output.

Table 26-41   *IP Trace Text Characters*

Char	Description
nn msec	For each node, the round-trip time in milliseconds for the specified number of probes.
*	The probe timed out.
?	Unknown packet type.
A	Administratively unreachable. Usually, this output indicates that an access list is blocking traffic.
H	Host unreachable.
N	Network unreachable.
P	Protocol unreachable.
Q	Source quench.
U	Port unreachable.

Related Commands

To locate documentation of related commands, you can search online at www.cisco.com.

trace (privileged)

## CHAPTER 27

Performing Basic System Management

This chapter describes the basic tasks that you can perform to manage the general system features of the Cisco IOS software—those features that are generally not specific to a particular protocol.

For a complete description of the basic system management commands in this chapter, refer to Chapter 28, "Basic System Management Commands." To locate documentation of other commands that appear in this chapter, you can search online at www.cisco.com.

Basic System Management Task List

This chapter describes the basic system management tasks you can perform. Perform any of the tasks in the following sections:

- Customize the Router Prompt
- Set the Router Name
- Create and Monitor Command Aliases
- Access Services
- Enable the Finger Protocol
- Hide Telnet Addresses
- Generate a Downward-Compatible Configuration
- Set Time and Calendar Services
- Delay EXEC Startup
- Handle Idle Telnet Connection
- Set the Interval for Load Data
- Limit TCP Transactions
- Configure Switching and Scheduling Priorities
- Modify the System Buffer Size

Refer to the "Basic System Management Examples" section at the end of this chapter for examples.

Customize the Router Prompt

By default, the prompt consists of the router name followed by an angle bracket (>) for EXEC mode or a pound sign (#) for privileged EXEC mode. To customize your prompt, use either of the following commands in global configuration mode:

Command	Purpose
prompt *string*	Customizes the prompt.
no service prompt config	Removes the configuration prompt (config).

Set the Router Name

One of the first basic commands is to name your router. The name is considered the host name and is the name that is displayed by the system prompt. If no name is configured, the system default name is Router. To name the router, use the following command in global configuration mode:

Command	Purpose
hostname *name*	Sets the host name.

For an example of configuring a router name, see the section "System Configuration File Example" at the end of this chapter.

Create and Monitor Command Aliases

You can create aliases for commonly used or complex commands. Use word substitutions or abbreviations to tailor command syntax for you and your user community.

To create and display command aliases, perform the tasks in the following sections:

- Create a Command Alias
- Display Command Aliases

Create a Command Alias

To create a command alias, use the following command in global configuration mode:

Command	Purpose
alias *mode alias-name alias-command-line*	Configures a command alias.

Display Command Aliases

To display alias names and the original command syntax, use the following command in EXEC mode:

Command	Purpose
show aliases [*mode*]	Shows all command aliases and original command syntax, or specifies the aliases in a particular command mode.

Access Services

You can access TCP, UDP, and BOOTP services (sometimes called *minor services*) from hosts on the network. These services are enabled by default.

To enable these services, use any of the following commands in global configuration mode:

Command	Purpose
service tcp-small-servers	Accesses minor TCP services such as echo, chargen, discard, and daytime.
service udp-small-servers	Accesses minor UDP services such as echo, chargen, and discard.
ip bootp server	Accesses the BOOTP service.

Enable the Finger Protocol

You can enable the Finger protocol so that people throughout the network can get a list of the users currently using the router. The information displayed includes the processes running on the system, the line number, connection name, idle time, and terminal location. To enable the Finger protocol, use the following command in global configuration mode:

Command	Purpose
service finger	Enables the Finger protocol requests.

Hide Telnet Addresses

You can hide addresses while attempting to establish a Telnet session. To configure the router to suppress Telnet addresses, use the following command in global configuration mode:

Command	Purpose
service hide-telnet-address	Hides addresses while establishing a Telnet session.

The hide feature suppresses the display of the address and continues to display all other messages that would normally display during a connection attempt, such as detailed error messages if the connection was not successful.

Use the **busy-message** command with the **service hide-telnet-address** command to customize the information displayed during Telnet connection attempts. If the connection attempt is not successful, the router suppresses the address and displays the message specified with the **busy-message** command.

Generate a Downward-Compatible Configuration

In Cisco IOS Release 10.3, IP access lists changed format. If you decide to downgrade from Release 11.0 to Release 10.2, you can configure the software to regenerate a configuration in the format of Release 10.2, thereby saving time and making your IP access lists compatible with the software.

To have the software regenerate a configuration in the format prior to Release 10.3, use the following command in global configuration mode:

Command	Purpose
downward-compatible-config *version*	Generates a backward-compatible configuration.

Set Time and Calendar Services

All Cisco routers provide an array of time-of-day services. These services allow the products to accurately keep track of the current time and date, to synchronize multiple products to the same time, and to provide time services to other systems. The following sections describe the time and calendar tasks:

● Understand Time Sources

● Configure NTP

● Configure SNTP

● Configure VINES Time Service

● Configure Time and Date Manually

● Monitor Time and Calendar Services

Understand Time Sources

The heart of the time service is the system clock. This clock runs from the moment the system starts up and keeps track of the current date and time. The system clock can be set from a number of sources and in turn can be used to distribute the current time through various mechanisms to other systems. When a router with a system calendar is initialized, the system clock is set based on the time in its internal battery-powered calendar; on other models, the system clock it is set to midnight on March 1, 1993. The system clock can then be set from the following sources:

● Network Time Protocol (NTP)

● Simple Network Time Protocol (SNTP)

● VINES Time Service

● Manual configuration

The system clock can provide time to the following services:

● NTP

● VINES Time Service

● User **show** commands

● Logging and debugging messages

NOTE   The system clock cannot provide time to the NTP or VINES Time Service if it was set using SNTP.

The system clock keeps track of time internally based on Coordinated Universal Time (UTC), also known as Greenwich Mean Time (GMT). You can configure information about the local time zone and summer (daylight savings) time zone so that the time is displayed correctly and relative to the local time zone.

The system clock keeps track of whether the time is "authoritative" or not (that is, whether it has been set by a time source considered to be authoritative). If it is not authoritative, the time will be available only for display purposes and will not be redistributed.

Network Time Protocol

The Network Time Protocol (NTP) is a protocol designed to time-synchronize a network of machines. NTP runs over UDP, which in turn runs over IP. NTP is documented in RFC 1305.

An NTP network usually gets its time from an authoritative time source, such as a radio clock or an atomic clock attached to a time server. NTP then distributes this time across the network. NTP is extremely efficient; no more than one packet per minute is necessary to synchronize two machines to within a millisecond of one another.

NTP uses the concept of a stratum to describe how many NTP hops away a machine is from an authoritative time source. A stratum 1 time server has a radio or atomic clock directly attached, a stratum 2 time server receives its time via NTP from a stratum 1 time server, and so on. A machine running NTP will automatically choose as its time source the machine with the lowest stratum number that it is configured to communicate with via NTP. This strategy effectively builds a self-organizing tree of NTP speakers.

NTP is careful to avoid synchronizing to a machine whose time may not be accurate. It avoids doing so in two ways. First of all, NTP will never synchronize to a machine that is not in turn synchronized itself. Secondly, NTP will compare the time reported by several machines, and will not synchronize to a machine whose time is significantly different than the others, even if its stratum is lower.

The communication between machines running NTP (known as *associations*) are usually statically configured; each machine is given the IP address of all machines with which it should form associations. Accurate timekeeping is made possible by exchanging NTP messages between each pair of machines with an association. However, in a local-area network (LAN) environment, NTP can be configured to use IP broadcast messages instead.

This alternative reduces configuration complexity because each machine can simply be configured to send or receive broadcast messages. However, the accuracy of timekeeping is marginally reduced because the information flow is only one-way.

The time kept on a machine is a critical resource, so we strongly recommend that you use the security features of NTP to avoid the accidental or malicious setting of incorrect time. Two mechanisms are available: an access list-based restriction scheme and an encrypted authentication mechanism.

Cisco's implementation of NTP does not support stratum 1 service; in other words, it is not possible to connect to a radio or an atomic clock. It is recommended that time service for your network be derived from the public NTP servers available in the IP Internet.

If the network is isolated from the Internet, Cisco's implementation of NTP allows a machine to be configured so that it acts as though it is synchronized via NTP, when in fact it has determined the time using other means. Other machines then synchronize to that machine via NTP.

When multiple sources of time (VINES, system calendar, and manual configuration) are available, NTP is always considered to be more authoritative. NTP time overrides the time set by any other method.

A number of manufacturers include NTP software for their host systems, and a publicly available version for systems running UNIX and its various derivatives is also available. This software allows host systems to be time-synchronized as well.

Simple Network Time Protocol (SNTP)

Simple Network Time Protocol (SNTP) is a simplified, client-only version of NTP for use on Cisco 1003, Cisco 1004, and Cisco 1005 routers. SNMP can only receive the time from NTP servers; it cannot be used to provide time services to other systems.

SNTP typically provides time within 100 milliseconds of the accurate time, but it does not provide the complex filtering and statistical mechanisms of NTP. In addition, SNTP does not authenticate traffic, although you can configure extended access lists to provide some protection. An SNTP client is more vulnerable to misbehaving servers than an NTP client and should only be used in situations where strong authentication is not required.

You can configure SNTP to request and accept packets from configured servers or to accept NTP broadcast packets from any source. When multiple sources are sending NTP packets, the server with the best stratum is selected. (See the "Network Time Protocol" section for a description of strata.) If multiple servers are at the same stratum, a configured server is preferred over a broadcast server. If multiple servers pass both tests, the first one to send a time packet is selected. SNTP will only choose a new server if it stops receiving packets from the currently selected server, or if a better server (according to the above criteria) is discovered.

VINES Time Service

Time service is also available when Banyan VINES is configured. This protocol is a standard part of VINES. Cisco's implementation allows the VINES time service to be used in two ways. First, if the system has learned the time from some other source, it can act as a VINES time server and provide time to other machines running VINES. It also can use the VINES time service to set the system clock if no other form of time service is available.

Calendar System

Some routers contain a battery-powered calendar system that tracks the date and time across system restarts and power outages. This calendar system is always used to initialize the system clock when the system is restarted. It can also be considered to be an authoritative source of time and be redistributed via NTP or VINES time service if no other source is available. Furthermore, if NTP is running, the calendar can be periodically updated from NTP, compensating for the inherent drift in the calendar time.

Configure NTP

NTP services are enabled on all interfaces by default. The optional tasks you can perform are documented in the following sections:

- Configure NTP Authentication
- Configure NTP Associations
- Configure NTP Broadcast Service
- Configure NTP Access Restrictions
- Configure the Source IP Address for NTP Packets
- Configure the System as an Authoritative NTP Server
- Configure NTP to Update the Calendar

Configure NTP Authentication

If you want to authenticate the associations with other systems for security purposes, use the commands that follow. The first command enables the NTP authentication feature. The second command defines each of the authentication keys. Each key has a key number, a type, and a value. Currently the only key type supported is **md5**. Third, a list of "trusted" authentication keys is defined. If a key is trusted, this system will be ready to synchronize to a system that uses this key in its NTP packets.

To configure NTP authentication, use the following commands in global configuration mode:

Step	Command	Purpose
1	**ntp authenticate**	Enables the NTP authentication feature.
2	**ntp authentication-key** *number* **md5** *value*	Defines the authentication keys.
3	**ntp trusted-key** *key-number*	Defines trusted authentication keys.

Configure NTP Associations

An NTP association can be a peer association (meaning that this system is willing to either synchronize to the other system or to allow the other system to synchronize to it), or it can be a server association (meaning that only this system will synchronize to the other system, and not the other way around). If you want to form an NTP association with another system, use one of the following commands in global configuration mode:

Command	Purpose
ntp peer *ip-address* [**version** *number*] [**key** *keyid*] [**source** *interface*] [**prefer**]	Forms a peer association with another system.
ntp server *ip-address* [**version** *number*] [**key** *keyid*] [**source** *interface*] [**prefer**]	Forms a server association with another system.

Note that only one end of an association needs to be configured; the other system will automatically establish the association.

See the section "Clock, Calendar, and NTP Configuration Examples" at the end of this chapter.

Configure NTP Broadcast Service

The system can either send broadcast packets or listen to them on an interface-by-interface basis. The estimated round-trip delay for broadcast packets can also be configured. Use one or more of the following commands in global configuration mode if you want to use NTP's broadcast feature:

Command	Purpose
ntp broadcast [**version** *number*]	Sends NTP broadcast packets.
ntp broadcast client	Receives NTP broadcast packets.
ntp broadcastdelay *microseconds*	Adjusts estimated delay.

See the section "Clock, Calendar, and NTP Configuration Examples" at the end of this chapter.

Configure NTP Access Restrictions

You can control NTP access on two levels by completing the tasks in the following sections:

● Create an Access Group and Assign a Basic IP Access List to It

● Disable NTP Services on a Specific Interface

Create an Access Group and Assign a Basic IP Access List to It

To control access to NTP services, you can create an NTP access group and apply a basic IP access list to it. To do so, use the following command in global configuration mode:

Command	Purpose
ntp access-group {**query-only** I **serve-only** I **serve** I **peer**} *access-list-number*	Creates an access group and applies a basic IP access list to it.

The access group options are scanned in the following order, from least restrictive to most restrictive:

1   **peer**—Allows time requests and NTP control queries and allows the system to synchronize itself to a system whose address passes the access list criteria.

2   **serve**—Allows time requests and NTP control queries, but does not allow the system to synchronize itself to a system whose address passes the access list criteria.

3   **serve-only**—Allows only time requests from a system whose address passes the access list criteria.

4   **query-only**—Allows only NTP control queries from a system whose address passes the access list criteria.

If the source IP address matches the access lists for more than one access type, the first type is granted. If no access groups are specified, all access types are granted to all systems. If any access groups are specified, only the specified access types will be granted.

For details on NTP control queries, see RFC 1305 (NTP version 3).

Disable NTP Services on a Specific Interface

NTP services are enabled on all interfaces by default. You can disable NTP packets from being received through an interface by using the following command in interface configuration mode:

Command	Purpose
ntp disable	Disables NTP services on a specific interface.

Configure the Source IP Address for NTP Packets

When the system sends an NTP packet, the source IP address is normally set to the address of the interface through which the NTP packet is sent. Use the following command in global configuration mode if you want to configure a specific interface from which the IP source address will be taken:

Command	Purpose
ntp source *interface*	Configures an interface from which the IP source address will be taken.

This interface will be used for the source address for all packets sent to all destinations. If a source address is to be used for a specific association, use the **source** parameter on the **ntp peer** or **ntp server** command shown earlier in this chapter.

Configure the System as an Authoritative NTP Server

Use the following command in global configuration mode if you want the system to be an authoritative NTP server, even if the system is not synchronized to an outside time source:

Command	Purpose
ntp master [*stratum*]	Makes the system an authoritative NTP server.

CAUTION Use this command with extreme caution. It is very easy to override valid time sources using this command, especially if a low stratum number is configured. Configuring multiple machines in the same network with the **ntp master** command can cause instability in timekeeping if the machines do not agree on the time.

For an example of configuring an authoritative NTP server, see the section "Clock, Calendar, and NTP Configuration Examples" at the end of this chapter.

Configure NTP to Update the Calendar

On systems which have calendars, you can configure NTP to periodically update the calendar.

Use the following command in global configuration mode if the system is synchronized to an outside time source via NTP and you want the calendar to be synchronized periodically to NTP time:

Command	Purpose
ntp update-calendar	Configures NTP to update the calendar.

For an example of configuring NTP to update the calendar, see the section "Clock, Calendar, and NTP Configuration Examples" at the end of this chapter.

Configure SNTP

SNTP is disabled by default. In order to enable SNTP on a Cisco 1003, Cisco 1004, or Cisco 1005 router, use one or both of the following commands in global configuration mode:

Command	Purpose
sntp server {*address* | *hostname*} [**version** *number*]	Configures SNTP to request NTP packets from an NTP server.
sntp broadcast client	Configures SNTP to accept NTP packets from any NTP broadcast server.

Enter the **sntp server** command once for each NTP server. The NTP servers must be configured to respond to the SNTP messages from the router.

If you enter both the **sntp server** command and the **sntp broadcast client** command, the router will accept time from a broadcast server but prefers time from a configured server, assuming the stratas are equal. To display information about SNTP, use the **show sntp** EXEC command.

Configure VINES Time Service

Use the following command in global configuration mode if you want to distribute the system clock to other VINES systems:

Command	Purpose
vines time use-system	Distributes the system clock to other VINES systems.

To receive VINES time service to control the system clock, use the following command in global configuration mode:

Command	Purpose
vines time set-system	Receives VINES time service.

Configure Time and Date Manually

If no other source of time is available, you can manually configure the current time and date after the system is restarted. The time will remain accurate until the next system restart. We recommend that you use manual configuration only as a last resort.

To set up time services, complete the tasks in the following sections as needed. If you have an outside source to which the router can synchronize, you do not need to manually set the system clock.

- Configure the Time Zone
- Configure Summer Time (Daylight Savings Time)
- Set the System Clock
- Set the System Calendar

Configure the Time Zone

Use the following command in global configuration mode to manually configure the time zone used by the Cisco IOS software:

Command	Purpose
clock timezone *zone hours* [*minutes*]	Sets the time zone.

For an example of configuring the time zone, see the section "Clock, Calendar, and NTP Configuration Examples" at the end of this chapter.

Configure Summer Time (Daylight Savings Time)

To configure summer time (daylight savings time) in areas where it starts and ends on a particular day of the week each year, use the following command in global configuration mode:

Command	Purpose
clock summer-time *zone* **recurring** [*week day month hh:mm week day month hh:mm* [*offset*]]	Configures summer time.

If summer time in your area does not follow this pattern, you can configure the exact date and time of the next summer time events by using one of the following commands in global configuration mode:

Command	Purpose
clock summer-time *zone* **date** *month date year hh:mm month date year hh:mm* [*offset*]	Configures summer time.
or	
clock summer-time *zone* **date** *date month year hh:mm date month year hh:mm* [*offset*]	

For an example of configuring summer time, see the section "Clock, Calendar, and NTP Configuration Examples" at the end of this chapter.

Set the System Clock

If you have an outside source on the network that provides time services (such as an NTP server or VINES time service), you do not need to manually set the system clock.

However, if you have do not have any time service source, use one of the following commands in EXEC mode to set the system clock:

Command	Purpose
clock set *hh:mm:ss date month year*	Sets the system clock.
or	
clock set *hh:mm:ss month date year*	

Set the System Calendar

Some routers have a separate system calendar in addition to the system clock. The calendar can set the system time and control the system clock, as well as enable the router to act as a time service for the network.

You can complete the tasks in the following sections to enable the calendar capabilities:

- Set the Router Calendar
- Set the Router as a Network Time Source
- Set the System Clock from the Calendar
- Set the Calendar from the System Clock

Set the Router Calendar

The calendar maintains time separately from the system clock. It continues to run when the system is restarted or power is turned off. Typically, it only needs to be manually set once, when the system is first installed. If time is available from an external source using NTP, the calendar can be updated from the system clock instead.

If you do not have an external time source, use the following command in EXEC mode to set the system calendar:

Command	Purpose
calendar set *hh*:*mm*:*ss day month year*	Sets the calendar.
or	
calendar set *hh*:*mm*:*ss month day year*	

Set the Router as a Network Time Source

Although the system clock is always initialized from the calendar when the system is restarted, by default it is not considered to be authoritative and so will not be redistributed with NTP or VINES Time Service. To make the calendar be authoritative, use the following command in global configuration mode:

Command	Purpose
clock calendar-valid	Enables the router to act as a valid time source to which network peers can synchronize.

For an example of making the calendar authoritative, see the section "Clock, Calendar, and NTP Configuration Examples" at the end of this chapter.

Set the System Clock from the Calendar

To set the system clock to the new calendar setting, use the following command in EXEC mode:

Command	Purpose
clock read-calendar	Sets the system clock from the calendar.

Set the Calendar from the System Clock

To update the calendar with the new clock setting, use the following command in EXEC mode:

Command	Purpose
clock update-calendar	Sets the calendar from the system clock.

Monitor Time and Calendar Services

To monitor clock, calendar, and NTP EXEC services, use any of the following commands in EXEC mode:

Command	Purpose
show calendar	Displays the current calendar time.
show clock [detail]	Displays the current system clock time.
show ntp associations [detail]	Shows the status of NTP associations.
show ntp status	Shows the status of NTP.
show sntp	Displays information about SNTP (Cisco 1003, Cisco 1004, and Cisco 1005 only).

Delay EXEC Startup

You can delay the startup of the EXEC on noisy lines until the line has been idle for three seconds. To do so, use the following command in global configuration mode:

Command	Purpose
service exec-wait	Delays startup of the EXEC.

This command is useful on noisy modem lines or when a modem attached to the line is configured to ignore MNP or V.42 negotiations, and MNP or V.42 modems may be dialing in. In these cases, noise or MNP/V.42 packets might be interpreted as usernames and passwords, causing authentication failure before the user can type a username/password. The command is not useful on nonmodem lines or lines without some kind of login configured.

Handle Idle Telnet Connection

You can configure the Cisco IOS software to set the TCP window to zero (0) when the Telnet connection is idle. To do so, use the following command in global configuration mode:

Command	Purpose
service telnet-zero-idle	Sets the TCP window to zero when the Telnet connection is idle.

Normally, data sent to noncurrent Telnet connections is accepted and discarded. When **service telnet-zero-idle** is enabled, if a session is suspended (that is, some other connection is made active or the EXEC is sitting in command mode), the TCP window is set to zero. This action prevents the remote host from sending any more data until the connection is resumed. Use this command when it is important that all messages sent by the host be seen by the users and the users are likely to use multiple sessions. Do not use this command if your host will eventually time out and log out a TCP user whose window is zero.

Set the Interval for Load Data

You can change the period of time over which a set of data is used for computing load statistics. Decisions, such as dial backup decisions, are dependent on these statistics. If you decrease the load interval, the average statistics are computed over a shorter period of time and are more responsive to bursts of traffic.

To change the length of time for which a set of data is used to compute load statistics, use the following command in interface configuration mode:

Command	Purpose
load-interval *seconds*	Sets the length of time for which data is used for load calculations.

Limit TCP Transactions

When using a standard TCP implementation to send keystrokes between machines, TCP tends to send one packet for each keystroke typed, which can use up bandwidth and contribute to congestion on larger networks.

John Nagle's algorithm (RFC 896) helps alleviate the small-packet problem in TCP. The first character typed after connection establishment is sent in a single packet, but TCP holds any additional characters typed until the receiver acknowledges the previous packet. Then the second, larger packet is sent, and additional typed characters are saved until the acknowledgment comes back. The effect is to accumulate characters into larger chunks and pace them out to the network at a rate matching the round-trip time of the given connection. This method is usually good for all TCP-based traffic. However, do not enable the Nagle slow packet avoidance algorithm if you have XRemote users on X Window sessions.

By default, the Nagle algorithm is not enabled. To enable the Nagle algorithm and thereby reduce TCP transactions, use the following command in global configuration mode:

Command	Purpose
service nagle	Enables the Nagle slow packet avoidance algorithm.

Configure Switching and Scheduling Priorities

The normal operation of the network server allows the switching operations to use as much of the central processor as is required. If the network is running unusually heavy loads that do not allow the processor the time to handle the routing protocols, you might need to give priority to the system process scheduler. To do so, use the following command in global configuration mode:

Command	Purpose
scheduler interval *milliseconds*	Defines the maximum amount of time that can elapse without running the lowest-priority system processes.

To change the amount of time that the CPU spends on fast switching and process level operations on the Cisco 7200 series and Cisco 7500 series, use the following command in global configuration mode:

Command	Purpose
scheduler allocate *network-microseconds* *process-microseconds*	For the Cisco 7200 series and Cisco 7500 series, it changes the default time the CPU spends on process tasks and fast switching.

CAUTION   Cisco recommends that you do not change the default values of the **scheduler allocate** command.

Modify the System Buffer Size

You can adjust initial buffer pool settings and the limits at which temporary buffers are created and destroyed. To do so, use either of the following commands in global configuration mode:

Command	Purpose
buffers {**small**	**middle**	**big**	**verybig**	**large**	**huge**	*type number*} {**permanent**	**max-free**	**min-free**	**initial**} *number*	Adjusts the system buffer sizes.
buffers huge size *number*	Dynamically resizes all huge buffers to the value that you supply.

CAUTION   Normally, you need not adjust these parameters; do so only after consulting with technical support personnel. Improper settings can adversely impact system performance.

During normal system operation, there are two sets of buffer pools: public and interface.

- The buffers in the public pools grow and shrink based upon demand. Some public pools are temporary and are created and destroyed as needed. Other public pools are permanently allocated and cannot be destroyed. The public buffer pools are small, middle, big, large, very big, and huge.

- Interface pools are static—that is, they are all permanent. One interface pool exists for each interface. For example, a Cisco 4000 1E 4T configuration has one Ethernet buffer pool and four serial buffer pools. In the **buffers** command, the *type* and *number* arguments allow the user to tune the interface pools.

See the section "Buffer Modification Examples" at the end of this chapter.

The server has one pool of queueing elements and six public pools of packet buffers of different sizes. For each pool, the server keeps count of the number of buffers outstanding, the number of buffers in the free list, and the maximum number of buffers allowed in the free list. To display statistics about the buffer pool on the system, use any of the following commands in EXEC mode:

Command	Purpose
show buffers	Displays all public pool information.
show buffers all	Displays all public and interface pool information.
show buffers alloc	Displays a brief listing of all allocated buffers.
show buffers [*type number*]	Displays interface pool information.
show buffers alloc dump	Dumps all allocated buffers.
show buffers interface	Displays all interface pool information.

Command	Purpose
show buffers interface *type number*	If the specified interface has its own buffer pool, it displays information for that pool.
show buffers interface *type number* **alloc**	Displays a brief listing of buffers allocated for this interface.
show buffers interface *type number* **alloc dump**	Dumps the buffers allocated to this interface.

Basic System Management Examples

The following sections provide system management examples:

● System Configuration File Example

● Clock, Calendar, and NTP Configuration Examples

● Buffer Modification Examples

System Configuration File Example

The following is an example of a typical system configuration file:

```
! Define line password
line 0 4
 password secret
 login
!
! Define privileged-level password
enable-password Secret Word
!
! Define a system hostname
hostname TIP
! Specify a configuration file to load at system startup
boot host host1-confg 192.168.1.111
boot host host2-confg 192.168.1.111
! Specify the system image to boot at startup
boot system sys1-system 192.168.13.111
boot system sys2-system 192.168.1.111
boot system rom
!
! Enable SNMP
snmp-server community red
snmp-server enable traps snmp authentication
snmp-server host 192.168.1.27 public
snmp-server host 192.168.1.111 public
snmp-server host 192.168.2.63 public
!
! Define TACACS server hosts
tacacs-server host 192.168.1.27
tacacs-server host 192.168.13.33
```

```
tacacs-server host 192.168.1.33
!
! Define a message-of-the-day banner
banner motd ^C
The Information Place welcomes you

Please call 1-800-555-2222 for a login account, or enter
your password at the prompt.
^C
```

Clock, Calendar, and NTP Configuration Examples

In the following example, a router with a system calendar has server associations with two other systems, transmits broadcast NTP packets, periodically updates the calendar, and redistributes time into VINES:

```
clock timezone PST -8
clock summer-time PDT recurring
ntp update-calendar
ntp server 192.168.13.57
ntp server 192.168.11.58
interface Ethernet 0/0
 ntp broadcast
vines time use-system
```

In the following example, a router with a calendar has no outside time source, so it uses the calendar as an authoritative time source and distributes the time via NTP broadcast packets.

```
clock timezone MET 2
clock calendar-valid
ntp master
interface fddi 0/0
 ntp broadcast
```

Buffer Modification Examples

The following example instructs the system to keep at least 50 small buffers free:

```
buffers small min-free 50
```

The following example instructs the system to keep no more than 200 medium buffers free:

```
buffers middle max-free 200
```

The following example instructs the system to create one large temporary buffer just after a reload:

```
buffers large initial 1
```

The following example instructs the system to create one permanent huge buffer:

```
buffers huge permanent 1
```

## CHAPTER 28

Basic System Management Commands

This chapter describes the commands used to perform basic system management tasks, such as naming the router and setting time services.

For basic system management configuration tasks and examples, refer to Chapter 27, "Performing Basic System Management."

alias

To create a command alias, use the **alias** global configuration command. Use the **no** form of this command to delete all aliases in a command mode or to delete a specific alias, and to revert to the original command syntax.

> **alias** *mode alias-name alias-command-line*
> **no alias** *mode* [*alias-name*]

Syntax	Description
mode	Command mode of the original and alias commands. See Table 28-1 for a list of options for this argument.
alias-name	Command alias.
alias-command-line	Original command syntax.

Defaults

Default aliases are in EXEC mode as follows:

Command Alias	Original Command
h	help
lo	logout
p	ping
r	resume
s	show
w	where

Command Mode

Global configuration

Usage Guidelines

This command first appeared in Cisco IOS Release 10.3.

You can use simple words or abbreviations as aliases. The aliases in the "Defaults" section are predefined. They can be turned off using the **no alias** command.

Table 28-1 shows the acceptable options for the *mode* argument in the **alias** global configuration command.

Table 28-1   *Mode Argument Options*

Argument Options	Mode
configuration	Global configuration
controller	Controller configuration
exec	EXEC
hub	Hub configuration
interface	Interface configuration
ipx-router	IPX router configuration
line	Line configuration
map-class	Map class configuration
map-list	Map list configuration
route-map	Route map configuration
router	Router configuration

See the summary of command modes in Chapter 1, "Using the Command Line Interface," for more information about command modes.

When you use online help, command aliases are indicated by an asterisk (*), as follows:

```
Router#lo?
*lo=logout  lock  login  logout
```

When you use online help, aliases that contain spaces (for example, telnet device.cisco.com 25) are displayed as follows:

```
Router# configure terminal
Enter configuration commands, one per line. End with Ctrl-Z.
Router(config)# alias exec device-mail telnet device.cisco.com 25
Router(config)# end
Router# device-mail?
*device-mail="telnet device.cisco.com 25"
```

When you use online help, the alias is expanded and replaced with the original command, as shown in the following example with the **td** alias:

```
Router(config)# alias exec td trace device
Router(config)# ^Z
Router# t?
*td="trace device" telnet terminal test tn3270
trace
```

To list only commands and omit aliases, begin your input line with a space. In the following example, the alias **td** is not shown, because there is a space before the **t?** command line.

```
Router# t?
telnet terminal test tn3270 trace
```

As with commands, you can use online help to display the arguments and keywords that can follow a command alias. In the following example, the alias **td** is created to represent the command **telet device**. The **/debug** and **/line** switches can be added to **telnet device** to modify the command:

```
Router(config)# alias exec td telnet device
Router(config)# ^Z
Router# td ?
    /debug      Enable telnet debugging mode
    /line       Enable telnet line mode
    ...
    whois       Whois port
    <cr>
Router# telnet device
```

You must enter the complete syntax for the **alias** command. Partial syntax for aliases are not accepted. In the following example, the parser does not recognize the command **t** as indicating the alias **td**:

```
Router# t
% Ambiguous command: "t"
```

Example

The following example creates the alias **fixmyrt** for the IP route198.92.116.16:

```
alias exec fixmyrt clear ip route 198.92.116.16
```

Related Commands

To locate documentation of related commands, you can search online at www.cisco.com.

show aliases

buffers

Use the **buffers** global configuration command to make adjustments to initial buffer pool settings and to the limits at which temporary buffers are created and destroyed. Use the **no** form of this command to return the buffers to their default size.

buffers {**small** | **middle** | **big** | **verybig** | **large** | **huge** | *type number*} {**permanent** | **max-free** | **min-free** | **initial**} *number*

no buffers {**small** | **middle** | **big** | **verybig** | **large** | **huge** | *type number*} {**permanent** | **max-free** | **min-free** | **initial**} *number*

Syntax	Description
small	Buffer size of this public buffer pool is 104 bytes.
middle	Buffer size of this public buffer pool is 600 bytes.
big	Buffer size of this public buffer pool is 1524 bytes.
verybig	Buffer size of this public buffer pool is 4520 bytes.
large	Buffer size of this public buffer pool is 5024 bytes.
huge	Default buffer size of this public buffer pool is 18024 bytes. This value can be configured with the **buffers huge size** command.
type number	Interface type and interface number of the interface buffer pool. The type value cannot be **fddi**.
permanent	Number of permanent buffers that the system tries to create and keep. Permanent buffers are normally not trimmed by the system.
max-free	Maximum number of free or unallocated buffers in a buffer pool. A maximum of 20,480 small buffers can be constructed in the pool.
min-free	Minimum number of free or unallocated buffers in a buffer pool.
initial	Number of additional temporary buffers that are to be allocated when the system is reloaded. This keyword can be used to ensure that the system has necessary buffers immediately after reloading in a high-traffic environment.
number	Number of buffers to be allocated.

Default

The default number of buffers in a pool is determined by the hardware configuration and can be displayed with the EXEC **show buffers** command.

Command Mode

Global configuration

Usage Guidelines

This command first appeared in Cisco IOS Release 10.0.

Normally you need not adjust these parameters; do so only after consulting with technical support personnel. Improper settings can adversely impact system performance.

You cannot configure FDDI buffers.

Examples of Public Buffer Pool Tuning

The following example keeps at least 50 small buffers free in the system:

```
buffers small min-free 50
```

The following example increases the permanent buffer pool allocation for big buffers to 200:

```
buffers big permanent 200
```

Example of Interface Buffer Pool Tuning

A general guideline is to display buffers with the **show buffers** command, observe which buffer pool is depleted, and increase that one.

The following example increases the permanent Ethernet 0 interface buffer pool on a Cisco 4000 to 96 because the Ethernet 0 buffer pool is depleted:

```
buffers ethernet 0 permanent 96
```

Related Commands

To locate documentation of related commands, you can search online at www.cisco.com.

load-interval
show buffers

buffers huge size

Use the **buffers huge size** global configuration command to dynamically resize all huge buffers to the value you specify. Use the **no** form of this command to restore the default buffer values.

buffers huge size *number*
no buffers huge size *number*

Syntax   Description

number   Huge buffer size, in bytes

Default
18,024 bytes

Command Mode
Global configuration

Usage Guidelines
This command first appeared in Cisco IOS Release 10.0.

Use only after consulting with technical support personnel. The buffer size cannot be lowered below the default.

Example
The following example resizes huge buffers to 20,000 bytes:

```
buffers huge size 20000
```

Related Commands
To locate documentation of related commands, you can search online at www.cisco.com.

buffers
show buffers

calendar set

To set the system calendar, use one of the formats of the **calendar set** EXEC command.

calendar set *hh:mm:ss day month year*
calendar set *hh:mm:ss month day year*

Syntax	Description
hh:mm:ss	Current time in hours (military format), minutes, and seconds
day	Current day (by date) in the month
month	Current month (by name)
year	Current year (no abbreviation)

Command Mode

EXEC

Usage Guidelines

This command first appeared in Cisco IOS Release 10.0.

Some platforms have a calendar which is separate from the system clock. This calendar runs continuously, even if the router is powered off or rebooted. After you set the calendar, the system clock will be automatically set from the calendar when the system is restarted or when the **clock read-calendar** EXEC command is issued. The time specified in this command is relative to the configured time zone.

Example

The following example manually sets the system calendar to 1:32 p.m. on July 23, 1997:

```
calendar set 13:32:00 23 July 1997
```

Related Commands

To locate documentation of related commands, you can search online at www.cisco.com.

clock read-calendar
clock set
clock summer-time
clock timezone
clock update-calendar

clock calendar-valid

To configure a router as a time source for a network based on its calendar, use the **clock calendar-valid** global configuration command. Use the **no** form of this command to specify that the calendar is not an authoritative time source.

> **clock calendar-valid**
> **no clock calendar-valid**

Syntax Description

This command has no arguments or keywords.

Default

The router is not configured as a time source.

Command Mode

Global configuration

Usage Guidelines

This command first appeared in Cisco IOS Release 10.0.

Some platforms have a calendar which is separate from the system clock. This calendar runs continuously, even if the router is powered off or rebooted. If you have no outside time source available on your network, use this command to make the calendar an authoritative time source.

Example

The following example configures a router as the time source for a network based on its calendar:

```
clock calendar-valid
```

Related Commands

To locate documentation of related commands, you can search online at www.cisco.com.

ntp master
vines time use-system

clock read-calendar

To manually read the calendar into the system clock, use the **clock read-calendar** EXEC command.

clock read-calendar

Syntax Description

This command has no arguments or keywords.

Command Mode

EXEC

Usage Guidelines

This command first appeared in Cisco IOS Release 10.0.

Some platforms have a calendar which is separate from the system clock. This calendar runs continuously, even if the router is powered off or rebooted. When the router is rebooted, the calendar is automatically read into the system clock. However, you may use this command to manually read the calendar setting into the system clock. This command is useful if the **calendar set** command has been used to change the setting of the calendar.

Example

The following example configures the system clock to set its date and time by the calendar setting:

```
clock read-calendar
```

Related Commands

To locate documentation of related commands, you can search online at www.cisco.com.

calendar set
clock set
clock update-calendar
ntp update-calendar

clock set

To manually set the system clock, use one of the formats of the **clock set** EXEC command.

clock set *hh*:*mm*:*ss day month year*
clock set *hh*:*mm*:*ss month day year*

Syntax   Description

Syntax	Description
hh:*mm*:*ss*	Current time in hours (military format), minutes, and seconds
day	Current day (by date) in the month
month	Current month (by name)
year	Current year (no abbreviation)

Command Mode

EXEC

Usage Guidelines

This command first appeared in Cisco IOS Release 10.0.

Generally, if the system is synchronized by a valid outside timing mechanism, such as an NTP or VINES clock source, or if you have a router with calendar capability, you do not need to set the system clock. Use this command if no other time sources are available. The time specified in this command is relative to the configured time zone.

Example

The following example manually sets the system clock to 1:32 p.m. on July 23, 1997:

```
clock set 13:32:00 23 July 1997
```

Related Commands

To locate documentation of related commands, you can search online at www.cisco.com.

calendar set
clock read-calendar
clock summer-time
clock timezone

clock summer-time

To configure the system to automatically switch to summer time (daylight savings time), use one of the formats of the **clock summer-time** global configuration command. Use the **no** form of this command to configure the Cisco IOS software not to automatically switch to summer time.

> **clock summer-time** *zone* **recurring** [*week day month hh:mm week day month hh:mm* [*offset*]]
>
> **clock summer-time** *zone* **date** *date month year hh:mm date month year hh:mm* [*offset*]
>
> **clock summer-time** *zone* **date** *month date year hh:mm month date year hh:mm* [*offset*]
>
> **no clock summer-time**

Syntax	Description
zone	Name of the time zone (such as PDT) to be displayed when summer time is in effect.
recurring	Indicates that summer time should start and end on the corresponding specified days every year.
date	Indicates that summer time should start on the first specific date listed in the command and end on the second specific date in the command.
week	Week of the month (1 to 5 or **last**).
day	Day of the week (Sunday, Monday,...).
date	Date of the month (1 to 31).
month	Month (January, February,...).
year	Year (1993 to 2035).
hh:mm	Time (military format) in hours and minutes.
offset	(Optional) Number of minutes to add during summer time (default is 60).

Default

Summer time is disabled. If **clock summer-time** *zone* **recurring** is specified without parameters, the summer time rules default to United States rules. Default of *offset* is 60.

Command Mode

Global configuration

Part III

Command Reference

Usage Guidelines

This command first appeared in Cisco IOS Release 10.0.

Use this command if you want to automatically switch to summer time (for display purposes only). Use the **recurring** form of the command if the local summer time rules are of this form. Use the **date** form to specify a start and end date for summer time if you cannot use the first form.

In both forms of the command, the first part of the command specifies when summer time begins, and the second part specifies when it ends. All times are relative to the local time zone. The start time is relative to standard time. The end time is relative to summer time. If the starting month is after the ending month, the system assumes that you are in the Southern Hemisphere.

Examples

The following example specifies that summer time starts on the first Sunday in April at 02:00 and ends on the last Sunday in October at 02:00:

```
clock summer-time PDT recurring 1 Sunday April 2:00 last Sunday October 2:00
```

If you live in a place where summer time does not follow the pattern in the first example, you could set it to start on October 12, 1997 at 02:00, and end on April 26, 1998 at 02:00, with the following example:

```
clock summer-time date 12 October 1997 2:00 26 April 1998 2:00
```

Related Commands

To locate documentation of related commands, you can search online at www.cisco.com.

calendar set
clock timezone

clock timezone

To set the time zone for display purposes, use the **clock timezone** global configuration command. To set the time to Coordinated Universal Time (UTC), use the **no** form of this command.

> **clock timezone** *zone hours* [*minutes*]
> **no clock timezone**

Syntax	Description
zone	Name of the time zone to be displayed when standard time is in effect
hours	Hours offset from UTC
minutes	(Optional) Minutes offset from UTC

Default
UTC

Command Mode
Global configuration

Usage Guidelines
This command first appeared in Cisco IOS Release 10.0.

The system internally keeps time in UTC, so this command is used only for display purposes and when the time is manually set.

Example
The following example sets the timezone to Pacific Standard Time and offsets eight hours behind UTC:

```
clock timezone PST -8
```

Related Commands
To locate documentation of related commands, you can search online at www.cisco.com.

calendar set
clock set
clock summer-time
show clock

clock update-calendar

To set the calendar from the system clock, use the **clock update-calendar** EXEC command.

> **clock update-calendar**

Syntax Description
This command has no arguments or keywords.

Command Mode
EXEC

Usage Guidelines

This command first appeared in Cisco IOS Release 10.0.

Some platforms have a calendar which is separate from the system clock. This calendar runs continuously, even if the router is powered off or rebooted.

If the system clock and calendar are not synchronized, and the system clock is more accurate, use this command to update the calendar to the correct date and time.

Example

The following example copies the current time from the system clock to the calendar:

```
clock update-calendar
```

Related Commands

To locate documentation of related commands, you can search online at www.cisco.com.

clock read-calendar
ntp update-calendar

downward-compatible-config

To generate a configuration that is compatible with an earlier Cisco IOS release, use the **downward-compatible-config** global configuration command. To remove this feature, use the **no** form of this command.

> **downward-compatible-config** *version*
> **no downward-compatible-config**

Syntax	Description
version	Cisco IOS Release number, not earlier than 10.2

Default

Disabled

Command Mode

Global configuration

Usage Guidelines

This command first appeared in Cisco IOS Release 11.1.

In Cisco IOS Release 10.3, IP access lists changed format. Use this command to regenerate a configuration in a format prior to Release 10.3 if you are going to downgrade from a Release 10.3 or later to an earlier release. The earliest release this command accepts is 10.2.

When this command is configured, the router attempts to generate a configuration that is compatible with the specified version. Currently, this command affects only IP access lists.

Under some circumstances, the software might not be able to generate a fully backward-compatible configuration. In such a case, the software issues a warning message.

Example

The following example generates a configuration file compatible with Cisco IOS Release 10.2:

```
downward-compatible-config 10.2
```

Related Commands

To locate documentation of related commands, you can search online at www.cisco.com.

access-list (extended)
access-list (standard)

hostname

To specify or modify the host name for the network server, use the **hostname** global configuration command. The host name is used in prompts and default configuration filenames. The **setup** command facility also prompts for a host name at startup.

> **hostname** *name*

Syntax   Description

name   New host name for the network server

Default

The factory-assigned default host name is *router*.

Command Mode

Global configuration

Usage Guidelines

This command first appeared in Cisco IOS Release 10.0.

The order of display at startup is banner message-of-the-day (MOTD), then login and password prompts, then EXEC banner.

Do not expect case to be preserved. Upper- and lowercase characters look the same to many internet software applications (often under the assumption that the application is doing you a favor). It may seem appropriate to capitalize a name the same way you might do in English, but conventions dictate that computer names appear all lowercase. For more information, refer to RFC 1178, *Choosing a Name for Your Computer.*

The name must also follow the rules for ARPANET host names. They must start with a letter, end with a letter or digit, and have as interior characters only letters, digits, and hyphens. Names must be 63 characters or fewer. For more information, refer to RFC 1035, *Domain Names—Implementation and Specification.*

Example

The following example changes the host name to **sandbox**:

```
hostname sandbox
```

Related Commands

To locate documentation of related commands, you can search online at www.cisco.com.

setup

ip bootp server

To access the BOOTP service available from hosts on the network, use the **ip bootp server** global configuration command. Use the **no** form of the command to disable these services.

> **ip bootp server**
> **no ip bootp server**

Syntax Description

This command has no arguments or keywords.

Default

Enabled

Command Mode

Global configuration

Usage Guidelines

This command first appeared in Cisco IOS Release 11.2.

By default, the BOOTP server is enabled.

When you disable the BOOTP server, access to the BOOTP ports causes the Cisco IOS software to send an "ICMP port unreachable" message to the sender and discard the original incoming packet.

NOTE	Unlike defaults for other commands, this command will display when you perform **show running config** to display current settings, whether or not you have changed the default using the **no ip bootp server** command.

Example

The following example disables the BOOTP service on the router:

```
no ip bootp server
```

ip telnet source-interface

Use the **ip telnet source-interface** global configuration command to allow a user to select an address of an interface as the source address for Telnet connections. Use the **no** form of this command to reset the source address to the default for each connection.

> **ip telnet source-interface** *interface*
> **no ip telnet source-interface**

Syntax	Description
interface	The interface whose address is to be used as the source for Telnet connections

Default

The address of the closest interface to the destination as the source address. If the selected interface is not "up," the Cisco IOS software selects the address of the closest interface to the destination as the source address.

Command Mode

Global configuration

Usage Guidelines

This command first appeared in Cisco IOS Release 11.1.

Use this command to set an interface's IP address as the source for all Telnet connections.

Example

The following example makes the IP address for Ethernet interface 1 as the source address for Telnet connections:

```
ip telnet source-interface e 1
```

Related Commands

To locate documentation of related commands, you can search online at www.cisco.com.

ip tacacs source-interface
ip tftp source-interface
ip radius source-interface

ip tftp source-interface

Use the **ip tftp source-interface** global configuration command to allow a user to select the interface whose address will be used as the source address for TFTP connections.

> **ip tftp source-interface** *interface*
> **no ip tftp source-interface**

Syntax	Description
interface	The interface whose address is to be used as the source for TFTP connections

Default

The address of the closest interface to the destination as the source address. If the selected interface is not "up," the Cisco IOS software selects the address of the closest interface to the destination as the source address.

Command Mode
Global configuration

Usage Guidelines
This command first appeared in Cisco IOS Release 11.1.

Use this command to set an interface's IP address as the source for all TFTP connections.

Example
The following example makes the IP address for Ethernet interface 1 as the source address for TFTP connections:

```
ip tftp source-interface e 1
```

Related Commands
To locate documentation of related commands, you can search online at www.cisco.com.

ip radius source-interface
ip tacacs source-interface
ip telnet source-interface

load-interval

To change the length of time for which data is used to compute load statistics, use the **load-interval** interface configuration command. Use the **no** form of this command to revert to the default setting.

> **load-interval** *seconds*
> **no load-interval** *seconds*

Syntax   Description

seconds   Length of time for which data is used to compute load statistics. A value that is a multiple of 30, from 30 to 600 (30, 60, 90, 120, and so forth).

Default
300 seconds (or 5 minutes)

Part III

Command Reference

Command Mode

Interface configuration

Usage Guidelines

This command first appeared in Cisco IOS Release 10.3.

If you want load computations to be more reactive to short bursts of traffic, rather than averaged over 5-minute periods, you can shorten the length of time over which load averages are computed.

If the load interval is set to 30 seconds, new data is used for load calculations over a 30-second period. This data is used to compute load statistics, including input rate in bits and packets per second, output rate in bits and packets per second, load, and reliability.

Load data is gathered every five seconds. This data is used for a weighted average calculation in which more-recent load data has more weight in the computation than older load data. If the load interval is set to 30 seconds, the average is computed for the last 30 seconds of load data.

The **load-interval** command allows you to change the default interval of five minutes to a shorter or longer period of time. If you change it to a shorter period of time, the input and output statistics that are displayed when you use the **show interface** command will be more current, and based on more instantaneous data, rather than reflecting a more average load over a longer period of time.

This command is often used for dial backup purposes, to increase or decrease the likelihood of a backup interface being implemented, but it can be used on any interface.

Example

In the following example, the default 5-minute average is set it to a 30-second average. A burst in traffic that would not trigger a dial backup for an interface configured with the default 5-minute interval might trigger a dial backup for this interface that is set for a shorter, 30-second interval.

```
interface serial 0
 load-interval 30
```

Related Commands

To locate documentation of related commands, you can search online at www.cisco.com.

show interfaces

ntp access-group

To control access to the system's Network Time Protocol (NTP) services, use the **ntp access-group** global configuration command. To remove access control to the system's NTP services, use the **no** form of this command.

> **ntp access-group** {**query-only** | **serve-only** | **serve** | **peer**} *access-list-number*
> **no ntp access-group** {**query-only** | **serve-only** | **serve** | **peer**}

Syntax	Description
query-only	Allows only NTP control queries. See RFC 1305 (NTP version 3).
serve-only	Allows only time requests.
serve	Allows time requests and NTP control queries, but does not allow the system to synchronize to the remote system.
peer	Allows time requests and NTP control queries and allows the system to synchronize to the remote system.
access-list-number	Number (1 to 99) of a standard IP access list.

Default

No access control (full access granted to all systems)

Command Mode

Global configuration

Usage Guidelines

This command first appeared in Cisco IOS Release 10.0.

The access group options are scanned in the following order from least restrictive to most restrictive:

1 peer

2 serve

3 serve-only

4 query-only

Access is granted for the first match that is found. If no access groups are specified, all access is granted to all sources. If any access groups are specified, only the specified access is granted. This facility provides minimal security for the time services of the system. However, it can be circumvented by a determined programmer. If tighter security is desired, use the NTP authentication facility.

Example

The following example configures the system to allow itself to be synchronized by a peer from access list 99. However, the system restricts access to allow time requests only from access list 42.

```
ntp access-group peer 99
ntp access-group serve-only 42
```

Related Commands

To locate documentation of related commands, you can search online at www.cisco.com.

access-list

ntp authenticate

To enable Network Time Protocol (NTP) authentication, use the **ntp authenticate** global configuration command. Use the **no** form of this command to disable the feature.

> **ntp authenticate**
> **no ntp authenticate**

Syntax Description

This command has no arguments or keywords.

Default

No authentication

Command Mode

Global configuration

Usage Guidelines

This command first appeared in Cisco IOS Release 10.0.

Use this command if you want authentication. If this command is specified, the system will not synchronize to a system unless it carries one of the authentication keys specified in the **ntp trusted-key** command.

Example

The following example configures the system to synchronize only to systems providing authentication key 42 in its NTP packets:

```
ntp authenticate
ntp authentication-key 42 md5 aNiceKey
ntp trusted-key 42
```

Related Commands

To locate documentation of related commands, you can search online at www.cisco.com.

ntp authentication-key
ntp trusted-key

ntp authentication-key

To define an authentication key for Network Time Protocol (NTP), use the **ntp authentication-key** global configuration command. Use the **no** form of this command to remove the authentication key for NTP.

ntp authentication-key *number* **md5** *value*
no ntp authentication-key *number*

Syntax	Description
number	Key number (1 to 4,294,967,295).
md5	Authentication key. Message authentication support is provided using the Message Digest (MD5) algorithm. The key type **md5** is currently the only key type supported.
value	Key value (an arbitrary string of up to eight characters).

Default

No authentication key is defined for NTP.

Command Mode

Global configuration

Usage Guidelines

This command first appeared in Cisco IOS Release 10.0.

Use this command to define authentication keys for use with other NTP commands in order to provide a higher degree of security.

NOTE   When this command is written to NVRAM, the key is encrypted so that it is not displayed when the configuration is viewed.

Example

The following example configures the system to synchronize only to systems providing authentication key 42 in its NTP packets:

```
ntp authenticate
ntp authentication-key 42 md5 aNiceKey
ntp trusted-key 42
```

Related Commands

To locate documentation of related commands, you can search online at www.cisco.com.

ntp authenticate
ntp peer
ntp server
ntp trusted-key

ntp broadcast

To specify that a specific interface should send Network Time Protocol (NTP) broadcast packets, use the **ntp broadcast** interface configuration command. Use the **no** form of this command to disable this capability.

> **ntp broadcast** [**version** *number*]
> **no ntp broadcast**

Syntax   Description

version *number*   (Optional) Number from 1 to 3 indicating the NTP version

Default
Disabled

Command Mode

Interface configuration

Usage Guidelines

This command first appeared in Cisco IOS Release 10.0.

Example

The following example configures Ethernet interface 0 to send NTP version 2 packets:

```
interface ethernet 0
 ntp broadcast version 2
```

Related Commands

To locate documentation of related commands, you can search online at www.cisco.com.

ntp broadcast client
ntp broadcastdelay

ntp broadcast client

To allow the system to receive NTP broadcast packets on an interface, use the **ntp broadcast client** interface configuration command. Use the **no** form of this command to disable this capability.

> **ntp broadcast client**
> **no ntp broadcast client**

Syntax Description

This command has no arguments or keywords.

Default

Disabled

Command Mode

Interface configuration

Usage Guidelines

This command first appeared in Cisco IOS Release 10.0.

Use this command to allow the system to listen to broadcast packets on an interface-by-interface basis.

Example

The following example synchronizes the Cisco IOS software to NTP packets broadcast on Ethernet interface 1:

```
interface ethernet 1
 ntp broadcast client
```

Related Commands

To locate documentation of related commands, you can search online at www.cisco.com.

ntp broadcast
ntp broadcastdelay

ntp broadcastdelay

To set the estimated round-trip delay between the Cisco IOS software and a Network Time Protocol (NTP) broadcast server, use the **ntp broadcastdelay** global configuration command. Use the **no** form of this command to revert to the default value.

> **ntp broadcastdelay** *microseconds*
> **no ntp broadcastdelay**

Syntax	Description
microseconds	Estimated round-trip time (in microseconds) for NTP broadcasts. The range is from 1 to 999,999.

Default

3000 microseconds

Command Mode

Global configuration

Usage Guidelines

This command first appeared in Cisco IOS Release 10.0.

Use this command when the router is configured as a broadcast client and the round-trip delay on the network is not 3000 microseconds.

Example

The following example sets the estimated round-trip delay between a router and the broadcast client to 5000 microseconds:

```
ntp broadcastdelay 5000
```

Related Commands

To locate documentation of related commands, you can search online at www.cisco.com.

ntp broadcast
ntp broadcast client

ntp clock-period

CAUTION	Do not enter this command; it is documented for informational purposes only. The system automatically generates this command as Network Time Protocol (NTP), determines the clock error, and compensates.

As NTP compensates for the error in the system clock, it keeps track of the correction factor for this error. The system automatically saves this value into the system configuration using the **ntp clock-period** global configuration command. The system uses the **no** form of this command to revert to the default.

> **ntp clock-period** *value*
> **no ntp clock-period**

Syntax   Description

value   Amount to add to the system clock for each clock hardware tick (in units of 2^{-32} seconds)

Default

171,798,692^{-32} seconds (4 milliseconds)

Command Mode

Global configuration

Usage Guidelines

This command first appeared in Cisco IOS Release 10.0.

If a **copy running-config startup-config** command is entered to save the configuration to NVRAM, this command will automatically be added to the configuration. It is a good idea to perform this task after NTP has been running for a week or so; this will help NTP synchronize more quickly if the system is restarted.

ntp disable

To prevent an interface from receiving Network Time Protocol (NTP) packets, use the **ntp disable** interface configuration command. To enable receipt of NTP packets on an interface, use the **no** form of this command.

> **ntp disable**
> **no ntp disable**

Syntax Description

This command has no arguments or keywords.

Default

Enabled

Command Mode

Interface configuration

Usage Guidelines

This command first appeared in Cisco IOS Release 10.0.

This command provides a simple method of access control.

Example

The following example prevents Ethernet interface 0 from receiving NTP packets:

```
interface ethernet 0
 ntp disable
```

ntp master

To configure the Cisco IOS software as a Network Time Protocol (NTP) master clock to which peers synchronize themselves when an external NTP source is not available, use the **ntp master** global configuration command. To disable the master clock function, use the **no** form of this command.

> **ntp master** [*stratum*]
> **no ntp master** [*stratum*]

CAUTION	Use this command with *extreme* caution. It is very easy to override valid time sources using this command, especially if a low stratum number is configured. Configuring multiple machines in the same network with the **ntp master** command can cause instability in keeping time if the machines do not agree on the time.

Syntax   Description

stratum   (Optional) Number from 1 to 15. Indicates the NTP stratum number that the system will claim.

Default

By default, the master clock function is disabled. When enabled, the default stratum is 8.

Command Mode

Global configuration

Usage Guidelines

This command first appeared in Cisco IOS Release 10.0.

Because Cisco's implementation of NTP does not support directly attached radio or atomic clocks, the router is normally synchronized, directly or indirectly, to an external system that has such a clock. In a network without Internet connectivity, such a time source may not be available. The **ntp master** command is used in such cases.

If the system has **ntp master** configured, and it cannot reach any clock with a lower stratum number, the system will claim to be synchronized at the configured stratum number, and other systems will be willing to synchronize to it via NTP.

NOTE	The system clock must have been set from some source, including manually, before **ntp master** will have any effect. This protects against distributing erroneous time after the system is restarted.

Example

The following example configures a router as an NTP master clock to which peers may synchronize:

```
ntp master 10
```

Related Commands

To locate documentation of related commands, you can search online at www.cisco.com.

clock calendar-valid

ntp peer

To configure the system clock to synchronize a peer or to be synchronized by a peer, use the **ntp peer** global configuration command. To disable this capability, use the **no** form of this command.

> **ntp peer** *ip-address* [**version** *number*] [**key** *keyid*] [**source** *interface*] [**prefer**]
> **no ntp peer** *ip-address*

Syntax   Description

Syntax	Description
ip-address	IP address of the peer providing, or being provided, the clock synchronization.
version	(Optional) Defines the Network Time Protocol (NTP) version number.
number	(Optional) NTP version number (1 to 3).
key	(Optional) Defines the authentication key.
keyid	(Optional) Authentication key to use when sending packets to this peer.
source	(Optional) Names the interface.
interface	(Optional) Name of the interface from which to pick the IP source address.
prefer	(Optional) Makes this peer the preferred peer that provides synchronization.

Default

No peers are configured by default. If a peer is configured, the default NTP version number is 3, no authentication key is used, and the source IP address is taken from the outgoing interface.

Command Mode

Global configuration

Usage Guidelines

This command first appeared in Cisco IOS Release 10.0.

Use this command if you want to allow this machine to synchronize with the peer, or vice versa. Using the **prefer** keyword reduces switching back and forth between peers.

If you are using the default version of 3 and NTP synchronization does not occur, try using NTP version number 2. Many NTP servers on the Internet run version 2.

Example

The following example configures a router to allow its system clock to be synchronized with the clock of the peer (or vice versa) at IP address 192.168.22.33 using NTP version 2. The source IP address is the address of Ethernet 0.

```
ntp peer 192.168.22.33 version 2 source ethernet 0
```

Related Commands

To locate documentation of related commands, you can search online at www.cisco.com.

ntp authentication-key
ntp server
ntp source

ntp server

To allow the system clock to be synchronized by a time server, use the **ntp server** global configuration command. To disable this capability, use the **no** form of this command.

ntp server *ip-address* [**version** *number*] [**key** *keyid*] [**source** *interface*] [**prefer**]
no ntp server *ip-address*

Syntax Description

Syntax	Description
ip-address	IP address of the time server providing the clock synchronization.
version	(Optional) Defines the Network Time Protocol (NTP) version number.
number	(Optional) NTP version number (1 to 3).
key	(Optional) Defines the authentication key.
keyid	(Optional) Authentication key to use when sending packets to this peer.
source	(Optional) Identifies the interface from which to pick the IP source address.
interface	(Optional) Name of the interface from which to pick the IP source address.
prefer	(Optional) Makes this server the preferred server that provides synchronization.

Default

No peers are configured by default. If a peer is configured, the default NTP version number is 3, no authentication key is used, and the source IP address is taken from the outgoing interface.

Command Mode

Global configuration

Usage Guidelines

This command first appeared in Cisco IOS Release 10.0.

Use this command if you want to allow this machine to synchronize with the specified server. The server will not synchronize to this machine.

Using the **prefer** keyword reduces switching back and forth between servers.

If you are using the default version of 3 and NTP synchronization does not occur, try using NTP version number 2. Many NTP servers on the Internet run version 2.

Example

The following example configures a router to allow its system clock to be synchronized with the clock of the peer at IP address 172.16.22.44 using NTP version 2:

```
ntp server 172.16.22.44 version 2
```

Related Commands

To locate documentation of related commands, you can search online at www.cisco.com.

ntp authentication-key
ntp peer
ntp source

ntp source

To use a particular source address in Network Time Protocol (NTP) packets, use the **ntp source** global configuration command. Use the **no** form of this command to remove the specified source address.

> **ntp source** *type number*
> **no ntp source**

Syntax

Syntax	Description
type	Type of interface
number	Number of the interface

Default

Source address is determined by the outgoing interface.

Command Mode

Global configuration

Usage Guidelines

This command first appeared in Cisco IOS Release 10.0.

Use this command when you want to use a particular source IP address for all NTP packets. The address is taken from the named interface. This command is useful if the address on an interface cannot be used as the destination for reply packets. If the **source** keyword is present on an **ntp server** or **ntp peer** command, that value overrides the global value.

Example

The following example configures a router to use the IP address of Ethernet 0 as the source address of all outgoing NTP packets:

```
ntp source ethernet 0
```

Part
III

Command Reference

Related Commands

To locate documentation of related commands, you can search online at www.cisco.com.

ntp peer
ntp server

ntp trusted-key

To authenticate the identity of a system to which Network Time Protocol (NTP) will synchronize, use the **ntp trusted-key** global configuration command. Use the **no** form of this command to disable authentication of the identity of the system.

> **ntp trusted-key** *key-number*
> **no ntp trusted-key** *key-number*

Syntax   Description

key-number   Key number of authentication key to be trusted

Default

Disabled

Command Mode

Global configuration

Usage Guidelines

This command first appeared in Cisco IOS Release 10.0.

If authentication is enabled, use this command to define one or more key numbers (corresponding to the keys defined with the **ntp authentication-key** command) that a peer NTP system must provide in its NTP packets, in order for this system to synchronize to it. This provides protection against accidentally synchronizing the system to a system that is not trusted, since the other system must know the correct authentication key.

Example

The following example configures the system to synchronize only to systems providing authentication key 42 in its NTP packets:

```
ntp authenticate
ntp authentication-key 42 md5 aNiceKey
ntp trusted-key 42
```

Related Commands

To locate documentation of related commands, you can search online at www.cisco.com.

ntp authenticate
ntp authentication-key

ntp update-calendar

To periodically update the calendar from Network Time Protocol (NTP), use the **ntp update-calendar** global configuration command. Use the **no** form of this command to disable the periodic updates.

> **ntp update-calendar**
> **no ntp update-calendar**

Syntax Description

This command has no arguments or keywords.

Default

The calendar is not updated.

Command Mode

Global configuration

Usage Guidelines

This command first appeared in Cisco IOS Release 10.0.

Some platforms have a calendar which is separate from the system clock. This calendar runs continuously, even if the router is powered off or rebooted.

If a router is synchronized to an outside time source via NTP, it is a good idea to periodically update the calendar with the time learned from NTP. Otherwise, the calendar will tend to gradually lose or gain time. The calendar will be updated only if NTP has synchronized to an authoritative time server.

Example

The following example configures the system to periodically update the calendar from the system clock:

```
ntp update-calendar
```

Related Commands

To locate documentation of related commands, you can search online at www.cisco.com.

clock read-calendar
clock update-calendar

prompt

To customize the prompt, use the **prompt** global configuration command. To revert to the default prompt, use the **no** form of this command.

> **prompt** *string*
> **no prompt** [*string*]

Syntax

string

Description

Prompt. It can consist of all printing characters and the escape sequences listed in Table 28-2.

Default

The default prompt is either Router or the name defined with the **hostname** global configuration command, followed by an angle bracket (>) for EXEC mode or a pound sign (#) for privileged EXEC mode.

Command Mode

Global configuration

Usage Guidelines

This command first appeared in Cisco IOS Release 10.3.

You can include escape sequences when specifying the prompt. All escape sequences are preceded by a percent sign (%). Table 28-2 lists the valid escape sequences.

Table 28-2 *Custom Prompt Escape Sequences*

Escape Sequence	Interpretation
%h	Host name. This is either *Router* or the name defined with the **hostname** global configuration command.
%n	Physical terminal line (TTY) number of the EXEC user.
%p	Prompt character itself. It is either an angle bracket (>) for EXEC mode or a pound sign (#) for privileged EXEC mode.
%s	Space.
%t	Tab.
%%	Percent sign (%).

Issuing the **prompt %h** command has the same effect as issuing the **no prompt** command.

Examples

The following example changes the EXEC prompt to include the TTY number, followed by the name and a space:

```
prompt TTY%n@%h%s%p
```

The following are examples of user and privileged EXEC prompts that result from the previous command:

```
TTY17@Router1 >
TTY17SRouter1 #
```

Related Commands

To locate documentation of related commands, you can search online at www.cisco.com.

hostname

scheduler allocate

To guarantee CPU time for processes, use the **scheduler allocate** global configuration command on the Cisco 7200 series and Cisco 7500 series. The **no** form of this command restores the default.

> **scheduler allocate** *interrupt-time process-time*
> **no scheduler allocate**

Syntax	Description
interrupt-time	Integer (in microseconds) that limits the maximum number of microseconds to spend on fast switching within any one network interrupt context. The range is 400 to 60,000 microseconds. The default is 4000 microseconds.
process-time	Integer (in microseconds) that guarantees the minimum number of microseconds to spend at the process level when network interrupts are disabled. The range is 100 to 4000. The default is 200 microseconds.

Default

Approximately five percent of the CPU is available for process tasks.

Command Mode

Global configuration

Usage Guidelines

This command first appeared in Cisco IOS Release 11.2.

This command applies to the Cisco 7200 series and Cisco 7500 series.

CAUTION   Cisco recommends that you do not change the default values.

Example

The following example makes 20 percent of the CPU available for process tasks:

```
scheduler allocate 2000 500
```

Related Commands

To locate documentation of related commands, you can search online at www.cisco.com.

scheduler interval

scheduler interval

To control the maximum amount of time that can elapse without running system processes, use the **scheduler interval** global configuration command. The **no** form of this command restores the default.

> **scheduler interval** *milliseconds*
> **no scheduler interval**

Syntax   Description

milliseconds   Integer that specifies the interval in milliseconds. The minimum interval that you can specify is 500 milliseconds; there is no maximum value.

Default

High-priority operations are allowed to use as much of the central processor as needed.

Command Mode

Global configuration

Usage Guidelines

This command first appeared in Cisco IOS Release 10.0.

The normal operation of the network server allows the switching operations to use as much of the central processor as is required. If the network is running unusually heavy loads that do not allow the processor the time to handle the routing protocols, give priority to the system process scheduler. High-priority operations are allowed to use as much of the central processor as needed.

On the Cisco 7200 series and Cisco 7500 series, use the **scheduler allocate** global configuration command.

Example

The following example changes the low-priority process schedule to an interval of 750 milliseconds:

```
scheduler interval 750
```

Related Commands

To locate documentation of related commands, you can search online at www.cisco.com.

scheduler allocate

service decimal-tty

To specify that line numbers be displayed and interpreted as decimal numbers rather than octal numbers, use the **service decimal-tty** global configuration command. Use the **no** form of this command to restore the default.

> **service decimal-tty**
> **no service decimal-tty**

Syntax Description

This command has no arguments or keywords.

Default

Decimal numbers on the 500-CS and Cisco 2500 Series.

Command Mode

Global configuration

Usage Guidelines

This command first appeared in Cisco IOS Release 10.0.

Example

The following example displays decimal rather than octal line numbers:

```
service decimal-tty
```

service exec-wait

To delay the startup of the EXEC on noisy lines, use the **service exec-wait** global configuration command. Use the **no** form of this command to disable the delay function.

> **service exec-wait**
> **no service exec-wait**

Syntax Description

This command has no arguments or keywords.

Default
Disabled

Command Mode
Global configuration

Usage Guidelines
This command first appeared in Cisco IOS Release 10.0.

This command delays startup of the EXEC until the line has been idle (no traffic seen) for three seconds. The default is to enable the line immediately on modem activation.

This command is useful on noisy modem lines or when a modem attached to the line is configured to ignore MNP or V.42 negotiations, and MNP or V.42 modems may be dialing in. In these cases, noise or MNP/V.42 packets may be interpreted as usernames and passwords, causing authentication failure before the user gets a chance to type a username/password. The command is not useful on nonmodem lines or lines without some kind of login configured.

Example
The following example delays the startup of the EXEC:

```
service exec-wait
```

service finger

To allow Finger protocol requests (defined in RFC 742) to be made of the network server, use the **service finger** global configuration command. This service is equivalent to issuing a remote **show users** command. Use the **no** form of this command to remove this service.

> **service finger**
> **no service finger**

Syntax Description
This command has no arguments or keywords.

Default
Enabled

Command Mode

Global configuration

Usage Guidelines

This command first appeared in Cisco IOS Release 10.0.

Example

The following example disables the Finger protocol:

```
no service finger
```

service hide-telnet-address

To hide addresses while trying to establish a Telnet session, use the **service hide-telnet-address** global configuration command. Use the **no** form of this command to remove this service.

> **service hide-telnet-address**
> **no service hide-telnet-address**

Syntax Description

This command has no arguments or keywords.

Default

Addresses are displayed.

Command Mode

Global configuration

Usage Guidelines

This command first appeared in Cisco IOS Release 11.2.

When you attempt to connect to a device, the router displays addresses and other messages (for example, Trying router1 (171.69.1.154, 2008)...). With the Hide feature, the router suppresses the display of the address (for example, Trying router1 address #1...). The router continues to display all other messages that would normally display during a connection attempt, such as detailed error messages if the connection was not successful.

The Hide feature improves the functionality of the Busy Message feature. When you configure only the **busy-message** command, the normal messages generated during a connection attempt are not displayed; only the busy-message is displayed. When you use the Hide and Busy features together, you can customize the information displayed during Telnet connection attempts. When you configure the **service hide-telnet-address** command and the **busy-message** command, the router suppresses the address and displays the message specified with the **busy-message** command if the connection attempt is not successful.

Example

The following example hides Telnet addresses:

```
service hide-telnet-address
```

Related Commands

To locate documentation of related commands, you can search online at www.cisco.com.

busy-message

service nagle

To enable the Nagle congestion control algorithm, use the **service nagle** global configuration command. Use the **no** form of this command to disable the algorithm.

>**service nagle**
>**no service nagle**

Syntax Description

This command has no arguments or keywords.

Default

Disabled

Command Mode

Global configuration

Usage Guidelines

This command first appeared in Cisco IOS Release 10.0.

When using a standard TCP implementation to send keystrokes between machines, TCP tends to send one packet for each keystroke typed. On larger networks, many small packets use up bandwidth and contribute to congestion.

John Nagle's algorithm (RFC 896) helps alleviate the small-packet problem in TCP. In general, it works this way: The first character typed after connection establishment is sent in a single packet, but TCP holds any additional characters typed until the receiver acknowledges the previous packet. Then the second, larger packet is sent and additional typed characters are saved until the acknowledgment comes back. The effect is to accumulate characters into larger chunks and pace them out to the network at a rate that matches the round-trip time of the given connection. This method is usually good for all TCP-based traffic. However, do not use the **service nagle** command if you have XRemote users on X Window sessions.

Example

The following example enables the Nagle algorithm:

```
service nagle
```

service prompt config

To display the configuration prompt (config), use the **service prompt config** global configuration command. Use the **no** form of this command to remove the configuration prompt.

> **service prompt config**
> **no service prompt config**

Syntax Description

This command has no arguments or keywords.

Default

The configuration mode prompts (*hostname*(config)#) appear in all configuration modes.

Command Mode

Global configuration

Usage Guidelines

This command first appeared in Cisco IOS Release 11.1.

Example

In the following example, the **no service prompt config** command prevents the configuration prompt from being displayed. The prompt is still displayed in EXEC mode. When the **service prompt config** command is entered, the configuration mode prompt reappears.

```
Router# configure terminal
Enter configuration commands, one per line.  End with Ctrl-Z.
Router(config)# no service prompt config
hostname bob
end
bob# configure terminal
Enter configuration commands, one per line.  End with Ctrl-Z.
service prompt config
bob(config)# hostname Router
Router(config)# end
Router#
```

Related Commands

To locate documentation of related commands, you can search online at www.cisco.com.

hostname
prompt

service tcp-small-servers

To access minor TCP/IP services available from hosts on the network, use the **service tcp-small-servers** global configuration command. Use the **no** form of the command to disable these services.

> **service tcp-small-servers**
> **no service tcp-small-servers**

Syntax Description

This command has no arguments or keywords.

Default

Enabled

Command Mode

Global configuration

Usage Guidelines

This command first appeared in Cisco IOS Release 11.1.

By default, the TCP servers for Echo, Discard, Chargen, and Daytime services are enabled.

When you disable the minor TCP/IP servers, access to the Echo, Discard, Chargen, and Daytime ports cause the Cisco IOS software to send a TCP RESET packet to the sender and discard the original incoming packet.

NOTE	Unlike defaults for other commands, this command will display when you perform **show running config** to display current settings whether or not you have changed the default using the **no service tcp-small-servers** command.

Example

The following example enables minor TCP/IP services available from the network:

```
service tcp-small-servers
```

service telnet-zero-idle

To set the TCP window to zero (0) when the Telnet connection is idle, use the **service telnet-zero-idle** global configuration command. Use the **no** form of this command to disable this service.

> **service telnet-zero-idle**
> **no service telnet-zero-idle**

Syntax Description

This command has no arguments or keywords.

Default

Disabled

Command Mode

Global configuration

Usage Guidelines

This command first appeared in Cisco IOS Release 10.0.

Normally, data sent to noncurrent Telnet connections is accepted and discarded. When **service telnet-zero-idle** is enabled, if a session is suspended (that is, some other connection is made active or the EXEC is sitting in command mode), the TCP window is set to zero. This action prevents the remote host from sending any more data until the connection is resumed. Use this command when it is important that all messages sent by the host be seen by the users who are likely to use multiple sessions.

Do not use this command if your host will eventually time out and log out a TCP user whose window is zero.

Example

The following example sets the TCP window to zero when the Telnet connection is idle:

```
service telnet-zero-idle
```

Related Commands

To locate documentation of related commands, you can search online at www.cisco.com.

resume

service udp-small-servers

To access minor User Datagram Protocol (UDP) services available from hosts on the network, use the **service udp-small-servers** global configuration command. Use the **no** form of the command to disable these services.

> **service udp-small-servers**
> **no service udp-small-servers**

Syntax Description

This command has no arguments or keywords.

Default

Enabled

Command Mode

Global configuration

Usage Guidelines

This command first appeared in Cisco IOS Release 11.2.

By default the UPD servers for Echo, Discard, and Chargen services are enabled.

When you disable the servers, access to Echo, Discard, and Chargen ports causes the Cisco IOS software to send an "ICMP port unreachable" message to the sender and discard the original incoming packet.

NOTE	Unlike defaults for other commands, this command will display when you perform **show running config** to display current settings, whether or not you have changed the default using the **no service udp-small-servers** command.

Example

The following example disables minor UDP services on the router:

```
no service udp-small-servers
```

show aliases

To display all alias commands, or the alias commands in a specified mode, use the **show aliases** EXEC command.

> **show aliases** [*mode*]

Syntax   Description

mode   (Optional) Command mode. See Table 28-1 in the description of the **alias** command for acceptable options for the *mode* argument.

Command Mode

EXEC

Usage Guidelines

This command first appeared in Cisco IOS Release 10.3.

All of the modes listed in Table 28-1 have their own prompts, except for the null interface mode. For example, the prompt for interface configuration mode is *Router(config-if)*.

Sample Display

The following is sample output from the **show aliases exec** commands. The aliases configured for commands in EXEC mode are displayed.

```
Router# show aliases exec

Exec mode aliases:
  h                     help
  lo                    logout
  p                     ping
  r                     resume
  s                     show
  w                     where
```

Related Commands

To locate documentation of related commands, you can search online at www.cisco.com.

alias

show buffers

Use the **show buffers** EXEC command to display statistics for the buffer pools on the network server.

show buffers [*type number* | **alloc** [**dump**]]

Syntax	Description
type number	(Optional) Displays interface pool information. If the specified interface *type* and *number* has its own buffer pool, it displays information for that pool. Value of *type* can be **ethernet**, **serial**, **tokenring**, **fddi**, **bri**, **atm**, **e1**, **t1**.
alloc	(Optional) Displays a brief listing of all allocated buffers.
dump	(Optional) Dumps all allocated buffers. This keyword must be used with the **alloc** keyword, not by itself.

Command Mode

EXEC

Usage Guidelines

This command first appeared in Cisco IOS Release 10.0.

Sample Displays

The following is sample output from the **show buffers** command with no arguments, showing all buffer pool information:

```
Router# show buffers

Buffer elements:
     398 in free list (500 max allowed)
     1266 hits, 0 misses, 0 created

Public buffer pools:
Small buffers, 104 bytes (total 50, permanent 50):
     50 in free list (20 min, 150 max allowed)
     551 hits, 0 misses, 0 trims, 0 created
Middle buffers, 600 bytes (total 25, permanent 25):
     25 in free list (10 min, 150 max allowed)
     39 hits, 0 misses, 0 trims, 0 created
Big buffers, 1524 bytes (total 50, permanent 50):
     49 in free list (5 min, 150 max allowed)
     27 hits, 0 misses, 0 trims, 0 created
VeryBig buffers, 4520 bytes (total 10, permanent 10):
     10 in free list (0 min, 100 max allowed)
     0 hits, 0 misses, 0 trims, 0 created
Large buffers, 5024 bytes (total 0, permanent 0):
     0 in free list (0 min, 10 max allowed)
     0 hits, 0 misses, 0 trims, 0 created
Huge buffers, 18024 bytes (total 0, permanent 0):
     0 in free list (0 min, 4 max allowed)
     0 hits, 0 misses, 0 trims, 0 created

Interface buffer pools:
Ethernet0 buffers, 1524 bytes (total 64, permanent 64):
     16 in free list (0 min, 64 max allowed)
     48 hits, 0 fallbacks
     16 max cache size, 16 in cache
Ethernet1 buffers, 1524 bytes (total 64, permanent 64):
     16 in free list (0 min, 64 max allowed)
     48 hits, 0 fallbacks
     16 max cache size, 16 in cache
Serial0 buffers, 1524 bytes (total 64, permanent 64):
     16 in free list (0 min, 64 max allowed)
     48 hits, 0 fallbacks
     16 max cache size, 16 in cache
Serial1 buffers, 1524 bytes (total 64, permanent 64):
     16 in free list (0 min, 64 max allowed)
     48 hits, 0 fallbacks
     16 max cache size, 16 in cache
TokenRing0 buffers, 4516 bytes (total 48, permanent 48):
     0 in free list (0 min, 48 max allowed)
     48 hits, 0 fallbacks
     16 max cache size, 16 in cache
TokenRing1 buffers, 4516 bytes (total 32, permanent 32):
     32 in free list (0 min, 48 max allowed)
     16 hits, 0 fallbacks

0 failures (0 no memory)
```

Table 28-3 describes significant fields shown in the display.

Table 28-3 *Show Buffers Field Descriptions*

Field	Description
Buffer elements	Buffer elements are small structures used as placeholders for buffers in internal operating system queues. Buffer elements are used when a buffer may need to be on more than one queue.
free list	Total number of the currently unallocated buffer elements.
max allowed	Maximum number of buffers that are available for allocation.
hits	Count of successful attempts to allocate a buffer when needed.
misses	Count of buffer allocation attempts that resulted in growing the buffer pool to allocate a buffer.
created	Count of new buffers created to satisfy buffer allocation attempts when the available buffers in the pool have already been allocated.
Public buffer pools:	
Small buffers	Buffers that are 104 bytes long.
Middle buffers	Buffers that are 600 bytes long.
Big buffers	Buffers that are 1524 bytes long.
VeryBig buffers	Buffers that are 4520 bytes long.
Large buffers	Buffers that are 5024 bytes long.
Huge buffers	Buffers that are 18,024 bytes long.
total	Total number of this type of buffer.
permanent	Number of these buffers that are permanent.
free list	Number of available or unallocated buffers in that pool.
min	Minimum number of free or unallocated buffers in the buffer pool.
max allowed	Maximum number of free or unallocated buffers in the buffer pool.
hits	Count of successful attempts to allocate a buffer when needed.
misses	Count of buffer allocation attempts that resulted in growing the buffer pool in order to allocate a buffer.
trims	Count of buffers released to the system because they were not being used. This field is displayed only for dynamic buffer pools, not interface buffer pools, which are static.
created	Count of new buffers created in response to misses. This field is displayed only for dynamic buffer pools, not interface buffer pools, which are static.

Continues

Part III

Command Reference

Table 28-3 *Show Buffers Field Descriptions (Continued)*

Field	Description
Interface buffer pools:	
total	Total number of this type of buffer.
permanent	Number of these buffers that are permanent.
free list	Number of available or unallocated buffers in that pool.
min	Minimum number of free or unallocated buffers in the buffer pool.
max allowed	Maximum number of free or unallocated buffers in the buffer pool.
hits	Count of successful attempts to allocate a buffer when needed.
fallbacks	Count of buffer allocation attempts that resulted in falling back to the public buffer pool that is the smallest pool but at least as big as the interface buffer pool.
max cache size	Maximum number of buffers from that interface's pool that can be in that interface buffer pool's cache. Each interface buffer pool has its own cache. These are not additional to the permanent buffers; they come from the interface's buffer pools. Some interfaces place all of their buffers from the interface pool into the cache. In this case, it is normal for the *free list* to display 0.
failures	Total number of allocation requests that have failed because no buffer was available for allocation; the datagram was lost. Such failures normally occur at interrupt level.
no memory	Number of failures that occurred because no memory was available to create a new buffer.

The following is sample output from the **show buffers** command with an interface *type* and *number*:

```
Router# show buffers Ethernet 0

Ethernet0 buffers, 1524 bytes (total 64, permanent 64):
    16 in free list (0 min, 64 max allowed)
    48 hits, 0 fallbacks
    16 max cache size, 16 in cache
```

The following is sample output from the **show buffers** command when **alloc** is specified:

```
Router# show buffers alloc

Buffer elements:
    398 in free list (500 max allowed)
    1266 hits, 0 misses, 0 created

Public buffer pools:
Small buffers, 104 bytes (total 50, permanent 50):
    50 in free list (20 min, 150 max allowed)
    551 hits, 0 misses, 0 trims, 0 created
Middle buffers, 600 bytes (total 25, permanent 25):
    25 in free list (10 min, 150 max allowed)
    39 hits, 0 misses, 0 trims, 0 created
```

```
Big buffers, 1524 bytes (total 50, permanent 50):
     49 in free list (5 min, 150 max allowed)
     27 hits, 0 misses, 0 trims, 0 created
VeryBig buffers, 4520 bytes (total 10, permanent 10):
     10 in free list (0 min, 100 max allowed)
     0 hits, 0 misses, 0 trims, 0 created
Large buffers, 5024 bytes (total 0, permanent 0):
     0 in free list (0 min, 10 max allowed)
     0 hits, 0 misses, 0 trims, 0 created
Huge buffers, 18024 bytes (total 0, permanent 0):
     0 in free list (0 min, 4 max allowed)
     0 hits, 0 misses, 0 trims, 0 created

Interface buffer pools:
Ethernet0 buffers, 1524 bytes (total 64, permanent 64):
     16 in free list (0 min, 64 max allowed)
     48 hits, 0 fallbacks
     16 max cache size, 16 in cache
Ethernet1 buffers, 1524 bytes (total 64, permanent 64):
     16 in free list (0 min, 64 max allowed)
     48 hits, 0 fallbacks
     16 max cache size, 16 in cache
Serial0 buffers, 1524 bytes (total 64, permanent 64):
     16 in free list (0 min, 64 max allowed)
     48 hits, 0 fallbacks
     16 max cache size, 16 in cache
Serial1 buffers, 1524 bytes (total 64, permanent 64):
     16 in free list (0 min, 64 max allowed)
     48 hits, 0 fallbacks
     16 max cache size, 16 in cache
TokenRing0 buffers, 4516 bytes (total 48, permanent 48):
     0 in free list (0 min, 48 max allowed)
     48 hits, 0 fallbacks
     16 max cache size, 16 in cache
TokenRing1 buffers, 4516 bytes (total 32, permanent 32):
     32 in free list (0 min, 48 max allowed)
     16 hits, 0 fallbacks

0 failures (0 no memory)
```

Address	PakAddr	Data Area	Off set	Data Size	Pool	Ref Cnt	Link Type	Enc Type	Flags (Hex)	Output Idb	Input Idb
604B37A0	604B37C0	40004A38	62	60	Big	1	65	3	0	Et0	
604C6DA0	604C6DC0	40007038	84	0	Ether	1	0	0	0		
604C6F60	604C6F80	400076E4	84	0	Ether	1	0	0	0		
604C7120	604C7140	40007D90	84	0	Ether	1	0	0	0		
604C72E0	604C7300	4000843C	84	0	Ether	1	0	0	0		
604C74A0	604C74C0	40008AE8	84	0	Ether	1	0	0	0		
604C7660	604C7680	40009194	84	0	Ether	1	0	0	0		
604C7820	604C7840	40009840	84	0	Ether	1	0	0	0		

```
.
.
.
```

show calendar

To display the calendar hardware setting, use the **show calendar** EXEC command:

> **show calendar**

Syntax Description

This command has no arguments or keywords.

Command Mode

EXEC

Usage Guidelines

This command first appeared in Cisco IOS Release 10.0.

Some platforms have a calendar which is separate from the system clock. This calendar runs continuously, even if the router is powered off or rebooted.

You can compare the time and date shown with this command with the time and date listed via the **show clock** command to verify that the calendar and system clock are in sync with each other. The time displayed is relative to the configured time zone.

Sample Display

In the following sample display, the hardware calendar indicates the timestamp of 12:13:44 p.m. on Friday, July 19, 1996:

```
Router# show calendar

12:13:44 PST Fri Jul 19 1996
```

Related Commands

To locate documentation of related commands, you can search online at www.cisco.com.

show clock

show clock

To display the system clock, use the **show clock** EXEC command.

> **show clock [detail]**

Syntax	Description
detail	(Optional) Indicates the clock source (NTP, VINES, system calendar, and so forth) and the current summer-time setting (if any).

Command Mode

EXEC

Usage Guidelines

This command first appeared in Cisco IOS Release 10.0.

The system clock keeps an authoritative flag that indicates whether the time is authoritative (believed to be accurate). If the system clock has been set by a timing source (system calendar, NTP, VINES, and so forth), the flag is set. If the time is not authoritative, it will be used only for display purposes. Until the clock is authoritative and the authoritative flag is set, the flag prevents peers from synchronizing to the clock when the peers' time is invalid.

The symbol that precedes the **show clock** display indicates the following:

Symbol	Description
*	Time is not authoritative.
(blank)	Time is authoritative.
.	Time is authoritative, but NTP is not synchronized.

Sample Display

The following sample output shows that the current clock is authoritative and that the time source is NTP:

```
Router# show clock detail

15:29:03.158 PST Mon Mar 3 1997
Time source is NTP
```

Related Commands

To locate documentation of related commands, you can search online at www.cisco.com.

clock set
show calendar

show ntp associations

To show the status of Network Time Protocol (NTP) associations, use the **show ntp associations** EXEC command.

> **show ntp associations** [**detail**]

Syntax Description

Syntax	Description
detail	(Optional) Shows detailed information about each NTP association.

Command Mode

EXEC

Usage Guidelines

This command first appeared in Cisco IOS Release 10.0.

Sample Displays

Detailed descriptions of the information displayed by this command can be found in the NTP specification (RFC 1305).

The following is sample output from the **show ntp associations** command:

```
Router# show ntp associations

     address         ref clock     st  when  poll  reach  delay  offset   disp
 ~172.31.32.2      172.31.32.1      5    29  1024   377    4.2    -8.59    1.6
+~192.168.13.33    192.168.1.111    3    69   128   377    4.1     3.48    2.3
*~192.168.13.57    192.168.1.111    3    32   128   377    7.9    11.18    3.6
* master (synced), # master (unsynced), + selected, - candidate, ~ configured
```

Table 28-4 describes significant fields shown in the display.

Table 28-4 *Show NTP Associations Field Descriptions*

Field	Description
(leading characters in display lines)	The first characters in a display line can be one or more of the following characters: * Synchronized to this peer \# Almost synchronized to this peer + Peer selected for possible synchronization - Peer is a candidate for selection ~ Peer is statically configured
address	Address of peer
ref clock	Address of peer's reference clock
st	Peer's stratum
when	Time since last NTP packet received from peer
poll	Polling interval (seconds)
reach	Peer reachability (bit string, in octal)
delay	Round-trip delay to peer (milliseconds)
offset	Relative time of peer's clock to local clock (milliseconds)
disp	Dispersion

Part
III

Command Reference

The following is sample output of the **show ntp associations detail** command:

```
Router# show ntp associations detail

172.31.32.2 configured, insane, invalid, stratum 5
ref ID 172.31.32.1, time AFE252C1.6DBDDFF2 (00:12:01.428 PDT Mon Jul 5 1993)
our mode active, peer mode active, our poll intvl 1024, peer poll intvl 64
root delay 137.77 msec, root disp 142.75, reach 376, sync dist 215.363
delay 4.23 msec, offset -8.587 msec, dispersion 1.62
precision 2**19, version 3
org time AFE252E2.3AC0E887 (00:12:34.229 PDT Mon Jul 5 1993)
rcv time AFE252E2.3D7E464D (00:12:34.240 PDT Mon Jul 5 1993)
xmt time AFE25301.6F83E753 (00:13:05.435 PDT Mon Jul 5 1993)
filtdelay =    4.23    4.14    2.41    5.95    2.37    2.33    4.26    4.33
filtoffset =  -8.59   -8.82   -9.91   -8.42  -10.51  -10.77  -10.13  -10.11
filterror =    0.50    1.48    2.46    3.43    4.41    5.39    6.36    7.34

192.168.13.33 configured, selected, sane, valid, stratum 3
ref ID 192.168.1.111, time AFE24F0E.14283000 (23:56:14.078 PDT Sun Jul 4 1993)
our mode client, peer mode server, our poll intvl 128, peer poll intvl 128
root delay 83.72 msec, root disp 217.77, reach 377, sync dist 264.633
delay 4.07 msec, offset 3.483 msec, dispersion 2.33
precision 2**6, version 3
org time AFE252B9.713E9000 (00:11:53.442 PDT Mon Jul 5 1993)
```

```
rcv time AFE252B9.7124E14A (00:11:53.441 PDT Mon Jul 5 1993)
xmt time AFE252B9.6F625195 (00:11:53.435 PDT Mon Jul 5 1993)
filtdelay =     6.47    4.07    3.94    3.86    7.31    7.20    9.52    8.71
filtoffset =    3.63    3.48    3.06    2.82    4.51    4.57    4.28    4.59
filterror =     0.00    1.95    3.91    4.88    5.84    6.82    7.80    8.77

192.168.13.57 configured, our_master, sane, valid, stratum 3
ref ID 192.168.1.111, time AFE252DC.1F2B3000 (00:12:28.121 PDT Mon Jul 5 1993)
our mode client, peer mode server, our poll intvl 128, peer poll intvl 128
root delay 125.50 msec, root disp 115.80, reach 377, sync dist 186.157
delay 7.86 msec, offset 11.176 msec, dispersion 3.62
precision 2**6, version 2
org time AFE252DE.77C29000 (00:12:30.467 PDT Mon Jul 5 1993)
rcv time AFE252DE.7B2AE40B (00:12:30.481 PDT Mon Jul 5 1993)
xmt time AFE252DE.6E6D12E4 (00:12:30.431 PDT Mon Jul 5 1993)
filtdelay =    49.21    7.86    8.18    8.80    4.30    4.24    7.58    6.42
filtoffset =   11.30   11.18   11.13   11.28    8.91    9.09    9.27    9.57
filterror =     0.00    1.95    3.91    4.88    5.78    6.76    7.74    8.71
```

Table 28-5 describes significant fields shown in the display.

Table 28-5   *Show NTP Associations Detail Field Descriptions*

Field	Descriptions
configured	Peer was statically configured.
dynamic	Peer was dynamically discovered.
our_master	Local machine is synchronized to this peer.
selected	Peer is selected for possible synchronization.
candidate	Peer is a candidate for selection.
sane	Peer passes basic sanity checks.
insane	Peer fails basic sanity checks.
valid	Peer time is believed to be valid.
invalid	Peer time is believed to be invalid.
leap_add	Peer is signaling that a leap second will be added.
leap-sub	Peer is signaling that a leap second will be subtracted.
unsynced	Peer is not synchronized to any other machine.
ref ID	Address of machine peer is synchronized to.
time	Last timestamp peer received from its master.
our mode	Our mode relative to peer (active / passive / client / server / bdcast / bdcast client).
peer mode	Peer's mode relative to us.
our poll intvl	Our poll interval to peer.
peer poll intvl	Peer's poll interval to us.

Table 28-5 *Show NTP Associations Detail Field Descriptions (Continued)*

Field	Descriptions
root delay	Delay along path to root (ultimate stratum 1 time source).
root disp	Dispersion of path to root.
reach	Peer reachability (bit string in octal).
sync dist	Peer synchronization distance.
delay	Round trip delay to peer.
offset	Offset of peer clock relative to our clock.
dispersion	Dispersion of peer clock.
precision	Precision of peer clock in Hz.
version	NTP version number that peer is using.
org time	Originate time stamp.
rcv time	Receive time stamp.
xmt time	Transmit time stamp.
filtdelay	Round trip delay in milliseconds of each sample.
filtoffset	Clock offset in milliseconds of each sample.
filterror	Approximate error of each sample.

Related Commands

To locate documentation of related commands, you can search online at www.cisco.com.

show ntp status

show ntp status

To show the status of Network Time Protocol (NTP), use the **show ntp status** EXEC command.

> **show ntp status**

Syntax Description

This command has no arguments or keywords.

Command Mode

EXEC

Usage Guidelines

This command first appeared in Cisco IOS Release 10.0.

Sample Display

The following is sample output from the **show ntp status** command:

```
Router# show ntp status

Clock is synchronized, stratum 4, reference is 192.168.13.57
nominal freq is 250.0000 Hz, actual freq is 249.9990 Hz, precision is 2**19
reference time is AFE2525E.70597B34 (00:10:22.438 PDT Mon Jul 5 1993)
clock offset is 7.33 msec, root delay is 133.36 msec
root dispersion is 126.28 msec, peer dispersion is 5.98 msec
```

Table 28-6 shows the significant fields in the display.

Table 28-6 *Show NTP Status Field Descriptions*

Field	Description
synchronized	System is synchronized to an NTP peer.
unsynchronized	System is not synchronized to any NTP peer.
stratum	NTP stratum of this system.
reference	Address of peer we are synchronized to.
nominal freq	Nominal frequency of system hardware clock.
actual freq	Measured frequency of system hardware clock.
precision	Precision of this system's clock (in Hz).
reference time	Reference timestamp.
clock offset	Offset of our clock to synchronized peer.
root delay	Total delay along path to root clock.
root dispersion	Dispersion of root path.
peer dispersion	Dispersion of synchronized peer.

Related Commands

To locate documentation of related commands, you can search online at www.cisco.com.

show ntp associations

show sntp

Use the **show sntp** EXEC command on a Cisco 1003, Cisco 1004, or Cisco 1005 router to show information about the Simple Network Time Protocol (SNTP).

show sntp

Syntax Description

This command has no arguments or keywords.

Command Mode

EXEC

Usage Guidelines

This command first appeared in Cisco IOS Release 11.2.

Sample Display

The following is sample output from the **show sntp** command:

```
Router# show sntp

SNTP server     Stratum   Version    Last Receive
171.69.118.9      5          3        00:01:02
172.21.28.34      4          3        00:00:36    Synced   Bcast

Broadcast client mode is enabled.
```

Table 28-7 describes the fields show in this display.

Table 28-7   *Show SNTP Field Descriptions*

Field	Description
SNTP server	Address of the configured or broadcast NTP server.
Stratum	NTP stratum of the server. The stratum indicates how far away from an authoritative time source the server is.
Version	NTP version of the server.
Last Receive	Time since the last NTP packet was received from the server.
Synced	Indicates the server chosen for synchronization.
Bcast	Indicates a broadcast server.

Related Commands

To locate documentation of related commands, you can search online at www.cisco.com.

sntp broadcast client
sntp server

sntp broadcast client

Use the **sntp broadcast client** global configuration command to configure a Cisco 1003, Cisco 1004, or Cisco 1005 router to use the Simple Network Time Protocol (SNTP) to accept Network Time Protocol (NTP) traffic from any broadcast server. The **no** form of the command prevents the router from accepting broadcast traffic.

> **sntp broadcast client**
> **no sntp broadcast client**

Syntax Description

This command has no arguments or keywords.

Default

The router does not accept SNTP traffic from broadcast servers.

Command Mode

Global configuration

Usage Guidelines

This command first appeared in Cisco IOS Release 11.2.

SNTP is a compact, client-only version of the Network Time Protocol (NTP). SNMP can only receive the time from NTP servers; it cannot be used to provide time services to other systems.

SNTP typically provides time within 100 milliseconds of the accurate time, but it does not provide the complex filtering and statistical mechanisms of NTP. In addition, SNTP does not authenticate traffic, although you can configure extended access lists to provide some protection.

You must configure the router with either this command or the **sntp server** command in order to enable SNTP.

Example

The following example enables the router to accept broadcast NTP packets and shows sample **show sntp** command output:

```
Router(config)# sntp broadcast client
Router(config)# end
Router#
%SYS-5-CONFIG: Configured from console by console
Router# show sntp

SNTP server     Stratum   Version    Last Receive
172.21.28.34       4         3        00:00:36    Synced  Bcast

Broadcast client mode is enabled.
```

Related Commands

To locate documentation of related commands, you can search online at www.cisco.com.

show sntp
sntp server

sntp server

Use the **sntp server** global configuration command to configure a Cisco 1003, Cisco 1004, or Cisco 1005 router to use the Simple Network Time Protocol (SNTP) to request and accept Network Time Protocol (NTP) traffic from a time server. The **no** form of the command removes a server from the list of NTP servers.

> **sntp server** {*address* | *hostname*} [**version** *number*]
> **no sntp server** {*address* | *hostname*}

Syntax   Description

Syntax	Description
address	IP address of the time server.
hostname	Hostname of the time server.
version *number*	(Optional) Version of NTP to use. The default is 1.

Default

The router does not accept SNTP traffic from a time server.

Command Mode

Global configuration

Usage Guidelines

This command first appeared in Cisco IOS Release 11.2.

SNTP is a compact, client-only version of the Network Time Protocol (NTP). SNMP can only receive the time from NTP servers; it cannot be used to provide time services to other systems.

SNTP typically provides time within 100 milliseconds of the accurate time, but it does not provide the complex filtering and statistical mechanisms of NTP. In addition, SNTP does not authenticate traffic, although you can configure extended access lists to provide some protection.

Enter this command once for each NTP server.

You must configure the router with either this command or the **sntp broadcast client** command in order to enable SNTP.

Example

The following example enables the router to request and accept NTP packets from the server at 172.21.118.9 and shows sample **show sntp** command output:

```
Router(config)# sntp server 172.21.118.9
Router(config)# end
Router#
%SYS-5-CONFIG: Configured from console by console
Router# show sntp

SNTP server    Stratum   Version   Last Receive
172.21.118.9      5         3       00:01:02    Synced
```

Related Commands

To locate documentation of related commands, you can search online at www.cisco.com.

show sntp
sntp broadcast client

## CHAPTER 29

Configuring the System Controller and Managed Shelves

The system controller is a Cisco IOS-based device that aids in the monitoring and management of a number of access servers and routers. Access servers and routers managed by the system controller are called shelves.

For a complete description of the system controller and managed shelves commands in this chapter, refer to Chapter 30, "System Controller Commands." To locate documentation of other commands that appear in this chapter, you can search online at www.cisco.com.

System Controller Configuration Task List

To configure the system controller and managed shelves, complete the tasks in the following sections:

- Configure Shelf Discovery and Autoconfiguration
- Configure the Virtual Console Feature
- Configure the Health Monitor Feature
- Configure Performance Data Collection
- Configure Syslog Disk Logging
- Configure the FTP Server Feature

See the end of this chapter for "System Controller and Managed Shelves Examples."

Configure Shelf Discovery and Autoconfiguration

The Shelf Discovery and Autoconfiguration feature allows a system controller to automatically discover new shelves and properly configure them to interact with the system controller. The system controller communicates with its managed shelves through the Shelf Discovery Protocol (SDP), which runs on top of UDP.

The Shelf Discovery and Autoconfiguration features provide the following benefits:

- Control of multiple platforms from one location
- Easier method of configuring commands on all shelves
- Consolidated list of managed shelves and all interfaces on managed shelves

When the system controller detects that a shelf has been added or reloaded, it sends the following configuration commands to the shelf:

- SNMP configuration commands
  - Enables SNMP
  - Configures the community string to match the string used by the system controller
  - Configures the system controller as a target for traps
- Logging configuration commands
  - Enables logging
  - Configures the system controller as a target for logging
  - Configures timestamps on messages
- NTP configuration commands
  - Specifies the system controller as the time source
  - Updates the system calendar using NTP time

Shelf Discovery and Autoconfiguration Task List

For a system controller to automatically discover and configure a shelf, both the system controller and the managed shelf must be configured. Perform the tasks described in the following sections:

- Configure the Shelf
- Configure the System Controller

Once you have configured the Shelf Discovery and Autoconfiguration feature on the system controller and managed shelves, you can increase the functionality of the system controller by configuring these additional features:

- Virtual Console
- Health Monitor
- Performance Data Collection
- Syslog Disk Logging
- FTP Server

Later sections in this chapter describe how to configure or use these features.

Configure the Shelf

To configure the shelf to use the system controller, use the following commands in global configuration mode:

Command	Purpose
syscon address *ip-address password*	Starts the SDP process on the shelf. This command causes the shelf to start looking for a system controller at the specified address.
syscon shelf-id *number*	If the shelf does not already have a shelf ID, this command configures a shelf ID for the system controller to use.

To monitor the SDP process, use the **show syscon sdp** and **debug syscon sdp** commands.

Configure the System Controller

To configure the system controller, use the following commands in global configuration mode:

Command	Purpose
syscon community *string*	Specifies the SNMP community string. During shelf autoconfiguration, this community string is automatically set on the shelf.
syscon password *password*	Specifies the password used in authenticating messages between the system controller and managed shelves. This password must match the password configured on shelves.

Use the following commands to monitor SDP events and status:

Command	Purpose
**show syscon discover [brief	full]**	Displays information about managed shelves.
show syscon sdp	Displays information about SDP.
debug syscon sdp	Debugs SDP.

Configure the Virtual Console Feature

The Virtual Console feature allows you to access dial and router shelves connected to a system controller. During a system controller session, you can connect to a router or dial shelf at the same privilege level as the current system controller session. By entering one command, you can Telnet directly to a shelf, provide a username and password, and then go to the same privilege level as the system controller.

The Virtual Console feature allows you to connect to all managed shelves through one session and easily switch between sessions. You do not have to reenable privileged EXEC mode every time you switch to another shelf session.

This feature is useful when you need to do quick tasks on different managed shelves.

The Virtual Console feature has the following security aspects:

- The system controller and managed shelves typically communicate over a private network. Thus, unauthorized access is limited.

- Shelf units will only allow **attach shelf** commands from the IP address for the system controller, as specified in the **syscon address** command.

- The system controller will only accept requests from the connected shelf.

To use the Virtual Console feature, you must first configure the Shelf Discovery and Autoconfiguration feature. Refer to the "Configure Shelf Discovery and Autoconfiguration" section for these tasks.

To use the Virtual Console feature, complete the tasks in the section that follows.

Use the Virtual Console Feature

To use the virtual console feature, use the following command beginning in user EXEC or privileged EXEC mode:

Command	Purpose
attach shelf *shelf-id*	On the system controller, connects to the managed shelf. Enters commands on the managed shelf.

You are connected to the managed system until one of the following occurs:

- You enter another **attach shelf** command.

- You enter the **exit** or **quit** commands at the EXEC prompt.

- You leave the session idle for a length of time (determined by the **exec-timeout** command on the shelf).

- You locally terminate the connection (^^x). (In a Telnet connection, ^^x will suspend the connection. With the **attach shelf** command, ^^x will break the connection.)

In every case except the first, control is returned to the system controller. In the first case, the connection to the current shelf is closed and a new connection to the specified shelf is opened.

Configure the Health Monitor Feature

The Health Monitor feature monitors key performance attributes of the shelves managed by the system controller.

The Health Monitor feature continually polls its managed shelves to obtain the information stored in the Health Monitor MIB. Management stations collect information for all the shelves from the system controller rather than by polling each shelf individually.

In addition, you can configure specific performance thresholds for all managed shelves through simple commands on the system controller. The system controller uses SNMP to automatically configure the following on each managed shelf:

- Expressions in the EXPRESSION-MIB to calculate the attributes
- RMON alarms to poll the attributes at specific intervals
- RMON events to send traps to the system controller when an attribute exceeds its specified threshold

When threshold traps are received by the system controller, they are converted to Health Monitor traps and sent to trap destinations configured in the system controller.

The Health Monitor feature provides the following benefits:

- Simplified configuration of SNMP-based monitoring functions. Entering a few commands on the system controller configures all of the managed shelves to send traps.
- Management systems poll only the system controller to get Health Monitor MIB data. The management systems do not have to poll the individual shelves. Thus, this feature reduces network traffic and system resources used by management systems.

Health Monitor Task List

To use this feature, you must first configure the Shelf Discovery and Autoconfiguration feature. Refer to the "Configure Shelf Discovery and Autoconfiguration" section for these tasks.

In addition, the SNMP Manager feature should be configured on the system controller. Use the **snmp-server manager** command to enable this feature. Refer to the "SNMP Manager" feature documentation from 11.3(1)T for details.

To configure the Health Monitor feature, complete the tasks in the following sections:

- Use the Health Monitor
- Monitor Shelf Attributes
- Supported MIBs and RFCs

Use the Health Monitor

When the Shelf Discovery and Autoconfiguration feature is enabled, the system controller automatically polls its managed shelves for Health Monitor MIB data. The system controller polls all the discovered shelves once a minute to obtain this data. Use the **show syscon mibpoll** EXEC command to display the current Health Monitor MIB data.

Optionally, you can configure the managed shelves to monitor certain attributes and notify the system controller when the attribute thresholds are exceeded, as described in the following section.

Monitor Shelf Attributes

To configure monitored attributes for the managed shelves, use the following commands in global configuration mode on the system controller:

Command	Purpose
syscon monitor {**io-mem** *percent* | **modem** *percent* | **trunk** *percent*}	Specifies attributes for the system controller to monitor.
syscon monitor traps	Enables Health Monitor MIB trap forwarding on the system controller.
snmp-server host *host* [**version** {1 | 2c}] *community-string* [**udp-port** *port*]	Specifies where the system controller sends the traps.
snmp-server enable traps	Enables trap generation on the system controller.

The Health Monitor MIB traps sent by the system controller are more readable than the traps sent to the system controller from the managed shelves. To send Health Monitor MIB traps to a management station, you should configure the **syscon monitor traps** command, the **snmp-server enable traps** command, and the appropriate **snmp-server host** command.

To view the status of the monitoring process, use the **show syscon monitor** EXEC command.

Supported MIBs and RFCs

This feature implements the Health Monitor MIB and utilizes MIB2 and POP-MGMT-MIB on the managed shelves.

Configure Performance Data Collection

The Performance Data Collection feature allows a system controller to collect and store SNMP MIB data from its managed router and dial shelves. The system controller then serves as a central point for network management data collection.

The system controller collects the raw data from the managed shelves periodically, saves the data, and provides a single access point for a central network management application. The data can then be uploaded to a network management station using FTP or TFTP.

Performance data is stored on a disk local to the system controller. The files are located at disk0:/performance/shelf-*shelfid/pollgroupname.unixtimestamp*. A new file is created each time the system controller collects data from a shelf.

The Performance Data Collection feature provides the following benefits:

- Remote network management stations can get performance data from one place, as a single file transferred via FTP or TFTP. This benefit reduces network traffic and resources in the management station because the station does not have to poll each individual shelf.

- The bulk transfer method of collecting data generates less traffic on the network than collecting the same amount of information using SNMP requests. The bulk transfer method also impacts the managed shelves less than SNMP polling.

Performance Data Collection Task List

To use this feature, you must first configure the following features:

- Shelf Discovery and Autoconfiguration. Refer to the "Configure Shelf Discovery and Autoconfiguration" section for these tasks.

- FTP Server. Refer to the "Configure the FTP Server Feature" section for these tasks.

- SNMP Manager. Refer to the "SNMP Manager" feature documentation from 11.3(1)T for details.

In addition, the system clock should be set to the current time before the data collection starts. Network Time Protocol (NTP) is the recommended method for obtaining the time.

To configure and use the Performance Data Collection feature, complete the tasks in the following sections:

- Configure Performance Data Collection on the System Controller

- What to Do Next

Configure Performance Data Collection on the System Controller

To configure Performance Data Collection on the system controller, use the following commands beginning in global configuration mode:

Step	Command	Purpose
1	**syscon poll-group** *name*	Specifies the name of the performance data set. This step will put the router in poll-group configuration mode.

Step	Command	Purpose
2	**oid** *object-id*	Specifies the MIB variables to collect. Repeat this command for each MIB variable.
3	**transfer-mode {bulk | poll}**	Sest the data collection method.
4	**shelf-type** *sysObjectID*	(Optional) Specifies the shelf types for the data collection. Repeat this step for each shelf type. The default is all shelf types.
5	**poll-interval** *minutes*	(Optional) Sets the data collection interval, in minutes. The default is 10 minutes.
6	**samples** *number*	(Optional) Specifies the maximum number of stored data sets. The default is 10.
7	**enable**	Enables Performance Data Collection.
8	**exit**	Exits poll-group configuration mode. This step ends the configuration of the performance data set.
9		(Optional) Repeats steps 1 through 8 for each additional poll group.
10	**end**	Returns to EXEC mode.
11	**more system:running-config** **show syscon perfdata**	Verifies that performance data is correctly configured.
12	**copy system:running-config** **nvram:startup-config**	Saves the configuration.

Configure the system controller to collect all the MIB variables that your network management station uses. Thus, the network management station can obtain all the information from the system controller without ever polling a managed shelf.

What to Do Next

After the system controller has collected the data, you must copy data from the system controller's disk (via FTP or TFTP) to the network management station. Use the **poll-interval** and **samples** commands to determine how long the data is stored on the disk before it is erased.

Configure Syslog Disk Logging

The Syslog Disk Logging feature allows you to collect, store, and retrieve all managed shelf syslog messages through the system controller. The system controller receives syslog messages from managed shelves and stores these messages in subfiles on its disk.

Each syslog message stored in a subfile contains the following information:

- Host IP address
- Facility
- Severity
- Timestamp (date and time) set by the managed shelf
- Message text

In addition, this feature provides an enhanced method of viewing messages in the logging history table. Messages can be displayed based on host IP address, time received, and order received.

The Syslog Disk Logging feature provides the following benefits:

- The system controller provides one storage and retrieval location for syslog messages from multiple hosts on the network.
- You can display syslog messages based on time, host name, or order received.
- Subfiles can store a large number of messages.
- Messages are preserved across system reloads. Without this feature, messages are stored in syslog history tables, which are lost when the system reboots.

Subfiles

Subfiles provide additional storage space for syslog messages. They contain the large logging history tables and preserve the tables even when the machine is reloaded.

The system controller creates subfiles using the same name as the root and a different extension for each subfile:

- The current subfile is called *name*.cur.
- The first archived subfile is *name*.1.
- The second is *name*.2.
- The last (oldest) archived subfile's extension is one less than the maximum number of subfiles (*number*-1). The complete subfile name is *name.number*-1.

The file space is preallocated before any messages are received to provide deterministic disk space allocation. When the system controller receives a new syslog message, the following events occur:

- The router determines if there is enough room in the current file (*name*.cur) to add the new data.
- If there is enough room, the data is added to the end of the current file.

- If there is not enough room, the last subfile is deleted (*name.number*-1).

    — The renaming subfiles are renamed to use the next (higher) extension.

    — A new *name*.cur is created.

    — The data is placed in the new current file.

Syslog Disk Logging Task List

To use this feature, you must first configure the Shelf Discovery and Autoconfiguration feature, which automatically configures the managed shelves to send syslog messages to the system controller. In addition, the **service timestamp log datetime** command is configured on all the shelves. Refer to the "Configure Shelf Discovery and Autoconfiguration" section for these tasks.

If you want messages generated by the system controller to be stored in the subfiles along with messages received from managed shelves, configure the system controller as the syslog server for its own messages using the **logging** *host* command.

To enable and use the Syslog Disk Logging feature, perform the following tasks:

- Create the Syslog-Server Subfiles
- Display Syslog Messages

Create the Syslog-Server Subfiles

Normally, the system controller just stores messages in the logging history table. However, to store a larger number of messages and preserve the messages across reboots of the machine, you need to create syslog server subfiles. To create these subfiles, use the following commands in global configuration mode:

Command	Purpose
logging syslog-server *size number dir-name*	Creates the syslog-server subfiles.
dir disk0:	Verifies that the files have been created.

A typical subfile configuration is five subfiles with a size of 500 KB. This configuration stores significant volumes of syslog data but still allows efficient searching. If the subfiles are too large or numerous, the **show syslog-server** command might be slow.

Display Syslog Messages

To view syslog messages stored in subfiles, use the following command in EXEC mode:

Command	Purpose
show syslog-server [**last** *number* I **since** [*date*] *hh:mm:ss*] [**source** *ip-address*]	Displays syslog messages.

Configure the FTP Server Feature

The FTP Server feature configures a router to act as an FTP server. FTP clients can copy files to and from certain directories on the router. In addition, the router can perform many other standard FTP server functions. For example, the FTP Server allows you to retrieve files, such as syslog files, from the disk file system on the router.

Supported FTP Commands

When the router receives a request for an FTP connection, the FTP Server process is started. The FTP Server prompts for a username and password.

After you supply a valid username and password, you can enter various commands. Not all FTP commands are supported by this FTP Server implementation. The FTP Server responds to the following FTP client commands:

!	cr	image	nmap	reset	sunique
append	debug	lcd	ntrans	rhelp	system
ascii	dir	ls	open	rstatus	tenex
binary	disconnect	macdef	prompt	runique	trace
bye	get	mdir	put	send	type
case	glob	mkdir	pwd	sendport	user
cd	hash	mls	quit	site	verbose
chmod	help	mode	quote	size	
close	idle	nlist	reget	status	

Refer to the documentation for your FTP client for detailed information on these commands. For example, if you are using a UNIX workstation as the FTP client, enter the **man ftp** command for descriptions of these commands.

To use the FTP Server feature, complete the task in the section that follows.

Enable the FTP Server

To enable the FTP Server, use the following commands in global configuration mode:

Command	Purpose
ftp-server enable	Enables the FTP Server.
ftp-server topdir *directory*	Restricts the region where the FTP clients can read or write files.

System Controller and Managed Shelves Examples

The following sections provide system controller and managed shelves examples:

- Shelf Discovery and Autoconfiguration Examples
- Virtual Console Examples
- Health Monitor Examples
- Performance Data Collection Examples
- Syslog Disk Logging Examples
- FTP Server Examples

Shelf Discovery and Autoconfiguration Examples

The following sample configuration enables a device to begin serving as a system controller. The system controller waits to be contacted by shelves and then provides them with the appropriate configuration.

```
syscon password syspassword
syscon community public
```

The follow example configures a shelf to use the system controller at 172.23.66.111. The shelf ID is 99. If you are using a Cisco AS5800, you do not need to specify a shelf ID with the **syscon shelf-id** command.

```
syscon address 172.23.66.111 syspassword
syscon shelf-id 99
```

After the shelf has contacted the system controller through SDP, the system controller configures the managed shelf with the following commands:

```
snmp-server community public RW
snmp-server enable traps
snmp-server host 172.23.66.111 traps version 2c public
snmp-server packetsize 1480
ntp server 172.23.66.111
ntp update-calendar
```

```
service timestamps log datetime msec
logging 172.23.66.111
logging trap
```

The following sample **debug syscon sdp** output on the managed shelf shows the shelf contacting the system controller. The shelf sends a Hello packet to the system controller at 172.23.66.111. The system controller responds with the autoconfiguration commands. The remaining lines show the Hello packets exchanged between the shelf and the system controller.

Shelf# **debug syscon sdp**

```
SYSCTLR: Hello packet sent to the SYSCTLR at 172.23.66.111
SYSCTLR: Command packet received from SYSCTLR
Feb 24 17:24:16.713: %SHELF-6-SYSCTLR_ESTABLISHED: Configured via system controller located
at 172.23.66.111
SYSCTLR: Rcvd HELLO from SYSCTLR at 172.23.66.111
SYSCTLR: Hello packet sent to the SYSCTLR at 172.23.66.111
SYSCTLR: Rcvd HELLO from SYSCTLR at 172.23.66.111
```

The following sample **debug syscon sdp** output on the system controller shows the system controller discovering the managed shelf. In the first few lines, the system controller receives a Hello packet from shelf 99 at 172.23.66.106. The system controller responds with a Hello packet. When the shelf sends another Hello packet, the system controller resets the timer and sends another packet.

Syscon# **debug syscon sdp**

```
SYSCTLR: Hello packet received via UDP from 172.23.66.106
%SYSCTLR-6-SHELF_ADD: Shelf 99 discovered located at address 172.23.66.106
Hello packet sent to the RS located at 172.23.66.106
SYSCTLR: Hello packet received via UDP from 172.23.66.106
Timer for shelf 99 updated, shelf is alive
Hello packet sent to the RS located at 172.23.66.106
```

Virtual Console Examples

In the following example, a user connects to a managed shelf from the system controller from user EXEC and privileged EXEC modes. Notice that the user connects to the shelf at the current user privilege level.

```
systemcont> show syscon
Shelf# 2  172.23.66.102 SDB update  09:09:16 PST Jan 27 1998
systemcont> attach shelf 2
Trying 172.23.66.102 ... Open

shelf2> show syscon
Current uptime 09:10:00 PST Jan 27 1998, system controller 172.23.66.100
Last hello packet received at 09:09:16 PST Jan 27 1998
8625 Total SDP packets
    0 packets with bad MD5 hash
    4311 Hello packets received
    4314 Hello packets sent
    0 Command packets received
    0 Command packets sent
shelf2> quit
```

```
[Connection to 172.23.66.102 closed by foreign host]
systemcont> enable
Password:
systemcont# attach shelf 2
Trying 172.23.66.102 ... Open

shelf2# show syscon sdp
Current uptime 09:10:45 PST Jan 27 1998, system controller 172.23.66.100
Last hello packet received at 09:10:14 PST Jan 27 1998
8627 Total SDP packets
    0 packets with bad MD5 hash
    4312 Hello packets received
    4315 Hello packets sent
    0 Command packets received
    0 Command packets sent
shelf2# exit

[Connection to 172.23.66.102 closed by foreign host]
systemcont#
```

Health Monitor Examples

The following system controller sample configuration monitors three attributes and forwards traps to myhost.cisco.com.

```
! The following commands are configured as part of the Shelf Discovery and
! Autoconfiguration feature.
!
syscon password syspassword
syscon community syscommunity
!
! The following lines configure the shelves to monitor IO memory on all the shelves and
! total modem and trunk utilization.
! If IO memory utilization exceeds 10%, the shelf sends a trap to the system controller.
! If the total utilization of all modems or trunk on all shelves exceeds 5%, the system
! controller generates a trap.
!
syscon monitor modem 5
syscon monitor trunk 5
syscon monitor io-mem 10
!
! The following commands enable forwarding of traps. When the system controller receives
! a trap from a managed shelf or generates one itself, it forwards the trap to the host
! called myhost using the community string public.
!
syscon monitor traps
snmp-server host myhost.cisco.com public
snmp-server enable traps
!
! The following line enables the SNMP manager process.
!
snmp-server manager
```

You can view the current configuration of Health Monitor on the system controller with the **show syscon monitor** command.

```
nnm3640-2# show syscon monitor

Health Monitor setup status on the shel(f,ves):
Shelf#  Shelf IP Address      Monitoring Type Threshold Value Status
    3   172.23.66.109         IO-Mem                10          Active

Health Monitor setup status on the system controller:
Monitoring Type Threshold Value Status
  Trunk          5           Active
  Modem          5           Active
```

The system will automatically configure each shelf to monitor its IO memory utilization. You can check the RMON configuration using the **show rmon alarms** and **show rmon events** commands on a managed shelf.

```
nnm7206-6# show rmon alarms

Alarm 596 is active, owned by IOMem
 Monitors ciscoExperiment.22.1.4.1.1.2.1.0.0.0 every 120 second(s)
 Taking absolute samples, last value was 66
 Rising threshold is 10, assigned to event 514
 Falling threshold is 0, assigned to event 0
 On startup enable rising or falling alarm

nnm7206-6# show rmon events

Event 514 is active, owned by IOMem
 Description is Send snmp trap to health_monitor
 Event firing causes trap to community syscommunity, last fired 00:04:02
```

Performance Data Collection Examples

The following partial sample configuration file configures Performance Data Collection on a system controller:

```
! Enable the FTP Server on the system controller and specify the top-level directory
! for FTP operations.
!
ftp-server enable
ftp-server topdir disk0:/performance
!
! Configure the device to act as a system controller and specify the passwords.
!
syscon password semtest
syscon community private
!
! Configure and enable the different poll groups.
!
```

```
syscon poll-group popmgmt
 oid cpmDS0Usage.1.*
 oid cpmActiveCallSummary.1.*
 oid cpmCallHistorySummary.3.*
 transfer-mode bulk
 poll-interval 25
 samples 5
 enable
syscon poll-group cmlineinfo
 oid cmLineInfo.1.*
 oid cmLineInfo.2.*
 oid cmLineInfo.3.*
 oid cmLineInfo.4.*
 transfer-mode bulk
 poll-interval 20
 samples 5
 enable
syscon poll-group cpmds0usage
 oid cpmDS0Usage.2.0
 oid cpmDS0Usage.3.0
 oid cpmDS0Usage.4.0
 oid cpmDS0Usage.5.0
 oid cpmDS0Usage.6.0
 oid cpmDS0Usage.7.0
 transfer-mode poll
 poll-interval 15
 samples 10
 enable
syscon poll-group callfailure
 oid cpmCallFailure.1.0
 oid cpmCallFailure.2.0
 oid cpmCallFailure.3.0
 oid cpmCallFailure.4.0
 oid cpmCallFailure.5.0
 oid cpmCallFailure.6.0
 oid cpmCallHistorySummary.1.0
 oid cpmCallHistorySummary.2.0
 transfer-mode poll
 poll-interval 20
 samples 10
 enable
syscon poll-group cmsysteminfo
 oid cmSystemInfo.1.0
 oid cmSystemInfo.2.0
 oid cmSystemInfo.3.0
 oid cmSystemInfo.4.0
 oid cmSystemInfo.5.0
 oid cmSystemInfo.6.0
 oid cmSystemInfo.7.0
 oid cmSystemInfo.8.0
 oid cmSystemInfo.9.0
 oid cmSystemInfo.10.0
 transfer-mode poll
 poll-interval 25
 shelf-type 108
```

```
 samples 12
 enable
syscon poll-group iftable
 oid ifEntry.3.*
 oid ifEntry.4.*
 oid ifEntry.5.*
 oid ifEntry.8.*
 transfer-mode poll
 poll-interval 20
 samples 10
 enable
```

The following **show syscon perfdata** output indicates that the system controller is collecting data from shelf 0:

```
SysCont# show syscon perfdata

Performance Data Collection:

          Poll       Last    Total     Get    GetBulk  Bulk Xfer
Shelf#    Group      File    Requests Requests Requests Requests  Errors
     0  popmgmt     891873300     5        0        0        5        0
        cmlineinfo  891873600     5        0        0        5        0
        cpmds0usage 891873000     1        1        0        0        0
        callfailure 891873600     1        1        0        0        0
        cmsysteminfo 891873300    1        1        0        0        0
        iftable     891873647   651        1      650        0        0
```

Use the **dir** command to view the data sets. Note that the file extension corresponds to the "Last File" time in the **show syscon perfdata** command.

```
SysCont# dir disk0:/performance/shelf-0
Directory of disk0:/performance/shelf-0/

128  -rw-       238   Apr 06 1998 14:29:59  cpmds0usage.891873000
192  -rw-       402   Apr 06 1998 14:34:59  cmsysteminfo.891873300
194  -rw-       385   Apr 06 1998 14:39:59  callfailure.891873600
196  -rw-    119967   Apr 06 1998 14:40:59  iftable.891873647

219791360 bytes total (218087424 bytes free)
```

You can watch the details of the data collection using the **debug syscon perfdata** command:

```
SysCont# debug syscon perfdata

PERF: Start 'cmlineinfo' timer, next cycle in 5 mins, 31 secs
PERF: Timer event: 'popmgmt', 15 minutes
PERF: Bulk file create: 'popmgmt', shelf 0, pc 60ACBB10
PERF: SNMP resp: Type 4, 'popmgmt', shelf 0, error_st 0
PERF: FTP transfer: 'popmgmt', shelf 0, pc 60ACBB10
PERF: SNMP resp: Type 5, 'popmgmt', shelf 0, error_st 0
PERF: Deleted disk0:/performance/shelf-0/popmgmt.891809700
PERF: Timer event: 'cpmds0usage', 15 minutes
```

```
PERF: Polling 'cpmds0usage', shelf 0, pc 60ADE004
PERF: SNMP resp: Type 6, 'cpmds0usage', shelf 0, error_st 0
PERF: Logged polled data to disk0:/performance/shelf-0/cpmds0usage.891873900
PERF: Timer event: 'iftable', 12 minutes
PERF: Bulk file create: 'iftable', shelf 0, pc 60BE16AC
PERF: SNMP resp: Type 4, 'iftable', shelf 0, error_st 0
PERF: FTP transfer: 'iftable', shelf 0, pc 60BE16AC
PERF: SNMP resp: Type 5, 'iftable', shelf 0, error_st 0
PERF: Deleted disk0:/performance/shelf-0/iftable.891883559
```

Syslog Disk Logging Examples

The following example creates five subfiles. Each subfile has a maximum size of 2,000 KB; thus, the total available size is 10,000 KB. The subfiles are named mysyslog.cur, mysyslog.1, mysyslog.2, mysyslog.3, and mysyslog.4.

```
Router# configure terminal
Enter configuration commands, one per line.  End with CNTL/Z.
Router(config)# logging syslog-server 2000 5 mysyslog
Router(config)# end
%SYS-5-CONFIG_I: Configured from console by console
Router# dir disk0:
Directory of disk0:/
    3  drw-         0   Jan 17 1998 07:03:53  syslogd.dir
    4  drw-         0   Jan 12 1998 11:02:29  performance
   12  drw-         0   Jan 12 1998 11:56:37  configs
  242  drw-         0   Jan 21 1998 17:51:29  mysyslog.dir
340492288 bytes total (336560128 bytes free)
Router# dir disk0:/mysyslog.dir
Directory of disk0:/mysyslog.dir/
    0  -rw-         0   Jan 21 1998 17:51:29  mysyslog.1
    0  -rw-         0   Jan 21 1998 17:51:29  mysyslog.2
    0  -rw-         0   Jan 21 1998 17:51:29  mysyslog.3
    0  -rw-         0   Jan 21 1998 17:51:31  mysyslog.4
    0  -rw-         0   Jan 21 1998 17:51:31  mysyslog.cur
340492288 bytes total (336560128 bytes free)
```

FTP Server Examples

The following example enables the FTP Server and limits client access to the syslogd.dir directory on disk0:

```
ftp-server enable
ftp-server topdir disk0:/syslogd.dir
```

After these commands have been entered, you can FTP to the router. In the following example, a user connects to the router and gets the file syslogd.1. Notice that the user starts in the directory specified by the **ftp-server topdir** command.

```
FTPclient% ftp FTProuter
Connected to FTProuter.cisco.com.
```


CHAPTER **30**

System Controller Commands

This chapter describes the commands used to configure a system controller and managed shelves.

For system controller configuration tasks, refer to Chapter 29, "Configuring the System Controller and Managed Shelves."

attach shelf

To start a session on a manager dial or router shelf, use the **attach shelf** EXEC command.

> **attach shelf** *shelf-number*

Syntax	Description
shelf-number	Number of the shelf to attach to. The number can range from 0 to 9999.

Command Mode
EXEC

Usage Guidelines
This command first appeared in Cisco IOS Release 11.3 AA.

If you are connected to a system controller, use this command to start a session with a managed shelf.

If you are already connected to a shelf unit, this command disconnects from the current shelf and connects to the specified shelf.

Example
In the following example, a user connects to a managed shelf from the system controller from user EXEC mode. Notice that the user connects to the shelf at the current user privilege level.

```
systemcont> show syscon
Shelf# 2  172.23.66.102 SDB update   09:09:16 PST Jan 27 1998
systemcont> attach shelf 2
Trying 172.23.66.102 ... Open

shelf2> show syscon
Current uptime 09:10:00 PST Jan 27 1998, system controller 172.23.66.100
Last hello packet received at 09:09:16 PST Jan 27 1998
8625 Total SDP packets
```

```
    0 packets with bad MD5 hash
    4311 Hello packets received
    4314 Hello packets sent
    0 Command packets received
    0 Command packets sent
shelf2> quit

[Connection to 172.23.66.102 closed by foreign host]
systemcont>
```

Related Commands

To locate documentation of related commands, you can search online at www.cisco.com.

syscon address
syscon shelf-id

enable (poll-group configuration)

To start data collection for a performance data set, use the **enable** poll-group configuration command. The **no** form of this command disables data collection.

> **enable**
> **no enable**

Syntax Description

This command has no arguments or keywords.

Default

The system controller does not collect data.

Command Mode

Poll-group configuration

Usage Guidelines

This command first appeared in Cisco IOS Release 11.3 AA.

Use this command to enable data collection for a specific poll-group. This command is required for performance data collection. You must also set the transfer mode with the **transfer-mode** command in order to collect data.

The **no** form of this command disables data collection, but it does not delete the poll-group configuration. To reenable data collection, reconfigure the **enable** poll-group configuration command. You do not need to reenter the other poll-group configuration commands.

Example

The following example configures and enables data collection for the cmlineinfo poll group:

```
SysCont# configure terminal
Enter configuration commands, one per line.  End with Ctrl-Z.
SysCont(config)# syscon poll-group cmlineinfo
SysCont(config-poll-gr)# oid cmLineInfo.1.*
SysCont(config-poll-gr)# oid cmLineInfo.2.*
SysCont(config-poll-gr)# oid cmLineInfo.3.*
SysCont(config-poll-gr)# oid cmLineInfo.4.*
SysCont(config-poll-gr)# transfer-mode bulk
SysCont(config-poll-gr)# enable
SysCont(config-poll-gr)# exit
SysCont(config)# exit
SysCont#
Jan 23 17:47:05: %SYS-5-CONFIG_I: Configured from console by console
```

Related Commands

To locate documentation of related commands, you can search online at www.cisco.com.

oid
poll-interval
samples
shelf-type
show syscon perfdata
syscon poll-group
transfer-mode

ftp-server enable

To enable the FTP server, use the **ftp-server enable** global configuration command. The **no** form of this command disables the FTP server.

> **ftp-server enable**
> **no ftp-server enable**

Syntax Description

This command has no arguments or keywords.

Default
Disabled

Command Mode
Global configuration

Usage Guidelines
This command first appeared in Cisco IOS Release 11.3 AA.

When the FTP server is enabled, you can use FTP to transfer files to and from the router. For example, you can FTP performance data sets or syslog data subfiles to a network management station.

In order for clients to access files on the FTP server, you must configure both this command and the **ftp-server topdir** command.

Example
The following example enables the FTP server and limits client access to the syslogd.dir directory on disk0:

```
ftp-server enable
ftp-server topdir disk0:/syslogd.dir
```

Related Commands
To locate documentation of related commands, you can search online at www.cisco.com.

ftp-server topdir

ftp-server topdir

To restrict the region where FTP clients can read or write files, use the **ftp-server topdir** global configuration command. The **no** form of this command completely disables access.

> **ftp-server topdir** *directory*
> **no ftp-server topdir**

Syntax   Description

directory   Top-level directory path for FTP server client operations

Default
Denies read and write access to any location

Command Mode
Global configuration

Usage Guidelines
This command first appeared in Cisco IOS Release 11.3 AA.

You must specify a top-level directory in order for clients to use the FTP server. If you do not configure this command, clients will not be able to access any files or directories on the router.

You must also configure the **ftp-server enable** command to enable the FTP server on the router.

Example
The following example enables the FTP server and limits client access to the syslogd.dir directory on disk0:

```
ftp-server enable
ftp-server topdir disk0:/syslogd.dir
```

Related Commands
To locate documentation of related commands, you can search online at www.cisco.com.

ftp-server enable

logging syslog-server

To create subfiles for syslog-server logging, use the **logging syslog-server** global configuration command. The **no** form of this command stops storage of syslog messages in the subfiles.

> **logging syslog-server** *size number dir-name*
> **no logging syslog-server**

Syntax	Description
size	Maximum size of a syslog-server subfile in kilobytes (KB). The range is from 10 to 10,000.
number	Maximum number of syslog-server subfiles. The range is from 2 to 10.

Syntax	Description
dir-name	Root name of the subfile directory.

Default

No subfiles are created.

Command Mode

Global configuration

Usage Guidelines

This command first appeared in Cisco IOS Release 11.3 AA.

Use this command to create subfiles to store syslog messages the system controller receives from its managed shelves. The system controller will create subfiles using the name specified with a different extension to differentiate the subfiles. The current subfile is *name*.cur. The first archived subfile is *name*.1; the second is *name*.2. The last (oldest) archived subfile's extension is one less than the maximum number of subfiles.

After the subfiles are created, the system controller will add any syslog messages it receives to the current subfile. If the current subfile is full, all of the subfiles are renamed to use the next (higher) extension and a new current subfile is created.

The **no** form of this command stops the storage of syslog messages in the subfiles. However, the subfiles are not erased and remain on the disk.

Example

The following example creates five subfiles. Each subfile has a maximum size of 2,000KB. Thus, the total available size is 10,000KB. The subfiles are named mysyslog.cur, mysyslog.1, mysyslog.2, mysyslog.3, and mysyslog.4.

```
Router# configure terminal
Enter configuration commands, one per line.  End with Ctrl-Z.
Router(config)# logging syslog-server 2000 5 mysyslog
Router(config)# end
%SYS-5-CONFIG_I: Configured from console by console
Router# dir disk0:
Directory of disk0:/
    3  drw-          0   Jan 17 1998 07:03:53  syslogd.dir
    4  drw-          0   Jan 12 1998 11:02:29  performance
   12  drw-          0   Jan 12 1998 11:56:37  configs
  242  drw-          0   Jan 21 1998 17:51:29  mysyslog.dir
```

```
340492288 bytes total (336560128 bytes free)
Router# dir disk0:/mysyslog.dir
Directory of disk0:/mysyslog.dir/
    0  -rw-          0    Jan 21 1998 17:51:29   mysyslog.1
    0  -rw-          0    Jan 21 1998 17:51:29   mysyslog.2
    0  -rw-          0    Jan 21 1998 17:51:29   mysyslog.3
    0  -rw-          0    Jan 21 1998 17:51:31   mysyslog.4
    0  -rw-          0    Jan 21 1998 17:51:31   mysyslog.cur
340492288 bytes total (336560128 bytes free)
```

Related Commands

To locate documentation of related commands, you can search online at www.cisco.com.

show syslog-server

oid

To specify MIB variables for the system controller to collect, use the **oid** poll-group configuration command. The **no** form of this command disables collection of the specified MIB variable.

> **oid** *object-id*
> **no oid** [*object-id*]

Syntax

object-id

Description

Object ID of the data to collect

Default

Only the sysUptime MIB variable is collected.

Command Mode

Poll-group configuration

Usage Guidelines

This command first appeared in Cisco IOS Release 11.3 AA.

Use this command to specify which MIB variables to collect for a specific data collection set. Enter this command once for each MIB variable you wish to collect. In order for the system controller to collect data, you must specify at least one object ID.

Part III

Command Reference

For descriptions of supported MIBs and how to use MIBs, see Cisco's MIB Web site on CCO at http://www.cisco.com/public/sw-center/netmgmt/cmtk/mibs.shtml.

The **no** form of this command disables data collection for the specified MIB variable. If you do not specify an object ID, data collection is disabled for every variable except sysUptime.

Use the following guidelines when specifying object IDs:

● Scalar MIB objects are specified with a ".n.0" instance. For example, **oid lsystem.57.0** or **oid 1.3.6.1.4.1.9.2.1.57.0** specifies avgBusy1.

● Columns and tables are specified with ".n.*" object IDs. For example, **oid ifEntry.2.*** specifies the ifDescr column of the ifTable, and **oid interfaces.2.*** specifies the ifTable.

NOTE   Columns are retrievable only in poll transfer mode.

● Tables for bulk transfer must be specified using the object ID with the table-defining "SEQUENCE OF ...." SYNTAX statement.

Example

The following example configures the system controller to collect the rows specified by cmLineInfo.1.*, cmLineInfo.2.*, cmLineInfo.3.*, and cmLineInfo.4.* using the bulk transfer mode:

```
SysCont# configure terminal
Enter configuration commands, one per line.  End with Ctrl-Z.
SysCont(config)# syscon poll-group cmlineinfo
SysCont(config-poll-gr)# oid cmLineInfo.1.*
SysCont(config-poll-gr)# oid cmLineInfo.2.*
SysCont(config-poll-gr)# oid cmLineInfo.3.*
SysCont(config-poll-gr)# oid cmLineInfo.4.*
SysCont(config-poll-gr)# transfer-mode bulk
SysCont(config-poll-gr)# enable
SysCont(config-poll-gr)# exit
SysCont(config)# exit
SysCont#
Jan 23 17:47:05: %SYS-5-CONFIG_I: Configured from console by console
```

Related Commands

To locate documentation of related commands, you can search online at www.cisco.com.

enable (poll-group configuration)
poll-interval
samples

shelf-type
show syscon perfdata
syscon poll-group
transfer-mode

poll-interval

To change the interval for data collection by system controller, use the **poll-interval** poll-group configuration command. The **no** form of this command returns the data collection interval to the default value.

> **poll-interval** *minutes*
> **no poll-interval**

Syntax	Description
minutes	Data collection interval, in minutes. The range is from 1 to 10,080. The default is 10.

Default

10 minutes

Command Mode

Poll-group configuration

Usage Guidelines

This command first appeared in Cisco IOS Release 11.3 AA.

Use this command to specify how often the system controller collects data for a particular performance data set from its managed shelves.

When the poll group is enabled or the first shelf in a poll group is discovered, the system controller acts as if the data collection started at midnight. The system controller will then collect data at the next scheduled data collection time. The data collection for a poll group is synchronized; the system controller collects data from all managed shelves for a poll group at the same time.

Example

The following example configures the system controller to collect data every 20 minutes. The system controller will store a maximum of five data sets for this poll group. Thus, data will be stored for 100 minutes after it is collected.

```
SysCont# configure terminal
Enter configuration commands, one per line.  End with Ctrl-Z.
SysCont(config)# syscon poll-group cmlineinfo
SysCont(config-poll-gr)# oid cmLineInfo.1.*
SysCont(config-poll-gr)# oid cmLineInfo.2.*
SysCont(config-poll-gr)# oid cmLineInfo.3.*
SysCont(config-poll-gr)# oid cmLineInfo.4.*
SysCont(config-poll-gr)# transfer-mode bulk
SysCont(config-poll-gr)# poll-interval 20
SysCont(config-poll-gr)# samples 5
SysCont(config-poll-gr)# enable
SysCont(config-poll-gr)# exit
SysCont(config)# exit
SysCont#
Jan 23 17:47:05: %SYS-5-CONFIG_I: Configured from console by console
```

Related Commands

To locate documentation of related commands, you can search online at www.cisco.com.

enable (poll-group configuration)
oid
samples
shelf-type
show syscon perfdata
syscon poll-group
transfer-mode

samples

To specify the maximum number of performance data sets to store on the disk for a poll group, use the **samples** poll-group configuration command. The **no** form of this command returns the value to the default.

> **samples** *number*
> **no samples**

Syntax

number	Maximum number of performance data log files to store on the system controller disk for a particular poll group. The value ranges from 2 to 1000. The default is 10.

Default

A maximum of 10 performance data sets are stored.

Command Mode

Poll-group configuration

Usage Guidelines

This command first appeared in Cisco IOS Release 11.3 AA.

Use this command to limit the number of performance data log files residing on the system controller disk for that poll-group. Once the limit is reached, the oldest file will be deleted after a new file is successfully written.

Use this command and the **poll-interval** command to determine how long it will take for a file to be deleted and how much disk space the files will require. If you set the sample number too low, files will be deleted soon after they are created, leaving you with little time to transfer the files to a network management station. If you set the sample number too high, the files may fill the disk.

Example

The following example configures the system controller to store a maximum of five data sets for this poll group. The system controller will collect data every 20 minutes. Thus, data will be stored for 100 minutes after it is collected.

```
SysCont# configure terminal
Enter configuration commands, one per line.  End with Ctrl-Z.
SysCont(config)# syscon poll-group cmlineinfo
SysCont(config-poll-gr)# oid cmLineInfo.1.*
SysCont(config-poll-gr)# oid cmLineInfo.2.*
SysCont(config-poll-gr)# oid cmLineInfo.3.*
SysCont(config-poll-gr)# oid cmLineInfo.4.*
SysCont(config-poll-gr)# transfer-mode bulk
SysCont(config-poll-gr)# poll-interval 20
SysCont(config-poll-gr)# samples 5
SysCont(config-poll-gr)# enable
SysCont(config-poll-gr)# exit
SysCont(config)# exit
```

Related Commands

To locate documentation of related commands, you can search online at www.cisco.com.

enable (poll-group configuration)
oid
poll-interval

Part
III

Command Reference

shelf-type
show syscon perfdata
syscon poll-group
transfer-mode

shelf-type

To specify which shelf types the system controller collects data from, use the **shelf-type** poll-group configuration command. The **no** form of this command removes the command from the configuration.

> **shelf-type** *sysObjectID*
> **no shelf-type** *sysObjectID*

Syntax

sysObjectID

Description

CISCO-PRODUCTS-MIB sysObjectID. This argument can have the following values:

- 108—Cisco 7206
- 109—Cisco AS5200
- 125—Cisco 7204
- 162—Cisco AS5300
- 188—Cisco AS5800

Although you can enter other values for this argument, the system controller will only collect data from devices that can be managed by the system controller.

Default

The system controller collects data from all discovered shelves.

Command Mode

Poll-group configuration

Usage Guidelines

This command first appeared in Cisco IOS Release 11.3 AA.

If this command is not configured, the system controller will collect data from all known shelves. However, if you configure this command with a particular shelf type, the system controller will only collect data from the specified shelves. To collect data from multiple shelf types, enter this command once for each shelf type.

The **no** form of this command removes the corresponding command from the configuration. If no other **shelf-type** commands remain, the system controller will collect data from all known shelves. If one or more **shelf-type** commands remain in the configuration, the system controller will collect data only from the remaining configured shelf types.

In order to turn off data collection for one shelf when you are currently collecting data from all shelves, enter the **shelf-type** command for each of the remaining shelves.

Example

The following example collects data from Cisco 7204 routers using the bulk transfer method:

```
SysCont# configure terminal
Enter configuration commands, one per line.  End with Ctrl-Z.
SysCont(config)# syscon poll-group cmlineinfo
SysCont(config-poll-gr)# oid cmLineInfo.1.*
SysCont(config-poll-gr)# oid cmLineInfo.2.*
SysCont(config-poll-gr)# oid cmLineInfo.3.*
SysCont(config-poll-gr)# oid cmLineInfo.4.*
SysCont(config-poll-gr)# transfer-mode bulk
SysCont(config-poll-gr)# shelf-type 125
SysCont(config-poll-gr)# enable
SysCont(config-poll-gr)# exit
SysCont(config)# exit
SysCont#
Jan 23 17:47:05: %SYS-5-CONFIG_I: Configured from console by console
```

Related Commands

To locate documentation of related commands, you can search online at www.cisco.com.

enable (poll-group configuration)
oid
poll-interval
samples
show syscon perfdata
syscon poll-group
transfer-mode

show syscon discover

To display information about discovered shelves, use the **show syscon discover** EXEC command.

show syscon discover [brief | full]

Syntax	Description
brief	(Optional) Displays a list of discovered shelves. This is the default.
full	(Optional) Displays detailed information about discovered shelves.

Command Mode

EXEC

Default

Brief

Usage Guidelines

This command first appeared in Cisco IOS Release 11.3 AA.

The **show syscon discover full** command includes output from the **show syscon perfdata** and **show syscon monitor** commands.

Sample Display

The following is sample output from the **show syscon discover brief** command:

```
Syscon# show syscon discover brief

Shelf# 3  10.0.1.2 Last update  11:15:29 PST Jan 22 1998
```

Table 30-1 describes the fields shown in this display.

Table 30-1 *Show Syscon Discover Brief Field Descritpions*

Field	Description
Shelf# 3	Identification number for this shelf.
10.0.1.2	IP address for this shelf.
Last update	Time and date of the last update from the shelf.

The following is sample output from the **show syscon discover full** command:

```
Syscon# show syscon discover full

Shelf# 3  10.0.1.2 Last update  11:16:27 PST Jan 22 1998 type products.108
ifIndex     Type   OperStatus    Speed        Last Changed
      1       1    down             9000          249
      2       1    down             9000          249
      3       1    down             9000          249
      4       1    down             9000          249
      5       1    down             9000          249
      6       1    down             9000          249
      7       1    down             9000          249
      8       1    down             9000          249
      9       1    down             9000          249
     10       1    down             9000          249
    ...

Performance Data Collection:

          Poll       Last      Total     Get     GetBulk   Bulk Xfer
Shelf#    Group      File    Requests Requests Requests   Requests Errors
    2   chassis    886010845    151       0         0        151      0
        popmgmt    886011146   5180     148      5032          0      0


Health monitor process is not running.
```

Table 30-2 describes the fields shown in this display.

Table 30-2 *Show Syscon Discover Full Field Descriptions*

Field	Description
Shelf# 3	Identification number for this shelf.
10.0.1.2	IP address for this shelf.
Last update	Time and date of the last update from the shelf.
type products.108	Type of shelf. The value can be one of the following: • 108 - Cisco 7206 • 109 - Cisco AS5200 • 125 - Cisco 7204 • 162 - Cisco AS5300
ifIndex	Interface index.
Type	Type of interface, corresponding to ifType.
OperStatus	Operational status of the interface.
Speed	Speed of the interface.
Last Changed	Value of ifLastChanged.

Continues

Part III

Command Reference

Table 30-2   *Show Syscon Discover Full Field Descriptions (Continued)*

Field	Description
Performance Data Collection...	Performance data collection information. The output corresponds to the output of the **show syscon perfdata** command. Refer to the **show syscon perfdata** command for field descriptions.
Health Monitor process...	Current status of the Health Monitor process. The output corresponds to the output of the **show syscon monitor** command. Refer to the **show syscon monitor** command for field descriptions.

Related Commands

To locate documentation of related commands, you can search online at www.cisco.com.

show syscon monitor
show syscon perfdata
show syscon sdp (system controller)
syscon community
syscon password

show syscon mibpoll

To display information about managed shelves contained in the Health Monitor MIB, use the **show syscon mibpoll** EXEC command.

> **show syscon mibpoll**

Syntax Description

This command has no arguments or keywords.

Command Mode

EXEC

Usage Guidelines

This command first appeared in Cisco IOS Release 11.3 AA.

This command displays the shelf statistics contained in the Health Monitor MIB on the system controller. The system controller collects this information from its managed shelves.

Sample Display

The following is sample output from the **show syscon mibpoll** command:

```
Router# show syscon mibpoll

Healthmon MIB count entry status:

Shelf ID 1 MIB entries last update 18:22:06 EDT Jan 12 1998.
T1E1 Lines     DS0s          Modems
Up      Down   Active Total  Total  Inuse   Unavailable
1       1      23     46     24     0       0


IO Mem         CPU    EgressPort     EgressPort
Used    Free   Busy1  InOctetUtil    OutOctetUtil
1378476 7010132 20    0              0


Healthmon MIB summary of count entry status:

Total   Total          Total         Total
Shelves T1E1 Lines     DS0s          Modems
        Up     Down    Active Total  Total  Inuse   Unavailable
1       1      1       23     46     24     0       0
```

Table 30-3 describes the fields shown in this display.

Table 30-3 *Show Syscon Mibpoll Output Field Descriptions*

Field	Description
Shelf ID	Shelf ID of the managed shelf.
last update	Last time the system controller polled these MIB variables on the managed shelf.
T1E1 Lines	
Up	Number of TI/EI lines up.
Down	Number of TI/EI lines with operational status down and administrative status up.
DSOs	
Active	Number of active DSOs.
Total	Number of DSOs.
Modems	
Total	Number of installed modems.
Inuse	Number of modems being used.
Unavailable	Number of modems that are not being used but cannot accept calls.

Continues

Table 30-3 *Show Syscon Mibpoll Output Field Descriptions (Continued)*

Field	Description
IO Mem	
Used	Number of bytes of IO memory that are currently in use by applications on the managed device.
Free	Number of bytes of IO memory that are currently available to use on the managed device.
CPU Busy1	Exponentially decayed moving average of the CPU busy percentage.
EgressPort InOctetUtil	Percent utilization of total number of octets received on all the active egress interfaces, including framing characters. A port is considered to be an egress port if the port speed is greater than 1,544,000bps.
EgressPort OutOctetUtil	Percent utilization of the total number of octets transmitted out on all the active egress interfaces, including framing characters. A port is considered to be an egress port if the port speed is greater than 1,544,000bps.
Total Shelves	Number of shelves polled.
Total T1E1 Lines	
Up	Total number of TI/EI lines up in all managed shelves.
Down	Total number of TI/EI lines with operational status down and administrative status up in all managed shelves.
Total DSOs	
Active	Total number of active DSOs in all managed shelves.
Total	Total number of DSOs in all managed shelves.
Total Modems	
Total	Total number of installed modems in all managed shelves.
Inuse	Total number of modems being used in all managed shelves.
Unavailable	Total number of modems unavailable for use.

Related Commands

To locate documentation of related commands, you can search online at www.cisco.com.

show syscon monitor
syscon monitor
syscon monitor traps

show syscon monitor

To display information about monitored shelf attributes, use the **show syscon monitor** EXEC command.

show syscon monitor

Syntax Description

This command has no arguments or keywords.

Command Mode

EXEC

Usage Guidelines

This command first appeared in Cisco IOS Release 11.3 AA.

This command is useful in determining the current status of monitored shelves.

Sample Display

The following example is sample output from the **show syscon monitor** command. The first group of lines show attributes being monitored separately on each shelf. The second group of lines show monitored attributes for all shelves combined.

```
Router# show syscon monitor

Health Monitor setup status on the shel(f,ves):
Shelf#   Shelf IP Address       Monitoring Type Threshold Value Status
    1    172.27.32.173          IO-Mem                 11         Active

Health Monitor setup status on the system controller:
Monitoring Type Threshold Value Status
  Trunk           12            Active
  Modem           50            Active
```

Table 30-4 describes the fields shown in this display.

Table 30-4 *Show Syscon Monitor output Field Descriptions*

Field	Description
Shelf#	Shelf ID of the managed shelf.
Shelf IP Address	IP address of the managed shelf.
Monitoring Type	Attribute being monitored, as set by the **syscon monitor** command.

Continues

Table 30-4 *Show Syscon Monitor output Field Descriptions (Continued)*

Field	Description
Threshold Value	Threshold value for the attribute. If the attribute exceeds this value, the shelf will send a trap to the system controller for individually monitored attributes, or the system controller will generate a trap for combined attributes.
Status	Current status of threshold monitoring on the managed shelf.

Related Commands

To locate documentation of related commands, you can search online at www.cisco.com.

show syscon mibpoll
syscon monitor
syscon monitor traps

show syscon perfdata

To display information about performance data collection, use the **show syscon perfdata** EXEC command.

show syscon perfdata

Syntax Description

This command has no arguments or keywords.

Command Mode

EXEC

Usage Guidelines

This command first appeared in Cisco IOS Release 11.3 AA.

The output from this command also appears in the **show syscon discover full** command output.

Sample Display

The following is sample output from the **show syscon perfdata** command:

```
SysCont# show syscon perfdata

Performance Data Collection:
```

```
           Poll      Last     Total    Get    GetBulk  Bulk Xfer
Shelf#     Group     File    Requests Requests Requests Requests   Errors
    2    chassis   886010845    151       0        0       151        0
         popmgmt   886011146   5180      148      5032       0         0
```

Table 30-5 describes the fields shown in this display.

Table 30-5 *Show Syscon Perfdata Field Descriptions*

Field	Description
Shelf#	Shelf ID.
Poll Group	Poll group.
Last File	UNIX timestamp for last performance data collection file.
Total Requests	Total number of sets of requested information.
Get Requests	Number of get requests sent by the system controller.
GetBulk Requests	Number of getbulk requests sent by the system controller.
Bulk Xfer Requests	Number of bulk transfer requests sent by the system controller.
Errors	Number of errors in transferring information.

Related Commands

To locate documentation of related commands, you can search online at www.cisco.com.

enable (poll-group configuration)
oid
poll-interval
samples
shelf-type
syscon poll-group
transfer-mode

show syscon sdp (managed shelf)

To display information about the Shelf Discovery Protocol, use the **show syscon sdp** EXEC command.

> **show syscon sdp**

Syntax Description

This command has no arguments or keywords.

Command Mode

EXEC

Usage Guidelines

This command first appeared in Cisco IOS Release 11.3 AA.

Sample Display

The following is sample output from the **show syscon sdp** command:

```
Shelf# show syscon sdp

Current time 10:46:32 PST Jan 28 1998, system controller 172.23.66.100
Last hello packet received at 10:45:38 PST Jan 28 1998
11773 Total SDP packets
    0 packets with bad MD5 hash
    5884 Hello packets received
    5889 Hello packets sent
    0 Command packets received
    0 Command packets sent
```

Table 30-6 describes the fields shown in the sample display.

Table 30-6 *Show Syscon SDP Field Descriptions*

Field	Description
Current time	Current time and date.
system controller	IP address of the system controller.
Last hello packet received	Time and date the last Hello packet from the system controller was received by the shelf.
Total SDP packets	Total number of SDP packets sent or received by the shelf.
packets with bad MD5 hash	Number of packets with a bad MD5 hash.
Hello packets received	Number of Hello packets received by the shelf from the system controller.
Hello packets sent	Number of Hello packets sent from the shelf to the system controller.
Command packets received	Number of packets containing commands received by the shelf.
Command packets sent	Number of commands sent by the shelf.

Related Commands

To locate documentation of related commands, you can search online at www.cisco.com.

syscon address
syscon source-interface

show syscon sdp (system controller)

To display information about the Shelf Discovery Protocol, use the **show syscon sdp** EXEC command.

show syscon sdp

Syntax Description

This command has no arguments or keywords.

Command Mode

EXEC

Usage Guidelines

This command first appeared in Cisco IOS Release 11.3 AA.

Sample Display

The following is sample output from the **show syscon sdp** command:

```
Syscon# show syscon sdp

3006 Total SDP packets
    6 Bad packets with bad MD5 hash
    1503 Hello packets received
    1497 Hello packets sent
    0 Command packets received
    0 Command packets sent
```

Table 30-7 describes the fields shown in the sample display.

Table 30-7 *Show Syscon SDP Field Descriptions*

Field	Description
Total SDP packets	Total number of SDP packets sent or received by the system controller.
Bad packets with bad MD5 hash	Number of packets with a bad MD5 hash.
Hello packets received	Number of Hello packets received by the system controller from managed shelves.
Hello packets sent	Number of Hello packets sent from the system controller to managed shelves.
Command packets received	Number of packets containing commands received by the system controller.
Command packets sent	Number of commands sent by the system controller.

Related Commands

To locate documentation of related commands, you can search online at www.cisco.com.

show syscon discover
syscon community
syscon password

show syslog-server

To display certain syslog messages in the syslog history table, use the **show syslog-server** EXEC command.

show syslog-server [**last** *number* | **since** [**date** *date*] *hh:mm:ss*] [**source** *ip-address*]

Syntax	Description
last	(Optional) Displays the newest syslog messages.
number	(Optional) Number of syslog messages to display. You can display up to the last 500 messages.
since	(Optional) Displays messages after the specified time.
date *date*	(Optional) Displays messages starting on this date. The format is either *month day year* or *day month year*. If you do not specify a date, only messages from the current date are displayed.
hh:mm:ss	(Optional) Displays messages starting at this time.
source *ip-address*	(Optional) Displays syslog messages from the specified host.

Command Mode

EXEC

Usage Guidelines

This command first appeared in Cisco IOS Release 11.3 AA.

Use this command to display syslog messages the system controller has stored in its logging history subfiles. If you do not specify any filter options, all of the messages in all of the subfiles are displayed. When you specify multiple filters for messages, only messages that meet all of the criteria are displayed.

Sample Display

The following example displays the last three messages the system controller received:

```
Router# show syslog-server last 3

Jan  7 21:44:09 [172.23.3.200] %CI-3-BLOWER: ps2 fan failure
Jan  7 21:50:09 [172.23.3.200] %CI-3-PSFAIL: Power supply 2 failure
Jan  7 21:50:10 [172.23.3.200] %CI-3-BLOWER: ps2 fan failure
```

The following example displays the last message from the host at 172.23.3.200:

```
Router# show syslog-server source 172.23.3.200 last 1

Jan  7 21:50:10 [172.23.3.200] %CI-3-BLOWER: ps2 fan failure
```

The following example displays the messages generated since 9:50 p.m. on January 7, 1998:

```
Router# show syslog-server since date 7 jan 1998 21:50:00

Jan  7 21:50:09 [172.23.3.200] %CI-3-PSFAIL: Power supply 2 failure
Jan  7 21:50:10 [172.23.3.200] %CI-3-BLOWER: ps2 fan failure
```

Table 30-8 explains the fields shown in these examples, using the first line from the first example for illustrative purposes.

Table 30-8   *Show Syslog-Server Command Output Field Descriptions*

Field	Description
Jan 7	Date of the syslog message.
21:44:09	Time the syslog message was generated.
[172.23.3.200]	IP address of the host generating the syslog message.
%CI-3-BLOWER	Error message.
ps2 fan failure	Message Text.

Related Commands

To locate documentation of related commands, you can search online at www.cisco.com.

logging syslog-server

syscon address

To specify the system controller for a managed shelf, use the **syscon address** global configuration command. Use the **no** form of this command to stop the management of the shelf by the system controller.

> **syscon address** *ip-address password*
> **no syscon address**

Syntax	Description
ip-address	IP address of the system controller
password	Password string

Default

No system controller is specified.

Command Mode

Global configuration

Usage Guidelines

This command first appeared in Cisco IOS Release 11.3 AA.

This command is required in order for the shelf to be managed by the system controller. The password must match the password configured on the system controller through the **syscon password** command.

Example

The following example configures a shelf to be managed by a system controller at 10.2.3.4 using the password green:

```
syscon address 10.2.3.4 green
```

Related Commands

To locate documentation of related commands, you can search online at www.cisco.com.

show syscon sdp (managed shelf)
syscon source-interface

syscon community

To set the SNMP community string the system controller uses to communicate with its managed shelves, use the **syscon community** global configuration command. The **no** form of this command sets the community string to public.

> **syscon community** *string*
> **no syscon community**

Syntax	Description
string	SNMP community string

Default

The community string is private.

Command Mode

Global configuration

Usage Guidelines

This command first appeared in Cisco IOS Release 11.3 AA.

This command is required in order to configure the system controller. The system controller automatically configures its managed shelves to accept this SNMP community string.

Example

The following example configures the system controller to use the community string purple when communicating with managed shelves using SNMP. The managed shelves will automatically be configured to accept the community string of purple from the system controller.

```
syscon community purple
```

Related Commands

To locate documentation of related commands, you can search online at www.cisco.com.

show syscon discover
show syscon sdp (system controller)
syscon password

syscon monitor

To specify attributes for the Health Monitor on the system controller to monitor, use the **syscon monitor** global configuration command. The **no** form of this command disables monitoring for the specified attribute.

> **syscon monitor** {**io-mem** *percent* | **modem** *percent* | **trunk** *percent*}
> **no syscon monitor** [**io-mem** | **modem** | **trunk**]

Syntax	Description
io-mem	Monitors shelf IO memory utilization
modem	Monitors total modem utilization for all shelves combined
trunk	Monitors total DS0 utilization for all shelves combined
percent	Percent utilization value for triggering traps

Default

The system controller does not monitor any attributes.

Command Mode

Global configuration

Usage Guidelines

This command first appeared in Cisco IOS Release 11.3 AA.

When you configure the **syscon monitor** command on the system controller, the system controller automatically configures each managed shelf to generate traps. The system controller will use SNMP to configure the following:

● Expressions in the CISCO-EXPRESSION-MIB to calculate the attributes

● RMON alarms to poll the attributes at specific intervals

● RMON events to send traps to the system controller when an attribute exceeds its specified threshold

For attributes that are total percentages for all shelves combined, the system controller uses the information in the Health Monitor MIB to calculate the current total percentage. For example, the system controller calculates the total modem usage percentage from the individual usage values in the Health Monitor MIB.

Enter this command once for each attribute you wish to monitor.

Example

The following example configures the managed shelves to monitor IO memory and shelf utilization. If IO memory utilization exceeds 80 percent or modem utilization exceeds 70 percent, the shelf sends a trap to the system controller.

```
syscon password blue
syscon community public
```

```
syscon monitor io-mem 80
syscon monitor modem 70
snmp-server manager
```

Related Commands

To locate documentation of related commands, you can search online at www.cisco.com.

syscon monitor
show syscon monitor
syscon monitor traps

syscon monitor traps

To enable Health Monitor MIB traps on the system controller, use the **syscon monitor traps** global configuration command. The **no** form of this command disables Health Monitor MIB traps.

> **syscon monitor traps**
> **no syscon monitor traps**

Part
III

Command Reference

Syntax Description

This command has no arguments or keywords.

Default

The system controller does not send traps.

Command Mode

Global configuration

Usage Guidelines

This command first appeared in Cisco IOS Release 11.3 AA.

This command enables the system controller to send Health Monitor MIB traps to network management stations. When the system controller receives a threshold trap from one of its managed shelves or generates a Health Monitor trap itself, it will forward the trap on to the management stations.

The traps are sent to the SNMP managers as specified by the **snmp-server hosts** command. You must configure this command in order to send traps from the system controller. In addition, enable trap generation using the **snmp-server enable traps** command.

Use the **syscon monitor** command to specify which threshold traps to configure on the shelves. If you do not specify enabled traps through the **syscon monitor** command, the system controller will not receive any traps from its managed shelves.

Example

The following example configures the router to send traps to the host myhost.cisco.com using the community string public. The system controller will generate modem utilization traps if the total modem utilization exceeds 70 percent.

```
syscon password blue
syscon community public
syscon monitor modem 70
syscon monitor traps
snmp-server host myhost.cisco.com public
snmp-server enable traps
snmp-server manager
```

Related Commands

To locate documentation of related commands, you can search online at www.cisco.com.

show syscon monitor
snmp-server enable traps
snmp-server host
syscon monitor

syscon password

To set the password used by the system controller to communicate with its managed shelves, use the **syscon password** global configuration command. This command also configures the device as a system controller. The **no** form of this command deletes the password and disables the system controller.

> **syscon password** *string*
> **no syscon password**

Syntax   Description

string   Password string

Default

No password is set.

Command Mode

Global configuration

Usage Guidelines

This command first appeared in Cisco IOS Release 11.3 AA.

This command is required to use any of the system controller features. The password must match the password specified on the shelves through the **syscon address** command. The managed shelves use this password to authenticate messages from the system controller.

Example

The following example configures the system controller to use the password yellow to communicate with its managed shelves:

```
syscon password yellow
```

Related Commands

To locate documentation of related commands, you can search online at www.cisco.com.

show syscon discover
show syscon sdp (system controller)
syscon community

syscon poll-group

To specify a performance data set for the system controller to collect, use the **syscon poll-group** global configuration command. The **no** form of this command stops data collection and removes the poll group from the configuration.

> **syscon poll-group** *name*
> **no syscon poll-group** *name*

Syntax	Description
name	Name of this performance data set

Default

The system controller collects no performance data.

Command Mode

Global configuration

Usage Guidelines

This command first appeared in Cisco IOS Release 11.3 AA.

Use this command on the system controller to configure performance data collection. The system controller periodically collects the specified MIB variables from managed shelves and stores the data on a disk local to the system controller. A new file will be created each time the system controller collects data from a shelf.

This command puts the router into poll-group configuration mode. You can enter any of the following commands:

- **enable (poll-group configuration)**

- **oid**

- **poll-interval**

- **samples**

- **shelf-type**

- **transfer-mode**

You must specify the desired Object IDs and the transfer mode. If you do not specify the **shelf-type** command, the system controller collects data from all discovered shelves. The default data collection interval is 10 minutes. The default maximum number of samples is 10. To begin the data collection process, configure the **enable** command.

Example

The following example configures the poll group cmlineinfo:

```
SysCont# configure terminal
Enter configuration commands, one per line.  End with Ctrl-Z.
SysCont(config)# syscon poll-group cmlineinfo
SysCont(config-poll-gr)# oid cmLineInfo.1.*
SysCont(config-poll-gr)# oid cmLineInfo.2.*
SysCont(config-poll-gr)# oid cmLineInfo.3.*
SysCont(config-poll-gr)# oid cmLineInfo.4.*
SysCont(config-poll-gr)# transfer-mode bulk
SysCont(config-poll-gr)# enable
SysCont(config-poll-gr)# exit
SysCont(config)# exit
SysCont#
Jan 23 17:47:05: %SYS-5-CONFIG_I: Configured from console by console
```

Related Commands

To locate documentation of related commands, you can search online at www.cisco.com.

enable (poll-group configuration)
oid
poll-interval
samples
shelf-type
show syscon perfdata
transfer-mode

syscon shelf-id

To specify a shelf ID for a managed shelf, use the **syscon shelf-id** global configuration command. The **no** form of this command removes the shelf ID.

> **syscon shelf-id** *number*
> **no syscon shelf-id**

Syntax

number	Shelf ID. The value ranges from 0 to 9999.

Default

No shelf ID is specified.

Command Mode

Global configuration

Usage Guidelines

This command first appeared in Cisco IOS Release 11.3 AA.

Use this command to specify a shelf ID for a managed shelf. Some platforms, such as the Cisco AS5800, use other commands to assign a shelf ID. In these situations, do not specify a shelf ID with the **syscon shelf-id** command. Use the platform-specific command instead.

Example

The following example configures a shelf ID of 5 for the managed shelf:

```
syscon shelf-id 5
```

Related Commands

To locate documentation of related commands, you can search online at www.cisco.com.

show syscon sdp (managed shelf)
syscon address

syscon source-interface

To specify the interface to use for the source address in SDP packets, use the **syscon source-interface** global configuration command. Use the **no** form of this command to return to the default source interface for a packet, the interface that transmitted the packet from the shelf.

> **syscon source-interface** *interface*
> **no syscon source-interface**

Syntax	Description
interface	Type and number of the interface to use for the source IP address

Default

SDP packets use the IP address of the output interface.

Command Mode

Global configuration

Usage Guidelines

This command first appeared in Cisco IOS Release 11.3 AA.

Use this command to ensure that all SDP packets sent by the managed shelf have the same source IP address.

Example

The following example configures a shelf to use the IP address of the Ethernet99/1/0 interface:

```
syscon source-address Ethernet99/1/0
```

Related Commands

To locate documentation of related commands, you can search online at www.cisco.com.

show syscon sdp (managed shelf)
syscon shelf-id

transfer-mode

To specify the transfer method for collecting performance data from shelves, use the **transfer-mode** poll-group configuration command.

$$\text{transfer-mode } \{\textbf{bulk} \mid \textbf{poll}\}$$

Syntax	Description
bulk	Bulk transfer (FTP)
poll	SNMP polling

Default

The system controller does not collect data.

Command Mode

Poll-group configuration

Usage Guidelines

This command first appeared in Cisco IOS Release 11.3 AA.

Use this command to specify which method the system controller uses to collect data from managed shelves. You must specify a transfer mode in order to collect performance data.

If you are collecting a large amount of data, use the bulk transfer method to avoid sending large numbers of SNMP packets. The bulk transfer method has less of an impact on the managed shelves and creates less network traffic than the poll transfer method.

The two methods generate different data formats. You may want to use the same transfer method for all of your poll groups so that all of the data is in the same format. Refer to the "Examples" section for examples of the two formats.

Bulk file formats have the following characteristics:

● Tables are always written in lexical order.

- MIB objects with a SYNTAX of OCTET STRING are stored as octet strings, not as ASCII characters.

Refer to the CISCO-BULK-FILE-MIB for more information on the format of the bulk files.

Examples

The following example configures the system controller to use the SNMP polling to collect the data:

```
syscon poll-group busyPerpoll
  oid lsystem.56.0
  oid lsystem.57.0
  oid lsystem.58.0
  oid interfaces.2.*
  transfer-mode poll
  enable
```

The following is a sample data collection file from the configuration:

```
sysUpTime.0
lsystem.56.0
lsystem.57.0
lsystem.58.0
interfaces.2
```

```
sysUpTime.0 1164196 lsystem.56.0 0 lsystem.57.0 0 lsystem.58.0 1 ifEntry.1.1 1 ifEntry.1.2
2 ifEntry.1.3 3 ifEntry.1.4 4 ifEntry.1.5 5 ifEntry.1.6 6 ifEntry.1.7 7 ifEntry.1.8 8
ifEntry.1.9 9 ifEntry.1.10 10 ifEntry.2.1 FastEthernet0/0 ifEntry.2.2 Ethernet2/0
ifEntry.2.3 Ethernet2/1 ifEntry.2.4 Ethernet2/2 ifEntry.2.5 Ethernet2/3 ifEntry.2.6
Loopback1 ifEntry.2.7 Tunnel8 ifEntry.2.8 Tunnel10 ifEntry.2.9 Dialer1 ifEntry.2.10 Lex30
ifEntry.3.1 6 ifEntry.3.2 6 ifEntry.3.3 6 ifEntry.3.4 6 ifEntry.3.5 6 ifEntry.3.6 24
ifEntry.3.7 1 ifEntry.3.8 1 ifEntry.3.9 22 ifEntry.3.10 6 ifEntry.4.1 1500 ifEntry.4.2 1500
ifEntry.4.3 1500 ifEntry.4.4 1500 ifEntry.4.5 1500 ifEntry.4.6 1514 ifEntry.4.7 1514
ifEntry.4.8 1514 ifEntry.4.9 1500 ifEntry.4.10 1500 ifEntry.5.1 100000000 ifEntry.5.2
10000000 ifEntry.5.3 10000000 ifEntry.5.4 10000000 ifEntry.5.5 10000000 ifEntry.5.6
4294967295 ifEntry.5.7 9000 ifEntry.5.8 9000 ifEntry.5.9 56000 ifEntry.5.10 10000000
ifEntry.6.1 ifEntry.6.1 ifEntry.6.2 ifE!
 ntry.6.2 ifEntry.6.3 ifEntry.6.3 ifEntry.6.4 ifEntry.6.4 ifEntry.6.5 ifEntry.6.5
ifEntry.6.6  ifEntry.6.7  ifEntry.6.8  ifEntry.6.9  ifEntry.6.10  ifEntry.7.1 2 ifEntry.7.2
1 ifEntry.7.3 2 ifEntry.7.4 2 ifEntry.7.5 2 ifEntry.7.6 1 ifEntry.7.7 1 ifEntry.7.8 1
ifEntry.7.9 1 ifEntry.7.10 1 ifEntry.8.1 2 ifEntry.8.2 1 ifEntry.8.3 2 ifEntry.8.4 2
ifEntry.8.5 2 ifEntry.8.6 1 ifEntry.8.7 2 ifEntry.8.8 2 ifEntry.8.9 5 ifEntry.8.10 2
ifEntry.9.1 817 ifEntry.9.2 817 ifEntry.9.3 817 ifEntry.9.4 817 ifEntry.9.5 817 ifEntry.9.6
0 ifEntry.9.7 0 ifEntry.9.8 0 ifEntry.9.9 0 ifEntry.9.10 758 ifEntry.10.1 0 ifEntry.10.2
575553 ifEntry.10.3 0 ifEntry.10.4 0 ifEntry.10.5 0 ifEntry.10.6 0 ifEntry.10.7 0
ifEntry.10.8 0 ifEntry.10.9 0 ifEntry.10.10 0 ifEntry.11.1 0 ifEntry.11.2 5729 ifEntry.11.3
0 ifEntry.11.4 0 ifEntry.11.5 0 ifEntry.11.6 0 ifEntry.11.7 0 ifEntry.11.8 0 ifEntry.11.9 0
ifEntry.11.10 0 ifEntry.12.1 0 ifEntry.12.2 555 ifEntry.12.3 0 ifEntry.12.4 0 ifEntry.12.5
0 ifEntry.12.6 0 ifEn!
 try.12.7 0 ifEntry.12.8 0 ifEntry.12.9 0 ifEntry.12.10 0 ifEntry.13.1
```

```
0 ifEntry.13.2 0 ifEntry.13.3 0 ifEntry.13.4 0 ifEntry.13.5 0 ifEntry.13.6 0 ifEntry.13.7 0
ifEntry.13.8 0 ifEntry.13.9 0 ifEntry.13.10 0 ifEntry.14.1 0 ifEntry.14.2 0 ifEntry.14.3 0
ifEntry.14.4 0 ifEntry.14.5 0 ifEntry.14.6 0 ifEntry.14.7 0 ifEntry.14.8 0 ifEntry.14.9 0
```

```
ifEntry.14.10 0 ifEntry.15.1 0 ifEntry.15.2 118 ifEntry.15.3 0 ifEntry.15.4 0 ifEntry.15.5
0 ifEntry.15.6 0 ifEntry.15.7 0 ifEntry.15.8 0 ifEntry.15.9 0 ifEntry.15.10 0 ifEntry.16.1
0 ifEntry.16.2 861338 ifEntry.16.3 0 ifEntry.16.4 0 ifEntry.16.5 0 ifEntry.16.6 0
ifEntry.16.7 0 ifEntry.16.8 0 ifEntry.16.9 0 ifEntry.16.10 0 ifEntry.17.1 0 ifEntry.17.2 7903
ifEntry.17.3 0 ifEntry.17.4 0 ifEntry.17.5 0 ifEntry.17.6 0 ifEntry.17.7 0 ifEntry.17.8 0
ifEntry.17.9 0 ifEntry.17.10 0 ifEntry.18.1 0 ifEntry.18.2 229 ifEntry.18.3 0 ifEntry.18.4
0 ifEntry.18.5 0 ifEntry.18.6 0 ifEntry.18.7 0 ifEntry.18.8 0 ifEntry.18.9 0 ifEntry.18.10
0 ifEntry.19.1 0 ifEntry.19.2 0 ifEntry.19.3 0 ifEntry.19.4 0 ifEntry.19.5 0 ifEntry.1!
 9.6 0 ifEntry.19.7 0 ifEntry.19.8 0 ifEntry.19.9 0 ifEntry.19.10 0 ifEntry.20.1 0
ifEntry.20.2 0 ifEntry.20.3 0 ifEntry.20.4 0 ifEntry.20.5 0 ifEntry.20.6 0 ifEntry.20.7 0
ifEntry.20.8 0 ifEntry.20.9 0 ifEntry.20.10 0 ifEntry.21.1 0 ifEntry.21.2 0 ifEntry.21.3 0
ifEntry.21.4 0 ifEntry.21.5 0 ifEntry.21.6 0 ifEntry.21.7 0 ifEntry.21.8 0 ifEntry.21.9 0
ifEntry.21.10 0 ifEntry.22.1 ccitt.0 ifEntry.22.2 ccitt.0 ifEntry.22.3 ccitt.0 ifEntry.22.4
ccitt.0 ifEntry.22.5 ccitt.0 ifEntry.22.6 ccitt.0 ifEntry.22.7 ccitt.0 ifEntry.22.8 ccitt.0
ifEntry.22.9 ccitt.0 ifEntry.22.10 ccitt.0
```

The following example configures the system controller to use the bulk transfer method to collect the same data:

```
syscon poll-group busyPerpoll
  oid lsystem.56.0
  oid lsystem.57.0
  oid lsystem.58.0
  oid interfaces.2.*
  transfer-mode bulk
  enable
```

The following is a sample data collection file from the configuration:

```
object 2.1.1.3.0 1188306
object 4.1.9.2.1.56.0 2
object 4.1.9.2.1.57.0 0
object 4.1.9.2.1.58.0 0
prefix 1.3.6.1.2.1.2.2.1
table 22 1 2 3 4 5 6 7 8 9 10 11 12 13 14 15 16 17 18 19 20 21 22
row 1 1 46617374457E6865726E6574302F30 6 1500 100000000 00602F861100 2 2 817 0 0 0 0 0 0
0 0 0 0 0 0.0
row 2 2 45746865726E6574322F30 6 1500 10000000 00602F861138 1 1 817 589642 5873 559 0 0 118
882201 8083 233 0 0 0 0.0
row 3 3 45746865726E6574322F31 6 1500 10000000 00602F861139 2 2 817 0 0 0 0 0 0 0 0 0 0 0 0.0
row 4 4 45746865726E6574322F32 6 1500 10000000 00602F86113A 2 2 817 0 0 0 0 0 0 0 0 0 0 0 0.0
row 5 5 45746865726E6574322F33 6 1500 10000000 00602F86113B 2 2 817 0 0 0 0 0 0 0 0 0 0 0 0.0
row 6 6 4C6F6F706261636B31 24 1514 -1  1 1 0 0 0 0 0 0 0 0 0 0 0 0 0.0
row 7 7 54756E6E656C38 1 1514 9000  1 2 0 0 0 0 0 0 0 0 0 0 0 0 0.0
row 8 8 54756E6E656C3130 1 1514 9000  1 2 0 0 0 0 0 0 0 0 0 0 0 0 0.0
row 9 9 4469616C657231 22 1500 56000  1 5 0 0 0 0 0 0 0 0 0 0 0 0 0.0
row 10 10 4C65783330 6 1500 10000000  1 2 758 0 0 0 0 0 0 0 0 0 0 0 0.0
```

Related Commands

To locate documentation of related commands, you can search online at www.cisco.com.

enable (poll-group configuration)
oid
poll-interval
samples
shelf-type
show syscon perfdata
transfer-mode

PART IV

Appendixes

ASCII Character Set

Some commands described in this documentation set, such as the **escape-character** line configuration command, require that you enter the decimal representation of an ASCII character.

Table A-1 provides code translations from the decimal numbers to their hexadecimal and ASCII equivalents. It also provides the keyword entry for each ASCII character. For example, the ASCII carriage return (CR) is decimal 13. Entering Ctrl-M at your terminal generates decimal 13, which is interpreted as a CR.

Table A-1 *ASCII Translation Table*

Numeric Values Decimal	Hex	ASCII Character	Meaning	Keyboard Entry
0	00	NUL	Null	Ctrl-@
1	01	SOH	Start of heading	Ctrl-A
2	02	STX	Start of text	Ctrl-B
3	03	ETX	Break/end of text	Ctrl-C
4	04	EOT	End of transmission	Ctrl-D
5	05	ENQ	Enquiry	Ctrl-E
6	06	ACK	Positive acknowledgment	Ctrl-F
7	07	BEL	Bell	Ctrl-G
8	08	BS	Backspace	Ctrl-H
9	09	HT	Horizontal tab	Ctrl-I
10	0A	LF	Line feed	Ctrl-J
11	0B	VT	Vertical tab	Ctrl-K
12	0C	FF	Form feed	Ctrl-L
13	0D	CR	Carriage return	Ctrl-M
14	0E	SO	Shift out	Ctrl-N
15	0F	SI	Shift in/XON (resume output)	Ctrl-O
16	10	DLE	Data link escape	Ctrl-P
17	11	DC1	Device control character 1	Ctrl-Q

Continues

Table A-1 *ASCII Translation Table (Continued)*

Numeric Values Decimal	Hex	ASCII Character	Meaning	Keyboard Entry
18	12	DC2	Device control character 2	Ctrl-R
19	13	DC3	Device control character 3	Ctrl-S
20	14	DC4	Device control character 4	Ctrl-T
21	15	NAK	Negative acknowledgment	Ctrl-U
22	16	SYN	Synchronous idle	Ctrl-V
23	17	ETB	End of transmission block	Ctrl-W
24	18	CAN	Cancel	Ctrl-X
25	19	EM	End of medium	Ctrl-Y
26	1A	SUB	Substitute/end of file	Ctrl-Z
27	1B	ESC	Escape	Ctrl-[
28	1C	FS	File separator	Ctrl-\
29	1D	GS	Group separator	Ctrl-]
30	1E	RS	Record separator	Ctrl-^
31	1F	US	Unit separator	Ctrl-_
32	20	SP	Space	Space
33	21	!	!	!
34	22	"	"	"
35	23	#	#	#
36	24	$	$	$
37	25	%	%	%
38	26	&	&	&
39	27	'	'	'
40	28	(	(	(
41	29	)	)	)
42	2A	*	*	*
43	2B	+	+	+
44	2C	,	,	,
45	2D	-	-	-
46	2E	.	.	.

Table A-1 *ASCII Translation Table (Continued)*

Numeric Values Decimal	Hex	ASCII Character	Meaning	Keyboard Entry
47	2F	/	/	/
48	30	0	Zero	0
49	31	1	One	1
50	32	2	Two	2
51	33	3	Three	3
52	34	4	Four	4
53	35	5	Five	5
54	36	6	Six	6
55	37	7	Seven	7
56	38	8	Eight	8
57	39	9	Nine	9
58	3A	:	:	:
59	3B	;	;	;
60	3C	<	<	<
61	3D	=	=	=
62	3E	>	>	>
63	3F	?	?	?
64	40	@	@	@
65	41	A	A	A
66	42	B	B	B
67	43	C	C	C
68	44	D	D	D
69	45	E	E	E
70	46	F	F	F
71	47	G	G	G
72	48	H	H	H
73	49	I	I	I
74	4A	J	J	J

Continues

Table A-1 *ASCII Translation Table (Continued)*

Numeric Values Decimal	Hex	ASCII Character	Meaning	Keyboard Entry
75	4B	K	K	K
76	4C	L	L	L
77	4D	M	M	M
78	4E	N	N	N
79	4F	O	O	O
80	50	P	P	P
81	51	Q	Q	Q
82	52	R	R	R
83	53	S	S	S
84	54	T	T	T
85	55	U	U	U
86	56	V	V	V
87	57	W	W	W
88	58	X	X	X
89	59	Y	Y	Y
90	5A	Z	Z	Z
91	5B	[	[	[
92	5C	\	\	\
93	5D	]	]	]
94	5E	^	^	^
95	5F	_	_	_
96	60	`	`	`
97	61	a	a	a
98	62	b	b	b
99	63	c	c	c
100	64	d	d	d
101	65	e	e	e
102	66	f	f	f
103	67	g	g	g

Table A-1 *ASCII Translation Table (Continued)*

Numeric Values Decimal	Hex	ASCII Character	Meaning	Keyboard Entry
104	68	h	h	h
105	69	i	i	i
106	6A	j	j	j
107	6B	k	k	k
108	6C	l	l	l
109	6D	m	m	m
110	6E	n	n	n
111	6F	o	o	o
112	70	p	p	p
113	71	q	q	q
114	72	r	r	r
115	73	s	s	s
116	74	t	t	t
117	75	u	u	u
118	76	v	v	v
119	77	w	w	w
120	78	x	x	x
121	79	y	y	y
122	7A	z	z	z
123	7B	{	{	{
124	7C	|	|	|
125	7D	}	}	}
126	7E	~	Tilde	~
127	7F	DEL	Delete	Del

APPENDIX B

References and Recommended Reading

This appendix contains the following lists of publications related to networks and networking:

- Books and Periodicals
- Technical Publications and Standards
- Cisco-Supported RFCs

Books and Periodicals

Apple Computer, Inc. *AppleTalk Network System Overview*. Reading, Massachusetts: Addison-Wesley Publishing Company, Inc.; 1989.

Black, U. *Data Networks: Concepts, Theory and Practice*. Englewood Cliffs, New Jersey: Prentice Hall; 1989.

————. *Physical Level Interfaces and Protocols*. Los Alamitos, California: IEEE Computer Society Press; 1988.

Case, J. D., J. R. Davins, M. S. Fedor, and M. L. Schoffstall. "Introduction to the Simple Gateway Monitoring Protocol." *IEEE Network*: March 1988.

————. "Network Management and the Design of SNMP." *ConneXions: The Interoperability Report,* Vol. 3: March 1989.

Clark, W. "SNA Internetworking." *ConneXions: The Interoperability Report*, Vol. 6, No. 3: March 1992.

Coltun, R. "OSPF: An Internet Routing Protocol." *ConneXions: The Interoperability Report*, Vol. 3, No. 8: August 1989.

Comer, D. E. *Internetworking with TCP/IP: Principles, Protocols, and Architecture*, Vol. I, 2nd ed. Englewood Cliffs, New Jersey: Prentice Hall; 1991.

Davidson, J. *An Introduction to TCP/IP*. New York, New York: Springer-Verlag; 1992.

Garcia-Luna-Aceves, J. J. "Loop-Free Routing Using Diffusing Computations." Publication pending in *IEEE/ACM Transactions on Networking*, Vol. 1, No. 1: 1993.

Green, J. K. *Telecommunications*, 2nd ed. Homewood, Illinois: Business One Irwin; 1992.

Hagans, R. "Components of OSI: ES-IS Routing." *ConneXions: The Interoperability Report*, Vol. 3, No. 8: August 1989.

Hares, S. "Components of OSI: Inter-Domain Routing Protocol (IDRP)." *ConneXions: The Interoperability Report*, Vol. 6, No. 5: May 1992.

Hughes Jr., L. J. *Actually Useful Internet Security Techniques*. Indianapolis, Indiana: New Riders Publishing; 1996.

Kaufman, C., R. Perlman, and M. Specinen. *Network Security: Private Communication in a Public World*. Englewood Cliffs, New Jersey: Prentice Hall, Inc.; 1995.

Kousky, K. "Bridging the Network Gap." *LAN Technology*, Vol. 6, No. 1: January 1990.

Leinwand, A. and K. Fang. *Network Management: A Practical Perspective*. Reading, Massachusetts: Addison-Wesley Publishing Company, Inc.; 1993.

Lippis, N. "The Internetwork Decade." *Data Communications*, Vol. 20, No. 14: October 1991.

Martin, J. *SNA: IBM's Networking Solution*. Englewood Cliffs, New Jersey: Prentice Hall; 1987.

Martin, J., with K. K. Chapman and the ARBEN Group, Inc. *Local Area Networks, Architectures and Implementations*. Englewood Cliffs, New Jersey: Prentice Hall, Inc.; 1989.

McNamara, J. E. *Local Area Networks: An Introduction to the Technology*. Bedford, Massachusetts: Digital Press; 1997.

Medin, M. "The Great IGP Debate—Part Two: The Open Shortest Path First (OSPF) Routing Protocol." *ConneXions: The Interoperability Report*, Vol. 5, No. 10: October 1991.

Meijer, A. *Systems Network Architecture: A Tutorial*. New York, New York: John Wiley & Sons, Inc.; 1987.

Miller, M. A. *LAN Protocol Handbook*. San Mateo, California: M&T Books; 1990.

O'Reilly, T. and G. Todino. *Managing UUCP and Usenet*, 10th ed. Sebastopol, California: O'Reilly & Associates, Inc.; 1992.

Perkins, D. and E. McGinnis. *Understanding SNMP MIBs*. Englewood Cliffs, New Jersey: Prentice Hall PTR; 1997.

Perlman, R. *Interconnections: Bridges and Routers*. Reading, Massachusetts: Addison-Wesley Publishing Company, Inc.; 1992.

Perlman, R. and R. Callon. "The Great IGP Debate—Part One: IS-IS and Integrated Routing." *ConneXions: The Interoperability Report*, Vol. 5, No. 10: October 1991.

Rose, M. T. *The Open Book: A Practical Perspective on OSI*. Englewood Cliffs, New Jersey: Prentice Hall, Inc.; 1990.

———. *The Simple Book: An Introduction to Management of TCP/IP-based Internets*. Englewood Cliffs, New Jersey: Prentice Hall, Inc.; 1991.

Ross, F. E. "FDDI—A Tutorial." *IEEE Communications Magazine*, Vol. 24, No. 5: May 1986.

Schlar, S. K. *Inside X.25: A Manager's Guide*. New York, New York: McGraw-Hill, Inc.; 1990.

Schneier, B. *Applied Cryptography: Protocols, Algorithms, and Source Code in C*. New York, New York: John Wiley & Sons, Inc.; 1995

Schwartz, M. *Telecommunications Networks: Protocols, Modeling, and Analysis*. Reading, Massachusetts: Addison-Wesley Publishing Company, Inc.; 1987.

Sherman, K. *Data Communications: A User's Guide*. Englewood Cliffs, New Jersey: Prentice Hall, Inc.; 1990.

Sidhu, G. S., R. F. Andrews, and A. B. Oppenheimer. *Inside AppleTalk*, 2nd ed. Reading, Massachusetts: Addison-Wesley Publishing Company, Inc.; 1990.

Spragins, J. D. et al. *Telecommunications Protocols and Design*. Reading, Massachusetts: Addison-Wesley Publishing Company, Inc.; 1991.

Stallings, W. *Data and Computer Communications*. New York, New York: Macmillan Publishing Company; 1991.

———. *Handbook of Computer-Communications Standards*, Vols. 1–3. Carmel, Indiana: Howard W. Sams, Inc.; 1990.

———. *Local Networks*, 3rd ed. New York, New York: Macmillan Publishing Company; 1990.

Sunshine, C. A., ed. 1989. *Computer Network Architectures and Protocols*, 2nd ed. New York, New York: Plenum Press.

Tannenbaum, A. S. *Computer Networks*, 2nd ed. Englewood Cliffs, New Jersey: Prentice Hall, Inc.; 1988.

Terplan, K. *Communication Networks Management*. Englewood Cliffs, New Jersey: Prentice Hall, Inc.; 1992.

Tsuchiya, P. "Components of OSI: IS-IS Intra-Domain Routing." *ConneXions: The Interoperability Report*, Vol. 3, No. 8: August 1989.

———. "Components of OSI: Routing (An Overview)." *ConneXions: The Interoperability Report*, Vol. 3, No. 8: August 1989.

Zimmerman, H. "OSI Reference Model—The ISO Model of Architecture for Open Systems Interconnection." *IEEE Transactions on Communications* COM-28, No. 4: April 1980.

Technical Publications and Standards

Advanced Micro Devices. *The Supernet Family for FDDI*. Technical Manual Number 09779A. Sunnyvale, California, 1989.

———. *The Supernet Family for FDDI*. 1989 Data Book Number 09734C. Sunnyvale, California, 1989.

American National Standards Institute X3T9.5 Committee. *FDDI Station Management (SMT).* Revision 6.1, March 1990.

————. Revised Text of ISO/DIS 8802/2 for the Second DIS Ballot, "Information Processing Systems—Local Area Networks." Part 2: Logical Link Control; 1987.

———— T1.606. "Integrated Services Digital Network (ISDN)—Architectural Framework and Service Description for Frame-Relaying Bearer Service"; 1990.

———— T1.617. "Integrated Services Digital Network (ISDN)—Signaling Specification for Frame Relay Bearer Service for Digital Subscriber Signaling System Number 1 (DSS1)"; 1991.

———— T1.618. "Integrated Services Digital Network (ISDN)—Core Aspects of Frame Protocol for Use with Frame Relay Bearer Service"; 1991.

ATM Data Exchange Interface (DXI) Specification, Version 1.0. Document ATM_FORUM/93-590R1; August 1993.

Banyan Systems, Inc. *VINES Protocol Definition.* DA254-00, Rev. 1.0. Westboro, Massachusetts, February 1990.

Bellcore. *Generic System Requirements in Support of a Switched Multi-Megabit Data Service.* Technical Advisory, TA-TSY-000772, October 1989.

————. *Local Access System Generic Requirements, Objectives, and Interface Support of Switched Multi-Megabit Data Service.* Technical Advisory TA-TSY-000773, Issue 1, December 1985.

————. *Switched Multi-Megabit Data Service (SMDS) Operations Technology Network Element Generic Requirements.* Technical Advisory TA-TSY-000774.

Chapman, J. T. and M. Halabi. *HSSI: High-Speed Serial Interface Design Specification.* Menlo Park, California and Santa Clara, California: Cisco Systems and T3Plus Networking, Inc.; 1990.

Consultative Committee for International Telegraph and Telephone. *CCITT Data Communications Networks—Services and Facilities, Terminal Equipment and Interfaces, Recommendations X.1–X.29.* Yellow Book, Vol. VIII, Fascicle VIII.2. 1980.

————. *CCITT Data Communications Networks—Interfaces, Recommendations X.20–X.32.* Red Book, Vol. VIII, Fascicle VIII.3. 1984.

DDN Protocol Handbook. Four volumes; 1989.

Defense Communications Agency. *Defense Data Network X.25 Host Interface Specification.* Order number AD A137 427. December 1983.

Defense Trade Regulations (Parts 120 to 126).

Digital Equipment Corporation. *DECnet/OSI Phase V: Making the Transition From Phase IV.* EK-PVTRN-BR. 1989.

————. *DECserver 200 Local Area Transport (LAT) Network Concepts.* AA-LD84A-TK. June 1988.

————. *DIGITAL Network Architecture (Phase V).* EK-DNAPV-GD-001. September 1987.

Digital Equipment Corporation, Intel Corporation, Xerox Corporation. *The Ethernet, A Local-Area Network, Data Link Layer and Physical Layer Specifications*. Version 2.0. November 1982.

Feinler, E. J., et al. *DDN Protocol Handbook*, Vols. 1–4, NIC 50004, 50005, 50006, 50007. Defense Communications Agency. Alexandria, Virginia; December 1985.

FIPS140, Federal Information Processing Standard.

Garcia-Luna-Aceves, J. J. "A Unified Approach to Loop-Free Routing Using Distance Vectors or Link States." ACM 089791-332-9/89/0009/0212, pp. 212–223; September 1989.

Hemrick, C. and L. Lang. "Introduction to Switched Multi-Megabit Data Service (SMDS), an Early Broadband Service." *Proceedings of the XIII International Switching Symposium* (ISS 90); May 27–June 1, 1990.

Hewlett-Packard Company. *X.25: The PSN Connection; An Explanation of Recommendation X.25. 5958-3402; October 1985.*

IEEE Project 802—*Local & Metropolitan Area Networks. Proposed Standard: Distributed Queue Dual Bus (DQDB) Subnetwork of a Metropolitan Area Network (MAN)*; February 1990.

IEEE 802.2—*Local Area Networks Standard, 802.2 Logical Link Control*. ANSI/IEEE Standard; October 1985.

IEEE 802.3—*Local Area Networks Standard, 802.3 Carrier Sense Multiple Access*. ANSI/IEEE Standard; October 1985.

Information Security and Privacy in Network Environments, Office of Technology Assessment (OTA)—Congress of the United States.

International Business Machines Corporation. *ACF/NCP/VS Network Control Program, System Support Programs: General Information*. GC30-3058.

———. *Advanced Communications Function for VTAM (ACF/VTAM), General Information: Introduction*. GS27-0462.

———. *Advanced Communications Function for VTAM, General Information: Concepts*. GS27-0463.

———. *Dictionary of Computing*. SC20-1699-7; 1987.

———. *Local Area Network Technical Reference*. SC30-3883.

———. *Network Problem Determination Application: General information*. GC34-2010.

———. *Synchronous Data Link Control: General information*. GA27-3093.

———. *Systems Network Architecture: Concepts and products*. GC30-3072.

———. *Systems Network Architecture: Technical overview*. GC30-3073-1; 1985.

———. *Token-Ring Network Architecture Reference*. SC30-3374.

International Organization for Standardization. *Information Processing System—Open System Interconnection; Specification of Abstract Syntax Notation One (ASN.1).* International Standard 8824; December 1987.

McGraw-Hill/Data Communications. *McGraw-Hill's Compilation of Data Communications Standards*, 3rd ed.; 1986.

National Security Agency. *Blacker Interface Control Document*; March 21, 1989.

Novell, Inc. IPX Router Specification, Version 1.10. Part Number 107-000029-001; October 16, 1992.

————. NetWare Link Services Protocol (NLSP) Specification, Revision 0.9. Part Number 100-001708-001; March 1993.

StrataCom. *Frame Relay Specification with Extensions.* 001-208966, Revision 1.0; September 18, 1990.

Transmission Control Protocol/Internet Protocol TCP/IP Version 2 Release 2.1 for MVS: Planning and Customization, SC31-6085 (or later version) .

Transmission Control Protocol/Internet Protocol TCP/IP Version 2 Release 2 for VM: Planning and Customization, SC31-6082 (or later version).

Xerox Corporation. *Internet Transport Protocols.* XNSS 029101; January 1991.

Cisco-Supported RFCs

Table B-1 lists the Requests for Comments (RFCs) supported by the Cisco Internetwork Operating System (Cisco IOS) software as of Cisco IOS Release 11.3, in descending numerical order. RFCs that have been superseded or replaced are identified, as are RFCs that are partially supported or supported only from Software Release 9.21 and on.

Table B-1 *Cisco-Supported Requests for Comments*

Standard Number		Standard Title
RFC 2125		PPP Bandwidth Allocation Protocol (BAP)
		PPP Bandwidth Allocation Control Protocol (BACP)
RFC 2037[1]		Entity MIB
RFC 2018		TCP Selective Acknowledgment Options
RFC 1997		BGP Communities Attribute
RFC 1994	Supersedes RFC 1334	PPP Challenge Handshake Authentication Protocol (CHAP)
RFC 1990	Supersedes RFC 1717	The PPP Multilink Protocol (MP)
RFC 1989	Supersedes RFC 1333	PPP Link Quality Monitoring
RFC 1918		Address Allocation for Private Internet Space

Table B-1 *Cisco-Supported Requests for Comments (Continued)*

Standard Number		Standard Title
RFC 1907		Management Information Base for Simple Network Management Protocol (SNMPv2)
RFC 1906		Transport Mappings for Version 2 of the Simple Network Management Protocol (SNMPv2)
RFC 1905		Protocol Operations for Version 2 of the Simple Network Management Protocol (SNMPv2)
RFC 1904		Conformance Statements for Version 2 of the Simple Network Management Protocol (SNMPv2)
RFC 1903		Textual Conventions for Version 2 of the Simple Network Management Protocol (SNMPv2)
RFC 1902		Structural Management for Version 2 of the Simple Network Management Protocol (SNMPv2)
RFC 1901	Supersedes RFC 1441-1450	Introduction to Community-Based SNMPv2
RFC 1889		RTP—A Transport Protocol for Real-Time Applications
RFC 1850		OSPF Version 2 MIB
RFC 1812		Requirements for IP Version 4 Routers
RFC 1795		DLSw: Switch-to-Switch Protocol
RFC 1793		Extending OSPF to Support Demand Circuits
RFC 1771		A Border Gateway Protocol 4
RFC 1745		BGP4/IDRP for IP—OSPF Interaction
RFC 1724		RIP Version 2 MIB Extension
RFC 1723		RIP Version 2 Carrying Additional Information
RFC 1722		RIP Version 2 Protocol Applicability Statement
RFC 1717	Replaced by RFC 1990	The PPP Multilink Protocol (MP)
RFC 1695		Definitions of Managed Objects for ATM Management Version 8.0 using SMIv2
RFC 1661	Supersedes RFC 1548	PPP (Point-to-Point Protocol)
RFC 1654		A Border Gateway Protocol (BGP-4)
RFC 1647		TN3270 Enhancements
RFC 1646		Cisco supports LU name selection method only
RFC 1638		PPP Bridging Control Protocol (BCP)

continues

Table B-1   *Cisco-Supported Requests for Comments (Continued)*

Standard Number		Standard Title
RFC 1634	Supersedes 1362 and 1551	Novell Routing over Various WAN Media (IPXWAN)
RFC 1633		Integrated Services in the Internet Architecture: An Overview
RFC 1631		The IP Network Address Translator
RFC 1618		PPP over ISDN
RFC 1604		Definitions of Managed Objects for Frame Relay Service
RFC 1587		The OSPF Not-So-Stubby Area (NSSA) Option
RFC 1583	Supersedes RFC 1247	OSPF Version 2
RFC 1577		Classical IP and ARP over ATM
RFC 1576		TN3270 Current Practices
RFC 1559		DECnet Phase IV MIB Extensions
RFC 1552		The PPP Internetwork Packet Exchange Control Protocol (IPXCP)
RFC 1549		PPP in HDLC Framing
RFC 1548	Replaced by RFC 1661	PPP (Point-to-Point Protocol)
RFC 1541	Supersedes RFC 1531	Dynamic Host Configuration Protocol
RFC 1531	Replaced by RFC 1541	Dynamic Host Configuration Protocol
RFC 1519		Classless Inter-Domain Routing (CIDR): an Address Assignment and Aggregation Strategy
RFC 1510		The Kerberos Network Authentication Service (V5)
RFC 1492		Access Control Protocol or TACACS
RFC 1490		Multiprotocol Interconnect over Frame Relay
RFC 1483[1]		Multiprotocol Encapsulation over ATM Adaptation Layer 5
RFC 1469		IP Multicast over Token-Ring Local Area Network
RFC 1450	Replaced by RFC 1907	MIB for SNMP Version 2
RFC 1403		BGP OSPF Interaction
RFC 1397		Default Route Advertisement in BGP2 and BGP3
RFC 1395		BootP Extensions
RFC 1393		Traceroute using an IP Option
RFC 1390		Transmission of IP and ARP over FDDI Networks
RFC 1382[1,2]		SNMP MIB Extension for X.25 Packet Layer
RFC 1381[1,2]		SNMP MIB Extension for X.25 LAPB

Table B-1 *Cisco-Supported Requests for Comments (Continued)*

Standard Number		Standard Title
RFC 1378[1]		PPP AppleTalk Control Protocol (ATCP)
RFC 1377		PPP OSI Network Layer Control Protocol (OSINLCP)
RFC 1376		PPP DECnet Phase IV Control Protocol (DNCP)
RFC 1370		Applicability Statement for OSPF
RFC 1362		Novell IPX Over Various WAN Media (IPXWAN)
RFC 1356		Multiprotocol Interconnect on X.25 and ISDN in the Packet Mode
RFC 1350		TFTP Version 2
RFC 1349		Type of Service in the Internet Protocol Suite
RFC 1348		DNS NSAP RRs
RFC 1334	Replaced by RFC 1994	PPP Authentication Protocols
RFC 1333	Replaced by RFC 1989	PPP Link Quality Monitoring
RFC 1332		PPP Internet Protocol Control Protocol (IPCP)
RFC 1331	Replaced by RFC 1548	PPP for the Transmission of Multi-protocol Datagrams over Point-to-Point Links
RFC 1323		TCP Extensions for High Performance
RFC 1315 [1,2]		MIB for Frame Relay DTEs
RFC 1305		Network Time Protocol (NTP) Version 3
RFC 1294[2]	Replaced by RFC1490	Multiprotocol Interconnect over Frame Relay
RFC 1293		Inverse ARP
RFC 1286		Definitions of Managed Objects for Bridges
RFC 1285 [1]		FDDI MIB
RFC 1269 [1]		Definitions of Managed Objects for the Border Gateway Protocol (Version 3)
RFC 1268		Application of BGP in the Internet
RFC 1267		BGP-3
RFC 1256		ICMP Router Discovery Messages
RFC 1253		MIB for OSPF Version 2
RFC 1247	Replaced by RFC 1583	OSPF Version 2
RFC 1236		IP-to-X.121 Address Mapping for DDN
RFC 1234		Tunneling IPX Traffic through IP Networks

continues

Table B-1   *Cisco-Supported Requests for Comments (Continued)*

Standard Number		Standard Title
RFC 1231 [1]		IEEE 802.5 Token Ring MIB
RFC 1220		Point-to-Point Protocol (PPP) Extensions for Bridging
RFC 1219		On the Assignment of Subnet Numbers
RFC 1215		Convention for Defining Traps for Use with SNMP
RFC 1213		Management Information Base for Network Management of TCP/IP-based Internets: MIB-II
RFC 1212		Concise MIB Definitions
RFC 1209		Transmission of IP Datagrams over SMDS Service
RFC 1196		Finger User Information Protocol
RFC 1195 [2]		Use of OSI IS-IS for Routing in TCP/IP in Dual Environments
RFC 1191		Path MTU Discovery
RFC 1188	Replaced by RFC 1390	Proposed Standard for the Transmission of IP Datagrams over FDDI Networks
RFC 1172		PPP Initial Configuration Options
RFC 1171	Replaced by RFC 1331	Point-to-Point Protocol for the Transmission of Multi-Protocol Datagrams over Point-to-Point links
RFC 1166		Internet Numbers
RFC 1164		Application of the BGP in the Internet
RFC 1163		Border Gateway Protocol (BGP)
RFC 1157		Simple Network Management Protocol (SNMP)
RFC 1156	Replaced by RFC 1213	MIB for TCP/IP
RFC 1155	Replaced by RFC 1212	Structure and Identification of Management Information for TCP/IP-Based Internets
RFC 1144		Compressing TCP/IP Headers for Low-Speed Serial Links
RFC 1141		Incremental Updating of the Internet Checksum
RFC 1139		Echo Function for ISO 8473 (PING)
RFC 1136		Administrative Domains and Routing Domains: A Model for Routing in the Internet
RFC 1122		Requirements for Internet Hosts—Communication Layers
RFC 1112		Host Extensions for IP Multicasting
RFC 1108	DCA Draft	IP Security Option (IPSO)
RFC 1101		DNS Encoding of Network Names and Other Types

Table B-1 *Cisco-Supported Requests for Comments (Continued)*

Standard Number		Standard Title
RFC 1091		Telnet Terminal-Type Option
RFC 1084		BootP Extensions
RFC 1080		Telnet Remote Flow Control Option
RFC 1079		Telnet Terminal Speed Option
RFC 1069		Guidelines for the use of Internet-IP Addresses in the ISO Connectionless-Mode Network Protocol
RFC 1060		Assigned Numbers
RFC 1058		Routing Information Protocol (RIP)
RFC 1055		Standard for the Transmission of IP Datagrams Over Serial Lines: SLIP
RFC 1042		Standard for the Transmission of IP Datagrams Over IEEE 802 Networks
RFC 1035		Domain Names—Implementation and Specification
RFC 1034		Domain Names—Concepts and Facilities
RFC 1027		Using ARP to Implement Transparent Subnet Gateways (Proxy ARP)
RFC 1009		Requirements for Internet Gateways
RFC 995	Replaced by ISO 9542	ES-to-IS Routing Exchange Protocol for Use in Conjunction with ISO 8473
RFC 994	Replaced by ISO 8473	Protocol for Providing the Connectionless-Mode Network Service
RFC 982		Guidelines for the Specification of the Top of the Structure of the Domain Specific Part (DSP) of the ISO Standard NSAP Address
RFC 951		Bootstrap Protocol (BootP)
RFC 950		Internet Standard Subnetting Procedure
RFC 925		Multi-LAN Address Resolution (PROXY ARP)
RFC 922		Broadcasting Internet Datagrams in the Presence of Subnets (IP_BROAD)
RFC 919		Broadcasting Internet Datagrams
RFC 906		Bootstrap Loading Using TFTP
RFC 904		Exterior Gateway Protocol (EGP) Formal Specification
RFC 903		Reverse Address Resolution Protocol (RARP)

continues

Table B-1 *Cisco-Supported Requests for Comments (Continued)*

Standard Number		Standard Title
RFC 896		Congestion Control in TCP/IP Internetworks
RFC 895		Standard for the transmission of IP datagrams over experimental Ethernet networks
RFC 894		Standard for the Transmission of IP Datagrams over Ethernet
RFC 891		Hello Protocol
RFC 879		The TCP Maximum Segment Size and Related Topics
RFC 877		Standard for the Transmission of IP Datagrams Over Public Data Networks
RFC 874		Telnet Protocol Specification
RFC 863		Discard Service (TCP discard)
RFC 862		Echo Service (TCP echo)
RFC 860		Telnet Timing Mark Option
RFC 858		Telnet Suppress Go Ahead option
RFC 857		Telnet Echo Option
RFC 856		Telnet Binary Transmission
RFC 855		Telnet Option Specification
RFC 854	MIL STD 1782	Telnet Protocol Specification
RFC 827		Exterior Gateway Protocol (EGP)
RFC 826		Address Resolution Protocol (ARP)
RFC 815		IP Datagram Reassembly Algorithms
RFC 813		Window and Acknowledgment Strategy in TCP/IP
RFC 793	MIL STD 1778	Transmission Control Protocol (TCP)
RFC 792		Internet Control Message Protocol (ICMP)
RFC 791	MIL STD 1777	Internetwork Protocol (IP)
RFC 783		Trivial File Transfer Protocol (TFTP) (version 2)
RFC 779		Telnet Send-Location Option
RFC 768		User Datagram Protocol (UDP)

1. This RFC is only partially supported by the Cisco IOS.
2. This RFC is supported from Software Release 9.21 on.

Where to Obtain RFCs

RFCs are maintained by Government Systems, Inc. (GSI). Both electronic and printed copies can be obtained. GSI can be contacted in the following ways:

- By mail:

  Government Systems, Inc.
  Attn: Network Information Center
  14200 Park Meadow Drive, Suite 200
  Chantilly, Virginia 22021

- By telephone:

  1–800–365–3642
  1–703–802–8376
  1–703–802–8376 (FAX)

- By electronic mail:

  NIC@NIC.DDN.MIL
  Network address: 192.112.36.5

INDEX

Symbols/Numerics

A

H

I

J-K

L

M

S

T

U

W

warning messages
    automatic, 769–770
    severity levels, 778
WCCP (Web Cache Control Protocol), 271
    configuring, 283–285
        example, 288–289
        support, 297–298
        task list, 285
    global statistics, displaying, 304–305
    monitoring, 286
    redirected packets, clearing counter, 291–292
Web browsers
    Cisco Web browser
        compatibility, 273
        configuring, 272–273
        HTML pages, customizing, 281
        task list, 271
    router home pages, accessing, 273–276
    SSIs, 278
        variables, 279–280
    user interfaces, customizing, 278–280
Web pages
    SSIs, 281
width
    ASCII characters, modifying, 210–211
    terminal screen, modifying, 159
width command, 223
word help, 42–43, 78
wraparound (commands), 51
write protection (Flash memory), 468
WWW (World Wide Web)
    Cisco Web browser interface
        accessing, 54–55
        command line, 59–61
        configuring, 272–273
        requirements, 57
        URL window, 61
    home page (routers), accessing, 57–59
    HTML pages
        customizing, 64
        SSIs (Server Side Includes), 61–63
    URLs, locating files, 312–313

X-Z

xmodem command, 461–463
Xmodem protocol, system images
    copying, 461–463
    recovering, 435–439
XRemote, exiting, 229

Y cables, master-slave arbitration, 523
Ymodem protocol, copying images, 461–463